WITHDRAWN

SCHOOLCRAFT COLLEGE LIBRARY

F 67 .S516 v.2

Sewall, Samuel, 1652-1730.

The diary of Samuel Sewall,
1674-1729

BRADNER LIBRARY
SCHOOLCRAFT COLLEGE
LIVONIA, MICHIGAN 48152

RESEARCH LIBRARY
OF
COLONIAL AMERICANA

RESEARCH LIBRARY
OF
COLONIAL AMERICANA

General Editor
RICHARD C. ROBEY
Columbia University

Advisory Editors
JACK P. GREENE
Johns Hopkins University

EDMUND S. MORGAN
Yale University

ALDEN T. VAUGHAN
Columbia University

DIARY

OF

SAMUEL SEWALL

1674–1729

Volume II

ARNO PRESS
A New York Times Company
New York – 1972

Reprint Edition 1972 by Arno Press Inc.

Reprinted from copies in
The State Historical Society of Wisconsin and
Columbia University Libraries

LC# 77-141102
ISBN 0-405-03311-7

Research Library of Colonial Americana
ISBN for complete set: 0-405-03270-6
See last pages of this volume for titles.

Manufactured in the United States of America

COLLECTIONS

OF THE

MASSACHUSETTS HISTORICAL SOCIETY.

Committee of Publication.

GEORGE E. ELLIS.
WILLIAM H. WHITMORE.
HENRY WARREN TORREY.
JAMES RUSSELL LOWELL.

COLLECTIONS

OF THE

MASSACHUSETTS HISTORICAL SOCIETY.

VOL. VI. — FIFTH SERIES.

SIC VOS NON VOBIS.

SOC. HIST. MASS.
MDCCXCI.

BOSTON:
PUBLISHED BY THE SOCIETY.
M.DCCCLXXIX.

F
67
.S516
1972
v.2

UNIVERSITY PRESS:
JOHN WILSON AND SON, CAMBRIDGE.

PREFACE.

THE Publishing Committee herewith presents to the Society the second volume of the Diary of Samuel Sewall, printed from the Manuscript in its Cabinet. The text of the volume includes the period from January 14, 1699–1700, to April 14, 1714. Another volume in print will complete the publication of the manuscript Diary. The Judge's Letter-Book will furnish the materials for a fourth volume.

The Committee has continued the same system of annotating the text which was adopted in the first volume. Resisting the prompting or opportunity to explain or illustrate the many interesting references which the Judge makes to matters of historical importance, to an extent which would expand the notes beyond the text, the method pursued, as the reader will observe, has been restricted to occasional comments, and to genealogical and local particulars and references, without quoting authorities easily accessible to the students of our history. The connection between Judge Sewall's family and that of Governor Dudley evidently embarrassed the former, alike in his official position as a magistrate, and in making entries in his diary concerning matters in which they were occasionally at variance. That Sewall should also have drawn upon himself the hostility of Cotton Mather, who, with his father, the President of the College, was in violent feud with Dudley, may help to show the perplexities of the Judge's position and course even when he seems to have tried to act as a moderator or an umpire. The Committee has therefore thought it advisable to reprint three very rare pamphlets which, as fully presenting matters of bitter strife in relation to the parties just named, will make annotation upon it unnecessary. A few fragmentary and miscellaneous papers in Sewall's hand precede these Tracts.

As the indices of names at the close of the volumes are necessarily so crowded, tables of the notes in both of them are here given for convenience of reference.

EDS.

TABLE OF CONTENTS OF NOTES.

VOL. I.

TABLE OF CONTENTS OF NOTES.

VOL. II.

MISCELLANEOUS ITEMS.

[Miscellaneous Entries on the Cover of the Journal.]

[The reference is to the " Bill" put up by Sewall on the Fast Day, Jan., 1697.   See p. 445.]

See p. 159 of this booke.

P. 163.   Mr. Rogers, May 1697.

[Sept. 26, 1686.]

America p. 48.

[References to his Captaincy of the Artillery Company.]
244. 6.

Mr. Cotton 168.

Sup'r Court

Com̄ons Address against Profaneness &c agreed to *Nemine con-tradicente.*   Feb. 15. 97. pag. 221.   Bill about regulating the Press, rejected, p. 225 —   21 Feb. 1697, p. 246.   Feby. 16. 170$\frac{2}{3}$.

A Bill to naturalize the Children of such officers and Souldiers, and others, the natural born subjects of this Realm, who have been born abroad, during the war; the Parents of such children having been in the service of this Government, read a 2^d time and com̄itted.

Mr. Eyre's Son dyed Apr. 18. 1700.

1697. June, 1.   Mr. Thomas Graves buried.

weigh'd
fol. 244 [?]

July 4. Mr. Moodey dyes.

November 8. Mr. Sam! Hooker, Farmington.

Dec.ʳ 12. Mr. John Baily dies ⎱ Brothers children fol. 245 Feb. 3,
Jan.ʸ 8 dear Unkle Quinsey dies ⎰ 170⅔

Febr. 9. Col. S. Shrimpton dies of an Apoplexy.

March, 1. Col. Barthol, Gedny dies.

April, 11. Mr. Morton dies

Dec.ʳ 7. 1692. Judges chosen

Ap. 2. 1694. Judge Richards dyes.

March, 6, 169⅘ Elisha Cooke Esqr chosen a Judge.

9.ʳ 5. 1699. Judge Danforth dyes.

June, 7. 1700. John Walley esqr made a Judge

July 7, 1701. L.ᵗ Gov.ʳ Stoughton dies.

Aug.ᵗ 1. 1701. John Saffin esqr made Judge

Aug.ᵗ 15. 1702. John Hathorne Leverett Esq made Judge.

An Elegie on Mrs. Alicia Lisle, which for high Treason was be-
headed at Winchester, September the 2.ᵈ 1685.[1]

> Let Rebels both and Loyalists draw nigh
> And view this Object of Disloyalty,
> A Lady which by a Rebellious Crew
> Was forc't in hast to bid the World adieu,
> And pay her head to Justice for her Crime
> Comitted now when she had pass'd her Prime.
> Not zeal blindfolded, nor the CAUSE, the **CAUSE**
> Can overturn Religion and the Laws.
>
>   &c. &c.

EPITAPH.

> Here lies Madam Lisle dead,
> Which for Treason lost her Head.
> She patroniz'd the CAUSE, the **CAUSE**,
> Against the Church and stablish'd Laws,
> Let all her Sex; both great and small
> Take here Example by her Fall:
> And henceforth ever Shunn to be
> Entangled by Presbytery;
> Which changeth into several shapes
> And hath brought forth Gomorrah's Grapes

----

[1] See Vol. I. p. 104.

Which have set England's Teeth on Edge
But now she is gone off the stage
Then here she is, and Let her Lie
A Beacon unto Loyalty.

This may be Printed   R. L. S.
To be sold by Randal Taylor

Survey your Ground first, lest your great Design
End in a Quagmire, or a hollow Mine.

Submit to Fate, turn Loyal now (for shame)
And strive no more to swim against the stream.

Aug. 30, 1686.   Speech to the South Company.

GENTLEMEN, — The reason of my being here, is not to comand you my self, but to commend you for your complying with the command of the honourable Council, and our Lieu! Mr. Elizur Holyoke, which I earnestly perswade you to persist in : by so doing you will exceedingly honour your selves and gratify me. So that if any of you study to shew me respect, let it be in that way. There are many Reasons with me why I inform'd the honourable Council of my inability to sustain that Character which somtime I have done in this Company ; which, as it would not be proper, so I have not now time to relate. I heartily thank you for the Respect I have had from you, which has been beyond my value. Am truly sorry for any inconvenience I have been the occasion of the last week to our Lieu! or any of the officers, and ask your pardon for it. The Drums have lately cost somthing the fitting, which I shall take care to discharge, that the Company be not in debt about it. And I have left with the Lieu! for the refreshment of the privat Souldiers, of which I crave your Acceptance.

And so wishing you a good day, I take Leave.

To JOSEPH DUDLEY, Esqr., Presd!

HONOURED SIR, — My not being at home when the Messenger came to my house yesterday gives the occasion of these Lines. Indeed I had then no expectation of any such thing ; but suposed on Thorsday it might have been. Am truly thankfull to your Honour for the respect you have put on me in nominating me for the keeping the Peace : but you shall still further oblige me in letting of it rest in a Nomination. What station I formerly had in the Government of this place it hath pleased God to cast me out of it just after the taking of a solemn Oath, which probably I had not done so soon, had not some small Circumstances turn'd the scale. And many of the Council reside in Boston : and those chosen Justices, Mr. Joyliff for one, are so aged and worthy, that now I am upon even ground, and in age his son, shall be perpetually asham'd to take place of him as a senior Justice, and shall be pleased to see him have his health and sit on the Bench. Besides, my Mother and wife are incessantly importunat with me to accept at least of part of that Retirement which God hath dismissed me to. I am glad that my Unkle Quinsey hath sworn and so, for ought I see, his sister is too : wish I may hear the like of other good men up and down the Country, which as have oportunity, I shall further. Only as I have serv'd this People as a Constable, and as a Justice of Peace, so now am desirous of making an Experiment, whether standing in the middle between those two Offices, be the hapier Life, as I think I have heard K. James the first should affirm. Have been willing to signify thus much, that so my non-acceptance may be managed by your Prudence for the best. I am your Hon[s] humble

Serv[t]   S. S.

JUNE 2, 1686.

To make a Salt-Petre Bed. *Impr:.* All the sword of the Ground is to be taken off or trenched in, and the Stones to be taken clean out as deep as the Trench. Then get the best and richest mould you can, and fill up the Trench according as you will make it in greatness — Length or depth, as you see cause. When the ground is made clean and fitting, turn over the ground and trench it in again, and as you trench it in mix it with strong Lime about a 10th or sixth part ; and the Seed-Petre, or Mother of Petre, and Hen, or Pigeon's Dung as much as you can get, the more the better. And after 'tis trenched in as above, Let all the Butchers Blood and Lees of Wine be mixed often with the uper part of the mould about half a foot down, that it be not lost or run away from the Bed or Bank. Let the Bank be made upon rising Ground, and a ditch about it, that the water rest not, nor run into the Petre-Bed ; with a dry House over it, to keep it from Rain.

Jan[y] 24th 170⅘ James Bayley Esqr. Ring and Glov[es].

April, 23. *feria quarta,* The Rever[d] and pious Mr. Samuel Torrey ; Gloves.

86. May, 12, 1707. Mrs. Lydia Scottow, Scarf and Gloves. 86 years old

69. Dec.ʳ 4. 1707. The Honble F. J. Winthrop, Governour of Coñecticut. Scarf, Ring, Gloves, Escutcheon. Gov. W. Tomb.

Dec.ʳ 12. Mrs. Mary Eliot, widow of my dear friend Capt.
75.   Jacob Eliot, and her self a very good woman. Scarf and Gloves. 75.

64. March, 22. 170⁷⁄₈ Mrs. Sarah Noyes; Scarf and Gloves.

54. Aug.ᵗ 17. 1708. Mrs. Mary Stoddard; Scarf and Ring.

73. Octob.ʳ 20. 1708. Capt. Anthony Checkley, Scarf and Gloves.

76. Febr. 11ᵗʰ 170⁸⁄₉ Mrs. Hañah Glover, Scarf and Gloves.

69. April, 30. 1709. James Russel Esqr. Scarf and Gloves.

May, 6. Mrs. Abigail Russel his widow. Scarf, Gloves.

64. May, 9. Major Thomas Brown, of Sudbury, Esqr Scarf and Gloves.

80. May, 26. Mrs. Sarah Pemberton, Scarf and Gloves.

74. June, 8. Mrs. Ruth Wyllys, Scarf, Gloves.

55. July, 26. Mr. Thomas Banister, Scarf and Gloves.

61. January, 10 ¹⁷⁰⁹⁄₁₀ Mr. John Hubbard; Scarf and Gloves.

63. Mrs. Elizabeth Savage, April, 16, 1710, Scarf and Gloves.

84. Madam —— Stoddard, July, 19, 1710. Scarf and Gloves.

72. Isaac Goose, Dec.ʳ 2. 1710. Scarf and Gloves.

58. John Foster esqr, Febr. 15. Scarf, Ring, Gloves, Escutcheon.

40. Mrs. Anne Allen, Febr. 28 ¹⁷¹⁰⁄₁₁, Scarf and Gloves.

68. Mrs. Abigail Foster; March, 8. 17¹⁰⁄₁₁, Scarf, Ring, Gloves, Escut.

57. Mrs. Sarah Banister, July, 3. 1711. Scarf and Ring, Gloves.

60. Mr. Elizur Holyoke, Aug.ᵗ 14. 1711. Scarf and Gloves.

72. Mrs. Mary Ardel, Octob.ʳ 20. 1711. Scarf and Gloves.

Mr. John Pole, Nov.ʳ 10. 1711. Scarf, Gloves, Escutcheon.

Mrs. Margaret Corwin Dec.ʳ 3. Scarvs and Gloves.

73. Mrs. M. —— Atkinson, Jan.ʳ 4. Scarvs and Gloves.

69. Jn° Walley Esqr., Jan.ʳ 17. Scarf, Ring, Gloves, Escutcheon.

77. John Fayerwether, Capt. Scarf and Gloves. Apr. 14. 1712.

Mrs. Elisa Whetcomb Aug.ᵗ 20. 1712. Scarf and Gloves.

80. Mrs. Sarah More, Nov.ʳ 26. Scarf and Gloves.

70. Samuel Hayman esqr, Dec.ʳ 18. Scarf and Gloves.

70. Mrs. Elisa Hutchinson Feb. 7. 1712, 13. Scarf, Ring, Gloves, Escut. Fun.ˡ Sermon.

76. Mrs. Elisa. Addington, March, 5ᵗʰ Scarf, Ring, Gloves.

6 – Mrs. Elisa. Stoddard Apr. 22. 1713. Scarf, good Ring, Gloves, Scutcheon.

6 – Mrs. Martha Patteshall Apr. 23. Scarf and Gloves. Old B. place

Mr. Thomas Brattle May, 21.

Col. Hunt.

SEWALL'S COMMONPLACE BOOK.

[In our first volume, pp. 56, 57, *note*, we called attention to presumed extracts from Sewall's Diary for a period (1677–85) for which we possessed no original. So also, we learn, there is a citation in Palfrey's History, III. p. 348, 349, about Mrs. Randolph, of this date.

We are now able to show that all these quotations are from Sewall's Commonplace Book, a volume in the possession of this Society, and we are thus relieved from the fear that some portion of the Diary might have been lost of late years. We are yet unable to trace the following quotation from Palfrey, III. 348. "May 2, [1681] Had discourse about putting the cross into colors. Captain Hall opposed, and said he would not till the Major [Denison] had it in his. Some spoke with the Major, it seems, that afternoon, and Mr. Mather was with him, who judged it not convenient to be done at this time. So is put a stop to it at present."

Again, "July 11, Captain Walley, instead of having no cross at all, as I supposed, had it unveiled.... Captain Henchman's company and Townsend hindered Captain Walley's lodging their colors, stopping them at the bridge."

Still, we trust, these citations will prove to be taken from some almanac or note-book or letter.]

[Sewall's Commonplace book contains various extracts from books arranged under appropriate heads. Most of the following are placed under that of "De Omene," and contain cross-references. A few items, however, occur separately, and we have endeavored to arrange them chronologically.

The book contains the following note of its beginning: "Samuel Sewall, his Booke, Decemb. 29, 1677. Bound by Jno. Ratcliff."

On the cover is this memorandum:—]

March 1, 77–8. Mr. Tho. Walley, Pastour of Barnst. Ch.ʰ dyed.

Ap. 16, 1678. Mr. Noah Newman, Pastour of Rehoboth Ch.ʰ dyed.

May 9. Mr. Joseph Brown, Fellow of Harvard Colledge dyed.

11. An House, 2 Women and 2 Children burnt at Concord.

June 22. Mr. Edm. Brown, Pastour of Sudbury Ch.ʰ dyed.

Oct. 11.   Sam¹ Simons, Esq. Dep. G: buried.

16.   Mr. Tho. Thacher, Past: 3ᵈ Chʰ Bost. dyed.

Nov. 24.   Mr. Joseph Rowlandson, Preacher at Wethersfield died.

Jan: 4.   Mr. Dan! Russell, Preacher at Charlestown died.

23.   Mr. Peter Hubbard, Pastour of Hingham Chʰ buried.

Feb. 1.   Mr. Ami-Ruhamah Corlett, Fellow of Harv. Col. died.

[Then we find a family record as follows:—]

(P. 87.)   John Sewall, the son of Samuel and Hañah S. was Born Apr. 2, 1677.[1]   Was Baptized Ap. 8 in the South-Meeting-House by the Reverend Mr. Thomas Thacher. I held the child when Baptized. Dyed Sept. 11, 1678, and lyeth buried in the New burying place, on the South side of the grave of his great Grandfather, Mr. Robert Hull.

June 11, 1678.   Samuel Sewall, second son of S. and Han. S. was Born.   Baptized p. Mr. Thomas Thacher June 16. I held him up.

Feb. 3, 1679.   Hañah Sewall was Born, just after a great snow. Baptized Feb. 8 in the New-Meeting-House, p. Mr. Samuel Willard. 1 held her up.   Mr. Thacher dyed in the Autumn, 1678.

May, 21, 1680.   I carry Sam. to Newbury, where his Grandmother nurses him till May 81, to see if change of air would help him against Convulsions; which hope it did, for hath had none there, nor since his coming home.

1681.   Thorsday, December 29th, Elisabeth, Daughter of Samˡˡ and Hañah Sewall is Born.   N. Two of the chief Gentlewomen in Town dyed next Friday night, viz. Mrs. Mary Davis and Mrs. Eliza. Sargent.

Sabbath-day, January 1, 1681.   Elisabeth is Baptized p. Mr. Samuel Willard, I holding her up.   Elisabeth Weeden was Midwife to my Wife bringing forth the four mentioned children.

[We next extract a few notes which are not in the consecutive entries:—]

(P. 8½.)   Mr. Nath. Higginson in a Letter of 4 Mar. 1679–80 writes Dr. Godwin dyed about a fortnight agoe.

---

[1] "Mr. Thomas Parker dyes that April."   Marginal note. — EDS.

(P. 12.) De Autophonia. 1677, Nov. 16. Friday, day after publick Thanksgiving, Jn? Tomlin Hanged himself in his Garret in the day time, fastning his Rope to a pin that held the Rafters at the pot.

Nov. 18. Sabbathday one Williams, an old Man, the Wiñisimet Ferry man cut his own Throat. *Vid Diar.*

Nov. 7, 1680. A Negro Man and Woman murdered themselves.

A certain dweller in the Town of Cambridge made away himself. In his bosom was a Writing to this effect that God did show mercy on great, grievous and desperat Siñers; and therefore he said that he hoped of mercy though he hanged himself.

(P. 12½.) 1678, Apr. 5th. Mr. Josiah Allen, a young Merchant of a very good estate and Account, was slain on board of Benj. Gillam's ship by the accidental firing of a fowling piece, out of a Boat of Joss. Gillam, as they were going from the jolly Ship. *vid. Diar.*

(P. 77½.) Mr. Edmund Quinsey married Mrs. Eliza. Eliot before Tho. Danforth, Esq. Dec. 8, 1680.

Dec? 18, 1680. Josiah Winslow, Esq. Gov? of Plymouth, dyeth after sore Pain with the Gout and Griping. His flesh was opened to the bone on's leggs before he dyed. Thorsday Xr. 23, buried.

Wednesday Xr. 22, '80. John Russell, the Anabaptist minister is buried, scarce having time to read his Print in favour of that Sect; come over in the last ships, Jener or Foy.

Friday, January 14, 1680–1. Benjamin Thwing, Carpenter, one of the South-Church, was goeing from Mount-Hope to Rhode-Island in a Canoo with an Indian, was overset by the wind and Ice, drowned. The Indian escaped.

Tuesday, Feb. 22. Eclips of the Moon. N. Mr. Samuel Worster, Deputy for Bradford, coming down to the Gen. Court, when he was within ¼ Mile of the first Houses of Lin, dyed: Mr. Gidney coming down from Salem saw him dead in the way, went to the next House where were two Men that first saw him; so gave a Warrant for a Jury and his Burial.

Tuesday, March 8, 1680–1. Mr. Edward Mitchelson, Marshall-General is Buried.

Sabbath-day, March 20, 1680–1. Tho. Woodbridge *exit.*

Major William Hathorn dyes April —.

The Reverend Mr. Urian Oakes dyeth, July 24, 1681, Sabbath-day night, suddainly, as to most, who are startled at the newes, being just before the Comencement and he so Learned, Godly, Orthodox a Man and so Discerning of the Times.

[On p. 38 is an account of Mrs. Dyer's monstrous birth, Oct. 17, 1638, "taken out of my Father Sewall's Copy." Also an account of a similar birth, Jany. 10, 1679–80, to the wife of Samuel Dible, of Windsor.]

[We next transcribe that portion which is continued through several pages, and seems to form a Diary for that period.]

(P. 60.) Thorsday, June 21, 1677. Mr. Torrey of Roxbury as he was in the Meetinghouse in Sermon-Time gave a Suddain and amazing Cry, being taken with a Fit of the Falling Sickness. It greatly disturbed the whole Assembly so that Mr. Allen was fain to cease from Preaching for a while.

July 8, 1677. Sabbath-Day. South-Meeting House, *mane*. In Sermon-Time a female Quaker slipt in covered with a Canvas Frock, having her hair dishevelled and Loose, and powdered with Ashes resembling a flaxen or white Perriwigg, her face as black as Ink, being led by two Quakers and followed by two more. It occasioned a great and very amazing Uproar.

June 3, 1680. Mr. Torrey hath another sore Fit in Lectur-time, old Mr. Eliot Preaching.

July 8, two Indians Kill'd and severall carried away by the Mohauks from Spy-Pond at Cambridge; it was done about 1 in the Morn. In the afternoon a Whirlwind ariseth (at first in a small Body) near Sam¹ Stones. Passeth on to Mat. Bridge (P. 73). Passeth by Mat. Bridges, (taking part of Stones Barn with it) Kills John Robbins who was at Hoe, breaking his Arm and jaw-bone. It hurled stones and brake off and transported Trees in an unusual mañer.

Vid. Xr. 16. Mis. Russell in Sermon-Time.

1680–1. Janʸ 25, 1680–1. Tuesday. Thoˢ Eams drops down dead in the Morning at Mr. Pain's stable, as he and others saw Hay thrown before their Horses. He was come to Court about Sherborn Controversy with respect to their Meeting House, its Situation.

Feb 1. Schollars get sooner out of School than ordinary by reason of the Bell's being rung for fire; which was quenched at the House where it begun.

Last night one Dyer of Braintrey shot an Indian to death as he was breaking his window and attempting to get into his House against his will, Saying he would shoot him a Dogg, bec. would not let him come in to light his Pipe. Man was abed. Indian's gun found charg'd, cockᵗ and prim'd in his Hand.

Tuesday night Febr. 1. Pet. Codnar an honest Fisherman goeing to come over the Draw-Bridge, (as is suᵖosed), missed it and was

Drowned: For Feb. 2, his dark Lantern was taken up out of the Crick by the wharf at Low-water. He is suposed to have fallen in about 7. the Tuesday night. Hath left a wife and Children.

Feb. 3. Lectr. Newes is brought of Mr. Deans son Robinson, his Killing a Lion with his Axe at Andover. Not many weeks agoe a young man at New-Cambridge was Kill'd by a Tree himself Felled.

Thorsday Feb. 10. See Mr. Eliot's Sermon.

Tuesday Feb. 22. Ecclips of the Moon. Mr. Samuel Worster, Deputy for Bradford, coming to the Court on Foot, dyes on the Rode about ¼ Mile short of the House at the end of the Town next Ipswich. Vid. P. 78. Newes comes this day of nine men being found dead at Pigeon-Iland near Shelter Iland: 't is feared it may be Jeremiah Jackson.

Vid. p. 79. Sylvanus Davis went out on Saturday to carry Corn and other necessaryes to the Fort at Casco, is driven on the Sand, essaying to put in again in the Sabbath day storm. So the Corn lost and Souldiers disapointed. Men saved.

(P. 78½.) Thorsday, Feb. 24, 1680–1. This morn, the Wife of Mr. Elias Row is found dead in her bed; much blood about her, so some think she was choak'd with it. A Jury was impanelled and 6 grave matrons and a Chirurg[eon], to view the Corps to see if any Violence had been offered her: found none; she and her Husband seldom lay together; she was given to Drink and quarrelling. Her death puts in mind of the Proverb wherein we say such an one hath drunk more than he hath bled to-day.

Friday Feb. 18. Mr. Sam¹ Legg cast away, was bound for Barbados.

Monday March 14. Mr. Noah Floid tells that 3 men essaying to goe from Mount-Hope to Warwick in a Canoo were all drowned about 3 weeks agoe.

Sabbath-day, March 20, 1680–1. Thomas Woodbridge is so burnt in his own Fire, that he Dyeth of the insupportable Torment in about 12 Houres time. Newbury.

Not long agoe an Irish woman living by my Father Hull's Pasture, was found dead, without dore, having her forehead on her hands, as she lay on the ground. Great Rumours and Fears of trouble with the Indians. Persons to Carry a competent number of Arms to Meeting.

N. At Coñecticot the Noise of a Drumme in the air, Vollies of

Shot, Report of Cannons have been Heard by divers; as pr. Letters rec'd this week. Ap. 1. '81.

Mr. Philip Nelson of Rowley wanders away and is lost from Ap. 5, to Satterday Ap. 9. Rowley and Newbury seeking him; on Satterday is found, having walked out of his place to take the air; it was between two Rocks on Crane-Neck. See Bro. Longfellow's Letter.

Goodwife Everit, Winthrop, and Capt. Richard Woode dye suddainly, *vid.* Diar. P. 102.

Sabbath-day, May the first, 1681. Mr. Angier of Cambridg, his Tenant dyes very suddainly and unexpectedly, having been at meeting and riding home with his Neighbour, Agur &c. Look in and smil'd on his wife through the Window, but sunk down before he got in at the doore, and his wife hearing a noise came out; but her Husband scarce spoke ten words before he utterly ceased to speak. The Newes of it came to us yesterday as we were at Diñer. About 3 weeks agoe a little Boy of Braintrey playing with a bean, [P. 84] in's mouth, got it into his wind-Pipe, of which in six or seven dayes he dyed.

Monday, May 2. Mr. Richard Hubbard of Ipswich Farms, dyeth suddainly in the afternoon, goeing to ly on's Bed after diñer was there found dead by his daughter accidentally goeing in thether. *teste* Guil. Gerrish, sen. (*p. me?*)

Satterday, May 7th, there was a Hurrican at Newbury, which blew down Rich. Bartlett's Barn, uncover'd Capt. Pierce's new house at the uper end of Chandler's Lane, blew down the chimneys.

Sabbath-day-night, July 24, 1681. The Reverend Mr. Urian Oakes, President of the College, and Pastour of Cambridge Church Died; scarce any Knowing of his Sickness till his Death was sadly told up and down the street, Monday July 25. *vid.* Diar. p. 109.

Thorsday, Xr. 1, 1681. The well-accomplish'd merch! and Accomptant, Mr. Paul Dudley dyed, being little above 30 yeers old.

Xr. 13, '81. Jonathan Jackson's wife hangs herself in the lower room of her dwelling House near my Father's ware-House.

Xr. 17. Foye arrives, in whom Mr. Randolph and his new wife and family.

Xr. 25. They sit in Mr. Joyliff's Pue; and Mrs. Randolph is observed to make a curtesy at Mr. Willard's naming *Jesus*, even in Prayer time. Since dwells in Hez. Usher's House, where Ministers used to meet.

Satterday, Feb. 11. Is a bloody-colour'd Eclips of the Moon, onely middle of the uper part of a duskish dark.

Feb. 15. Tuesday, 14, past midnight, or Wednesday morn; — the Day the General Court was to sit upon adjournment, — Major

Tho. Savage dyeth suddenly, very suddenly, having been well at the Wedding on Tuesday, and sup'd well at home afterward, and slept well till midnight or past.

Feb. 15, Wednesday. 2 Houses and Barns burnt at Cambridge. Dep! Gov! hardly escaped. Sometime in the Court's sitting, there is a child born near the north Meeting-House, which hath no Tongue at all; or the Tongue grown fast to the roof of the Mouth; one finger too much on one Hand, and one too little on the other: And the Heels right opposite one to another, the (P. 88½) Toes standing to the Right and left outward.

Mar. 24, '81–2. Goodw. Fox dyes suddenly. The Town was sadly alarm'd the Tuesday night before at the Fire at Mr. Wing's, which, had the Wind promoted, a great part of the Town had been consumed, it being near or in the Center.

Thorsday, Novemb. 9, 1682. Cous. Dan! Quinsey Marries Mrs. Anne Shepard Before John Hull, esq. Sam¹ Nowell, esq. and many Persons present, almost Capt. Brattle's great Hall full; Capt. B and Mrs. Brattle there for two. Mr. Willard begun with Prayer. Mr. Tho. Shepard concluded; as he was Praying, Cous. Savage, Mother Hull, wife and self came in. A good space after, when had eaten Cake and drunk Wine and Beer plentifully, we were called into the Hall again to Sing. In Singing Time Mrs. Brattle goes out being ill; Most of the Comp! goe away, thinking it a qualm or some Fit; But she grows worse, speaks not a word, and so dyes away in her chair, I holding her feet (for she had slipt down). At length out of the Kitching we carry the chair and Her in it, into the Wedding Hall; and after a while lay the Corps of the dead Aunt in the Bride-Bed: So that now the strangeness and horror of the thing filled the (just now) joyous House with Ejulation: The Bridegroom and Bride lye at Mr. Airs, son in law to the deceased, going away like Persons put to flight in Battel.

Satterday night, Nov! 11. Twelve Jurors come before my Father, to give Oath as to the Cause and Manner of one Johnson, a Turnour, his imature death; which was by letting a Barrel of Cider into a Trap-dore Cellar;¹ the Board he stood on gave way, he fell in, and the end of the Barrel upon his Jaw and Kill'd him outright. Jury came to swear about eight a clock.

One Blood of Concord about 7 days since or less was found dead in the woods, leaning his Brest on a (P 89½) Logg: Had been seeking some Creatures. Oh! what strange work is the Lord about to bring to Pass.

---

¹ "Just by Cous. Quinsey's." Marginal note. — EDS.

The Wednesday fortnight before Mrs. Brattles Death, Mr. Gardener of Salem, who lives p. the Meeting-House, going into his Shop after Lecture to open it, as he was hanging up a net of Cotton-wool, fell down dead over his Threshold: which made a great Hubbub.

Nov: 12, at night or even, Capt. Benj. Gillam's Mate is drowned off the outward wharf.

Friday, Nov: 17. one Smith is drowned, coming up from Mr. Edwards, sailing for Lond[on]. Not many weeks before, a Man fell into the Dock, up by my Father's Ware-House, and was drowned: and Josiah Belcher, Sen' was drowned at Weymouth.

Sabbath-day, Nov: 19. Mr. Edw. Winslow, Ship M:, dyed suddenly: He took Physick the Friday before and John Alcock discours'd with him, he seeming to him no iller than Men ordinarily are when taking Physick. A Woman dyed suddenly at the North end of the Town.

Tuesday, Nov: 28, '82. One Horton coming from Nevis, makes the Land this day, and stands in; but the Rain and Snow take him so that in the night drives him over Rocks and Sholes, cast Anchor; but all Cables break. So about 3 a clock at night, that violent Storm strands the Ship on Nahant Beach, about ¼ mile to the Northward of Pulling Point Gut; the Ship about 100 Tun. Persons on Board 13, 3 whereof drowned; 4 perished in the Cold, not being able to grope out the way to Mr. Winthrops: and 6 onely escaped: 3 of the above if not all four, lay frozen like sticks, in a heap. One of the six was so frozen that will hardly escape. Very little goods saved. About 200 £ in P ⅝ lost.

Febr. 9. 1682–3. A considerable deal of Snow being on the Ground, there falls such plenty of warm Rain as that the Waters swell so as to do much damage. Ipswich Dam and Bridge is carried away by the Flood and Ice violently coming down; so that they now go over in a Boat, Horse and Men. Rowly Mill Dam also spoyled, and generally much harm done in (P. 90) Dams and Bridges; so that 'tis judged many Thousands will scarce repair the Loss. Woburn hath suffered much. Roxbury Bridge carried away just as persons on it; so that a woman was near drowning.

Satterday, March 22, 1683–4, there was an extraordinary high Tide, which did much hurt at Boston and Charlestown, coming into Houses and Ware-Houses that stood low. All that I hear of at Cambridge, Charl. and here, say 'tis higher than ever any was known before.

Wednesday, Oct: 29, a Maid's Brains shot out, her head broke all to pieces, at Salem.

Friday Nov: 28, 1684. W: Allen, a Plumer, receives a blow by a piece that was used for a Scaffold falling on's head, of which he dyes at night. Boston. About a fortnight agoe, one at Sparks, the Ordinary at Ipswich near the Meetinghouse, falls down stairs or the like, and dies. About that time Jn° Poor of Newbury perrisheth in the Snow, near the Fresh-Meadows, about a Mile from my Father's Farm.

(P. 90½) Wednesday, Nov: 15, 1682. Mr. Sherman Ordains Mr. Nath. Gookin Pastor of Cambridge-Church: Mr. Eliot gives the Right hand of Fellowship, first reading the Scripture that warrants it. Mr. Sherman, Eliot and Mather laid on Hands. Then Mr. Gookin ordain'd Deacon Stone and Mr. Clark Ruling Elders. The Presence of God seem'd to be with his People. Mr. Jonathan Danforth, the Dep! Governours onely Son, lay by the Wall, having departed on Monday Morn, of a Consumption. Tis a comfortable day and much People at the Ordination. I go and come on foot in Comp: of Mr. Zadori, the Hungarian, whom I find to be an Arminian.

(P. 92.) Wednesday, Apr. 25, 1688. I went to Gov: Bradstreet, to enquire about the Custom of Swearing in New England: He told me That of lifting up the Hand had been the Ceremony from the begiñing; that He and some others did so swear on board the Ship, 1630. And that He never Knew an Oath administred any other way after he came on Shoar.

Sir, it is all one to touch a Book and swear by a Book. Fox. Martyrol. Henry the 4th, p. 702 and 701. &c &c &c. [Various authorities are cited, the passage above being among other citations under the head of "De Juramento."]

(P. 108½.) Mr. Joshua Gee, sometime Captive in Algeer, tells me June 11, 1694, that the Turks observe an Hebdomadal Revolution as we do; Our first day of the week is their first day of the week; And they call the days by their Order in the Week; One, Two &c. If they have any notable piece of work to doe, they chuse to begin it upon the first day of the Week, bec. God began his Works on that day.

[There is also a full account of the trial of Rev. Thomas Chiever, Jr., of Malden, which is briefly mentioned in Vol. I. pp. 130, 131.]

(P 132 of orig.)   At MALDEN, Wednesday, Apr. 7th. 1686.

A Council of the 3 Ch^{hs} of Chr^t in Boston, met. Persons were Mr. James Allin, Joshua Moody, John Wiswall, Mr. Elisha Cook, Mr. Isaac Addington, Mr. Henry Allin, Mr. Increase Mather, Mr. Cotton Mather, Major John Richards, Mr. Adam Winthrop, Mr. Daniel Stone, Lt Richard Way, Mr. Saml Willard, Sam Sewall, Jacob Eliot. Met at the House of Father Green; Mr. Allin went to Prayer, when discoursed whether should have 2 Moderators or one; Mr. Allin put it to vote, and carried for one, being but a small Company. Then voted for a Moderator by Papers. Mr. Increase Mather was chosen, had more than ten votes and but 15 Persons in all. Discoursed of our work, then went into the Publick. Mr. Moderator prayed. When had heard some Debates there, went to our Quarters, had the witnesses and Mr. Tho. Chiever face to face. Mr. Chiever, the Father, desired to be present, was admitted and bid wellcom, except when Council debated in private all alone (Mr. Sam. Parris present throughout, though not of the Council).

In the evening Mr. Chiever the Pastor was sent for, Mr. Moodey and others acquainted him how grievous his carriage had been and that day not so humble and in such a frame as ought; told him expected not an Answer, but that should sleep on't. Debated considerably what to do till about 10 at night Mr. Moderator pray'd, went to Bed. Mr. Moderator and his son to Mr. Wigglesworth's, some to Mr. Chiever, Major Richards and self Kept the House. In the Morn, Thorsday, Ap. 8, Mr. Moderator went to prayer: read over what was drawn up, then discours'd about it. Sent for Mr. Chiever, to see what had to say; then not finding satisfaction, all agreed on the following Declaration and Advice.

The Elders and Messingers assembled in Council at Maldon, April 7, 1686, at the Request of the Church there, after humble Invocation of the Name of God for his Guidance in the solemn Case propos'd unto them, do declare and advise as follows.

1. We find that Mr. Tho. Chiever, the present Pastor of the Church in Maldon, has been accused as Guilty of great Scandals, by more than 2 or 3 witnesses; and that since his being in Office-Relation Particularly, he is by two or three Witnesses charged with speaking such words as are scandalous breaches of the Third Comandment, as apears by the Testimony of Mrs. Eliza. Wade and Abigail Russell. He is moreover accused with Shamefull and abominable Violations of the Seventh Comandment. There are several who have testifyed that they heard him use light and obscene expressions (not fit to be named) in an Ordinary at Salem, as by the Testimony of Samuel Sprague, Jacob Parker, Isaac Hill: Also as he was travailing

on the Rode, as p. the Testimony of Thomas, Esther and Eliza. New-hall.

2. We find that although Mr. Chiever has been convicted of very scandalous Evils since his being a Preacher in Maldon, the Church there has declin'd all Testimonies against him as to Scandals comitted before his Ordination; as also some other Testimonies respecting matters very criminal since that; because they judged the Witnesses on account of Prejudices and otherwise, incompetent; upon which Consideration we have also waved these Testimonies.

3. We find that in Aug! 9, 1685, Mr. Chiever made an Acknowledgement of some Evils to the Brethren of that Church, whereto he stands related; and that the most part of them were willing to take up with a slender satisfaction: But that on the next Lord's-day, he manifested before the Congregation so little sense and sorrow for his great sins, as that the generality of the Brethren were more dissatisfied than formerly.

We find by our own enquiries since we met together, that Mr. Chiever has absolutely deny'd some things, which are by sufficient Witnesses prov'd against him. Mr. Chiever's filthy words testifyed by Tho., Esther, and Elizabeth Newhal, he utterly deny'd to Lᵗ Samˡ Sprague, also to Cornet Green and his son, saying that Thomas Newhal was forsworn. Likewise he did to Capt. Sprague and Tho. Skiñer utterly deny that ever he spake the words at Salem, so fully prov'd against him.

Also we find, that as to some particulars he pretends he does not remember them: Nor have we seen that humble penitential frame in him when before us, that would have become him: but have cause to fear that he has been too much accustomed to an evil course of Levity and Profaneness.

These things considered, we conceive it to be Duty and accordingly advise the Church of Maldon, to Suspend Mr. Tho. Chiever from the Exercise of his ministerial Function; and also to debar him from partaking with them at the Lord's Table, for the space of Six Weeks, untill which time the Council will adjourn themselves, to meet at Boston. And that in case he shall in the mean while manifest that Repentance which the Rule requires, they should confirm their Love to him, and (if possible) improve him again in the Lord's Work among them.

And this, our Advice, is grounded on these Scriptures and Reasons. (1). Among the Lord's People in the dayes of the O. Testament, no man might be permitted to execute the Priest's office that had a blemish: He might not come nigh to offer the offerings of the Lord. Levit. 21, 17, 21, which teaches that Men under moral blemishes, are unfit for holy ministrations, untill they be, in a way of Repentance, healed. (2) It is in the New Testament required, that an Elder should be sober and of good behaviour, and moreover he must have a good Report of them that are without, 1 Tim. 3, 2, 7. (3) Christ's Discipline ought to be exercised impartially, without respect to Persons. 1 Tim. 5, 21. Nor does Mr. Chiever's standing in a Sacred Office-Relation any way lessen, but greatly aggravate his sin. (4) There is no probability that Mr. Chiever's Ministry will be blessed for good to Souls, untill such time as his Conversation shall declare him to be a true penitent. Mat. 5, 13.

Finally, we exhort and advise our beloved Brethren of the Church of Maldon to set a day apart, solemnly to humble themselves by Fasting and Prayer before the Lord under this awfull dispensation, and for whatever failings have attended them, as to the management of their Differences, in this hour of Temptation which they have been subject unto. Particularly, for not observing the Rules of Christ, in endeavouring to prevent Evils by giving seasonable notice to Mr. Chiever of their Dissatisfactions. And for that want of Love, and for that bitterness of Spirit, which appears in sundry of them. So we pray the God of Love and Peace and Truth to dwell among you.

INCREASE MATHER, Moderator,
In the Name, and with the unanimous
Consent of the whole Council.

Note. Mr. Chiever was ordained July 27, 1681, Wednesday, Mr. Oakes dying the Sabbath before.

———

Thorsday, Ap. 8. the Bell was rung; went in publick. Mr. Moderator pray'd, read the Council's Report. Mr. Wigglesworth spake, thank'd him and the Council; said had cause to condemn themselves, as for other sins, so their sudden laying Hands on Mr. Chiever; and now God was whiping them with a Rod of their own making. Mr. Chiever the Father, stood up and pathetically desir'd his son might speak, but Mr. Moderator and others judg'd it not convenient, he not having by what he said given the Council encouragement. Mr. Allin pray'd; went to Diñer; Council adjourned to that day 6 weeks. Came Home well.

ZADORI'S LETTER.

[In Vol. I. p. 97, of Sewall's Diary, mention is made of "Zadori." The reference was obscure, and no light upon it presented itself to us as the sheets passed through the press. We have since received from abroad the following letter, which, however, does but little to clear the obscurity attaching to a scholar of that name who, it seems, made a visit to Boston. The text of the manuscript copied for us seems in some places to be doubtful, and other difficulties stand in the way of a confident translation. We offer such an one as may serve the occasion. — EDS.]

Bodl: MS. Tanner xxxv. f. 105.

Letter addressed : —

"To the most Reverend Father in ^{God} William, by the grace of blessed Jesus Lord Arch-Bishop of Canterbury these humbly present. London." [1]

Vir fidelis & Dei timens, Christique amantissime, Salve !

Non omnes quos tellus fert mortales despicato terræ pulveri adhærescunt, Amplissime Præsul, sed numerosa eorum portio, relictis rusticanæ turbæ flagellis, opificumque instrumentis, altioribus animum applicat, potiorisque sui partis, animæ puta, perfectionem indefesse quæritat. Ingenerasse scilicet Natura hominibus quosdam Videtur igniculos, qui desiderium sciendi stimulorum instar magnoperè excitant. Unde fieri consuevit, ut rerum altiorum avidiùs cupidi mortales, nullâ scientiâ satiari valeant, verum quantò propiùs in cognitione rerum, cum Divinarum, tum humanarum perfectioni accessit animus, tantò majus desiderium sciendi capiat incrementum. Quod maximè laudabile esse, non possumus non asserere, cum sui parare perfectionem sit longè laudatissimum. Puto hinc me facile impetraturum à beata Tua Reverentia excusationem, quod per duos planè annos inter Vos, mansuetioribus musis feci rem. Quis enim adeo excoecatus, qui tam religiosissimum Orbis Christiani sidus, & perenne literarum decus, immensamque Patriæ & sæculi spem, facile relinquat ? Si præsertim loquar de memetipso, Proh Deum immortalem ! quanta nos Hungaros, in hac decrepita mundi senectâ, ruina literarum operit, quam

---

[1] William Sancroft was at this time Archbishop of Canterbury.

turpe & securum militiæ nostræ ocium irrupit. Videre siccis puto nemo posset oculis. Ubi non nisi Mars gaudet prœliis, & nos inter tot tantaque funesta bella pendemus potiùs quam sedemus. Ducimur, & portamur per vastam eremum. Rapimur, dispergimur, in diversa trahimur : ità ut nec coeptum opus deserere, nec suprà vires ferre valeamus. Et ipse cùm anno hoc ipso Patriam versùs iter facere meditarer, intempestivè nimis impedivit Hungariæ recens conditio, ità ut contraria via coactus sum [?] ire, quasi è tergo Hungariam intueri plurimum delectarer. Ego igitur, mi Pater Reverendissime (quod solum possum) Deum Optimum, Maximum, qui Te mihi providit, obnixè deprecor, ut quando Tibi talem debitorem dedit, qui nunquàm solvendo sit futurus, beneficentiam istam quam mihi 29 die Maji, anni 1682, tam effusus impendebas, ipse Tibi dignetur pro sua benignitate rependere, tum ut nos ab hoc ærumnoso & procelloso sæculo in suam requiem, pro sua miseratione perducat, ubi non erit opus epistolis, ubi non distinebit nos paries, ubi non arcebit à colloquio janitor, sed gaudio perfruemur æterno. Nunc pro tempore apud Novos-Anglos in America hospitor, quid mecum hic faciant ignoro. Gens revera hæc est non modo pietati addicta, & christiana charitate imbuta, verum & Regiæ Majestati addictissima. Nam toto hoc tempore, quibus apud hos hospitor peregrinus, nil tale quid audivi sicut in Scotia & Anglia à quibusdam sceleratissimis, contrà Sacræ Regiæ Majestatis Thronum, blasphemia verba ex impuris palatis eructantibus. Teror corde vehementer quod nil sit in me, vel penes me, quo tantam beneficentiam Sanctæ Tuæ Reverentiæ pensare possem, qui sum eroque ad finem usque hujus vitæ Tuæ dominationi addictissimus ac fidelis servus. Is igitur qui Dominationi Vestræ talem debitorem dedit, qui nunquàm solvendo sit futurus, Te donis suis locupletet, & in multos annos Ecclesiæ suæ conservet, Serenissimam Sacræ Regiæ Majestatem, Nobilissimos Proceres, adeôque Omnes Potentissimi Regni vestri Ordines protegat, & omni benedictionum genere quam pinguissimè cumulet ; ad veræ pietatis & Regni Christi propagationem ævo largissimo tueatur. Et tandem post seros vitæ laudabiliter exactæ annos, ad nunquàm intermoritura & desitura cœlestis vitæ gaudia, solenni Angelorum comitatu introducat. Ubi cum Deo Patre ingenito [?] & uniprocedente Paracleto, gaudio perfruemini æterno.

Ità animitùs precatur clàm qui hæc palam Vobis peroptat.

Salutis Vestræ avidissimus Stephanus Zadori Pannonio-Hungarus de S. P.

Scribebam hospes & peregrinus celeri cursu defessa manu ad lucernam jamjam lectulo imminens Bostonii Novi-Anglorum, anno vitæ meæ 29. anno verò beatissimi beatæ Mariæ Virginis Filii Jesu 1682. 10. 8bris.

TRANSLATION.

Faithful and God-fearing man, most loving of Christ, Health!

Most Illustrious Primate, — Not all the mortal men whom the world sustains cling to the mean dust of the earth, but a considerable portion of them, turning from the vexations of the rustic crowd and from the tools of the workshops, devote their minds to higher objects, and unweariedly strive for the perfection of their nobler part, namely, the soul. For Nature seems to have generated in men certain sparks which intensely rouse as with a goad the craving for knowledge. Whence it is wont to happen that men, keenly craving higher things, can find satisfaction in no attainment, but the nearer the mind approaches towards perfection in the knowledge alike of divine and human things, the more does a desire for such knowledge take increase. We cannot refrain from asserting that this is greatly praiseworthy, inasmuch as it is superlatively laudable to be perfecting one's self. So I think I may readily claim from your Blessed Reverence an excuse for having for two full years devoted myself among you to the more gentle muses. For who would be so blind as slightingly to desert the most devout star of the Christian Sphere, the perennial glory of letters, and the loftiest hope of his country and his age? If especially I may speak of myself, By the Immortal God! what a wreck of literature is visited upon us Hungarians in this decrepit old age of the world, how has a base and confident ease broken in upon our military vigor. I think no one can see this with dry eyes, when only Mars revels in battles, and we, amidst so many and such direful wars, hang in suspense rather than rest. We are dragged and borne over a vast desert. We are caught up, dispersed and scattered, so that we can neither abandon a work undertaken, nor bear it on beyond our strength [?]. And when I myself was this very year contemplating a journey to my country, the recent condition of Hungary inopportunely opposed me, so that I was compelled to go in a contrary direction, as if it were my highest pleasure to behold Hungary behind me. I, therefore, Most Reverend Father, (it is all that I can do,) earnestly beseech the Great and Good God, who has provided you for me, that, since he has given to you such a debtor as can never pay his debt, he in his benignity will vouchsafe to repay to you that beneficence which you so lavishly bestowed upon me on the 29th of May, 1682, and then that in his own mercy he may guide us out of this oppressed and stormy era to his own repose, where there will be no need of letters, where no wall will separate us, where no janitor will restrain our intercourse, but we shall enjoy delights forever. Now for a season I am living as a guest with the New-Englanders in America; I know not what they may do with me here. Verily this is a people, not only devoted to piety and imbued with Christian charity, but most loyal also to the Royal Majesty. For during this whole time, in which [?][1] I, a stranger, have been their guest, I have heard nought such as I had heard in Scotland and England from some most wicked men, belching from impure lips blasphemous words against the throne of the Sacred Royal Majesty. I am greatly grieved at heart, that there is nothing in me, or in my power, by which I can repay such kindness of your Sacred Reverence, — I, who am, and will be even to the end of this life, a most devoted and faithful subject of your Lordship. May He, therefore, who has made me such a debtor to your Lordship as can never pay his debt, enrich you with his gifts, and preserve you for many years to his Church; may He also protect the most Serene Majesty of his Sacred Royalty, the most noble Lords, and all orders of your most potent kingdom, and heap upon them most richly every kind of blessing; may he watch over them for the propagation of true piety and of the kingdom of Christ, to the most distant age [?]. And at length, after the late years of a nobly-spent life, may he bring you to the never-dying and endless joys of the celestial state in the holy fellowship of the Angels, where, with the uncreated God the Father, and the one-proceeding [?] Paraclete, you shall find the fruition of eternal bliss. So, heartily in secret prays he who openly craves for you such things, Stephen Zadori, of Pannonian Hungary, de S. P. — most desirous of your welfare.

As a guest and a stranger, I write with a running pen, with a wearied hand, by lamplight, just before going to bed [?], at Boston, in New-England, in the 29th year of my life and in the year of the most Blessed Jesus, son of the Blessed Mary, 1682, October 10th.

---

[1] This conjectural rendering of an ungrammatical text reads *quo* for *quibus*. Another conjectural version would be, "Among those with whom I have been a stranger-guest."

INTRODUCTORY NOTE.

THE three following pamphlets have been reprinted, because they deal with a controversy in which Sewall was deeply interested and in which he took a part, and also because of their great rarity. For a copy of the first, we are indebted to Colonel Joseph L. Chester, of London, who procured a transcript of an example in the British Museum; for the second and third, we are indebted to the courtesy of the John Carter Brown Library and the Harvard College Library, respectively.

It will be noticed that the first is a violent attack on Governor Dudley; the second, an able defence of him; and the third, a renewed attack.

They are entitled, respectively, " A Memorial of the Present Deplorable State of New England," &c., " A Modest Enquiry," &c., and " The Deplorable State of New England," &c.

In view of the charge made in the preface to the " Modest Enquiry," it may be safely assumed that the first tract was *not* published in Boston as it pretended to be, but was prepared here, and printed in London, where it appeared in July, 1707. Sewall writes under date of Nov. 1, 1707 (*post*, ii. 197), " after coming from Council, I read the Book printed against the Governour *in London*. I had not seen it before." So again under date of Nov. 21, 1707 (*post*, ii. 200). " Some " (of the Council) " began to be hot to send for the Book wherein the Affidavits are, and Mr. M.'s letter; and to burn it: others were for deliberation."

Of the merits of the controversy we say nothing; a few points of interest may be indicated. Thus it is evident that Rev. Cotton Mather was the inciter, and perhaps the compiler, of the first pamphlet. The R. A. whose letter is on p. 42*, is possibly R. Armstrong, as that name best agrees with the " Mr. Ar—nge " on p. 81*.

It seems evident that many thought that Cotton Mather had been guilty of duplicity; but at all events the mask was now dropped. Quincy writes (Hist. Harv. Univ., i. p. 201), " the election of Leverett " (as President) " was insupportably grievous to Increase Mather and his son. They had anticipated that the choice would have fallen upon one or the other of them. Between them there was no rivalry. For the disappointment of both, they were not prepared. Their indignation was excited against Dudley, who, as they thought, had buoyed up their hopes until he had arranged measures and agents to insure their defeat."

In view of these pamphlets, we may perhaps conclude that the dissimulation was the other way. It looks rather as if Cotton Mather, aspiring to the presidency of the college, had pretended friendship to Governor Dudley; and, concluding that the election would be settled in 1707, he gave vent to his malice by sending to England the manuscript of this first pamphlet.

At all events, the reception of copies of it in Boston must have terminated all hopes of further friendship between the Mathers and Dudley. Their abusive letters of Jan. 20, 1707–8, reveal their bitterness of soul. (See Collections, first series, Vol. III. pp. 126–138.)

The "Modest Enquiry" was the immediate retort; and the anecdote concerning Cotton Mather, printed on p. 81*, must have been a bitter pill to his admirers.

The preface to the third tract is signed A. H.; possibly, as Palfrey suggests, the Alexander Holmes whose name is appended to the petition on the last page. He does not seem to have been a resident here, and was perhaps one of the persons "trading thither." The most noticeable item therein is Samuel Sewall's protest (on p. 111*) against the statement that the Council has passed a vote *unanimously.* He dwells upon it in his Journal (*post*, ii. 202).

It is Palfrey's opinion (Hist., IV. 310, note) that Mather was "concerned in the composition" of this third pamphlet; and, as Sewall quarrelled with him some years before (see Journal, *post*, ii. 45–46), this may account for the slurs on p. 124*. "Nevertheless, we doubt not but in the large Province of Massachusetts there may be found an Hundred Men as fit to be Counsellors, as S. S. or J. C. or P. T." These names we interpret to be, Samuel Sewall, Jonathan Corwin, John Cushing or Joseph Church, and Penn Townsend.

We trust our readers will find in these pamphlets a sufficiently lively picture of the questions which agitated the colony at that date to warrant the space which we have given to them.

EDS.

A

MEMORIAL

Of the Prefent Deplorable State of

New-England.

A
MEMORIAL

Of the Prefent Deplorable STATE of

New-England,

With the many Difadvantages it lyes under,
by the *Male-Adminiftration* of their
Prefent GOVERNOUR,

𝕵𝖔𝖘𝖊𝖕𝖍 𝕯𝖚𝖉𝖑𝖊𝖞, Efq.

And his Son *P A U L,* &c.

TOGETHER WITH

The feveral *Affidavits* of People of Worth,
Relating to feveral of the faid Governour's Mercenary and Illegal Proceedings, but particularly his
private Treacherous Correfpondence with Her Majefty's Enemies the *French* and *Indians.*

To which is Added, A *Faithful,* but *Melancholy* Account
of feveral Barbarities lately Committed upon Her Majefty's Subjects, by the faid *French* and *Indians,* in the Eaft and Weft Parts
of *NEW-ENGLAND.*

Faithfully Digefted from the feveral Original Letters, Pa-
pers, and M S S. *by* Philopolites.

Printed in the Year, MDCCVII. and Sold by *S. Phillips*
N. Buttolph, and *B. Elliot.* Bookfellers in *Bofton.*

A

MEMORIAL

Of the Prefent Deplorable S T A T E of

New-England.

THE Inhabitants of *New-England* had for many years before the Late Happy *Revolution*, Enjoy'd the Liberty and Property of as Free and Eafy a *Charter* as a People could Defire; and this too, with as much Satisfaction and Loyalty on their part, as Malice and Envy on that of their Enemies; who, from a Perfecuting Spirit, looking upon this their *Charter* with an evil Eye, took up an Implacable Refolution of Robbing them of it. They had no fooner Effected this, but a vaft Scene of Mifery appear'd; and they found among the principal Inftruments of this Mifchief, *One,** whom their own Womb had brought forth, and whofe Breafts had Nourifh'd!* But the Unhappy (or rather Happy) Reign of the Late K. J. running Precipitantly upon its own Ruin, made well for the deliverance of *New-England;* without which doubtlefs the People had fell a facrifice to *French* and Popifh Slavery.

[2] We fhall not Recriminate here the Mifmanagements of the then Governour Sir *Edmund Androfs,* fince that Gentleman is now in a Future State; but by the way, we think it highly Neceffary to fay fome Matters of Fact, of the prefent Governour *Dudley,* who, (under the faid Sir *E. Androfs*) acted as Prefident of the Council, and One of the *Quorum* in all his Affairs.

* The prefent Governour, J. Dudley, Efq. is a Native of New England, Born at or near a place call'd Roxbury, 2 Miles from Bofton:

The Behaviour of this Man, as foon as he arrived, ftruck in with the firft Opportunity to difcover him of a Mercenary Intereft. Indeed, the People were fomething Surpris'd to fee the publick Offices and Places of Truft fnatch'd from them, and Conferr'd on Strangers on one hand, and the Avarice and Beggary of a Crew of Mercenary Fellows, Supported by Extortion on t'other. But, when the Prefident was pleafed, out of an Active and Paffive Principle, to tell our Countreymen, in open Council, *That the People in* New-England *were all Slaves; and that the* only *Difference between Them and Slaves, was their not being* Bought *and Sold: And that they muft not think the Privileges* of Englifhmen *would follow them to the end of the World.* I say, when the People heard this, they lookt upon themfelves in a manner Loft. On one Hand they faw their Enemies invefted with a full Power in the Government; on t'other they faw themfelves not only turn'd out of the Publick Miniftry, but under a Neceffitous Fear of being Quiet, left their Eftates fhould be Siezed, and themfelves Imprifoned. On this fide they faw their Wives and Children, their Fathers, Mothers, &c. Butchered daily by a Handful of Barbarous Indians; on t'other fide, little or no Refiftance made by their Armies, which were Commanded by thofe of the *Romifh* Religion; infomuch that it feem'd rather an intended Maffacre, than a Defire of putting an End to a Diabolick and Bloody War. They faw then, that they had to their Coft, brought forth a *Prophet*, who told them they were Slaves; and they then faw his Prophecy fulfilling: In fine, they faw all this, but perceiv'd no way to efcape; till throwing up their Cryes to Heaven, they were animated by Divine Power, to Refcue themfelves and Children from the approaching Ruin.

[3] Under the Preffure of all thefe Grievances, they Unanimoufly arofe, upon the coming in of the late King *William*, of Bleffed Memory, Siezed the Government for His Majefty's Ufe; and, amongft the reft of the Authors of their Miferies, not unjuftly Imprifon'd this their prefent Governour.

From that time *New-England* took Heart, and concluded that Heaven was removing from them all the Plagues in their Land. They indeed Thankfully Rejoiced to fee themfelves Reftored to their Ancient Liberty, as afterwards in a great Meafure they were by another Miniftry.

And thus much for the former Actions of the Author of the following Matters of Fact, which has rendered His Love to his Native Country, His Veneration for the Liberty and Property of a Free People, His Fidelity, Juftice, and Loyalty, in delivering the Oppreffed, and detecting the Queen's Profefs'd Enemies, but the Reverſe of Good Mens Actions, and ought to be Remembered only as ſo many Monuments of Infamy.

But to come down to our Memorial, and inform the World of the modern Miſmanagements of this unhappy Gentleman, we humbly Declare, That

THE Trade with the *French* and *Indians*, being ſo countenanced by the Governour, that without ſpeedy Remedy, the Country is in great Danger of being Ruined, which will plainly Appear as follows:

Firſt, In the Year 1705, The Governour ſent his Son *William Dudley*, with Captain *Vetch*, to *Canada*, under a pretence of Redeeming Captives; but brought very few back to *Boſton* of thoſe that were there, and them of the Meaneſt ſort, leaving the Principal of the ſaid Captives behind, to give them occaſion of going again, that they might have a Pretence to Colour their Treacherous Deſign of Trading, as Appears by the ſaid *Vetch's* Acknowlecgment of going to Settle a Correſpondency with the Enemy, and carrying a Cargo out with him of 800 l. which, according to their Diſpoſal, [4] might amount to near 3000 l. as particularly Shot, which was Sold at 13 *Sous per* Pound; whereof they carried a conſiderable Quantity, also Rigging, Pitch, Iron, and other Neceſſaries, fit for ſupplying the *Indians* and *French;* and this done under a Colour, of the ſaid *Vetch's* going to get in a Debt due to him, from the *French*, of 800 l. with the Governour's Approbation.

Secondly, For Settling a Correſpondency with the *French* Governour at Port-Royal, for Exchange of Priſoners; Whereas it was indeed, only a Cover for an Illegal Trade; when, at the ſame time, the *French* there, were drove to ſuch extreme Hardſhips, for want of Ammunition Proviſion, &c. that moſt of their Principal People were forced to go out a Privateering on our Coaſts, who were, afterwards taken and brought into *Boſton;* particularly one *Battis*, a Man of great Note and Service among the Enemy, who had been a Barbarous, Murdering Fellow, to the *Engliſh:* He, with all the other *French* Priſoners, were ſent to *Canada* and *Port-Royal*, and Diſcharged; but great part of our People that were Priſoners, were left behind at the ſame time, and that, becauſe our Governour had been falſe in his Promiſe, to the *French* Governour, who had reſtrained the *Indians* from diſturbing our Fiſhery, and indeed would not allow them any Ammunition for a conſiderable time, till our Governour taking that Opportunity of the *Indians* great Want, countenanced a trade with them, and ſupply'd them by the Veſſels that were ſent as Tranſports (as aforeſaid) to fetch

Prifoners; when at the fame time they were made Veffels of Merchandize, as appears by the *Indian* Traders on their Tryal.

Thirdly, The Country are at a vaft Charge, in maintaining an Army Yearly, to March feveral Hundred Miles up into the Country, to Deftroy the *Indians* Corn, the better to difenable them to Subfift; for they have been fo Reduced (as by Information of the Captives) that a great part of them would Perifh for Want, were it not for the Supply they had from the faid *Indian* Traders; who particularly, Sold about Eight Quarts of *Indian* Corn for one large *Beaver* Skin; which Trade has been all along countenanced by the Governour, which fufficiently Appears, by his being always Unwilling [5] the Prifoners taken in that Trade fhould be Fined, or Punifhed, even owned by *Vetch*, as in his Petition more at large, is fet forth.

Fourthly, The Country was at a great Expence, in Erecting a Fortification at *Cafco Bay*, and maintaining a number of Soldiers for fecuring the fame, thereby to fupprefs the Enemy, and keep fure Footing in that part of the Country, and the Governour, through fome Defign or Neglect, did fuffer thofe Soldiers to remain there without any Commiffion Officer, to the great Diffatisfaction and Dread to the Soldiers; infomuch, that they Declared to Captain *Cally*, (a Member of the Affembly at *Bofton*) that when the Enemy came upon them, they would Surrender the Fort, and dare not Refift for want of a Commiffion. Then Captain *Cally* made Application to the Affembly, which he found Sitting when he came to *Bofton*, and they reprefented to the Governour, that fpeedy care might be taken, that fome Perfon might be Commiffionated to Command that Fort, which, with a great deal of Difficulty, was at laft Obtained.

Fifthly, And further, as to the Governour's countenancing this Private and Illegal Trade, the Country has been at vaft Expence, occafioned thereby; infomuch, that at one Seffions the laft Summer, the Affembly were forc'd to raife 33000 Pounds, for Supporting and Maintaining the Charge they were put to, by the Enemies Invafions, after they had a Supply; that whereas, if things were rightly Managed, and the Enemy kept back for want of thofe Supplies, one Third Part of the faid Sum might have anfwer'd the End. The *Indians* that were Supply'd by thofe Traders, are the only People that deftroyed our *Eaftern* Parts, the Fifhery, and the Coaft of *Accady;* and alfo the very fame that were at Deftroying of *New-found-land;* particularly one *Efcombuet*, a Principal Commander among them, who is generally one that Heads the *Indians*, when they come to Deftroy the *Englifh* in *New-England*.

Sixthly, The Governour, with his Son *Paul*, not being Content with what Money they come fairly by, and over greedy of Gain, are very Screwing and Exacting upon the People, particularly upon fundry Inhabitants, taking away their Priviledge in catching [6] of Whales, a Priviledge they have Enjoyed many years before ; that is, (under a Pretence of drift Fifh) what Whales are taken by Her Majefty's Subjects, he takes from them by Force, not giving them the Liberty of a Tryal at *Common Law*, but for his own Ends, decides the Matter in the Admiralty, where his Son *Paul* is the Queen's Attourny and Advocate, thereby Encroaching the whole to themfelves, a thing never heard of before, and very much to the Prejudice of Her Majefty's good fubjects there, and that without Remedy.

Seventhly, As to the Addrefs the Governour Obtained, pretended to come over from the General Affembly at *Bofton*, in his favour, for his Continuance, it was no more than what he Clandeftinely procured, by fending to his particular Friends ; fuch, who being either Related to him, or bore Commiffions under him, dare not deny his Requeft, and was never approved nor allowed of by the Affembly ; but on the Contrary, had not the Majority of the Country, waited in Expectation of Her Majefty's Favour, in fending another Governour, they would largely have fignified their Refentments and Diffatisfaction, in the Adminiftration of *Dudley's* Government.

Eighthly, While the Great and General Affembly at *Bofton* were Sitting, there arrived a Flagg of Truce from *Canada*, with a haughty Demand of the Governour, for all the *French* Prifoners, charging of him with breach of Promife, which was the occafion of the *French* Governour's not fending feveral of the Prifoners, particularly a Minifter that was taken Captive at *Derefield*, detained by the *French*, who might have been Difcharged with fundry others.

Ninthly, The Lower Houfe, miftrufting the *French* Flagg of Truce coming upon a Trading Defign, as well as for Prifoners, ordered the Flagg of Truce to be diligently Searched, who found on Board their Veffel fundry new Arms and Ammunition, hid in Private Places, particularly new Bullets, hid among Pease, and yet denied by the Commander, who was an *Englifh* Renagado, which Ammunition being brought before the Affembly, were generally concluded to be Bought in *Bofton ;* whereupon, the Governour in- [7] terpofing, the Matter was hufhed up and Conniv'd at, to the great Diffatisfaction of the Affembly, and Country in general.

This being realy the State of *New-England,* and its Provinces, it may very well be called Deplorable, when it is render'd the very Scene of Arbitrary Power, with all that's Miferable : But to proceed, before I come down to the feveral Affidavits upon these Heads, it is Convenient to Recite fome Letters from the Inhabitants of that Place, who, under a deep Senfe of their Approaching Ruin, have breath'd forth their Complaints in the following Words.

Bofton, New-England October 2 : 1706.

SIR!

*I*NASMUCH, *as you have Expected from me, a true and brief Reprefentation of feveral Matters, relating to this Province, I fhall, with all poffible Faithfulnefs, endeavour it. Our Prefent Governour is not without a number of thofe, whom he has by Promotions and Flatteries made his Friends; but this hinders not a much more confiderable number, from wifhing, that we had a Governour, who would put an end unto the horrid Reign of Bribery, in our Adminiftration, and who would not infinitely Incommode Her Majefty's Service, by keeping the People in continual Jealoufies of his Plots, upon their moft Valuable Interefts.*

What the difpofition of the People towards him is, you may guefs by this : There was lately prepared an Addrefs from hence, to the Queen, *upon many important Articles; but by certain Arts there was got into it a Claufe, to defire of the* Queen, *that this Governour might be continued, the Reprefentatives Voted all the reft of the Addrefs, but this Claufe they abfolutely Rejected; they could not get above Five or Six Votes for it, fo the whole Addrefs, (which was contrived by a Party for nothing but that Claufe) fell to the ground.*

[8] There happened lately a number of Perfons, namely, Boreland, Vetch, Roufe, Lawfon, Philips *and* Cauplin *to be taken managing an unlawful Trade with the* French *and* Indians, *the Commodities wherein they Traded, were fuch, that the late Act of Parliament made their Crime to be* High Treason, *and we had no Act of the Province relating to that Matter, but was defectively Exprefsed: Our merciful Affembly was mighty loathe to proceed unto fo fevere a Judgment as that of Death, upon thefe Offenders. The Offenders Petitioning for it, the General Affembly were (very much by the Governour's influence) drawn into it, to take the Tryal of them into their own Hands; and as only Guilty of an High Mifdemeanour, the Vote for it was obtained in a Thin Houfe, upon an hurry at breaking up; and fome Claufes in the Charter were fo Construed, as to Countenance it. Upon their coming together again, they would fain have revoked their Votes, as fear-*

ing, that the very Perfons who had been their Tempters into it, would turn their Accufers, and improve it by way of Complaint, for the Enemies of our Charter to work upon ; but the Governour would by no means permit the Revocation of that wrong Step, (if it were one) fo the Tryal proceeded, and the Offenders were Fined in feveral Sums, by an Act of the Governour and Affembly.

It is now faid, that the ingrateful Men who were faved from the Gallows, by the Tendernefs of the Government, are now cutting our Throats, and Petition home againft the Government, for Fining them inftead of Hanging them ; yea, it is alfo faid, that the very Perfon who was the chief Caufe of drawing the Affembly into this extraordinary Proceeding, intends to make an ill ufe of it, againft the Country ; if you are fenfible of any thing of this nature carrying on, we pray you to add unto the reft of your Offices, that of an Interceffion, that an harmlefs People, furpriz'd into any Error, may not be Punifhed any otherwife, than by the removal of fuch as have been the Caufes of it ; and fo much for that.

[9] Sir, *You would do a vaft Service to the Crown, if you would fet forward the defigns of reducing* Canada, *and poffeffing* Nova Scotia, *a much lefs Fleet than what annually goes into the* Indies, *coming early enough in the Spring, may eafily do the former, even in the way thither ; and a* Scotch Colony *might be of good Confequence to do the latter ; but if any affiftance from* New England *fhould be expected in this matter, it is of abfolute neceffity that the Country have a Governour whom the People may fomewhat Rely upon.*

Sir, *You are Born to do the* Queen *and the Nation Service ; you are fpirited for great undertakings ; you are highly beloved and efteemed among our People in this Land, and where-ever you have come,'tis wifhed that you may do fome confiderable Action in this Affair.*

I have been earneftly Sollicited to Addrefs one of the moft Illuftrious Patriots of the Englifh *Nation, my Lord High Treasurer, with fome of thefe Intimations : That Noble Perfon is known to be fuch a Patron to all good Men, and fuch a defence of Oppreffed Innocence and Liberties, that we all fly to him as our unqueftionable Refuge. I am well fatisfied there would need nothing (to fpeak Humanely) to make this Country Eafy and Happy, but for that excellent* Perfon *to have an exact Reprefentation of our Circumftances ; nothing hinders me from attempting it, but the hazard of doing what may be thought a prefumption in one fo much a ftranger to him, neverthelefs, I am defired by fome confiderable* Perfons *to move you, that you would wait upon his Lord-*

ſhip, and fully acquaint him with the Matters now laid before you.

May the Almighty proſper you ;
I am, Sir,
Your Obliged Servant, &c.

Sir

I may inform you of one Action lately done among us, which I know you will be pleaſed withal. Upon the advice of [10] the extream Diſtreſs whereto the French Invaſion had brought *St. Chriſtophers* and *Nevis*, the People of *New-England*, in a moſt Chriſtian manner expreſſed their Charity towards thoſe, who perhaps would have hardly done the like for them, on a like Occaſion. We made a Collection for the Relief of their Neceſſities, the Collection was, as I am told, between 7 and 800 l. in this Collection, there were two Churches in *Boſton*, the *South* and the *North*, one gave ſomewhat above a 100 l. the other gave a little under it. Certainly, a Country ſo ready to ſerve Her Majeſty, and to help their fellow Subjects, ought to have a room in the Thoughts of all good Men in the *Engliſh* Nation.

The foregoing Letter carrying with it ſo many undeniable Truths, the World muſt of conſequence concede with the general Exclamations of the now Diſtreſſed *New-Englanders.* Indeed the publick had not been allarm'd with theſe Diſtant Calamities, had the inexorable Authors of them adhered to reitterated Grievances, from thoſe who too ſeverely ſuffer'd under their Protection. The Author of this Letter, who is a Perſon of a character beyond the reach of Envy, and one who is a great Bleſſing to his Native Country, had not invoked the protection and Aſſiſtance of others, without a due ſenſe of the Danger his innocent Neighbours and Country-men were expos'd to. To Report all the Letters of Complaint from theſe Provinces, would be too Voluminous and tireſome to the Reader ; we will only mention one more, which, tho' ſhort and plain, carries nothing but Veracity with it.

Sir

A LL the People here are Bought and Sold, betwixt the Governour and his Son *Paul ;* they are ſo Mercenary, there is no Juſtice to be had without Money : There is not one Publick Place in the Government that is worth Money, but what the Governour or *Paul* goes Halves with : In ſhort, the whole Country is very uneaſy, and the People here are ſo univerſally ſet againſt him, that Her Majeſty can ſcarce give a greater Inſtance

of Her tender Care and Regard to them, than by a re-
[11] moval of him, which to my certain knowledge, would be
foon followed by a Sincere and Hearty Acknowledgment of
Her Majefty's Singular Favour to them, in that particular.

R. A.

In the foregoing Letters we find feveral things Worthy our
Remark ; but I fhall only mention the Three following :

(1.) *That without Money, there is no Juftice to be had in* New-
England ; So that the meaner fort, Doubtlefs, is in a Deplorable
Condition ; the faces of their Poor being ground to Duft ; their
Widows Houfes laid Wafte, and the hopes of their Offspring cut
off. From whence we may infer, that *New-England* having a
Governour, whofe God is the Mammon of this World ; whofe
Principles act Counter to the Defign of his Power ; and whofe
Drift is the Ruin of his own Country ; the Inhabitants thereof
have nothing but Juftice on their part to Petition Her Majefty to
throw him afide.

(2.) *A general uneafinefs under, and oppofition to this Governour, thro' the whole Country.* And this, methinks, might ftop
the Mouths of fome People here, (who, not knowing the Nature
of this affair, no otherwife than as their Intereft leads them to
fide with the Governour, or by Virtue of a bare Friendfhip Contracted with him whilft he Refided in *England*) and put a
Period to all their Objections in his Behalf ; efpecially One,
unhappily let flip from the Mouth of a Gentleman too well
known for his great Learning and Parts, to be thought fo over-
fighted, and that is to this Effect. *If a Governour muft be
removed for every trivial Complaint, there wou'd be no End of
fuch Removals ; and Her Majefty's Miniftry would be wholly
taken up with turning out, and putting in.* I will not pretend to
affirm the Reafon that produc'd this hafty Plea for our Criminal
Governour ; but fure I am, the Author of it knows too much
Law, than to extenuate the like Crimes in others. And a weak
Argument I take it to endeavour the influencing our Superiors in
Redreffing Grievances of the Subject, when the feveral matters
of Fact Sworn to, are laid down before them : But [12] to fay
no more, this Gentleman has not been the firft that has over-fhot
himfelf in Defending things of this Nature. And

(3*dly*) *A fervent Defire to be eas'd of Oppreffion, i:e.* That
they might be capable of acknowledging with Refpect and
Gratitude, the mighty advantages of fuch a Deliverance to the
Queen of Great Brittain ; to a *Queen* who is all Juftice and Piety,
Peace and Union ; and a Queen who will not only hear the Peti-

tions of her Subjects, but maintain them in their Rights and Priviledges. Let not *New-England* doubt then of finding Redrefs, from fo Great and Gracious a Miftrefs, notwithftanding the fubtle Defigns and Evafions of Evil-minded Men. And fo we come to prefent the Reader with a further Account of the faid Mifmanagements, by another Hand.

SOMETIME in the Spring of the Year, 1706, Mr. *Dudley*, the prefent Governour of the Province of *Maffachufets Bay*, and *New-Hampfhire*, writ a Letter from *Bofton*, Directed to Mr. *Richard Waldron*, and my felf, to ufe our Intereft to prevail with the Council at an Affembly, to Draw up an Addrefs to the *Queen*, That Her Majefty would pleafe to continue the faid *Dudley* in the Government of *New-Hampfhire:* Whereupon the faid *Waldron* (after he had Communicated the Letter to me) drew up an Addrefs, and fhew'd it to the Affembly, and prevailed with them to pafs it in Both Houfes, with little Alteration. And this is the Addrefs that is now come over from the Province of *New-Hampfhire*. The Affembly was much againft it, but we thought it would be beft for us to do any thing that would pleafe the Governour at that time; confidering, that we were always in danger of the Enemy, and concluded, it was much in his Power, under God, to preferve us, having often heard him fay, that he would ftop the Courier of the *Indians* and *French*, (when he pleas'd) in a Month or Six Weeks time; and I did then, and do ftill believe, that he could prevent the *Indians* and *French* from coming upon us, and Killing us as they did; for I know that he had Correfpondence with a *Fryer* or *Jefuit*, or one fo called, a *Frenchman* that Lives among the *Indians*, and hath great influence over them, who writes himfelf *Galen Emefary*. The Governour to my certain Knowledge, did order fundry things that were fent him; [13] and confidering the great Correfpondence (he told me) he had with the Governour of *Port-Royal*, it caufed a firm belief in me, that he could do what he would with the Enemy: Thefe, with other Motives, prefs'd us forwards to get the Addrefs paffed, concluding all thefe things would add to our Peace, if rightly improved; and the *Indians*, about that time, and for many Months before, had done little or no Mifchief, and for my part, I did really believe, that it was the Governour's Intereft that caufed our quiet, but foon found we were Miftaken, finding out, that much about the fame time that *Waldren* and myfelf were forwarding the Addrefs to Her Majefty, to continue Mr. *Dudley* Governour, he was countenancing a private Trade with the *Indians* and *French*, our Enemies, as we found by woful Experience: For foon after thofe Traders went to the *Eaftward*, the *Indians* came fharply down upon us about the latter end of *June* laft, Killed Six People, Wounded two, and carried away two from the Town of

Almfbury, and a little before they Killed Lieutenant *John Shap-leigh*, at the Town of *Kittery*, and a whole Family, as a Man, Wife and Children, all Killed and Scalped out of the Townfhip of *Dover;* and one Man Killed with Swan-fhot out of the Town-fhip of *Hampton;* and Nine Killed, one Wounded, and one carried out of the Townfhip of *Exeter*. All thefe Barbarities were committed before I came from thence, which was about the beginning of *September* laft; God knows how many have been thus Barbaroufly Murther'd fince. Captain *Vetch*, and Captain *Lawfon*, oftentimes told me, that they had oftentimes acquainted the Governour with their defign of going to the *Eaft-ward* upon Trade, and had the confent of him, and did folemnly proteft that they would not have gone without it : And I do believe, and it is generally believed in *New-England*, that the Governour did know of this Trade, and no doubt but that he was to have a fhare of the Profit. When thefe Traders came from the *French* and *Indians*, one of their Veffels ftopped at the Ifle of *Shoals*, near the Province of New-*Hampfhire*, the Mafter's Name was *Roufe*, who brought to that place from *Port-Royal* Seven Prifoners; and Capt. *Jethro Furbur* being at the faid Ifles of *Shoales*, at the faid time when the Veffel came in, heard the faid Prifoners affirm, That the *Eaftern* Indians had no Shot, nor Bul-lets, nor Lead to make any, and it was very fcarce with the *French*, infomuch that they could not fupply them, fo that the *Indians* were [14] like to Starve for want of Ammunition ; for great part of their Livelihood depends on their Guns to Kill Wild Beafts and Fowl, *&c.* whereby we find it was not the Governour's Intereft he had with the Enemy, to prevent their coming upon us, but it was for want of Ammunition : And thofe Prifoners that were brought from *Port-Royal*, which Capt. *Furber* fpoke with at the Ifles of *Shoals*, did further affirm, That they heard the Governour of *Port-Royal* fay, That he had given his Letter to the Governour of *Bofton*, that he would not fupply the Indians with Powder nor Shot, but that he would do all he could to prevent the *Indians* coming upon the *Englifh*, and had been as good as his Word ; but that the faid Governour of *Bofton*, or his People, had fupplied the *Indians* with more Ammu-nition than he was able to do ; for the Traders from *Bofton* brought it by Tuns ; and that if this Trade had not been incour-aged by the Governour, we fhould have had no Men Killed, nor indeed any Difturbance amongft us. It is my Belief, and it feems very plain to me, that the Governour intends to forward the *French* and *Indian* Enemy to Deftroy all they can, and keep the Country allarm'd, thereby to put them to fuch vaft Charges, as will Ruin the whole Government, by Killing fome and Impov-erifhing the reft. There was never fuch Taxes on the Poor People as now ; 33000 l. being raifed a little before I came away, and many great Sums not long before that. I was credibly

Informed that fome Perfons were forced to cut open their Beds, and Sell the Feathers to Pay their Taxes. I don't remember that ever there was any of the *Indian* Enemy Kill'd or Taken fince Mr. *Dudley* came over Governour, except an Old Woman, and two others I took to be Girls by their Scalps ; and fome few taken near *Port-Royal* taken by Major *Church.* So that inftead of being Deftroyed, I wifh they be not preferv'd : For, Six Months before it came to pafs, the Governour *Mr. Dudley* told me, what Methods the *Indians* would take when they came again, and it proved accordingly. He told me, That the *Indians* would not come in any great Body as they ufed to do, but they would come in fmall Numbers, no Number above Thirty, and fo Line the Woods from *Dearfield,* which is the South-Weft fide of the *Maffachufets* Government, and all along the Woods, juft within the Towns to Cafko Bay, which is the North-Eaft Part of Inhabitants at this time. And this Method I am afraid will be continued till the Country is for a great part Deftroyed, if Mr. *Dudley* be continued Governour. As for the Addrefs he ob- [15] tained of the militia of *Maffachufet's* Bay, it was a forc'd thing ; for the Officers are beholden to him for their Commiffions, and if any Refus'd to Sign what the Governour got drawn, he could put them out, and put in others as he pleafed.

Thus having given the Publick an Exaɛt Relation of the prefent State of *New-England,* it remains only that we Produce a Confirmation of all that hath been faid. To which end we will begin with the feveral Affidavits and Depofitions already made, and which are as follows.

[16]

The feveral Affidavits *as they were laid before the* QUEEN *and* Council, *relating to the* Governour *of* New-England's *Mercenary and Illegal Proceedings, but particularly his private Correfpondence with Her Majesties Enemies, efpe-cially the* French *and* Indians

The Two Affidavits of Mr. *John Calley.*

JOHN CALLEY *of* Marble-head *in the County of* Effex *in* New-England, *now in* London *Mariner, Depofeth and faith, That he doth and hath good reafon to Believe, That Her Majefties* Colonies *of* New-England *are in great Danger of being Ruined by reafon of Governour* Dudleys *Countenancing a Trade, and Correfpondence with the* French, *and* Indian *Enemies, and many other his Irregular praƐtices: Alfo faith, that the faid Governour did in the Year,* 1705, *fend his Son* William Dudley *with Captain* Samuel Vetch *to* Canada *under a Pretence of Redeeming Captives; who accordingly went and brought back only a few of the meaneft of the Englifh Captives; Leaving the chiefeft of them there for an Occafion of their returning again to* Canada *to Trade, and fettle a Correfpondence with the* French; *and that the faid* Vetch *did carry out with him a Cargo of about* 800 *lib. Value in Iron, Pitch, Rigging, Shot, &c: Which Cargo upon a Moderate Computation, might produce near* 3000 *lib. And that the faid* Vetch *did alfo pretend that he went with Governour* Dudley's *Approbation to get in a Debt of* 800 *lib. ContraƐted in time of Peace; And due to him from the* French, *of which matters and things he this Depo-nent, hath been credibly informed, and Believes them to be true. And further faith that it did appear to the General As-* [17] *fem-bly of the* Maffachufets *Colony in* New-England, *that Captain* William Roufe *was (the better to colour a Trade with the* French, *and* Indians) *fent to* Port-Royal *with a Flag of Truce, under Pre-tence of fettling a Correfpondence with the* French *Governour there for exchanging Prifoners; and did Trade not only with his own Veffel, but had alfo at the fame Time two other Trading Veffels with him, under his own DireƐtion, and did bring back Furrs, &c. To above* 2000 *lib. Value; and that the faid* Dudley *did allow one* Difhey Foe, *a French Prifoner on Parole, to go in the fame Veffel with the faid* Roufe, *who aƐted as Interpreter between the faid* Roufe *and the* Indians, *in Trading with them;*

and that the said Flag of Truce meeting with one of the two other Veſſels, the said Foe *was put into the same with ſeveral Goods, and Merchandiſes, out of the said Flag of Truce, with which the said* Foe *was Trading; and that the said* Foe *returned again to* Boſton, *and that when the said Furrs,* &c. *were brought to* Boſton, *it was alledged, that they were brought to Pay* French *Mens Debts in* New-England, *but that it was proved that the said Furrs,* &c. *were moſtly purchaſed by the Goods carried out in the Veſſel of the said* Rouſe *and were seized, yet cleared afterwards; And the said* Rouſe *declared to the said Aſſembly, that he had done nothing but by Governour* Dudleys *approbation; and that it appeared to the said General Aſſembly, that the Enemies diſtreſs through want of Ammunition, Proviſion,* &c. *before they were by the Engliſh ſupplied, occaſioned many of them to go out a Privateering on the Engliſh Coaſt, ſome of which were taken and brought into* Boſton, *and were afterwards with other* French *Diſcharged and ſent to* Canada, *and* Port-Royal, *and among others one* Battis *a Priſoner Kept for Murders,* &c. *by him committed upon the Engliſh in cold Blood, and under a Flag of Truce, and he being a Man of great note and Service among the French and uſually joyned with the* Indians, *whilſt the Engliſh Priſoners were ſtill detained, becauſe Governour* Dudley *had as was alledged, falſified his Promiſe to the French Governour, who had reſtrained the* Indians *from Diſturbing the Engliſh Fiſhery or otherwiſe; and would not allow them any Amunition for a conſiderable time, nor until they were ſupplied by the Engliſh Veſſels ſent under the pretence of fetching Priſoners, about which Letters were produced from the French Governour. And this Deponent further ſaith, that it appeared to the said General Aſſembly, that the endeavours of the Country, by a chargeable maintaining an Army, and ſending them yearly ſeveral hundred Miles to deſtroy the* Indians *Corn, thereby to diſtreſs and ſubdue them, have (by their being ſupplied in their great Neceſſities, by ſuch* [18] *Traders, for great Prices) been in a great meaſure fruſtrated, and that if the said* Indians *had not been ſo ſupplied many more of them muſt have periſhed thro' want; and that Governour* Dudley, *generally ſhewed an unwillingneſs that ſuch Traders when taken, ſhould be puniſhed, or Fined; and further ſaith, that the above said Colony, was at a great Expence to Erect a Fort at* Caſco *bay, and to maintain Souldiers for Securing the same to ſuppreſs the Enemy, and to keep ſure Footing in that Part of the Country, yet that Governour* Dudley *ſuffered thoſe Souldiers to remain there without any Comiſſion Officer, to the great diſſatisfaction and dread of the said Souldiers, inſomuch that they declared to this Deponent, a Member of the said Aſſembly, that if the Enemy ſhould come upon them they would Surrender the said Fort, and dared not Reſiſt for want of a Comiſſion; and that he, this Deponent coming into the Aſſembly then Sitting at* Boſton; *and Informing them thereof, the said*

Assembly Represented to the Governour, the necessity of speedily Commissionating some person to command that Fort, which after some considerable time was obtained: And this Deponent further saith, that the said Colony, hath by reason of such Illegal Trade been put to vast Expences to secure themselves from the Invasions of the Enemy; and that in one Sessions the last Summer was raised by the said Assembly, about 33000 *lib. When as otherwise one-third part thereof might have been sufficient. And further saith, that the Indians, that have been thus Supplyed are the only People, that destroy the Eastern parts of the Countrey; the Fishery and Coast of* Accady, *and are, as this Deponent hath been credibly Informed, and doth believe the very same* Indians *that were at the destroying of* New-Found Land, *and headed by one* Escombuct, *that usually heads the* Indians *when they come to destroy the* New-Englanders. *And this Deponent further saith, that he hath been credibly Informed and hath good reason to believe; that Governour* Dudley *doth several ways Illegally exact from Her Majesties Subjects several Sums of Money, and Deprives them of the Priviledges in catching of Whales by force, taking Whales from the Fishers under Pretence of Drift-fish; and obstructs the course of Justice; and Particularly that one* Clap *took by force a Whale from one* Newcomb, upon which the said Newcomb sued Clap, and obtained Judgment against *him, and for which he was cast into Prison, and then was cleared by Governour* Dudley, *without any satisfaction made to said* Newcomb. *And this Deponent further saith, that he is informed that an Address hath been sent to Her Majesty, Representing, as if the People of* New-England *Prayed for the continuing the said* Dudley, *their Governour; but that* [19] *he doth in part know, and hath been informed, and hath great grounds to believe, that the far greatest part of Her Majesties Subjects in* New-England *are very weary under his administration, and that the said Governour* Dudley *did cause to be Prepared an Address to Her Majesty, for his Continuance, and the same to be sent up and down the Country, to get hands thereunto, and that the same was only Signed by such persons as were in Commission under him, or influenced by him. And that he this Deponent doth know that an Address was presented to the House of Representatives, to be Sign'd, Praying for several Favours from Her Majesty, but because in the said Address a prayer for his Continuing Governour was inserted, the whole Address was by the said House Rejected: And that he doth believe, that if an Address to Remove him hath not been presented, it was because they had an Expectation that Her Majesty, would suddenly favour that Countrey with a better Governour: And further saith, that whilst the Assembly was Sitting there arrived a Flag of Truce from the* French *Governour, with a haughty Demand of the* French *Prisoners, in* New-England, *and charging Governour* Dudley *with Breach of his Promise, and his permitting* English

*Trading Veſſels on their Coaſts; whereupon the Houſe of Repre-
ſentatives Suſpecting the Flag of Truce to come upon account of
Trade, Ordered the Veſſel to be ſearched, and that there was found
on Board the ſame New Arms and Ammunition, hid in private
places, particularly ſhot among Peas, yet denied by the Commander
thereof, who was an* Engliſh *Renegado; part of which being
brought before the ſaid Houſe, it was Generally concluded, that they
had been newly bought in* Boſton; *but the Governour Interpoſing,
the matter was huſhed up to the great diſſatisfaction of the General
Aſſembly, and Country in General; and altho' the Aſſembly
moved the Governour for a ſtrict Guard to be kept on the Veſſel or
Flag of Truce, nothing was done. This Deponent further ſaith,
that the Houſe of Repreſentatives, Inſiſted not only upon far
greater Fines to be laid on the foreſaid Traders, and others Concerned; but alſo that they ſhould ſtand upon the Gallows, and
ſuffer Twelve Months Impriſonment, and continued inſiſting upon
the ſame about Three Weeks, but Governour* Dudley, *not conſenting
thereto, by his Wearying out the ſaid Houſe, and perſuading them
to Moderate* [20] *their ſentence; to the great diſſatisfaction of the
Council, and the ſaid Houſe; at laſt the Houſe altered their Sentence; to the Fines they now Stand Charged with.*

John Calley.

Jur. 2 die Jun. 1707
  coram me
       Thomas Gery.

JOHN CALLEY, *of* Marble-head *in the County of* Eſſex *in*
New-England, *now in* London, *Mariner, Depoſeth and ſaith,
That about the middle of the Month of* May, 1706, *This Deponent
was choſen an Aſſembly-Man, or Repreſentative for the ſaid Town
of* Marble-head, *to ſit in the Great and General Court of Aſſembly
at* Boſton, *for the* Province *of the* Maſſachuſets-Bay *in* New England, *on the laſt* Wedneſday *of the ſaid Month of* May; *and
accordingly this Deponent took the* uſual *Oath and was a Member
of the ſaid Court of Aſſembly; and that in the beginning of the
ſaid Seſſions, the Houſe of Aſſembly, or Repreſentatives, being
Informed by ſome Captives redeem'd out of Captivity from the*
French *and* Indians *That there were ſome Engliſh Perſons Trading in the Eaſtern parts of* New-England *with the* French *and*
Indians; *and that one Captain* Samuel Vetch *was returned to*
Cape Ann, *from ſuch Trading; whereupon this Deponent was
Authorized by the Governour, Council, and Aſſembly, to Search for
the ſaid Perſons ſo Trading as aforeſaid, and to Seize their Goods,
Veſſels, and Effects, and in Purſuance of his Commiſſion this
Deponent at* Marble-head *aforeſaid, found one* John Curtys *Pilot
of the ſaid Veſſel, Coming privately on ſhore, to go to Mr.* John

Borland *of* Bofton *Merchant, who was concerned in the faid Veffel and Goods, and Seized the faid* Curtys, *whom this Deponent Carried to* Bofton, *where he was Examined before the Governour, and Council: And there gave an Account upon Oath of the faid Voyage and Trading, as by his Teftimony, given in upon the Tryal appears; and afterwards this Deponent Seized the Sloop or Veffel called the Flying-Horfe,* Archibal Furgifon *Mafter; and the Refolution,* Thomas Barrow *Mafter; wherein* [21] *was found fundry Parcels of Goods brought back again in the Flying-Horfe and not Difpofed of in the Trade abovefaid, and this Deponent put the Veffel and Goods into the Poffeffion of Mr.* William Pain, *Deputy Collector of Her Majefty's Cuftoms at* Bofton *aforefaid; and amongft the Bills of Loading, Orders, and Papers, found on Board the Flying-Horfe, it appeared that the faid John* Borland, Samuel Vetch, *and* Roger Lawfon *were Owners of the faid Sloop Flying-Horfe, and the Cargo put on Board her for the Voyage aforefaid: Which Amounts to the Value of Eight Hundred Pounds, as the faid Curtys Informed this Deponent; whereupon by a Vote of the Houfe of Affembly, a Meffenger was fent for the* faid Vetch, Borland, *and* Lawfon, *and upon their Examination before the faid Houfe, and other Evidences that were Produced againft them, the faid* Borland, Vetch, *and* Lawfon, *Were Committed to Prifon for Treafon, in Aiding, and Affifting, Her Majefties Enemies Contrary to a Late Act of Parliament made in* England: *And this Deponent further faith, that he was fent in the* Province Galley *to look for other Perfons that had likewife been, and were Trading with the* French *and* Indians, *and it appeared that* William Roufe, John Philips, *and* Ebenezer Coffin, *had alfo been Concern'd for Illegal Trading with the* French *and* Indians: *And upon their Examinations and Evidences Produced againft them, they were Committed by the faid Houfe of Reprefentatives for Treafon as the other were, who were all Continued in Prifon upon their* —— *for feveral Weeks, the General Court or Affembly, ftill Sitting, and that the Prifoners Petitioned the faid Court, to be Tryed for High Mifdemeanours only: Which the Lower Houfe would not confent to, for fome Weeks when the Countrey-men in the General Court being wanted at Home, upon prefent Occafions, and to Guard their Families, being then Invefted in feveral Places by the* French *and* Indians, *who had been fupply'd by the faid Traders with fhot and other Neceffaries, as by the Evidence appear'd, but were ftill detained by the Governour from their Lawful bufinefs, who was altogether averfe for Trying them for Treafon, and ufed Strenuous Arguments, and his utmoft endeavours to Try them for High Mifdemeanours, Alledging (amongft other things) that they had Power by the Charter to Try them fo, and to lay Fines, and Mulcts, and Imprifonments upon them; Which would be of much greater advantage to the Country, than to Try them for Treafon. And the faid Governour having Wearied out the Affembly, and Keeping them only on that*

*Affair; and when many of the moſt Prudent Men of the Aſſembly
were gone, to their ReſpeЄtive dwellings, he over perſwaded the Remainder (which [22] could but juſt make a Houſe) to alter their Vote,
to Try them for High Miſdemeanors inſtead of Treaſon. As they
were at firſt Committed, which by his means was conſented unto,
and they were all afterwards ConviЄted of High Miſdemeanours,
and fined, as by their Tryal Appears wherein the Governour ſtill
interceeded for the moderating thereof, and by his means they were
Reduc'd to the ſeveral Sums, they now ſtand Fined for.*

Collonell *Partridges* Affidavits.

WILLIAM PARTRIDGE of *Portſmouth* in the Province
of *New-hampſhire* in *New-England;* now in *London,*
Eſq : Depoſeth that Sometime in the Month of *January,* 1702,
Col. *Joſeph Dudley* Governour of the ſaid Province, and of the
Maſſachuſets-Bay, did Diſpoſe of two Great Guns out of Her
Majeſties Fort, at *New-caſtle,* in the Province of *New-Hampſhire,*
and received the money for the ſame: And this Deponent further
ſaith, that one Mr. *Theodore Atkinſon,* being an Officer appointed
to Receive a Duty the General Aſſembly had laid upon all Boards
and Staves exported out of the ſaid Province of *New-Hampſhire,*
(and Naval Officer there) was threatened by Mr. *Paul Dudley*
the Governour's Son, and the Queens Attorney to have turned
him out of his Place, for not paying the Money due the Preceeding Year, as agreed for. And this Deponent Paid Ten or
Twelve Pounds in Part of what was behind, that the ſaid Officer
might not be turned out of his Place, which Sum the ſaid *Atkinſon* afterwards repay'd to this Deponent ; And that a year or
two afterwards the ſaid *Paul Dudley* told this Deponent, that the
Governour ſhould turn the ſaid *Atkinſon* out of his Place, for that
he had not Pay'd him all that was agreed for, whereupon this
Deponent acquainted the ſaid *Atkinſon* therewith, who reply'd
that there was not above Five or Six Pounds behind, and he
would Pay it the next Poſt : And that ſometime in the Month of
Auguſt laſt, as this Deponent was coming away, to his beſt remembrance, the ſaid *Atkinſon* told him he had Paid [23] Twenty
Pounds a year, for both his Offices : And this Deponent further
ſaith, that having occaſion to run the Bounds of a Piece of Land
he had bought in *Portſmouth;* he wrote to the ſaid Mr. *Paul
Dudley* to procure the Governour's Order to the Sheriff, to accompany the Perſons Appointed to run the Line or Bounds between
this Deponent, and the Adjacent Freeholder, for fear of any
Diſturbance, and he would be at the Charge thereof ; but ſent no
Money, and the ſaid *Paul Dudley* ſent this Deponent word that

it could not be done, or to that Purpofe : And the next Poft this Deponent ordered his Friend in *Bofton* to Pay the faid *Paul Dudley* Ten Pounds, and thereupon an Order came to this Deponent by the next Poft ; and the Bufinefs was afterwards done in three or four Hours time ; and the Charge to the Officers and Sheriff was not above the Sum of Twelve Shillings : And this Deponent further faith, that upon the Fifth Day of *Auguft* laft, fome of the Men belonging to Her Majefties Ship the Deptford, then Riding in the River of *Pifcataqua ;* came on fhore at the Town of *New-Caftle*, aforefaid, and took from thence by the Captains Order as they faid one *Jethro Furber* Mafter of the Ship called the *William* and *Richard*, and forthwith fet Sail and Carried him to *Bofton*, in another Province ; where Captain *Stuckley* Commander of the Deptford, and Captain *Mathews* Commander of the Dover, entred a Complaint againft the faid *Furbur*, in the Court of Admiralty at *Bofton*, for Shipping two of their Men : whereupon this Deponent wrote to Col. *Dudley* the Governour, how that Captain *Stuckley* had Carried away the Mafter of his Ship, Loaded with dry Fifh, bound to *Leghorn ;* having cleared the Cuftom-Houfe and obtained the Governours Pafs to the Fort, and earneftly defired Relief : And Inclofed to the Governour a Proteft againft the faid *Stuckley*, but fent no Money either to the Governour, or his Son ; neither could he obtain any Relief ; whereupon this Deponent took Horfe and went to *Bofton* and applyed himfelf to the Governour, acquainting him, that the Fifh on Board his Ship was a Perifhing Comodity ; and if any Water fhould come into the Ship the Cargo would be utterly loft ; for as foon as Captain *Stuckley* carried away his Mafter, the reft of the Men run away from the faid Ship, into the Woods ; And this Deponent was informed the faid Ship fwung to and again, in the Tyde, and was like to Sink, and could not get a Man on Board her : And this [24] Deponent further informed the faid Governour, that there was a great Fleet of Englifh and Dutch Men of War in the Straits, and if his Mafter could Sail before they came out, his Ship would be out of Danger of being taken, but if the Mafter was Detained, he fhould Lofe his Ship and Cargo : And that if the Mafter had done anything Amifs he ought to be Tryed at *Pifcataqua*, and not at *Bofton ;* but this Deponent could not get no Relief from the Governour ; and thereupon went to the faid *Paul Dudley*, the Queens Advocate, of the Court of Admiralty, and Offered Ten Thoufand Pounds Bond, with good fecurity to Pay whatever the Courts Sentence fhould be ; Provided his Mafter and Ship might go : But all in vain, and his Veffel was Detained above Three Weeks, and when fhe came into the Straights, the Men of War was come out Seven Days before fhe Arrived there, and afterwards was taken, and further faith not.

[25]

Collonel *Partridge's* Affidavits.

WILLIAM PARTRIDGE of *Portſmouth*, in the Province of *New Hampſhire*, in *New-England*, maketh Oath, that he doth believe that *Joſeph Dudley* Eſq; preſent Governour of *New England*, did Countenance a Trade with the *French* and *Indian* Enemies, and ſaith, that he the ſaid Dudley did keep Correſpondence with one *Gallen Emiſſary*, a *French* Fryar or Jeſuit, that Lives among the Indians; and the ſaid Dudley owned to this Deponent, that he had a great Correſpondence with the Governour of *Port-Royal;* And this Deponent ſaith, that Captain *Vetch*, and Captain *Lawſon* often told this Deponent, that they had acquainted the ſaid Dudley with their Voyage to the Eaſtward, when they Traded with the *French* and *Indians*, and that he Conſented thereto; and that ſoon after they had ſo Traded, the *Indians* came down and Killed Lieutenant *John Shapeley* at the Town of *Kittery;* and a Man, his Wife and Children in the Townſhip of *Dover;* and Killed one Man with Swan-ſhot out of the Townſhip of *Hampton;* and Killed Nine; and Wounded one out of the Townſhip of *Exeter;* and about the latter end of *June* laſt Killed Six, and Wounded Two; and carried away Two out of the Townſhip of *Almeſbuy;* all which Perſons were Killed and taken in this Deponent's Neighbour-hood, as this Deponent hath heard, and verily believes, being informed ſo by thoſe that were at moſt of their Funerals. And this Deponent further ſaith, that there was not to his Knowledge, any of the *Indian* Enemies Killed ſince the ſaid *Dudley* was Governour, except an Old Woman and two others, that ſeemed by their Scalps to be Girls. And this Deponent further ſaith, that the ſaid *Dudley* told this Deponent Six Months before the Invaſion by the *Indians*, that when they came again they would not come in any great Body, as they uſed to do, but not above Thirty in a Company, and ſo Line the Woods from *Dearfield* to *Caſko Bay*, which is above a Hundred Miles, which Method the ſaid *Indians* did after take in their ſaid Invaſion; but how the ſaid *Dudley* came to know that they would ſo do, this Deponent knoweth not; but ſaith, that the ſaid *Dud-* [26] *ley* often told this Deponent, that he could ſtop the Career of the *French* and *Indians* when he pleaſed, in a Month or Six Weeks time

Will: Partridge.

Jurat Viceſſimo primo die Junij
   Anno, 1707.   *Cor. me*
        W. Rogers

Mr. *Thomas Newton's* Affidavit.

THOMAS NEWTON of *Boſton* in *New-England*, at preſent in *London*, Gent. maketh Oath, that he hath Lived in *New-England* for near Sixteen Years laſt paſt, and during that time has been well acquainted with Collonel *Joſeph Dudley*, the preſent Governour of the Province of *Maſſachuſetts-Bay* and New *Hampſhire:* And that ſince the ſaid Collonel *Dudley* was Governour there, this Deponent was credibly Informed, that ſeveral Perſons having purchaſed Lands at *Naſhobah* and *Nip-muck*, within his Government, and wanting a Confirmation of their Titles, by an Act of the General Court, (as is uſual in ſuch Caſes) they could not obtain the Governour's aſſent thereto, without giving him Money, and part of their Lands. And this Deponent further ſaith, that he being Deputed by *William At-wood* Eſq; to be Deputy Judge of the Court of Vice Admiralty, as well as of the Collony of *Rhode Iſland*, as for the Provinces of *Maſſachuſets-Bay*, and New *Hampſhire*, was prohibited by the ſaid Governour from going to *Rhode Iſland*, and Condemning ſome Prizes brought in there, unleſs this Deponent would procure the Governour One Hundred Pounds, and that his Son ſhould go Advocate thither; and threatned this Deponent to raiſe the *Poſſe Comitatus* upon him, if he offered to proceed without [27] his Order, or Licenſe under his Hand. And this Deponent alſo further ſaith, That one Mr. *Stephen Minot*, having Built a very Convenient Houſe for a publick Inn or Tavern, upon a place called the Neck, the Governour having a Tennant who kept a Publick Houſe near to it, Prohibited the Juſtice to grant a Licenſe to the ſaid *Minot*, tho' it was Requeſted by the General Aſſembly; but the ſaid *Minot* could not obtain a Licenſe for his Houſe, until he complied with the Governour upon hard Terms. And this Deponent moreover ſaith, that Sentence in the Court of Vice-Admiralty being given by this Deponent for a Saylor, againſt a Maſter of a Veſſel for Wages, from which the ſaid Maſter appealed to the High Court of Admiralty in *England*, but not giving Bond to Proſecute as is uſual in ſuch Caſes, Proceſs was granted againſt the ſaid Maſter, and the Mareſchal took him into Cuſtody thereupon. Yet the Governour abuſed the Officer, and diſcharged the ſaid Maſter contrary to Law, and by that means the Saylor loſt his Wages, and his Charges and Coſts: And laſtly, this Deponent ſaith, that the people in *New-England* in general, are much diſſatisfied with the ſaid Colonel *Dudley*, and would rejoyce to have him removed from his Government; and further ſaith not.

[28]

Colonel Partridge's *Certificate.*

WHEREAS an Addrefs *from Her Majefties* Affembly, *in the Province of* New-Hampfhire, *in* New England, *has been lately fent over, Praying Her Majefty's Continuance of Colonel* Dudley *Governour of the faid Province ; Now the Truth and Occafion of Procuring and fending the fame, was thus :*

" *Coll.* Dudley, *who is not only Governour of* New-Hampfhire,
" *but alfo of the* Maffachufets-Bay, *and lives at* Bofton, 60 *Miles*
" *from* New-Hampfhire, *Wrote to fome Principal Gentlemen, to*
" *Prevail with the Affembly of* New-Hampfhire, *to Prefent an*
" *Addrefs to Her Majefty for the Purpofe aforefaid, and in Compli-*
" *ance with this Defire, and in Order to Prevail with the Affem-*
" *bly, the faid Gentlemen Prepar'd an* Addrefs *accordingly, and*
" *fhow'd it to the* Affembly, *who, in fome time after, though with*
" *Difficulty and Reluctancy, were prevailed on to Sign the fame,*
" *with little Alteration. The Chief,* [29] *and indeed the Only*
" *Inducement to which, was the Apprehenfion they were then under,*
" *that it was better for them to do anything that would Pleafe the*
" *Governour ; and that it was in his Power to Contribute much to*
" *the Advantage and Security, or to the Mifchief and Prejudice*
" *of that Province ; and not any Opinion they had of the Conduct*
" *and Integrity of the faid* Dudley, *who is generally Difliked and*
" *Ill-Thought of in both* Provinces, *where he is Governour ; and*
" *has given too much Reafon and Occafion to Sufpect his Regard*
" *to the Good and Welfare of thofe Places, efpecially when his own*
" *Intereft ftands in Competition, or a fair Opportunity offers, for*
" *his Profit and Advantage.*

All which is humbly Certified and Submitted.

Wm. Partridge.

---

[30] Thus far the Affidavits of the Illegal and Difloyal Practices of our Governour. Can any Man that loves not a *French* Intereft, call thofe Trivial; or say, they are not worthy of the fevereft Refentments? With what Face Men now a-days can go about to Juftify Crimes that have fo near an affinity to High Treafon, is a wonder to me; and yet pretend at the fame time to be Loyal and True to their Country. Crimes of the moft pernicious Confequence to a State ; and which, among all Nations, have been Punifh'd with the utmoft feverity. The *Athenians,* notwithftanding the Liberty they gave to fome of their Rulers, yet they appointed a Reckoning Day among them ;

fo that thofe that thought themfelves not accountable whilft in
Authority, found at laft a very ftrict Account to be given to
certain Auditors, and a worfer Punifhment inflicted on them if
Criminal, than the abufed Clemency of this Age can produce :
To do Juftice and Right is the moft invaluable Jewel in *Magna
Charta;* and a Bleffing which no People in the World can boaft
of, like thofe of the *Brittifh* Nation. The *New-Englanders* are of
the fame Tribe; have the fame Liberty to, and the fame Property in the Enjoyment of the many Legal Priviledges in that
Charter contained : They are *not Slaves*, as their conceited
Governour once told them ; but have ftill a right Legally to
oppofe his Pride and Covetoufnefs ; have ftill a Right to Petition
for a Better, that will not be Brib'd to do Evil ; they have a
Right to tell the World, and that loudly, That for a Governour
to furnifh the Enemy with Powder and Shot, *&c.* to deftroy his
own Country-men, is a Wretch not only fit to be Difcarded, but
to be for ever forgotten among Mankind.

The Cryes fent up to Heaven, by the many poor Souls lately
moft inhumanely Butchered by the Mercilefs *Indians*, with our
own Inftruments, have reached the Ears of the Almighty, and
will certainly draw down Redrefs from him, who is not only *Rex
Magnus & Rex Solus*, but *Judex Supremus*, who hath *Imperium
fine Fine*, as well as *fine Limite*, to whom we commit all that
hath been already faid.

And now to Conclude all, (that our Readers may have a juft
Senfe of the-unaccountable Cruelties acted by the *Indians*, upon
our *Englifh* in *New-England*) we fhall prefent them with the
following Particulars, lately fent over to us by a very great and
good Man.

[31]

An Account of feveral Barbarities lately committed by the Indians *in* New-England ; *Intermix'd with fome Memorable
Providences.*

ASTONISHING Deliverances have been fent from Heaven,
to many of our Captives. They have been many a time
upon the Point of deftruction ; but, *Thefe poor ones have Cryed
unto the Lord*, and He has Remarkably delivered them.

'Tis a Wonderful Reftraint from God upon the Bruitifh Salvages, that no *Englifh Woman* was ever known to have any
Violence offered unto her *Chaftity*, by any of them :

'Tis wonderful, that no more of the Captives have been Murdered by them, neither when they were Drunk nor when the Caprichio's, and the Cruelties of their Diabolical Natures were to be Gratified.

'Tis Wonderful, that when many of the Captives have been juft going to be Sacrificed, fome ftrange Interpofition of the Divine Providence has put a ftop to the Execution, and prevented their being made a Sacrifice. The Stories are numberlefs. Take a few of them.

[32] A Crue of Indians had been three Days without any manner of Suftenance. They took an Englifh Child, and hung it before the Fire to Roaft it for their Supper ; but that thefe Canibals might Satiate their —— I want a Name for it, —— as well as their Hunger, they would Roaft it Alive. The Child began to Swell. A Cannow arrived at that Inftant, with a Dog in it. The leffer Devils of the Crue, propofed their taking the Dog inftead of the Child ; they did fo, and the Child is yet Living ! Her Name is *Hannah Parfons*.

A Man had Valiantly Killed an Indian or two before the Salvages took him. He was next Morning to undergo an horrible Death, whereof the Manner and the Torture was to be affigned by the Widow *Squa* of the Dead Indian. The French Priefts told him, they had indeavoured to divert the Tygres from ther bloody Intention, but could not prevail with them ; he muft prepare for the terrible Execution. His cries to God were hard, and heard ; when the Sentence of the *Squa*, was demanded, quite contrary to every ones Expectation, and the Revengeful Inclination fo ufual and well-known among thefe Creatures, fhe only faid, *His Death won't fetch my Hufband to Life ; Do nothing to him !* So nothing was done to him.

A Woman was carried afide, by her Monfter of a Mafter; he faftened a Rope about her Neck ; it was in vain for her to contend, the Hatchet muft prefently have difpatched her, if thé Halter had failed ; fhe had no Remedy but to Cry unto God : Her Mafter throws up the end of the Rope over a Limb of a Tree ; he afcends to hale her and tye her up ; and then a fine Exploit for the Wretch ! *a memorable Name !* However the Limb happily breaks down he falls ; full of madnefs he goes to repeat his brave action : An Indian Commander juft in the Nick of Time comes in upon him ; Reproaches him very bitterly; Takes her away from him ; and fends her to *Canada*.

But we ought not to pafs over the marvellous Difplay of the Power of God, in fupporting and preferving the poor Captives

when they Travelled thro' the horrid Wildernefs, oftentimes
much more than a fcore of Miles in a day, and thro' very deep
Snows ; [33] and with vaft Loads on their Backs, and griev-
oufly pinched with Hunger, having fcarce one bit of any Refrefhment, for whole days together.   Poor, Weak, fick Women have
done fo !

One cannot well imagine any other than Supernatural and
Angelical affiftances, in fome of the inftances.

The Indians came upon the Houfe of one *Adams* at *Wells*,
and Captivated the Man and his Wife, and affaffinated the children ; whereof one, who had an Hatchet ftruck into his Skull,
and was left for dead, was ftrangely recovered.   The Woman
had Lain in about Eight Days.   They drag'd her out, and tied
her to a Poft, until the Houfe was rifled.   They then loofed her,
and bid her walk.   She could not ftir.   By the help of a Stick
fhe got half a ftep forward.   She look'd up to God.   On the
fudden a new ftrength entred into her.   She travelled that very
Day Twenty Miles a Foot : She was up to the Neck in Water
fix times that very Day in paffing of Rivers.   At night fhe fell
over head and ears, into a Slough in a Swamp, and was hardly
got out alive.   She got not the leaft Cough nor Cold by all this :
She is come home alive unto us.
Many more fuch Inftances might be mentioned.   We will
fuperfede them all, with a Relation of what befel *Mrs. Bradley*
of *Haverly.   Ab una Difce omnes.*

This Vertuous Woman had been formerly for Two Years
together a Captive in the Hands of the Barbarous Indians ; a
fubject of wondrous Afflictions, of Wondrous Deliverances.
Her Hufband at length found her out, and fetch'd her home, and
their Family went on happily for fix years together after it.   But
the Clouds return after the Rain.

On *February* 6, 1703-4, She with her Sifter, and a Maid or
two, and fome Children, (a Man being alfo in the Room) were
talking about the Indians, and behold, one of the Fierce *Tawnies*
looked in, with a Gun ready to Fire upon them.   The *Englifhman* pull'd him in, and got him down, and Mrs. Bradly took the
opportunity to pour a good quantity of fcalding Soap, (which
was then boyling over the Fire) upon him, whereby he was kill'd
immediately.   Another of the Tawnies follow'd at the Heels of
his [34] Brother, who ftabb'd the Englifhman to the Heart.
Unto him fhe difpenfed alfo a quantity of her Sope, which not
killing him, fhe with the other Women and Children ran into the
Chamber.   The Houfe was fired by the Indians, and Mrs. *Bradly*
with her Companions found it neceffary to retire behind the

Houfe. One of the Women fell into the Hands of the Indians; and they that remained were Mrs. *Bradly* and her Sifter; each of them having a Child of Mrs. *Bradlies* with her. The Sifter was difcerned by the Indians, who commanded her to come out unto them, and threatned that they would elfe cut her to pieces. Mrs. *Bradly* very generoufly bid her fit ftill, and wait for a better time to efcape; and offered her, that inafmuch as the Indians knew of but one there, fhe would be that one, and go out in her ftead. She did fo, and thereby her obliged Sifter and the Child with her were preferved; but Mrs. *Bradly* was no fooner come to the Salvages, but they employ'd a Head-breaker on the Child that fhe brought unto them.

She was not entred into a Second Captivity; but fhe had the great Encumbrance of being Big with Child, and within Six Weeks of her Time! After about an Hours Reft, wherein they made her put on Snow Shoes, which to manage, requires more than ordinary agility, fhe travelled with her Tawny Guardians all that night, and the next day until Ten a Clock, affociated with one Woman more who had been brought to Bed but juft one Week before: Here they Refrefhed themfelves a little, and then travelled on till Night; when they had no Refrefhment given them, nor had they any, till after their having Travelled all the Forenoon of the day Enfuing; and then too, whatever fhe took, fhe did thro' Sicknefs throw it up again.

She underwent incredible Hardfhips and Famine: A *Moofes* Hide, as tough as you may Suppofe it, was the beft and moft of her Diet. In one and twenty days they came to their Head-Quarters, where they ftayed a Fortnight. But then her Snow-fhoes were taken from her; and yet fhe muft go every ftep above the Knee in Snow, with fuch wearinefs, that her Soul often Pray'd, *That the Lord would put an end unto her weary Life!* until they came to another Place, where they ftay'd for three Weeks together.

[35] Here in the Night, fhe found herfelf ill, and having the help of only one Woman, who got a little Hemlock to lay about her, and with a few fticks made fhift to blow up a little Fire, fhe was in half an Hour Delivered of the Infant, that fhe had hitherto gone withal. There fhe lay till the next Night, with none but the Snow under her, and the Heaven over her; in a mifty and rainy feafon. She fent then unto a French Prieft, that he would fpeak unto her *Squa Miftrefs*, who then, without condefcending to look upon her, allow'd her a little Birch-Rind, to cover her Head from the Injuries of the Weather, and a little bit of dried Moofe, which being boiled, fhe drunk the Broth, and gave it unto the Child.

In a Fortnight fhe was called upon to Travel again, with her Child in her Arms: every now and then, a whole day together, without the leaft Morfel of any Food, and when fhe had any, fhe fed only on Ground-nuts and Wild-onions, and Lilly-roots. By the laft of *May*, they arrived at *Cowefick*, where they Planted their Corn; wherein fhe was put unto a hard Tafk, fo that the Child extreamly Suffered. The Salvages would fometimes alfo pleafe themfelves, with cafting *hot Embers* into the Mouth of the Child, which would render the Mouth fo fore, that it could not Suck for a long while together. So that it Starv'd and Dy'd.

There they ftaid until they Wed their Corn, but then fome of our Friend-Indians coming on them, kill'd Seven of them, whereat away they fled for *Canada*, and never faw their Corn-field any more. But they made a Forty-Days Ramble of it, before they reach'd thither, in which, if at any time, her Heart began to faint, her Miftrefs would be ready to ftrike the Mortal Hatchet into her Head.

[36] The *French* being thought more Civil to the Englifh than to the Indians, her Miftrefs thereat Provoked, refolved, that fhe would never Sell her to the *French*. According fhe kept her a Twelve-month with her, in her Squalid *Wigwam :* Where, in the following Winter, fhe fell fick of a Feavour; but in the very heighth and heat of her Paroxyfms, her Miftrefs would compel her fometimes to Spend a Winters-night, which is there a very bitter one, abroad in all the bitter Froft and Snow of the Climate. She recovered; but Four Indians died of the Feavour, and at length her Miftrefs alfo. Another Squa then pretended an Heirfhip unto her, with whom fhe lived, and faw many more ftrange Deliverances. They had the Small Pox in the Family; but fhe never had it. She was made to pafs the River on the Ice, when every ftep fhe took, fhe might have ftruck through it if fhe pleafed. Many more fuch Prefervations might come into her Story.

At Laft, there came to the fight of her a Prieft from *Quebeck*, who had known her in her former Captivity at *Naridgowock*. He was very Civil to Her, and made the *Indians* Sell her to a French Family, for Fourfcore Livers, where tho' fhe wrought hard, fhe Lived more comfortably and contented.

She poured out her continual Supplications to Heaven; Some-times Two or Three of her own Sex, would by Stealth, come to joyn with her in Supplicating to the Glorious LORD. She had her Mind often Irradiated with Strong Perfwafions and Affur-ances, that fhe fhould yet *See the Goodnefs of God*, in this Land of the Living. Her tender and Loving Hufband, accompanied Mr. *Sheldon*, in his Laft Expedition. He found her out, and fetch'd her home, a Second time; She arriv'd with thofe of the

Laſt Return from the Captivity; and affectionately calls upon her Friends, *O magnifie the LORD with me, and let us Exalt his Name together.*

[37] Becauſe of its having ſome Affinity with the foregoing Relations, and that we may at once diſcharge ourſelves of what we can relate concerning our Captives, we will proceed with a Coppy of a Letter ſent unto one of the Miniſters in *Boſton*.

[38]

A Letter from a Captive at *Port-Royal*.

Sept. 18. 1703.

'*Reverend Sir,*

'THE Occaſion of my now Writing to you is becauſe I lye
' under a Vow and Promiſe to the Great and Almighty
' God, to declare and make known his Wonderful Goodneſs and
' Mercy to me, and likewiſe to have His Name Bleſſed and
' Praiſed in your Congregation on my Behalf. I ſhall briefly
' Inform you.

' Being taken a Priſoner ſometime laſt *January* by the *French*:
' in going to *Port-Royal* we met with very Tempeſtuous Weather,
' and were faſt in an Harbour near Cape *Sables*. And here two
' *Frenchmen* had Orders from their Captain to take me with
' them, and go to *Port-Royal* by Land. They took with them
' but little Bread ; and we Travelled one Night in the Woods in
' a miſerable Condition. I had myſelf no Shoes or Stockings,
' but a piece of Skin wrapt about my Feet ; and the Snow being
' very deep, we could not Travel, being Weak for want of Pro-
' viſion, and loſt in the Woods, not knowing which way to go.

[39] ' One of the *Frenchmen* Loaded his Gun, and Preſented
' at me, telling me, *That it was impoſſible to find Port-Royal, I*
' *muſt Dye, and they muſt Eat me.* Then I begged Leave to
' Pray unto God, before he Kill'd me, and he Granted it. As I
' was at Prayer, it ſtruck into my Mind, That I had formerly
' heard yourſelf declare in your Pulpit, what Great and Wonder-
' ful Things hath been done by Prayer ; particularly, *That it had*
' *ſtopped the Mouths of Lions, and that it had Quenched the Vio-*

' *lence of the Fire.* So I earneftly begged of God, that he would
' manifeft his great Power to me, by turning the Hearts of thofe
' that were about to take away my Life.

 ' The Words were no fooner out of my Mouth, but the *French-*
' *man* feeming to have Tears in his Eyes, bid me rife up ; he
' would try one Day longer. And he bid me go and get Wood for
' a Fire. It prefently grew Dark ; and then I made an Efcape
' from them, and hid myfelf in the Woods, until the next Day
' that they were gone ; and then I found the way out of the
' Woods, unto the Water-fide, where I got *Clams.*

 ' Thefe *French-men* found the way to *Port-royal,* and there
' told what they had done. The Governour put them in Prifon,
' and fent out Two Men, and Charged them not to return, until
' they had found me, Dead or Alive. In Four Days after thefe
' *Frenchmen* left me, they found me Alive, and brought me Pro-
' vifion, and a Pair of Shoes, and carried me to *Port-royal.*

 [40] ' Thefe and many other Favours have I received from
' my Good God in the time of my Imprifonment; Bleffed and
' for ever Praifed be his Holy Name for it. Pray, Sir, give me
' Directions what I fhall do for the Great and Good GOD.

W. C.

---

[41]

OUR Eaftern Indians had no fooner, with all poffible Affurance renewed their League of Peace with us, but being
moved by the Inftigation of the *French,* they Perfidioufly and
Barbaroufly Surprifed Seven more of our naked and fecure Plantations ; and coming at once into the fcattered Families, they did,
on *Auguft* 10,–11, 1703 : Reward the Hofpitable Civilities that
were fhown them, with the Murder of above Seventy *Englifh*
People, and the Captivity of near an Hundred. Upon this there
Enfued Leffer Depredations, and Captivations, as the Treacherous Enemy found Opportunity for them.

 About half a year after thefe Calamities thus begun on the
Eaftern Parts of the Country, the *Weftern* had a tafte of the fame
Cup given to them. On *Feb.* 29, 1703–4. An Army confifting,
as it was judg'd, of about 400 *French* and Indians, made a Defcent
upon the little Town of *Deerfield,* the moft Northernly Settlement on *Connecticut-River,* which had long been a watchful and

an ufeful Barrier for the reft of the Plantations in the Neighbourhood.

They Surprifed the Place about an Hour or Two before Break of Day, and in a little time, not without Lofs to themfelves, Butchered and Captivated above 150 of the People.

Mr. *John Williams*, the Worthy Minifter of that Pious and Holy Flock, was carried into Captivity, with Five of his Children; two of which were Slain; and his Defirable Confort beginning to Faint at about a Dozen Miles of the doleful Journey, they there, like themfelves, cruelly Murdered her, and left her for the Funeral which her Friends afterwards beftow'd on her. Before they reach'd unto *Mont Real*, a Journey difpatch'd by the Parcels now divided in Twenty Days, more or lefs, near Twenty more of the Captives loft their Lives; for the manner was, that if any found themfelves not able to Travel thro' the Deep Snows now on the Ground, the Salvages would ftrike their Hatchets into their Heads, and there leave them weltring in their Blood.

F I N I S.

A

Modeſt Enquiry

INTO THE

Grounds and Occaſions of a Late

PAMPHLET,

INTITULED, A

MEMORIAL

OF THE

Preſent Deplorable State

O F

New-England.

By a Diſintereſted Hand.

L O N D O N:

Printed in the Year, 1707.

A

Modern Enquiry

INTO THE

Grounds and Occasions of a Late

P A M P H L E T

INTITULED,

MEMORIAL

OF THE

Present Deplorable State

OF

New-England.

By a Diſintereſted Hand.

L O N D O N,

Printed in the Year 1707.

A Modeſt Enquiry into the Grounds, &c.

A Pamphlet call'd, *The Memorial of the Preſent Deplorable State of NEW England,* having been received in Town with various Opinions, according to the different Intereſts, or capacities of its Readers ; Curioſity led me to look into it : And firſt beginning with the Title-Page,* I find it made up (as the Author calls it) of ſeveral *Original Papers Letters and Manuſcripts, Printed in the year* MDCCVII, *and Sold by* S. Philips &c. *Bookſellers in* Boſton. Which ſaid Pamphlet appear'd in Town about the Tenth of *July* laſt : upon which finding Mr *Cally's* † Affidavit was made the ſecond of *June* 1707, Mr *Partridge's* on the Twenty-firſt of the ſame Month and Year (both which are there Printed) and having ſeen this *Memorial* about the middle of *July* following, which does not give a *Months* time for the ſending it to NEW ENGLAND, Printing it there, and returning it again,) I could not help concluding, that no manner of credit ought to be given to it, upon the ſingle reputation of the Author. However to act impartially, I begin with his firſt Page, extolling the former happy ſtate of the *Province* in the *Charter* they enjoy'd before the Revolution : ‡ which ſufficiently ſhews how they regard the *Charter* they now have ; and conſequently what an Opinion they retain not only of that Power that took from them their *Old Charter,* but alſo of *K. William,* who was too wiſe, to return them their *Idol,* which he knew had been often *affrontingly* uſ'd in preceding Reigns. I know not what the Author means by the *unhappy, or rather happy reign of the late K. J.* ſo will leave it to be explain'd by himſelf as it ſhall hereafter ſerve his turn.§

NOW comes a heavy Charge againſt the late Governour Sir *Edmond Androſs,* made up of falſity and nonſence ; theſe are his words, *We ſhall not recriminate here the miſmanagement of the then Governour Sir* Edmond Androſs, *ſince that Gentleman is NOW in a future ſtate.* ‖ Which obliges me to give a ſhort account of the Revolution in *NEW ENGLAND.*

The firſt account of the Revolution in ENGLAND, came to NEW ENGLAND by Merchants Letters from *Barbadoes ;* upon which the People (without any regard to Authority) confin'd the Governour Sir *E. Andros,* and *Col. Dudley* the preſent Governour ; and would by no means liſten to the wholeſome advice that was given [2] by the Governour, to maintain the Peace of the

---

* Title-Page.   † Pag. 16. Pag. 25.   ‡ Pag. 1. Lin. 2.
§ Pag. 1. Lin. 13.   ‖ Pag. 2. Lin. 1.

Province; and let all things remain upon the fame foot they were,
till they had a more authentick account, and alfo Orders from
England; to which the Governour declar'd himfelf moft willing
to conform.   Thefe juft Arguments could not prevail, they had
got the Government into their own hands; they had formerly
been told by *Hugh Peters,* and fome fuch Paftors, that *Dominion
is founded in Grace;* and knowing themfelves to be *the elect
people of God,* they refolved to perfect what they had began;
fo over thefe two Gentlemen are fent Prifoners, who upon a full
hearing before His Majefty K. WILLIAM in Councel (to the
mortification of their Accufers) are Honourably acquited.   In
confideration of whofe *faithful Services,* and *fevere Ufage, Sir
E. Androfs* was made by K. WILLIAM Governour of *Virginia,
&c,* and *Col. Dudley Lieutenant-Governour* of the *Ifle of Wight;*
fince which Her *prefent Majefty* as a Demonftration of the fame
good opinion of *Col. Dudley* was pleas'd to let his Commiffion
for Governour of *New England,* be one of the *firft Acts* of her
Reign; and alfo very lately to conftitute Sir *E. Androfs's* Lieutenant-Governour of *Guernfey;* Happy in Her Majefty's Favour
and good Efteem of him; Honour'd by the Inhabitants of the
Ifland, who wonderfully admire Her Majefties Choice; and bleft
with a confiderable Eftate, *the due reward of his long Service
and Merit;* this is Sir *Edmond Androfs's prefent ftate,* his NOW
future ftate is to me incomprehenfible.

The Legend of Accufations that make up almoft two Pages,
and are laid down with fo much Acrimony againft the *prefent
Governour's* proceedings, when *Prefident* of the Council of *New
England,* fhall not be taken notice of, that having been difallow'd
when *Urged* before Her Majefty in Council; I fhall only make
this remark that *K. William* the Reftorer of our Liberties, would
never have diftinguifh'd this Gentleman by his Favours, had not
his *Innocency* been clearly prov'd, not only from his *Accufation* at
the beginning of the *Revolution,* but alfo from the *Memorial* deliver'd in againft him by Sir H. A. when *K. William* had appointed him Governour of *New England,* which *Memorial* as it
put the Governour to a large Expenfe, it was alfo attended with
the happinefs of her Prefent Majefty's giving her *Sanction,* to
what *K. William* so Judicioufly began.

THUS have I done with the Preamble, and am now come to
the *Memorial* it felf, drawn up in *Nine Articles,* each of which I
in- [3] tend to fpeak to feparately; but can't do it in any regular method; part of fome Articles being neceffary to explain
others.   Therefore I have incerted it *Verbatim,* that the Reader
comparing the Anfwer with the Memorial, may be better able to
judge of the Validity of the Accufation.

The *MEMORIAL.*

" *FIRST* in the year 1705, the Governour fent his Son *Wil-*
" *liam Dudley* with Captain *Vetch*, to *Canada*, under a pre-
" tence of Redeeming Captives ; but brought very few back to
" *Boſton* of thoſe that were there, and them of the meaneſt ſort,
" leaving the Principal of the ſaid Captives behind, to give them
" occaſion of going again, that they might have a Pretence to
" colour their Treacherous Deſign of Trading, as appears by the
" ſaid *Vetch's* acknowledgment of going to ſettle a Correſpondence
" with the Enemy, and carrying a Cargo out with him of 800 *l.*
" which according to their diſpoſal ; might amount to near 3000 *l.*
" as particularly Shot, which was ſold at 13 *Sous per Pound;*
" whereof they carried a conſiderable Quantity ; alſo Rigging,
" Pitch, Iron and other Neceſſaries, fit for ſupplying the *Indians*
" and *French;* and this done under a Colour of the ſaid *Vetch's*
" going to get in a Debt due to him from the *French* of 800 *l.*
" with the Governour's Approbation.

Secondly. " For ſetling a Correſpondency with the *French*
" Governour at *Port Royal*, for Exchange of Priſoners ; whereas
" it was indeed only a Cover for an Illegal Trade ; when at the
" ſame time the *French* there, were drove to ſuch extream Hard-
" ſhips, for want of Ammunition, Proviſion, *&c*, that moſt of their
" Principal People, were forced to go out a Privateering on our
" Coaſts, who were afterwards taken and brought into BOSTON ;
" particularly one *Battis,* a Man of great Note and Service among
" the Enemy, who had been a Barbarous, Murdering Fellow to
" the *Engliſh :* He with all the other *French* Priſoners were ſent
" to *Canada* and *Port-Royal*, and Diſcharged ; but great part of
" our People that were Priſoners, were left behind at the ſame
" time, and that becauſe our Governour had been falſe in his
" promiſe to the *French* Governour, who had reſtrain'd the *In-*
" *dians* from diſturbing our Fiſhery, and indeed [4] would not
" allow them any Ammunition for a conſiderable time, till our
" Governour taking the opportunity of the *Indians*, great Want,
" countenanced a Trade with them, and ſupply'd them by the
" Veſſels that were ſent as Tranſports (as aforeſaid) to fetch
" Priſoners ; when at the ſame time they were made Veſſels of
" Merchandize, as appears by the *Indian* Traders on their Trial.

Thirdly. " The Country are at a Vaſt Charge, in maintaining
" an Army yearly, to march ſeveral Hundred Miles up into the
" Country, to deſtroy the *Indians* Corn, the better to diſinable
" them to ſubſiſt ; for they have been ſo reduced (as by Informa-

" tion of the Captives) that a great part of them would perish
" for want, were it not for the supply they had from the said
" *Indian* Traders ; who particularly, sold about Eight Quarts of
" *Indian* Corn, for one large Beaver-skin ; which Trade has been
" all along countenanced by the Governour, which sufficiently
" appears by his being always unwilling the Prisoners taken in
" that Trade should be Fined, or Punished, even owned by *Vetch*,
" as in his Petition more at large is set forth.

Fourthly. " The Country was at a great Expense in Erecting
" a Fortification at *Casco-Bay*, and maintaining a number of Sol-
" diers for securing the same, thereby to suppress the Enemy, and
" keep sure Footing in that part of the Country ; and the Gov-
" ernour through some design or neglect, did suffer those Soldiers
" to remain there without any Commission-Officer, to the great
" dissatisfaction and dread to the Soldiers ; Insomuch that they
" declared to Captain *Cally* (a Member of the Assembly at *Boston*)
" that when the Enemy came upon them, they would surrender
" the Fort, and dare not resist for want of a Commission. Then
" Captain *Cally* made Application to the Assembly, which he
" found sitting when he came to *Boston*, and they represented to
" the Governor, that speedy care might be taken, that some
" Person might be Commissionated to Command that Fort, which
" with a great deal of difficulty was at last Obtained.

Fifthly. " And further as to the Governour's Countenancing
" this Private and Illegal Trade, the Country has been at vast
" Expence, occasion'd thereby ; insomuch that at one Sessions the
" last Summer the Assembly were forc'd to raise 33000 Pounds,
" for supporting, and maintaining the Charge they were put to,
" by the Enemy's Invasions, after they had a Supply ; that
" whereas if things [5] were rightly managed, and the Enemy
" kept back for want of those Supplys, one third part of the said
" Sum might have answered the End. The *Indians* that were
" supply'd by Those Traders, are the only People that destroy'd
" our Eastern parts, the Fishery, and the Coast of *Accady ;* and
" also the very same that were at Destroying of *Newfound-land*,
" particularly one *Escombuet*, a Principal Commander among them,
" who is generally one that Heads the *Indians*, when they come
" to Destroy the *English* in *New England*.

Sixthly. " The Governour with his Son *Paul*, not being con-
" tent with what Money they come fairly by, and over-greedy of
" Gain, are very Screwing and Exacting upon the People, par-
" ticularly upon sundry Inhabitants, taking away their Priviledge
" in catching of Whales, a Priviledge they have enjoy'd many
" Years before ; that is (under the pretence of *Drift-Fish ;*) what
" Whales are taken by Her Majesty's Subjects, he takes from

" them by Force, not giving them the liberty of a Trial at Com-
" mon Law, but for his own Ends decides the matter in the
" Admiralty, where his Son *Paul* is the Queen's Attorny and
" Advocate, thereby Encroaching the whole to themfelves, a
" thing never heard of before, and very much to the Prejudice
" of Her Majefty's good Subjects there, and that without
" Remedy.

Seventhly. " As to the Addrefs the Governour obtain'd, pre-
" tended to come over from the General Affembly at *Bofton* in
" his favour, for his Continuance, it was no more than what he
" Clandeftinely procured, by fending to his Particular Friends ;
" fuch who being either Related to him, or bore Commiffions
" under him, dare not deny his Requeft, and was never approved
" nor allowed of by the Affembly ; but on the contrary had not
" the Majority of the Country waited in expectation of her
" Majefty's favour, in fending another Governour, they would
" largely have fignify'd their Refentments and Diffatisfaction, in
" the Adminiftration of *Dudley's* Government.

Eighthly. " While the Great and General Affembly at *Bofton*
" were Sitting, there arrived a Flag of Truce from *Canada*, with
" a haughty demand of the Governour, for all the *French* Prifon-
" ers ; charging of him with breach of Promife, which was the
" occafion of the *French* Governours not fending feveral of the
" Prifoners, particularly a Minifter that was taken Captive at
" *Derefield*, detain'd [6] by the *French*, who might have been
" difcharg'd with fundry others.

Ninthly. " The Lower Houfe miftrufting the *French* Flag of
" Truce coming upon a Trading Defign, as well as for the Prifon-
" ers, order the Flag of Truce to be diligently fearched, who
" found on Board their Veffel fundry New Arms and Ammuni-
" tion hid in private places, particularly New Bullets hid among
" Peafe, and yet denied by the Commander, who was an *Englifh*
" Renegade, which Ammunition being brought before the Affem-
" bly, were generally concluded to be Bought in *Bofton*, where-
" upon the Governour interpofing, the matter was hufhed up and
" conniv'd at, to the great diffatisfaction of the Affembly and
" Country in General.

The *Firft* and *Second* Articles are moftly concerning the affair
of the private Trade, which fhall not be medled with by me, it
lying at prefent before *Her Majefty* undetermin'd ; but if any
Perfons are curious to know that matter, I prefume that Mr
Phips Agent for *that Country* will fully fatisfie them, if they are
not perverfely bent againft whatever makes out the Governour's
Innocency. The Gentlemen that carried on that Trade, was fo

far from finding any *Favour* from the Governour, (which they
might have affur'd themfelves of, if he had had any concern with
them) that the Extremity of the Laws of *New England* were put
in force againft them, and a *heavy Sentence* paffed upon them,
from which Sentence they *Appeal'd* to Her Majefty, who refer'd
them to the *Lords Commiffioners for Trade,* where the caufe was
argued in the behalf of the Petitioners, by that *Learned* and *Judicious Lawyer,* Mr *Weft* fo much to the fatisfaction of the Lords
Commiffioners, that a Report was made in their favour. Upon
which Her Majefty in Councel, was gracioufly pleas'd to order all
the *Acts* and *Proceedings* againft them to be *Repeal'd,* and declar'd *null* and *void.*

The Third Article Deplores the miferable ftate of the Country
in the vaft Charge they are at by defending themfelves againft
the *Indians.* Much can't be faid upon this occafion, for as War
in all Countries is attended with Expenfe, it is not to be expected
New England can be wholly exempted from it, but whoever will
confider the largenefs of the Country to be defended, (the Frontier being more than 200 Miles) and the number of the Enemys
to encounter with, muft admire the Excellency of the Governours
Adminiftration ; that fo much is done with fo little Expence,
either of Blood or Treafure.

[7] The *Fortifications* at *Cafco Bay* mentioned in the *Fourth*
Article was repair'd and made Tenable by the prefent *Governour,*
who took care to keep a *good Garrifon* in it, for the Defence of
the Country on that fide ; formerly Coll. *March* afterwards Capt.
Moody commanding in it. How it came to be without a Commiffion Officer, or whether it was fo (as this Gentleman complains)
I can't find upon the ftricteft enquiry, neither am I obliged to
believe it ; but admitting it ; feveral occafions, as marching out
with a Detachment, or the like, are not only Juftifiable but
neceffary. The Summ of this heavy Charge is, that upon the
firft notice that an Officer was wanting, the Governour fent one,
and the *Fort* is ftill in the poffeffion of the Government. Either
the Garrifon (admitting they had no Commiffion Officer) muft be
ignorant of *Military Difcipline,* or inclin'd to Mutiny ; otherwife
they ought to have fubmitted to the command of a *Serjeant,*
whofe *Halberd* was a fufficient Authority for fuch a Command
upon any *Emergency.*

The *Fifth* Article tells you the Summ that was given laft Year
for fupporting the Expenfes of the War *&c,* which the *Third*
Article makes very heavy, but does not name. And here it is
done fo obliquely, that the Author would endeavour to *infinuate,*
as though the Summ of 33000 *l.* was raifed more than once laft
Year ; which if it had been, he would have told you in plain

words. If I will believe that fo much was given as above mention'd, 'tis intirely upon the reputation of the Author, who in
fome cafes ought to produce Teftimonials. But admitting it ;
confider what is to be done with it, and the Wonder will be on
the other fide.   33000 *l. New England* Money, deducting the
Difcount, is reduced to lefs than 22000 *l. Sterling.* Any Man
that confiders the pay of the *Army* which confifts of 1900 Men ;
Maintaining the *Garrifons,* Providing *Magazeens,* The conftant
Charge of the *Province Gally,* The accidental occafions of hiring
Tranfport Ships, together with the other *Incidentals* that muft
neceffarely accrue ; will rather admire how fo fmall a Summ could
anfwer fuch large and expenfive Occafions. I am fearful the
Governour whofe *Sallery* comes alfo out of the above mentioned
Summ, is able to fpeak *fealingly* of the *frugality* of the Country.
If lefs Summs had done under preceeding Governours in time
of War, our Author would not have fail'd letting the World know
it.   I acknowledge fome damage has been formerly done in the
Eaftern Parts of *New England* by the *Indians,* and that *Efcombuet* did command thofe *Indians,* who in conjunction with the
[8] French made the Defcent upon *Newfound-Land,* and be it
alfo remembr'd to the Honour of the Governour, that this very
Efcombuet upon his drawing off from the Fort at *Newfound-Land,*
releafed feveral Englifh Captives, upon promife that all endeavours fhould be us'd at the *Britifh Court,* for removing Coll.
Dudley from the Government of *New England.* That an *Indian*
who is a *profefs'd* Enemy to the *Englifh American Settlements,*
and *thefe* Gentlemen, fhould *Joyntly* endeavour the removal of the
Governour, is worth obferving, I fhall only make this remark on
it, that as *Efcombuet* ufed formerly to make thofe *Devaftations* in
New England, which by the *Wifdom* and *Vigilance* of the Governour are now *Prevented,* fo thefe Gentlemen (he being kept at a
diftance) are lefs capable to carry on any affairs with him, if they
are fo inclined.

The *Sixth* Article contains a very Grevious Accufation againft
the Governour and his Son, and if the Facts were true, might
demand Juftice, but as it is, it ferves only to demonftrate the
Innocency of the Governour, and the *Malice* of the *Accufers.*
They fay *he Decides the Priviledge of Whale Fifhing, claim'd by
the People,* and yet *that it is Decided in the Admiralty ;* when all
the World muft know, that the Governour if he has any Intereft
in any of the Courts of Juftice, it muft be in the Common Law
Courts, and not in the *Admiralty,* where the Judge has an *Independant* Commiffion from *England,* and no manner dependency
upon the Governour. As for Mr. *Paul Dudley's* being *Advocate,*
let Coll. *B—ld* the Judge clear himfelf if he be any ways byaff'd
thereby. But it muft be allowed far more probable, that the fame
Mr. *Paul.Dudley,* as the Queen's Attorney General, and the de-

pendance of the Courts upon the Governor, could much better Byaſs any other Court than that ; ſo that nothing can better demonſtrate the Governours innocency, than bringing forth Groundleſs matters in charge againſt him. If any Encroachments have been made upon the People by the Court of Admiralty, let the Judge anſwer it ; but whether it be ſo or not, this Article (as the others) is an abuſe upon the Governour.

How it hapened that no Addreſs from the General Aſſembly at *Boſton* was preſented to Her Majeſty, by the return of the laſt Fleet I know not ; but am certain that the Honourable the Aſſembly are little beholden to this Author for the Reaſons by him given in the Seventh Article, ſo many occaſions calling for one ; as Congratulating Her Majeſty upon the Great and Glorious [9] Succeſſes of the preceding Year, a Gratefull tender of their Allegiance and Duty to Her Majeſty, *&c.* which makes me conclude that ſome Occaſions have interven'd, beſides what this Memorialiſt has given. 'Tis wonderful that this Honourable Body are full of *Reſentments, and Diſſatisfaction in the Adminiſtration of Coll.* Dudley, and yet not write one word of Complaint againſt him, and the Reaſon that is given is yet more remarkable, *Viz. They expected Her Majeſty would ſend another.* If the Governour's Adminiſtration is or has been oppreſſive, the Aſſembly are Deficient in their Duty to Her Majeſty, in not making their Complaints, as on the contrary to the Governour, in not giving him his due praiſe if merited. The four Addreſſes annex'd to this, as they recommend the Governour to Her Majeſty, worthy the Station She has been pleaſ'd to Honour him with, and unanimouſly beg Her Gracious Continuance of him, ſo I muſt conclude the delay of an Addreſs from the Aſſembly, has not been thus long retarded by any diſſatisfaction to the Governour, but however will not take upon me to be their Advocate for ſuch a ſurpriſing omiſſion. Having no manner of reaſon to ſuſpect that the Honourable Aſſembly have leſs regard for the Governour now, than they had when they preſented their laſt Addreſs to Her Majeſty, I have alſo annexed that with the others.

As to the *Eighth Article ;* upon the coming of the Flag of Truce, there was a general Exchange of Priſoners, when unhappily five or Six Children were got amongſt the *more diſtant Indians,* ſo could not be exchang'd ſo early as the others, but were included in the Article. The Miniſter taken at *Derefield* was the Reverend Mr *Williams,* who alſo was exchang'd at the ſame time with the other Priſoners, but by a *Particular Agreement,* which obliges me to explain the Story of *Battis* mention'd in the Second Article. This Man after he was taken Priſoner, was accuſed of ſeveral Murders, but no ſufficient proof being made out againſt him, he remained a Priſoner of War ; the Governour who knew him to be an *acceptable Leader* amongſt the *Indians*, not being willing to part with him though *often* demanded ; till underſtanding that the Reverend Mr *Williams* could have his *Enlargement* upon no other terms ; the Governour in reſpect to Mr *Williams* ſubmitted to it. This Author that accuſes the Governour, for *diſcharging Battis*, and at the ſame time deplores the hard Fate of Mr *Williams's Captivity*, could not be ignorant of the Return of Mr *Williams*, as well as of Mr *Battis's* Diſcharge.

[10] The *Ninth Article* as it commends the *Vigilancy* of the Aſſembly, ſo it no ways concerns the Governour, but becauſe the Reader may think the *Arms* and *New Bullets* that were found in the French Ship of Truce, were ſufficient to Arm the whole French Settlement, take the account as it is.   Upon a Suſpition that ſome Clandeſtine Trade was managed by this Truce Ship, the *Aſſembly* Deputed ſome of their *Own Body* to ſearch the Ship, who found in it Five *Fuzee's,* which they brought with them, and fifteen Pounds of Small-ſhot ; enough to ſhoot a few Sea Fowle in their return, (as indeed that was the true meaning) but not to annoy an Enemy, or defend themſelves.   The *Governour's interpoſing and getting the matter huſh'd up to the diſſatisfaction of the Aſſembly, and Country in general,* as this Memorialiſt ſays, is trifling, and needs no other Reply but Laughter.

I would willingly have omitted reciting any other parts of this Pamphlet, the Author having, as he ſays, including in the *Preceeding* Nine Articles, all the * Modern *Miſmanagements of the Governour,* and alſo the *Particular Grievances* that afflict the *Province :* But a little afterwards he tells you that out of the † *Vaſte* number of Letters of *Complaints* that are come over againſt the Governour, the TWO that he has Publiſh'd are Eminently diſtinguiſhable ; the firſt for the ‡ *Character* of the Gentleman that writ it, who is a *Great Bleſſing* to his *Native Country.* The other for the ‖ *Shortneſs, Plainneſs,* and *Veracity.*   Therefore I rather ſubmit to let them have a place here, than leave it to any Prejudiced Perſon to ſay that Partiality Curtail'd ſuch material Evidences.

* Pag. 3. Lin. 19.   ‡ P. 10. Lin. 19.
† P. 10. Lin. 24.   ‖ P. 10. Lin. 26.

Bofton. New England, *Octob.* 2d, 1706.

SIR,

*I*NASMUCH *as you have expeated from me, a true and brief
Reprefentation of feveral Matters relating to this Province, I
fhall with all poffible faithfulnefs endeavour it. Our prefent
Governour is not without a number of thofe whom he has by Promotions and Flateries made his Friends; but this hinders not a
much more confiderable Number, from wifhing that we had a
Governour who would put* [11] *an end unto the horrid Reign
of Bribery in our Adminiftration, and who would not infinitely
incommode her Majefty's Service, by keeping the People in continual jealoufies of his Plots upon their moft Valuable Interefts.*

*What the difpofition of the People towards him is, you may
guefs by this. There was lately prepar'd an Addrefs from hence
to the Queen, upon many Important Articles, but by certain Arts
there was got into it a Claufe, to defire of the Queen, that this
Governour might be continued; the Reprefentatives Voted all the
reft of the Addrefs, but this Claufe was abfolutely rejeaed; they
could not get above five or fix Votes for it, fo the whole Addrefs
(which was Contrived by a Party for nothing but that Claufe) fell
to the Ground.*

There happened lately a Number of Perfons, namely, Bouland,
Vetch, Roufe, Lawfon, Philips, *and* Cauplin, *to be taken managing
an unlawful Trade with the* French *and* Indians, *the Commodities wherein they Traded were fuch, that the Aa of Parliament
made their Crime to be High Treafon; and we had no Aa of the
Province relating to that Matter, but was defeaively expreft:
Our Merciful Affembly was mighty loath to proceed unto fo fevere
a Judgment as that of Death upon thefe Offenders. The Offenders Petitioning for it, the General Affembly were (very much by
the Governour's Influence) drawn into it, to take the Tryal of them
into their own hands; and as only Guilty of an High Mifdemeanour, the Vote for it was obtain'd in a Thin Houfe, upon a
hurry at Breaking up, and fome Claufes in the Charter were fo
conftrued as to Countenance it. Upon their coming together again,
they would fain have revoked their Votes, as fearing that the
very Perfons who had been their Tempters into it, would turn their
Accufers, and improve it by way of Complaint, for the Enemies
of our Charter to work upon; but the Governour would by no
means permit the Revocation of that wrong ftep, (if it were one)
fo the Tryal proceeded, and the Offenders were Fined in feveral
Sums, by an Aa of the Governour and Affembly.*

*It is now faid that the Ingrateful Men who were faved from
the Gallows, by the Tendernefs of the Government, are now cutting*

our Throats, and Petition home againft the Government, for Fining them inftead of Hanging them ; yea it is alfo faid, that the very Perfon who was the chief caufe of drawing the Affembly into this Extraordinary Proceeding, intends to make an ill ufe of it againft the Country ; If you are fenfible of any things of this nature carrying on, we [12] *pray you to add unto the reft of your Offices, that of an Interceffion, that an harmlefs People, furpriz'd into an error, may not be punifh'd any otherwife, than by the removal of fuch as have been the caufe of it ; and fo much for that.*

Sir, You would do a vafte Service to the Crown, if you would fet forward the Defigns of reducing Canada, *and Poffeffing* Nova Scotia, *a much lefs Fleet than what Annually goes into the* Indies, *coming early enough in the Spring, may eafily do the former, even in the way thither ; and a* Scotch *Colony might be of good Confequence to do the latter ; but if any affiftance from* New England *fhould be expected in this matter, it is of abfolute neceffity that the Country have a Governour whom the People may fomewhat rely upon.*

Sir, You are born to do the Queen and the Nation Service ; you are fpirited for great Undertakings, you are highly beloved and efteemed among our People in this Land, and wherever you have come ; 'tis wifhed you may do fome confiderable Action in this Affair.

I have earneftly folicited to Addrefs one of the Moft Illuftrious Patriots of the Englifh *Nation, my* Lord High *Treafurer, with fome of thefe Intimations. That Noble Perfon is known to be fuch a Patron to all Good Men, and fuch a Defence of Oppreffed Innocence and Liberties, that we all fly to him as our Unqueftionable Refuge. I am well fatisfy'd there would need nothing (to fpeak Humanely) to make this Country eafie and happy, but for the Excellent Perfon to have an exact Reprefentation of our Circumftances ; nothing hinders me from attempting it, but the hazard of doing what may be thought a Prefumption in one fo much a ftranger to him : Neverthelefs I am defired by fome Confiderable Perfons to move you, that you would wait upon his Lordfhip, and fully acquaint him with the Matters now laid before you.*

> May the Almighty profper you,
> I am Sir,
> Your Obliged Servant &c.

[13] Poftfcript,

Sir, *I may inform you of one Action lately done among us, which I know you will be pleas'd withal : Upon the advice of the*

Extream Diſtreſs, whereto the French *Invaſion had brought* St. Chriſtophers, *and* Nevis ; *the People of* New England *in a moſt Chriſtian manner, expreſs'd their Charity towards thoſe, who perhaps would have hardly done the like for them on a like occaſion. We made a Collection for the Relief of their Neceſſities, the Collection was I am told, between* Seven and eight hundred Pounds, *in this Collection there were two Churches in* Boſton, *the* South *and the* North, *one gave ſomewhat above a* 100 l. *the other gave a little under it. Certainly a Country ſo ready to ſerve her Majeſty, and to help their fellow Subjects, ought to have a room in the thoughts of all Good Men in the* Engliſh *Nation.*

The Reverend Mr *C. M.* Author of the foregoing Letter has gain'd ſo much upon the blind Obedience of the Inferiour ſort of People in *New England,* by his ſeeming Sanctity, and has ſo inſinuated himſelf into the opinion of ſome of good Credit *here,* under the notion of a *Patriot,* that in order to let them *ſee the Man,* it becomes neceſſary to ſay a few words of him in General, and of this Letter in Particular. He begins with promiſes of all *Poſſible Faithfulneſs* in his Relation, and then tells you that the Friends of the Governours, by Promotion or Flattery, are made ſo *numerous,* that one might naturally conclude he muſt carry whatever he propoſes ; thoſe that oppoſe the Governours Proceedings having as he intimates no other power than Wiſhes, whereas in the ſecond Paragraph the Scene is quite chang'd ; for an Addreſs being prepared to Her Majeſty upon *many Important Articles,* it was *Rejected* for the ſake of a Clauſe brought in, to deſire Her Majeſty's *Continuance of the Governour.* 'Tis pitty the *Important* Affairs of the Province ſhould be retarded upon any Private Account : But afterwards to ſhew you thoſe *Important Articles* were not of the laſt conſequence, he tells you the *whole Addreſs* was *contrived by a party for nothing but a Clauſe about the Governour.* When it beſt anſwers the Ends of theſe People, then the Governour's Intereſt is ſo great that all things are tranſacted at his pleaſure, whereas at other times they wont allow him to have Intereſt enough to ſupport the Dignity of his Station. I have in the Anſwer to the Seventh Article ſaid what I thought neceſſary about the Aſſembly's not Addreſſing Her Majeſty.

[14] The Third and Fourth Paragraphs are wholly upon the *Indian* Trade, ſo muſt expect the ſame Anſwer that was given to the Two *firſt Articles* of the Memorial. Be pleas'd only to obſerve that whereas in ſeveral parts of the Pamphlet the Governour is cenſur'd about the Tryal of the Gentlemen accus'd of the Trade, here 'tis plain 'twas wholly done by the Aſſembly, for which reaſon this Gentleman calls them the *Merciful Aſſembly,* and ſpeaking of the Tryal calls it the *Tenderneſs of the Govern-*

ment &c and in truth they ought to take it all to themſelves.
For the Traders were at firſt committed by the *Lower Houſe of
Aſſembly* upon ſuſpicion *&c*, and the ſecond time by the *ſame
Houſe* for *High Miſdemeanour* without Col. *Dudley's Knowledge*
or *Privity*, neither was their any mention of Treaſon in either
of their Commitments duly atteſted : But to be more clear, the
Laws of *New England* then in force could make it no more than
High Miſdemeanour, though ſince, that defeet is provided againſt
by the *Direction of the Governour ;* for an act is paſt in *New
England*, declaring ſuch proceedings *High Treaſon.*

'Tis of no ſignification to inſinuate that the Aſſembly were
drawn into this Proceding by the Governour, the Governours
Intereſt (as the ſecond Paragraph of this Letter ſays) not being
able to get more than ſix Voices upon a more Important Occaſion.

The Pride and Vanity of the Man is very remarkable in his
Fourth Paragraph preſuming to Intrench upon the Office of his
Superior's in laying down Military Scheames, oppoſite to thoſe
that are now Tranſacting in his Native Country, and propoſing
the advantage (upon ſucceſs) to thoſe that in all probability will
have no hand in the attempt.

I will not pretend to gueſs who is meant by this Paragraph,
Sir, You are born to do the Queen and Nation Service &c. But
will aſſure you, Sir. that Col. *Dudley* before he left *England* had
abundance of Letters from *New England* fill'd with the *like
Rhetorick*, ſome of them near of kind to the Gentleman that
writ this : Therefore let not the Gentleman to whom this is directed, propoſe to himſelf if ever he becomes Governour, (as I
ſee no likelihood of it) to be better uſed than Col. *Dudley* and
his Predeceſſors have been ; If he will be alſo ſteady in the
performance of his Duty to Her Majeſty and the Nation.
The ſame *Cauſes* will always be attended with the ſame *Conſe-
quences ;* and the *Hereditary Rancour* that appears in this
[15] Holy Man's Letter, as well as in many of his Actions, will
Everlaſtingly be *Oppoſite* to Government, even though it were
Angelical.

What Mr *C. M.* ſays in his laſt Paragraph is ſo exceeding juſt
that 'tis ſurpriſing to find it from the ſame Pen. — All Mankind
muſt concur with the Honourable Character that he there gives
my Lord Treaſurer, he is juſtly by him ſtiled, *A Patron to all
Good Men. A Defence of Oppreſſed Innocency and Liberty.* 'Tis
for theſe and his many other valuable Qualities, that Her Majeſty
in Her *Conſummate Wiſdom*, has thought fit to place him in ſo
exalted a Station ; and 'tis from his *Patronage*, that all thoſe that

wifh well to *New England*, affure themfelves that that *Province* will *Flourifh* in fpight of *Faction*, and the Governour be *confirm'd* to the confufion of his Oppofers. Whether the Addrefs (at the End of this) from the whole Body of the Clergy of *New England*, *Gratefully* acknowledging Her Majefty's Favour, in *Appointing* and *Continuing*, Col. *Dudley* their Governour, (the like of which was never before feen from that Venerable Body under any Adminiftration) ought to be lefs regarded than the Venomous Letter of one Malecontent Prieft, let Impartiality determine.

I have done with the Letter, but the Poftfcript, though Foreign to the Occafion will admit of this remark ; That a *Body of People* that have been fo liberal in their Charity to their *Suffering Neighbours*, muft (Generally fpeaking) be better Chriftians, (however Characteriz'd by Mr *C. M.*) than to trouble Her Majefty, with Groundlefs Complaints againft the prefent Governour, whofe fteady Loyalty, Great Knowledge, and unparallel'd Clemency, is endeavouring to make them *Happy*, and *Flourifhing*, even againft the *Oppofition* of fome Turbulent Spirits, that can't endure Conformity either in Church or *State*.

Mr *C. M.* would have been more ingenuous, being he thought fit to mention this Charity, if he had given a faithful account of it, and told you, that the Tendernefs of the Governour, (whofe defigns of doing good are very extenfive) had by a Brief, (the Copy of which you'l find at the End) excited the People to this Act of Charity : And after the Money was Collected, faw it laid out in Provifions, and fent to them ; which in their unhappy Circumftances, was of the utmoft confequence. Whilft this Reverend Gentleman, is fpeaking of this Charity of the Province to St. *Chriftophers* and *Nevis* in their Diftrefs, be pleas'd to obferve his own Charity : *The People of* New England *in a moft Chriftian manner exprefs'd* [16] *their Charity towards thofe, who perhaps would have hardly done the like for them upon a like occafion.*

A small Tract of Religion coming to my Hands a few years fince, Written by the Reverend Mr. *C. M.* I could not without fome remark take notice of a Paffage in the Preface, which is to this effect, That being arrived at the Thirty fecond year of his Age, he had alfo Publifh'd Thirty two Volumns ; However I concluded that experience would rectifie a little youthful vanity, which I thought was atton'd for, by the ability and inclination the Man had to do Good ; but I find him in Spirituals as failable as in Politicks, or he would not have attempted a *Pretended Vifion*, to have converted Mr *Frafier a Jew*, who had before conceiv'd fome good Notions of Chriftianity : The Confequence was, that the *Forgery* was fo plainly detected that Mr *C. M.* confeft it ; after which Mr *Frafier* would never be perfwaded to hear any more of Chriftianity.

The Particular I am now going to fpeak to, fhould have been omitted, but without it the Doctors way of *Aequivocating* could not be fo well known. The ftory is this : A Gentlewooman of *Gayety*, near *Bofton*, was frequently vifited by the Reverend Mr. *C. M.* which giving offence to fome of his Audience, he promifed to avoid her Converfation. But *Good* intentions being fruftrated by *Vicious* Inclinations, he becomes again her humble Servant ; this *Reciprocal* promife being firft made, that *NEITHER OF THEM SHOULD CONFESS THEIR SEEING EACH OTHER :* However it becoming again publick, his Father accufed him of it, who after two or three HEMS to recover himfelf, (like Col. *Partridge* at the Council-Board) gave this *Aequivocal* Anfwer, *INDEED, FATHER, IF I SHOULD SAY I DID SEE HER, I SHOULD TELL A GREAT LYE.* This is the Gentleman diftinguifhable for his *Character ;* next comes the Letter, *Short*, and *Plain*, and nothing in it but Veracity.

SIR,

ALL *the People here are bought and fold betwixt the Governour and his Son* Paul ; *they are fo Mercenary that there is no Juftice to be had without Money ; there is not one Publick place in the Government, that is worth Money, but what the Governour or* Paul *goes halves with. In fhort, the whole Country is very uneafie, and the People here are fo univerfally fet againft him, that Her Majefty can fcarcely give a greater influence of Her tender care and regard to them, than by a removal of him, which to my certain knowledge would be* [17] *foon follow'd by a fincere and Hearty Acknowledgment of Her Majefty's fingular Favour to them in that Particular.*

R. A.

I am forry I am obliged to take notice of Mr *Ar—ngs* Letter, but as it is produced in Evidence, againft the Governour and his Son, and as the Author of the *New England* Memorial draws *Inferences* from this, and the foregoing Letter, it becomes neceffary upon this occafion to look into it, but with the utmoft tendernefs and compaffionate regard, for the prefent Circumftances of the Gentleman, which I am told are very contracted, I think Mr *Ar—nge* is very little beholden to his Correfpondents in *London* for fo publickly expofing a Letter, which muft be attended with very uneafie confequences to him, if the Clemency of the Governour and his Son is not very remarkable. Nothing to an Impartial Reader can be a greater argument of the Uprightnefs of the Governour and his Son, than to find that the *Rancour* of this Man, has not thought fit to give one particular inftance, to

Corroborate his General Accufation. He fhould have told us in particular who are the People *that are Bought and Sold*, and given fome inftances of corruption in *Judicial Proceedings*, or any other *parts* of the Governour's *Adminiftration* and have nam'd ' the Sums of Money *Criminally* Gain'd and *Divided*. Sure I am, it is not the effects of his good nature, that makes him forbear mentioning any of the Particulars by me enquired after.

His *advifing* Her Majefty to remove the Governour, *affuring* Her, that to *his Own certain knowledge* 'twill be very acceptable to the People, is fuch an exceeding inftance of the Impudence of the *Man*, that can fcarcely be parallel'd even amongft the whole body of the *Seditious*. And then he concludes, the Province will become *fincere and hearty Acknowledgers of Her Majefty's fingular Favour to them in that Particular*.

I fhould injure the refpect that's due to the *Honourable* the *Council* and *Affembly* of *Maffachufetts Bay*, to imagine they will neglect inquiring into the Authority this Man has, for thus *Saucily* advifing Her Majefty, nay even telling Her, that *Sincerity* and hearty *Acknowledgments*, are only to be expected to Her Majefty from *New England*, upon the Terms by *Him* Prefcribed.

The Two preceeding Letters produce three fubfequent Inferences, *viz.*

[18] I. *THAT WITHOUT MONEY THERE IS NO JUSTICE IN NEW ENGLAND.**
What a Difmal Character is here given of the whole People of that Flourifhing Country, *Clergy* and *Laiety*, *Merchant* and *Peafant &c*, are all involved in this *heavy* Accufation. If this be true, no wonder that a Governour *Fearing God and hating Covetoufnefs*, is made uneafie in the Faithful Difcharge of his *Office*.
† II. *A GENERAL UNEASINESS UNDER, AND OPPOSITION, TO THIS GOVERNOUR THROUGH THE WHOLE COUNTRY.*
Speak for your felves ye Collective Bodies of the People: The Honourable the *Affembly*, the *Reverend the Clergy*, ye *Merchants* and *Traders* at *Bofton*, and alfo ye the *Honourable*, the *Council* and *Reprefentatives* of *New Hamtfhire;* fpeak I fay, for your *Selves*, and tell the World, that Infatuation hung over your Heads, to make you Recommend to Her *Majefty* a Man againft whom there is a ‡ *General Uneafinefs through the whole Country*, to be continued Governour amongft you. But if you

---

* Pa. II. L. 7.   † P. II. L. 17.   ‡ P. II. L. 17.

are fenfible thefe *Accufations* are *Calumnies* and are well affur'd (as you fay in your feveral Addreffes you are) that your Governours Adminiftration * *has* and *always will have a Tendency to the Promotion of Her Majefty's Intereft,* and alfo to the *Eafe and Satisfaction, of all Her GOOD Subjects,* that his *Wifdom. Diligence Courage* and *Fidelity,* are Exemplary, with many other Qualifications becoming a Governour : Then fpeak like your felves (in Juftification of your Injur'd Governour, and your own Reputations, thus barbaroufly attackt) with a Voice that fhall for the future filence all thofe Difpifers of Authority.

III. *A FERVENT DESIRE TO BE EASED OF OP-PRESSION.*†

'Tis for this very End that Her *Majefty* and Her *Allyes* are now engaged in War. Let not the People of *New England* fufpect that Her Majefty whofe Compaffionate Affiftance is extended towards all the oppreffed Nations about her, will be wanting to her *GOOD* Subjects of *New England,* neither will I imagine they'l (for the *FUTURE*) neglect any opportunities of returning their *Duty* and *Gratitude* to Her Majefty.

I am obliged to follow the Steps of the Author ‡ who *Prefents the Reader with a farther account of the Mifmanagements of the Governour* by *another Hand,* that is to fay, by Mr *P—dge,* a mighty *Affiftant in carrying on this work,* as appears by this *long* account, (taking up almoft four pages) his *two Affidavits,* his *Certificate,* and alfo his *Speech* before Her Majefty in *Council.* The reafon that [19] this Gentleman gave for embarking in this caufe fhall be known in its place. This *Farther account* tells you of a Letter fent to Mr *Waldron* § and himfelf, by the Governour ; recommending it to the *Province of New Hampfhire,* to draw up an Addrefs to her Majefty, which was done ; and fo generally accepted, that Mr *Waldron* had no manner of occafion to ufe any art with the Council, and Reprefentatives, to perfwade them to what they were fo dutifully inclin'd. This *Farther account* is almoft full of Repetitions of what has been fpoke· to already, which I fhall omit, only taking notice of his new matter. The Governours Correfpondence with ‖ *Gallen Emefary* was fo Beneficial to the Province, in foreknowing the intended Defigns of the *French* and *Indians,* which capacitated him to provide againft them, that I doubt not but the feveral Prefents that the Governour (to this Gentlemans knowledge) fent him, are Retaliated by the Country.

'Tis very wide to draw any Conclufion from this following accufation ¶ becaufe Captain *Furber* told Mr *P—dge,* that the *French* Prifoners told him that they had heard the Governour of *Port-Royal* fay, that he had promis'd that he would not let the

---

* *The Addreffes.*
† P. 11. L. 3.
‡ P. 12. L. 11.

§ P. 11. L. 7.
‖ *The Addreffes.* P. 12. L. 36.
¶ P. 13. L. 35.

Indians have Powder and Shot, that therefore he did not do it, when he had it to fpare. Thofe *Indians* are his Mafter's Subjects, or at leaft his Allies, and let no Man believe that any of the King of *France's* Governours, are fo *good natur'd*, as not to put Arms into the hands of thofe, that they can depend upon, will ufe them to annoy their Mafter's Enemies in time of War. Neither let it be fufpected that the *French* don't take care to fupply their Plantations, with Warlike Stores, (without expecting to buy them of their Enemies Clandeftinely) though fometimes the Accidents of the Sea may retard them, which I fuppofe was the cafe when the Governour of *Port Royal* (if at all) made thefe promifes. I know not how many of the Enemy have been kill'd fince the prefent Governours time, having feen no Lift, but I believe more than * *an Old Woman* and two *Girls*, which is all this *Farther account* allows. † Several were kill'd at *Derefield;* ‡ Our *Indians* kill'd *Seven* at *Cowftick*,§ another kill'd an *Indian* or *two* before he was taken ; ‖ Mrs *Bradley* fcalded one Fellow to Death with hot Soap, and alfo *difpofed a Quantity of her Soap to another*, with the like Heroical intention, but it not fucceeding at the firft, she ran from him.

Thefe Particulars I find in the Pamphlet now under confideration ; As for the Governours foreknowing that the Enemy would not (or to fpeak properly durft not) appear in a Body like [20] an Army ; but in fculking Parties of Twenty, or Thirty, it fpeaks fo much the Honour and good Intelligance of the Governour than nothing need be faid of it. The Addrefs from the Militia of *Maffachufetts* Bay, is a very honourable one, and worthy the Gentlemen that fign'd it. they being moft of them the principal Men of the Country ; let Mr *P—dge* (who is gone over) tell them they durft not do otherwife, and I fhall be furpriz'd, if I don't hear of his Correction.

Five Affidavits, and one Certificate, come next ; two of them by *John Calley*, Mariner ; one by *Thomas Newton*, Gent. and the other two, and the· Certificate, by *William Partridge*, Efq ; all which are now before Her Majefty. They are too mighty things for me to meddle with ; but a Word or two of the feveral Occafions, that may feem to have ruffled thefe Gentlement, may not be improper. Mr *P—dge* has publickly given the Reafon of his Anger againft the Governour ; which is, becaufe the Governour did not interpofe his Authority, to difcharge *Jethro Furber*, Mafter of a *Veffel* belonging to the faid *P—dge*, who was in Confinement, and under a Profecution in the Admiralty Court at *Bofton*, at the Suit of Her Majefty ; for enticing away feveral Sea-men out of Her Majefties Ship the *Deptford*, Captain *Stuckley* Commander. The Governour could act no part in this Affair, the Caufe lying in a Court independant of him : But if it had

* P. 16. L. 26.   † P. 41. *Lin.* 19.   ‡ P. 35. *Lin.* 94.
§ P. 32. L. 10.   ‖ P. 33. L. 33.

been never fo much in his Power, it would have given ground
for a very juft Complaint againft him, to countenance any Perfons, againft whom there is full proof of enticing the Men out of
Her Majefties Ships of War ; the want of whom, may expofe
them to great danger from the Enemy or otherwife.

Mr. *John C—y* has been ferviceable in taking two Prizes in
America; whether the Governour was too fevere upon him, in
directing the Collector to take them into his Care for Her Majefty's Ufe, after Mr *C—y* appropriated them to his own ufe, I
leave to others to determine.

* Mr. *N—ton* accufes the Governour, for not permitting him to
go to *Rhode Ifland,* to condemn fome Prizes (being deputed thereunto by *W. At—d* Efq.) unlefs the faid Governour had a Hundred Pounds procur'd him by the faid *N—n.* The Governour
might have prevented his going, very juftly ; but however, if the
Hundred Pounds had been paid for that leave, it would have
been a principal part of the Affidavit.

[21] From the Affidavits, we come to fome Remarks made by
this Author : Firft, † *Can any Man that loves not a* French
Intereft, call thofe trivial ? Yes truly, I make no manner of
doubt, but a Man may be very honeft, and a hearty Lover of
Great-Britain, and alfo of *New England ;* and yet fee through
the Malice, and Falcity of thefe Accufations. The Author need
not have gone fo far back, as to the ‡ *Athenians,* to have found
out Prefidents for punifhing great Officers for Male-Adminiftration ; fuch Examples might be feen in the Annals of *England ;*
but we muft not revive the old *Abington* Law, of punifhing Men
before they are prov'd guilty. Have a little patience Gentlemen,
there is a Day appointed for hearing all that can be faid againft
the Governour ; Her Majefty is *Juft,* She'll hear both fides, and
then *decree Righteous Judgment.* § *To do Juftice and Right, is
the moft Invaluable Jewel in* Magna Charta. I am not prefum-
ing to queftion the Righteoufnefs of our Laws ; but the Law of
Mofes is much older. The Spirit of Perverfenefs is mighty
vifible in the Gentlemen, or elfe he would not have gone to
Athens, to find out Prefidents for *Englifh* Men ; or quoted Magna
Charta, to prove the Neceffity of Keeping the Ten Command-
ments.

‖ 'The Cries fent up to Heaven, by the many poor Souls
' lately moft inhumanly butchered by the mercilefs *Indians* ——
' will certainly draw down Redrefs from him, who is not only
' *REX MAGNUS & REX SOLUS,* but *JUDEX SUPRE-*
' *MUS,* who hath *IMPERIUM SINE FINE,* as well as *SINE*
' *LIMITE.*' Undoubtedly, God Almighty hath heard and regarded, the Cries and Sufferings of thofe poor People ; and alfo,

---

* *Pag.* 26. † *Pag.* 30. *l.* 2. ‡ *Pag.* 30. l. 9.
§ *Pag.* 30. l. 15. ‖ *Pag.* 30. *l.* 28.

without any manner of queſtion, the fame of the *Proto-Martyr*
of the Country, the poor *Weaver*, whoſe only Crime was, that he
was not a *Cobler*. And here the *Attributes* of *God* are exprefs'd
in a Language, that it may be, fome of that Country may call
Popery ; but there is fomething fo agreeable, and melting in the
Chiming of Words, as *Rex Magnus*, and *Rex Solus*, *Sine Fine*,
and *Sine Limite*, that it could not well be omitted ; otherwiſe the
Author might from the *Common-Prayer-Book*, have quoted more
proper Attributes, and much more intelligible to the People.

    * I am now come to the Account of feveral Barbarities *&c.*
committed by the *Indians*, intermix'd with fome memorable
Providences, which fill ten Pages to very little purpofe, there
being in them nothing uncommon to Frontiers, that are con-
tiguous to undiſciplin'd barbarous People, fuch as *Tartars, Indians*, or the like.

    † [22] I can't be very much furpris'd, that when a Crew of
Indians that had taken an Engliſh Child, and had eat no Victuals
for 3 Days, were rather determin'd to eat the Child, than one
another. This Nature induced them to do, but the Humanity
of the Heathens is remarkable, that a Dog falling in their way,
they compaſſionated the Child ; the Dog though but half a Meal
to them, fupply'd that occaſion ‡ and *Hannah Parſons* is yet
living. If an Indian had fallen in the way of half a Dozen
hungry Chriſtians, even though they were come to a *Fulneſs* of
Grace, and *Ripe* in the Lord ; yet if they had Eat no Victuals
for three days, I make no doubt but he would have been diſpos'd
of, according to the Regular Form of Leggs, and Shoulders, for
the more Expeditiouſly ſupplying themſelves, by Boyling and
Roaſting ; and yet the Deliverance would have remain'd Remarkable (*i. e.*) that *Providence* threw this Fellow into the way of their
Neceſſities —— An § Engliſhman killing an Indian, and being
taken was to be murder'd at the direction, and in what manner
the *Squa* (*i. e.*) the Widdow of the Indian was pleas'd to preſcribe ;
but ſhe (having more Humanity than fome that call themſelves
Chriſtians) forgave him —— ‖ A *New England* Woman was
going to be hang'd by an Indian, but the limb of the Tree broke
as ſhe was tying up, and another Indian interpoſing, ſhe was
likewiſe fav'd. I paſs over feveral other Particular hardſhips that
fome Chriſtians during their Captivity have endured from Hunger
Weather, and long Sojourning, but ¶ Mrs *Bradly* of *Haverly's*
Cafe muſt be particularly taken notice of, becauſe 'tis recommended with an —— *AB UNO DISCE OMNES*. She poor
Woman, paſt through feveral Varieties of Affliction during her
Captivity. The Story of her delivering her ſelf from danger by
killing, one Fellow with ſcalding Sope, and lathering another

---

has been told already ; afterwards fhe went through feveral difficulties, as Hunger, and the like. Being near her time in the
midft of Winter ; fhe had no Habitation but amongft Ice and
Snow ; but fhe had an * *Eafie Labour* in this *hard Weather,* and
her felf and child did well after it. I find no other Particulars
till her Liberty, which was thus, † Her good Hufband Mafter
Bradley, accompanying Mr *Sheldon* in his laft Expedition, unexpectedly found his Wife and brought her home to *Haverly;*
Even this Particular is not the moft furprizing, it being no uncommon thing for a Man to find his Wife, where he leaft expected
her.

· I have purpofely omitted feveral of thefe Cafes, as the *Captives*
Wandering in the Defarts, and going through feveral Perils by
Land and Water, enough having been faid of it already. It be-
hoves [23] every Man to Compaffionate thefe unhappy Prifoners ;
but when they fhall be heap'd together to endeavour to Incenfe
the People againft their Governour, (to whofe good Conduct 'tis
owing that fewer are in this Diftrefs now than in Former Wars,)
it takes off from that Humanity that fuch deplorable Cafes call
for.

I can't end this Difcourfe without taking a little notice of the
Hard Fate of the Gentlemen that are Governours of Her Majefties Plantations abroad, whilft they in their feveral Stations are
promoting the Honour of Her Majefty, and the Intereft of the
feveral Provinces committed to their Care, to have a Malecon-
tented Party *HERE* undermining and mifreprefenting them.

The Cafe of Coll. *Dudley* is an Unufual Inftance. He (if ever
any Governour) ought to have expected all due acknowledgments
from the People of *New-England.* What confiderable Services
has he done for the Honour of Her Majefty, and the good of the
Country, fince he has been made Governour. Piracies that were
formerly fo familiar, and fo much a Scandal to the Country, are
now intirely Rooted out ; Naval Stores, by his great Application
exceedingly encreafed, to the benefit of the Province in Particular, and all Her Majefties Subjects in General ; The Country
more Effectually Defended now than in former Wars : And
though the want of the *Spanish* Trade has put a Check to the
Great Increafe of Bullion at prefent ; yet *New England* never
appear'd more flourifhing than at this time. Juftice was never in
that Province more Impartially adminiftred, Her Majefties Prerogative preferv'd, (which I hope is not a Crime) and the Subjects
Property maintained.

To Sum up all, His long Experience and known Abilities, has
render'd him fo perfect a Mafter of all the true Interefts of Her

* P. 35. *Lin.* 4.　　　　　　† P. 36. *Lin.* 27.

Majefty, and the Country ; and his Eftate and Settlement there puts it fo much in his Power, that perhaps no Man in the World, can govern that Province at a lefs Charge to the Crown, or burthen to the People than he has done.

Thus have I concluded what I intended, whether it will gain acceptation, or accompany the MEMORIAL, in the common ufes of wraping up Tobacco, and fuch like neceffary Occafions ; as it is not in my Power to Determine, fo am I not Solicitous about it.

[24]

London, Sept. 6.

To the Queen's moft Excellent Majefty.

The humble Addrefs of the Minifters of the Gofpel, in New England.

' WE your Majefties moft Loyal and Dutiful Subjects, and
' Minifters of the Gofpel, in the feveral Parts of *New*
' *England,* cannot but with utmoft Joy and Thankfulnefs, ac-
' knowledge and be fenfible of your Majefty's great and true
' Zeal, for the promoting of Religion and Virtue (which are the
' Glory and Security of any Nation) in your Majefty's Realms at
' Home, and your Dominions Abroad, ever fince your Majefty's
' Acceffion to the Throne of your Royal Anceftors : And that
' not only in your Majefty's own rare and excellent Example,
' your Majefty's feveral Proclamations for the Encouragement of
' Piety and Virtue ; but alfo in thefe great and juft Wars of the
' Lord, which your Majefty at firft undertook, and ftill are en-
' gaged in, for thofe two high and noble Reafons, the Security of
' our Holy and Precious Religion, and alfo of our Civil Liberties.
' May it pleafe your Majefty, we do alfo in a more efpecial
' manner, with all Thankfulnefs, find and admire your Majefty's
' great Moderation and Gracious Indulgence, towards fuch of
' your Majefty's good Subjects, as diffent from the Church of
' *England,* as by Law eftablifhed ; and alfo your Royal Affurance
' from the Throne, that you will inviolably maintain the TOL-
' ERATION within your Kingdoms ; and we humbly affure your
' Majefty, that in thefe Parts of your Dominions, we fhall in our
' feveral Stations, endeavour, by God's Affiftance, to infpire our
' People, as well with Principles of Peace, Charity, and Loyalty,
' as all other Chriftian Graces and Virtues, that under your
' Majefty's moft Aufpicious Reign, we and they may lead Quiet
' and Peaceable Lives in all Godlinefs and Honefty.

'We alfo take this occafion; with all Thankfulnefs to ac-
' knowledge your Majefty's Favour to this People, in appointing
' and continuing Colonel *Dudley*, your Captain-General, and Gov-
' ernour over us, whofe Government here has been very much to
' your Majefty's Honour and Intereft, and to the Happinefs of
' [25] your Majefty's Subjects of this Province, moft efpecially
' in this difficult and diftreffing time of War.

' May it pleafe your Majefty, we do moft humbly and joyfully
' give Thanks to the God of Heaven, for thofe many great and
' glorious Victories and Salvations, which he has been pleas'd to
' blefs your Majefties Arms withal, more efpecially under the
' Conduct of his Grace the Duke of *Marlborough*, againft the
' great Enemy of the Proteftant Religion, and Liberties of *Eu-*
' *rope*, infomuch, that our Nation is now, through your Majefty's
' Wife and Happy Influence, become the Head among the Na-
' tions.

' And we moft humbly and devoutly pray, that, that God, by
' whom Kings and Queens Reign, and unto whom alone belongs
' Salvation, would preferve your Majefty's Sacred Perfon, direct
' your Wife Councils, profper your Juft Arms, and make you
' more and more victorious, until your Majefties Enemies be
' afham'd and found Liars : And your People like *Ifrael* of old,
' fhall dwell in Safety alone, and be a happy People faved by the
' Lord, and become a Quiet and Peaceable Habitation, a Name
' and a Praife in the whole Earth.   We are

Your Majefties moft Loyal and Dutiful Subjects.

N.B. This is the firft Addrefs that was ever made by the
Clergy of that Country to the Crown of *England*.

London. *Auguft* 12.

To the Queen's moft Excellent Majefty.

The Humble Addrefs of the Principal Merchants and Traders of
Boston *in* New England.

WE *Your Majefty's moft Loyal and Dutiful Subjects, Mer-*
chants and Traders in this Your Majefty's Town of Bofton
in New-England, *beg leave moft humbly and Joyfully to congratu-*
late Your Majefty in thofe Great and Glorious Succeffes and Vic-
tories, wherewith it has pleas'd Almighty God to blefs the Arms
of Your Majefty, and Your Allies, ever fince your Majefty's Happy
Acceffion to the Throne, more efpecially the laft Summer, againft

the great and inveterate Enemy, not only of the Religion and Profperity of Your Majefty's Kingdoms in efpecial, but even of the Proteftant Religion and Liberties of Europe *itfelf.*

And we humbly hope and pray, that as Your Majefty has never yet been difappointed in Your firm Reliance and expectation of the Divine [26] *Favour and Blefing, in profecuting fo juft and necefary a War, fo Your Majefty may quickly fee a Glorious Ifue thereof, and long Live to enjoy the Happy Effects of all Your Majefty's great Defigns in the Peace and Profperity of Your own Kingdoms, and the whole Chriftian World.*

We do moft humbly, and with all Thankfulnefs acknowledge Your Majefty's great Care and Favour to ourfelves, and Your Majefty's People of this Province, in protecting and encouraging our Trade and Merchandize, and altho', for the prefent, by reafon of the War, it may labour under fome Difficulty, yet we doubt not but when Your Majefty (which God grant) has prevented the French King's engrofing the Trade and Wealth of the World, we here in Your Majefty's Dominions Abroad, with Your Majefty's good Subjects at Home, fhall become a Flourifhing and Happy People.

We humbly alfo beg leave to reprefent to Your Majefty, That the Government of Coll. Dudley, *Your Majefty's Commander in chief over this Province, has been and is yet very acceptable to us, and Your People here, and thro' his great Care, Courage and Wifdom, as well Your Majefty's Honour and Intereft, as the Peace and Profperity of Your Majefty's People of this Province, has been greatly fecur'd and advanc'd in this time of War.*

We moft humbly pray for the continuance of Your Majefty's Care and Favour towards us, and for Your Majefty's long Life and Happy Reign over us, and fhall endeavour, by all imaginable Methods, to approve ourfelves, Your Majefty's moft Loyal, and Dutiful Subjects.

Bofton Octob. 18. 1706.

To the Queen's Moft Excellent Majefty.

The humble Addrefs of your Majefty's Military Officers in the feveral Parts of your Majefty's Province of the Maffachufetts Bay, *in* New England.

WEE *Your Majefty's moft Loyal and Dutiful Subjects having the Honour to be employed in Your Majefty's Militia in this Province, moft humbly beg leave among the Crowd of Your Majefty's Loyal Subjects to Congratulate Your Majeft's Glorious*

Succefs in your juft Wars. And alfo to reprefent to Your Majefty, that through the great favour of Almighty God, and the conftant Diligence, Wifdom, and Courage of Col. Dudley, *Your Majefty's Captain General and Governour, Your Majefty's People and Intereft in this Province, efpecially* [27] *in the Frontiers, have been to admiration taken care of, protected and faved in our late and yet continuing heavy and diftreffing War, even beyond what hath been in former Wars. And that his Excellency's difpofal of the Forces at all times, and the Charge thereupon neceffarily arifing, has been with great Juftice and Wifdom, and to the great Eafe, Quiet and Satisfaction of Your Majefty's People in thefe Parts. Under the fenfe of which, we are humbly bold to afk the continuance of Your Majefty's favour to our Governour, being well affur'd that his Government over us, will be for Your Majefty's Honour and Intereft, and to the Peace and Satisfaction of Your Majefty's good Subjects within this Province. We humbly beg leave to affure Your Majefty that we continually wifh and pray for Your Majefty's long Life and happy Reign : And that Your Majefty's great and Juft Wars in* Europe, *and alfo in* America, *may have a Glorious and happy Iffue.*

And are Your Majefty's moft Loyal and moft Dutiful Subjects.

N.B. This was fign'd by the Field-Officers, and all the Captains of Twelve Regiments, being the whole Militia of this Province.

To the Queen's moft Excellent Majefty.

The humble Addrefs of the Council and Affembly of your Majefties Province of the Maffachufetts-Bay *in* New-England.

Moft Gracious Soveraign,

' IT is upwards of two Years fince the Arrival of Colonel
'   Dudley, your Majefties Captain-General, and Governour in
' chief here : For whofe Appointment to that Station, we for-
' merly humbly Addrefs'd your Majefty, with the Thanks of this
' Province ; and we have been made fenfible of his careful Man-
' agement of your Majefties Interefts, and the Government of
' your good Subjects ; particularly of his great Application, and
' the Coft expended, to have ftedyed the *Eaftern Indians* in their
' Obedience to the Crown of *England,* and your Majefty's Sov-
' eraignty over them, whereof they have formerly made their

' repeated Recognition and Submiffion thereto ; and more lately
' renewed the fame, in two Attendencies upon his Excellency,
' with Proteftations of all good Fidelity. Yet notwithftanding,
' thro' the Influence of the *French* Emiffaries refiding among
' them, they have for Twelve Months paft, broken out, and con-
' tinued in open Rebellion and Hoftility ; and with the Affiftance
' of *French* Officers and Souldiers, from the feveral Parts, have
' committed divers Outrages, and barbarous Murders, upon many
' of your Majefties good Subjects.

' Which Irruption of the *Indians*, has oblig'd the Governour
' to Garrifon all the Frontiers of more than Two Hundred Miles
' extant ; and to fend forth greater and leffer Parties into the
' Defert, in places almoft inacceffible, if [28] poffible, to find out
' thofe bloody Rebels in their obfcure Receffes under covert of a
' vaft hideous Wildernefs (their manner of living being much
' like that of the Wild Beafts of the fame) and to give Check to
' their Infolencies.

' And there are not lefs than Nineteen Hundred Effective
' Men, now in Arms under pay, upon our Eaftern and Weftern
' Frontiers ; befides the Veffels and Men, neceffarily imploy'd for
' guarding of the Sea-Coaft, againft the Infeftings of the *French*
' from *Canada*, *Port-Royal*, and the *Weft-Indies*, who indeavour
' to intercept our Supplies, and difturb our Fifhery : So that we
' are at an exceeding great, and almoft infupportable Charge ;
' and fee not the end thereof. We are ready to think it highly
' reafonable, That the neighbouring Governments being fecur'd
' thereby, fhould bear a juft Quota of the faid Charge. Which
' is humbly fubmitted to your Majefties great Wifdom to direct.

' We have therefore accounted it our Duty, by an Exprefs,
' humbly to reprefent and lay before your Sacred Majefty, the
' very diftreffing Circumftances of your Majefties good Subjects,
' within this your Province, who have hitherto chearfully under-
' gone the fore Fatigue and Charge of their Defence and Pur-
' fuits, made after the Enemy and Rebels ; and that in the
' greateft Severities and Heights of the Winter, expofing them-
' felves to the laft Sufferings. Being fenfible, that the Advances
' made by the Governour in the Service have been abfolutely
' neceffary ; and that his Care has been, to keep the Expenfe as
' low as the Emergencies would bear ; And we doubt not of a
' good Concurrence at all times, of the Council and Affembly,
' with the Governour, to advance both the Men and Money
' neceffary, to the utmoft of their Ability.

' We crave alfo by this Opportunity, humbly to exprefs to your
' Majefty, our juft Refentment and Deteftation of the Piracies
' and Robberies lately committed by Captain *Quelch* and Com-
' pany : And we hope the fpeedy Juftice that has been done upon
' thofe vile Criminals, will vindicate the Government from the
' Imputation of giving any Countenance to, or favouring of fuch

' wicked Actions. A full and particular Account of the whole
' Procefs, and of the diligent Care taken to recover and fecure
' the Treafure fo ill gotten, will be humbly laid before your
' Majefty by our Governour.

' May it pleafe your Majefty, There are feveral Articles and
' Stores of War, neceffary for the Safety and Defence of your
' Majefties Intereft, within this Province, that cannot be fupply'd
' here ; which we have moft humbly offer'd to your Majefty, in a
' Memorial accompanying this our Addrefs.

' And if your Majefty of your Royal Bounty, fhall be gracioufly
' pleas'd to order, That they be fupply'd out of your Majefties
' Stores, it will greatly encourage us in the Service of your Sa-
' cred Majefty : being always refolv'd to maintain the Honour
' and Dignity of your Majefties Crown and Government over us ;
' and, by the Favour of Almighty God, to maintain our Station
' in this Province ; which we hope, upon the reftoring of Peace,
' will, by the increafe of People and Trade therein, render it felf
' a further Honour and Advantage to your Majefty and the
' Crown of *England ;* for whofe long and profperous Reign over
' us, and a happy Succeffion of Proteftant Princes, We fhall ever
' pray.

Madam, *Your Majefties moft Loyal and Dutiful Subjects.*

In the Name, and by order of the Council

Bofton,   Ifaac Addington, *Secretary.*

July 12th.   *In the* NAME, *and by Order of the Affembly*

1704.   James Converfe, *Speaker.*

[29]

London, Auguft 9.

To the Queen's Moft Excellent Majefty.

The humble Addrefs of Your Majefty's Council and Reprefentatives of Your Majefty's Province of *New Hampfhire,* in *New
England* Conven'd in General Affembly. This 25th day of *July*
1706.

Moft humbly Sheweth,

THAT *Your Majefty's Loyal Subjects, the Inhabitants of this
Province, having been always Happy fince your Majefty's
Acceffion to the Crown, under your Majefty's Protection, and Government, are humbly bold to acquaint your Sacred Majefty. That
notwithftanding the very great Troubles this little Province lies*

*fo immediately expos'd unto, by the barbarous Salvages and French,
our Neighbours, yet, by the good Providence of Almighty God, the
Courage, Care and Prudence of Colonel* Dudley, *your Majefty's
Captain General, and Governour we have been exceedingly preferved, beyond what has been in former Wars, and are perfectly
fatisfied with the difpofal of the People and Arms of the Province, and the juft Expenfe [of?] our Money at all times, under our
prefent Governor's Management, and humbly pray, if it may con-
fift with your Majefty's Pleafure, that he may be continued in the
Government of this Province, which we are well affured, will
always have a Tendency to the Promotion of your Majefty's Intereft here, as well as the Eafe and Satisfaction of all your Majefty's
good Subjects Inhabitants herein.*

*And we further pray to be admitted, as the meaneft of your
Majefty's moft dutiful Subjects, humbly to Congratulate your
Majefty's Glorious Succefs againft the common Enemy, which, that
they may be perfected, and that your Majefty's Victorious Arms
may give a happy and lafting Peace to* Europe *is the Prayer
of,* &c.

[30]

By his Excellency *JOSEPH DUDLEY* Esq, Captain General
and Governour in chief, in and over her Majefties Provinces of
the *Maffachufetts Bay,* and *New Hampfhire* in *New England.*

WHEREAS the *Ifland of St. Chriftopher's fome few Weeks
fince, has been Infulted and Ravaged by the French: And
Her Majefties good Subjects of that Ifland reduced to the laft
Extremity, by the Spoyles the Enemy has made in burning of
their Houfes and Mills, deftroying and carrying off their Stocks
and Eftate; So that they are left deftitute both of Habitation and
Subfiftance; moft having loft everything they had.*

I HAVE therefore, at the Defire of the Reprefentatives in
their late Seffion, and with the Advice of Her Majefties
Council, Iffued forth this BRIEF, Hereby Recommending to
the Commiferation and Pity of all Charitable Well difpofed
Chriftians, within this Province, and the Province of *New Hampfhire* the deplorable Circumftances and diftreffing Wants of their
faid Chriftian Brethren and fellow Subjects; And Exciting them
to put on bowels of Chriftian Compaffion and Charity, for the
Relief of the Pinching Neceffities of their diftreffed Friends and
Countrymen. Which will be very acceptable to GOD, profitable
to our Selves, and be remembered with the like grateful Acknowledgment and Refpect from this Ifland, as formerly.

The Money that fhall be Contributed and Collected for this pious Ufe, to be put into the Hands of *Samuel Sewell*, Efq. ; and *Andrew Belcher* Efq ; by them to be Invefted in Provifions *&c*, and forthwith forwarded by the Direction of My Self and the Council.

And the Minifters of the feveral Towns are Directed to Read and Publifh this in their Congregations ; And to ftir up their People, notwithftanding their deep Poverty, to a Cheerful and Liberal Contribution to this good Work.

Given at the Council Chamber in Bofton *the* 17th. *Day of* April, 1706. *In the Fifth Year of the Reign of our Sovereign Lady QUEEN* ANNE.

J. DUDLEY.

By Order of the Governour and
Council. *Ifaac Addington*, Secr.

FINIS.

THE

Deplorable State

OF

New-England,

By Reafon of a *Covetous* and *Treacherous*

𝕲𝖔𝖛𝖊𝖗𝖓𝖔𝖚𝖗,

AND

Puſillanimous COUNSELLORS

ble
With a Vindication of the Hon Mr. *HIGGINSON*,
Mr. *MASON*, and ſeveral other Gentlemen from the
Scandalous and Wicked *Accuſation* of the VOTES, Or-
dered by Them to be Publiſhed in their *BOSTON*
News-Letter.

To which is Added,

An ACCOUNT of the Shameful *Miſcarriage* of
the Late EXPEDITION against

PORT-ROYAL.

LONDON, Printed in the Year 1708.

To the Right Honourable, the

Earl of *Sunderland,*

Her MAJESTY's Principal

Secretary of State.

My LORD

THIS Deplorable Narrative, Contains but a fmall Part of the Grievances of *New-England*, under their Prefent Governour, who is a perfect Reverfe to Our Gracious QUEEN, whofe Perfon he Reprefents.

New-England in K. *Charles* the Firft's Time, was firft Inhabited by *Proteftants* of the Church of *England*: When feveral Learned and Pious Parifh Minifters, were Silenc'd here, for Refufing to Read the *Book of Sports* on the Lord's Day, and many of them Imprifoned: the Love that feveral Gentlemen of Quality had for their Minifters, induced 'em to Sell their pleafant Seats and Leave their Native *Country*, to go to an *uninhabited Wildernefs*, where they had Caufe to Fear the *Wild Beafts*, and *Wilder Men*. [1]*For if Religion be Worth any Thing, 't is Worth every thing.*

So that this Country (by the Blefling of GOD, who always Rewards a Vertuous People with Temporal Bleffings) was lately become a Great NATION ; but Col: *Dudley*, in King *Charles* the Second's Reign, was Intrufted with the Precious *Depofitum*, their Greateft Treafure, their Religious Priviledges, and Civil Liberties, which were conveyed to them by CHARTER, but were both Betray'd by him. Yet notwithftanding the faid *Dudley* has, by his Cunning Infinuations, Obtained the Favour to be made the Prefent Governour by Her now Majefty, of the *Maffachufet's* Colony in *New-England.* But his Male-Adminiftration, hath Caufed feveral Confiderable Merchants and Inhabitants there, Believing their Country to be in Imminent Danger by

---

[1] Here begins the second page. The running title is: " The Epistle Dedicatory | to the Earl of Sunderland." — EDS.

[by] fuch a Governour, to Petition Our moft Gracious Sovereign for his Removal, Charging him with Crimes of the Higheft Guilt; which the Petitioners did Humbly Hope, would have foon Remov'd him had not the great Piety of the Queen inter-pofed (who has always had a fpecial Regard to the feveral Min-ifters in her Dominions., Upon the faid Governour's Council, producing an *Addrefs*, faid to be from the Minifters of *New-England*, Commending his Government, and Praying his Con-tinuance: Which *Addrefs* is a part of his Crime, being Obtained by the Threats and Promifes of his *Agents*, and with Difficulty Subfcribed by fome Minifters in the Country, but the moft Con-fiderable amongft them, and the Minifters of *Bofton*, Refuf'd it, who Deteft his Perfon, and Pray for his Removal.

[1] And this is Apparent; for in their *Addrefs* the Minifters Thank'd the Queen for the Tolleration *Act*, and the *Affurances* of *Tollerating them in their Religion*, which is the *ONLY* Eftab-lifh'd Religion of their Country. And 't is much more Reafon-able That the *Kirk* of *North Britain*, in their Addreffes to the *Queen*, fhould Thank Her Majefty for Tollerating *Prefbytery* among them, which is their National *Church Government*, they having formerly had fome Sort of *Epifcopal Government* among them: But *thefe* People never had any other *Church Government* than they *Now* have.

Befides what is now Offer'd, there are feveral other Reafons for his Removal. He is a *Native of the Country:* His Relations, and thofe he calls his Friends, are it feems, the fitteft Men for all the *Civil and Military Pofts*. His Son, whom he calls the *Queen's Attorney-General*, being the only *Minifter of State*, under him, by which any can have Accefs to his Perfon for *com-mon Juftice.* . . . . . . This is the *Third Time* that he has been Trufted with Power from the *Crown* in *America* and he has con-ftantly Abuf'd it, to the Difhonour of the Government, and almoft Ruin of the People he was fent to Govern.

My LORD,

YOUR Lordfhip's Great Abilities have Raifed you to be a *Great Minifter of State*, in this Critical Juncture. Your Lordfhip's *Known Hatred* of Oppreffion, and *Love* of Liberty, and the *Englifh* Government, makes up Your *Finifh'd Character*. My Lord, *New-England* is in your Lordfhip's *Prov-ince*, and under Your Care, [2] and Flyes to your Lordfhip for Protection; and Humbly Prays your Lordfhip to Reprefent their *Diftreffed Cafe* to our moft Gracious QUEEN. A Queen, that would have all Her Subjects, (even in the Remoteft Parts

---

[1] Here begins the third page, unnumbered. — EDS.
[2] Beginning of the fourth page. — EDS.

of Her Dominions) Eafy and Happy. In doing which, your
Lordfhip will Oblige a whole Country of *Proteftants*, to fend up
their Fervent Prayers to Heaven for your Lordfhip's Long Life
and Happinefs ; and lay a Lafting Obligation upon

> *My LORD, with the utmoft Refpect,*
> *and Sincerity, your Lordfhips moft Humble*
> *moft Obliging, and moft Faithful Servant,*

A. H.

☞ The Reader is Defired to take Notice, that the following Sheets being Printed before the Epiftle Dedicatory was
Writ, we could not Conveniently Infert in their proper Place,
thefe Material Advices lately fallen into our Hands, *viz.*

Boston, July, 17, 1708.

OUR prefent General Affembly have Acted like Men. They
have Turned out of the Council, feveral of *D——'s*
Creatures. And the Country has Chofen better Reprefentatives than they had the Laft Year. The prefent Houfe of
Commons here has Voted an Addrefs to the Queen, in which
they Declare, That they Declined fending a former Addrefs, becaufe there was an Article in it, Applauding the Governour's
Conduct, and Praying his Continuance, *&c.*

---

¹TO THE

READER.

*I*F the New-England Counfellors, (*as well as their Governour*) *are Publickly Expofed in a Land a Thoufand Leagues Diftant from them, they have no Reafon to Complain of Hard Dealing,* Lex Talionis *Requires that it fhould be fo; for it is nothing but what they themfelves have done, by Gentlemen who are on feveral Accounts Superior to them. We Wifh they may be Senfible of the great Hurt their Country is like to Suffer by their Means. They have Difcouraged their Friends from ever Appearing again in their Behalf, when if they fhould, they, to Pleafe their Governour, will in Print,* Brand *them for* Scandalous and Wicked Accufers.

Their Fault is very much Aggravated, in that after they Saw an Invoice *which mentions an Hundred Thoufand Nails, fent to the* Queen's *Enemies at* Port-Royal, *Allowed by the Governour under his Own Hand, they Caufed their Abufive* Vote *to be Printed. Only we Hear,*² *that their* Secretary, *who is a Prudent Man, and one of their* Counfellors, *was againft the Publication of their Scandalous* Vote.

But we likewife Hear, that fome of them moved that feveral Affidavits, *which had been laid before Her* Majefty *in* Council, *and were after that Printed here in* London, *might be Burnt, becaufe they Complained of their Governours Notorious Briberies, and other Male-Adminiftrations. Probably the fame Perfons will make the like* Propofal *again, if a New Governour does not* Negative *them out of his* Council, *which we Suppofe he will, unlefs the* Reprefentatives *of the* Province (*as in Duty they are Bound*) *fhall fave him the Trouble.*

The Reader may Depend upon it, that as to Matter of Fact, *there is nothing in this* Narrative *but Exact Truth; what is therein Related, is not only Affirmed by Gentlemen Worthy of Credit lately come from* Bofton, *but by Letters from as Eminent Perfons as any in* New England.

---

¹ Here begins the fifth page. — EDS.
² Here begins the sixth page. — EDS.

[1]

The Deplorable STATE

O F

New-England.

SECTION I.

SOME Late *Votes* paffed in the Affembly at *Bofton*, and
Printed in the *Bofton* News-Letter, Caufe us to Reflect
with fome Wonder on the *Deplorable State of the Plantations.*

They that are fent over as *Governours* thither, appear as Perfons of Suitable *Abilities*, and Approved *Loyalty*. They are in
Favour with fome Minifters of *State*, who Recommend them to
the King or Queen for the Time being ; and are in Fee with
their *Clarks*, by whofe Means, their Bufinefs is done the more
Effectually. When they arrive with their *Commiffions*, they Exprefs themfelves in Obliging Terms ; and the Ravifh'd People,
who are quite Giddy with Joy, if they have Governours, which
they may Hope, will not *Cut their Throats*, make them Noble
Prefents, and fend Home an *Addrefs of Thanks* for fuch Admirable Governours.

Their next Work is, by all poffible Artifices, to get into all
Offices about the Country, fuch as are, or they know, will be,
meer *Creatures* to them ; or at leaft, fuch as are not Furnifhed
either with *Courage* or *Conduct*, to make any *Complaints* Home
againft them, in Cafe of any Male-Adminiftration.

After this, let the Governour do what he will, either there will
be no Body *Strong* enough to Repair unto the Crown with due
Remonftrances ; or if any Body *do*, the Governour has many
Ways to Moleft him and his, and to Defeat all his Undertakings.
Yea, 'tis Ten Thoufand to One, but at the [2] very Time,
when an Oppreffed Perfon is Solliciting his own and an Oppreffed
People's Caufe, the Governour may have fo Modell'd the *General
Affembly*, that they fhall pafs wretched *Votes* to his Advantage,

and *Kiſs the Hand* which all the open Eyes in the Country ſee *Stabbing of them.*

One would have thought, the People of *N. England* ſhould have been Senſible of their Good Fortune in it, that when they are Betrayed in Miſerable Circumſtances by an Hungry Governour, who has been willing to Enrich himſelf and his Family, on the Ruines of his Country, ſome Gentlemen of Note, have Interpoſed with Humble *Addreſſes* to Her Majeſty on their Behalf. They have no *Agent* here, but what is Entirely in the Intereſt of their Governour. When the whole *Houſe* of Repreſentatives ſent over hither, an *Addreſs* to the Queen, relating to Matters of the Greateſt Importance, the *Agent* whom they had Imploy'd and Rewarded with ſome Hundreds of Pounds, Refuſed to Preſent the Addreſs, becauſe it would not ſuit with the Governour's Intereſt, and Wrote them Word, *That no Addreſs muſt be Preſented, except Signed by the Governour.* And yet after this, the ſame Gentleman could Preſent *Addreſſes* for the Continuance of the Governour, which were Signed by *Private Hands,* and Procured by *Ways* and *Means* little to the Honour of thoſe Concerned. Some Gentlemen here, knowing the Oppreſ'd, and Betray'd Condition of that poor People, have Addreſs'd on their Behalf; and have ſaid nothing in their Addreſs, but what they had the *Oaths* of ſeveral Good Men, to Support the Truth of what was Aſſerted: But, lo! to their Surprize, they find themſelves in the *Boſton News-Letter* Expoſed, as having been the Authors of, *Scandalous and Wicked Accuſations!* The *Counſellors* of *N. England,* have done as much as lyes in them for ever to Diſcourage all Gentlemen here from Appearing for the Country, let never ſuch Difficult Circumſtances be brought upon it; but we will Pity them, as Trapann'd into, *they know not what themſelves!* However, if they will allow no Body here to Speak for their *Country,* they can't forbid us to Speak for *Ourſelves,* which they have now made but too Neceſſary for us.

[3] Letters from *New-England* Inform us, That the Great and Only Reaſon, why ſome of the Council there will *firmly believe* more Charitably of their Governour *Dudley,* than many others do, is, *Becauſe his Family and Intereſt is there, and therefore 'tis unreaſonable to Believe, that he would do any thing that ſhould hurt the Country.*

But, Was not his *Family and Intereſt* there in Sir *Edmund Androſs's* time? And yet a Book Publiſhed here, by the Agents of *New-England,* after the Revolution, Intituled, *The Revolution in* New-England *Juſtified,* has given the World a ſad Story of what a Colonel *Dudley* may do, towards the Ruining a Country which has his *Family* and *Intereſt* in it. Read that Hiſtory, and you will find, that after Col. *Dudley* had been an Agent for the Country, he Tack'd about, and Join'd with the Inſtruments that overthrew their *Charter,* and Accepted an Illegal and Arbitrary

Commiffion from K. *James*, by which he held the Government, until the Arrival of Sir *Edmund Andros*, and then was, as *Prefident* of the Council, and *Chief Judge* of the Territory, a *Chief Tool* of all the enfuing Barbarous, and Infamous Adminiftration. They Governed without an *Affembly*, when *Laws* were Propofed in the Council, tho' the *major part* of the Council fhould happen to Diffent, yet if the *Governour* were Pofitive there was a *Prefident* at the Board, by whofe Allowance the Laws were Immediately *Engroffed, Publifhed, and Executed:* And Judge *Dudley* did not Contradict it, when fome of the Principal Gentlemen in the Country were told at the Council Board, *You have no more Priviledges left you but this, that you are not Bought and Sold for Slaves.* By the Sequel we fhall fee *not this* neither. A *Juncto*, (wherein how often this Chief Judge, was of the *Quorum*, is now forgotten) made a World of Laws, which Pillaged that Poor People Defperately. They Levied a Tax on the whole People without any Affembly; and when the Principal Perfons, and fome others in *Ipfwich* on that Occafion, with all poffible Modefty moved, that the King fhould be Humbly Petition'd for the Liberty of an Affembly, they were Committed to Prifon for an *High Mifdemeanour*, and were Denied an *Habeas Corpas*, and Drag'd many Miles out of their own County, to Anfwer it at a Court [4] in *Bofton*, where *Jurors* were pickt for the Turn, that were neither *Free-holders*, nor fo much as *Inhabitants*. They were all Fined feverely, and laid under great Bonds for their *Good Behaviour;* befides which, the Hungry Officers Extorted Fees of near Two Hundred Pounds, where they would not have rifen to Ten Pounds, had any Law of *England*, or Juftice been Obferved. The Townfmen of many other Places were ferved in the like Fafhion ; and our Judge *Dudley* was a Principal Actor in all this Wickednefs. It was now Denied, that any Man was Owner of a Foot of Land in all the Colony. Judge *Dudley* gave it as his Judgment under his Hand. *Writs of Intrufion* were prefently ferved upon the Chief Gentlemen in the Country, to Compel them, and others by the Terror of their Example, to take *Patents* for the Lands which they had Quietly Poffeffed for Fifty or Sixty Years together. For thefe *Patents* there were fuch Exorbitant Prices Demanded, that Fifty Pounds would not Purchafe for its Owner, an Eftate not worth Two Hundred ; nor could all the Money and Moveables in the Territory, have Defrayed the Charges of Pattenting the Lands.

If the *Harpies* were at any time a little out of Money, they Invented Pretences to Imprifon the Beft Men in the Country, and tho' there Appeared not the leaft Information of any Crime againft them, yet they were put unto intollerable Expences, and the Benefit of the *Habeas Corpus* was Denied unto them. Judge *Dudley* knows this, and we fuppofe he has not Forgotten either

Colonel *Saltonftal*, or Major *Appleton*. Pickt *Juries* were commonly ufed, for the Trouble of Honeft and Worthy Men, and they were Hurried out of their own Counties to be Tried, when *Juries* for the Turn were not likely to be found there. Judge *Dudley* knows this; and we fuppofe, he Remembers the Famous Mr. *Morton*.

In Short, all things were going to Wreck, but yet Colonel *Dudley* was like to Inrich himfelf and his Family in the General Ship wreck. There lies the Myftery!

Thefe things, and many more fuch things, are Afferted in the Book aforefaid, not only by the Oaths of many Honeft Gentlemen, but alfo a Declaration Signed by the Honourable Hands of Judge *Stoughton*, and Major General *Winthrop*, and [5] Colonel *Shrimpton*, and other Members of the Council.

The World has Heard how narrowly Col. *Dudley* Efcaped a *De-Witting* for thefe his Follies, from the Inraged People in the *Revolution*. Being then fent over a Prifoner to *England*, he with the reft, were there fet at Liberty. He returned, with a Commiffion for the place of *Chief Judge* in the Province of *New-York*, where his firft Work, after his Arrival was, to Condemn to Death, the Lieutenant Governour of the Province, and another Gentleman, for not Surrendering the Government before the Arrival of Governour *Slaughter* with his Commiffion. The Condemnation and Execution of thefe Two Gentlemen, was a Bloody Bufinefs: It was afterwards Examined in the Parliament, where Colonel *Dudley* underwent a Confufion, which will never be worn off; and Mr. *Conftantine Phips*, Profecuted the Matter with fo much Demonftration, that Eminent Perfons in both Houfes, Declared it, *A Barbarous Murder;* King, Lords, and Commons, did as good as Declare it fo, and by an *Act* of *Parliament* Revoked the *Attainder* of the Murdered Gentlemen. On this Occafion, Judge *Stoughton*, (who yet was always known to be as Partial to Col. *Dudley*, and his Intereft, as any Man in *New-England*) faid to fome of his Friends, what he had been heard formerly to fay unto others, *Alas, to get a little Money, he would make his own Father hold up his Hand at the Bar.* There, Gentlemen, you have again the *Key* to Explain the Matter; which becaufe you can't fee thro', you *firmly Believe* as you do!

After many Years abfence from his Family, my Lord *Bellamont*, the Governour of *New-England* Dies. Col. *Dudley*, by many fair Promifes, both to Gentlemen here, and at his own Home, obtains Recommendations for a Succeffion in the Government. He had not been long in the Government, before the following M E M O R I A L was fent over to *London*.

[6]

A
MEMORIAL,

On the Behalf of the Province of the Maſſachuſet's *Bay,*
in NEW-ENGLAND; *Relating to the Adminiſtra-*
tion of their Preſent Governour, Colonel Dudley.

I. ONE Principal Grievance, which Comprehends many un-
" der it, is, The Courſe of *Bribery*, which runs thro' the
" Governour's Adminiſtration, whereby the Queen's Gov-
" ernment is greatly Expoſed in a Country where *Bribery* has
" rarely, if ever before this, been known to be Practiſed. The
" Governour having brought in his Son to be Attorney General,
" this Corruption is more Effectually carried on between them,
" unto the great Oppreſſion of the People.
" Only Two Inſtances, among many, ſhall be Reported in this
" *Memorial.*
" 1. Certain People having Purchaſed Land at a New Planta-
" tion called *Naſhoba*, and wanting a Confirmation of their Title,
" by an Act of the General Aſſembly, (as is Uſual in ſuch Caſes)
" they could not have the Governour's Aſſent unto the Act,
" without a *Bribe* of a Thouſand Acres of the beſt Land, and in
" the Center of the Plantation, and to the Ruin of the reſt.
" [7] " 2. Alſo, A Tract of Land at *Nipmuck*, belonging to
" Nine or Ten Partners, when Both Houſes in the General
" Aſſembly had paſſed the *Bill*, to Allow their Title, (as was Re-
" quired by an Old Law of the Country) the Governour would
" not Sign the Act, until he had a Bribe of Twenty Pounds, and
" One whole Share of the Land, which was Valued at One
" Hundred and Fifty Pounds more.
" But, if a *Commiſſion of Enquiry* could be Obtained, there
" would be ſuch Practiſes of this Nature Diſcovered, as are
" hardly to be Parallel'd.

" II. The Governour, meerly to Gratify his own Arbitrary
" Will and Pleaſure, did for ſome while Refuſe to fill up the nec-

" effary Number of *Judges;* by which Means, the *Courts* dropt,
" and the *Courfe of Juftice* was Obftructed ; and the Oppreffed
" People were Defeated in their *Suits,* to the Damage of many
" Hundreds of Pounds.

" III. There have been odd *Collufions* with the Pyrates of
" *Quelch's* Company, of which one Inftance is, That there was
" Extorted the Sum of about Thirty Pounds from fome of the
" Crue, for Liberty to Walk at certain times in the *Prifon* Yard ;
" and this Liberty having been Allow'd for Two or Three Days
" unto them, they were again Confined to their former Wretched
" Circumftances.

" IV. An Army of Volunteers went out, and did Good Ser-
" vice upon the *French* and *Indian* Enemy at *Acady.* They were
" Incouraged by an Act of the Governour and General Affembly,
" which Promifed the Soldiers a Certain Share of the Plunder.
" When the Soldiers returned, fome Officers, without their Con-
" fent or Knowledge, and before the Divifion of the Plunder,
" made the Governour a Confiderable Prefent out of it : Where-
" upon he fo managed the Matter with the faid Officers, as to
" Cheat and Cut off the Soldiers of near One Half that the Act
" of the Affembly had Promif'd them ! When the Houfe of
" Reprefentatives Applied themfelves to the Governour on this
" Occafion, they could get nothing from him. *By this means,*
" *no* [8] *more Volunteers are like to appear in Her Majefty's*
" *Service.*

" The Governour's manner is, To trample on the Affembly
" with grofs Indignities ; and fuch as they never have received
" from their former Governours. Nor can they have any Re-
" drefs of Grievances, though many have been from Time to
" Time Reprefented.
" And when Bills for the Payment of the juft Debts of the
" Province, are Prefented to him to be Signed, he has Declared,
" he would not Sign them, except he were himfelf Gratified with
" Sums Demanded of them.
" On thefe, and many more fuch Accounts, it is humbly Con-
" ceived, That it would be much for Her Majefty's Intereft, if a
" more Acceptable Governour were placed over that Province.

This was the *Memorial;* but becaufe here was no Body to
Profecute it, it fell to the Ground.

Much about the fame time, there came to Light a little more
of Colonel *Dudley's* Defigns upon the *new Charter* of the Province. It feems, he was as willing to do the fame Kindnefs for
this, that he did for the *old One;* and that he was at this very

time doing for the Colony of *Connecticut;* which, if it were Accomplished, would lay the Country Open to an Innundation of Calamities. His Son *Paul*, (the great Inftrument of his Oppreffions) Writes over to his Friend in *London*, a Letter, wherein are thefe following Words.

[9]

Bofton, 12*th* Jan. 170⁴₃.

Dear KINSMAN,

I Confefs I am Afhamed almoft to Think, I fhould be at Home fo long, and not let you know of it, till now. Tho' after all, a New-England Correfpondence is fcarce worth your having. ------ *I Refer you to* * *Mr.* ----- *for an Account of every thing, efpecially about the* Government, *and the* Colledge; *both which, are Difcourfed of here, in Chimney Corners, and Private-Meetings, as confidently as can be. If there fhould be any Occafion, you muft be fure to ftir your Self and Friends, and fhow your Affection and Refpect to my Father, who* Loves you well, *and Bid me* Tell you fo.----- *This Country will never be worth Living in, for Lawyers and Gentlemen, till the* CHARTER IS TAKEN AWAY. *My Father and I fometimes Talk of the Queen's Eftablifhing a* COURT OF CHANCERY [10] *in this Country; I have Writ about it, to Mr.* Blathwayt: *If the Matter fhould Succeed, you might get fome Place worth your Return; of which I fhould be very Glad. If I can any ways Serve you or your Friends, Pray Signify it to (Dear SIR)*

Your Affectionate Friend,
and Humble Servant,

Paul Dudley.

* See P. Dudley's Original Letter to Mr. W. Wharton Printed at London with fome Neceffary Queries.

This *Apocryphal Epiftle* of *Paul*, [not a Saint *Paul*, we can Affure ye!] needs no *Commentary!* ------ But,

Thefe are *Old* Stories, we muft now come to fome *New* Ones.

[11]

SECT. II.

B Y Letters from *New-England*, we are Informed how Matters paſt in the laſt Seſſions of their General Aſſembly, which was in *October* and *November* 1707. One would have Imagined, that the *Maſt-Fleet*, which brings us our Letters of Intelligence, had been the *Conſolidator*, coming back with Intelligence from the *World in the Moon:* For ſuch things could never have happen'd, but among a People very *Lunatick.* —— And, Firſt let us begin, as in Good Manners Bound, with the *Upper Houſe,*

Their Governour *Dudley*, produced to the Council, the Copy of an Addreſs to the Queen's Majeſty, Signed by above Twenty Gentlemen in *London*, in which, out of the Reſpect to a Country for which they were more Generouſly Concerned, than ſome that were under greater Obligations, they Petitioned for *Dudley*'s Removal from his Government ; Alledging, among other Weighty Reaſons, *That he had Countenanced a Private Trade and Correſpondence with Her Majeſty's Enemies, the* French, *and the* Indians *which are in their Intereſts.* He Required his Counſellors *immediately* to Clear him from theſe Imputations. He came upon them with his Demand, on the *Saturday* next, when they were (as they uſually then are) in the Hurry of Breaking up. 'Tis the Time, when the Governour commonly makes any thing to Paſs, that either Houſe muſt be either *Trick'd* or *Tir'd* into. Three or Four of the Council, particularly *Brown, Sewal,* and *Pain,* Pray'd, That ſince the Thing was both New and Weighty, it might be put off till *Monday.* The Governour, with a Boiſterous Fury, Required them to do it *immediately ;* And they did it *immediately :* At once they Ruſhed into a *Vote,* wherein they ſay,

[12] *Upon Reading the Addreſs, Offer'd Her Majeſty, againſt his Excellency, our preſent Governour, Signed,* Nath. Higginſon, *&c. We firmly Believe, and are of Opinion, the Allegations therein, of the Governour's Trading, or allowing a Trade with Her Majeſty's Enemies, the* French, *and* Indians *in their Intereſts, is a Scandalous and Wicked Accuſation.* Paſſed Unanimouſly.

Iſaac Addington, *Secret.*

The Council being Brow-beaten into ſuch a Vote, one of that Board, namely, Mr. *Samuel Sewal,* who is alſo a *Judge* of the Superior Court ; but a Perfon of Unfpotted Integrity, thought him-felf Bound in Confcience to Exhibit a Remonftrance againft this Rafh Vote : His Relation as a Brother-in-Law to the Governour, did not get the Upper-Hand of his Confcience ; but he Prefented his Remonftrance to the Board, and had it Enter'd on *File ;* from whence one of our Correfpondents has Obtained a Copy. 'Tis as follows.

Tuefday, November, 25, 1707.

" THE Reafons of my With-drawing my Vote, from what was
" Paffed in Council upon *Saturday, November* the Firft, re-
" lating to an *Addrefs* Offer'd to Her Majefty, Sign'd, *Nath.*
" *Higginfon,* &c.

" I. Becaufe my Motion, for leaving the Confideration of it,
" till the *Monday* following, was not Admitted ; and it was En-
" ter'd upon, and pafs'd about Noon, in a very fhort Time ; being
" a Matter of great Concernment to our Leige Lady, Queen
" ANNE, to the Province, to his Excellency our Governour, and
" to the Council and Reprefentatives.

[13] " II. The Governour's *Perfonal Intereft* was much in it,
" and therefore I humbly Conceive, the Vote ought to have
" been Debated and Framed by the Members of the Council,
" apart by themfelves, in the Abfence of the Governour.

" III. The Words [*firmly Believe*] and [*always Apparent*]
" were never Pleafing to me. And *now,* I do not *firmly Believe,*
" that the Governour did no way Allow Mr. *Borland,* and Capt.
" *Vetch,* their Trading Voyage to Her Majefty's Enemies, the
" *French.*
" *Qui non vetat Peccare, cum poffit, Jubet.*

" Not that I Sufpect, the Governour defign'd to Hurt the
" Province ; but to *Gratify Grateful Merchants.* And I readily
" and Thankfully Acknowledge the Governour's Orders for the
" Defence of the *Frontiers,* to be truly Excellent ; * both refpect-
" ing the Suitablenefs of the Orders themfelves, and the Quick-
" nefs of their Difpatch : And I Blefs God for the Succefs that
" has Attended them.

---

* The Gentleman, with his ufual Goodnefs, is willing to make the Beft of any Good Thing. His Meaning is, That when the New-Englanders had the Good Fortune to be Advifed of the Approach of the Enemy, the Governour would (which was a wonderful piece of Sagacity) Order a Number of Soldiers to Repair to the Frontiers !

" IV. I have been Acquainted with Mr. *Nathaniel Higginfon*
" thefe Fourty Years ; and I cannot Judge, the Offering this
" Addrefs to Her Majefty, to be in him a *Scandalous and Wicked*
" *Accufation*, unlefs I know his Inducements. And I fear, this
" Cenfure may be of ill Confequence to the Province in time to
" come ; by Difcouraging Perfons of Worth and Intereft, to
" Venture in Appearing for them, tho' the Neceffity fhould be
" never fo Great.

" Samuel Sewall.

[14] Tho' this Gentleman had thus Recalled his Vote, (and
another Gentleman prefent in the Council, never had a Vote put
to him) and he Infifted on it, as we are Informed, that it would
be a *Direct Falfehood in Matter of Fact.* Now to call this, *an
Unanimous Vote*, yet we find it was after this Ordered to be
Printed in the *Bofton News-Letter*, with a PASSED UNANI-
MOUSLY. We cannot Conceive how the Council could Order
a Direct Falfhood to be Printed, if their Souls were their own.
Or, if they would fo Mifreprefent Judge *Sewall* and Colonel *Higginfon* (Brother to Mr. *Nathaniel Higginfon*) it may be, they did
alfo Mifreprefent themfelves, in faying, *they firmly Believe*, when
it is ftrange if they do *really Believe it.*

Notwithftanding their News-Letter fays, their Vote was Paffed
Unanimoufly, Worthy Gentlemen in *New-England* have given
us fuch a Character of their *Winthrop*, their *Hutchinfon*, their
Fofter, and of fome others of them, as that we cannot *Firmly
Believe*, that they ever Confented to have the Honourable Mr.
Higginfon fo Stigmatized in the *Bofton* Infamous News-Letter.
Nor, is it to be Imagined, that they are all fo *Paradoxical*, as we
hear fome of them are ; for you cannot with a Beetle, beat it
into fome of them, but that if a Vote obtain a *Majority*, it is to
be called an *Unanimous Vote.* We have been Told, (and we
Thought fo, by hearing them Talk, who came from thence) that
they Speak as Good *Englifh* at *Bofton*, as they do in *London :*
But we perceive, in the *Council Chamber* there, they begin to
forget the *Englifh* Tongue ; and they have loft the Senfe of the
Word *Unanimous.*

One may Guefs at the Politick Reafon, which Drew too many
of them into that Undeliberate, Inconfiderate Vote aforefaid ;
by what One of them, (a principal Stickler for Ma*jority* being
Unanimity) utter'd in a Barber's Shop, with fo much Opennefs,
that the Noife of it has reach'd over hither to *London*, That it
was Beft for us, *to keep this Governour*, (*tho' he had done very
bad things*) *for he had fufficiently Spunged upon the People, and
had now got Money enough ; he was now fatisfied.* [No, Sir, by
your Leave, 'tis the Thirft of a Dropfy !] *And* [15] *had privately promis'd the Council, he would do fo no more. Whereas*

if another Governour come, he will come Hungry, and we muſt be Squeezed over again!

Had the Gentlemen of the Council Cauſed their Vote to run in ſome Softer Terms; as, That they were Sorry ſuch Eminent Perſons, as Mr. *Higginſon*, and Mr. *Maſon*, &c. had been Impoſed upon by ſuch Informations, as produced their *Addreſs* to Her Majeſty.   This had been ſomewhat like *Gentlemen*, tho' not like *Counſellors :*   For ſome of them Own, they had never ſeen any of the *Affidavits* made before the Queen and Council, nor any of thoſe other Things anon to be produced, when they Paſſed their Haſty Vote.   But for them now to run upon theſe Eminent Perſons, with a Clamour of *Scandalous and Wicked Accuſations ;* yea, Publickly to Stigmatize them in their Infamous News-Letter, as being *Scandalous and Wicked Accuſers !*   Truly therein they have not Honoured themſelves.   The *Higginſon* they Vilify, is a Perſon every way much Superior to the Beſt of them :   The Honour and Figure he has Obtained by his good Conduct in the *Eaſt-Indies*, will not be Impaired by any Affronts from the *Weſt-Indies*.   The *Maſon* whom they Throw Dirt upon, was a Member of their Council, before a great part of them were ſo ; and Served their Agents with no ſmall Aſſiſtances.

'Tis Unintelligible !   Why will the *Maſſachuſet* Counſellors permit themſelves to be made the Tools of their Governour's particular Deſigns ?   Why will Counſellors that are Choſen by the People, be leſs Concerned for, leſs Faithful to the People, than the Counſellors in the other Plantations, who are not by the Choice of the People brought unto the Board ; where yet we ſee, they often Prove Thorns in the Sides of Evil Governours ? Will you give your Friends, at a Thouſand Leagues diſtance from you, Leave to Adviſe you ?   We make no doubt, there are Wiſe and Good Men at your Board.   We make no doubt, you are often Over-Voted by ſome of your Brethren, coming from your Country Towns, who are not Over-Stockt with more than One of thoſe Qualities.   But where is your Courage ?   In Truth, 'tis the leaſt of your Talents ; you muſt get a little more of it.   You ſhould be ready to ſay before the Governour's Face, [16] what you Talk ſo freely behind his Back, that the Report of it reaches over the *Atlantick*.

You know, That when the Governour will have any thing paſs among you, all your Humble Intreaties to have a few Hours Time to Think upon it, ſignify nothing ; he will have it go *juſt now*, and you *let it go*.   So you are ever now and then puſh'd into you know not what yourſelves, and you durſt not Liſp your Diſſatisfaction.   You know, That when Officers are to be Elected ; the Governour muſt Iſſue out a Notification for a *General Council*, to come together at the Day ; but *on* the Day the thing is rarely done ; 't is put off Two or Three Days till you are Diſperſed, and a *Nick of Time* is taken, in which Elections are carried on, which we hear, much Difoblige the Publick; and Juftices are Created, which have brought the Queen's Commiffions under fuch Difparagement, that we hear many of the Beft Gentlemen among you, Scorn to Accept of them.

You know, that things are managed with Tricks, Frauds, and Juggles, without Numbers; and yet, you durft not Open your Mouths. You cannot but know, That your Governour ever now and then, will Violently Affert a Thing, and you Affent to it; Anon, in the very fame Seffions of the Court, he will as Violently Affert a Thing Diametrically Oppofite unto it, (as the Service of fome ill Caufe may drive him to) and you durft not fay, that you don't Affent to *that* alfo.

We Underftand, that your former Governour, the Earl of *Bellamont*, did not ufe to Treat you fo; and was it for this, that you offered fuch an Indignity unto that Noble Perfon, as to Vote, *The taking off his Speech from the File*, as foon as Colonel *Dudley* (being one of *Tory* Principles, which my Lord was not) at his firft coming moved you to it, and made you the Tools of his Malice againft the Earl of *Bellamont*, for fticking fo Clofe to him in the Parliament, upon the 𝕭𝖆𝖗𝖇𝖆𝖗𝖔𝖚𝖘 𝕸𝖚𝖗𝖉𝖊𝖗 (as he would always call it) of *Leifter* and *Milburn?* Your Governour with a Torrent of *Language*, and Mixture of *Coakfing* and *Bouncing*, and Confident Affertions of Things (True or Falfe, 'tis all one, you can't Difprove them) has been *too many* for you. We Ad- [17] vife you, to Unite more together, a fufficient Number of you, and prefent Strong Remonftrances on fuch Occafions, if the Succeffor (which we are Satisfied he will not) fhould go on in the late Methods. And we Advife you, That you would not be fo monftrously Afraid of the Governour's putting his *Negative* upon you, the laft *Wednefday* of *May*. Should you be Negatived out of the Council, for your Fidelity to your Country, it would be a much greater Honour to you, than to be there; and no great Honour to them that are left behind: But you are already Chofen, and Sworn to Serve till others are Chofen; if the Reprefentatives are not Satisfied in the Reafons of the Governour's Negative, they will Declare, That they will not Proceed unto another Choice. We would Beg their Pardon, that we prefume to give them this Advice: Then do you pluck up your Spirits: Nothing but an Act of the Affembly, can Remove a Chofen Counfellor. You may appear, and Affert your Seat at the Council Board. And you may do it with fuch apparent Evidences of being Acted by nothing but a Zeal for the Publick, that you may do it without any Difhonourable Charge of being Immodeft, or Intruders. Without Confulting the Stars, we can foretell to ye, That if you Refolve to keep always in the Obfequious Strain, you'll at laft Rowfe the Reprefentatives, both to Remove feveral of you, and to Difpute feveral Powers which you pretend unto; and efpecially that of being able to *Sit by yourfelves* in the time of the General Affembly ; and by your Vote (without the Governour's) to hamper the People with a Third Negative, (befides the Queen's, and the Governour's) which your Agent here fays, *Your Charter never intended for you.*

---

[18]

S E C T.   III.

W E have feen how the *Blanching* Bufinefs went on in the *Council*, Shall we now fee how it Proceeded among the *Reprefentatives?* We have been Told a very Odd Thing, That the Counfellors will fometimes *Outwardly* Comply with a Vote, which they *Inwardly* Approve not, in hopes that it will never be Carried in the Lower Houfe. But, if this were an Honeft, yet it is no Prudent Experiment: There is more than a *little* Danger in it. The Story of the Upper Houfe, has the Truth of it enough Confirm'd by Judge *Sewall's* Inftrument of Revocation, if we had not had the more Ample Relation, both from Packets and Paffengers newly Arrived here. For the Story of the Lower Houfe, we have it with a Confirmation (if it be poffible) more Authentick. For here are come over Letters from a great part of the Houfe, unto that Honourable Friend of *New-England*, and of all Good Men, Sir *Henry Afhurft;* one Signed by Seven, and afterwards another Signed by about Thrice that Number; both to the fame Effect. By thefe we Underftand, how Notorioufly the World is Impofed upon.

On the *Fifth* of *November*, the *Plott* begun to Operate. A Meffage was brought by Sundry *Counfellors*, from their Board, to incite the Houfe, that they would Concur with *Their Vote* for the Governour's Vindication. But the Houfe for diverfe Days, declined to Meddle with it ; and then the like Meffage was brought again to the Houfe, by a Greater Number of *Counfellors*. The Houfe being thus at Length Drawn in, to Confider this Dirty Matter, there Appeared Mr. *John Nelfon*, who having fent unto *Port-Royal*, one Hog's-Head of Dry Goods, a Parcel of *Iron Potts* and *Scythes*, &c. by a [19] Flag of Truce, whereof Capt. *Roufe* was Commander, now Declared, That he had the Governour's Allowance for it, and Capt. *Roufe* being Examined, made the fame Declaration.

But this was a Trifle to the Next : The Gentlemen aforefaid, we Believe had no Traiterous Defign of Supplying the Queen's Enemies. But, when the Fort at *Port-Royal* had no Dry Lodgings for the Souldiers ; nothing but a few Thatch'd things, that alfo Rendered it more Combuftible to the Fire of the Befiegers ; Now, to Supply the *Fort* with Nails to Shingle and Board their *Barecks !* There Appeared Mr. *Samuel Baker,* who Produced unto the Houfe the Original Invoyce, of things which he Shipp'd for the Governour and the Commiffary at *Port-Royal ;* with an Allowance for them, under Governour *Dudley's* own Hand. There is no need of Tranfcribing all the Articles ; thefe are enough.

Eighty Thoufand of *Shingle Nails.*
Twenty Thoufand, *Ditto,* Board.
One Dozen of Black Hafted Table *Knives.*
One Hundred Weight of Good *Butter.*
Two Barrels of *Mackerel.*
One Piece of Good *Searge.*
One Cafk of *Paffado-Wine.*
Some *Rice,* &c.

I Know no Inconvenience in the Particulars above, and therefore Allow it.

J. DUDLEY.

Thefe things were Ship'd on Board a *French* Veffel, Called *A Flag of Truce,* (*Anglice,* of *Trade*) Capt. *De Chafeau* Commander. It was done at the very time, when the Governour and Affembly, were Fining *Veatch,* and Company, for a Trade as little Criminal : And when an Act of the *Maffachufet* Province had made it *Capital.* Some of the Counfel would fain have perfuaded the Houfe, that there was a *Cyphre* (their own *Namefake* in the *Council,*) Added unto the 8, and the 2, of the Nails. But *Baker's* Confeffion, had Spoilt that Idle Whim. The Governour's Friends, his Ma- [20] jors, Captains, Juftices, and Feather-Caps in the Houfe, and the *Meaner Slaves of the Trencher,* ufed all Imaginable Artifices to Vindicate him : And yet, when it came to a Vote on *November the* Nineteenth, *Whether, after ftrict Enquiry, the Houfe could Clear his Excellency of Managing, or Countenancing a Private Trade with the* French *and* Indian *Enemies,* The Vote Paffed in the Negative, with a very great Majority. About Forty Five Members, more than Two to One, of the Houfe, Voted, That they could not Clear him. He had, according to the New *Maffachufet* Senfe of the Word, *An Unanimous Condemnation.*

On the Day following, there was a long Conference of Two Hours, held between the Two Houfes, and chiefly Manag'd by the Governour. At this Conference there Occur'd feveral pretty little Things, which might be Diverting enough at the *Coffee-Houfe*, but fcarce Worthy to be Inferted in a more Serious Narrative. We'll Mention only Two of them.

A Counfellor, who had been a mighty Decrier of the Governour, while he was under his *Negative*, upon his Re-admiffion, becomes an Efpoufer of his Intereft. This Gentleman greatly Expofed himfelf, by faying to the Affembly, *There is no Trade, but there are fome Returns : I Pray, What Returns were there ! How can you fay, this was a Trade carried on?* This became a By-Word in the Town. They fay, the Merchants of *Bofton* often to their Sorrow, *Trade without Returns :* And we could Wifh, That every Body here in *London*, who has Traded for *Bofton*, could fay, *There had always been Returns.*

Again, The Governour in his Flourifhes, tells the Affembly, *To Support the Queen's Enemies with an Unlawful Trade, is to fend them your Beef and your Pork, and not fuch things as are in this Invoyce.* An Unlucky Old Man in the Houfe, (they fay from a Town call'd *Woburn*) Reply'd '*Tis very True, an't like your Excellency, and your* Butter, *and your* May-krill !—— Which gave fuch a Sting, That the Affembly faw, that if he be an *Happy Man, who Catches a* Mackrel, yet an *Unhappy Man may be Catched with a Mackrel.*

The next Day after this Conference, and after the Governour's Violent Proteftations of his own *Innocence*, (as the [21] Letters of the *Reprefentatives* Affure us) the following Vote was again Prefs'd upon the Houfe, *That we firmly Believe, and are of Opinion, that the Allegations in the Addrefs* (to which the Vote of the Council referr'd) *of the Governour's Trading, or Allowing a Trade with Her Majefty's Enemies the* French, *and the* Indians *in their Interefts, is a Scandalous and Wicked Accufation.* Still the Vote Paffed, as formerly, in the *Negative.* The Squeamifh Reprefentatives, it feems, had not fuch Stomachs of *Oftriches*, as to Digeft an *Hundred Thoufand Iron Nails* at once ; nor would they Believe (no, tho' Counfellors told them fo!) that *Nails* were not *Iron.* The Governour's Friends were now at their Wit's Ends ;—— And in Humble wife, befought the Houfe, That they would Confine their Vote unto the Particular Trade of *Vetch, Borland* and *Lawfon.* And it was Urged, that *Borland* and *Lawfon*, had Cleared the Governour; (the Sham of the *Grateful* Merchants you fhall hear anon !) Hereupon the Flexible Honeft Men, perfectly Worried, and Wearied out of their Lives, by Three Week's Alterations, did fo many go over, as to make a fort of a Vote of it. But the Conclufion of their Letters to Sir *Henry Afhurft*, (a Gentleman whom *New-England* can never fufficiently Requite) is, *Yourfelf, and all Perfons may judge, how far the Vote of this Houfe doth extend to the Vindicating of his Excellency from being a Countenancer of Trade with the Queen's Enemies !*

We have already Intimated, how the Governour comes to have fo many Friends in the Houfe; that are fo fet upon doing him Juftice, Right or Wrong. Befides the Careffes of the *Table*, which are enough to Dazzle an Honeft Countryman, who Thinks every Body Means what he Speaks; The Influence which Preferments and Commiffions have upon little Men, is inexpreffible. It muft needs be a Mortal Sin, to Difoblige a Governour, that has Inabled a Man to Command a *whole Country Town*, and to Strut among his Neighbours, with the Illuftrious Titles of, *Our Major*, and, *The Captain*, or, *His Worfhip*. Such magnificent Grandeurs, make many to Stagger Egregioufly! If it be but Propofed in the Affembly, that any Mifmanagements of the Governour be Enquired into, we are Informed, that fome of thofe Officers [22] have been fo Infolent, as to move, *That he who made the Propofal fhould be fet in the Pillory!* We perceive, the well-affected part of the Affembly, take much Notice of this! And it feems, there was in this Affembly, one Occafion Odder than the reft, to take Notice of it.

There was a Reprefentative of *Ipfwich*, who formerly falling in with the Interefts of the Country, fo Provoked Colonel *Dudley*, that in a Printed Pamphlet, Publifhed by him, (or, the Perfon who Wrote for him, fo as to make it He) he Reproached the Country. That fuch a Figure fhould be made in the Affembly, by one who was then a Practifing *Sow-Gelder*. This Practifing *Sow-Gelder* (as Mr. *Dudley* calls him) was a Member of this Affembly, and unto the Surprize of the Whole Houfe, Tack'd about, and gone over to Colonel *Dudley's* Interefts; tho' 'tis not many Months ago, that we have (now in *London*) his Hand with others, unto an Honeft Letter, to that Honourable Perfon, Sir *Henry Afhurft*, to Solicit his Endeavours to Deliver the Country from a Plot againft the *Charter*, and all the Courts of Juftice in it, with a Sham Court of *Chancery*, (or rather of Bribery) which Governour *Dudley* was then Purfuing. We are told, he has (for we know not what Reafons) a Number in the Houfe, who Refign themfelves up to him, for him to do almoft what he will with them; they follow *his* Dictates. The Main Things that have been Carried in the late Affembly at *Bofton*, otherwife than they fhould have been, were owing to his Dexterous Operations. Every Body faid, *This man has in his Eye*, a Bribe, *as the Reward of his Apoftacy*. He'll certainly be made a *Juftice*, as foon as his Drudgery in gaining the *Vote* aforefaid, is over! It came to pafs; —— As foon as the *Sham-Vote*, which has Abufed the World in your Foolifh News-Letter yonder, was Gained, the Governour draws the Council in, to Confent, unto their own Immortal Honour, that this Gentleman *Sow-Gelder* fhould be made a *Juftice of Peace!* Fy, Gentlemen, What d'ye do? —— And fo the *Worfhipful* of your County of *Effex*, have the Practifing *Sow-Gelder* aforefaid, (it was Mr. *Dudley* who taught us to call him fo !) fit on the Bench with them. Whether the *Cattle* are in lefs Danger, or the *People* in more, fince this Promotion, we who [23] are Strangers to the Man, except by hearfay, know not ; we fuppofe there never was a *Sow-Gelder* made a Juftice, except in *New England*, and that not till *Dudley* was their Governour.

But, it were Good Advice for the People of *New-England*, in Chufing Reprefentatives, to beware of Chufing too many, who have their Obligations to their Governours, for their Preferments and Employments. The fewer you have in your Affemblies under fuch Temptations, the more Faithfully are your Affairs like to be carried on. You will Pardon Strangers, if their Good Will to you, make them fo far Meddlers, as to Offer you their Opinion.

[24]

SECT. IV.

THE Houfe of Reprefentatives then *Firmly Believe, and are of Opinion,* That their Governour was not Concerned in Trading with *Veatch, Borland,* and *Lawfon.* Others do Firmly Believe the Contrary. Becaufe, diverfe Traders have Own'd, and faid before many Witneffes, that their Governour did Know, and Allow of what they did ; *Vetch* doth himfelf Confefs it, in his Petition to the Queen. And when One of them Swears in the Governour's Vindication, he only means, that the Governour was not Concern'd as a Merchant, or a Partner with them. He Ship'd nothing ; there was nothing Shipp'd on his Account. All this is nothing to the Purpofe. And tho' Col. *Dudley* fhould be Clear of having any thing to do with thefe Three Grateful Merchants, yet there is another who is able to make Difcoveries.

In the fame Condemnation with the Three aforefaid, there was at this time, under Imprifonment, by Vertue of the Sentence which the *General Affembly* had Illegally, (and it now appears Oppreffively) paffed upon him, for a part in an Unlawful Trade, one Captain *Roufe.* The laft General Affembly growing Senfible of his Condition, Voted his being let out upon Bail, that he might enjoy his Liberty. But, for a Reafon, which he will tell in due time, the *Vote* was in a great Meafure Eluded.

It is Reported by fome now in *London*, That the Affembly's Vote to fet *Roufe* at Liberty, was made very Infignificant, by means of one faid to be a *Tory* Judge, one *Leveret*. And they fay, that *Dudley* has made that *Tory* Lawyer, to be Prefident of their *Colledge*. No Queftion but the Lawyer will bring up Hopeful Young Divines, to be fent hither for my Lord of *London* to Ordain them. We hear that they have Sung the *Gloria Patri* in their Colledge-Hall already, and that feveral [25] of their Clergy ftood up at it. An Aufpicious beginning under their Lawyer Prefident, who, we alfo hear, was Chofen a Lieutenant of their Artillery Company at *Bofton*, the laft Summer. Such Reports as thefe, make their Friends here, think that the People in *New-England* are running Mad.

But to Proceed with Captain *Roufe*. Several of his Letters are come to *London*, whereby we Underftand, "That he having " been fent unto *Port-Royal*, on a Service for the Publick, in " which he did Good Service, returned Home under a Languifh- " ing Sicknefs. A way being by this firft Voyage open'd for a " Private Trade between *Port-Royal* and *Bofton*, he was Invited " into a New Trading Voyage; being told, *He had Eaten the* " *Sowre, he fhould now Eat the Sweet*. Governour *Dudley* told " him, *His main Bufinefs was to Steer clear of the Officers of the* " *Cuftom-Houfe*. And the Matter was Propofed fo Advantage- " oufly, that *fome Body* preffed him to make the Governour a " Prefent of an Hundred Pounds, for the Liberty and Advantage " which was to be Allow'd him. Becaufe he lay Sick, he *had* " Nothing, and *faw* Nothing aboard, but what had been Shipp'd " by others Concerned in the Voyage. He went and made the " Beft of his Goods ; and for *this*, and nothing but *this*, he under- " gone a Fine of *Twelve Hundred Pounds*.

" Diverfe Perfons, and efpecially a certain *Lady*, came to him " feveral times in the Prifon, before his Trial ; and this as from " the Governour, to Perfuade him and the reft, to Petition the " Affembly, to take their *Trial* into their own Hands ; (which " the Governour had himfelf Propofed unto the Affembly) with " many fair Promifes, that in a Week's time, or very Quickly, " the Governour would fo Manage the Affembly, as to bring " them abroad again, without any further Trouble. Continual " Communications paffed between *Roxbury* and the Prifon ; and " thofe Good Offices were done, for which *Paul Dudley*, the Gov- " ernour's Son, received of *Borland* and *Lawfon*, (as they have " Affirmed) at one time, a Prefent of *Eighteen Pounds*. They " came with frequent Meffages, to keep Captain *Roufe* in a Good " Pliant, Silent Humour, and prevent his Telling of Tales. Juft " before his Trial, a Meffenger came from the Governour [26] " to him, to Defire him, *That if the Governour fhould Speak any* " *Sharp Things to him, he would not Retort any thing, or Mif-* " *confterue it ; for he might Affure himfelf, he was his Hearty*

" *Friend.* He would carry on the General Affembly as far as
" was Convenient, but then, at laft, bring off the Matter, and
" prevent their doing any Harm. Capt. *Roufe* accordingly kept
" Counfel; the Trial went on, and the Fine anon, proves as we
" told ye, *Twelve Hundred Pounds.* The Governour's Son, could
" not Demand of *Roufe,* as he did of *Cauphin,* a Prefent of
" Twenty Pounds to the Governour, for bringing his Fine fo low.
" After this, Capt. *Roufe* is frequently Sollicited to make the
" Governour a Prefent of *Five or Six Hundred Pounds;* with
" Affurances, that the Governour would find a way for his Lib-
" erty, tho' he were now Imprifon'd by an Act of the Affembly.
" He ftill Refufed it: refolving to wait for Her Majefty's Difal-
" lowance of that Illegal Act. He Wrote Letters to the Gov-
" ernour, Intreating him to procure a Mittigation of his Hard
" Circumftances, becaufe he had done nothing, but with Counte-
" nance from his Excellency. The Governour told the Meffen-
" ger, that *Roufe* muft Write another fort of Letter to him;
" which the Meffenger Explained, with telling him, that he muft
" Write, *That the Governour had no Concern with what was done.*
" But this he would never do. We hear that he continues Wait-
" ing for an Opportunity, to bring more fully to Light, many
" other things, befides thefe that have been Mentioned.
   Thefe being the main Strokes of what Captain *Roufe* has
thought fit as yet to Declare of his Cafe; we don't Wonder, that
the Practifing *Sow-Gelder* thought fit to Caftrate the Vindicating
Vote of *Roufe's* Name. But we may well Wonder, that the
Houfe would be drawn into a Vote, that was Defign'd for a
Blind, and a Sham, to Impofe on People at a Diftance; and yet,
at fuch a Diftance as we are, we can fee thro' it! At the fame
time, the Counfellors and Reprefentatives, even the moft Antient
Blanchers among them, would (as we are Affured) freely fay to
the Expoftulators of their Conduct, which they every where met
withal, *That if the Governour had put them upon Clearing him
from* [27·] *grofs Briberies and Corruptions, they could not have
Cleared him.* Well, but why don't they Search into thofe things?
For they have a Tendency to Debauch and Ruin the Country,
and make it a Vile, and a Forlorn Country. We are told, their
Anfwer is, 'Tis *too Big* a Thing for them to Manage: They
Wifh the Queen would Grant a *Commiffion of Enquiry.* And
People have been Afraid to Tell what they Know; for the Gov-
ernour and his Son, between them, have (thought they) Num-
berlefs Ways to come up with 'em; and, 'tmay.be, they will
Prefs their Sons to the *Caftle,* or elfewhere; from whence they
fhall be Sold unto Merchant-Ships, and fent out of the Country.
Or, they may fhortly have fome Caufe in Court, where the
Queen's Attorney (the Governour's Son) Reigns *Lord and King;*
and will take Effectual Care that the Caufe go againft them.
Others go on, *That thofe are little things; they do fo in* England;

fuch things muft be borne with! Which is indeed, a Cruel Re-
proach on the Queen's Government. And Laftly, the Sharpeft
of all will tell ye, *Oh! the Governour is our Father; we muft
not be fuch Sons of* Cham, *as to Uncover the Nakednefs of our
Father.* And thus until the New Governour Arrive, who being
a Man of Integrity, will Honour himfelf by a Strict Enquiry
into fuch Things, there is like to be no Distinct Account brought
in, to Inform the World,

What Wicked *Bribes,* by a Juggling Management between the
Governour and his Son, [for, as we Told you before, *You muft
go to my Son!*] are Extorted on all the Occafions in the World!
How Prifoners have been let out of Prifon for a Bribe!

How Men in the Officers Hands, upon a *Judgment for Debt,*
have by the Governour's Arbitrary Command, been fet at Liberty!

How Criminals in the Hands of Juftice, being Frighted with
a Prospect of their Punifhment, into a Willingnefs to go to Sea,
the Governour fends an Order to the Keeper to Sell 'em for Ten
Pounds; and fo they are fent away to Sea!

What a Wicked Trade is carried on, of *Selling Men* from the
Caftle, *&c.* to Merchant-men; by which, poor Men have their
Sons Kidnapp'd into the *Indies,* where the *French* [28] Catch
'em, and they Perifh in their Prifons! And what intolerable
Penfions are Paid by Officers for their Places; (by which, and
the like means, the War, which impoverifhes the whole Country,
has Inriched the Governour) which introduces a World of Mif-
management! And, Whether a Lieutenant, whofe Salary is but
Sixty Pounds a Year, muft not Pay Thirty Pounds a Year Pen-
fion to Son *Paul,* or be turn'd out! *Cum multis alijs.*

What would have been the Punifhment of fuch things in Old
King *Alfred's* Days? Thefe things make a *louder* Cry, than
can be Stifled by the Noife of all your *filly Addreffes.*

We don't Wonder to fee *Addreffes* for fuch a Governour's Con-
tinuance, come over hither, Signed by his *Commiffion Officers.*
They are but Addreffes for their own Continuance. The Royal
Wifdom is not fo to be Impos'd on.

But We can't but Smile to fee the *Clergy* of *New-England* fo
Eafily drawn in to Sign *Addreffes* of this Nature. We are Glad,
that we can't fee the Hands of the moft eminent Minifters, to
thefe *Addreffes.* By which we gather, That the Governour has
fent his Emiffaries here and there into Country-Towns, and Sur-
prizes their Honeft Minifters alone, and fo many Arts of Infinua-
tion are ufed, that they have not Prefence of Mind enough, to
Refufe a *Subfcription* unto any thing that is Offered them. We
do not fee the Minifters of *Bofton,* nor the Judicious Minifter of
Roxbury, (your Governour's Paftor) to any of those Addreffes
which you have been Wheedled into, not at all to your Credit
here.

Certainly, when thefe Honeft Gentlemen come to fee the Practices of their Governour Difcovered, they will with Grief and
Shame Reflect upon the Addreffes, by which they have too far
made themfelves *Parties* to fuch a Governour.   Some of them will
Confider, Whether they had not beft follow the Noble Pattern
which their Judge *Sewall* has given them.   Gentlemen, Such
things as by common Fame, you know to be in the Conduct of
your Governour, are not things which muft needs Render *a Man
acceptable to God, and to all Good Men.* —— That Expreffion
were fitter for Pens of *Roman-Catholicks*, than of *New-England*
Minifters.   You ought, with fome Remorfe to make a Retracta-
tion of [29] fuch a Paffage as that, which we hear (by Letters,
for we have not feen it) is in one of your *Addreffes.*   We hope
you Teach your People better things !

You are generally, fo far as we hear, Good, Pious, Faithful
Men, and Bleffings to your People.   But if we may be worthy to
Advife you, we think you would do well to Refolve, that you
will never Sign *Addreffes* of this Nature, till you have had Opportunity in fome *Convention* (if you have fuch Things, for we are
Strangers to your Methods) to Difcourfe with one another, how
far it may be Convenient.

We have heard, that of Old Time, there were fome *Oxen*, who
had the Wifdom to Refolve, that they would no one of them,
have any Talk with *Monfieur* the *Lyon*, apart :   Allow us to tell
you, if you go on Signing fuch *Addreffes*, you will ftrangely Un-
dermine your own Authority among your People, and Sacrifice
your own Reputation to your Governours.   You'll Tempt 'em to
fay, *That you'll fet your Hands to any thing!*   Your Predeceffors
would not have done, as you have done.   And, what a *Sword*
do fuch *Addreffes* put into your Refolute Governours Hands !
He may now Opprefs you, or any of yours, to the laft Degree,
and you have Tied yourfelves up from Complaining of him.
Were not GOD Merciful to you, in removing fuch a Governour,
you had *Inflaved* your Country before you are aware of it.   If
you'll permit fuch as are no *Clergymen*, to Addrefs you with
Stories out of Old *Councils*, we could tell you, That the Firft
Council of *Orleans*, A. C. 52, made a ftrange Decree, *That if a
Bifhop Ordain a Slave, to be a Prieft, knowing him to be a Slave,
fhall pay double the Price of him to his Mafter.*   We know not
well, what fort of a World it was, when this *Decree* was made.
All that we move you to, Gentlemen, is, That at your next General Council, you would make a Decree, *That none of you fhall
be Slaves, or, do any thing that fhall faften the Fetters of Slavery
upon your People.*   We believe, That if you had known your
Addreffes would have come too late, (as fome of them have) and
Expofed you to be Laughed at, you would have had more Wit,
than to have done as you have.   We fuppofe you have heard
what befell the Lord *Verulam* for permitting his Servant to take

a Bribe, and what we [30] lately done to Sir *J. T.* becaufe he did like your Governour take a Bribe to promote the Paffing a Bill. Certainly, if you had known your Governour had been guilty of fuch Briberies, and other Male-Adminiftrations, as not only Chriftian, but Heathen Princes have Punifh'd with the greateft Severity, you would not have Signed your *Ignorant Addrefes*.

Before we Proceed to give an Account of the late Shameful Expedition of the *New-Englanders*, againft *Port-Royal.* We fhall take fome farther Notice, of what Gentlemen worthy of Credit do Affure us. One Writes, That a Gentleman in *New-England*, when he firft heard, that Colonel *Dudley* had Obtained a Commiffion to be Governour there, faid, *That he could not Believe, that a Man who had been a Traytor to his Country, and an Apoftate from the Religion in which he had been Educated; and that had Murder'd two Men at* New-York, *better, and more Righteous than himfelf, would prove a Good Governour.*

Another Letter fays, That the Mifery of that People of late, has been in their *Counfellors*, as well (tho' not fo much) as in their *Governour.* The Priviledges which they enjoy by their prefent *Charter*, are Great and Singular : For, no Man, but fuch as the People fhall Nominate by their Reprefentative, can be of the Governour's Council. Nor, may there be any *Judge*, or *Juftice of the Peace*, but what the Council thus Chofen by the Reprefentatives of the People, fhall Confent unto. So that they may, and Ought to be *Shields* to the People, by keeping ill Men from being in Places of Power. Yet we hear, that their Governour has made a Number of very Unfit Men to be their *Juftices;* and this with the Confent of his Council, without which he could make none. So that it feems, thefe Great Priviledges fignify very little, through the Pufillanimity, and Unfaithfulnefs of their Governour's *Counfellors*, who will, too many of them, Confent to almoft any thing that he would have them. Witnefs, befides the Things already mentioned, among other innumerable Inftances, fo many of them Confenting to have a Fort Built at *Pemaquid*, and a ftated Salary settled upon the Governour, and other Officers, by which they had like to have Enflaved their Country at once.

[31] The Reprefentatives are alfo to be Blamed, in that they do not *Change their Counfellors.* We know, that they want Men fit for Government. Neverthelefs, we doubt not but in the large Province of *Maffachufet's*, there may be found an Hundred Men, as fit to be Counfellors, as *S. S.* or *J. C.* or *P. T.* [we deal more Tenderly with *them*, in giving but the Firft Letters of their Names, than they have Dealt with the Honourable *Nathaniel Higginfon*, whom they have, by Name at large, Vilified, as a *Scandalous and Wicked Accufer*.] And others, who by their Obfequioufnefs to *D.* have juftly Forfeited the Love of the People.

Had their Reprefentatives the Wifdom frequently to *Change*

their Counsellors, it would make them more Careful to Study the Interest of their People, and not that so they may Please their Governour, and Stigmatize better Men than themselves, in their *Boston* News-Letter, only because they *Slandred* D. *in a matter of Truth.*

We are also Advised from *New-England*, That *D.* has Exposed himself to the whole Colony of *Connecticut.* They Dislike him there more Universally than in the *Massachuset's.* For he is not in a Capacity to *Bribe* Men there with his *Commissions*, Civil or Military. But he has joyned a Hellish Malice with the worst Men, and greatest Enemies of the *Charter* belonging to that Colony, in seeking to Disturb them in the quiet Possession of their Lands. A Commission was Obtained, in which *Dudley* was Chief, but others, who pretended to have a Right to Great Tracts of Land, were put into the *Commission*, with Power to be Judges of their own *Pretensions;* the like to this has been seldom known. But when that Honourable Gentleman, who has Condescended to be their Agent, discovered the Fraud of this Affair before the Queen in *Council*, Praying that Her Majesty would put some Remarkable *Discountenance* on said *Dudley*, that *Commission* was soon Vacated, to his no little Confusion.

[32]

SECT. V.

THAT Honourable Person before-mentioned, who is here Appearing on the Behalf of one of the *N. English* Colonies, which Colonel *Dudley* has been seeking to Enslave, saw cause to Conclude his Petition, with a Complaint against him in these Terms; *Your Majesty's Name and Authority is Abused to Serve some Dark Designs of his own.* It seems he is used to *Dark Designs;* but if ever *Dark Designs* were to be Suspected, it has been in the Business of that Late Expedition to *Port-Royal;* an Expedition, that besides the everlasting Disgrace of it, has entirely Ruined the Country, and made it highly Necessary for another Governour to be sent thither, to Rescue that poor People, if it be possible, from Extirpation. We have pretty *Broad Hints* of an *Unlawful Trade* carried on with the Fort at *Port-Royal.* And besides the things already mentioned, it is well known, that when *Flags of Truce* passed between *Port-Royal* and *Boston*, the Officers of the *Custom-House* at *Boston*, were Obftructed from going aboard thofe Flags of Truce, that fo the Trade carried on with the Enemy, might be Concealed. And when Goods have been Seized on Board the *Flags of Truce*, they have been again taken out of the Hands of the Officers. But we muft now proceed to a Sadder Story. The Short of the Story is this. But the *Dark Defigns* muft be left for another Judgment.

When the War firft broke out, the People of *New-England*, efpecially the Trading part of the Country, and thofe that were more immediately Concerned in the *Fifhery*, were very Uneafy to fee *Port-Royal*, which was then of no confiderable Strength, advancing into a Capacity of Diftreffing, if not Ruining the Province. It is fo near, and fo Seated, as to have all imaginable Advantage to Animate, and Supply [33] the *Indians*, by *Land;* and by *Sea*, with *Privateers*, to Deftroy their *Fifhery*, and Ruin all their other Trade, by Intercepting and Taking their Veffels, both Outward and Inward Bound. Their Fort was but an *Embryo*, and it was thought they might have been eafily Suppreffed.

The *New-Englanders* understood by a *Port-Royaller* falling into their Hands, that at *Port-Royal* they had not yet Heard of the War broken out. Whereupon Governour *Dudley* was earneftly Sollicited, and his Leave Intreated by fome, to go and Deftroy that Neft of *Hornets*, which was like to be fo Grievous a growing Plague to the Country ; with Offers to raife Volunteers fufficient for that Purpofe : But the Propofal was Rejected ; which made People Sufpect fome *Dark Defigns*, and that *Port-Royal* was referved for fome fpecial Advantages not Obvious to the Vulgar.

Afterwards, when the Governour could no longer withftand the Cry of the Country, Colonel *Church* was allow'd to go. The Affembly procured a Mortar-piece, and provided Bombs, and other things Convenient, and had fome Eye upon the Fort, which was not then finifh'd. Yet the faid *Church* had not only the Taking of the *Fort* left out of his Orders, but was pofitively *Forbidden* to Meddle with it. And he hath fince Affirm'd to many Gentlemen, that he could with all the Eafe imaginable have Taken the Fort, but that he had been fo Strictly and Menacingly *Forbidden* to meddle with it, that he Durft not ; but only Ravaged the Naked Country. *Church's* Soldiers were all *Volunteers*, and an *Act of the Affembly* for their Encouragement had Promifed them a certain Share of the Plunder : But the Chief Commanders firft made a large Prefent out of it to the Governour ; and then *He*, joining with them, Cut off the Army of Half that the *Publick Faith* had Engaged them ; which it was feared, would have proved a lafting Difcouragement to all *Volunteers* for the Service of the Crown and the Country : And the Houfe of Reprefentatives Remonftrated unto the Governour, this among other Grievances ; but were Rejected with Obftinate Contempt.

The Reaſon Pretended by the Governour, for Prohibiting Church's meddling with the Fort was, *That he had laid the* [34] *Matter before the Queen, and had yet received no Orders about it.* Tho' the ſame Objection ſtill continued, yet the People being extreamly Deſirous that a Period might be put to their Miſeries from *Port-Royal*, and a Way open'd for the Deliverance of many Scores of Poor *Engliſh* Captives, likely to Languiſh for ever in the *Indian Wigwams*, Moved for another Expedition above a Year ago. The Governour now gives a Commiſſion for *Taking the Fort;* but whether with any *Dark Deſigns*, we are yet *in the Dark*. After the Inſtructions were drawn up, there was a Clauſe *Tack'd* at the End of 'em, which gave the Army Leave to come off when they would, if they ſhould imagine, they could not preſently Finiſh their Buſineſs to their Minds. It was the Tacking of this unobſerved Clauſe at laſt, that Confounded all, and brought on a Story, which all the Letters from *New-England* we have yet ſeen, ſay, *They Bluſh to Write it.* And that is the Reaſon why we can give but a Short Account of it. In Short, There was an Army of as Likely Men as can be Imagined, the beſt part of Two Thouſand of them ; and as well provided with Ammunition, Proviſion, and all things Neceſſary, as a Willing Country could Afford. But, when it comes to Execution, quite Contrary to the beſt Advice of them who Knew the Place, they Landed ſeveral Miles off the Fort, when they might have Landed cloſe by, and probably at once have taken it. However, Land they did ; and Drove the Enemy before them, and Chaſed them into the Fort with much Courage and all the Encouragement that could be. The Men, to do them Juſtice, Fought like Men, and would have done any thing in the World. —— But, lo, the Iſſue ! The *Deptford* Man of War, which was *Commodore* of the Fleet, had Expreſs Orders from the Governour, *That he ſhould not Expoſe the Queen's Ship.* Which Orders he afterwards Expoſed in the *Coffee-Houſes.* An Engineer was fetch'd from *New-York,* where the People from the beginning fore-told what would be the Concluſion. The Governour's Youngeſt Son, *Wm. Dudley,* was there too, in the Quality of a Secretary of War ; and tho' he were little more than a *Boy,* yet he was a *Son,* and the Army ſoon Cry'd out of being *Boy-ridden.* The General, a Man of no Conduct, having Signaliz'd ſome- [35] thing of a *Belluine* Courage in ſome *Indian* Encounters, the *Mob,* 't is ſaid, was ſet upon having him to be a Commander. They landed as we ſaid : but then they never made a *Formal Demand* of the Fort ; they never Threw up a *Shovel-full* of Earth. The Buſineſs was ſo managed, between certain Perſons, that altho' at a *Council of War,* one Day it was Voted, That the *Fort* ſhould be attack'd, it was by 'nd by, Unvoted again. The Engineer had wrought upon ſundry Captains, to make 'em Believe, *That the Taking of the Fort* was Impracticable. They moſt of them gave it under their

Hands to their Wife General, *That it was their Opinion, it was best for 'em to Draw off.* The Soldiers began also to be Dispirited, for some had Blabb'd among them a Secret, which, when it came to be Known, made 'em out of their Witts. Tho' it was Known and Publifhed here in *London*, before the Fleet was returned from *Port-royal.* The General Affembly had Agreed, and Engaged, That if the Fort were Taken, it fhould immediately be Demolifhed; and without this Affurance the Army would never have Proceeded. But *fome Body* now, Indifcreetly let 'em Underftand, that the Governour had fome *Dark Defigns* to put a Trick upon them, and had given him Orders not to *Demolifh* the Fort: Whereupon the Inraged Army faid, *They had now nothing to do, but Fight themfelves into a Prifon!* They were moftly Good Livers at Home, and could not bear the Thoughts on't, that Half the Army, (no Man Knowing, whether it might not be his own Share) fhould be Confined there one long Winter in a remote Garrifon, and perhaps, Two Winters after that; or until they fhould Buy themfelves a Releafe upon as Hard Terms, as the poor Country-Soldiers have, to get out of the Caftle at *Bofton.* Well: A Packet is Difpatch'd unto the Governour of *Bofton*, to Signify their Opinion, and to Pray his Excellency's further Pleafure. But in Three or Four Days after the Sailing of the Packet, and before it was Poffible for them to Hear from *Bofton*, they drew off in great Confufion, and Weigh'd Anchor, and came away. But as they were in the midft of their Difperfion, there came Orders to ftop as many of them, as were together, at *Cafco Bay.* From thence [36] they fent Three Perfons to Acquaint the Governour with the Miferable Affair; whereof one was the *Engineer* aforefaid. They had a very Melancholly, and almoft a Tumultuous Reception by the People; and when they were, at their firft Landing, upbraided with Cowardice, their Answer ftill was, *The Fault was at Home; and they had gone as far as their Orders would bear them out!* With fundry fuch Reflections, which bore Hard upon the Government. The Council were Informed of this Difcourfe; but there was no Notice taken of it. And tho' they were Chidden by the Governour, in the Council Chamber, yet we underftand, they were Hugg'd and Careff'd by him, below Stairs, to the great Scandal of the People. The People were now in a mighty Ferment. It was the Univerfal Opinion, That if the Army had only ftaid, and Plaid at *Coits* in their Camp (far enough from the Fort) at *Port-royal*, the Fort would have been within a few Days Surrendered to them. The Soldiers within were Mutinous to the laft Degree; Deferters Daily came over. Provifions would have grown Scanty in a little Time. [Tho' the Lodgings of their Men were not now Thatch'd! (the Reafon why, we told ye before) yet a Red-hot Bullet or Two, flung into the Fort, might have fet 'em on Fire.] Ten Thoufand Things might have happened. But, like Men afraid of having the Fort fall into their Hands, they ran back to *New-England* as faft as their *Canvas* Sails would carry them. The Good *Women* in *Bofton*, could not forbear their Outcries, when they met in the Streets, on this Occafion Says one of them, *Why, our Cowards imagined that the Fort at* Port-Royal *would fall before them like the Walls of* Jericho. Another Anfwers, *Why did not the Block-heads then ftay out Seven Days to fee! What ail'd the Traitors to come away in Five Days time after they got there!* The Cry of the People muft be Satisfied. Another Ship of War was fitted out, and Recruits of Soldiers were fent unto the Fleet, which now lay at *Cafco-Bay.* Which after Tedious and Expenfive Delays of many Weeks, fet fail from thence again to *Port*-royal; but with the greateft Averfion that ever was in the Hearts of Men: and not until they had been further weakened by many and numerous Defertions. While they were on their Voyage [37] to *Port-royal,* a Man of War arrived from *Portugal;* the brave Commander (a *New-Englander*) was ready to Venture his Ship and Life too on this Occafion ; and Chearfully Complyed with Orders which were with fome ado Obtained, for him to go to *Port-Royal* after them. Our Fleet arriving there a Second Time, found that in the time of their withdraw to *Cafco,* the *Port-royallers* had much Recruited themfelves ; and had Taken and carried in fome *Englifh* Veffels, laden with Provifion ; and had alfo Difpatch'd away their Galley for *France.*

Therefore, after a little Skirmifh on the oppofite Shore, and fome Follies not to be mention'd, away they come for *Bofton,* without Orders, and before Capt. *Paddon* could have Opportunity to come up with 'em. So that the Second Expedition was as Bad or more Worfe than the firft.

After the Expedition was thus Shamefully Finifh'd, there was another Difficult *Card* to Play : that was, to *Satisfy the General Affembly,* which was then Quickly to fit. The way pitch'd upon was, to make a Pretended *Court-Marfhal,* to Enquire into the Caufe of the Mifmanagements at *Port-Royal.* This Court was the Ridicule of Town and Country. No Body was Try'd at it, or fo much as Accufed. All was carried on in *Hugger-mugger.* We can Hear of nothing done: but the Prefenting of the Secretary of War, *Will. Dudley,* with all the Plunder which was taken ; and amounted to between One and Two Hundred Pounds, and then leave to go Home ! It is plain, the General was not to be Impeached there : 't is well, if it has not Ruined the Governour, as well as the diftreffed Country, yet we hear the Governour, before the fitting of the faid Court, gave him an Order for an Advantageous Poft at the *Eaft-ward ;* to Build a Fort at *Saco,* becaufe he would not take one at *Fort-royal ;* as High and Rich a Poft, as he was ever capable of.

And fo much for *Port-royal,* until the *dark defigns* come into further Light. And then it will be Known whether Governour

D. when he faw the Country was Violently fet upon going, and fo Interrupting his Trade with the *French*, had not a Secret Defign that the Fort at *Port-royal* fhould have been made (as the Fort at *Pemaquid* would have been) a [38] Convenient Place for the *Fur-Trade* with the *Indians*, whereby himfelf, and fome Friends of his here, in *Britain*, would have got no little Riches. In the mean time, under his Admirable Conduct, an impoverifh'd Country has, (as we are credibly informed) been put to above Two and Twenty Thoufand Pounds Charge, only to be Laughed at by their Enemies and Pitied by their Friends.

To the *QUEEN's* moft Excellent Majefty.

The Humble Petition of Your Majefty's moft *Loyal* Subjects, Inhabitants in Your Majefty's Dominions, in *America*, or Trading thither.

SHEWETH,

*T**HAT Colonel* Jofeph Dudley, *whofe Arbitrary and Tyranical Proceedings had Expofed him to the juft* Refentments *of his Country-men, before the Happy* Revolution, *hath been neverthelefs fo Fortunate, as to Obtain the Government of the* Maffachufet's *Colony, in* New-England.

That Your Petitioners *are Certainly Informed of diverfe Grievous Corruptions and Oppreffions, and Unjuft and Partial Practices of the faid* Dudley, *on which they might Ground many Complaints, againft him, but they are fo Senfible of the imminent* Danger *which Threatens* Your Majefty's *Subjects in that and the Neighbouring Colonies, thro' his Male Adminiftration, that they at this time Beg Leave Humbly and Singly to reprefent to Your Majefty.*

That the faid Dudley *hath Countenanced a private Trade and Correfpondence with* Your Majefty's *Enemies, the* French *at* Canada, *and the* Indians *which are in their* Intereft, *Furnifhing them with Ammunition and Provifion.*

[39] *That the Perfons managing the faid Correfpondence, pretended a Voyage to* New-found-land, *and being Accufed of* High Treafon, *by the* General Affembly *of* New-England, *the faid Governour by his Intereft and Power, delayed their Profecution, till the Ammunition which he had furnifh'd the Enemy was ufed by*

them, to the Deftruction *of* Your Majefty's *good Subjects, and that Colony, thereby put to* Three and Thirty Thoufand Pounds Charge.

That many of the beft, *and moft* prudent *members of the Lower Houfe* of Reprefentatives, *being tired with his* Delays, *and Neceffitated to go Home and defend their* Plantations *from the Enemy, he prevailed with thofe that remained, who were fcarce a Houfe, that the Accufations againft his Agents, fhould be changed from* Treafon *to* Mifdemeanour ; *and they being* Convicted, he Laboured *to Mitigate their Fines. All which was fo apparent to the People of* New-England, *that they threatned to pull down his Houfe.*

That he had the Confidence neverthelefs, to Apply to the General Affembly *for an* Addrefs *to* Your Majefty *in his Favour, but his Application was received with a general Murmur and Contempt, and nothing done therein.*

And altho' he hath fince Endeavour'd to obtain Your Majefty's Good Opinion *by Collecting a Number of Names of Perfons under his Command and Influence to give him a* Character.

Your Majefty's *Petitioners who Apprehend their Wives, Families, and Eftates to be in Imminent danger under fuch a Governour, do therefore Humbly Pray, that this matter may be fpeedily Enquired into, and that* Your Majefty *would Pleafe to give fuch* Directions *thereupon, as to* Your Majefty's *Great Wifdom fhall feem meet.*

And Your Petitioner's fhall ever Pray, *&c.*

Wm. Partridge, Thomas Newton, Nathan Higginfon, Tho. Allen, Alex. Holmes, John Calley, *&c. &c. &c.*

DIARY

OF

SAMUEL SEWALL.

1674—1729.

VOL. II.

1699-1700—1714.

DIARY OF SAMUEL SEWALL.

Jan 14 $\frac{1699}{1700}$ Elder Jonas Clark, of Cambridge, dies, a good man in a good old Age, and one of my first and best Cambridge friends. He quickly follows the great Patron of Ruling Elders, Tho. Danforth, Esqr.

15. This day fortnight Lawrence Copeland of Braintry was buried; 'tis counted that he liv'd to be at least one hundred and ten years old. *Teste Arnoldo*[1] *octogenario olim ejusdem vicino.*

Jan^r 17. $\frac{1699}{1700}$. A great fire brake out at Charlestown last night though very rainy. Three Houses burnt; viz. the widow Cutlers and two more: on the left hand of the way as one goes to Cambridge, upon the side of the hill. Other Houses on the oposite side of the Ally very narrowly escaped. Elder Clark is buried this day. Snowy all day long.

Gave Mr. Willard two volums of Rivets works.[2]

Jan^r 17 about 5 p. m. Dame Hañah Townsend dies in the 93^d year of her Age. Cook, Hutchinson, Sewall, Addington, Chiever, Maryon *pater*, Bearers. Jan^r 19. 1699–1700.

---

[1] Probably this was Joseph Arnold, of Braintree, whose death does not appear on our books. He married in 1648, and his wife died in 1693; hence we infer he was alive at this time, and an octogenarian. — Eds.

[2] Andrew Rivet, a Poictevin, born 1572, died 1647. He was a professor at Leyden, D.D. at Oxford, and "three volumes of his devotional and controversial writings have been published." — Eds.

Jan^ᵣ 24th   The Lt Govr calls me with him to Mr. Willards, where out of two papers Mr. Wm Brattle drew up a third for an Accomodation to bring on an Agreement between the New-Church [Brattle Square] and our Ministers; Mr. Colman got his Brethren to subscribe it.

This day Jany 24. was a Council at the Governers. Assembly is proroug'd to the 13 March.

Jany 25th   Mr. I. Mather, Mr. C. Mather, Mr. Willard, Mr. Wadsworth, and S. S. wait on the Lt Govr at Mr. Coopers: to confer about the writing drawn up the evening before.   Was some heat; but grew calmer, and after· Lecture agreed to be present at the Fast which is to be observed Jany 31.

Jan^ᵣ 30.   Lt Govr, [Stoughton] Winthrop, Cooke, S. S. hold the Court in Somers's great Room below stairs; finish the Court by 7. at night: Note, good going over the ferry as in Sumer almost, no Ice.

Jany 31.   Fast at the New Church.   Mr. Colman reads the Writing agreed on.   Mr. Allin Prays, Mr. Colman preaches, prays, blesses.   p.m.   Mr. Willard prays, Mr. I. Mather preaches, Mr. Cotton Mather prays, Sing the 67 psalm without reading.   Mr. Brattle sets Oxford Tune. Mr. Mather gives the Blessing.   His Text was, Follow peace with all men and Holiness.   Doct. must follow peace so far as it consists with Holiness.   Heb. 12. 14.

Mr. Colman's Text was Rom. 15. 29.   Mr. Fisk, Hobart, Belchar and many Ministers and Scholars there. Mr. Torrey absent by reason of sickness and the bad wether yesterday.   Of the Council, Lt Govr, Mr. Russell, Mr. Cooke, Col. Hathorne, Sewall, Addington, Sergeant (Foreseat) Col. Foster, Lynde, Saffin, E^m Hutchinson, Walley, Townsend, Byfield.   Mr. Willard pray'd God to pardon all the frailties and follies of Ministers and people; and that they might give that Respect to the other churches that was due to them though were not just of their Constitution.   Mr. Mather in's Sermon, and Mr. Cotton Mather in's prayer to the same purpose. Mr. Willard and C. Mather pray'd excellently and pathetically for Mr. Colman and his Flock. Twas a close dark day.[1]

Febr. 1. A pretty deal of Thunder Rain and Hail the last night.

Col. Hambleton[2] comes to Town this day from Pensilvania.

Cousin Wm Savil died last night of a Fever.

Febr. 2. Cous. Savil is buried. Tis so very cold that none of us venture to goe. Visit my Lord [Bellomont].

Seventh-day, Febr. 3. 1699, 1700. Capt. Win, in the Advice, a 4th Rate, arrives from England 6 weeks passage from the Spit-head. Govr heard nothing of him till he came and deliver'd his Packets. Came to Nantasket the day before; on Friday. He says, the King redeems all the Captives at Maccaness [Mequinez, in Morocco]. Peace.

Tuesday, Febr. 6. A Council is held at my Lord's. The Advice of Councillors asked about sending the Pirats on Board.[3] I motioned that by that time the Prisoners

---

[1] We learn, from Lothrop's "History of the Brattle Street Church," that the church records give few more details about this affair. This church was one established late in 1699, by a few of the more liberal men of the day. It was called the "Manifesto Church," from its printed declaration of principles. Rev. Benjamin Colman, a native of Boston, then in England, was invited to become the first pastor, and accepted. It was necessary to establish fellowship with the other churches, and hence the proceedings in which Sewall participated. — Eds.

[2] Probably Andrew Hamilton, Governor of New Jersey, 1699–1701; Deputy-Governor of Pennsylvania, 1701–1709. He was made Deputy-Postmaster for all the Plantations, in 1692. — Eds.

[3] As in the matter of the witchcraft trials, Sewall here disappoints us by his silence in regard to most interesting matters. This meeting was in reference to the famous pirate, Captain William Kidd, whose memory is stamped indelibly upon the popular imagination in New England. Kidd was licensed May 16, 1691, at New York, to marry Mary, widow of John Oort (N. E. Hist. Gen. Register, VI. 63). June 8, 1691, he was commissioned by Bradstreet to attack a privateer then on our coast. (Palfrey, IV. 180.) He probably sailed between New York and England for some years, and becoming acquainted with Colonel Livingston, Lord Bellomont, and others,

could be got from N. York, Coñecticut, Rode-Island : the
Assembly might sit if his L⁴ship saw meet, and they would
willingly rid themselves of them. Govʳ seem'd displeas'd.
I had ask'd before, What Pirats, and the Govʳ said them
and their Associates. Govʳ mention'd Kid, Gillam, Bradish, Witherly, to be sent aboard presently for better security. Council voted to leave it to the Govrs. Discretion
whom to send aboard : only the Govʳ had said to some
that enquired, He intended not [to let] them out upon
Bail. I think only I, Col. Townsend and Capt. Byfield
were in the Negative. I said I was not clear in it. The
grounds I went upon were because I knew of no power I
had to send Men out of the Province. Capt. Byfield said,
He was for their going aboard : but reckon'd twas not so
safe to send them presently as to keep them in Goal.
Voted also the Treasure to be deliver'd to such as the
Govʳ should apoint. Govʳ nominated Lᵗ Hunt and Capt.

he made an agreement to go out to the East Indies, as captain of a lawful
privateer, to suppress piracy. This was in October, 1695. Here he turned
pirate himself, making his rendezvous on the coast of Madagascar, and cap-
turing native vessels. He returned to Hispaniola, where he left his ship,
and came to New York in a sloop, whence he proceeded to Boston, in June,
1699. After an examination, he was committed a close prisoner with divers
of his crew. Sewall has already recorded (I. 498, 503) that, by the aid of
one Kate Price, two of these men, Joseph Bradish and Tee Witherly, escaped in June, and were recaptured in October. Bellomont says, "We
have found that the jailer was Bradish's kinsman, and he confessed that he
and one of his crew went out of the prison door."

Nov. 30, 1699, Bellomont wrote home, "These pirates I have in gaol
make me very uneasy for fear they should escape. I would give £100 they
were all in Newgate." (N. E. Hist. Gen. Register, VI. 84.) At his request, as there was no provincial law for punishing piracy with death, a
frigate was sent for the prisoners, and they sailed in February, 1699–1700.
Kidd was tried for piracy and for the murder of one of his crew, and, being
found guilty, was executed.

The whole affair was brought into politics. Not only was Bellomont,
one of the original owners of Kidd's vessel, now in high position, but Lord
Chancellor Somers and some other distinguished noblemen were sharers in
the enterprise, and the King was to have a tenth of the profits. Macaulay,
in his twenty-fifth chapter, has eloquently described the attack upon Somers
and his triumphant acquittal. — Eds.

Win, capt. of the Advice. Present Mr. Cooke, Col. Hutchinson, Mr. Secretary, S. S. Mr. Russel, Col. Lynde, Capt. Foster, Mr. Sergeant, Mr. Saffin, Mr. E^m Hutchinson, Col. Townsend, Capt. Byfield, Major Walley. Have reckon'd them as came to mind. Lt Govr, Maj^r Genl Winthrop, Col. Phillips, not there.

High Wind, and very cold at Nwest.

Febr. 7th Council is called to advise about the Indians, being Rumors of a War by the Maquas. One Tobie, who murder'd several at Oxford, stirs them up, and brings wampam to our Indians. On Wednesday night, Jany ult, the night it Thundered, Sixteen Men with women and children ran away from Woodstock. Govr Winthrop has sent 40 Men thither. Have writt a Letter to answer his with Thanks; and to desire him to surprise Tobie if he can.

Friday, Febr. 9th. Will, formerly Capt. Prentices Negro, now living with Maylem, a Horse run away with him, threw him upon the hard frozen Ground, or Timber, near Houchins's corner, and kill'd him; died in a little while. I saw him panting as came from visiting Capt. Foxcroft. He was much delighted in Horses, and now dies by a Horse. About 1664. he sav'd his Master Prentice from a Bear. Went with Col. Townsend and me to Albany. Rid Post one while.

Capt. Belchar was at the Meeting, come home from burying his daughter Vaughan,[1] who died in child bed. Child died first. Wast the most beautifull of all his Daughters. I wonder'd to see him at Mr. Bromfield's, the wether had been so excessive cold. Said, I was sorry for the croping of his desirable Flower.

Febr. 6, 7, 8. were reputed to be the coldest days that have been of many years. Some say Brooks were frozen

---

[1] This was Mary, daughter of Andrew Belcher, and wife of George Vaughan, of Portsmouth. — EDS.

for carts to pass over them, so as has not been seen these Ten years. Ground very dry and dusty by the high wind.

Febr. 12. A considerable snow falls.

Jany 11th was a storm of Snow; which occasiond Mr. C. Mather to take for his Text, White as the snow of Salmon : Quickly melted away. Have not as yet had any path to make upon the Lords Day.

Febr. 12. Justices met with the Selectmen at the Stone-House, Davis's, to take away some misunderstanding between us; and to agree to take Lists of each quarter of the Town to reform and prevent disorders.

Tuesday, Febr. 13. I got up pretty early, being forc'd to it by a laxness. Had sweet comunion with God in Prayer, and in reading the two last Sermons I heard in London, about Assurrance &c. This came to my hand by accident, the book being fallen upon my wood in the closet. Had read before, my own Notes upon Ephes. 5, 15, 16, 7: 16. 1679. at Mrs. Oliver's. The Lord inlighten my Understanding, and incline my Will.

Febr. 14. I visit Mr. Tho. Thornton in the Afternoon between 3 and 4. He made a shift to say he was willing to dy, but wanted Patience. Hop'd should dy next night. I spake to him what I could. Holp him up while he drank something comfortable.

At three past midnight he alter'd much.

Febr. 15, 3 p.m. Mr. Tho. Thornton dyes very quietly; which Mr. Gee acquaints me with. Is very near 93 years old.[1]

Febr. 16. pleasant wether. Kid, Bradish, Gillam,[2] With-

---

[1] The Rev. Thomas Thornton came to Yarmouth, Mass., about 1663, and thence to Boston, in 1677. — EDS.

[2] Of the third of these names, we find that James Gillam proved to be a man who killed Captain Edgecomb, of the Mocha frigate, and persuaded the crew of that vessel to turn pirates. In searching his house a letter was found from Kidd's wife to Captain Pain, an old pirate of Rhode Island,

erly are sent on board the Advice Frigat. Warrant was
dated Febr. 13. but no mention of the Council in it. But
the Gov^{rs} name only, in pursuit of the King's Com̄and.

Febr. 22. I had thoughts of sitting up to see the
eclipse : but the cloudy thick sky discouraged me : yet
kept a candle burning, and went to the Window at two of
the clock ; the wether was still thick with clouds, that I
could see nothing : only seem'd very dark for a full Moon.

In the evening I visited Mrs. Williams in her Languishing. Am invited to a Fast there on Friday.

Wednesday, Febr. 28. We ship off the Iron chest of
Gold, Pearls &c., 40 Bails of East-India Goods, 13 hogs-
heads, chests and case, one Negro Man, and Venturo
Resail, an East-Indian born at Ceilon.[1] Wether was doubtfull in the morning, which made us irresolute : but at
last we set about it, and accomplish'd it very hap̄ily. I
look upon it as a great Mercy of God, that the Storehouse has not been broken up, no fire has hap̄end. Agreed
in the Weight of the Gold with our former Weight, and
had so comfortable a day at last to finish our work. Mr.
Bradstreet, and Capt. Winn's Clerk took an account at the
Crane ; but Capt. Winn would not give a Rec^t till had
them on board the sloop Antonio, which ridd off just
without the Outward Wharf. Gave a Rec^t for the Gold
at Capt Belchar's as soon as it was weighed. Cousin
Wells and his wife visit us. I went to his L^{d}ship to

---

showing that the latter had some of Kidd's money in his hands. (Register,
VI. 84.) — EDS.

    [1] This treasure was of course Kidd's. When he was captured at Boston,
the searchers found a bag of gold dust and ingots worth £1,000, and a bag of
silver. On information, they sent to Mr. Gardiner, of Gardiner's Island, in
the Sound, and obtained gold, silver, and jewels left there by Kidd, worth
£4,500, and six bales of goods, one valued at £2,000. The total capture
was thought to be worth £14,000. Kidd afterwards told Lord Bellomont
that if he was allowed to go to the place where he left his ship, and to St.
Thomas and Curaçoa, he would recover £50,000 to £60,000, hid by himself,
which no one else could recover. See the interesting notes in N. E. Hist.
Gen. Register, VI. 77–84, and Palfrey, IV. 184. — EDS.

speake to Him about some paym^{ts} to be made of about
£16.

March, 4. 1699. Capt. Gullock is sent to Prison for his
contempt of the Governm^t in giving in to the Govr and
Council an Insolent writing under his hand, and justify-
ing it.

March 5, Tuesday, $\frac{1699}{1700}$. Mr. Sergeant, Capt. Frary,
Capt. Hill, Capt Checkly and my self goe to Cambridge
over the Ferry, and acquaint Mr. Pemberton with the
Church's Call, and their desire of his Acceptance. He
makes a very sensible Answer as to the Weight of the
Work, his own inability; hôp'd God would hear his earnest
Prayer, and help him to make a right Answer. Din'd at
Remington's, Mr. Flint, Fitch, and Blower din'd with us:
visited Mr. Brattle, came home round: Saw a man plowing at Muddy River; breaking up a Pasture with two
oxen and a horse.

March 7th Mrs. Williams dies.

March, 11th 1699. 1700. Town-Meeting, chose Seven
Select-men; Mr. Daniel Oliver, Mr. Isa Tay, Mr. Joseph
Prout, Mr. Jno Maryon jun^r Capt. Tim^o Clark, Mr. Elizur
Holyoke, Mr. Obadia Gill, Mr. James Taylor Treasurer,
Wm Griggs Town-Clerk. 5 overseers of the Poor; Elisha
Hutchinson esqr. 38, Mr. Saml Lynde, 33, Mr. Jno Eyre
31, Mr. Nathl Oliver 30. Capt. Nathl Byfield, 23. Consta-
bles, Benja Fitch, 90. Henry Hill, 83. William Man 63.
Wm Welsteed 61. Joseph Billing, 57. Wm Clark jun^r 45.
James Gooch, 40. Joseph Dowden 67. Jose Winthrop
constable of Rumney-Marsh.

Surveyors of High Ways. Tho Walker, Stephen Minott,
Jacob Melyen, Jno Goodwin sen^r

Voted to raise Money;

Stock to set poor on work	£500
To maintain impotent poor	400
Schools, Bells, &c.	300
To mend the Way over the Neck	200
	£1400. 0. 0

Capt. Byfield was Moderator; had Candles, broke up at 8. Began at 10 m. Mr. Colman began with Prayer. Capt. Byfield dismiss'd the Assembly with Prayer.

Tuesday, March, 19. $\frac{1699}{1700}$. Three young men: viz. Robert Cunable, Wm Salter, and Tho Comer, went in a Canoo a Guñing before day-light, and were drowned. Wind high, and wether cold. Only James Tileston was saved.

March 21. Mrs. Martha Collins dieth.

March, 23. She is buried between 5 and 6. p.m. Bearers Lt Govr Stoughton, Mr. Russel, Sewall, Lynde, Byfield, Hayman. Mr. Cook was at the funeral. Col Phillips not well. Had Gloves and Rings. The under-bearers were honest men. I took my cousin Moodey, minister of York, over with me. Mr. Leverett there. Mr. Bradstreet the minister. Snow'd hard as we came home.

Monday, March, 25, 1700. Set out with Mr. Cooke for Plimouth, visited Mr. Torrey, staid near 3 hours, then to Mr. Norton's where Maj^r Genl Winthrop came to us late, so got late to Sittiate to Mr. Cushings, lodg'd there just by the ruins of Mr. Chauncey's house. Maj^r Genl. had apointed to visit said Cushing. Were so belated that fail'd Maj^r Thomas, who with some other Gentlemen waited for us at the old Ferry on Marshfield side.

Tuesday, March 26. The wind is very bleak that it was ready to put me into an Ague, having rid late the night before. Had a noble Treat at Maj^r Thomas's. Mr. Sheriff and his Gentlemen were so wearied that they were afraid of some Miscarriage at the Ferry. Began the Court about five. Wednesday and Thorsday were extravagantly stormy. On Friday Mr. Cooke comes home but the wind was strong in my face, and cold that I durst not venture. Satterday was also very cold and chose rather to keep the Sabbath at Plimouth than by the way. Staid at Plimouth. At Noon was a Contribution for one that had his house burnt. Mr. Little invited me to sup with him, which I did.

Monday, April, 1.   I was in a great quandary whether
I had best to avoid the wind, come home by water and
leave my Horse, or no.   At last I went on board Elisha
Hedge's decked sloop laden with Oyle He put in there
in the storm from Yarmouth and lay till now for a wind.
Came aboard about 2 hours by Sun, and landed at Mrs.
Butlers Wharf before 3 p.m.   Having had a very speedy
and pleasant Passage, wherein I have experienced much
of God's parental pity towards me, and care over me.   I
could not have got home to day by Land: and I fear my
health would have been much impair'd, if I had come but
part of the way.   Jonathan Wheeler ridd in the Rain
from Milton.   I have now kept one Sabbath with those
who first kept Sabbaths in New England.[1]

March, 31. 1700.   At coming ashoar I met with the L^t
Govr at Mr. Secretarys, and had their welcome.

Apr. 8. 1700.   Mr. Turfrey is made Capt of Saco-Fort,
and Truck-master with the Indians, in stead of Capt. Hill.

Apr. 9. 1700.   Snow covers the Ground.

Sabbath, Apr. 14.   I saw and heard the Swallows proclaim the Spring.

Fifth-day, Apr. 18. 1700.   Mr. Cooke, Mr. Addington,
Mr. Willard, Mr. Estabrooks and his Son Daniel come to
my house and here adjust their Matters in difference relating to Mrs. Abigail Estabrookes and her Father — and
brother in Law.   Mrs. Abigail pass'd a Deed to Daniel
last Sumer, and he a Mortgage to her: Abigail being dissatisfied in the Mortgage, makes a Deed of the same Land
to Capt. S. Checkly and Records it: It was a surprise to
me to see it, and I express'd my Dislike of it in Terms
that Mr. Willard could hardly bear.   Said twas contrary to
all Goodness, or words to that purpose.   However I press'd
that Daniel would give up his Deed, and Abigail her

---

[1] We must interpret this remark as merely meaning that Sewall spent the
Sunday at Plymouth. To take a literal meaning, we should infer that he
had met some survivor of the Pilgrims; but this seems improbable. — EDS.

Mortgage; and that Capt. Checkly should give Daniel a Deed; that so this Fraudulency might not remain to be seen. It rain'd hard, and Mr. Estabrook and his son lodg'd here. Ap. 19. I gave Mr. Estabrooks 20.ˢ to buy his Grand son Benjamin a Coat.

Apr. 19. Sam. is sent for to be a Bearer to Mr. Eyre's Son, a very likely child, who dyed yesterday. I had that very day, Ap. 18, accidentally lit upon, and nail'd up the verses on Jnᵒ; who dyed Novʳ 30. 1696.

April, 22. 1700. Mr. Sheriff Gookin, by Execution, delivers me and Cous. Aña Quinsey, Mr. H. Usher's House and Ground on the Comon, And we introduce Madam Usher, *mane*. Ap. 23, 24. Tenant Wiar goes out. Apr. 26. Mrs. Usher removes thither to dwell. I send her a Cord of Wood that came from Muddy-River.

Extract of a Letter from Mr. Hugh Adams dated at Charlestoun in Carolina Feb. 23. $1\frac{699}{700}$.

I have Scripture Grounds to fear and expect that some more terrible impending Judgments are hovering over Carolina to be rained down in snares, fire and Brimstone and an horrible Tempest, as the portion of our cup for the yet tolerated and practised abominations, and Sodom like Sins of this Land. It is hard to describe the dreadfull and astonishing aspect of our late terrible Tempest of Mortality in our Charleston; which began towards the latter end of August, and continued till the middle of November. In which Space of time there died in Charlestown, 125, English of all sorts; high and low, old and young. 37, French. 16, Indians, and 1 Negro. Three Ministers; viz. Mr. Jnᵒ Cotton [1] dissenter, Mr. Samuel Marshal conformist, Mr. Preolo French Minister. Mr. Gilbert Ashly an Anabaptist preacher, Mr. Curtice a Presbyterian preacher dyed all in the begining of the Mortality for their peoples contempt of their Gospel Labours. After whose decease, the Distemper raged, and the destroying Angel slaughtered so furiously with his revenging Sword of Pestilence, that there died (as I have read in the Catalogue of the dead) 14. in one day, Septʳ 28.ᵗʰ and raged as bad all October: So that the dead were carried in carts, being heaped up one upon another.

---

[1] This was the Rev. John Cotton, formerly of Plymouth. See Vol. I. p. 473. — EDS.

Worse by far than the great Plague of London, considering the smallness of the Town. Shops shut up for 6 weeks; nothing but carrying Medicines, digging graves, carting the dead; to the great astonishment of all beholders. Out of Mr. Cotton's church there died himself, Septr 17th, Mr. Jn° Alexander Merch^t, Mr. Curtice preacher, Mr. Matthew Bee, Schoolmaster, Mr. Henry Spry (besides his Serv't man, his youngest child, and an Indian Woman). But lastly, which may grieve you most of all, our precious godly Mother Avis Adams departed this Life Octb^r 6th last, being infected by means of tending Mr. Cotton all the time of his Sickness, which was but three days. — Dearly beloved Brother, I intreat you to prepare for the near-approaching of Temptation and Persecution, which Christ will bring upon all the World to try them that dwell upon the earth. When the Lord will search Jerusalem with candles, and punish the men that are settled on their Lees ; when Christ will weigh all Professors in the Balance of the Sanctuary. Then wo to them that shall be found out of Christ at that day. Take this favourably as a plain token of my Love to your soul and body. I must needs confess, I have but little Comfort in this Life, only what the Lord himself is pleased to give my Soul out of his spiritual Brests of Divine Consolation, and Loving-kindness and favours, which is better than life itself.— Although we may see one another no more in this world: yet I hope to meet you in Christ with Comfort and Joy at the morning of the Resurrection.

To Mr. John Adams Shop-keeper in Boston
℘ Capt. Green Q. D. C.

Monday, Apr. 29, 1700. Sam. Sewall, Josiah Willard Jn° Bayly, Sam. Gaskill, and —— Mountfort goe into the Harbour a fishing in a small Boat. Seeing Rich'd Fifield coming in, some would needs meet the ship and see who it was: Ship had fresh way with a fair wind ; when came neare, Capt. call'd to them to beware, order'd what they should doe. But they did the clear contrary, fell foul on the ship, which broke their Mast short off, fill'd the Boat with water, threw Willard and Gaskill into the River. Both which were very near drown'd ; especially Gaskill, who could not swim. It pleas'd God Fifield's Boat was out, so he presently man'd it and took them in. Gaskill was under water, but discover'd by his

Hat that swam atop as a Buoy. Sam, Jn° Bayly and Mountfort caught hold of the Ship and climbed on board in a miserable fright as having stared death in the face. This is the second time Sam has been near drown'd with Josiah Willard. Mother was against his going, and prevented Joseph, who pleaded earnestly to go. He sensibly acknowledged the Good Providence in his staying at home, when he saw the issue.

1. A Narrative of the Portsmouth Disputation between Presbyterians and Baptists at Mr. Williams's Meeting-house.

2. Bp. of Norwich's Sermon of Religious Melancholy.

3. Amintor, a defence of Milton with Reasons for abolishing the 30th Jan.y [1]

4. An Account of the first Voyages into America by don Barthol de las Casas   4s.

5. Account of a Jew lately converted and baptis'd at the Meeting near Ave Mary-Lane.

The President desires me to send for the above mentioned Books.

Monday May 13. 1700. Mr. Wheelwright dies. This day p.m. I set out towards Kittery, Lodge at Salem.

May 14. Get to Newbury a little before sunset, visit my sick Father in bed, call in the Major Genl whom Father salutes. Kiss'd my hand, and I his again. Mr. Tapan came in and pray'd with him and us.

May, 15. Walks into the west end of the house with his staff, breakfasts there. I read the 17th Luke, and went to Prayer. My father would have stood up but I persuaded him to sit still in his chair. Took leave and went on to Portsmouth. Majr Genl and I lodge at Col. Parkers. Most Gentlemen out of Town, some at Mr. Wheelrights funeral and som at Business. Mr. Hirst and Geoffries welcom'd us to Town. May 16th goe to Spruce-

---

[1] Written by John Toland. — EDS.

Crick and hold Court at Mr. Curtis's. Cousin Moodey comes thither and tells me of his son born that morn when sun about 2 hours high. Return in the night to Portsmouth.

May, 17th Benj Moss jun^r is sent to me to acquaint me that my dear Father died the evening before. It rains hard. Holds up about 5 p.m. I ride to Hampton, lodge at Mr. Cottons, where am very kindly entertained.

May, 18th ride to Newbury in the Rain; when breaks up, Bro^r and Sister come from Salem. Bury my Father, Bearers, Col. Peirce, Mr. Nich. Noyes, Mr. Sam. Plumer, Mr. Tristram Coffin, Major Danl Davison, Major Thomas Noyes, had 8 Underbearers.

Sabbath, May. 19. Mr. Tapan in the afternoon preach'd a funeral Sermon from Prov. 19. 20. Said my Father was a true Nathanael: Mention'd 3 or four other deaths which occasion'd his discourse: gave a good character of most of them. May, 20. Rains hard, holds up in the afternoon. Major Genl and Mr. Cooke come to Newbury in the night.

May 21, ride to Ipswich: sheriff, Mr. Harris, and Major Epes meet us at Rowley. Give no Action to the Jury till after diñer. Lodge at Mr. Rodgers's where am very kindly entertain'd.

May 23. Mr. Rogers preaches very well of the Divine Efficiency in Mans Conversion, from Philip. 2. 13. Invite the Ministers to diñer, There are Mr. Hubbard, Rogers, Mr. Gerrish, Mr. Payson, Mr. Capen, Mr. Green, Mr. Rolf; last did not dine.

May 24th set out for Salem about an hour by sun, Mr. Joseph Woodbridge with me, Got to Brothers a little before Nine, met there Mrs. Añe Woodbridge. Proved my Fathers Will. May 25. 1700 went homeward in company Mrs. Anne as far as Col. Paiges. Got home about 3 aclock, found all well, Blessed be God. My Wife provided Mourning upon my Letter by Severs, All went in mourning save Joseph, who staid at home because his Mother lik'd not his cloaths. Sister Short here, came from Newbury the morn father died, and so miss'd being at the funeral. It seems about a 14night before, upon discourse of going to Meeting, my Father said, He could not goe, but hôp'd to go shortly to a Greater Assembly. The Lord pardon all my sin of omission and commission towards him, and help me to prepare to Dye. Accept of any little Labour of Love towards my dear Parents. I had just sent four pounds of Raisins, which with the Canary were very refreshing to him.

Worthy Mr. Hale of Beverly was buried the day before my father. So was Mr. John Wadsworth of Duxbury, who died May, 15th 1700. I used to be much refreshed with his company when I went to Plimouth; and was so this last time. He gave me an account of the begiñing of their Town, and of his Fathers going over to fetch Mr. Partridge.

Friday, June, 7th 1700. *mane*, the Govr nominates Major Jno Walley for a Judge of the Superr court, gives time of consideration till after diñer, Then give in Yes and No in papers. Said Walley had all present save his own and one No. Col. Hathorne was absent. I think had 25 Papers written YES. Chose Mr. John Clark a Justice Peace in Boston and many other; Justices of Inferior Courts, Coroners &c. Mr. Jno Wheelwright chosen Justice of Peace at Wells. Things were carried with Peace and comfortable unanimity.

Lords-day, June, 16, 1700. Mr. Daniel Oliver has his son Daniel baptised.

June, 17. Mr. John Eyre makes his Will in the morning, and dies in the Afternoon, an hour or 2. before Sunset. Born Febr. 19th 165¾. I visited him on Satterday in the Afternoon: He was sitting up in his little Room, Took me by the hand at first coming in, Desired me to pray for him when took leave.

Fourth-day, June, 19. 1700. Mr. Jn° Eyre is entomed
in the new burying place. Nine of his children are laid
there to handsel the new Tomb : Bearers, Sewall, Addington, Townsend, Byfield, Dumer, Davis : Scarvs and
Rings. Lt Govr and many of the Council there. Mr.
Thomas Brattle led his mourning widowed Sister. When
I parted, I pray'd God to be favourably present with her,
and comfort her in the absence of so near and dear a Relation. Having been long and much dissatisfied with the
Trade of fetching Negros from Guinea; at last I had a
strong Inclination to Write something about it; but it
wore off. At last reading Bayne, Ephes.[1] about servants,
who mentions Blackamoors; I began to be uneasy that I
had so long neglected doing any thing. When I was thus
thinking, in came Bro^r Belknap to shew me a Petition he
intended to present to the Genl Court for the freeing a
Negro and his wife, who were unjustly held in Bondage.
And there is a Motion by a Boston Comittee to get a Law
that all Importers of Negros shall pay 40^s p̄ head, to discourage the bringing of them. And Mr. C. Mather re-
solves to publish a sheet to exhort Masters to labour their
Conversion. Which makes me hope that I was call'd of
God to Write this Apology for them; Let his Blessing
accompany the same.[2]

---

[1] Paul Baynes, "Commentary on the First Chapter of the Ephesians,"
1618. — Eds.

[2] The reference is here to Sewall's anti-slavery tract, published June 24,
1700. Although it was reprinted in the Proceedings of our Society for October, 1863, from a very rare copy presented by our President, it seems extremely proper to reproduce it in this place. We have been compelled to
expose Sewall's weakness; let us put equally upon record this proof that on
one most important subject he was far in advance of his fellows. — Eds.

" The Selling of Joseph.

A MEMORIAL.

" *Forasmuch as* Liberty *is in real value next unto* Life: *None ought to part with
it themselves, or deprive others of it, but upon most mature Consideration.*

" The Numerousness of Slaves at this day in the Province, and the Uneasiness of them under their Slavery, hath put many upon thinking whether the

July, 8. 1700. Hañah rides in the Coach with her Mother to Mr. Thachers at Milton, to stay there awhile.

Foundation of it be firmly and well laid; so as to sustain the Vast Weight that is built upon it. It is most certain that all Men, as they are the Sons of *Adam*, are Coheirs; and have equal Right unto Liberty, and all other outward Comforts of Life. *GOD hath given the Earth* (with all its Commodities) *unto the Sons of* Adam, *Psal* 115. 16. *And hath made of One Blood, all Nations of Men, for to dwell on all the face of the Earth, and hath determined the Times before appointed, and the bounds of their habitation: That they should seek the Lord. Forasmuch then as we are the Offspring of GOD* &c. *Act* 17. 26, 27, 29. Now although the Title given by the last ADAM, doth infinitely better Mens Estates, respecting GOD and themselves; and grants them a most beneficial and inviolable Lease under the Broad Seal of Heaven, who were before only Tenants at Will: Yet through the Indulgence of GOD to our First Parents after the Fall, the outward Estate of all and every of their Children, remains the same, as to one another. So that Originally, and Naturally, there is no such thing as Slavery. *Joseph* was rightfully no more a Slave to his Brethren, than they were to him: and they had no more Authority to *Sell* him, than they had to *Slay* him. And if *they* had nothing to do to Sell him; the *Ishmaelites* bargaining with them, and paying down Twenty pieces of Silver, could not make a Title. Neither could *Potiphar* have any better Interest in him than the *Ishmaelites* had. *Gen.* 37. 20, 27, 28. For he that shall in this case plead *Alteration of Property*, seems to have forfeited a great part of his own claim to Humanity. There is no proportion between Twenty Pieces of Silver, and LIBERTY. The Commodity it self is the Claimer. If *Arabian* Gold be imported in any quantities, most are afraid to meddle with it, though they might have it at easy rates; lest if it should have been wrongfully taken from the Owners, it should kindle a fire to the Consumption of their whole Estate. 'Tis pity there should be more Caution used in buying a Horse, or a little lifeless dust; than there is in purchasing Men and Women: Whenas they are the Offspring of GOD, and their Liberty is,

"' . . . . *Auro pretiosior Omni.*'

" And seeing GOD hath said, *He that Stealeth a Man and Selleth him, or if he be found in his hand, he shall surely be put to Death.* Exod. 21. 16. This Law being of Everlasting Equity, wherein Man Stealing is ranked amongst the most atrocious of Capital Crimes: What louder Cry can there be made of that Celebrated Warning,

"' *Caveat Emptor!*'"

" And all things considered, it would conduce more to the Welfare of the Province, to have White Servants for a Term of Years, than to have Slaves for Life. Few can endure to hear of a Negro's being made free; and indeed they can seldom use their freedom well; yet their continual aspiring after their forbidden Liberty, renders them Unwilling Servants. And there

Sister and Betty come to Town from Salem : July, 10th
They go home.   Waited on Mr. Mather this day, at three

---

is such a disparity in their Conditions, Colour & Hair, that they can never
embody with us, and grow up into orderly Families, to the Peopling of the
Land: but still remain in our Body Politick as a kind of extravasat Blood.
As many Negro men as there are among us, so many empty places there are
in our Train Bands, and the places taken up of Men that might make Husbands for our Daughters.   And the Sons and Daughters of *New England*
would become more like *Jacob*, and *Rachel*, if this Slavery were thrust quite
out of doors.   Moreover it is too well known what Temptations Masters are
under, to connive at the Fornication of their Slaves; lest they should be
obliged to find them Wives, or pay their Fines.   It seems to be practically
pleaded that they might be Lawless; 'tis thought much of, that the Law
should have Satisfaction for their Thefts, and other Immoralities; by which
means, *Holiness to the Lord*, is more rarely engraven upon this sort of Servitude.   It is likewise most lamentable to think, how in taking Negros out of
Africa, and Selling of them here, That which GOD has joyned together
men do boldly rend asunder; Men from their Country, Husbands from their
Wives, Parents from their Children.   How horrible is the Uncleanness,
Mortality, if not Murder, that the Ships are guilty of that bring great
Crouds of these miserable Men, and Women.   Methinks, when we are be-
moaning the barbarous Usage of our Friends and Kinsfolk in *Africa:* It
might not be unseasonable to enquire whether we are not culpable in forcing
the *Africans* to become Slaves amongst our selves.   And it may be a question whether all the Benefit received by *Negro* Slaves, will balance the
Accompt of Cash laid out upon them; and for the Redemption of our own
enslaved Friends out of *Africa*.   Besides all the Persons and Estates that
have perished there.

"Obj. 1.   *These Blackamores are of the Posterity of* Cham, *and therefore
are under the Curse of Slavery.*   Gen. 9. 25, 26, 27.

" *Answ.*   Of all Offices, one would not begg this; *viz.* Uncall'd for, to be
an Executioner of the Vindictive Wrath of God; the extent and duration of
which is to us uncertain.   If this ever was a Commission; How do we know
but that it is long since out of Date?   Many have found it to their Cost,
that a Prophetical Denunciation of Judgment against a Person or People,
would not warrant them to inflict that evil.   If it would, *Hazael* might
justify himself in all he did against his Master, and the *Israelites*, from
2 *Kings* 8. 10, 12.

" But it is possible that by cursory reading, this Text may have been
mistaken.   For *Canaan* is the Person Cursed three times over, without the
mentioning of *Cham*.   Good Expositors suppose the Curse entaild on him,
and that this Prophesie was accomplished in the Extirpation of the *Canaan-
ites*, and in the Servitude of the *Gibeonites*.   *Vide Pareum*.   Whereas the
Blackmores are not descended of *Canaan*, but of *Cush*.   Psal. 68. 31.   *Princes
shall come out of Egypt* [Mizraim], *Ethiopia* [Cush] *shall soon stretch out her
hands unto God.*   Under which Names, all *Africa* may be comprehended;

in the Afternoon.   I told him the Honor of Athanasius,
Maluit sedem quām Fidei syllabam mutare: Worthies

---

and their Promised Conversion ought to be prayed for.   *Jer*. 13. 23.   *Can
the Ethiopian change his skin?*   This shows that Black Men are the Posterity
of *Cush:* Who time out of mind have been distinguished by their Colour.
And for want of the true, *Ovid* assigns a fabulous cause of it.

> " ' *Sanguine tum credunt in corpora summa vocato
> Æthiopum populus nigrum traxisse colorem.*'
> > Metamorph. lib. 2.

"Obj. 2.   *The Nigers are brought out of a Pagan Country, into places where
the Gospel is Preached.*

"*Answ.*   Evil must not be done, that good may come of it.   The extraordinary and comprehensive Benefit accruing to the Church of God, and to
Joseph personally, did not rectify his brethrens Sale of him.

"Obj. 3.   *The* Africans *have Wars one with another: Our Ships bring
lawful Captives taken in those Wars.*

"*Answ.*   For ought is known, their Wars are much such as were between
Jacob's Sons and their Brother *Joseph.*   If they be between Town and Town;
Provincial, or National: Every War is upon one side Unjust.   An Unlawful
War can't make lawful Captives.   And by Receiving, we are in danger to
promote, and partake in their Barbarous Cruelties.   I am sure, if some Gentlemen should go down to the *Brewsters* to take the Air, and Fish: And a
stronger party from *Hull* should Surprise them, and Sell them for Slaves to
a Ship outward bound: they would think themselves unjustly dealt with;
both by Sellers and Buyers.   And yet 'tis to be feared, we have no other
kind of Title to our *Nigers.*   *Therefore all things whatsoever ye would that
men should do to you, do ye even so to them: for this is the Law and the Prophets.*
Matt. 7. 12.

"Obj. 4.   Abraham *had Servants bought with his Money, and born in his
House.*

"*Answ.*   Until the Circumstances of *Abraham's* purchase be recorded, no
Argument can be drawn from it.   In the mean time, Charity obliges us to
conclude, that He knew it was lawful and good.

"It is Observable that the *Israelites* were strictly forbidden the buying,
or selling one another for Slaves.   *Levit.* 25. 39. 46.   *Jer.* 34 8. ...... 22.
And GOD gaged His Blessing in lieu of any loss they might conceipt they
suffered thereby.   *Deut.* 15. 18.   And since the partition Wall is broken
down, inordinate Self love should likewise be demolished.   GOD expects
that Christians should be of a more Ingenuous and benign frame of spirit.
Christians should carry it to all the World, as the *Israelites* were to carry it
one towards another.   And for men obstinately to persist in holding their
Neighbours and Brethren under the Rigor of perpetual Bondage, seems to
be no proper way of gaining Assurance that God ha's given them Spiritual
Freedom.   Our Blessed Saviour has altered the Measures of the ancient
Love-Song, and set it to a most Excellent New Tune, which all ought to be

of N. E. left their Houses in England, and came hither
where there were none to preserve Religion in its Purity.
Put him in mind how often God had renewed his Call to
this work which was to be consider'd.[1] That were 19 in
the Council; and had every vote.

Seventh-day, July, 13. My dear Mother comes hither
by water from Newbury in one of the Poors. Set sail on
Thorsday morning, and lodg'd aboard two nights in Marblehead Harbour: Capt. Norden and others would have
had her come ashoar: but the wind was high and chose to
keep on board. Jonathan Woodman jun[r] waited on her
to my house about 5. *p. mer'*[m] Saw her not till just
night; when brought in Mr. Cooke, Mr. Sergeant, E[m]
Hutchinson to drink, as they came from the Neck.

July, 17th The L[d] Bellomont our Gov[r] sets sail for
New-york.

July, 25th 1700. Went to the Funeral of Mrs. Sprague,
being invited by a good pair of Gloves.

Aug[t] 2. 1700. Betty comes to Town from Salem.
Aug[t] 3. Bro[r] comes to Town in the morning. I bring

---

ambitious of Learning. *Matt.* 5. 43, 44. *John* 13. 34. These *Ethiopians*,
as black as they are; seeing they are the Sons and Daughters of the First
Adam, the Brethren and Sisters of the Last ADAM, and the Offspring of
GOD; They ought to be treated with a Respect agreeable.

" ' *Servitus perfecta voluntaria, inter Christianum & Christianum, ex parte
servi patientis sæpe est licita, quia est necessaria : sed ex parte domini agentis,
& procurando & exercendo, vix potest esse licita : quia non convenit regulæ illi
generali : Quæcunque volueritis ut faciant vobis homines, ita & vos facite eis.*
Matt. 7. 12.

" ' *Perfecta servitus pœnæ, non potest jure locum habere, nisi ex delicto gravi
quod ultimum supplicium aliquo modo meretur : quia Libertas ex naturali æsti-
matione proxime accedit ad vitam ipsam, & eidem a multis præferri solet.*'
                                        Ames. Cas. Consc. Lib. 5. Cap. 23. Thes. 2, 3.

"*BOSTON* of the *Massachusetts;*
Printed by *Bartholomew Green*, and *John Allen*, June, 24th. 1700."

[1] Quincy (Hist. Harvard University, I. 109) gives some more details. The
Rev. Increase Mather wished to be president of Harvard without living at
the college. The Legislature voted £220 per annum to a resident president. — EDS.

him going to the Ferry.   About 2 *post merid*, Mr. Adam
Winthrop dies.   Between 3 and 4 I receiv'd a Letter from
the Justices of Northamptonshire, i. e. Partrig, Parsons,
and Hawley to notify us that there is no Business requir-
ing our going to Springfield this hot wether.   We are
very glad to be thus fairly discharged from this long and
tedious journey.

BOSTON, 5th Augt 1700.

MADAM, — I present you with my greatest Respects and (nothing
unknown intervening) will wait on you between the hours of eight
and Nine this evening. Subscribe not my Name, you are not unac-
quainted with the hand : for as formerly, so I will remain an admirer
of your person and Virtues. I expect the favour of your presence,
as I am Madam your humblest Servt   STREPHON.[1]

Augt 7th 1700.   Mr. Adam Winthrop is buried.   Bearers Col. Hutchinson, Middlecott, Foster, El^m Hutchinson,
Col. Townsend, Capt. Dumer.   I rode with the Lt Govr in
his Coach.

Lords day Augt 18. 1700.   Henry Cole, Joseph's School-
fellow, dies about 3 aclock *post mer.* of vomiting, Flux and
Fever.   Has been sick 12 or 13. days.   His Father sent
for me, and I pray'd with him in the morning.   At 2
aclock I look'd on him and pray'd God to grant him that
Favour and Loving Kindness of his that was better than
Life.   He thank'd me.   In the morn, I ask'd him what I
should pray for, He answer'd, that God would pardon all
his Sin.   Neighbour Cole had two Cows, and one of them
is dead also.   Henry was a forward towardly Scholar, and
used to call Joseph every morning to goe to School.

Augt 30. 1700.   A young hopefull Scholar is buried,
Edward Mills's son by Minot.

Wednesday, Augt 28. 1700.   Mr. E[benezer] Pemberton is ordained [Minister of the South Church] : He

---

[1] Compare this letter with the following one under date of Jan. 13, 1700–1.
post, p. 29. — EDS.

preached; then Mr. Willard Preached: Mr. Willard gave
the charge: He, Mr. I. Mather, and Mr. Allen laying on
Hands. Mr. I. Mather gave the Right Hand of Fellowship. Mr. Wigglesworth and Mr. Torrey were in the
Pulpit, Mr. Hubbard of Ipswich and many Ministers below. A very great Assembly. All was so managed, as I
hope does bode well, that the Blessing of God will accompany Him and us.

Sept. 4th. 1700. Capt. Byfield and I took with us Peter
Weare, and went to Mr. Googe to warn him to leave my
house at Cotton Hill. He acknowledged I had spoken to
him about the 12 of Aug[t], and he would quit the house
by the 12 or 14th of November next.

Thorsday Sept. 26th 1700. Mr. John Wait and Eunice
his wife, and Mrs. Debora Thair come to Speak to me
about the Marriage of Sebastian, Negro serv[t] of said Wait,
with Jane, Negro servant of said Thair. Mr. Wait desired
they might be published in order to marriage Mrs. Thair
insisted that Sebastian might have one day in six allow'd
him for the suport of Jane, his intended wife and her
children, if it should please God to give her any. Mr.
Wait now wholly declin'd that, but freely offer'd to allow
Bastian Five pounds, in Money p̄ añum towards the suport
of his children p̄ said Jane (besides Sebastians cloathing
and Diet). I persuaded Jane and Mrs. Thair to agree to
it, and so it was concluded; and Mrs. Thair gave up the
Note of Publication to Mr. Wait for him to carry it to
Wm Griggs, the Town Clerk, and to Williams in order to
have them published according to Law.

As attests Sam Sewall J.

Lords Day Sept. 29th 1700. Mr. Willard, by reason of
sickness keeps house, and Mr. Pemberton preaches forenoon and Afternoon.

Note. from 11 to 2 p.m. it snows hard, covers the
Houses and Ground, lodges on the Trees. Was very cold
yesterday and to day. Oct. 2. Haña comes home.

BOSTON, 8ʳ 6ᵗʰ 1700.

SIR, — Speaking with my Son after your being here, I understand
it will be inconvenient for you to come abroad this evening by reason
of the solemnities of the day preceding.   Besides, there is a Meeting
of some of the South church occasioned by Mr. Willards sickness ; at
which I am obliged to be.   Therefore I shall not expect you, neither
would I have you come till to morrow night.   I thought good to
signify thus much to you, who am, Sir, your friend and Servᵗ
S. S.

To Mr. Grove Hirst, Merch'ᵗ in Boston, at Capt. Ballentine's.

8ʳ 8ᵗʰ 1700.   Is a Fast at the New-Meetinghouse to
pray for Mr. Willard's Life.   Mr. Colman, Wadsworth
pray.   Mr. Pemberton preaches: Philip. 1. 24.   Mr.
Allen, Cotton Mather Pray. 20ᵗʰ Psalm two staves and ½
sung L.   Lᵗ Govʳ, Mr. Russel, Cook, Addington, Eᵐ
Hutchinson, Townsend there.   Mr. Fisk, Danforth, Walter, Brattle, out of Town.   Pretty considerable congregation, it being so sudden, and first intended in privat.

8ʳ 10ᵗʰ 1700.   Mr. Hirst asking my pardon, I told him
I could forgive him, if he would never forgive himself ;
He fully assented to the condition : and said moreover
that if ever he did the like again he would not expect or
desire to be forgiven.

Octʳ 17ᵗʰ 1700.   Capt. Theophilus Frary expires about
3 aclock past midnight.[1]

---

[1] Deacon Frary has been repeatedly mentioned by Sewall. He married
Hannah, daughter of the first Jacob Eliot, and his wife inherited a part of the
Eliot lands at the South End.   Eliot's house stood at the south-west corner
of our Washington and Boylston Streets, and this part of the estate passed
to the Frarys.   The Frarys also owned on the south side of Frog Lane, now
Boylston Street.   Theophilus Frary had several sons, all of whom, undoubt-
edly, died young, as his will leaves his property to his three daughters.
These were Hannah, who married first Isaac Walker, Jr., and secondly Andrew Belcher; Abigail, who married —— Arnold; and Mehitable, wife of
Samuel Lillie.

Abigail Arnold had an only child, Hannah, who married Samuel Welles.
This estate remained in the Welles family until it was sold to Joseph C.
Dyer (Suff. Deeds, Lib. 227, f. 18), who conveyed it to the present proprie-
tor for $20,560.   The Boylston Market Association was incorporated by
Chap. 48 of Acts of 1808-9.   The building cost about $37,000 besides the

In the following Evening Mr. Grove Hirst and Elizabeth
Sewall are married by Mr. Cotton Mather. Present, I and
my wife, Mr. Hirst and his wife, Bro^r St. Sewall of Salem
and his son Sam, Brothers and Sisters of Bridegroom and
Bride. Madam Usher, Capt. Ephra Savage, Capt. Dumar
and wife, Capt. Ballentine, Mrs. Mary Clark, Esther
Wyllye, Margaret Stewart &c. Sung the 128. Psal. I
set York Tune, not intending it. In the New Parlor.

Octr 18. Mr. Pemberton and Mr. Colman and his wife
dine with us. Sent and Spent 21. Cakes.

Octob^r 20. 1700. In the Afternoon I and my wife, Mr.
Hirst and his Bride, Sam. ánd Eliza Hirst, Will. Hirst and
Hañah Sewall, Jameś Taylor and Esther Wyllie, Joseph
and Mary Sewall, walk to Meeting together.

Octr 30th Mr. Hirst comes and carries his daughter
Betty to Salem. Mr. Grove Hirst and his wife accompany
them.

Novemb^r 4th 1700. A Council was called at the Town-
House. Present, The honorable William Stoughton Esqr.
Lt Govr, Elisha Cooke, Elisha Hutchinson, Saml Sewall,
Isaac Addington, Jno Foster, Peter Sergeant, John Wal-
ley, Eliakim Hutchinson, Penn Townsend, Nathanael By-
field, esqrs. Lt Govr ask'd Advice whether Benjamin
Bedwell should be tryed by Comissioners of Oyer and
Terminer; or at the Court of Assize and Genl Goal Delivery, to be held at Plimouth next March. Twas carried
for the latter. A Proclamation was ordered to prevent
endangering the Town by Fire-Works.[1]

Francis Hudson, Ferry-man, dyed last Lords-Day, Nov^r
3. Was one of the first who set foot on this Peninsula.[2]

---

cupola, which was built by subscription. Ward Nicholas Boylston, for whom
it was named, gave a clock. The building was moved back eleven feet in
1870. — EDS.

[1] The next day being the anniversary of the Gunpowder Plot. — EDS.

[2] Francis Hudson, aged sixty-eight years, made a deposition June 10, 1684,
before Bradstreet and Sewall, as to the purchase of land from Blackstone.
This deposition is in Suff. Deeds, XXIV. 406, and has been often printed;

Novr 10. 1700. Lords-day Madam Elizabeth Sergeant died in the Afternoon, half an hour past three. Was taken last Thorsday Señight at night. Hath been delirious a great part of the Time, and hardly sensible since Friday.

Novr 11th Salem Court is adjourned by reason of Mr. Cooks Indisposition of Body.

Novr 12. Last night a considerable Snow fell which covers the Ground several Inches thick. This morn Mr. Thomas Broughton expires about 87. years old: once a very noted Merchant in Boston, Select-man &c. About 3 years agoe he join'd to the North church. On Satterday-night I was with him when the President pray'd with him.

Novr 14. Madam Eliza. Sergeant is entombed, Bearers, Cooke, Hutchinson Elisha, Sewall, Addington, Foster, Walley. She was born Apr. 11. 1660. Maj^r Genl Winthrop was at the Funeral. He came last night from New-London.

Novr 14. 1700. about ½ hour past one in the Afternoon, Mr. Joseph Eliot dieth.[1] He was abroad on the Lords day at Meeting. I saw him in the street near his own house, about 8 in the morning. The Lord fit us for his good pleasure.

Novr 15th 1700. Mr. Tho. Broughton buried in the old burying place. Bearers, Sewall, Foster, E^m Hutchinson, Byfield, Howard, Fayerwether. No scarf. No Gloves. Went back again to the house.

Novr 16. Mr. Joseph Eliot was buried. Bearers, Capt. Alford, Capt. Checkley, Mr. Danl Oliver, Mr. Beñet, Mr. Cutler, Mr. Gibbs. 38. years old.

---

it can be read in Shurtleff's "Description," pp. 296, 297. The other deponents were, — John Odlin, aged eighty-two: William Lytherland, aged seventy-six; and Robert Walker, aged seventy-eight. As to Walker, see Diary, Vol. I. pp. 47, 179. — EDS.

[1] This was Joseph, son of Deacon Jacob Eliot, and grand-nephew of Rev. John Eliot. His wife, Silence, died June 8, 1744, aged seventy-eight. — EDS.

This day John Soams, the Quaker, dies. Was well this day señight.

Nov.̅ 20th Mrs. —— Lynde (formerly Richardson) was buried: Bearers, Cook, Sewall, Addington, Dum̅er, Dering, Gibbs. Scarf and Ring.

Nov.̅ 21. 1700. Day of publick Thanksgiving. At 3. *post merid^m* Mr. Willard comes abroad and Prays to the great Refreshment of the Congregation. This the first time since his sickness. In the evening I made these verses on it, viz,

> As Joseph let his brethren see
> Simeon both alive, and free:
> So JESUS brings forth Samuel,
> To tune our hearts to praise Him well.
> Thus He with beams of cheerfull light,
> Corrects the darkness of our night.
> His Grace assists us in this wise
> To seise, and bind the Sacrifice.

Monday, Nov.̅ 25th 1700. Prime brôt me a horse to Wiñisim̅et, and I ridd with him to Salem.

Nov.̅ 26th Sup'd at Mr. Hirst's in company of said Hirst, his wife, Mrs. Betty Hirst, Mr. Noyes and my Brother. Nov.̅ 28. Court rose. Mr. Higginson was not at Lecture nor abroad this Court; so miss'd the pleasure of dining with Him. Visited him at his house and his sick wife. Madam Bradstreet, Mrs. Batter in Bed. Mrs. Jn° Higginson the 2^d Set out to come home about ½ hour past two in the Afternoon: came by Charlestown. Very cold going, abiding there, and Returning. Yet hope have taken very little hurt through the Goodness of God.

Major Walley has a swell'd face that keeps him from Meeting on the Sabbath xr. 1. 1700.

Nov.̅ 30th My Aunt Quinsey dieth of the Jaundice befôr break of day.

Thursday, xr. 5th 1700. Sam. and I ride to the Funeral of Aunt Eli. Quinsey. Because of the Porrige of snow, Bearers — Mr. Torrey, Fisk, Thacher, I, Danforth, Wilson,

Belchar — rid to the Grave, alighting a little before they came there. Mourners, Cous. Edward and his Sister rid first, then Mrs. Aña Quinsey, widow, behind Mr. Allen; and cous. Ruth Hunt behind her Husband; then Sam. and I. None of the Gookings there. Mr. Torrey prayed. Bearers had Rings and Wash-Lether Gloves. I had Gloves and a Ring. Cous. Edmund invited us; for I lodg'd there all night, with Mr. Torrey, Sam. with his Cousin. All else went home. Cousin Savil was at Weymouth and came not. Funeral about 4. p.m̄.

Dec.ʳ 6ᵗʰ. Mr. Torrey and I and Sam. about 12 set forward and ride home; Find all pretty well, about 2 or 3 aclock, and good satisfaction as to our Lodging there. It Rain'd quickly after our getting home. Very foggy thawing wether.

Justice Cushing of Hingham died on Tuesday and, as is said, was buried this Thorsday.[1]

Jan.ʸ 2. $\frac{1700}{1701}$ Went afoot to Dorchester, carried Mr. Willard's Fountain open'd. Eat Yokeheg [yolk of egg?] in Milk. Lᵗ Govʳ orders me to wait on him next Tuesday morn. Jan.ʸ 1. $\frac{1700}{1701}$ Just about Break-a-day Jacob Amsden and 3 other Trumpeters gave a Blast with the Trumpets on the com̄on near Mr. Alford's [in Margin — Entrance of the 18ᵗʰ Century]. Then went to the Green Chamber, and sounded there till about sunrise. Bell-man said these verses a little before Break-a-day, which I printed and gave them. [in Margin — My Verses upon New Century.]

---

[1] This was Daniel, oldest son of the emigrant Matthew Cushing, and Town Clerk of Hingham. The nephew of this Daniel was John, Justice of the Superior Court, and father of John, also Justice of same Court, whose son William was Judge of the United States Supreme Court, and declined the Chief-Justiceship. In other lines were Nathan, also of our Supreme Court; Caleb, J. S. J. C., now living; and Luther S., Judge C. C. P., the well-known author of Cushing's Manual of Parliamentary Practice, and his brother, Edmund L. Cushing, C. J. S. C. of N. Hampshire. Others of the family have been distinguished in other professions, but these examples show the legal tendency of the family. — Eds.

Once more! our God vouchsafe to shine:
Correct the Coldness of our Clime.
Make haste with thy Impartial Light,
And terminate this long dark night.

Give the poor Indians Eyes to see
The Light of Life: and set them free.
So Men shall God in Christ adore,
And worship Idols vain, no more.

So Asia, and Africa,
Eurôpa, with America;
All Four, in Consort join'd, shall Sing
New Songs of Praise to Christ our King.

The Trumpeters cost me five pieces $\frac{8}{8}$. Gave to the College-Library Dr. Owens two last Volumes on the Hebrews. Sent them by Amsden. When was about to part with Dr. Owen, I look'd, to read some difficult place; pitch'd on v. 11ᵗʰ of the 8ᵗʰ Chapter — Know the Lord — I read it over and over one time and another and could not be satisfied: At last this came in my mind Know the Lord, i.e. Know the Messiah, to whom the word Lord is very much a̍propriated &c. *vide locum.* Now my mind was at quiet, and all seem'd to run smooth. As I hope this is Truth, so I bless God for this New-years Gift; which I also writt in a spare place, and gave it with the Book to the College.

Satterdȧy, Janʸ 4. $\frac{1700}{1701}$ Mrs. Thair is this morn taken with an Apoplexy after she had been up and employ'd a while; was at our pump for water. Dies about six in the Evening.

Between 2 and 3 in the Afternoon Mr. Sergeant, Col. Townsend, and I take the Affidavits of Barth[olemew] Green, Jnᵒ Allen and Timᵒ Green. Present Mr. T. Brattle, Mr. Mico, and Tuthill notified. Mr. Nathˡ Oliver, Mr. Hern, Mr. Keeling: Mr. Hirst and my Son. I do not remember any more. Mr. Keeling, upon enquiry, what he call'd for pen and Ink for, whether twas to take notes or no: He own'd it was. Then I said I

would also send for one to write, naming Mr. Barnard; so
he forbore, and said he would not write.

Jan.ʸ 7ᵗʰ Mrs. Thair is buried : By reason of the Court,
Stars were seen before we went; but comfortably Light
by remains of the Day.   Moon-shine and Snow.

Bearers, Cook, Sewall, Addington, Oakes, Melyen,
Maryon, Jn.ᵒ Buried in the new burying place, close to
the Alms-house Ground.   [The Granary.]

Friday, Jan.ʸ 10. ₁₇₀₁⁰⁰. Mr. John Wait came to me,
and earnestly desired me to hasten consumating the Marriage between his Bastian and Jane, Mrs. Thair's Negro.
This day I waited upon the Lᵗ Governour at Dorchester
and spent about two hours in looking over and ordering
Corporation Bonds, but brought none away with me.   I
shewed Mr. Green's paper, and asked his Honor's Leave to
use his Name.   Shew'd it in the morn to Col. Townsend
at his own house, and to Mr. Sergeant at his, the night
before.   I had promised that nothing should be tack'd to
their Names, but they should first have a sight of it.

BOSTON, Jan.ʸ 13 ₁₇₀₁⁰⁰.

MADAM, — The inclosed piece of Silver, by its bowing, humble
form, bespeaks your Favor for a certain young Man in Town.   The
Name [Real] the Motto [Plus ultra] seem to plead its suitableness
for a Present of this Nature.   Neither need you to except against
the quantity : for you have the Mends in your own hand ; And by
your generous Acceptance, you may make both it and the Giver
Great.   Madam, I am
                              Your Affectᵗ Friend   S. S.

Jan.ʸ 14ᵗʰ Having been certified last night about 10.
oclock of the death of my dear Mother at Newbury, Sam.
and I set out with John Sewall, the Messenger, for that
place.   Hired Horses at Charlestown : set out about 10.
aclock in a great Fogg.   Din'd at Lewis's with Mr. Cushing of Salisbury.   Sam. and I kept on in Ipswich Rode,
John went to accompany Broʳ from Salem.   About Mr.
Hubbard's in Ipswich farms, they overtook us.   Sam. and

I lodg'd at Cromptons in Ipswich.   Bro^r and John stood
on for Newbury by Moon-shine.   Jany 15th Sam. and I set
forward.   Brother Northend meets us.   Visit Aunt Northend, Mr. Payson.   With Bro^r and sister we set forward
for Newbury: where we find that day aᵖointed for the
Funeral: twas a very pleasant Comfortable day.

Bearers, Jn° Kent of the Island, Lt Cutting Noyes,
Deacon William Noyes, Mr. Peter Tappan, Capt. Henry
Somersby, Mr. Joseph Woodbridge.   I follow'd the Bier
single.   Then Bro^r Sewall and sister Jane, Bro^r Short and
his wife, Bro^r Moodey and his wife, Bro^r Northend and his
wife, Bro^r Taᵖan and sister Sewall, Sam. and cous. Hañah
Taᵖan.   Mr. Payson of Rowley, Mr. Clark, Minister of
Excester, were there.   Col. Pierce, Major Noyes &c. Cous.
John, Richard and Betty Dumer.   Went ab^t 4. p.m.
Nathan^l Bricket taking in hand to fill the Grave, I said,
Forbear a little, and suffer me to say That amidst our
bereaving sorrows We have the Comfort of beholding this
Saint put into the rightfull possession of that Happiness
of Living desir'd and dying Lamented.   She liv'd comend-
ably Four and Fifty years with her dear Husband, and
my dear Father: And she could not well brook the being
divided from him at her death; which is the cause of our
taking leave of her in this place.   She was a true and
constant Lover of Gods Word, Worship, and Saints: And
she always, with a patient cheerfullness, submitted to the
divine Decree of providing Bread for her self and others
in the sweat of her Brows.   And now her infinitely
Gracious and Bountiful Master has promoted her to the
Honor of higher Employments, fully and absolutely discharged from all mañer of Toil, and Sweat.   My honoured and beloved Friends and Neighbours!   My dear
Mother never thought much of doing the most frequent
and homely offices of Love for me; and lavish'd away
many Thousands of Words upon me, before I could return
one word in Answer: And therefore I ask and hope that

none will be offended that I have now ventured to speak one word in her behalf; when shee her self is become speechless. Made a Motion with my hand for the filling of the Grave. Note, I could hardly speak for passion and Tears. Mr. Tappan pray'd with us in the evening. I lodg'd at sister Gerrishes with Joseph. Bro[r] and Sam. at Br. Tapans. Jan[y] 16th The two Brothers and four sisters being together, we took Leave by singing of the 90th Psalm, from the 8th to the 15th verse inclusively. Mr. Brown, the Scholar, was present. Set out ab[t] 11. for Ipswich, got time enough to hear Mr. Rogers preach the Lecture from Luke 1. 76. about ministerial preparation for Christ. Sung the nine first verses of the 132. Psalm. Mr. Rogers prai'd for the prisoner of death, the Newbury woman who was there in her chains. This is the last Sermon preached in the old Meeting-house. Eat Roost Fowl at Crompton's. Delivered a Letter to the Widow Hale; got very comfortably over the Ferry to Brothers, whether Mr. Hirst quickly came to welcome us and invite us to dine or breakfast next day, which we did, the morning being cold: Visited Madam Bradstreet and Major Brown, and told them of the death of their fellow-passenger. Rec'd me very courteously. Took horse about one p.m̄. Baited at Lewis's; Stop'd at Govr Usher's[1] to pay him a visit. He and his Lady being from home, we pass'd on, and got to Charlestown about Sun-set, very comfortably. Found all well at home through the Goodness of God.

Lords-Day, Jan[y] 29th $\frac{1700}{1701}$ Ipswich people Meet the first time in their New- Meeting-House, as Deacon Knowlton informs me at Cousin Savages Meeting Jan[y] 22th

Jan[y] 29th. $\frac{1700}{1701}$. Sam. and I went to Dedham Lecture, and heard Mr. Belchar preach excellently from Mat. 9. 12.

---

[1] John Usher, Lieutenant-Governor of New Hampshire, 1692-7 and 1702. He lived in Medford, in a house which was enlarged by Col. Isaac Royal. An engraving of it is given in Brooks's History of Medford, p. 49. Usher's descendants still continue the name in Rhode Island. — EDS.

Dined at said Belchars. Gave him and some young men with him my New-years verses: He read them and said Amen. Said twas a good Morning's Work.

Jany 30. Mr. Willard preaches from Eccles. 9. 2.— he that sweareth and he that feareth an Oath. Spake very closely against the many ways of Swearing amiss. Great Storm.

Febr. 1. $\frac{1700}{1701}$ p.m. Waited on the Lt Govr and presented him with a Ring in Remembrance of my dear Mother, saying, Please to accept of the Name of one of the Company your Honor is preparing to go to. Mr. Baily, Oliver, and Chip were there when I came in.

Febr. 3. $\frac{1700}{1701}$ Little Richd Fifield, a child of $\frac{1}{2}$ a year old, died very suddenly last Friday, and was buried this day. Mr. Simon Willard, and S. Sewall [the son] Bearers. Very windy and cold after the Rain.

Satterday, Febr. 15 $\frac{1700}{1701}$. News comes by Myles from England in a Gazett of Decr 2^d of the D.[uke] of Anjou, the new K.[ing] of Spain, taking his journey for Spain setting out from Versalles. Cardinal Albani, born 1650, is made Pope, takes the name of Clement the Eleventh. Gazett is printed here this day. Just about 3 in the Afternoon I went to the Maj^r General's; look'd upon Mingo who lies extream sick; then discoursed him in the Hall on the right hand where his pictures hang.

Tuesday, March, 4. $\frac{1700}{1}$. Mrs. Anne Woodbridge is buried at Roxbury.

Satterday, March. 8. $\frac{1700}{1}$. Ballard, from Barbados, brings News of the death of James Taylor at Barbados; Capt. Crow writes also of the Report they heard that Jamaica was Sunk; which much saddens the Town.

Thorsday, March, 13. Turin,[1] that was blown off to Barbados, arrives. Was at Mr. Taylor's funeral Jany the

---

[1] Undoubtedly a Turell. The name of Capt. Daniel T. is spelled in the town records, Turin, Turinge and Turell. — EDS.

last Friday, (the day little Fifield died) And gives a more distinct account of the fears of Jamaica being sunk: and of Rumors of Wars between England and France: the Preparations at Martinico; and sending six Companies to St Christophers.

Satterday, March. 15th $\frac{1700}{1}$ The Town is fill'd with the News of my Ld Bellomont's death, last Wednesday was señight. The Thorsday after, a Sloop set sail from N. York to Say-Brook; Mr. Clark, a Magistrate, carries it to New-London; from thence Mr. Southmayd brought it by Land last night, Capt. Belchar acquainted Mr. Secretary with it about 9 aclock last night. Upon this the Assembly is prorogued to Wednesday, the 16th April, at 9 *mane*.

Tuesday, March, 18th Last night I heard several Claps of Thunder: Great Fogg to day.

Wednesday, March, 19. We hear by the way of Virginia, that War is proclaimed between England and France.

Satterday, March 22. 4. p.m. The awfull News of the Lord Bellomont's death March 5th, 6. in the morn, $\frac{1700}{1}$; is confirmed by Letters received by the Posts! The Town is sad.[1]

Apr. 7th 1701. Last Satterday News was brôt by the Post of my Lord's Interment, March 27: So 46. Guns were ordered to be fired at the Castle, and 22. at the Sconce: were fired about 6–. p.m. Have warm discourse about the sitting of the Court. Lt Govr would have it dissolv'd; most of the Council are for its sitting. The Artillery Company give three Volleys in the middle of the Town when they came out of the field, with regard to my Lord. Col. Townsend wears a Wigg to day.

---

[1] Lord Bellomont died at New York. Palfrey writes, IV. 196, "Perhaps he died of sheer disappointment and mortification, for he knew how he was maligned in England; and the King's ministers, who should have been his vindicators, had given him recently no sort of attention." — EDS.

Monday, Apr. 14.ᵗʰ I ride and visit Mr. Trowbridge, who is still very feeble, and has been many months confin'd. From thence to Mr. Hobart's, with him to Sudbury, where we dine at Mr. Sherman's. From thence to Mr. Brinsmead's. He was much refresh'd with our company. Day was doubtfull: But got very well thither, and when by Mr. Brinsmead's fire, it Rain'd and hail'd much. Lodg'd at Mr. How's.

Apr. 15.ᵗʰ Mr. Torrey, Mr. Danforth of Dorchester, Mr. Swift came to us from Framingham to visit Mr. Brinsmead: He said twas as if came to his Funeral: If he were ready wish'd it were so. After diñer Mr. Hobart and I come home.

I staid and baited at the Greyhound, and got home between 8 and 9 very comfortably.

Satterday, May. 3. Mr. Daniel Olivers little Son is buried.

May, 28. 1701. Mr. Cooke, Addington, Walley, and self goe in my Coach and meet the Lieut Gov.ʳ; met the Guard and his Honor near the first Brook. Mr. Belchar preaches; Lᵗ Govʳ, notwithstanding his Infirmities, was an Auditor.

May, 29.ᵗʰ The election [of Councillors, or Magistrates] is sent in. Lᵗ Govʳ Ap̄roves all but Mr. Corwin, and to him he demurrs, taking some time of Consideration. Mr. Corwin said he acquiesced in it, and quickly went away, saying I humbly take my leave.[1] Mr. Eliakim [Hutchinson] pray'd he might be excused; he could not accept, He had sold most of his Interest in the Province of Main; and perceiv'd there was a desire among the Deputies that persons on the place might serve. In the evening Mr Cooke, Secretary, major Brown, Mr. Sergeant and I waited on Mr. Eliakim Hutchinson, and perswaded him not to decline serving. He treated us with Canary.

---

[1] The election of Corwin was, however, approved June 3d, as the Council record shows. — EDS.

All the rest were sworn that were present. Major Walley and I wait on Mr. Belchar at Mr. Wadsworth's and give him the Thanks of Lt Govr and Council for his Sermon, and desire a copy. This day a Burlesqe comes out upon Hull-street, in a Travestie construing my Latin verses.

Mr. Howard's Daughter [Sarah] is married. The President [1] refused to be among the Ministers at their annual Meeting.

Monday, June. 2 – 1701. Mr. Pemberton preaches the Artillery Sermon, from Luke. 3–14. Dine at Monk's. Because of the Rain and Mist, this day, the election is made upon the Town-house, Sewall. Čapt. ; [2] Tho. Hutchinson Lieut. ; Tho. Savage jun^r, Ensign. ; Tho. Fitch, 1 Sergt. :

---

[1] The President of Harvard College was at that time, and long after, regarded as the head of the Ministers of the Province. — EDS.

[2] Sewall was now captain of the Ancient and Honorable Artillery Company, an organization which is still flourishing. Although two editions of its History, by Z. G. Whitman (1820 and 1842), are in print, a few words may be given to this Boston company.

It was founded and chartered in 1638, mainly by the exertions of Captain Robert Keayne, who had been admitted a member of the Honorable Artillery Company of London, May 6, 1623. Others of the early members belonged to the same English corps, and the claim of our company to be a regular off-shoot therefrom is acknowledged in the recent history of the London Company, by Captain G. A. Raikes. (London, 1878.)

During the Andros period, the company was in abeyance; but in April, 1691, Colonel Elisha Hutchinson was chosen commander, and Cotton Mather preacher. From that time until the Revolution, the company held regular meetings. Then there was a necessary intermission until 1786, and Major William Bell was the commander chosen. The company has since flourished, and at present musters a large number of members. It enjoys various privileges, and it is to be hoped that it will long preserve the remembrance of the many distinguished men who have belonged to it.

The sermons annually delivered before the company have been by eminent divines, and a large number of them are in print. A copy of Mr. Pemberton's is in the Boston Athenæum, with the following title: —

"The Souldier Defended and Directed: as it was Delivered in a Sermon Preached to the Artillery Company in Boston, on the day of their Election of Officers, June 2d, 1701. By Ebenezer Pemberton, Pastor of a Church in Boston. Boston: Printed by B. Green and J. Allen, for Samuel Sewall, Junior, 1701." pp. 42, and one page advertisement. — EDS.

Oliver Noyes 2 : Hab. Savage 3 : Charles Chauncey 4.
Call'd down the Council out of the Chamber, set their
chairs below; Col. Pynchon gave the Staves and Ensign.
I said was surpris'd to see they had mistaken a sorry
pruning Hook for a Military Spear; but paid such a def-
erence to the Company that would rather run the venture
of exposing my own inability, than give any occasion to
suspect I slighted their call.   To Serg^t Fitch, Doubted not
but if I could give any thing tolerable words of com̄and,
he would mend them in a vigorous and speedy performance : was glad of so good a Hand to me and the
Company (Mr. Noyes abroad in the Gally).   To Hab.
S[avage]   The savages are souldiers *ex Traduce;* in imi-
tation of his honr^d father, Uncle, and Grandfather, hop'd
for worthy performances from him.   To Ch. Chauncy,
Had such a honor for your Grandfather and father, that
was glad was join'd with me in this Relation.   Drew out
before Mr. Ushers, gave 3 volleys.   Drew into the Town-
house again; sent Serg^t Chauncy for Mr. Pemberton,
who said he was glad to see the staff in my hand; pray'd
with us.   Had the company to my house, treated them
with bread, Beer, wine Sillibub. —— They order'd Capt.
Checkly and me to Thank Mr. Pemberton for his Sermon,
which we did on Tuesday, desiring a copy.   June, 4.
Bro^r comes to Town, I Treat him at Plyes : goes home.

Tuesday, June, 10th Having last night heard that
Josiah Willard had cut off his hair (a very full head of
hair) and put on a Wigg, I went to him this morning.
Told his Mother what I came about, and she call'd him.
I enquired of him what Extremity had forced him to put
off his own hair, and put on a Wigg? He answered, none
at all.   But said that his Hair was streight, and that it
parted behinde.   Seem'd to argue that men might as well
shave their hair off their head, as off their face.   I answered men were men before they had hair on their faces,
(half of mankind have never any).   God seems to have

ordain'd our Hair as a Test, to see whether we can bring
our minds to be content to be at his· finding : or whether
we would be our own Carvers, Lords, and come no more
at Him.   If disliked our Skin, or Nails; 'tis no Thanks to
us, that for all that, we cut them not off : Pain and danger restrain us.   Your Calling is to teach men self Denial.
Twill be displeasing and burdensom to good men :   And
they that care not what men think of them care not what
God thinks of them.   Father, Bro^r Simon, Mr. Pemberton,
Mr. Wigglesworth, Oakes, Noyes (Oliver), Brattle of Cambridge[1] their example.   Allow me to be so far a *Censor
Morum* for this end of the Town.   Pray'd him to read the
Tenth Chapter of the Third book of Calvins Institutions.[2]
I read it this morning in course, not of choice.   Told him
that it was condemn'd by a Meeting of Ministers at Northampton in Mr. Stoddards house, when the said Josiah was
there.   Told him of the Solemnity of the Covenant which
he and I had lately enterd into, which put me upon discoursing to him.   He seem'd to say would leave off his
Wigg when his hair was grown.   I spake to his Father of
it a day or two after : He thank'd me that had discoursed
his Son, and told me that when his hair was grown to
cover his ears, he promis'd to leave off his Wigg.   If he
had known of it, would have forbidden him.   His Mother
heard him talk of it ; but was afraid positively to forbid
him ; lest he should do it, and so be more faulty.

June, 12.   Mr. Willard marries Mr. Pemberton and
Mrs. Mary Clark.   All Mr. Willard's family there, as I am
informed, and many others.   Come to our Meeting the
next Sabbath.

Monday, June, 30.   Lt Govr said would go to the Comencement once more in his life-time ; so would adjourn

---

[1] It is to be inferred that the worthies here named wore no periwigs.
— EDS.

[2] The subject of this chapter is, " *Comment il faut user de la vie présente
et ses aides.*" — EDS.

the Court to Friday; and did so. But was very much pain'd going home. ˙ Mr. Nelson, Secretary, and I visit him on Tuesday to dissuade him from going, lest some ill consequence should haṗen. He consented, and order'd us to present his Bowl. After Dinner and singing, I took it, had it fill'd up, and drunk to the president, saying that by reason of the absence of him who was the Firmament and Ornament of the Province, and that Society, I presented that Grace-cup *pro more Academiarum in Anglia.* The Providence of our Soveraign Lord is very investigable; in that our Grace Cups, brim full, are passing round; when our Brethren in France are petitioning for their *Coup de Grace.* President made no oration.

Friday, July 4. The court understanding the Lt Gov$^{r's}$ growing illness, were loth to press him with business, and sent Mr. Secretary, Mr [Sewall?] Mr. Speaker and Mr. White to discourse his Honor, and propound an Adjournment. He agreed to it very freely. I said the Court was afflicted with the sense of his Honors indisposition; at which he rais'd himself up on his Couch. When coming away, he reach'd out his hand; I gave him mine, and kiss'd his. He said before, Pray for me! This was the last time I ever saw his Honor. July 7th, Mr. Cooke, Walley and I set out for Ipswich. About the time got thither the Lt Govr died.

July 8. Went to Newbury, eat Sturgeon at Major Davison's. Went to Hampton; from thence, having time, Major Walley and I with our Men, Bairsto and Hasting, went to Exeter; eat at Capt. Gilmans, Lodg'd at Mr. Clark's. July 9. Mr. Clark piloted us to Squamscot, where saw Govr Bradstreets daughter, Mrs. Wiggins. To Portsmouth. Lodg'd at Packers. In the Room where was told of my Fathers death, Govr Partridge told me of Mr. Stoughtons death Wednesday p.m̄. Mr. Epaphras Shrinton writt it by the post. July, 10. Went to Kittery, Major Vaughan accompanied us. Lodge there at Spruce-creek.

July 11. Major Wally and I ride to the Bank [Straw-berry]. July 12. Bairsto and I alone goe to Newbury betime, over Carr's Bridge. Dine at Bro‍ʳ Tap̄ans visit Acch. Woodman; lodge at sister Gerrishes.

July 13. Lords-day, Major Noyes shews me the Proc-lamation of the 10ᵗʰ publishing the Lᵗ Governours death,¹ and confirming Military officers.

July. 14, p.m. Mr. Cooke and Walley being now come to Town, rid towards Ipswich; I turn'd off to Cousin Dummers, visited her. Then to the Falls, Broʳ piloting us, lodge in sister Moodey's Brick House; which has an excellent foundation.

July, 15ᵗʰ Funeral-day of Lᵗ Govʳ To Ipswich; Try Esther Rogers. Jury next morn ask'd advice, then after, brought her in Guilty of murdering her Bastard daugh-ter. July, 17. Mr. Cooke pronounc'd the sentence. She hardly said a word. I told her God had put two Children to her to nurse: Her Mother did not serve her so. Esther was a great saviour; she, a great destroyer. Said did not do this to insult over her, but to make her sensible.

18. Rid to Salem in a little time, Sun almost down when went from Ipswich; yet got thither before the Bell rung. Lodg'd at daughter Hirst's. 19ᵗʰ ride home with my wife in a Calash with Joseph. Were in great danger by the pin of the Axeltree traping out, but Sam and Bair-sto spied it and cried out before the wheel was quite worn off. 22. rid to Dorchester Lecture, only I was in the Lᵗ Governours Pue. 27. Go into mourning for the Lᵗ Govʳ 30ᵗʰ Court sits. Augᵗ 1. Choose Major Genˡ [Win-throp] chief-justice, Mr. Saffin Justice, Mr. Cooke Judge

---

¹ William Stoughton, Lieutenant-Governor of the Province, was born at Dorchester, in 1632. His career and character will be found described in Sibley's "Harvard Graduates," pp. 194–208. He was a graduate of Harvard, and bestowed upon it the first Stoughton Hall, land in Dorchester, and other gifts. He was never married. — EDS.

Probats, without any mentioning the inconvenience of
that authoritye resting in one mans breast. Capt. Byfield judge of Bristol-Court. Mr. Saffin had 14. They
that sign'd his Comission are W. Winthrop, James Russell, Elisha Cooke, Jn° Hathorne, Wm Browne, Elisha
Hutchinson, Jonathan Corwin, Jn° Higginson, Peter Sergeant, Jn° Foster, Joseph Lynde, E^m Hutchinson, Penn
Townsend, Benj^a Browne, John Thacher.[1]

Have much adoe to get a number to sign the Maj^r Gen^ls
Comission. If had not withdrawn his paper, supose he
would not have had a number; 'tis said Several Deputies
have entered their dissent against the Agency.

Augt 11. Go down to the Castle to try to compose
the differences between the Capt. and Col. Romer: Order
that the Line next the Chanel be presently finished with
the Brick-Work.[2] I told the young men that if any in-
temperat Language proceeded from Col. Romer, twas not
intended to countenance that, or encourage their imita-
tion: but observe his direction in things wherein he was
Skillful and ordered to govern the work: or to that effect.
Lest should be thought the Council had too much wink'd
at his cursing and swearing, which was complained of.

---

[1] The Council was placed, by the death of both the Governor and Lieutenant-Governor, in supreme control. There were twenty-seven members,
but many were residents of places remote from Boston. The Council held
power from July 7, 1701, till the arrival of Gov. Joseph Dudley, June 11,
1702. As Stoughton was also Chief Justice of the Superior Court, Saffin
was elected to fill the vacancy, and Winthrop was promoted to be Chief.
— EDS.

[2] We have already spoken of Col. Romer (Vol. I. 488). Shurtleff, 492,
493, gives the copy of an inscription which was on a slab placed over the
entrance to the fort. In the " Description " he terms it a *white* slab; but in
the " Boston Transcript " of Oct. 17, 1861, he calls it a *slate* stone. He refers
to the fact that one-half of the stone, divided vertically, was preserved, but
does not say where it was. Very recently a fragment, doubtless the one he
means, although his description is to be taken as the heraldic *dexter* side,
was discovered amid some rubbish in the cellars of the Boston Athenæum.
It has been transferred, for safe-keeping, to the gallery of the Massachusetts
Historical Society. — EDS.

Augt 19th Sign an order for Capt. Crow to cruise to Tarpolin Cove because of some suspected vessels there, as Govr Cranston informs.

Mr. Saffin takes his Oath, Mr. Secretary administers it, and Mr. Russel and Col. Hutchinson attest it. This morning, *Vae Malum*, Capt. Hunting accidentally shoots himself dead.

Mr. E.^{m} Hutchinson cut his hand last Satterday between his left Thumb and fore finger; It bled pretty much to-day. Came to Council but would not sign, because his right hand was occupied in holding his Left, to prevent bleeding. Mr. Sergeant sign'd for him at his Request.

Septr 8.   rid to Rehoboth with Mr Cooke, Major Walley; Mr. Saffin went last week.

Sept. 9. to Bristow.   Mr. Saffin and others met us near the Ferry.   Peter Walker charg'd Mr. Saffin with urging a man to swear that which he scrupled to swear.

Septr 11.   Mr. Saffin tampered with Mr. Kent, the Foreman, at Capt. Reynold's, which he denyed at Osburn's. Coñived at his Tenant Smith's being on the Jury, in the case between himself and Adam [a negro], about his Freedom. 7.^{r} 12.   Broke fast at Mr. Brenton's.   Mr. Cooke and I rid to Billinges, near $\frac{1}{2}$ the way in the night. 7^r 13.   home between 12 and 1.   Vessel arrives from England that brings News of Sir Henry [Ashurst] opōsing Col. Dudley's being Govr: 4 of the Council; viz: Winthrop, Cooke, Hutchinson Elisha, Sergeant are said to have written to him.

Septr 17th.   Wentworth arrives, in whom comes Capt. Richards and wife, Dudley Woodbridge, N. Henchman, Martin, Bonus, &c.   Brings a Letter to the Lt Govr with a Bill of Lading for 50 Barrels powder given by the King.

Monday, 7.^{r} 29.   Training of the Foot Company: In the Afternoon, I waited on Mr. Mather to desire his Apointm.^{t} of a Meeting of the Coṁissioners [of the Society

for Propagating the Gospel]. He tells me he is going to
Lin tomorrow; and shall not return till next week: I
tell him I will wait on him then.

Monday, Oct. 6. 1701. Very pleasant fair Wether;
Artillery trains in the Afternoon [Sewall in command].
March with the Company to the Elms; Go to prayer,
March down and Shoot at a Mark. Mr. Cushing I think
was the first that hit it, Mr. Gerrish twice, Mr. Fitch,
Chauncy, and the Ensign of the Officers. By far the
most missed, as I did for the first. Were much contented
with the exercise. Led them to the Trees agen, perform'd some facings and Doublings. Drew them together;
propounded the question about the Colours; twas voted
very freely and fully. I inform'd the Company I was told
the Company's Halberds &c. were borrowed; I understood
the Leading staff was so, and therefore ask'd their Acceptance of a Half-Pike, which they very kindly did; I
deliver'd it to Mr. Gibbs for their Use.

They would needs give me a Volley, in token of their
Respect on this occasion. The Pike will, I supose, stand
me in fourty shillings, being headed and shod with Silver:
Has this Motto fairly engraven:

> *Agmen Massachusettense*
> *est in tutelam Sponsæ*
> *AGNI Uxoris.*
> 1701.

The Lord help us to answer the Profession. Were
treated by the Ensign in a fair chamber. Gave a very
handsome Volley at Lodging the Colours. The Training
in Sept. was a very fair day, so was this.

Thorsday, Octob. 9th. 1701. Peter Sergeant Esqr. marries my Lady Mary Phips.

Oct. 10th. Send my wife and me Gloves and Cake. Col.
Hutchinson, Mr. Addington, Foster, Townsend, Bromfield,
Stoddard, Burroughs, visit the Bridegroom and Bride, and

sup there with Roast-Beef, Venison Pasty, Cake and
cheese, Betty came yesterday to see us. Bro^r and his
daughter came, and go home to day. Mr, Sergeant dwells
at my Ladies house and Major Hobbie comes into his
[afterwards the Province House].

Wednesday Octr 15. Court meets, draw up a new
Address ; send that and their former with the Memorial to
Mr. Constantine Phips,[1] with 100£ Sterling Money of
England, for to recompence his former service.

Octr 18., or thereabout, Mr. Foster and Cooke had a hot
discourse about Mr. [President] Mather; Capt. Foster
moving for a Quarter's Salary. I spake that he might
have it.

8^r 18. The Court is prorogued to the tenth of De-
cemb^r at 9 *mane*.

Octr 19. Mr. Sergeant and his Bride come to our
Meeting forenoon and afternoon.

Octr 20. [In Margin — Opprobrium. Mr. Cotton
Mather speaks hard words of me.] Mr. Cotton Mather
came to Mr. Wilkins's[2] shop, and there talked very sharply
against me as if I had used his father worse than a Neger ;
spake so loud that people in the street might hear him.
Then went and told Sam, That one pleaded much for Negros, and he had used his father worse than a Negro, and
told him that was his Father. I had read in the morn Mr.
Dod's saying ; Sanctified Afflictions are good Promotions.
I found it now a cordial. And this caus'd me the rather

---

[1] Sir Constantine Phips was an eminent lawyer, Lord Chancellor of Ire-
land in 1714, and died in 1723. His grandson was made Lord Mulgrave in
the Irish peerage in 1767; in England, the third baron was made Earl of
Mulgrave in 1812, and *his* son was created Marquess of Normandy in 1838.
No connection is known to have existed between Sir Constantine and Sir
William Phips, despite the fables of the peerages, beginning with Archdall's.
See also Vol. I. p. 204, *note.* — EDS.

[2] Mr. Richard Wilkins has already been mentioned in our first volume,
p. 452, *note.* — EDS.

to set under my Father and Mother's Epitaph, — Psal. 27. 10.[1]

It may be it would be arrogance for me to think that I, as one of Christ's Witnesses, am slain, or ly dead in the street.

Octr 9. I sent Mr. Increase Mather a Hanch of very good Venison; I hope in that I did not treat him as a Negro.

8^r 20. Mr. Pemberton and his wife visit Daughter Hirst; pray with her.

Octob^r 22. 1701. I, with Major Walley and Capt. Saml Checkly, speak with Mr. Cotton Mather at Mr. Wilkins's. I expostulated with him from 1 Tim. 5. 1. Rebuke not an elder. He said he had consider'd that: I told him of his book of the Law of Kindness for the Tongue, whether this were correspondent with that. Whether correspondent with Christ's Rule: He said, having spoken to me before there was no need to speak to me again; and so justified his reviling me behind my back. Charg'd the Council with Lying, Hypocrisy, Tricks, and I know not what all [in Margin — Surreptitious]. I ask'd him if it were done with that Meekness as it should; answer'd, yes. Charg'd the Council in general, and then shew'd my share, which was my speech in Council; viz. If Mr. Mather should goe to Cambridge again to reside there with a Resolution not to read the Scriptures, and expound in the Hall: I fear the example of it will do more hurt than his going thither will doe good. This speech I owned. Said Mr. Corwin at Reading, upbraided him, saying, This is the man you dedicat your books to! I ask'd him If I should suppose he had done somthing amiss in his Church as an Officer; whether it would be well for me to exclaim against him in the street for it. (Mr. Wilkin would fain

---

[1] " When my father and my mother forsake me, then the Lord will take me up." — EDS.

have had him gon into the iñer room, but he would not.)
I told him I conceiv'd he had done much unbecoming a
Minister of the Gospel, and being call'd by Maxwell to
the Council, Major Wally and I went thither, leaving
Capt. Checkly there. 2 Tim. 2. 24. 25. Went to the
Council, Sign'd Mr. Mather's order for £25. Hamer'd
out an Order for a Day of Thanksgiving.

Thorsday, Oct.ʳ 23. Mr. Increase Mather said at Mr.
Wilkins's, If I am a Servant of Jesus Christ, some great
Judgment will fall on Capt. Sewall, or his family.

Oct.ʳ 24. Rainy Day, yet Judge Atwood comes from
Rehoboth to Boston. 25. Visits several, and me among
the rest. This day in the morn. I got Mr. Moody to
copy out my Speech, and gave it to Mr. Wilkins that all
might see what was the ground of Mr Mather's Anger.

Writ out another and gave it to Joshua Gee. I perceive Mr. Wilkins carried his to Mr. Mathers; They seem
to grow calm. (On Friday received Mr. Fitch's Letter
and Blessing.) Receive the News of Sister Sewall's being
brought to Bed of a Son, which is the Sixth; and the
fifteenth Child. Messenger came in when Judge Atwood
here. Son Hirst comes to Town. Was in danger to be
cast away coming over the Ferry, the wind was so very
high. Mr. Chiever visits me this Afternoon.

Octob.ʳ 28. 1701. Mr. William Atwood Takes the Oaths
and subscribes the Declaration and Association, to qualify
himself to exercise his Authority here as Judge of the
Admiralty.[1] He ask'd for a Bible: but Mr. Cooke said

---

[1] Very little has been written about the officers of the Crown during our
colonial period. In Washburn's Judicial History of Massachusetts, pp. 175,
185, it is stated that the first Judge of Admiralty was Wait Still Winthrop,
commissioned in 1699. Atwood succeeded him, with Thomas-Newton for
Deputy. In 1703 the district seems to have been divided, Roger Mompesson taking New York, and Nathaniel Byfield Massachusetts, Rhode Island,
and New Hampshire.

In 1715 Byfield was superseded by John Menzies, a Scotchman, who died
at Boston Sept. 20, 1728. Robert Auchmuty then held till Byfield was re-

our Custom was to Lift up the hand; then he said no more, but used that Ceremony. His Comission was first read before the Council. At going away, he thanked me for, The Selling of Joseph, saying twas an ingenious Discourse.

Thus a considerable part of Executive Authority is now gon out of the hands of New England men.[1]

Nov.ʳ 1. 1701. Bastian has a Daughter born, he being at the Castle; He calls her Jane. Nov.ʳ 2. She is baptised by Mr. Allen; Bastian holds her up. Deacon Isa. Tay is Ordained at the same time; Mr. Allen and ——— Wadsworth [Rev. Benjamin Wadsworth, colleague minister of First Church] lay their hands on him. Joseph went to that Meeting in the Afternoon, and brought us this word. Hañah Davis, and Bumsteds daughter are taken into our Church. Monday, Nov.ʳ 11. 1701. Maj.ʳ Gen.ˡ Winthrop, Mr. Cooke, Sewall, Saffin set out for Salem to keep Court. Going in the Calash and benighted, I lodge at Hart's and go thence in the morning early. Major Walley is released, and promises not to ask to stay at home again, till I have had my Turn.

A complaint was prefer'd against Woodbridge at Newbury Court, Jury`cleer'd him. James Wise, the Complainant, Apeals. Action was dismiss'd; because a man being Acquitted by a Jury, ought not to be Try'd again. Rioters that were fined Ten pounds apiece, were now fined twenty shillings, great pains having been used to bring them quite off; but the Jury confirm'd their former Judgment and were directed by the Court only to say Guilty.

---

commissioned, in 1728–29. Byfield held till his death, in 1733, with Nathaniel Hubbard for Deputy in Bristol for part of the time.

Auchmuty succeeded Byfield until 1747, when Chambers Russell was appointed Judge, with George Cradock, and later with William Reed, Deputy.

Robert Auchmuty, Jr., was Russell's successor, and held until the Revolution. — EDS.

[1] A sentence burdened with much sad feeling for the writer as he marked the steady transfer of authority to crown officials, while local government was impaired. — EDS.

The Salem Justices were much disgusted at this management and sentence: I dissented from it as too small a Plaister for so great a Sore.

Satterday, Novr 15th Went home. Major Genl Winthrop, Mr. Cooke, Saffin, Mrs. Añe, by Charlestown, I was forced to go to Wiñisiṁet; because my Horse was to be had back by Cous. Sam. Sewall. Had very comfortable going and coming home. Find all well. I lodg'd at my Son and Daughter Hirst's. *Laus Deo.*

Boston, N. E. Novr 19. 1701. The Court gave Sentence that the Law for Reviews bars Mr. Cooke &c. their Action against Col. Paige,   Mr. Saffin was of that opinion also. Super. Court adjourn'd to Friday respecting Mr. Pain. In the Court held at Boston July 27. 1686, When Col. Paiges case was Tryed: Jury

Gervase Ballard	Francis Foxcroft
Benj. Alford	John Bird
Tho Clark	
Tobias Davis	
Willm Blake	
Joseph Crosby	
John Hersey	
Tho. Fuller	
Edw. Adams	
Nathan^l Stearns	

At the Court of Appeals, Novemb^r 2. 1686.

Joseph Lynde	
Samson Sheaf	Dudley
Francis Burroughs	Stoughton
William White	Bulkley
Daniel Brewer	Wharton
John Breck	Gedney
John Minott	Randolph
Peter Woodward	W. Winthrop
William Dean	Jno Usher
Samuel Goff	Edw. Tyng.
John Haṁond	
John Morse	

Nov[r] 23. 1701. John Joyliffe Esqr. dies. He had been
blind, and laboured under many Infirmities for a long
time.[1] Mr. Brunsdon died the night before: and one
Birds-eye a few days before; 3 men. Jn° Arnolds wife is
also dead. I wish it do not prove a sickly time after long
Health.

Mr. Nicholas Noyes of Newbury, aged about 86 years,
died on the Lords-Day 9[r] 23. 1701. Mr. Oliver Purchas,
late of Lin, now of Concord, is to be buried this week.
Bearers of Mr. Joyliffe; Mr. Cooke, Addington, Sergeant,
Anth. Checkly, El[m] Hutchinson, Mr. Saffin.

Sabbath, Nov[r] 30. I went to the Manifesto church to
hear Mr. Adams; Mr. Coleman was praying when I went
in, so that I thought my self disapointed. But his Prayer
was short; When ended, he read distinctly the 137, and
138th Psalms, and the seventh of Joshua, concerning the
conviction, sentence, and execution of Achon. Then sung
the second part of the Sixty ninth Psalm. Mr. Brattle
set it to Windsor Tune. Then Mr. Adams pray'd very
well, and more largely: And gave us a very good Sermon from Gal. 4. 18. Doct. It is just and comendable
&c. Mr. Adams gave the Blessing.

In the Afternoon Mr. Adams made a short Prayer, read
the 139th Psalm, and the six and twentieth chapter of the
Acts; Then Agripa said —— Sung. Mr. Coleman made
a very good Sermon from Jer. 31. 33.— and will be their
God, and they shall be my people.

Pray'd, sung — Contribution. Gave the Blessing. I
spent this Sabbath at Mr. Colman's, partly out of dislike
to Mr. Josiah Willard's cutting off his Hair, and wearing

---

[1] John Joyliffe was one of the connecting links with the first settlers.
He married, in 1657, Anna, widow of Robert Knight, and previously widow
of Thomas Cromwell, that rich privateer, who settled in Boston. Cromwell
is mentioned by Winthrop in his Journal, II. 264, as having been, in 1636,
a common seaman in the "Massachusetts," and thus one of the first generation here. — EDS.

a Wigg: He preach'd for Mr. Pemberton in the morning; He that contemns the Law of Nature, is not fit to be a publisher of the Law of Grace: Partly to give an Example of my holding Comunion with that Church who renounce the Cross in Baptisme, Humane Holydays &c. as other New-english Churches doe. And I had spent a Sabbath at the Old Church, and at Mr. Mathers. And I thought if I should have absented my self in the *forenoon* only, it might have been more gravaminous to Mr. Willards friends than keeping there *all day.* I perceive by several, that Mr. Coleman's people were much gratified by my giving them my Company, Several considerable persons express'd themselves so. The Lord cleanse me from all my Iniquity &c. Jer. 33. 8. and 16. which chapter read in course xr. 5ᵗʰ 1701.

Decʳ 24. 1701. Sam sets out for Newbury with Capt. Somersby; went away about ½ hour past 12.

Janʸ 2. 170½. My Wife had some thoughts the Time of her Travail might be come, before she went to bed: But it went over. Between 4 and 5 m. I go to prayer, Rise, make a Fire, call Mrs. Ellis, Hawkins, Mary Hawkins calls Midwife Greenlef. I go to Mr. Willard and desire him to call God. The Women call me into chamber, and I pray there. Jnᵒ Barnard comes to me for Money: I desire him to acquaint Mr. Cotton Mather, and Father.

Janʸ 2. 170½. My Wife is well brought to Bed of a Daughter just about two p.m., a very cold day: Was got into Bed without a fainting Fit.

Sabbath-day night my wife is very ill and something delirious. Pulse swift and high. I call Mr. Oakes about Two aclock or before. Grows a little better.

Janʸ 6. 170½ Nurse Hill watch'd last night. Wife had a comfortable night.

MEMORANDUM.

Sarah Sewall was born Novr 21. 1694. Baptised p̄ Mr. Willard Novr 25. Died Decr 23. Was buried xr. 25. 1696. A dear amiable Son of Samuel Sewall and Hañah his wife, was Still-born May, 21. 1696.

Judith Sewall was born upon Friday, Jany 2. at two in the Afternoon, Hañah Greenlef Midwife, Judd Nurse. Lords-Day, Jany 4. p.m., Was baptised by the Rever^d Mr. Ebenezer Pemberton. It being his Turn: because The Rev^d Mr. Willard administered the Lord's super just before. So is a New Midwife, and a New Baptiser. What through my wives many Illnesses, more than ordinary, her fall upon the stairs about 5 weeks before; from which time she kept her chamber; her thoughtfullness between whiles whether she were with child or no; her Fears what the issue would be, and the misgiving of our Unbelieving hearts, GOD hath been wonderfully Mercifull to us in her comfortable Delivery; which I desire to have Recorded.

Note. This is the Thirteenth Child that I have offered up to God in Baptisme; my wife having born me Seven Sons and Seven Daughters. I have named this little Daughter Judith, in Remembrance of her honoured and beloved Grandmother Mrs. *Judith Hull*. And it may be my dear wife may now leave off bearing. For my former Children, See p. 124. 125 [in Journal, *ante*, Vol. I. pp. 383, 384].

Jany 8. 170½ Mr. Incr. Mather preaches the Lecture from Gen. 18. 24. Doct. The Wicked many times fare the better for the sake of the Godly, Hopes for England and N. E. because many Righteous ones in both. About 4. Alice Macdoñel is buried. Mr. Lynde and I were there as Overseers of the poor. This day agreed with Nurse Randal to suckle Judith.

Friday Jany 9. 170½ Buy a Wicker Cradle for Judith of Tho Hunt; which cost Sixteen Shillings.

My wife puts on her Cloaths, and sits up in the Bed.

Jan.ʸ 10. My Wife gets on to the Pallat Bed in her Cloaths, and there keeps, while Linen Curtains are put up within the Serge; and is refresh'd by it.

Jan.ʸ 12. 170½ The Harbour is open again, and pretty well freed from the Ice. Jan.ʸ 13. m. I pray'd earnestly by my self and in the family for a Nurse; Went and expostulated with Mr. Hill about his daughters failing me; in the chamber: In the mean time, one of his family went and call'd the Nurse and I brought her home with me; which was beyond my expectation. For Mr. Jesse huff'd and ding'd, and said he would lock her up, and she should not come. I sent not for her, So I hope twas an Answer of Prayer.

Friday, Jan.ʸ 16. My Wife Treats her Midwife and Women: Had a good Dinner, Boil'd Pork, Beef, Fowls; very good Rost Beef, Turkey-Pye, Tarts. Madam Usher carv'd, Mrs. Hañah Greenlef; Ellis, Cowell, Wheeler, Johnson, and her daughter Cole, Mrs. Hill our Nurses Mother, Nurse Johnson, Hill, Hawkins, Mrs. Goose, Deming, Green, Smith, Hatch, Blin. Comfortable, moderat wether: and with a good fire in the Stove warm'd the Room.

Jan.ʸ 17. We hear that Mrs. Sam. Brown of Salem is dead, and the first child she had. She earnestly desired a child, having been a pretty while married. Col. Turner's sister.

Jan.ʸ 18. Storm of snow: but not very cold.

Jan.ʸ 20. between 11 and 12. Farnum the Father, was pecking Ice off the Mill-wheel, slipt in and was carried and crush'd, and kill'd, with the wheel. Elder Copp and Mr. Walley came to call cousin Savage at my house.

Note. Last night were under awfull aprehensions, lest the House was on fire, there was such a smoke and smell in the cellar like as of a Colepit. Got Joseph Clark to view it and neibour Cole. Could find nothing. Cole supos'd **twas a Steem** by reason of the cold. Many watch'd but found nothing. And blessed be God, the House is still standing.

Jan.ʸ 22. ₁₇₀½ Sam. comes home in company of his unkle Moodey, Broʳ and Sister Hirst. Jan.ʸ 23. Broʳ Moodey goes home.

Satterday, Jan.ʸ 24. 4 *post meridiem.* Mary Bowtel of Cambrige was burnt to death in her own fire, being in a Fit as is supos'd. Her right arm, and left Hand, were burnt quite off; her bowels burnt out, &c. Coroner Green told us this at Charlestown, Jan.ʸ 27. Tis very remarkable that two such awfully violent Deaths should fall out in one and the same week at Boston and Cambridge.

Jan.ʸ 30. ₁₇₀½ Cousin Moodey of York comes to see me : upon enquiry about a Hebrew word, I found he had no Lexicon ; and I gave him my Buxtorf.

Jan.ʸ 31. ₁₇₀½ William Parsons of 88 years, is buried. Was in the fifth-monarchy fray in London :[1] but slipt away in the Crowd.

Febr. 1. William Willard and William Blin were baptised by Mr. Willard. At the funeral Mr. Chiever told me he enter'd his 88ᵗʰ year 25. Jan.ʳ, and is now the oldest man in Boston.

Feb.ʳ 2. Very sore storm of Rain and Hail and Snow. Hunting is cast away on the Rocks of Marblehead. Comes from the Bay; his company and he lost.

A man dround in the Cellar of the Queens-head Tavern : went to take out the plug, and dropt in. It seems had the falling sickness. No Sun-shine this day.

Wednesday, Feb.ʳ 11ᵗʰ. The Gazette that Andover

---

[1] This riot in London occurred Jan. 6, 1661. The ringleader was Thomas Venner, formerly a cooper at Salem, a freeman in 1638, and a member of the Artillery Company. Some time after 1651, he went to England, and April 9, 1657, he began a little riot in London in favor of a republic and against the assumption of the crown by Cromwell. But in 1661 he incited a more formidable riot; and, after a stout resistance, he was captured and hanged. See Palfrey, II. 304 and 434. — EDS.

Adress presented Octob.^r 9th relating to their Dr. Wales, I read it at Col. Hutchinson's in hearing of 12 or 13 of the Council, were there waiting for the Maj.^r Gen^{ls} Rising. This Gazett comes by way of New-York. Febr. 14. This last week has been a week of extraordinary cold Wether. Last night I dream'd I was in company with Mr. Stoughton and Mr. N. Higginson.

Thorsday, Febr. 19. Mr. I. Mather preached from Rev. 22. 16 — bright and morning Star. Mention'd Sign in the Heaven, and in the Evening following I saw a large Cometical Blaze, something fine and dim, pointing from the Westward, a little below Orion.

Febr. 21. Capt. Tim.^o Clark tells me that a Line drawn to the Comet strikes just upon Mexico, spake of a Revolution there, how great a Thing it would be. Said one Whitehead told him of the magnificence of the City, that there were in it 1500 Coaches drawn with Mules. This Blaze had much put me in mind of Mexico; because we must look toward Mexico to view it. Capt. Clark drew a Line on his Globe. Our Thoughts being thus confer'd, and found to jump, makes it to me remarkable. I have long pray'd for Mexico, and of late in those Words, that God would open the Mexican Fountain.

Febr. 21. This day Goodw- Pope, and John Wait dye.

Febr. 22, $\frac{170\frac{1}{2}}{}$ My Wife goes to Meeting in the Afternoon, after long Restraint.

Febr. 23. Goodw. Pope is buried. Capt Byfield and I and the Select-Men, and about 12 women there; Cowel, Wheeler, Calef &c. One or two Bacons, her Grandsons, followed next.

Febr. 25. Archibald Macquerry has a son born at Charlestown without Arms.

Jn° Wait is buried; Genl Court Sat, and I think none of the Council at the Funeral.

Febr. 26. Sixteen of the Council sign an order for making Dracot a Town.

Feb. 28. Yesterday Mr. Cookes Petition to enable him to sue Col. Paige for his Farm, was brought forward. I moved that Col. Paige might be Notified and 4 more. Mr. Cooke seemed displeas'd, and in way of Displeasure said twas to delay his Business: was sorry I was so far engag'd *in it*. For this, and because of Sherbourn case, I chose to stay from Council this Forenoon; that might avoid being present when suspected, or charg'd with Prejudice. Sam. brings word of a Ship from England 19 weeks; last from Fayall, In whom is Mr. Brenton.

Capt Scott arrives, in whom comes Mr. Brenton, Febr. 28. $\frac{1}{1702}$.

March, 11. $\frac{1}{1702}$ In the Afternoon, there are great Southerly Gusts and Showers; Considerable Thunder and Lightening. Last night between 10 and 11, A great Fire brake out in Mr. Thomson's Warehouse upon the Dock: Seven or Eight of the chief Warehouses were burnt and blown up. 'Tis said the Fire began in that part which Monsr. Bushee hires. About half a Ship's Loading was lately taken into it.

Satterday, March, 14. $\frac{1}{1702}$ at 5 p.m. Capt. John Alden expired; Going to visit him, I hapened to be there at the time.

May, 1. Whitehorn arrives: Came from Falmouth March, 12. Ld Cornbury[1] came out with. Rains in the Afternoon, after much Drought. May, 2. Great storm, very fierce Wind. A Briganteen is driven up the Harbour, and into the Mill-Crick with such Fury that she carrys away the Drawbridge before her.

May. 4, 1702. Artillery Comp^a Trains, Rainy day; So we exercise on the Town-House in the morn. Mr. Pitkin, Capt Whiting, Comissioners for Connecticut about Runing the Line, Dine with us. Mr. Colman and Adams,

---

[1] The new Governor of New York. He was grandson of the first Earl of Clarendon, and cousin of Queen Anne. — EDS.

Major Hobby, Capt. Pelham, Southack, Ephr. Savage,
Mr. Paul Dudley, Will Dumer, Edw. Hutchinson, &c. In
the Afternoon went into Comon; Major Hobby, Will
Dumer, Ned Hutchinson, Oliver Williams and another,
Listed. Major Hobby was introduced by Col. Hutchinson, He and I vouch'd for him. Mr. Elisha Cooke jun^r
mov'd to be dismiss'd, which when he had paid his Arrears, was granted by Vote with a Hiss. Went to Pollards to avoid the Rain. March'd out and shot at a Mark.
Before they began, I told the Comp^{any} that I had call'd
them to shoot in October, and had not my self hit the
Butt; I was willing to bring my self under a small Fine,
such as a single Justice might set; and it should be to
him who made the best Shott. Mr. Gerrish and Ensign
John Noyes were the competitors, At Pollards, by a Brass
Rule, Ens. Noyes's Shot was found to be two inches and
a half nearer the centre, than Mr. John Gerrishes; His
was on the right side of the Neck; Ensign Noyes's on the
Bowels a little on the Left and but very little more than
G. on the Right of the middle-Line When I had heard
what could be said on both sides, I Judg'd for Ensign
Noyes, and gave him a Silver cup I had provided engraven

May. 4. 1702.

Euphratem Siccare potes.[1]

Telling him, it was in Token of the value I had for that
virtue in others, which I my self could not attain to.
March'd into Comon and concluded with Pray'r. Pray'd
in the morn on the Townhouse, Praying for the Churches
by Name. After Diner, We Sung four staves of the 68th
PS. viz. first Part and the 9. and 10th verses of the 2^d with
regard to the plentifull Rain on the 1 and 2 May and
now, after great Drought; Mr. Dering mov'd we might

---

[1] See Rev. XVI. 12. The drying up of Euphrates, as a prophetic symbol,
engaged much of Judge Sewall's interest. See Vol. I. p. 69, *note*. But the
cup was probably used for other liquids. — Eds.

sing. Some objected against our singing so much; I answer'd, Twas but *Four Deep*. Were Treated at Major Savages.

Satterday, May 9. 1702. By this days Post we hear that my Lord Cornbury arriv'd, a Thorsday was señight, at New York. May, 9. This day, several of the Gentlemen of the Council go to the Castle. As they came up, Miller was going down. And a little after they pass'd him his ship overset. A Swisse Boy drown'd.

Visit Sister Moodey twice in Kittery Circuit. May 19th Mr. James How, a good Man of Ipswich, 104 years old, is buried. Died I think on Lords-Day night, just about the time the News of the Kings Death was brought from Madera.

May, 28. Burrington from New-found-Land brings Prints of the King's death March, 8. at 8 m. Queen's Speech to her Lords at St James's. Lords Spiritual and Temporal, their Address; Queen's Speech to the Parliament; Several Addresses; and at last the Gazette containing the Proclaiming the Queen, came to Hand: Then we resolv'd to proclaim her Majesty here: Which was done accordingly below the Town-house. Regiment drawn up, and Life-Guard of Horse; Council, Representatives, Ministers, Justices, Gentlemen taken within the Guard; Mr Secretary on foot read the order of the Council, the Proclamation, and Queen's Proclamation for continuing Comīssions. Mr. Sheriff Gookin gave it to the people. Volleys, Guns. Went into chamber to drink, and there had the sad news of the Taking of 3 Salem Catches by the Cape-Sable Indians; one of them Col. Higginson's: David Hills, and one of the Masters kill'd. This arrived at Salem this day, and was sent per Express, one of the men swore it before the Council. Proclamation was made between 3 and 4. At 5. p.m. Madam Bellingham dies, a vertuous Gentlewoman, *antiquis Moribus, prisca fide*, who has liv'd a widow just about 30 years.[1] May, 31. 146. Ps. sung, and Mr. Pemberton preaches a Funeral sermon for the King, from the 3[d] and 4th verses of that Psalm.

June, 1, 1702. Artillery election-Day. Mr. Colman preaches from Heb. 11. 33. Sermon is well liked of. Had much adoe to persuade Mr. Willard to dine with me. Said Ministers were disgusted because the Representatives went first at the Proclaiming the Queen;[2] and that by order of our House. But at last he came: I went for him, leaving my Guests. No Mather, Allen, Adams there. But there were Mr. Torrey, Willard, Simes, Thacher, Belchar and many more. No Mr. Myles, Bridge, [Ministers of King's Chapel.] No Capt of Frigat. Tho the last were invited. June. 10. 1702. Comittee Tryes Powder, and firing so much and long distempered me; that partly by that, and partly by my Wives intolerable pains, I had a most restless night. June, 11. Thorsday, before I was dress'd, Sam. Gave the Word that Gov[r] [Joseph Dudley] was come. Quickly after I got down, Maxwell sumoned me to Council, told me the Secretary had a Letter of the Governours Arrival yesterday, at Marblehead. Mr. Addington, Eliakim Hutchinson, Byfield and Sewall, sent per the Council, go with Capt Crofts in his Pinace to meet the Governour, and Congratulat his Arrival; We get aboard a

---

[1] This was another of the links to the first generation. The lady was Penelope, sister of Herbert Pelham, and second wife of Governor Richard Bellingham, who was himself the last survivor of the patentees named in the Charter. Winthrop, II. 43, mentions the scandal about his marriage. She was "ready to be contracted to a friend of" Bellingham's, "who lodged in his house, and by his consent had proceeded so far with her, when on the sudden, the Governour treated with her, and obtained her for himself." Not only was there this romance, and a considerable disparity in years, he being about fifty years and the lady twenty, but Bellingham also solemnized the marriage himself. There is no reason, however, to conclude that the marriage was not as happy as less remarkable ones have proved. — EDS.

[2] Mr. Sewall was as ready as were the Ministers themselves, to take note of every token of the curtailment of their prerogatives and privileges with the changes which followed upon the administration under the Provincial charter. — EDS.

little before got within Point Alderton; Capt Heron introduced us; After had all saluted the Gov.ʳ I said,

Her Majesty's Council of this Province have com̄anded
us to meet your Excellency, and congratulate your safe
Arrival in the Massachusetts Bay, in quality of our Governour: Which we do very heartily; not only out of Obedience to our Masters who sent us; but also of our own
accord. The Cloaths your Excellency sees us wear, are a
true Indication of our inward Grief for the Departure of
K. William. Yet we desire to remember with Thankfullness the Goodness of God, who has at this time peaca-
bly placed Queen Anne upon the Throne. And as Her
Majestys Name imports Grace, so we trust God will shew
Her Majesty Favour; and Her Majesty us. And we look
upon your Excellency's being sent to us, as a very fair
First-Fruit of it, for which we bless God and Queen Anne.

I was startled at 2 or 3 things; viz. The Lᵗ Governour
[Thomas Povey] a stranger, sent, whom we knew nor
heard anything of before:[1] When the Govʳ first mention'd
it, I understood him of Mr. Addington. I saw an ancient
Minister, enquiring who it was, Governour said, twas
G— Keith,[2] had converted many in England, and now
Bp. London had sent him hether with Salery of 200.
Guineys per añum. I look'd on him as Helena aboard.[3]
This man crav'd a Blessing and return'd Thanks, though
there was the chaplain of the Ship, and another Minister
on board. Governour has a very large Wigg. Drink
Healths, About one and Twenty Guns fired at our leav-

---

[1] Palfrey, IV. 247, says that Povey was probably a brother of the Secre-
tary to the Board of Trade. He was, when now appointed, captain in the
Queen's own regiment of footguards, and was selected without notifying the
Board of Trade. He returned to England in 1705. — Eds.

[2] George Keith had been a minister among the Friends, but had conformed to the Church of England. — Eds.

[3] We leave to future commentators the explanation of this reference to
Helen. Possibly Sewall foresaw in Keith the cause of ecclesiastical discords
in the future. — Eds.

ing the Centurion; and Cheers, then Capt Scot and another Ship fired. Castle fired many Guns; Landed at Scarlet's Wharf, where the Council and Regiment waited for us; just before came at the North-Meetinghouse Clock struck five. Was the Troop of Guards, and Col. Paige's Troop. March'd to the Townhouse. There before the Court; Ministers, and as many else as could crowd in, the Governour's and Lt Gov^{rs}. Comissions were published; they took their Oaths laying their hands on the Bible, and after Kissing it. Had a large Treat. Just about dark Troops Guarded the Govr to Roxbury. He rode in Major Hobby's Coach Drawn with six Horses richly harnessed. By mistake, my coachman stayed in the yard, and so Joseph and I went alone. Foot gave 3 very good Volleys after the publication of the Comissions, and were dismiss'd. Mr. Mather crav'd a Blessing and Mr. Cotton Mather Return'd Thanks.

June 12. as Governour came to Town, he alighted and call'd at my House, Thank'd me for my Kindness to his family. I was much indispos'd by my Throat being sore, and I feverish.

June. 13. Ships Sail.

June. 28. Govr partakes of the Lords Super at Roxbury: In the Afternoon goes to Boston to hear Mr. Myles, who inveighed vehemently against Scism. June. 29. Refused to let us give our Yes and No in Papers. June, 30. War is proclaim'd. Address sign'd a 2^d time, which I again declined. New Justices are much talk'd of.

Satterday, July, 4. It is known in Town that the Lt Governour has his Comission for Captain of the Castle; and Charles Hobby, for Colonel of Boston Regiment. July, 6. Col. Hutchinson, by order, delivers the Castle to the Lt Govr. In the Afternoon Paul Dudley esqr.[1] is Apointed the Queen's Attorney. Judges of Middle-

---

[1] Son of the Governor. — EDS.

sex and Suffolk sworn. And Justices of Suffolk (Mr. Sergeant, Hutchinson, Belcher Swear Not.) Lt Govr laying his Hand on, and kissing the Bible. Council is adjourn'd to Wednesday. July, 9. Waited on the Govr to Marblehead, to Salem. Were Treated at Sharp's. July. 10. Went to Ipswich, in the Rain part of the Way. Troop met us. I and Mr. White lodg'd at Mr. Rogers's, as had done at Son Hirst's the night before. July 11. about 10. Govr sets out for Newbury, and I for Boston ; Serene, windy day. Came with B. Marston and Wakefield to Phillips's. Dined there with Capt Winthrop, his lady, Madam Wainwright, Mrs. Belcher of Newbury. Little Colman ; Mrs. Añe Winthrop Lyes in there. Capt Adam Winthrop accompanied me home. Find all well. *Laus Deo.* July, 14. 1702. A man is killed on board her Majesty's Ship the Swift, by a Gun from the Castle. July, 15. Goe to Dedham Lecture, come home with Maj^r Genl and his Son and Daughter from Coñecticut.

July. 17. Visit Madam Dudley : Sup with her, cous. Dumer and wife, daughter, Col. Townsend, Bromfield and wife, and Kate Dudley.

July 20. Sam. visits Mrs. Rebecka Dudley.

July, 21. Mr. Borland's House, the Raising of it is begun. July, 20. Mr. Paul Dudley dined with us. I ask'd him if he had any service for Sam., to Roxbury : He told me he would be welcom there. July, 22. I went with the Major Genl Winthrop to the Lieut Govr At our privat Meeting I read the first sermon of Mr. Flavel's Fountain of Life.

July, 24. 1702. When I had read to Mrs. Mary Rock the 2^d half of Dr. Sibbs's 3^d Sermon [1] Glance of Heaven, In

---

[1] Dr. Richard Sibbes, an eminent Puritan divine, became, in 1618, preacher to the Society of Gray's Inn; and, in 1628, Master of Catherine Hall, Cambridge. "From the year 1630 onwards for twenty years or so, no writings in practical theology seem to have been so much read among the

discourse about her father and Mother, She told me her Mother had not been with child in eight years ½. Was very fearfull about coming to N.-E. but at last had a day of Prayer, many Ministers: and she resolv'd to follow their advice, come what would. And about 12-moneths after her arrival here, she had this daughter viz. 7^r 1633. which was her last.[1] July, 30. I, my wife, Sam. Hannah visit Madam Dudley, Mrs. Rebekah to whom Sam. gives a Psalm-Booke. Augt 4. 1702. Govr Dudley invites me and my wife to Din̄er and Lecture, Sends his Coach for us; Mr. Whiting and his cousin Foxcroft dine there, Mrs. Willard. Mr. Walter preach'd a solid Sermon from the days of Darkness. Exhorted to prepare for death.

Augt. 8. 1702. My dear sister Moodey dies a little before sun-rise. I and cous. Dum̄er dine at Roxbury.

Augt. 9. I put up a Note. Augt. 10. I goe to Winnisimet and there meet Bro^r Goe with him to Salem: lodge at Son Hirst's. Augt 11. Set out from Salem as the School-Bell rung. Baited at Crompton's. Note. at Wenham pond Reproved David Simons for being naked about his Flax; threatened to Fine him. He submitted.

When came to Rowley, our Friends were gone. Got to the Falls about Noon. Two or three hours after, the Funeral was, very hot sunshine. Bearers, Woodman, Capt. Greenlef, Dea., Wm Noyes, Jno Smith, Jon^a Wheeler, Nathan^l Coffin. Many Newbury people there though so buisy a time; Col. Pierce, Major Noyes, Davison, Tristram Coffin, Mr. Tap̄an, father and Son, Mr. Payson of Rowley, (though muffed) Mr. Hale their Minister, Cousin Dum̄er and family, Mr. Bennet, Bradstreet. About a mile or more to

---

pious English middle classes as those of Sibbes." His portrait is in Middleton's "Evangelical Biography." — Eds.

[1] This seems to be the second wife of Joseph Rock, one of the founders of the Old South Church. She died Sept. 13, 1713, in her eighty-first year. The reference to her parents may enable genealogists to trace her pedigree. — Eds.

the Burying place. Bro^r Moodey led his Mother, Sam,
his Sister Mary; then Dorothy and Mehetabel went together (Sarah was so overpowered with Grief that she
went to Town and was not at the Funeral.) I led Sister
Gerrish; Bro^r, Sister Short, —— Sister Northend. Aunt
Northend was there. Bro^r Tap̄an, Sister Sewall and her
son John; Jacob and Joe Tap̄an and many cousins: Capt
Boynton.

Our dear sister Mehetabel is the first buryed in this
new Burying place, a Barly-earish, pure Sand, just behind
the Meetinghouse. Bro^r went home im̄ediately. I went
back to the House, lodg'd there all night with Bro^r
Moodey. Gave Wheelers wife a piece of $\frac{8}{8}$ to buy her a
pair Shoes. Gave cousin Lydia a piece of $\frac{8}{8}$. Augt. 12.
pray'd with them and sung the 146 Psalm. Went to Jn°
Smith's and took the Acknowledgment of the Deed for
the Land of the Meeting-house and Burying place. Rid
with Mr. Woodman and Smith to Andover, which is a
good In-land Town, and of a good Prospect. Some
warned us not to goe to the ordinary, because Mr. Peters
was dangerously sick of the Bloody Flux: So went to
Mr. Woodman's Daughters, and there din'd on Pork and
Beans: Afterward had Fowls rosted and dress'd very
well. Right conducts me to Wooburn through the Land
of Nod.[1] This is the first time I have seen it. Got late
to Fowl's at Wooburn: Sick there, which made me uneasy. Augt. 13. Visit Mr. Fox, view the Hop-yards,
come home, very hot. Met Mr Converse, the Father,
and discours'd him under a Shady Tree. Wont give his
Grand-children till after his death for fear of giving

---

[1] "The Land of Nod" is fully explained in Sewall's "History of
Woburn," pp. 540–43. See also Vol. I. pp. 190, 191. It consisted of three
thousand acres of land in Wilmington, and was owned by Charlestown men.
Francis Willoughby bought enough shares to own eleven hundred acres, and
Lawrence Hammond, who married his widow, sold them, in 1683, to John
Hull. Thence, of course, Sewall gained the ownership. Charlestown, in 1704,
claimed the land, and contested Sewall's right, but ineffectually. — EDS.

offence.   Express'd his Grief that Govr Dudley put men
in place that were not good.   Call'd at Mr. Woodbridges
and drank a Glass of very good Beer.   Told him he had
got so pleasant a situation he must not remove till he
went to heaven.   Got home in Lecture-time.   After Lecture Council sits.   Doe somthing about Judges of Probat.
Adjourn.   Augt. 14.   Nominate Col. Townsend for Inferior Court, Suffolke ;   Col. Hathorne for Superiour, Council advise because new : said would always do so.   Adj :
till Satterday.   Note.   I said Nomination of Hathorne
pleas'd me   I gave my voice for him in '92., when this
Court was first erected :   And County of Essex had
thought themselves postpon'd because no Judge of the
Court out of their County.   Govr said that was one Consideration made him name him.

Satterday, Augt 15. p.m.   Govr brings home Sam.,
then takes me into the Calash to the Townhouse.   Col.
Hathorne and Townsend chosen :   Govr delivers him his
Comission, then me and Maj^r Walley.   Said would never
insert himself any way to influence any proceeding before ;
which has many times done with great Vehemency ; ex-
horting us to doe Justice.   Addington, Hathorne, Sewall,
Walley sent for Mr. Elisha Cooke jun^r : constituted him
our Clerk, and gave him the Oaths.   So now the Superior
Court and Inferior Court Suffolk are both open'd this
day ;   which is a considerable celebration of my son
Joseph's Birth-day.   The Lord cause his face to shine
on us !

See June, 7. 1700.

Augt 19. 1702.   I give Mr. Joseph Prout, the Town
Clerk, the names of my Son and Mrs. Rebekah Dudley to
enter their Purpose of Marriage.

Augt 20.   Williams publishes them.   Mr. Leverett is
Sworn after Lecture Judge of the Superior Court.

Augt 21.   I gave Madam Cooke a Ring, cost 19s of
Cous. Dumer, in Remembrance of my dear Sister Moodey,

whom Mr. Cooke visited in May last. Madam Cooke said
had got rid of Mr. Cooke. I answer'd, we should much
want his Caution, Discretion, and Constancy. Was very
thankfull for the present I made her Husband in the
Ring. Walter Negro has his Thigh cut off; viz. his Legg
above the knee.

Satterday, 7ʳ 5. I set out for Dedham about 3. p.m̄.
to shorten my Bristol Journey. Got thither just about
Sun-set. Lodg'd at Fishers. 7ʳ 7ᵗʰ About ¼ after 7. m.
Mr. Leverett, Capt Saunders, and I set out (Amos Gates
waits on me); set forward. Got to Rehoboth when the
Sun was ¾ of an hour high. Lodg'd at the Bear. Rose
about 2. past midnight, were on Horseback by 5 because
of the Likelihood of Rain. Had a very comfortable journey. Got to our Quarters at Osburns before 8 mane.
Govʳ was gon over to Narraganset. All the Justices
there : Mr. Isaac Addington, the Chief Justice, said had
been no court open'd in the Queens Reign : so his commission was read, then mine, then Walleys, then Hathorn's then Leverett's. Court Treated Govʳ, Lᵗ Govʳ,
Gentlemen, Council &c. at Osburn's : cost us 15s apiece.
Horses and Servants were paid for by the Governours
Steward.

7ʳ 9. Col. Byfield Treats at Osburn's.

Septʳ 10. Court were of Opinion that Adam's Freedom could not be Tryed by Mr. Saffins complaint, and
Adam being kept from the court by the Small Pocks, No
proceedings at all could be had thereupon.

Mr. Mackentash, who bought Col. Byfields Farm at the
Mount, makes a noble Treat at Major Church's which is
his hired house. Got to Rehoboth by dark; Mr. Leverett and I Lodged at Mr. Greenwood's; Col. Hathorn and
Sam. at Mr. Smith's.

7ʳ 11ᵗʰ Went to Billinges in the Cart-way; Had a
very good Diñer, Venison &c. Got home in good time.
Capt Williams with his Red-Coats met us between Ded-

ham and the Turning to Fowl-Meadow. Capt Belchar and sundry Boston Gentlemen met us at Dedham. Note. Wednesday, at Osburn's, about Break-a-day, I heard one riding as I lay awake. (Mrs. Sparhawk having miscarried, I lodg'd there.) Thought I, I fear there may be some bad News from Boston. The man knock'd, and when he could make any hear, he·ask'd if Capt. —— were there: I took it he said me. They answer'd yes. He said must come away presently: for his daughter was very bad. Then I said to my self, I must undertake a sorrowfull Journey, as from Salem to Boston, upon the advice of my Still-born son: But God dismiss'd me from the burden of that sorrowfull Surprise, having laid it on Capt Brown of Swansey. We saw the Funeral as went over the Ferry on Thorsday.

7ʳ 13. Lords-Day, Mr. Bradstreet baptiseth Simon, the Jew, at Charlestown, a young man whom he was Instrumental to convert.

Septʳ 15. Mr. Nehemiah Walter marries Mr. Samˡ Sewall and Mrs. Rebekah Dudley, in the Dining Room Chamber about 8 aclock. Mr. Willard concluded with prayer, Sung the last part of the 103 Psalm. Mr. Tho. Dudley reading and setting of it out of my Turkey-Leather Psalm book. Present Govʳ, Lady, family (all save. Mr. Paul, who was call'd away just then with the news of Capt. Larimore's prises, Brothers Letter of it the Govʳ read to us). I and my family, all save Betty and Judith. Mr. Willard and wife, Mr. Lynde and wife, Mr. Jnᵒ White, Mrs. Mary Hubbard. Got home about 11 aclock.

Thorsday, Octʳ 1. 1702. The Govʳ and Council agree that Thorsday Octʳ 22. be a Fast-Day. Governour moved that it might be Friday, saying, Let us be English-men. I spake against making any distinction in the Days of the week; Desired the same Day of the Week might be for Fasts and Thanksgiving. Boston and Ipswich Lecture Led us to Thorsday. Our Brethren at Connecticut had

Wednesday; which we aplauded. Governour, it seems, told the Secretary, He himself would draw up the Order, which he did at Cousin Dumers by Candle-Light. Some of the Council were there, but the Gov did not ask their voice. I suggested to Maj Gen that the Drought might be mention'd; Mr. Winthrop spake, but the Gov refused: I think at our house where the Gov Dined with Mr. Increase Mather, and Mr. Tim Woodbridge; the Gov said was a better Harvest than had been these Twenty years.

Oct 6. 1702. Rode with the Gov to Cambridge, saw his field on the Neck, and Hicks &c. building a large sluice to the Dam. Drove a Pin. Din'd with Mr. Foxcroft; only us three at Table. Mr. Brattle came to us and smoked a pipe. As came home, call'd at Mrs. Clark's, and bespake a Bed for my self during the sitting of the Gen Court, in case I came not home. She granted it. As came home saw Bastion and the Negro digging the Drain. Brought home my Daughter Hirst in the Governour's Chariot, Mr. Hirst went to Salem.

Tuesday, 8 13. Went with the Gov to Hogg Island, son and daughter Sewall, Mrs. Anne, Mrs. Mary Dudley there, Tho. Dudley, Capt. Southack, Mr. Paul Dudley, Mr. Tho. Richards, Col. Townsend, Mr. Brattle, Col. Povey the Lieut Gov, Cous. Jer. Dumer had a good Treat there. I was sorry Mr. Addington and Mr. Pemberton, and Mr. Roberts were not there, and therefore Returning Thanks closed thus; Bring us to thy Entertainment in Heaven, where not one of the Company shall be wanting. Son Hirst got to the House just as were coming away, Gave him a good Plate to Winisimet, where he with Col. Paige and Chris. Taylor eat it.

8 14th I carry my Daughter Hirst in the Hackney Coach (Hañah and Mary in Company) to the Salutation, ferry over, and her Husband carryes her to Salem. Cambridge Court, 8 15, 1702. Mr. Secretary, Mr. Cooke,

El^m Hutchinson and I ride in my coach to Roxbury in Lecture Time, Goe with the Govr about 2 p.m̄. Dine; into the College yard. Goe up into Library, one Deputy is sworn. Govr make a speech to the Council and Assembly about his visiting the Eastern parts, building Pem̄aquid Fort, settling Salaries for Govr, Judges &c., building the Govr a House. Came home in the Coach as went out. Young Peleg Sanford, Major Walley's Prentice, was buried this day at Boston. Mr. Cotton Mather preached the Lecture there.

Monday, Octr 26. 1702. Waited on the Govr to Wooburn, dined there: From thence to Billericay, Visited languishing Mr. Saml Whiting, I gave him 2 Balls of Chockalett and a pound Figgs, which very kindly accepted. Saw the Company in Arms led by Capt. Tomson. Went to Chelmsford, by that time got there twas almost dark. Saw Capt. Bowles and his Company; Gave a Volley and Huzza's. Sup'd at Mr. Clark's; I and Col. Pierce in his study. Some went on to Dunstable by Moonshine. Octr 27. Went to Dunstable in the Rain, Din'd and lodg'd at Col. Tyng's. Saw and drunk of Merrimack. No Indians come in. Octr 28. Went to Groton, saw Capt. Prescot and his company in Arms. (Govr had sent to them from Dunstable that would visit them). Lancaster is about 12 Miles Southward from Groton. Concord is 16 Miles $\frac{3}{4}$ and Ten-Rod from Groton. Got thither about 2. Horses and Men almost tired by our very hard riding. Dine at Capt. Prescot's. Lodge at Mr. Estabrooks with Col. Foxcroft. Their Foot Company, and Troop, in Arms, Seem'd to be numerous and well apointed.

Octr 29. Breakfast at Capt. Minott's, Set out for Cambridge. In Company Col. Pierce, Thomas, Partrigge, Foxcroft, Capt. Cutler, son Sewall, young Mr. Tyng. At Mr. Hancocks Mr. Secretary, Leverett met us. Mr. Dyer, Col. Byfield; at Russel's Mr. Dudley. There the Calash met the Govr and weary Major Brenton rid in it with the

Govr to the Town: Col. Hobbey rid his Horse. Dined with the Govr at Mr. Leveretts, Madam Leverett the Grandmother. Went home with Col. Hutchinson, Walley, Foster. Col. Foster invited us to drink at his house. Found all well, and David Sinclair rocking Judith; he came to our house after I was gon my Journey.

Novr 2. 1702. John Adams, a very good man, and John Drury, a desirable young man, dye of the small pocks.

Anthony Checkley dyed last week of the same disease.[1]

Novr 3. 1702. Capt. Tim^o Prout died last night, aged more than 80 years.

Mr. Chief Justice Addington opens the Court at Boston. Mr. Wadsworth prays. Mr. Sheriff Dyar officiats with his white Wand. Sits on the Bench for want of a Seat. Col. Hutchinson, Hobby, Mr. Wadsworth dine with us. Mr. Palmer dines with us of's own accord, and no other Justice peace except Mr. Attorney.

Novr 9. 1702. Go to Salem with Cousin Jane. Dine at Lt Lewes's, where meet Bro^r Sewall, Mr. Dudley comes in also: Ride in company with them to Salem. Lodge at Son Hirst's.

Novr 10. Mr. Leverett comes from Cambridge; open the Court in the Meetinghouse, because the Townhouse is very near a house that has the Small Pocks; so that people are afraid to goe there; and Sharp is not willing to let us have his chamber. Sat in the Deacon's seat, Col. Hathorne on my Right Hand, and Mr. Leverett on my Left. After the Reading of the Queen's Proclamation, I

---

[1] This was, of course, Anthony Checkley, Attorney-General of the Province, though Savage puts his death in 1708. All other authorities seem to agree on 1702. His daughter Hannah married Captain John Adams, of Boston, who, by a first wife, was grandfather of the patriot, Samuel Adams. This Captain John Adams is said (Register, VII. 41) to have died intestate before Jan. 20, 1712. He *may* have been the John Adams mentioned in our text, or the one who died *may* have been his son John, born in 1687, of whom we hear nothing. — EDS.

spake to the Grand-Jury, having written it down before-
hand in my Daughters chamber.

Novr 13. 1702. Visit Mr. Higginson now in his 87th
year. Dine at son Hirst's; Mr. Dudley, and cousin Elsa
Hirst there. Set forward in our way home; viz. Mr. Leverett and Dudley; visit Mr. Kitchen by the way, who
makes us very welcom. Rain takes us before get to the
Sluice. I had no Boots, and the Southerly wind much
disturbed my Cloak: so I lodg'd at Lewes's: Mr. Leverett and Dudley stood on.

Novr 14. 1702. Rid to Wiñisimmet and so home, very
pleasant day. Find all well. *Laus Deo.*

xr. 8. 1702. p.m. writt to Mr. R^d Henchman clause of
my Speech to the Grand-jury, Novr 10. at Salem, referring to the Lord's-Day. Epitaph of my Grand-Daughter. Sence of Rev. 14. 13. Write *Lib. Cop. Phœnom.*
Enclos'd the Gazett that had the Queens Proclamation
against Profaneness.

Novr 30. Rid to Salem to visit my Daughter Hirst,
who was brought to bed of a dead child Novr 28.

From Lewis's in company of Mr. Lyde. Got thither
about 2 hours by Sun. Daughter very glad to see me.
xr. 1. My Daughter being threatened with the headache,
I send Chapman to Cambridge to Dr. Oliver for a Plaister: He follow'd the Dr. to Boston, and brought word of
Mrs. Mathers death. Laid on a Plaister; Daughter grows
better: but then again had an ill turn; yet grew fine and
well agen by Satterday and cheerfully dismiss'd me. Had
a very comfortable Journey home. Son Hirst brought me
going to the Butts. At Lewis's fell in with Maj^r Epes,
Major Wainright and Mr. Fitch, going to Ipswich. Maj^r
Wainwright tells me of the death of Mr. Brakenbury.

xr. 8. Mr. Robt Gibbs dies, one of our Select men, a
very good man and much Lamented; died suddenly of
the Small Pocks. His death, and the death of Jno Adams,
the Master, Isaac Loring, and Peybody, is a great stroke

to our church and congregation. The Lord vouchsafe to dwell with us, and Not break up Housekeeping among us! Xr. 9. Mr. Gibbs buryed.

I first heard of Mr. Calamy's History.[1]

xr. 16. I went out early with David to carry two of Mr. Mathers History[2] to my Bro^r to Charlestown: Heard the church [Kings Chapel] Bell ring for Capt. Crofts. He dyed last night.

xr. 19. Is buried in the New burying place in Capt. Hamilton's Tomb. Corps was first had into the church and a Funeral Sermon preach'd. For Debauchery and Irreligion he was one of the vilest Men that has set foot in Boston. Tis said he refused to have any Minister call'd to pray with him during his Sickness, which was above a fortnight.

xr. 23. I go to Roxbury, dine with my Daughter Sewall, Mr. Dudley &c in their Chamber, where their Stove is.

Sixth-day, Decr 25. Govr and Lt Govr partake of the Lords Super; the undersheriff Hawksworth's child was baptised.

Decr 24. Govr din'd at our house, but went not to Lecture: it was very cold: Decr 17. din'd at Col. Hobbies, but went not to Lecture; was at both places at least in part of Lecture time.

xr. 26. Son Sewall comes to Town, dines with us. Grows ill, and we keep him all night.

---

[1] This may refer to the younger Calamy's Abridgement of Mr. Baxter's History of his Life and Times, which was published in 1702. — EDS.

[2] The famous "Magnalia." Cotton Mather records in his Diary (see Proceedings of Massachusetts Historical Society for December, 1862) the birth-pangs by which his folio volume was ushered into life. Under date of Oct. 30, 1702, he writes: "Yesterday I first saw my 'Church History' since the publication of it. A gentleman arrived here from Newcastle, in England, that had bought it there." The author makes the event the occasion for a day "for Solemn Thanksgiving unto God for his watchful and gracious providence over that work."

Doubtless Sewall availed himself of the earliest importation of copies. Its price in London was one pound. — EDS.

xr. 25.   Jonathan Stoddard 7 years and 8 months old:
Subael Dumer 10 years and 8 months old, were buried.

Dec.ʳ 30. 1702.   I was weigh'd in Col. Byfield's Scales:
weight One Hundred One Half One Quarter wanting 3
pounds, i.e. 193 pounds Net.   Col. Byfield weighed Sixty
three pounds more than I: had only my close coat on.
The Lord add, or take away from this our corporeal
weight, so as shall be most advantagious for our Spiritual
Growth.   July 31. 1721 [in Margin].   I weighed 228 £
p̄ cous. Sam¹ Sewall's Scales.

Friday, Jan.ʸ 8. 170⅔   Between 5. and 6. m.   Mr. Edward Turfrey dyes of the Small Pocks; was dying all
night in a mañer, having strong Agonies.   He was a person of great Abilities.   His death is a great Loss to the
Town and Province: but more especially to Mr. Addington, to whom Mr. Turfrey was extraordinarily Serviceable,
having liv'd with him above Ten years.   If real Worth
and Serviceableness and Youth wont give a discharge in
this warfare, what shall?   He is universally Lamented.

Lords-day, Jan.ʸ 17. 170⅔   L.ᵗ Gov.ʳ calls a Council, about
5 in the even.   Shews us his Intelligence from Eastham
of 3 Sloops and a whale bote or 2, Taken at Cape Cod by
a French Sloop last Friday.   Order Capt. Southack to take
up a Sloop and endeavour to come up with them.   Send
away an Express to the Gov.ʳ   Jan.ʸ 18.   Last night Capt.
Hunt's Son went to bed well, and next morn not rising at
his usual hour, his Mistress sent to see what was the matter, and he was found stark dead.   Just now about Ebenezer Bird, a young man of Dorchester, is kill'd by a fall from
a Horse.   Jan.ʸ 24. 170⅔   Mr. Simon Willards Twins, Samuel and Abigail, were baptised: and Samuel Valentine,
Mr. Lynde's Grandson, and Richard.   Very cold Day.

Jan.ʸ 26. 170⅔   Mr. Secretary, Major Walley, and Sewall, went to Charlestown to hold Court.   Had good going
over the Ferry, notwithstanding the cold wether we have
had.   Met Mr. Leverett there.   Col. Hathorn is not well

and stays at home. Chief Justice prays at Opening of the Court; Mr. Bradstreet not being well. Mr. Stoddard's Son dyed last night.

Jany 27. 170¾ Mr. Tim.° Woodbridge Prays at opening of the Court at Charlestown: but dines not with us. Jany 28. 170¾ The Chief Justice prays at the opening of the Court. Daughter Hirst comes to Charlestown.

Jany 29. Joseph goes with the Hakney coach and brings his Sister Hirst to Boston. Mr. Secretary and I visit the Govr and congratulate his safe Return.

Feb^r 1. I visit my sick Brother at Salem, find him very ill. Monday Night worse.

Feb^r 3. Had a good night, and I return home. Note, I carried the News to Salem that was brought by Andrew Wilson from Oporto, Eight weeks, of the extraordinary success of our Fleet against the Flota in the River of Vigo; which we first heard of in part by way of Cork.[1] Read it to Bro. Mr. —— Burchsted, a German Doctor, administers to my Brother. Jonathan gives me this Account of Brothers children.

Salem, Feb^r 3. 170¾. The children of Major Stephen Sewall are, Margaret, Samuel, Susaña, Jonathā, Jane, Mehetabel, Mitchel, Henry and Stephen.

Feb^r 5th 170¾ Col. Elisha Hutchinson, Col. Penn Townsend, Capt. Andrew Belcher, and Samuel Sewall rid to Roxbury in the Hackney coach; Capt. Jeremiah Dumer, Mr. Edward Bromfield on horseback: Went on purpose to speak to the Governour against having Illuminations, especially in the Town house; That so the profanation of the Sabbath might be prevented. I said twould be most

---

[1] The reference is to a great success gained Oct. 22, 1702, by an English and Dutch force under the Duke of Ormond, and an English fleet under Sir George Rooke. The Spanish galleons, with a great treasure on board, had taken refuge in Vigo bay. The English attack was entirely successful; and, though much of the treasure was thrown overboard, a great booty was captured. (Stanhope's Queen Anne, I. 67.) — EDS.

for the Honor of God; and that would be most for the
Honor and Safety of Queen Anne. Governour said twould
be hard for him to forbid it, considering how good the
Queen was, what successes God had given her. I answered, It could not be introduced into the Town-house
without his Excellency's Order, for under his Excellency
the Government of the Town was (partly) comitted to us.
Govr answer'd not a word. Others urged our Law, the
Grief of Good People, his best Friends. And I think all
was said between us, that could be said. Got well home
about 9 at night, and had a very comfortable Journey,
and sufficient Light Notwithstanding the Fogg, and absence of the very New Moon.

Feb^r 6. between 8 and 9. m. The Bells begin to Ring,
to celebrate Queen Anne's Birth-Day, being the last of
the Week.

Col. John Pynchon died Jany 17. 170⅔, about Sun-Rise,
as Mr. Holyoke tells me Sabbath-Day. Ebenezer Franklin of the South Church, a male-Infant of 16 months old,
was drown'd in a Tub of Suds, Feb^r 5. 170⅔.[1]

Feb^r 11th 170⅔ The Govr under his hand remits the
Fines of several sentenced to pay 5s apiece for drinking
at Mrs. Monk's on Satterday night last about 9 aclock.
Had warn'd Mrs. Monk an hour before. Said Monk also
remitted her 25s, and the writing given to the Sheriff to
Notifie Col. Townsend and Mr. Bromfield.

Feb^r 12. 170⅔. Carry Daughter Hirst to Salem in Mr.
Austin's Calash. Visit Bro^r, Col. Hathorne. Bro^r Hirst
and sister and daughter sup with us. Saw not Mr. Noyes,
but writ to him.

Feb^r 13. Return home very comfortably, notwithstanding much of the way was bad. Had like to have overset
two or 3 times, but God upheld me. When came home,

---

[1] This child, born Sept. 20, 1701, was an elder brother of Benjamin
Franklin. — EDS.

ask'd the reason of the Gates being open, and am told Mr. Josiah Willard had the Small Pocks at Cambridge; our coach went to fetch him to Town: but he fainted and could not come.

Tuesday, Feb. 16. 170⅔ 2. p.m̄. Town-Meeting at Boston to chuse Representatives. Mr. Colman pray'd. Chose S. Sewall Moderator, Voters 459. Sam¹ Legg Esqr. 451. Capt. Sam¹ Checkley 446. Mr. Tho. Oakes, 440. Capt. Ephraim Savage 435. This was the most unanimous Election that I remember to have seen in Boston, and the most Voters.

Febr. 22. Mrs. Willard and several of her children had like to have been cast away coming from Cambridge by Water, wind was so very high; put ashore at last on Muddy-River Marsh: Got to the Govʳˢ by that time twas dark. This morning as I was praying alone, I was much affected to think how concern'd and inquisitive I was in my Journeying about my Way; whether I was in the right or no; and yet not so constantly and effectually inquisitive about my Way to Heaven, although I was equally hastening to my Journey's End; whether in the right or wrong way. May He who is the Way, the Truth, and the Life, bring me into and always keep me in the right Way!

Lords-Day, Febr. 28. 170⅔ Mr. Jabez Fox dies of the Small Pox in the forenoon.[1]

Lords-Day, March. 7. 170⅔ Nurse Randal is taken with an Ague in her Brest, which much indisposes her: Whereupon my wife begins to wean Judith though it be a few days before we intended. The wether is grown cold.

March, 16. 170⅔ Though all things look horribly win-

---

[1] The Rev. Jabez Fox, of Woburn, was connected by marriage with Sewall, his wife being Judith Reyner, sister of the Rev. John Reyner, Jr., who married Judith Quincy. See Vol. I. Introd. p. xxiii. Mrs. Fox married secondly Colonel Jonathan Tyng, and died June 5, 1756, in her ninety-ninth year. — EDS.

terly by reason of a great storm of Snow, hardly yet over, and much on the Ground : yet the Robbins cheerfully utter their Notes this morn. So should we patiently and cheerfully sing the Praises of God, and hope in his Mercys, though Storm'd by the last efforts of Antichrist.

March, 20th. A Message is sent in to desire the House might attend with an Answer of the Gov^{rs} Speech; which the Speaker, Maj^r Converse, Read. Then a Message sent do desire it might be printed, which the Govr readily assented to. Only afterward desired to read it first.

March 22. Judith is very well weaned, and by a late addition can now shew eight Teeth. Little Jane, Bastian's daughter, died last night 2 hours after midnight. God is pleased to dispense himself variously. Our little daughter gave us very little Exercise after 3 or 4 nights. Then her cousin Mary Moodey could receive her without any noise.

March, 22. Mr. Banister and I Lotted our Fence on Cotton-Hill : He took E, which was prick'd with a pin on a Label of paper for East-End ; and W. for West end was left in my hand for me. He chose to put it to Lot. We saw Pits sail up and fired, laden with Salt.

March, 27. 1703. Have not yet given Sermons to Lothrop, Perce, Thomas, Thacher, Appleton, Hamond.

March, 29. Set out for Plimouth with Major Walley, and Mr. Leverett; Get thither a little before night. The souldiers gave us a Volley, and those on board Huzzas, at our entrance into Town ; kept at Rickets.

Ap. 1. went into Meetinghouse.[1] Note. March *ult.* Mr. Russel preach'd the Lecture.

Ap. 2. Came home, dined at Cushings. I stay'd and Lodg'd at Mr. Torrey's. He told me of Bridgewater Troubles as to Mr. Brett. Ap. 3. came home alone, went with Joseph Hunt, and viewed part of the 300 Acres.

---

[1] Frequent similar entries in the Journal refer to Sewall's private religious exercises when away from home. — EDS.

Found all well at home. Was surprised to find a Letter giving account of the Death of the Rever'd Mr. Israel Chauncy of a Fever and Convulsions at Stratford. March, 14. 170⅞ 8 or 9 m. Had not recᵈ my Letter. But am now thank'd for it by his son Charles.

April, 12. 1703. I set out with my son S. and Daniel Allen; meet with Sherman at Spring's, proceed to Sawen's, there bait, thence to Capt. Mosses, where we dine, thence to Kibbee's, look upon the Line next Mr. Lynde, and assert my Right; Thomas Holbrook, the Father, and Capt. Moss offering to take their Oaths to confirm my Bounds.

Tuesday Apr. 13. Mr. Sherman lays out my Farm of 150 Acres, beginning at Mr. Lynde's and extending to Winthrop's Pond.[1] Tho. Holbrook, sent Moss and Joseph Twitchel with us approving what was done, helping to carry the Chain and lay Stones for Bound-Marks.

Wednesday, Apr. 14. Renew'd the Bounds of the Farm Moses Adams lives on. Tho. Holbrook, Sergeant Moss, and Samˡ Moss with us, also Capt Moss, Sawen, Deacon Larned &c.

Thorsday Apr. 15. I heard Mr. Sherman had run a Line within mine at Kibbee's; I got Deacon Moss, Tho. Holbrook, Ebenezʳ Leland to go with me: Fairbank was also there. Went to my Bounds, asserted them, in the presence of Mr. Lynde's Tenants whom I sent for, then ordered Kibbe to pull up the Stakes. Told Mr. Lynde's Tenants what my Bounds were, and that within them was my Land; forwarn'd them of coming there to set any Stakes, or cut any Wood. This hinder'd my coming home one day. Sup'd at Cous Gookin's with Pickerill —

---

[1] This farm was situated in the present town of Holliston, formerly Bogistow. Morse, in his "History of Sherborne and Holliston," p. 325, says that John Hull owned a farm here which was divided among Sewall's children. In 1728 (History, p. 326), the Sewalls gave eleven acres of land for the use of the first minister to be settled there. — EDS.

Friday, Apr. 16.   My son and I come home : Visit Mr. Hobart, who is glad to see us, Dine there, and then come with him by Tho. Stedman's ; where is a privat Meeting. Then ride to Bairstow's and gave Lion 2 Reals, he is stoning the Cellar ; saith he began the day before.   It seems my daughter Sewall had been there a little before.   Got home about 4 aclock, found all well, only Judith had fallen this day and hurt her forhead.   *Laus Deo.*

Town-Meeting to chuse Representatives, April, 27. 1703. 2 p. m.   Voters about 244.   Capt. Legg had 242.   Checkly, 240.   Oakes, 238.   Savage, 232.

Meeting was much less ; but Voters rather more unanimous than last time.   Feb. 16.   Mrs. Ann and Kate Dudley dined here to day.

Tuesday, May, 11th   set out for Newbury by Charlestown, with Sam Robins.   Din'd at Perkins's, Beverly : Got to Newbury about 1 h ½ by sun ; Lodg'd at Sister Gerrishes.

May, 12.   To Portsmouth with Mr. Leverett.

May. 13.   To Kittery ; after our getting thither it Rain'd sorely —

May, 14th   To Newbury, lodg'd at Bror Tapans.   15th at sister Gerrishes.   16. Heard Mr. Tappan preach.   17. Visited Mr. Tapan, Bror Shortt : when there was a great and sore Tempest of Thunder, Rain, Hail.   When over, ridd to Ipswich, lodg'd at Mr. Rogers.

18th   Held Court, Mr. Rogers prayed.   Mr. Hubbard, Col. Apleton, and Rogers dined with us.

19.   About an hour before sun-set rode to Salem with Col. Hathorne, Cook, Lynde —— 20. Visited Bror Hirst sick of the Gout : came homeward with Cousins Sam. and Margaret.   Fain to put in at Hart's and Shelter our selves from a vehement Tempest of Wind, Rain, Hail, Thunder. Got hom about 5. p.m.   Found all well through the wonderfull Goodness of God.   This day Mr. Stoddard comes to Town, being to preach the Election Sermon.   May, 21.

Companies are warned to attend on their Election Day. Note. May, 20.. Barth. Green's New Frame being cover'd but not enclosed, was blown down.

Election-Day, May, 26, 1703.

chosen

Wait Winthrop	P. Townsend
J. Russell.	J. Higginson
Negative Tho. Oakes	A. Belcher
E. Cooke	E. Bromfield
J. Hathorne	J. Thacher
E. Hutchinson	J. Walley
S. Sewall	J. Saffin, Neg.
I. Addington	J. Bradford, Neg.
W. Brown	E^m Hutchinson
J. Ph[illips]	J. Hamond
J. Corwin	B. Brown
J. Foster	J. Lynde
Negative, P. Sergeant	Sam! Partridge
D. Pierce	S. Hayman

Not finished till about 9 or 10 at night.

May 27. Govr sends in for the Deputies; in a speech shows his Resentment of their Election, One of the Massachusetts and three of Plimouth being changed : Saith he will expunge Five; viz. Elisha Cooke, Peter Sergeant, Tho. Oakes, John Saffin, John Bradford. Some poor; one Superañuated, Some might have served the Queen better than they did.

May 28. Some Papers being sent to the Deputies, they decline Receiving them or entering on other Business till the Council be fill'd. Send in a Bill that are ready to compleat the Election: consented. Capt. Hayman sworn, Chosen, Capt. Samuel Legg, Mr. Saml Appleton, Col. Ephraim Hunt, Mr. Nathan^l Pain, Mr. Isaac Winslow. Governour signs his Approbation: Capt. Legg is sent for in and sworn.[1]

---

[1] It will be noted that five members of the Council were rejected by the Governor, and five new ones chosen. See the vote in " Whitmore's Civil

Mr. Sam¹ Shrimpton, who dyed May 25. is now buried
May. 28. By reason of the great Rain, Col. Phillips,
Capt. Hayman, and I went not out of the Council Cham-
ber, at Noon : but din'd together on Bread and Cheese from
Monk's.

May 31. Col. Hunt comes to Town and is sworn of
the Council.

June, 1. 1703. Town-meeting is held in the old Meetinghouse because of the Gen! Assembly, 2. p.m. Voters
206. Elizur Holyoke 154: by which was chosen a Representative for Boston. Jn° Love Constable, only one
vote otherwise. Note. Col. Hobby had 45. votes for a
Representative. Mr. Cooke invited many of the Council
to drink with him. When came found a Treat of salmon,
Neat's Tongues, Lamb &c. 'Twas near Ten before got
home. Mr. Addington, Legg, Rusel, Phillips, Hayman,
Lynde, Byfield not there, only Mr. Corwin of Salem.

June, 8. Mr. Pain is sworn in the Afternoon, This day
there was much agitation about Nominating a Justice for
the Superʳ Court, Council pleaded, till there was a Vacancy they could not do it. If any place was vacant it
was that of the Chief Justice, and were ready to speak to
that. Govʳ would have a Justice Nam'd and consented to
in the first place; else said he should lose one of the
Court. Nothing was done. Mr. Taylor chosen Treasurer.
Court adjourned to the last of June 9 *mane*.

Adam is again imprison'd to be Tryed at Suffolk Sessions. Trial order'd by the Genˡ Assembly.

Superanuated Squier, wigg'd and powder'd with pretence,
Much beguiles the just Assembly by his lying Impudence.
None being by, his bold/sworn Attorneys push it on with might and main
By which means poor simple Adam sinks to slavery again.

List," p. 64, and the remarks in Palfrey, IV. 254, 255. This act of the
Governor was, of course, hostile to the Assembly, and the trivial and unjust
reasons assigned by him could not have had any soothing effect upon the
friends of the rejected Councillors. — Eds.

June, 9. 1703.   Gov: and L⁺ Gov: set out for Ipswich in order to goe and meet the Indian sachems.

June, 11ᵗʰ between 12 and 1. Mr. Bromfield is struck down by the Boom of a Sloop swinging upon the Dock; which took his Left shoulder Blade.   The Collar Bone on that side is dislocated or broken.   The Concussion causes great pain in his back, is fain to sit in a great Chair not being able at present to ly down; between 7 and 8, Even.

Friday, June, 18. 1703.   My sons House was Raised at Muddy-River; The day very comfortable because dry, cloudy, windy, cool.   I sent for Mr. Wigglesworth and his Wife from Deacon Barnard's in the Coach; to discourse with my Wife about her and Judith's Maladies.   After they were sent back, being late in the Afternoon, I went alone in the Hackney-Coach to Roxbury, took Mr. Walter with me.   By that Time got there, had just done their Work, and were going to Diñer in the new House.   Mr. Walter crav'd a Blessing, Return'd Thanks.   Many were there from Muddy-River, Dedham, Roxbury.   I drove a Pin before Dinner.   After Diñer sung the 127ᵗʰ Psal. and 8ᵗʰ v. 28ᵗʰ St. David's Tune, I set and read the Psalm. Brought home Madame Dudley and my Daughter.

Thorsday June, 24.   I am kept from Mr. C. Mather's Lecture by my swoln face.   Mr. Secretary visits me. June, 25. Mr. P. Dudley visits me.   Madam Eyre invites me to her Meeting, by her Daughter; but my Indisposition detains me at home.   Yet I grow much better.

June 27.   Goe to the publick Assembly and take no harm.   *Laus Deo.*

June 28. 1703.   I have my son Joseph to Cambridge in Austin's Calash, where he is examined by Mr. Jonathan Remington in presence of the President and Mr. Flynt. He Answer'd well to Mr. Remingtons Critical Examination—Mr. Willard gave him for his Theme.   *Omnis in*

Ascanio chari stat cura Parentis ; [1] And advised him and
3 others to be studious, saying, = Wigglesworth, Tuft,
Russel.

> *Qui Cupit optatam cursu pertingere metam*
> *Multa tulit fecitque puer, sudavit et alsit.* [2]

Second-day of the Week July 5ᵗʰ 1703. I had my son
to Cambridge again in Austin's Calash. Paid Andrew
Bordman his Cautionary Three pounds, in order to my
Son Joseph's being Admitted. Went to Mr. Flynt's Cham-
ber, where Col. Wainright's Son and others were upon
Examination. When that was doing, and over, Mr. Willard call'd for Joseph's Theme. Read it, gave it to Mr.
Flynt, Then in Mr. Flynt's Study, The President and
Fellows sign'd his Laws ; President said, your Son is now
one of us, and he is wellcom. I thanked him ; and took
Leave. Coming home I order'd Mr. Sheriff [3] to take up a
Scurvy post out of the middle of the High way, that had
been a Nusance for many years. Gave his Son a shilling
for his pains. Got home well. *Laus Deo.* Was pretty
much Rain at Charlestown ; yet we went almost quite
dry, being but a small Sprinkling where we were.

Com̄encment day July, 7ᵗʰ 1703. Mr. Secretary, Ma-
jor Walley, Major Brenton and I went by Charlestown to
the hether edge of Maldon, and so met the Govʳ in his
Return homeward from Casco-Bay. Note ; in the after-
noon Mr. Wells [4] of Almsbury, is made a Master of Art.
Mr. Belcher of Newbury Testified his Education under
Mr. Andros at Ipswich, that he was a good Latin and
Greek Scholar. Came to Charlestown in company with

---

[1] Virg. Æn. I. 646. — EDS.

[2] Hor. Ep. ad Pis. 412, 413; with variations. — EDS.

[3] Samuel Gookin was Sheriff of Middlesex, 1702–1715. — EDS.

[4] The Rev. Thomas Wells leads as the first on the now lengthened roll of
those whom Harvard College has in honor adopted among her Alumni, without having passed through her training. — EDS.

Mr. Thomson and Mr. Webster.   Mr. T. tells me his Unkle at Virginia is dead.

July, 8. p.m.   Mr. Winslow is sworn and takes his
place at the Board.   Bombazeen [an Indian Sachem]
comes to Town as an Express with Rumors of 15. Frenchmen landed near Pemaquid, and of a Frenchman of War.

July 10.   From New-York we hear of a ship arrived
there June 29; that came out with a great Fleet from
Plimouth May, 2.ᵈ in which were five ships bound for
New-England.

July 12 Bombazeen and his companion before the Council with Serjᵗ Bean.

Monday, July, 19. 1703 my daughter Mrs. Rebecka
Sewall is brought to Bed of a son, about six-a-clock in
the Afternoon.   My wife and daughter Hirst were there,
Madam Dudley, Hubbard, Roberts &c.   Mrs. Baker Midwife.   Mr. Winchcomb first told the Govᵣ of it, at the
Council Table, and then me.   Stephen brought the News
to Town.   I ride home with the Govᵣ and send the Hackney-Coach!   See my daughter and Grandson: Bring
home my wife, Madam Roberts, daughter Hirst.   July,
22.   Governour, A Gentleman sent from New-York, Mr.
Mackentosh, Mr. Dudley, Mr. Belchar, Dedham, Mr. Hirst
dine at our House.

July, 23.   Deputies after many days Toil, have at last
this day come off, and let fall that clause in the Act about
restraining the power of the Govᵣ and Council as to inci-
dental Charges, so as they might not exceed Thirty pounds.
Mr. Secretary obtain'd leave of the Govᵣ to make this
Minute of Council; viz. Whereas yesterday was apointed
for chusing of Officers, and was adjourned to this day, the
Secretary alleged that through decay of his health, he was
unable to sustain the place of Chief-Justice any longer,
pray'd to be dismiss'd and offered his Comission at the
Board; whereupon the Govᵣ said he would not expect
any further service from him at the present, and that he

with the Council would Endeavour to fill the Chair so soon as conveniently they might. This the substance.[1]

Mr. Addington much startled at the words *at present* and urg'd to have them left out: but the Governour did not yield to it. This was done in open Council, in the forenoon.

July, 24. 1703. Joseph takes leave of his Master and Scholars in a short Oration.

Bristol Business is Non-concurr'd by the Deputies.

Governour's note to me to instruct a Meeting of the Judges next Monday is in my Court Book.

Augt. 2 – 1703. It is said the Colours must be spread at the Castle every Lords Day in honour of it:

Yesterday was first practiced. If a ship come in on the Lord's day, Colours must be taken down. I am afraid the Lord's Day will fare none the better for this new pretended honor.

Monday, Aug.t 2. Thomas, the Governour's Coachman, having offended him, He sends him aboard Capt. Southacks in order to make him a Sentinel under Major March at Casco fort. I mov'd the Govr to Try him a little longer: but would not; said He might send any man a Souldier.

Ab.t 5 p.m. My Wife, Madam Willard, Daughters Hañah and Eliza — visit Daughter Sewall at Roxbury. Wednesday, Aug.t 4. I carried Mary to Mr. Wigglesworth's and left her there; to see if he could help her against her Sickness and Infirmity.

Augt. 6. I visited Mary as I promis'd her. Mr. Wigglesworth thinks her distemper is of a Convulsive nature.

Aug.t 5. Mr. Thomas Bridge preaches his first Lecture-Sermon from Hab. 3. 2.

---

[1] This minute is still on the Council records. But, though Addington thus obtained leave of absence, no changes were made until Feb. 19, 1707–8, when Wait Still Winthrop was made Chief Justice; and, on the following day, Jonathan Corwin was appointed Justice in place of John Leverett, who became President of Harvard College. — EDS.

Aug.ᵗ 7. 1703. News comes from N. York that my Lord Cornbury has rec'd his comissions, and that the Militia of Coñecticut and the Jersies is granted him.

From the Eastward, Fear of the French and Indians, some being seen.

Aug.ᵗ 10. 1703. I went to Roxbury and saw my daughter who is still in very great pain. Went and saw the Drean. Gov.ʳ Dudley tells me that Mr. Usher has got Partridge's place; that all Actions Tried here must be sent over to England; an account of them. Will have a Sessions in September. This day, Aug.ᵗ 10 — is a Corporation-Meeting at Cambridge; chuse Mr. Josiah Willard a Tutor: chuse Mr. Tho. and W.ᵐ Brattle into the Corporation, in stead of Mr. Allen and Mr. Walter, who have abdicated as they reckon.[1]

Aug.ᵗ 11. News comes of the Onset of the Enemy.

I went to Cambridge Aug.ᵗ 11. to make sure a study for Joseph in Mr. Remington's Chamber: came home with Mr. Torrey, call'd at the Gov.ʳˢ, where a Master that came by water from Black-point, gave account of the Fires kindled by the Indians in several places; brought a little youth that narrowly escaped the enemies hands.

Aug.ᵗ 12. at night, News comes from Wells that have buried 15. durst not go to bury their uttermost [outermost]: Lost as they fear 60. Enemy numerous.

This morn. the L.ᵗ Gov.ʳ set out for Portsmouth, Capt. Tuthill goes to the Castle.

---

[1] President Quincy, in his History of Harvard University (I. 150), after quoting this passage, adds: "By comparing the names of the seventeen members of the Corporation, chosen by virtue of the act which passed 9th of July, 1700, with those who, as the records show, attended its meetings during the Vice-Presidency of Willard, it is apparent that Mr. Walker and Cotton Mather were the two who were thus construed to have 'abdicated.' Neither of them attended any meeting of the Corporation after the exclusion of President Mather. But the name of Allen appears occasionally among those present at the board, quite down to the change introduced by the revival of the first charter of the College, at the time of the accession of Leverett to the presidency." — Eds.

Aug.ᵗ 13. Council is call'd to read the sad Letter from Capt. Willard and Wheelwright. Capt. Southack is sent away with a chaplain and chirurgeon.

Aug.ᵗ 9. I read the Transaction of the Gov.ʳ with the Indians, at the coffee house. Aug.ᵗ the 12ᵗʰ borrowed it; Abstract of it follows.

CASCO-BAY, June, 30. 1703.

The Queen of England in six months time of War with French King and Spanish King, has Taken more Towns and done more Exploits, than the great and valiant King William did in Twelve years. And besides all this which she hath don by Land, her Fleet by Sea hath taken 40. Sails; Taken much Money, the Royal Crown sent the Spanish King from N. Spain. Notwithstanding all this I offer peace. Twas once very dark here about 20 or 30 years ago; was great Troubles, and also great Troubles among our selves. New Hundred now, new Century, and would have the Old Hundred to be forgotten, and never talk'd of any more; New Hundred, new Queen, new Governour now will be all in new friendship. When any French March through the Country, Stop them or give notice to the Fort: For it is easy if there be but Ten Indians in some parts of the Country to fetch away whole familyes, and they not able to defend them selves. I have very particular Intelligence from Kebeck and Port Royal, they have two partys out at this time, would have you keep back those partyes according to the Treaty of peace made two years agoe. I do it not to boast of my self, but I Trust in God. I have Twelve Hundred and fifty men impress'd in N. England, ready to march at Six hours warning: they are enough to disturb all the Indians in the Country. Indians are able like Wolves to disturb men, but not to do them any damage; they are not able to hurt us in the least, and I value them not, no more than the paring of my nails. And the great Queen of England has order'd me 17. sail of Men of War all superior to the Gosport; which I may improve to do any thing upon the French or any of our Enemies. And I am confident that time will come that nothing, nor no one will remain but English here and Indians. For the Indians part they may remain a hapy people if they will themselvs.—I have the Assistance of the Noble Gov.ʳ of N. York, who is a Kinsman of the great Queen of England.—I acknowlege have kept their promise in not passing Saco River.—If arrest and stop French partys will give them a good Reward for it. And methinks I see among you some that I know that are fit to be made Officers to bear Comission for the Queen of England, to bear Rule among you, who shall be my Officers, and shall be Rewarded from

time to time, as my other officers at Boston, or any where else are;
every month they shall be paid off as our own people: — have nothing more in the world to say but to persuade them that I am an honest man and their Brother: — our boys and youth will go and do
beyond their prudence or strength; but these old men these Sachems here present, they and I are old men and should be discreet
and wise, so as that when we dye we might be carried to our Graves
with honor.   Let them consider two hours and give me their Answer — Gave them a good Ox and 20 — bushels corn for diñer: They
return'd Thanks for their noble diñer and all other Kindnesses
offer'd to them.   Then, said his Excellency here is a Peace, and Satisfaction to the two Nations.

INDIANS ANSWER.

First breach was at Penobscut, which was the first thing in the
morning.   The 2[d] was the Frenchmen and Indians, they broke the
peace in doing that mischief at Casco: but we do affirm that we did
not know of their coming, but of their going back we knew of it: but
we calling to remembrance what was don at Penobscut before, and
so we thought fit not to meddle of neither side.

TWO BEVERS.

Again they say that what his Excellency was pleased to tell them,
was not the same as their French was, i. e. to make war as the
French would have them.   His Excellency's desire is that we should
be peaceably on both sides, for which we return him many a hearty
Thanks and tell him we resolve to doe it.

TWO BEVERS.

His Excellency was pleas'd to desire them in the next place that if
any of the English should be Taken by the French and carried over
their Ground or through their Country, that we should bring them
back again, and not suffer them to be carried through as Captives;
but that we should do well to bring them back again.   But if we
should do so, such a thing as that would make us seem guilty, and so
thereby we might be thought to be concern'd, when we are not.

TWO BEVERS.

There is about the Mohawks a great many ready to fight, not certain of the number, but hope to know in a day or two, for have sent
scouts to Albany.

Two Bevers.

Again they wonder that his Excellency would be pleas'd to tell them, or desire any of them to come upon wages upon any account. For they desire it not. But their desire is to be as Neuters; not to medle nor make, nor to stir or act in any thing one way or other.

Three Bevers.

Now they desire to come and pay their Respects to the Govr, since have said all they have to say.

Govr will have them stay and hear his Answer a little — Action at Penabscot and Casco much alike: But Govr N. E. hated the Action as to the Frenchmans death: Govr French nourished and imbraced the Casco breach; sent them to do the thing. If resolve to sit still and be quiet, I shall remain perfectly satisfied in all things and desire to remain as an entire and dear Brother unto them.

May stop the French from Marching through their Country and yet remain Neuters still; they mistake if think otherwise: Be call'd Captains and Officers; why this is pure honor meant to them not that they should be expos'd to march or fight, but to be as my Brother, as I am to them. And if I would honor them so far as to make them Captains and to send them a present now and then, why it is honor: not that I desire they should be expos'd to fight upon any occasion. Tell Moxes I am willing to honor Moxes' son that was with me, with the place of a Captain here: not that I expect him to be expos'd to fight; no not so much as to fire a piece: but that we may live as Brothers and that I may send him a piece of Cloth once a year. —— Penecook Indians not return till after Harvest.

Then the Govr and Sachems repaired to the heaps of stones, and put up each man a stone again.

Second-day of the week, Augt 16, 1703. In the Afternoon I had Joseph in a Calash from Charlestown to Cambridge, carried only his little Trunk with us with a few Books and Linen; Went into Hall and heard Mr. Willard expound the 123 [Psalm]. 'Tis the first exercise of this year, and the first time of Joseph's going to prayer in the Hall.

Augt 23. 1703. I went to Cambridge to see Joseph settled in his study, help'd to open his Chest. Joseph was

at home the Sabbath, and went up on foot by Charlestown. This day several very unusual Circles were seen
about the sun. Mr. Leverett first told me of them, but I
saw them not.

Septr 3. Mr. Banister's eldest daughter is buried. She
died very suddenly of convulsions. — Sept. 4. Mrs. Emm
Lynde is buried. Bearers, Maj^r Genl Winthrop, Mr. Russel, Col. Hutchinson, Sewall, Capt. Belchar, Col. Savage.

Septr 6. 1703. Artil. Training, I Train'd in the Forenoon, As I was going, Mr. Oakes met me and ask'd if I
had not heard the News? He said French King; he had
his Neck broken by a fall from his Horse, as he was viewing an Army Rais'd to goe against those of the Ceveñes.
One Bodwin brings the Report, who comes from New
Castle, and had it at Sea from Comodore Taylor.

Tho. Oakes had a Tin Granado shell broke in his Hand,
which has shattered his hand miserably, his two last fin-
gers are already cut off: This was in the Afternoon, as
came from Council, was told of it.

Septr 9. Genl Court is prorogued to Wednesday, Oct.^r
27, 1703, 9 *mane*. Great Rain. Govr went not to the
Lecture. Septr 11th 1703. Col. Hathorn and I set out
for Wrentham, lodge at Lt Wear's. Sept. 12. Hear Mr.
Man. Dine with him. 7^r 13 See Wullamanuppack pond,[1]
out of which Charles River runs. Dine at Rehoboth, to
Bristow. 7^r 16. return to Rehoboth, sup there and ride
in the night to Woodcock's. Breakfast at Billinges. Bait
at Dedham, got home by four p.m. Go to Major Walli-
ces to their Meeting.

7^r 19. Hear of the Taking of Providence[2] by the

---

[1] Wrentham was first known by the Indian name of Wollomapaugh. —
EDS.

[2] " New Providence was again recolonized by the British, in 1686, and
continued in their hands till 1703, when a formidable combined force of
French and Spaniards effected a landing, carried off the Negroes, destroyed
Nassau, and drove into the woods the inhabitants, the most of whom, on the

French; surpris'd it in the night July 20. 7ᵉ 20. Wadsworth arrives from Dublin 7 weeks: Brings no News of the French King's death, so that conclude he is alive. I, my wife, Joseph, Mary, visit son and daughter at Muddy-River. I bring Joseph going in his way to Cambridge from Gates's into the Highway. Tuesday, 7ᵉ 28. very cold, and snow to cover the ground. 7ᵉ 29ᵗʰ The Snow is now three or four inches deep, and a very cold Norwest wind: a sad face of Winter, to see the Houses and Ground so cover'd with snow, and to see so much Ice.

7ᵉ 25. The Beams and Joyce of the old Hall Floor are laid.

7ᵉ 28. Keats comes to Ground piñing.

8ᵉ 13. 1703 Capt. Rich'd Sprague is buried. Mr. Russell, Capt. Hayman, Capt. Belchar, Mr. Leverett, Capt. Cary, Capt. Fowl Bearers: is buried in Mr. Morton's Tomb. I was there. Most of the Scholars, Joseph for one: My Gloves were too little, I gave them him. Govʳ there.

[Volume III. of the Manuscript Journal.]

[We ——— Janʸ 19. 170¾ Four Men kill'd at Casco-Bay belonging to Capt. Gallop; go out of the Boat; Beñet the Master out of the Sloop; Indians had their canoes, and lay there in wait.

Janʸ 24. express brings the News.

Ice would not suffer him to go to the Fort; so lay by Hog-Island.

By the good Providence of Almighty God, and the Prudence, Courage and Conduct of your Majʳ Capt. Genˡ, the enemy has hitherto been prevented of making such Impressions upon us as sometimes heretofore they have

---

invaders having departed, retired to Carolina." Edward's British West Indies, IV. 219, 220, fifth ed. — EDS.

done: of whose Conduct we pray the continuance may it consist with your Majesties good pleasure.

ELISHA HUTCHINSON
p̄ order of the Com̄ittee.

Augt. 24th unanimously voted p̄ the Council, send down for concurrence. [In margin, Not voted by the Deputies.] Augt 28   In the House of Depts Read Augt 29. read.

Septr 4th Read and voted a Concurrence with the Amendm'^t. Sent up for concurrence.

Council unanimously insist on the former *die prædict*. sent down.   Deps.   *die prædict*   Read.]¹

MASSACHUSETS; Anno Domini 1703.

Novr 26   Harrison the Controller, and Mr. Wm Pain are examined before the Govr and Council by Mr. Russell's Motion.²   When mention was made of putting them to their Oath, Harrison said he was ready to swear, but then it must be by laying his hand on the Bible: Govr said, So he ought, and order'd Mr. Secretary to fetch the Bible.   Mr. Pain also slip'd on his hand.   Mr. Harrison first look'd into it to see that 'twas the Bible.   When had sworn, seem'd to ap̄laud himself, and said he would have this forwarded and upheld.   When Questions were asked him, he answer'd, By that Booke it is True.

Sabbath, Novr 28.   A very sore storm of snow, which makes Assemblys very thin.   Not one Woman in Roxbury Meeting.

---

¹ These first few entries seem to be out of their chronological order, and are therefore bracketed by us. — EDS.

² This refers to a matter recorded in Massachusetts Archives, Vol. LXII. f. 446.   One Nathaniel Carey, a waiter under James Russell, Commissioner of the Impost, &c., had seized some rum from Michael Shaller, of Boston, a distiller, for non-payment of excise.   Wishing to keep it safely, he deposited it at the Custom-house, by leave of Mr. Ralph Harrison, comptroller, and Mr. William Payne, deputy-collector.   But when he went for it these latter claimed it as a customs prize, and refused to deliver it. — EDS.

Decᵣ 11. Poor little Hull Sewall dies in Mr. Phips's house at Muddy-River about 6. in the evening, of Convulsions. About 8. at night the Govʳ sends us word of it. Decᵣ 14ᵗʰ Corps is brought to Town in the Governours Slay. Decᵣ 15. is born to our Tomb, and set upon a Box that his great Grandfathers Bones now put into it at Williams's desire, some being wash'd out. On the Box is made with Nails, 1683. Bearers were Mr. Nathanˡ Oliver and David Stoddard. — Govʳˢ Lady and my wife rode in the Coach. Son and daughter followed the little Corps in Mourning : then Grandfathers, Joseph and Hannah, Mr. Hirst and his wife. Several of the Council here, and Mr. Cotton Mather, Mr. Nehemiah Walter. Provided new oak Plank for the entrance of the Tomb. Madam Leverett and Usher there. Gave no Gloves.

Decᵣ 23. Dr. Mather marries Mr. Thomas Hutchinson and Mrs. Sarah Foster. A very great Wedding. Mr. Secretary and I not bidden, nor Mr. Bromfield. Mr. Hirst and his wife were invited ; but Mr. Hirst was at Portsmouth, and my daughter being very big with child, excus'd her going in Want of her Husband's company. I knew not she was invited till the time was past.

Decᵣ 23. Mr. Brisco, now my son's Tenant, comes to the Council-Chamber when I was left there almost alone, and desired me to Marrie his Daughter, which I did at his house. Sung the 90ᵗʰ Psalm from the 12ᵗʰ v. to the end, with earnest desires that this Match might prove better than the former.

Decᵣ 30. Col. Hutchinson makes a very great Entertainment : Mr. Bromfield and wife are now invited : Mr. Secretary and I pass'd by, and I do not know who beside.

Decᵣ 26. Sabbath ; very sore vehement Storm of Snow ; exceeding high Tide, which did much hurt in Cellars and lower Rooms, and carried many Stacks of Hay quite away. It seems Roxbury Meeting was held at Mr. Walter's Dwelling-house. The Christmas keepers had a very pleasant day, Govr and Mr. Dudley at Church, and Mr. Dudley made a pretty large Entertainment after.

Decr 20. Five men that were getting home wood at Saco, are surpris'd by the enemy, three after found slain. Seven others that were at a distance, escaped to Wells: from whence the News came to Town.

Decr 23. Jany 1. 170¾ I carried 2 Duz. Mr. Willard's Books about swearing, to Mr. Phillips; Duz. to Buttolp; Duz. to Eliott; Duz to Boon.

Jany 5. Meeting at Mrs. Stevens; I pray there. Lindsey arrives at Marblehead this day; came from Isle Wight 29th Jn° Barston in her.

Jany 7th Col. Hutchinson's case is put to the Jury of which Mr. Hirst Foreman. Jany 8. They bring in a conditional verdict, If Madam Warren had power to alienat before Division &c. Court would not accept of it; but said that was it they were to Try: and sent them out again: Then they brought in for Col. Hutchinson, costs. Col. Hutchinson said upon the Bench, He would not be Try'd by Infer. or Sup'or Court; He would be Try'd by the Jury; they were his Judges.

Jany 14th 170¾ Got an Overseers Meeting at Col Foste[r] [manuscript imperfect] and pass my Account but could not get through with it; met with so[me] gross mistakes or such as fear'd were so; and had not time. Col Foster offers me to carry all I have done, into Leger parcells.

Jany 16. A storm of snow; but not so vehement as those in Novr and Dec. In the Afternoon Dr. Jer. Dum̄er preaches from Luke 13, *ult.* Mr. Pemberton baptizes Mr. Daniel Oliver's son Daniel. My wife not abroad. The last Lecture and this Lord's Day Major Walley apears in his Wigg, having cut off his own Hair. Jany 19. reckon'd with the Tenants of the Saw-mill at Braintry, and took their Bonds for the Arrears, and cancell'd the Leases. In the morning walk'd with Major Walley, Capt. Tim° Clark, Mr. Calef, constable Franklin, to visit disorderly poor; Met at my house. Capt Clark took up his Wigg: I said would have him consider that one place; The Bricks are fallen &c. But here men *cut down* the sycamores.[1] He seem'd startled.

Second-Day; Jan.ʸ 24. 170¾ I paid Capt. Belchar £8–15–0. Took 24ˢ in my pocket, and gave my Wife the rest of my cash £4.3–8, and tell her she shall now keep the Cash; if I want I will borrow of her. She has a better faculty than I at managing Affairs: I will assist her; and will endeavour to live upon my Salary; will see what it will doe. The Lord give his Blessing.

Jan.ʸ 31. Second day of the week, about four hours before day, my Daughter Hirst was delivered of a Living lively Daughter. Her mother went to her after the forenoon exercise Jan.ʸ 30. Mother Hirst came the evening before. We have an Answer of Peace to our many Prayers. *Laus Deo.* Mrs. Wakefield was Midwife. Madam Usher, Pemberton, Hubbard, Welsteed, Nurse Johnson assisted. Nurse is from Salem.

Jan.ʸ 31. George Pierce brings the News, of a Girl being kill'd at Nickawañuck; [Berwick, Me.] 30 Indians assaulted a Garrison there; were received bravely by the English, one of them kill'd, and the rest by Capt. Brown with a small party of men 10 or 12, put to flight, sundry of them wounded; left many of their own Accoutrements, for haste, and carried nothing away of ours. This was done last Friday.

Febr. 1. 170¾ Third of the week, I went to Dorchester Lecture, and heard Mr. Danforth preach from those words, All is vanity. Din'd with Madam Taylor and Mr. Trott.

---

[1] Isaiah IX. 10. "The bricks are fallen down, but we will build with hewn stones: the sycamores are cut down, but we will change them into cedars." — EDS.

Before Lecture, I rid into the Burying place, and read
Mr. Stoughton's Epitaph, which is very great.[1]

Febr. 3. 170¾ Mr. Neh. Hobart dines with us in the
chamber. Has not been in Town of many weeks before.
I Lent him Forbes[2] on the Rev. Gave him 4 Quires paper
and box wafers. Told him I was like to have some Bickerings with Mr. Noyes;[3] and he should be Judge of the
Controversy. I set up this Problem, that Christ set his
Right Foot on the New-World; his Left, on the Old.
Rev. 10. Pray'd him to assign otherwise if he saw convenient.

Febr. 4th 170¾ I paid Sarah Mountfort her Legacy
with the Three and Twenty pieces of Gold. Mr. Secretary took eight pieces, which 1 ounce and 12d weight, and
gave £8–11–3. Sarah Mountfort had Fifteen pieces,
which weighed —— 16–8–9 Three ounces, 2d, weight,
and 12 Grains by Cousin Dumers Scales £25–0–0. Mr.
Secretary took the Acquittance seal'd and Deliver'd in
presence of her Brother Wadsworth, and Tom Maccarty.

Lord's-Day, February the 6th 170¾ I went to Mr. Col-
man's that I might see my little Grand-daughter baptised;
Besides me there were Mr. Brattle, Mr. Clark and Capt.
Anth. Checkley in the Fore-Seat. Mr. Colman read the
15th and 16. Psalms, and the last chapter of the first
Epistle of Peter. Text was Mat. 26. 38. Went on with
the Discourse had begun in the morning for the Lord's
Supper. Pray'd excellently at Baptisme, for the Child,
Mother, all. Child is call'd Mary My —— [daughter]
would have it so for the sake of Mrs. Mary Hirst, her

---

[1] All who desire to do so may verify the Judge's remark by reading the
still legible inscription on the stately monument of Stoughton, or in the careful transcript printed by Sibley, " Harvard Graduates," I. 205, 206. Harvard College, some years since, repaired this memorial of its benefactor. —
EDS.

[2] Patrick Forbes, of Corse, Bishop of Aberdeen, died 1635. — EDS.

[3] On disputed points in the interpretation of prophecy. — EDS.

Husband's [Moth]er, who was present, and my little daughter Mary. Nurse brought the Child, and Mr. Grove Hirst the father held it up. Though the Child had cry'd before, did not cry at Mr. Colman's pouring on the Water. Daughter reckons herself very ill.

Febr. 7. Nurse Hawkins, who watch'd with her, tells me my daughter had a very good night. *Laus Deo.*

Febr. 5. Seventh-day of the week; I fasted and pray'd to God that Satan might not be comissioned any longer to buffet me and my wife; for my self and family in the advancing year: and Province &c. for Daughter Hirst, and little Mary to be dedicated to Him the next day.

Lt Tristram Coffin dyed Febr. 4th 170$\frac{3}{4}$. Joseph Frazon, the Jew, dyes at Mr. Major's, Mr. Joyliff's old house; Febr. 5th Satterday, is carried in Simson's coach to Bristow; from thence by Water to Newport, where there is a Jews-burying place.[1]

Febr. 8th a Garrison-house is surpris'd at Haverhill by 6 or 7 Indians.

Febr. 18. 19. 20. My wife lodges with my daughter Hirst to comfort her. Febr. 20. Major William Bradford dies in the 80th year of his Age: He was a Right New-England Christian. Mrs. Lewis dies at Boston. Isaac Goose jun^r is baptised this day. Febr. 22. A great funeral for Mrs. Lewis.

Febr. 25. I went to Charlestown Lecture; heard Mr. Bradstreet preach from 1 Cor. 7. 31.; made a good Sermon. As return'd in the Ferry-boat, I was told Capt. Stephens had done nothing. The Lord pity us.

Febr. 24th 170$\frac{3}{4}$ This day the new Parishoners meet in

---

[1] Arnold (History of Rhode Island, I. 479) says that the Jews petitioned, in 1684, for protection. They contributed for a century to the prosperity of the colony, making Newport their centre. Not one of their descendants now remains there, but Abraham Touro (a son of their last priest), who died at Boston, in 1822, left a fund of $15,000 for the support of the synagogue and cemetery on Touro street, Newport. — Eds.

the house built for their Minister, and call the Precinct
Byfield, as Bro^r Moody tells me, March 4th. 170¾ before
his going home.

March, 5. The dismal News of the Slaughter made at
Deerfield is certainly and generally known, Mr. Secretary
came to me in the morning, and told me of it : I told Mr.
Willard ; by which means our Congregation was made a
Bochim. [Judges, II. 1–5.] Tis to be observ'd that the
great slaughters have been on the Third day of the week ;
our Court day. This was Febr. 29th 170¾ My Tenant
Kibbee was arrested this day.

March, 16. 170¾ Mr. Dean Winthrop, of Pulling Point,
dies upon his Birth-day, just about the Breaking of it.
He was Taken at eight aclock the evening before, as he
sat in his chair, sunk first, being set up, he vomited, complain'd of his head, which were almost his last words.
Hardly spake anything after his being in bed. 81 years
old. He is the last of Govr Winthrop's children ——
statione novissimus exit.[1] March, 20. is buried at Pulling
Point by his son and Three Daughters. Bearers Russel,
Cooke ; Hutchinson, Sewall ; Townsend, Paige. From the
House of Hasey. Scutcheons on the Pall. I help'd to
lower the Corps into the Grave. Madam Paige went in
her Coach. Maj^r Genl and Capt. Adam Winthrop had
Scarvs, and led the widow. Very pleasant day ; Went by
Wiñisimet.

March, 24, 170¾ William Daws, Mason, dyes about 2
p.m. A good old man, full of days, is got well to the end
of his weary Race.[2] Arthur Mason's Negro dyes this day,
being run over by his own cart on Tuesday. Is a great
Loss, being faithfull and in his full strength.

---

[1] Diffugiunt stellæ: quarum agmina cogit
   Lucifer, et cœli statione novissimus exit.
                              OVID, *Met.* II. 114. — EDS.

[2] He was the progenitor of the noted Boston family. See Dawes Genealogy, by H. W. Holland, Boston, 1878. — EDS.

March, 25, 1704.   Col. Hathorne and I travel to Braintry, lodge at Cousin Fisk's.   March, 26.   Hear Mr. Fisk
preach Forenoon and Afternoon : Note. One Sheffield,
a very good aged Christian, of about 90 years old, was
there, who, as was expected, was never like to have come
abroad more.   Was accordingly given Thanks for.   George
Allen waits on me.

March, 27ᵗʰ. Bait at Mr. Cushing's. He shews us Accord Pond,¹ hardly ¼ of a mile out of the Rode.   Dine at
Barkers in company of Major Eels, his son, Mr. Stoddard, Dr. Samsons and others.   Sheriff Warren meets us
there ; before we get away, Major Walley and Leverett
come in.   We get to Plimᵒ ½ hour before Sun-set.

March   the Court.

March, 29ᵗʰ. Went into the Meetingh— in the
Adjourn'd *sine die* before Noon.   Din'd and got to Cushings about sunset.   In the evening Mr. Cushing desired
me to pray, which I did, and sang three staves of the 137
Psal. omitting Edom.   Mr. Cushing told us, Mr. Danforth
us'd to sing.   I shew'd Mr. Leverett Accord Pond as came
along.

March, 30. Call'd and visited Mr. Torrey. Call'd at
the Governours, He told us the particulars of the dreadfull Storm in England in Novr.²   Came home about 4 p.m̄ :
found all well.   *Laus Deo.*

April, 1. 1704. Visited my valetudinarious son at Brooklin ; gave Baker a shilling to drive a Naïl for me in the
great Stairs.   Call'd at the Govʳˢ as I came home to condole the Loss of Mr. Samuel Dudley at Suratt, Febr. 22.

---

¹ Accord Pond is at the angle of Abington, Scituate, and Hingham, and
is named as early as 1640.   It was one of the points by which to run the
boundary of Plymouth Colony.   As we write we notice a petition for leave
to supply Hingham with water from this pond. — EDS.

² This storm, which has been called "the most terrible storm that had
been known in England," as described by Defoe, in a volume entitled "The
Storm," published in 1704. — EDS.

170⅔ : was taken with the small Pocks Febr. 16th, of which
he died the 22th., the day Madam Willard had like to have
been cast away and her family, coming from Cambridge
by Water. I told the Govr I hoped this young Gentleman might have been a Suport to his family; for countenance was one of the Goodliest I had known. Said to
Mr. William Dudley that to get more Acquaintance with,
and Conformity to Christ, as his Elder Brother, was the
best and only way to Repair such a Loss. Read Brothers
Letter to the Govr about a Scout-Shallop: He said Southack and Gallop were hastening. The News of Mr. Saml
Dudley's death was inclosed to Col. Foxcroft by Mr.
Shepard, Govr of the East-India Company: Letter dated
Decr 3. 1703. Col. Foxcroft deliver'd it to the Govr the
evening following, Thorsday, March 30. 1704, 2 or 3 hours
after Major Walley and I took leave of his Excellency.

April, 2. 1704. Ship arrives from England Seven weeks
passage; came out with the Fleet that had the King of
Spain[1] on board to carry to Portugal. Brings Prints of
the November Storm, and the December Mercury.

April, 3. Artil. Company chuses Mr. Henry Gibbs of
Watertown[2] to preach their Sermon; chuse Capt. Checkley
and me to join Comiss'd Officers to acquaint him with it,
and desire him to undertake it.

April, 5th. Capt. John Ballentine, Lt Tho Savage and
Ens. Tho. Fitch, Sewall and Checkly, set out at 2 p.m.
round for Watertown: Find Mr. Gibbs at home, Acquaint
him with our Message, press him earnestly: but can get
no Answer, He will give an Answer the 13th after Lecture. I invited him to dine with me. Had comfortable

---

[1] The Archduke Charles, a claimant of the Crown of Spain, and recognized by the Allies as King. — EDS.

[2] Rev. Henry Gibbs, of Watertown, H. C. 1685, died Oct. 21, 1723, leaving issue. His father was Robert Gibbs, of Boston, who was fourth son
of Sir Henry Gibbs, and great grandson of Robert Gibbs, of Honington,
County Warwick. See Heraldic Journal, III, 165–167. — EDS.

going and returning : Call'd at Brooklin as came home.
Baited at Remington's. I used Dr. Witsius's[1] Title of's
Oration *De Theologo Modesto ;* told him the more Modesty
we saw the more vehement we should be in our Assaults.

Apr. 6 & 7th very cold North-east Stormy Wether, and
Tuesday was the Catechising : so that we took the only
day could be had to go in this week.

April, 10. 1704. The Seven and Thirty French privateers are brought to Town, who were put a-Shore at
Marshfield last Friday in the vehemency of the Storm.
Feria quarta, Apr. 12. In the morning I saw and heard
three Swallows playing over my head. I think I never
observ'd them so soon in the year before. Rowse came
in from London, 7 weeks passage, Apr. 10. *Feria Sexta,*
Ap. 14. p.m. Tho. Wallis dieth. *Feria septima,* Apr. 15.
1704. Mr. Nathan¹ Oliver dieth between 3 and 4 in the
morning. He was born 20 days before me. Joseph
comes to see us. *Feria Secunda,* April, 17th. 1704, I go
to Salem to see my Broʳ Hirst ; Speak with Mr. Noyes,
who conceives that the Witnesses were slain at the conclusion of the Peace of Ryswick, 1697. Passing away of
the 2ᵈ Wo. at the conclusion of the Peace of Carlowitz
with the Turk. [1699.] Resurrection of the Witnesses
by the Convulsions following the death of Charles 2ᵈ K—
of Spain ;[2] The 1260 days Expire, and then the Witnesses
Rise ; namely the 1260 Days of the Ten-horn'd Beast, his
power to make war. Antichrist's Reign begins at the
Time of the great Whore's mounting the Beast, the 10
horned beast, viz. Año 1073. Hildebrand papa. At the
death of Valentinian, the Ten-horn'd Beast set up ; viz.
anno, 458. Taken from Mr. Noyes's mouth at Broʳ
Sewall's.[3]

---

[1] A Dutch Divine: born, 1636; died, 1708. — EDS.

[2] Charles II. died in 1700. His dying without issue gave rise to the War
of the Spanish Succession. — EDS.

[3] The " bickerings " which Judge Sewall, according to his expectations,

Apr. 18.th Go home in company of Major Brown, Corwin, Higginson, Lynde, Gerrish to the parting way, where turn'd off to Mr. Wigglesworth [of Malden], where I din'd: then home by Charlestown: Went to the Funeral of Mr. Nathan^l Oliver: Bearers, Sewall, Walley; Legg, Dūmer; Cooper, ——. Govr was there.

April, 24. 1704. I went to Cambridge to see some Books on the Revelation, and there met with Mr. Pignet:[1] went into Hall and heard Mr. Willard expound Rom. 4. 9. 10. 11 and pray. I gave Mr. Willard the first News-Letter[2] that ever was carried over the River. He shew'd it the Fellows. I came home in company with Mr. Adams.

April, 25. My daughter Hañah and I carefully removed all Eben^r Mountfort's Linnen &c out of his crazy,

---

had with the Rev. Nicholas Noyes, of Salem, on these prophetical mysteries, concern such profound and perplexing matters that the professional attainments of the Editors do not qualify them to attempt any arbitration in the case. — EDS.

[1] This is a mysterious name, unknown to our annals. — EDS.

[2] "The Boston News Letter," the first Anglo-American newspaper, appeared on Monday, April 24, 1704, and continued to be published until 1776, on the evacuation of Boston by the British troops. Its first publisher and proprietor was John Campbell, a bookseller, and also postmaster, in which last office he continued till his death, in 1728. Nicholas Boone was associate publisher. Bartholomew Green, John Allen, and again Green, were, successively, its printers. Issued weekly, on Monday, it answered the needs of the time, and even with difficulty secured a supporting constituency. No price for subscription or for a single copy is mentioned upon it. It was a half-sheet, small folio, "Published by Authority," — i. e., by allowance of the provincial authorities. The first number contained but one advertisement, and that was the publisher's. He solicits advertisements of "Houses, Lands, Tenements, Farms, Ships, Vessels, Goods, Wares, or Merchandises, &c., to be Sold or Lett: or Servants Runaway: or Goods Stole or Lost," to be "Inserted at a reasonable rate: from Twelve Pence to Five Shillings, and not to exceed." "Reasonable terms" are offered to "All persons in Town or Country" for the Weekly, "agreeing with John Campbell, Postmaster, for the Same." The publishing office was near the site of the present Joy's Building, then occupied by the First Church. A few matters of public intelligence, the announcement of a sermon preached by Mr. Pemberton on "Doing one's own business," "which his Excellency has ordered to be printed," and the fact that "The Rev. Mr. Lockyer dyed on Thursday last," make up the contents of this first Boston "News Letter." — EDS.

unfaithfull Trunk, and laid them up orderly in the new
Chest I bought of Bro^r Nichols for that purpose. Col.
Perce died the 22 Ap. in the Afternoon. Son and daugh-
ter Sewall lodg'd here last night.

Lord's-Day, Apr. 23. There is great Firing at the
Town, Ships, Castle upon account of its being the Coro-
nation-day, which gives offence to many; See the Lord's-
day so profan'd. Down Sabbath, Up St George.

April, 27, 1704. Little Judith is carried on Horseback,
Jane Green attending her, unto the house of Mr. Robert
Avery of Dedham, for to be healed of her Rupture. Had
Mrs. Wigglesworth's advice. In the morning, not thinking
of her departure, I first got her to say after me, Create in
me a clean heart, O God; and renew a right spirit within
me. It was near sun-set, when they went away, which
made us uneasy: But Mrs. Avery was in a readiness
with Horses and Company; and the spring advancing
apace made us consent. I intended 4. p.m. to be the
latest for their setting out.

May, 13. I visit little Judith; find her well: visit Mr.
Belchar.

May, 15th Set out for Ipswich with Major Walley;
Mr. Leverett falls in at Lewis's; go by Salem: from
thence Col. Hathorne goes with us, Sheriff Gedny waits
on us: got thither in season. Lodge at Mr. Rogers'.
When came away gave Mrs. Martha a Turkey-Leather
Psalm-book.

May, 17. Made a shift to get to Rowley, Lodg'd at
Bro^r Northend's, who came to Ipswich and invited me.

May, 18. heard Mr. Payson and Hale; No Meeting at
Byfield, had not timely notice.

May, 19. ride to Newbury; Dine at Sister Gerrishes;
See Cousin Joseph's wife, give her Mr. Cole's Sermons.[1]

---

[1] Probably Thomas Cole, Principal of St. Mary's Hall, Oxford. He was
ejected by the King's Commissioners, in 1660, and afterwards took charge of
a congregation in London. — EDS.

Knew not of the Clause about Perriwigs till I got to Rowley. I read the Discourse of Adoption to my Aunt Northend. Lodge at Bro˞ Taping's. May, 21. Goe and hear Mr. Belchar; Dine there. After dinner the aged Ordway [1] comes to see me, complains bitterly of his cousin John Emery's carriage to his wife, which makes her leave him and go to her Sister Bayly.

May, 22. visit Cousin Joshua Pierce, the widow Pierce, widow Coffin. Went with Bro˞ Moodey to his house, dine there, went to Perkin's in Beverly, lodge there: because of the extream heat, I travel'd from Ipswich thither in the night. May, 23, went early to Salem, convers'd with Mr. Noyes, told him of the Quaker Meeting at Sam. Sawyers, a week ago, profaneness of the young Hoags, professing that heresy. Visited Bro˞ Hirst still confin'd by the Gout. Came home with daughter Sewall, she rides single, Sam. Sewall *de Stephano*, waits on her. Refresh at Lewis's, where Mr. Paul Dudley is in egre pursuit of the Pirats. He had sent one to Boston; and seeing me call'd him back again; At such a sudden I knew not what to doe: but charg'd Tom. Cox and one Jarvis with him, and order'd them to deliver him to Mr. Secretary Addington. For my daughter's sake I went by Charlestown, and parted with her where Cambridge way turns off. George Allen and I got home about Sun-set. *Laus Deo.* Mr. Bridge and Mr. Bridgham welcom'd me by the New Burying place, met them there. May, 27th Mr. Secretary and Capt. Belcher, Mr. E^m Hutchinson and Palmer, Mr. Bromfield and I ride to Cambridge to meet the Gov˞ Staid till about 7, then supos'd would not come till Monday, and so came home. But the Gov˞ came that night. I knew not of it till 'twas too late to visit his Excellency on Monday morn. Went to Council, and met

---

[1] Probably James Ordway, of Newbury, said by Savage to have been born in 1620, and to have died after 1702. — EDS.

with the Govr there.   May, 29th Govr orders another
Proclamation to be issued out, respecting the Pirats.
Several bring in Gold ; Capt. Tuttle brings three parcels ;
two given him by Wm Clark *de Johane;* one by Capt.
Quelch.   May, 31, 1704.   Mr. Addington, Walley and
Sewall Give the Depts the Oaths; but one Councellor at
Roxbury, *viz.* Capt. Belcher.   Mr. Jonathan Russell
preaches.   Deputies send in a Resolve that none is to be
accounted chosen who has not the major part of the
Voters : Election finished about eight : Govr and Lieut.
Govr went away long before.

June 1.   Govr signs the Allowance of all but Mr. Sergeant and Cook; them He does not allow.[1]

June 2.   Debated in Council whether or no should not
fill up the Council: Most seem'd for it.   Some against it,
as Col. Townsend, Foster, Hutchinson.

Wednesday, June 7th. 1704.   Col. Nathan^l Byfield, Mr.
Palmer and my self have rec'd an Order from the Govr to
search for and seize Pirats and their Treasure, and to
hold a court of Enquiry for this end at Marblehead; because Capt. Quelch in the Charles Galley arrived there :
we set forward this day for Salem, having James Noyes
and Joseph Gerrish to wait on us.   We got to Salem
about 8 aclock   There Sam. Wakefield, the Water Baily,
inform'd Col. Byfield of a Rumor there was that Capt.
Larrimore was now with the Larramore Gally at Cape-
Anne ; and that two of Quelch's company designed
to go off in her.   Upon this we made out a Warrant
to the said Wakefield to goe and see into this matter
and seize the Men if true.   Despatch'd him about midnight.

Thorsday, June 8.   We went to Marblehead in the
Rain, and held our Court at Capt. Brown's by the Fire-

---

[1] It seems, by the Council records, that on the thirteenth of June, Simeon
Stoddard and Samuel Hayman were chosen instead. — Eds.

side; took Major Sewall with us, who return'd to Salem the same night.

Friday, June, 9ᵗʰ about 6. m. An Express from Cape-Anne, gives an Account of 9. or 11. Pirats, double arm'd, seen in a Lone-house there. This Express found us a-bed. We rose imediately, Sent for Col. Legg, and directed him to send warrants to the Northward Companies within his Regiment; to send such parties as they could raise, to Cape-Anne upon this Extraordinary occasion. And writt to Col. Wainright to do the Like in his Regiment, intimating that we were moving thither our selves to be Witness of their forwardness for Her Majesties Service. Sent this by James Noyes to shew it to Capt. Fisk of Wenham, as he went along. Col. Byfield and I rode to Salem; there met Dr. Gatchman, took his Affidavit for some better foundation for our Actions. Sent him post to the Govʳ Broʳ got a shallop, the Trial, and his Pinace, and about a score of his Compᵃ to go by water. Mr. Dudley went by water from Marblehead with Col. Legg. Col. Byfield and I proceeded with Sheriff Gedney and Capt. Turner and part of his Troop by Land : call'd on Lᵗ Brisco at Beverly; that Troop resolv'd to go by Jabacko [Chebacco]. Manchester Company was mustering upon the top of a Rock; shook hand with Mr. Webster. When drew nigh the Town of Glocester a Letter from Mr. Dudley and Legg met us, to acquaint us that Larramore¹ Sail'd in the morning and took in the Pirats at the head of the Cape. Messenger seem'd to discourage our going forward. However, we sent back the Sheriff to post their Letter to the Govʳ, and as many of Salem Troops as would go back, persuad-

---

¹ This was, probably, the Captain Thomas Larrimore mentioned in a letter printed in the New England Historical and Genealogical Register, IV. 348. It is from John Leverett to Isaac Addington, under date of July 11, 1702. He writes: "His Excellency also commands me to acquaint your honor that he hath ordered Capt. Thomas Larrimore with his crew in Mr. Marston's Sloop to joyn Capt. Gilbert's in their Cruise." — EDS.

ing them to return. Mr. Dudley had sent to stay Ipswich Regiment and direct their Return. When came to Capt. Davis's, waited Brother's arrival with his Shallop Trial, and Pinace: When they were come and had Din'd, Resolv'd to send after Larramore. Abbot was first pitch'd on as Captain. But matters went on heavily, 'twas difficult to get Men. Capt. Herrick pleaded earnestly his Troopers might be excus'd. At last Brother offer'd to goe himself: then Capt. Turner offer'd to goe, Lieut Brisco, and many good Men; so that quickly made up Fourty two; though we knew not the exact number till came home, the hurry was so great, and vessel so small for 43. Men gave us three very handsom cheers; Row'd out of the Harbour after sun-set, for want of wind. Mr. Dudley return'd to Salem with Beverly Troop. Col. Byfield and I lodg'd at Cape-Ann all night; Mr. White pray'd very well for the Expedition Evening and morning; as Mr. Chiever had done at Marblehead, whom we sent for to pray with us before we set out for Glocester. We rose early, got to Salem quickly after Nine. Din'd with Sister, who was very thoughtfull what would become of her Husband. The Wickedness and despair of the company they pursued, their Great Guns and other warlike Preparations, were a terror to her and to most of the Town; concluded they would not be Taken without Blood.[1] Comforted our selves and them as well as we could. Call'd at Lewis's. Col. Byfield went to Cambridge; Mr. Dudley and I to Boston, Joseph Gerrish waiting on us. June. 12th Joseph Gerrish comes to my Bed-Chamberdoor and Tells of Brother's good success. He dispatched Chapman in the night to the Govr. He came to the Isles Sholes about 7. m. June 10, kept his men rank'd with

---

[1] It is somewhat surprising that so little remains on record in regard to Quelch's affair. We find nothing worth mention in the State archives. Yet it seems to have created a very lively scare in Essex county, and Sewall evidently feels that the capture was a perilous exploit. — EDS.

their Arms on both sides the shallop in covert; only the
four Fishermen were in view: as drew near saw the Boat
goe ashoar with six Hands, which was a singular good
Providence of God. Wormwall and three of the Pirats
were of the six. When were so near that were descryd,
Larramores Men began to run to and fro and pull off the
Aprons from the Guns, draw out the Tomkins [Tompions],
Brother shew'd his men. Ask'd Larramore to come aboard.
He said he could not, his Boat was gon ashore. Bro^r told
him he would come to him: imediately man'd the Pinace,
and did it as soon almost as said it, He, Capt. Turner,
Abbot step'd aboard. Brisco attempted; but one swore
no more armed Men should come there. Bro^r got the
Capt ashore to discourse him, got him there to sign two
orders; one to send the L^t and one of the Pirats ashore;
the other for Abbot to comand the Galley till they return'd; and so quickly finish'd his business thorowly
without striking a stroke, or firing a Gun. See the
News-Letter.[1] Twas all order'd and Tim'd and effected
by the Singular all-powerfull gracious Providence of
God.

---

[1] As Judge Sewall here refers to the "News Letter," a file of which he
may have kept for reference, we extract from the copy in the cabinet of
the Historical Society all that relates to the capture and trial of the pirates.
The date of the paper is June 9 to 16, 1704. — EDS.

"*God Save the Queen.*

"MARBLEHEAD, June 9. The Honourable Samuel Sewall, Nathaniel
Byfield, and Paul Dudley Esqrs. came to this place yesterday, in obedience
to His Excellency the Governour, his Order for the more effectual discover-
ing and Seizing the Pirates lately belonging to the Briganteen Charles, John
Quelch Commander, with their Treasure. They made Salem in their way,
where Samuel Wakefield the Water-Baily informed them of a Rumor that
two of Quelches's Company were lurking at Cape Anne, waiting for a Passage off the Coast: The Commissioners made out a Warrent to Wakefield to
Search for them, and dispatched him away on Wednesday night. And
having gain'd intelligence this Morning, that a certain number of them well
Armed, were at Cape Anne designing to go off in the Larrimore Galley, then
at Anchor in that Harbour. They immediately sent men from the several

June, 27ᵗʰ *feria tertia*, Madam Richards dies about 3 hours after midnight. Heard not of it till at Mr. Stod-

---

adjacent Towns by Land and Water, to prevent their escape, and went thither themselves, to give necessary orders upon the place.

" GLOCESTER, upon Cape Anne, June 9. The Commissioners for Seizing the Pirates and their Treasure, arrived here this day, were advised that the Larrimore Galley Sail'd in the Morning Eastward; and that a Boat was seen to go off from the head of the Cape, near Snake Island, full of men, supposed to be the Pirates. The Commissioners seeing the Government mock'd by Capt. Larrimore and his Officers, resolved to send after them. Major Stephen Sewall who attended with a Fishing Shallop, and the Fort Pinnace, offered to go in pursuit of them, and Capt. John Turner, Mr. Robert Brisco, Capt. Knight, and several other good men Voluntarily accompanied him, to the Number of 42 men, who Rowed out of the Harbour after Sun-sett, being little Wind.

" SALEM, June 11. This Afternoon, Major Sewall brought in to this Port, the Larrimore Galley, and Seven Pirates, viz. Erasmus Peterson, Charles James, John Carter, John Pitman, Francis King, Charles King, John King, whom he with his Company Surprised and Seized at the Isles of Sholes the 10th. Instant, viz., four of them on Board the Larrimore Galley, and three on Shoar on Starr Island, being assisted by John Hinckes and Thomas Phipps Esqrs., two of Her Majesties Justices of New Hampshire, who were happily there, together with the Justices, and the Captain of the place. He also Seized 45 Ounces and Seven Pennyweight of Gold of the said Pirates.

" Capt. Thomas Larrimore, Joseph Wells Lieutenant, and Daniel Wormmall Master, and the said Pirates are Secured in our Gaol.

" GLOCESTER, June 12. Yesterday Major Sewall passed by this place with the Larrimore Galley, and Shallop Trial, standing for Salem, and having little wind, set our men ashore on the Eastern Point, giving of them notice that William Jones, and Peter Roach, two of the Pirates had mistook their way, and were still upon the Cape, with strict charge to search for them, which our Towns People performed very industriously. Being strangers and destitute of all Succours, they surrendered themselves this Afternoon, and were sent to Salem Prison.

" BOSTON, June 17. On the 13 Instant, Major Sewall attended with a strong guard brought to Town the above mentioned Pirates, and Gold he had Seized, and gave His Excellency a full Account of his Procedure in seizing them. The Prisoners were committed to Goal in order to a Tryal, and the Gold delivered to the Treasurer and Committee appointed to receive the same. The service of Major Sewall and Company was very well Accepted and Rewarded by the Governour.

" His Excellency was pleased on the 13 Currant to open the High Court of Admiralty for Trying Capt. John Quelch late Commander of the Briganteen Charles and Company for Piracy, who were brought to the Barr, and the Articles exhibited against them read. They all pleaded Not Guilty, excepting three viz. Matthew Primer, John Clifford and James Parrot, who

dard's noble Treat in the evening. Mr. Secretary invited the Govr, Lt Govr, several of the Council to Diñer at North's, the Stone-house. I there. In the morning I heard Mr. Cotton Mather, Pray, preach, Catechise excellently the Condemned Prisoners in the chamber of the prison.

June, 29. Madam Richards buried, in her Husbands

---

were reserved for Evidences, and are in Her Majesties Mercy. The Prisoners moved for Council, and His Excellency assigned them Mr. James Meinzes. The Court was adjourned to the 16th. When met again, Capt. Quelch preferr'd a Petition to His Excellency and Honourable Court, craving longer Time, which was granted Monday Morning at Nine of the Clock, when said Court is to Sit again in order to their Tryal."

An extract from "The Boston News Letter" of June 26, 1704.

"Boston, June 24. On Monday last, The 19. Currant, The High Court of Admiralty Sat again, when the Tryal of John Quelch late Commander of the Briganteen Charles, and Company for Piracy and Murder, Committed by them upon Her Majesties Allies the Subjects of the King of Portugal, was brought forward, and the said Quelch was brought to the Bar, being charged with nine several Articles of Piracy and Murder whereupon he had been Arraigned and Pleaded, Not Guilty: The Queen's Attorney opened the case, and the Court proceeded to the Examination of the Evidences for Her Majesty. And the Council for the Prisoner, and the Prisoner himself being fairly heard, The Court was cleared, and after Advisement, the Prisoner was again brought to the Bar; and the Judgment of the Court declared. That he was guilty of the Felony, Piracy and Murder, laid in said Articles: Accordingly Sentence of Death was pronounced against him.

"The next day being Tuesday, John Lambert, Charles James, John Miller and Christopher Scudamore, were brought to the Bar, who pleaded Not Guilty: And were severally tryed as Quelch was, and found guilty and Sentenced to Dy in like manner.

"Then was brought to the Bar, William Whiting and John Templeton being Arraigned, They pleaded Not Guilty, and the Witnesses proving no matter of Fact upon them, said Whiting being Sick all the Voyage, and not active, and Templeton a Servant about 14 years of Age, and not charged with any action, were acquitted by the Court, paying Prison Fees. Next 15. more being brought to the Bar and Arraign'd, viz. Will. Wilde, Benj. Perkins, James Austin, Nich. Richardson, Rich. Lawrence, John Pitman, Will. Jones, Erasmus Peterson, John King, Francis King, Charles King, Peter Roach, John Dorothy, Denis Carter and John Carter, who severally pleaded Guilty, and threw themselves on the Queen's Mercy. And Sentence of Death was past upon them, in like manner as those above named. 'Tis said some of them will be Executed the next Friday, and the whole proceeding be put out in Print."

Tomb at the North-burying place. Bearers, Russel, Cook; Hutchinson Elisha, Sewall; Sergeant, Foster. Scarfs and Rings, Scutcheons on the Coffin.[1]

Feria Sexta, Junij, 30, 1704. As the Governour sat at the Council-Table twas told him, Madam Paige was dead;[2] He clap'd his hands, and quickly went out, and return'd not to the Chamber again; but ordered Mr. Secretary to prorogue the Court till the 16th of August, which Mr. Secretary did by going into the House of Deputies. After Diñer, about 3. p.m. I went to see the Execution.[3] By the way (cous. Ephr. Savage with me) James Hawkins certifies us of Madam Paiges death; he was to make a Tomb. Many were the people that saw upon Broughton's Hill. But when I came to see how the River was cover'd with People, I was amazed: Some say there were 100 Boats. 150 Boats and Canoes, saith Cousin Moody of York. He told them. Mr. Cotton Mather came with Capt. Quelch and six others for Execution from the

---

[1] This was Anna, daughter of Governor John Winthrop, of Connecticut, and second wife of John Richards, of Boston, whose first wife was widow of Adam Winthrop. The reference to escutcheons reminds us that in Gore's Roll of Arms (Heraldic Journal, I. 117) is a description of Richards's arms impaling Winthrop, and ascribed to this lady. — EDS.

[2] She was his niece, wife of Edward Lane, and then of Benjamin Paige, being the daughter of Benjamin Keayne and Sarah Dudley. Savage points out an error in Hutchinson's History, I. 375, where she is called sister, instead of niece, of Governor Joseph Dudley. — EDS.

[3] This execution took place on the Boston side of the Charles River flats. It is thus described in the " Boston News Letter " three days afterwards. — EDS.

" On Friday was carried to the Place of Execution Seven Pirates to be Executed, viz.; Capt. John Quelch, John Lambert, Christopher Scudamore, John Miller, Erasmus Peterson, Peter Roach and Francis King: all of whom were executed except the last named, who had a Reprieve from his Excellency. And notwithstanding all the great labour and pains taken by the Reverend Ministers of the Town of Boston ever since they were first Seized and brought to Town, both before and since their Trial and Condemnation, to instruct, admonish, preach and pray for them: yet as they led a wicked and vitious life, so to appearance they dyed very obdurately and impenitently, hardened in their sin. His Excellency intends to send an Express to *England,* with an Account of the whole matter to her Majesty."

Prison to Scarlet's Wharf, and from thence in the Boat to the place of Execution about the midway between Hanson's point and Broughton's Warehouse. Mr. Bridge was there also. When the scaffold was hoisted to a due height, the seven Malefactors went up; Mr. Mather pray'd for them standing upon the Boat. Ropes were all fasten'd to the Gallows (save King, who was Repriev'd). When the Scaffold was let to sink, there was such a Screech of the Women that my wife heard it sitting in our Entry next the Orchard, and was much surprised at it; yet the wind was sou-west. Our house is a full mile from the place.[1]

July, 1, 1704. *Feria Septima.* News is brought from New-york of Trade to be had with the American Spaniards. This comes in seasonably upon Quelches Spightfull admonition yesterday.[2] Melyen told me of it on the Lords Day.

---

[1] The painful particularity with which Judge Sewall describes this scene, of which he was a spectator, suggests to us, by contrast, the great change in our modern views and usages in the execution of the sentence of the law inflicting capital punishment. All that the civil and religious acts and exercises of those times could effect to give publicity to the final scene, closed the whole series of similarly demonstrative and distressing spectacles and observances which preceded it. The processes connected with the indictment and the trial in court were intended to be made very solemn and awful by devotional services. The judges prayed, and, in passing sentence, often preached, as we have noticed on a previous page (p. 39), when the Judge reminded Esther Rogers of quite another Esther mentioned in the Bible. On the Sunday preceding an execution, or on the day of the Thursday lecture, the doomed culprit, heavily chained, was the subject of direct and special prayer and exhortation, and often of sharp objurgation, in the meeting-house, crowded with curious, excited, and morbid spectators. Then followed the public procession with the dread ministrations of law through the streets, the criminal being drawn in a cart, with his coffin behind him. Women, shrieking and swooning, as we read in the text, mingled in the hurrying and gazing throng which extended from the foot of the scaffold as far as the wretched spectacle was visible, and then a broad-side, in the style of gallows literature, was peddled abroad. — EDS.

[2] In what we should call an "Extra," of the "News Letter," we find an account of the behavior, and last, dying speeches, of these pirates. In this it is said: "There were Sermons Preached in their Hearing Every Day: And Prayers daily made with them. And they were Catechised. And

July, 2.ᵈ Lords Day, Madam Paige is buried from her own house, where Mrs. Perry is Tenant, between 6 and 7. p.m. Bearers Lᵗ Govʳ Povey, Usher; Sewall, Addington; Col. Phillips, Foxcroft. Rings and Scarves. The Tomb was near Messengers. The Govʳ, his Lady and family there. Note. By my Order, the diggers of Mᵐ Paiges Tomb dugg a Grave for Lambert, where he was laid in the Old burying place Friday night about midnight near some of his Relations: Body was given to his Widow. Son and others made Suit to me.[1]

July, 3, *Feria Secunda*, I read the three first sheets of the Trial of the Pirats. July, 4. Send David to Cambridge with Joseph's cloths. July 15. *Feria quarta*. Last night very refreshing Thunder shower. Rains this morning. Goe to Cambridge with Mr. Tho. Brattle in Stedman's Calash. Spent the forenoon in the Meetinghouse. Waited on the Govʳ from Dinner Time till the last Question: Then follow'd the Govr in. Mr. Gibbs[2] was holding the last Question. Dr. Dumer[3] rose up and in very fluent good Latin ask'd Leave, and made an oposition; and then took Leave again with Comendation of the Respondent. Came home with Col. Townsend.

Mr. Dudley[4] made a good Oration in the morning. men-

---

they had many occasional Exhortations.'' The exhortation of the ministers on the scaffold is given, and the prayer of one of them, of considerable length, is reported *verbatim*. In Captain Quelch's dying speech, there appears none of the bravado to which Sewall alludes, though he warned the by-standers to beware '' how they brought Money into New England to be hanged for it.'' — EDS.

[1] We do not know why Lambert should thus have been allowed burial apart from the other pirates. He may have had respectable connections here. — EDS.

[2] Perhaps Henry Gibbs, who graduated in 1685. — EDS.

[3] Jeremy Dummer, of the Class of 1699, in Harvard College, had received the degree of *Philosophiæ Doctor*, at Utrecht, in 1703. — EDS.

[4] Probably William Dudley, of the Class of 1704. It was an old custom to honor, by mention at the annual commencement, the benefactors of the College. — EDS.

tion'd Benefactors, Harvardus, Stoughtonus, Spragus,[1] Decease of Col. Pierce. Captivity of Mr. Williams. Judges as at the first, Councellors as at the Beginning [Isaiah i. 26.]

July, 10th. 1704. Went to Benj Child beyond the Pond, to bespeak his driving my wife to Brooklin to morrow. As came home visited my old friend Mr. Bailey, who has been confin'd some Moneths by the Stone. He was very glad to see me. Mr. Stoughton's Executors have made offers to him for compliance, which he has taken up with. Rid over the Neck with my Brother.

July, 11th. 1704. Son and daughter Hirst, Joseph and Mary, rode with me in the coach to Brooklin, and there dined at my Son's with the Governour, his Lady, Mr. Paul Dudley and wife, Mr. Neh. Walter and wife, Dr. Dumer, Mrs. Anne Dudley, Mrs. Mary Dudley, Mr. Flint and others. Call'd in as went to Hartford. Sung a Psalm.

July, 12. *feria quarta*, went to Dedham in company of Mr. Gray, and David Jeffries; find Judith well, carried her a little Basket and some Cakes. Mr. Belcher preach'd from Lam. 3. Why doth living man complain. Din'd at Mr. Avery's with Judith. Harvest begun.

July, 13. 1704. Thin Lecture at Boston by reason of the Heat. In the afternoon Jenkyns arrives, 9 weeks from England; brings News of the Arrival of all our Fleet there.

July, 16. Lords-day morn, Miles arrives, who came out with Jenkins.

July, 21, 1704. Mr. Thomas Weld, who proceeded Master of Arts this Comencement, July 15th, died this day at his unkle Wilson's at Braintry. July, 22, *Feria septima*, is buried from his unkle Weld's at Roxbury. Mr. Bromfield and I were there, rode with Madam Bromfield

---

[1] Richard Sprague, of Charlestown, who bequeathed to Harvard College £300, Massachusetts currency. He died in 1703. See Quincy's History of Harvard University, I. 409. — EDS.

in the Calash. Mr. Walter prayed in the Orchard. Mr.
Bromfield and I follow'd the Relations; then Mr. Dan-
forth and Mr. Walter. Mr. Bailey is very bad and in his
chamber; as Mr. Bromfield told me, who went to see him.
Govr is gon to Dedham. It begins to be known that the
Bills of Credit are counterfeited, the Twenty-Shilling
Bill.[1]

July, 24, 1704. Mrs. Zachary,[2] the Quaker's wife, who
died in child-bed, is brought in a black Walnut Coffin to
the South-end of the Town, carried down the 7-Star Lane,[3]
and then into Bishop's Lane, and buried in the inner Corner of Mr. Brightman's Pasture [4] and Orchard. It seems

---

[1] See Province Laws, Vol. II. pp. 503, 666. — EDS.

[2] Probably this was the wife of Daniel Zachary, whose will, dated
March 10, 1704–5, proved Jan. 16, 1705–6, is in Suff. Wills, Lib. XVI. f. 97.
He was a merchant, mentions a lot of land in Philadelphia worth £120, and
names his son, Lloyd Zachary, and sisters Elizabeth Stephens and Winifred
Brabins. The boy was to be with his uncle and aunt Hill until ten years
old, when he was to go to the testator's brother, Thomas Zachary, in London.

It will be noted that the Quaker meeting-house was, at this time, in
Brattle Square. In 1709, the Quakers bought a lot on Congress Street, opposite Lindall Street, where afterward the Transcript building stood. Here
was their cemetery; the first, probably, used by them. Shurtleff doubts if
they had any earlier one, and this burial on Hawley Street confirms this idea.
— EDS.

[3] Now Summer Street. Bishop's Alley is now Hawley Street. — EDS.

[4] In regard to Brightman's pasture, we learn, from the "Book of Posses-
sions," that Robert Reynolds owned the southerly corner of Milk and
Washington Streets. Thence southerly on the latter street came Edward
Fletcher, Richard Waite, Charity White, Francis East, Nathaniel Eaton,
Richard Hogg, John Marshall, and Nathaniel Woodward on the corner of
Summer and Washington Streets.

East, on Milk Street, from Reynolds, were John Stevenson, Nathaniel
Bishop, Nicholas Parker, James Pen, John Kenrick, &c.

East, on Summer Street, from Woodward, were John Palmer, Jr., Amos
Richardson, John Palmer, Sen., Gamaliel Waite, &c.

In the centre were William Hudson, Robert Scott, and others; but Bishop
and Parker bounded south on Hudson, and Richardson bounded north on
Hudson.

Oct. 5, 1695 (Suff. Deeds, Lib. XVII. f. 150), Jonathan Curwin, of
Salem, and wife, Elizabeth, and Sampson Sheaffe, with wife, Mehitable,
sold Henry Brightman one and three-fourth acres of land, undoubtedly part
of Hudson's lot. It was bounded, north, by land late of Nathaniel Bishop;

one spake much at the Grave. Proclamation is issued out against the Forgers of the Bills &c.

July, 25, 1704. Major Walley and I rid together in Heton's Calash to Cambridge Court: there met Col. Hathorne and Mr. Leverett. Major Walley and I came home together. Old Bell rung 9 as we got to the Ferry. Gave Heton 6 shillings. Between 10 and 11 by that time we got home. The Forgers are discover'd.

Mr. Barnard of Andover married Lydia Goff last week and din'd with us.

July, 31, 1704. Capt. Ephr. Savage, Mr. Antram and I ride to Dedham, Dine there with Capt. Barber, I visit Judith. From Dedham to Medfield. There I meet Mr. Gookin, his wife and Son. Have Mr. Gookin for our Pilot to his house. Call at Capt. Mors's about an hour in night; and he tells us of the Indians assaulting Lancaster. This was very heavy News to us now in a Fronteer Town; yet we went on, lodg'd at cousin Gookin's, and were kept safe. Tuesday and Wednesday did our business, and came home on Thorsday.

Augt 25th *feria Sexta*, Mr. Richard Wilkins being blind

---

south, on Amos Richardson; west, on Bishop's Lane (now Hawley Street); east, on Thomas Marshall and Robert Keayne. This was Brightman's great pasture.

March 7, 1705–6. (Suff. Deeds, Lib. XXII. f. 475) Joshua Eaton, of Reading, and wife, Ruth, sold Henry Brightman the little pasture of thirty-eight rods six feet, being land formerly Nathaniel Bishop's, bounded, south, by. Brightman; west, by Bishop's lane; north, by Joshua Davis; east, by Mumford.

Henry Brightman left a widow, Abiel, and sons, Henry and Joseph, both victuallers. By Suff. Deeds, Lib. XXX. f. 98, and Lib. XXXII. f. 49, it seems the Little pasture was 110 feet on the south line, 150½ feet on Bishop's alley, 40 feet on Davis, 137½ feet east, on Brown.

Also Brightman's widow had a house which was 27 feet on Marlborough (Washington) Street, north, 25 feet on John Gray, and with it a yard and another house and lot, which came to the west side of Bishop's Alley, there measuring 15 feet.

We conclude, then, that Brightman's pasture was on the east side of Hawley Street, the second lot from Summer Street, and reached, probably, across Franklin Street. — EDS.

and helpless, goes to Milton to live and dye there with his daughter Thacher. Mr. Gray and others ride after the coach. He call'd and took leave as he went along : I and my wife went to him as he sat in the Coach.

Aug^t —— at the South Church, Mr. Tho. Bridge pray'd, Mr. Pemberton preach'd : just as had done his Sermon and stood up to pray, a Cry of Fire was made, by which means the Assembly was broken up, but it pleas'd God the Fire was wonderfully Quench'd. The wind was South-wardly, so that if it had proceeded from the Tavern Ancor,[1] probably the old Meeting House and Townhouse must have been consumed and a great part of the Town beside. Ministers express'd great Thankfullness in the Afternoon for this Deliverance. Dr. Incr. Mather pray'd, Mr. Willard preach'd and then pray'd. Mr. Thacher and Mr. Danforth sup'd with us.

Augt. 29. rode to Roxbury Lecture. Visited Mr. Bayley. Mr. Walter preach'd from [Psalm] 119–71. It is good for me that I have been Afflicted : Kept from sin, made more fruitfull, shew me wherefore Thou contend-est with me. Waited on Madam Dudley home, presented her with Mr. Fowl's Books for Govr and self. Saw my Daughter there. Son was getting in Hay.

Feria septima, Septr 9. 1704. Col. Hathorne and I set out for Bridgewater, Sam. Moodey waits on me. Bait at Braintry. A Taunton man, Mason, overtakes us and becomes a very good Pilot to us through the wilderness. Dine late at Waldo's upon the edge of Bridgewater. Got to Howard's about a quarter of an hour before Sun-set. Septr 10. Mr. Keith administred Baptisme and the Lords super, whereby my Missing the Administration of it at home, was supplied.

Septr 11 Rode to Taunton ; from thence Capt. Leñard

---

[1] We have mentioned (Vol. I. pp. 89, 461) the Blue Anchor Tavern. As it was on Washington Street, the second estate north of Little, Brown, & Co.'s book-store, a south wind would have carried the flame as Sewall says. — EDS.

and Mr. King accompanied us through very bad way. Dined at Luther's. I was threaten'd with my sore Throat: but I went to Bed early at Mr. Sparhawk's, pin'd my Stocking about my Neck, drunk a porringer of Sage Tea, upon which I sweat very kindly. The pain of my Throat was the more painfull to me, for fear of my being rendred unable to goe to Court next morning; and then the Court must have fallen, for was only Major Walley with us. Sept.ʳ 12. I was so well recover'd as to go to the Court, not losing any time. Sept.ʳ 13. grew very well. Sept.ʳ 14. Adjourn'd the Court *sine die*. Dined at Col. Byfield's with the Justices at Papasquash.¹ From thence the Gentlemen accompanyed us to the Ferry: Lodg'd at Mr. Smith's at Rehoboth. Sept.ʳ 15. Baited at Slack's; Dined at Billenges. At Dedham met the Comĩsioners going to New-York, Col. Townsend, Mr. Leverett: Gave Mr. Leverett my Letter to Mr. Williams: In it was a Letter of Credit for some Money not exceeding Ten Ounces. Visited my Dear little Judith. Got home about Sunset or a little after. *Laus Deo*.

Monday, 7r. 11ᵗʰ Mr. Robert Hawkins dies in the Afternoon. 7r. the 12th buried; Hill, Williams, Checkley, Belknap, Cole, Emory, Bearers. Great Funeral.

Sept.ʳ 12ᵗʰ Mrs. Tuthill falls through a Trap Door into the cellar, breaks her right Thigh just above the knee, so that the bones pierce through the skin.

Sept.ʳ 19. Mrs. Tuthill dies.

Thorsday, 7ʳ 14th. Mr. William Hubbard,² of Ipswich, goes to the Lecture, after to Col. Apletons: Goes home, sups, and dyes. that night.

Thorsday, 7ʳ 21. 1704. Mrs. Mary Tuthill, widow, buried; Govʳ, Lᵗ Govʳ, Capt. Smith at the Funeral. Bear-

---

¹ A part of the town of Bristol, R. I. — EDS.

² Rev. William Hubbard, born in England, 1621. By request of the Colonial authorities he wrote a history of New England, his compensation being £50. He published other historical and biographical works. — EDS.

ers, Elisha Hutchinson, Sewall; Addington, E^m Hutchinson; Legg, Belchar. Laid in a brick Grave of the South Burying place,[1] southwest corner of it. Mr. Neh. Hubbard dined with us this day.

Wednesday, Octob.^r 4. 1704. Went to Dedham Lecture in company with Mr. Danl Oliver. Mr. N. Hobart fell in with us two miles before we got to Town. Visited Judith. Text, Wisdom is the principal thing. Grace is Glory in the Bud; Glory is Grace full-blown. Din'd with Mr. Belchar. Got home about 7 at night.

Octob.^r 12. Mr. Cotton Mather prays for the College and other schools. Mr. Ezk. Lewis marries the widow Kilcup, Octob.^r 12.

Octob.^r 13. Deacon Dyer of Weymouth, Mr. Torrey's Right Hand, is to be buried to-day. Dy'd with a Fall from's Horse.

Octob.^r 14th 1704. visited Col. Savage. He has kept house 7 weeks. Mr. Wigglesworth came to Town the 9th Inst^t and ə^dministers to him. I pray'd God to bless his sickness to him; and his Physick for his Restauration. He seem'd refresh'd with my company.

Octr 24. Went to Roxbury Lecture. Mr. Walter, from Mat. 6. 1. Shew'd we should have a care of Wrong Ends in doing Duties. Led my daughter Sewall home. Then visited Mr. Walter; told Mr. Mather of Alcasar, Dan. 12. 7;[2] and scattering power of the Holy people; not

---

[1] The tombstone of Mary, relict of John Tuthill, is still in the Granary, bearing a coat of arms, as is shown in the Heraldic Journal, II. 132. She was sixty-seven years old, and was probably the mother of Zechariah Tuthill, Lieutenant of Castle William. Of her daughters, Sarah married James Gooch, Susanna married Abraham Blish, and Mary was the wife of Deacon Thomas Hubbard. — EDS.

[2] The text is, "Blessed is he that waiteth and cometh to the thousand three hundred and five and thirty days."

And here, à propos of prophecies, we would say that, in Vol. I. p. 97, Sewall mentions Zadori, and we inserted in the text the words [it may be a writer on Prophecies]. But we find that the late Rev. Samuel Sewall printed in the "American Quarterly Register" for 1838, p. 180, the following extract

to be understood of the Jews, as he had set it in his Problema Theologicum.

Nov[r] 13. set out for Salem with Major Walley; Lodg'd at Lewis's, being taken with a Storm of Rain.

Nov[r] 26. Major Davis dies of a Flux about 6. in the evening after the Sabbath. I knew not that was sick till about 24 hours before.

Nov[r] 30 Major Davis buried; Bearers, Elisha Hutchinson esqr: Sewall, Addington, Foster, Jeffries, Joseph Parson. Mr. Torrey lodg'd here last night, and went home this day, Nov[r] 30.

Dec[r] 1. Went to Charlestown Lecture. After Lecture discoursed with Capt. Chamberlain, Phillips, and Mr. Austin, all of the Comittee could meet with, to persuade them not to go on with their Action against me.[1]

Dec[r] 2. Visited my son and Daughter at Brooklin.

Dec[r] 7th Mr. Clark of Chelmsford dies of a Fever; was taken very suddenly the Friday before, after he had been at a Funeral; buried the 11th.

Dec[r] 10th Mr. Richard Wilkins[2] dies at Milton; is

---

from Sewall's "Common-place Book," p. xc. *verso*, now in our possession, distinguishing it from the "Journal:" —

"Wednesday, Nov. 15, 1682. Mr. Sherman ordains Mr. Nath. Gookin, Pastor of Cambridge Church; Mr. Eliot gives the Right Hand of Fellowship, first reading the Scripture that warrants it. Mr. Sherman, Eliot and Mather laid on Hands. Then Mr. Gookin ordain'd Deacon Stone and Mr. Clark Ruling Elders. The presence of God seemed to be with his People. Mr. Jonathan Danforth, the Deputy Governours onely Son, lay by the wall, having departed on Monday Morn of a Consumption. 'Tis a comfortable day, and much People at the Ordination. I go and come on foot in Company of Mr. Zadori, the Hungarian, whom I find to be an Arminian." — EDS.

[1] About Sewall's claim to the "Land of Nod," see p. 62 *ante*. — EDS.

[2] Richard Wilkins and his "daughter Thatcher" (referred to, *ante*, p. 115) have caused us some trouble. Undoubtedly she was Susanna, second wife of Rev. Peter Thatcher, and widow of Rev. John Bailey or Bayley. Bailey's first wife, Lydia, died April 12, 1690, and he died, as his tombstone in the Granary witnesses, Dec. 12, 1697. His widow, Susanna, mentioned in his will, married, Dec. 25, 1699, Rev. Peter Thatcher, of Milton. Her tombstone, at Milton, bears the following inscription: "Here lies the remains of Mrs. Susanna Thacher, second wife of the Rev. Peter Thacher,

brought in the coach to Boston, Decr 12; buried Decr 13 in the uper end of the South-burying place.[1] I went to the Burying as I came from Charlestown Court. Son

---

who died Sept. 4, 1724, æt. 59 yrs." She was, therefore, younger than Comfort, if we are to trust Dunton. Her will (Suff. Wills, lib. 23, fol. 380) mentions her dear kinsman, Mr. John Baily, of Boston; sister, Madam Rebecca Brown; kinswoman, Mrs. Margaret Pain; sons, Oxenbridge and Peter Thatcher; daughters, Gulliver and Niles; nieces, Elizabeth, Ann, and Comfort Alison; kinswoman, Susanna Glover.

Her children named were her step-children, being Thatcher's children by his first wife. Her sister, Rebecca Brown, was undoubtedly Rebecca Bayley, who married William Brown, of Salem, as Savage reports, and as undoubtedly was sister of Rev. John Bayley.

Her kinswoman, Mrs. Margaret Pain, was unquestionably Margaret (Stewart), wife of William Payne (see Mass. Hist. Soc. Proceedings, for January, 1875, p. 415), and this gives us the necessary proof. For, as has been shown in Dunton's Letters, published by the Prince Society, Mrs. Wilkins and Mrs. Stewart were sisters; and, therefore, Mrs. Payne and Mrs. Thatcher were first cousins.

As to her three nieces, Elizabeth, Ann, and Comfort Alison, who gave a release for their bequests, to be seen in Suff. Deeds, lib. 38, fol. 212, less can be found. Dunton has much to say about Richard Wilkins, who was his landlord at Boston, and his daughter, Comfort, who was born about 1660. From the name of the niece, Comfort Alison, we may presume that Comfort Wilkins was their mother. The name of Alison is very uncommon here. Savage records that James Allison, of Boston, by wife, Christian, had James in 1650, and John in 1653. Nov. 27, 1690, Samuel Veazie, of Boston, in his will (Suff. Wills, lib. 11, fol. 243), mentions kinswoman, Christian Allison, daughter of James Allison, of New York, mariner.

Dec. 1, 1701, James Allison, of Jamaica, merchant, having died intestate at Boston, administration was granted to William Clarke. (Suff. Deeds, lib. 14, fol. 420.) — EDS.

[1] It may be convenient to note that there were then three grave-yards in Boston; the Copp's Hill, the King's Chapel, and the Granary. The last was established about 1660, and was, in the early part of the eighteenth century, called the South Yard. In 1754, the more southerly one, on the Common, was established (called, in 1810, the Central Yard); and, in 1810, the South Burying-ground, on Washington Street, between Newton and Concord Streets, was laid out. The name of the " South Yard" has thus been migratory. Probably there were other private yards at the South End, for it seems that, some five years ago, in widening Eliot Street near Carlton Place, there were found a number of tombstones, which, though not in situ, probably had not been removed far. One of these stones was for the infant son of Edmund Perkins, dated in 1682; the latter being the progenitor of the very distinguished Boston family of the name. — EDS.

Samuel there. Several of the Council and Ministers, Mr. Chiever, Williams, Gloves [to ?] Bearers.

Dec͛ 25. Monday, a Storm of Snow, yet many Sleds come to Town, with Wood, Hoops, Coal &c as is usual.

Dec͛ 30. Satterday, Daughter Sewall of Brooklin is brought to Bed of a Daughter, Rebeka. 31. is baptised.

Jan.ʸ 2. Madam Leverett dies; was taken with an Apoplexy last Thorsday, 2 or 3 Hours after her coming from Lecture. Mrs. Mason dies also this night.

Jan.ʸ 3 Tedman, the Brazier, opens his Shop and dies.

Emons, the shomaker, dies; is older than Benj Emons, his Brother.[1]

---

[1] Little is in print concerning the Emmons family, though it is still flourishing in Boston.

The first of the name was Thomas, of Newport and Boston, according to Savage, who had three sons, Obadiah, Samuel, and Benjamin. From the dates of their children, they probably stood in this order. Samuel was a shoemaker; but as administration was granted to his widow Oct. 27, 1685 (Suff. Wills, Lib. IX. f. 251), this could not be the man. Probably it was Obadiah, whose death we do not find.

In the next generation Benjamin, son of Benjamin, had a wife, whose obituary is as follows: —

"Boston News Letter," Oct. 16, 1740. "On the 8th inst. at night, died Mrs. *Mary Emmons*, wife to Mr. *Benjamin Emmons*, in the 67th Year of her Age, and had lived with her Husband 46 Years. She was the only Daughter of Capt. *Simon Amory*, of Barnstable, in Old England, a worthy Gentleman, Member of the first Church in Boston. Her parents dying when she was very young, her Uncle Drinker, who was for some time Teacher of the Baptist Church here, took the care of her and brought her up in a religious manner. She was a Member of the First Church in Boston about 40 years. She was a loving wife, a tender mother, a quiet and peaceable neighbour, and a good Christian; one who walked with God, and whose Life and Conversation was very inoffensive. She has left one only Son and two Grandsons."

Another branch claims especial notice. Samuel Emmons, by wife, Mary Scott, had a son, Nathaniel, born Feb. 9, 1669–70, who doubtless married Mary Warmall, Sept. 15, 1698. He had three children, — a son, Nathaniel, born in 1699, who died young; and a second Nathaniel, born in November, 1703. Administration was granted to the widow, Mary, Feb. 1, 1721.

The son, Nathaniel Emmons, was one of the early portrait-painters in Boston. He died May 19, 1740, aged thirty-six years and seven months, and was buried in the Granary. Administration on estate of Nathaniel Emmons, painter-stainer, was granted to the widow, Mary, June 3, 1740 (Suff. Wills,

Monday, Janʸ 1. 170⁴⁄₅ Col. Hobbey's Negro comes
about 8 or 9 *mane* and sends in by David to have leave to
give me a Levit[1] and wish me a merry new year. I admitted it: gave him 3 Reals. Sounded very well.

Janʸ 5ᵗʰ I dine at Mr. Paul Dudley's with the Govʳ,
Lᵗ Govʳ, Capt. Sam. Appleton, Mr. Colman, Mr. White,
Mr. Antho. Stoddard.

Janʸ 6. Begins to be some heat between the Govʳ and
the Deputies. At last the Govʳ sends in Mr. Secretary,
Mr. Eᵐ Hutchinson and Mr. Stoddard, to prorogue the
Assembly to the 21. Febr. at 10. m. At first the Deputies seem'd to be against Prorogation; afterward sent in
Capt. Checkly to say, That by reason of the thinness of
their House, Shortness and Coldness of the days, inclined
to a Prorogation. Speaker intimated their Desire of a
Fast.

Monday, January, 8. I went to the Funeral of Mrs.
Johaña Mason. She was a vertuous, pious woman, in the
70ᵗʰ year of her Age. Then went to the Council-Chamber, and from thence with the Governour to the Funeral
of Madam Sarah Leverett; Bearers, Govʳ Dudley, W.
Winthrop; Elisha Hutchinson, S. Sewall; Peter Sergeant,
Eᵐ Hutchinson. Had very warm discourse with the Govʳ
about Philip Morse, after came from the Tomb, at Mr.
Cook's.

Thorsday, Janʸ 11ᵗʰ The Govʳ and his Lady essaying to come from Charlestown to Boston in their Slay,
4 Horses, two Troopers riding before them, First the
Troopers fell into the water, and then the Govʳ making a

Lib. XXXV. f. 32; 392). The inventory amounts to £634: among the items
are eight mezzotint pictures, 64s.; two pictures, 20s.; one hundred brushes,
£8.10; two pictures, 15s.; sundry picture frames, 10s.; sundry colours, ground,
£5; and the Hon. Judge Sewall's picture, £20. This was, of course, the
portrait now in possession of Samuel Sewall, of Burlington, Mass., which
has been engraved, and is quite familiar to collectors. — EDS.

[1] Levet — a blast of a trumpet. — EDS.

stand, his four Horses fell in, and the Two Horses behind were drown'd, the Slay pressing them down. They were pull'd up upon the Ice, and there lay dead, a sad Spectacle. Many came from Charlestown with Boards, planks, Ropes &c. and sav'd the other Horses. Tis a wonderfull Mercy That the Govr, his Lady, Driver, Postilion, Troopers escaped all safe.

January, 19. 170⁴⁄₅ The Govr coming to Town, the way being difficult by Banks of Snow, his Slay was turn'd upon one side against the Fence next Cambridge, and all in it thrown out, Governour's Wigg thrown off, his head had some hurt; and my Son's Elbow. The Horses went away with the foundation and left the Superstructure of the Slay and the Riders behind.

Jany 26. Mr. Hirst and I went to Brooklin to see my Little Grand Daughter, Rebeka Sewall: He and I were on Horseback; in Simson's slay were Madam Willard, daughter Hirst, Hañah, and Mrs. Betty Hirst. Had some difficulty in going because of some deep descents between Banks of Snow. But went and came very well. Blessed be God. Din'd there. Before we came away, we sung the 113th Psalm. W [indsor?] While we were gon, Mr. Edw. Gouge was buried; Mr. E^m Hutchinson call'd at our House to take me with him to the Funeral. The poor Man Liv'd Undesired, and died Unlamented.

January, 29. I buy the two Folios of Mr. Flavell's works for £3.10–0 and gave them to Mr. Foster for his helping me in my Account last winter, to send to the Corporation [for Propagating the Gospel].

Jany 30. Major Walley and I ride to the Ferry in Simson's Slay, and at Charlestown, with Mr. Leverett, hold the Super^r Court. At Somers's I mention Justus Heurnius; [1] Mr. Leverett told me he would bring one if in the Li-

---

[1] Probably his "De Legatione Evangelica ad Indos Capessenda Admonitio." Leyden, 1618. — EDS.

brary; I promised to Lend him Judge Hales's[1] Origination of Mankind. Jan.ʸ 31. We interchange those two Books; which is the first time I ever saw Amiable Heurnius : I first found him quoted by Alsted[2] in his Treatise *De Mille Annis.* Febr. 6. Tuesday, Many go to the Council Chamber and there drink Healths on account of its being the Queen's Birth-Day. Maxwell did not call me, and I even staid at home, and went and heard Mr. Willard's Catechising Lecture. It seems the Govʳ order'd the Inferiour Court to be Adjourn'd upon the Account of it. Cousin Jer. Dumer, Philosophiæ Dr., going out of the Townhouse about 8 at night, fell by reason of the Ice, hit his left Temple against a piece of Brick-batt, Cut a great Gash at which much blood Issued: He was so stun'd as to be as dead when Mr. John Winthrop took him up. I dont remember that I knew the Govʳ was in Town till next day.

Febʳ 11ᵗʰ Mr. Pemberton preaches of the undoubted Interest children have in the Covenant, and baptiseth his son Ebenezer, who was born Febr. 6ᵗʰ Mrs. Hañah Savage, Mr. Phillip's daughter, is taken into the Church, though next Sabbath be the usual Season. It seems she desired it, as being likely then to be detain'd at home by child-birth.

Tuesday, Febʳ 13ᵗʰ Last night I had a very sad Dream that held me a great while. As I remember, I was condemn'd and to be executed. Before I went out I read Dr. Arrowsmith's[3] Prayer p 274 —— which was a comfort

---

[1] Sir Matthew Hale: " The Primitive Origination of Mankind, considered and explained, according to the Light of Nature. London, 1677." — EDS.

[2] Johann Heinrich Alsted, a German Protestant divine, 1588–1638. He was Professor of Philosophy and Divinity at Herborn, in Nassau, and was at the Synod of Dort. His " De Mille Annis Apocalypticis " appeared in London, in 1630. —EDS.

[3] John Arrowsmith, D. D., Master of St. John's and Trinity Colleges, successively, and Regius Professor of Divinity in the University of Cambridge. He died in 1659. Neal says of him: " He was an acute disputant and a judicious divine, as appears by his ' Tactica Sacra,' a book of great reputation in those times." — EDS.

to me. A Council was warn'd to meet at Noon. I was
there one of the first: Governour came in and quickly put
Capt. Lawson's Petition into my hand; and upon my
speaking somthing to it, He fell to a vehement chiding
about Philip Morse's business, and then with great Loud-
ness and passion spake to the affair of Capt. Lason's; several times said He would dy if ever any such thing was
done in England except in case of Felony or Treason, or
the like. I objected against that ridiculous part of the
Petition of his being forc'd by Mr. Clark or me to retire
into the neighbouring Province; as being a great Re-
proach to the whole Governm^t. No body apeared, I expected my Accuser face to face. Govr mov'd that a day
might be set for a Hearing: but the Council being but 7,
besides my self, declared they did not understand what
was contain'd in the Petition belong'd to them to deal in,
i. e. settling a Maintenance. Govr said, then it must be
left to another time.

Feb^r 14. I got a copy: Mr. Secretary told me he had
no Money paid for entring of it. Feb^r 14. Mrs. Odlin
buried; I went to the Funeral.

Feb^r 17. Richardson tells me that the Charlestown
Gent have sued me again. Here is Wave upon Wave.
The Good Lord be With me when so many, almost all, are
against me. Hern tells me the Petition was first in Mr.
Dudleys hand, and Mr. Secretary tells me 'tis Weavers
writing. When I ask'd Hern who drew it, He answer'd
all, i. e. Dudley, Newton, Valentine and he. Newton denys
it; but I perceive will stand Neuter. Febr. 23. Jer.
Dumer, Dr. Philosoph., went with me to Col. Lynde's at
Charlestown: I pleaded first to the Jurisdiction of the
Court; then to the writ, that it could not ly, because I
was in Possession. [In margin, — Land of Nod.] Went
to Lecture. Din'd at Col. Lyndes with Mrs. Everton,
Major Davison.

Febr. 24. Singing of Birds is come.

March, 2. Deputies present the Govr with Two Hundred pounds. Towards night the Govr called upon the Council to consider George Lason's Petition;[1] If he might have a Protection, he was ready to come. [In margin, — Great Dispute.] Council excepted against their meddling with settling estates of Maintenance; knew not that it was his Petition. Spoke pretty much to it.

March, 3. Govr said he would now take their vote whether they would hear Lason : Twas carried in the Negative, not one that I observ'd, speaking for it. I read a Clause out of Dalton[2] shewing when an officer might break open a House. Mention'd the Act of Parliam^t about cutting Poles where the Fine is but Ten shillings; yet a suspected person's house might be entred. In presence of 2 Justices Peers house might be broken up and yet peer must not be attach'd or imprison'd. Because the Govr had said, Must be Treason or Felony. And upbraided me, because had broken up the house, and then taken his parol till morning. Should have sent him to Prison with 20 Halberts. No Law for a man to live with his wife. I said Govr [Thomas] Dudley's saying was, A bargain's a Bargain and must be made Good; If we look'd to the Form of Marriage should find twas a great deal Lason had promis'd. Govr seem'd to reject it with disdain, and ask'd Col. Hutchinson when he lay with his wife? Col. Hutchinson answer'd, The Question should not have been when he lay with his wife; but when he

---

[1] A search of the remaining records fails to disclose any particulars as to Lason's case. George Lason, described as a mariner, and once termed "late commander of the Baron Frigate," had several suits about this time for money alleged to be due him. May 10, 1706, Martha Lason, wife of George L., represented to the Superior Court that her husband had gone to England, and that he intrusted all his property to David Josse, of Boston, who was to pay her six shillings per week for her subsistence. She could not collect this allowance, and so prayed for relief, which was granted. — EDS.

[2] Doubtless the law book entitled "The Country Justice," by M. Dalton, published first in the time of James I., and often reprinted; or else a work by the same author, on "The Office and Authority of Sheriff." — EDS.

lay with another woman. I said, The people were ready to pull down Lason's house, high time for the Government to interpose. Mr. Henchman had not complain'd of the Watch for knocking him up the other night. Lason's house was on fire, and he was not aware of it; high time for the Government to awaken him. Last night mention'd the Queen's Proclamation, and Governours to do to the utmost to supress Imorality and profaneness: None had yet shew'd me any Law I had broken. Govr mention'd Dalton.

March, 4. Lord's-Day. A great deal of snow falls after a great deal of Rain the night before.

March, 9. Govr sails for Piscataqua in a Briganteen belonging to Capt. Belchar and Mr. Pepperil.

March, 13. I go to Charlestown Court. Col. Phillips tells me his wife could not sleep for thinking of the Danger the Govr was in by reason of the vehement storm on Satterday night.

March, 14. go to Charlestown Court: take David with me to carry my Books.

March, 15. between 10 and 11. m. I rec. Brother's Letter giving an account of the extraordinary danger the Govr had been in, and their wonderfull Deliverance that was at Glocester, and were going to fetch him to Salem.

March, 17. Mr. E^m Hutchinson carrys me in his chariot to meet the Govr; was got home and at Diñer: After Diñer were call'd in: Told the Govr I did congratulat His Excellency and the Province upon the great Salvation God had wrought for him.[1] Went and visited Mr. Bayly who was very glad to see us.

---

[1] "The governor, in the month of March this year [1705], returning by water from his other government of New Hampshire, before the brigantine in which he had taken his passage came up with Cape Ann, was surprized with as violent a storm as had been known and of as long continuance. There being advice brought to Boston of his sailing from Portsmouth and no further intelligence of him, it was generally apprehended that the vessel

Satterday, March, 24. 170$\frac{4}{5}$. Between 1 and 2 p. m. I set out with Sam. Robinson for Weymouth. Call at Cousin Quinsey's and carry Shepard of the Virgins,[1] and take Dalton away with me to Weymouth, where I made use of it in convicting Ichabod Holbrook for Drunkenness, whom I saw drunk as rode into Town the 24th, and convicted and sentenced him at Capt. Frenches. March 26, 1705. Lodg'd at Mr. Torrey's, He was full of grief by reason of the dangerous illness of Mrs. Torrey's eldest daughter, the wife of his Nephew Torrey. Lord's Day, March 25, 1705. p. m. Mr. Torrey after sermon baptised two children, pray'd that God would fit us by this Ordinance for the Other. Administred the Lord's Super, did not pray after his delivering the wine, but only sung a Psalm. When came home said he was never so weary before; could neither speak or stand any longer. Col. Hunt was in the seat with me.

March, 26. set out for Barker's, a souldier from Deerfield accompanied us with his Fusee.[2] At Barkers the Sheriff met us, and Major Walley and Mr. Leverett came up : So went cheerfully along, and got to the sheriff's House in good season, where were entertain'd.

March, 28. I got up betime and begun my Birth-day in the Meetinghouse. Finished the Court this day.

March, 29. Thorsday, came homeward, Din'd at Cushing's : Call'd at Mr. Torrey's, Took my Dalton. Mr. Leverett and I visit Madam Shepard. Got home in good

---

must have foundered. At length came news of his arrival in the harbour of Glocester, having been four days at anchor on the back of the cape, expecting every hour to perish. In a proclamation for a public thanksgiving, a few days after, notice is taken of his wonderful preservation from shipwreck." Hutchinson's History, II. 148. — Eds.

[1] Parable of the Ten Virgins, opened and applied by Thomas Shepard, late worthy and faithful pastor of the Church of Christ, at Cambridge, in New England. — Eds.

[2] Notwithstanding this mention of a soldier from Deerfield, it is clear that Sewall was leaving Weymouth, probably for Plymouth. — Eds.

season, and found all well; never had a more comfortable
Journey.

March, 30. Went to the Funeral of young Mr. Allen,
Mr. Daniel Allens son, a very hopefull youth, Mr. Georges
Aprentice. Gov[r] and his Lady there. Bearers Willard,
David Stoddard; Bronsdon, Colman; Banister, Foxcroft.
Mr. Willard's Meeting was diverted by it, to a Moneth
hence. After Funeral, call'd at Mr. Clark's; I congratu-
lated her Recovery. Mr. Winthrop and Madam Eyre and
many more there.

Lord's Day, April, 1. My daughter Hirst is join'd to
Mr. Colman's Church. The good Lord Accept her in
giving up her Name to his Son.

April, 12, 1705. Thanksgiving Day. The Night was
so cold that was a very great Frost, thick Ice, and the
street frozen like winter. Remain'd frozen at Noon in
the shady places of the street. Mr. Melyen had a great
Tub of water frozen so hard, that it bore two men standing upon it in his sight.

April, 17. Council; Capt. Tuthill's Allowance of 80.£
would not pass: so Gov[r] would pass none of the Quarter-
Roll for the Castle.

April, 18. 1705. Gov[r] sets out for Piscataway, his
Lady in the Calash with him. Brother met his Excellency at Lindsey's. Got to Town that night and lodg'd
at son Hirst's.

April, 18. 1705. Sam. Robinson planted 8 Trees at
Elm pasture, one white-oake.[1] Three Trees at Phipenys;
Elm, White oak, Ash; one Elm at Morey's pasture.

---

[1] The following extracts are from the Town Records of Boston. — Eds.

March 11, 1700 [O. S.]. Town Records, Vol. II.

" It was voted, That all the land on both sides of the way, between the
oak and Walnut and the Fortification, the Town's right and title therein, be
given to such persons as shall undertake sufficiently to make and maintain
the highway for ever, not less then fifty foot wide; and that Sam[ll] Sewall,
esq. and Capt. Bozoon Allen be a Committee to agree with persons accord-

Monday, April, 23. Sam. Robinson sets four Poplars in the Foreyard, to shade the windows from the Western sun in Sumer. Remov'd the little Peach-Trees. As were setting the Trees, heard and saw several Swallows; which are the first I remember to have seen this year. Widow Holland visits us. Guns fired about Noon: Flags, and Ships Colours flying.

April, 26. 1705. Mr. Paul Dudley buries his little son Thomas: He was taken with a swelling in's Groin and stopage of his Water. On the coffin was nail'd a little Plate of Lead with this Inscription

Thomas Dudley.

Pauli Dudlœi Armigeri[1] *et Luciœ uxoris Filius primogenitus, Nepos Josephi Dudlœi Gubernatoris Novœ Angliœ. Natus est* 13. *Aprilis* 1705. *Obi't* 25 *ejusdem.*

---

ingly; and to make application to the proprietors for their approbation and Consent, that if any appear to accept of the Land upon these Conditions, they may have an unquestionable Title.

"D? Elisha Cook esq᷼ , Isaac Addington, esq, Sam˭ Sewall, esq᷼ , Penn Townsend, esq᷼ , Capt. Sam˭ Checkley, were by a Vote of the Town, chosen a Committee to draw up instructions for the Selectmen and Overseers of the poor, and present the same to the Town (the next Gen˭ Town meeting) for their Approbation. And it was further voted, That the same Committee, together with the Selectmen, shall consider about repairing or building or hiring a House for Mr. Ezek˿ Cheever, which they judge may be best."

March 20th, 1701 [O. S.]. Town Records, Vol. II. p. 253.

"Samuel Sewall, Esqʳ and Hannah his wife grants unto the Town of Boston, a certain strip or slip of land fenced and layd out for a High way or Street, running through their field or pasture at the northerly end of Boston, called by the name of Hull Street, containing in Length about thirty rodds, in breadth at the easterly end Twenty two foot next the Green Lane, and at the westerly end Twenty five feet. Reserving liberty to fence in two foot in breadth thereof upon the southerly side. As p. a deed under their hand and seales doth more fully appear, and Entred with the Records of deeds for the county of Suffolk, Lib. 20, pa. 265."

[1] The inscription describing Paul Dudley as "armiger," reminds us that, though Governour Thomas Dudley and Governour Joseph Dudley both used a coat-of-arms, it has thus far been found impossible to connect the emigrant with any English family of the name. Much has been writtten on the subject, but no satisfactory conclusion has been obtained. See Aldlard's "Sutton-Dudley's," and the Heraldic Journal. — EDS.

Only Mr. Addington and I of the Council were at the
Funeral.   Mr. Colman,   Mr. Woodward, Mr. Williams
Ministers.   Mr. Brattle, Mr. S. Lynde Justices.

April, 28.   Went to the Funeral of Sarah Beñet, her
Maiden Name was Harris : Mr. Perry her uncle.   Then to
the Funeral of Capt. Bozoon Allen's wife, Mr. Balston's
Daughter.[1]   A pretty many Graves are open'd : The Lord
grant that I may be cloathed upon, and so ready to be un-
cloath'd.

Friday, May. 4, 1705.   I visited my Son and daughter
at Brooklin; Little Grand-daughter.   Came home in the
Rain.

May, 8.   Went to Roxbury Lecture : visited Mr. Bayly;
join'd with Mr. Torrey in praying for him in his Chamber.
His Sister Doggett of Marshfield there.   Col. Allen died
last Satterday night.   Persons kill'd and carried away at
York and Spruce Crick last Friday.   New-found-Land;
Many of the people kill'd and captivated there.

May, 30, 1705.   Election.   Mr. Secretary, Sewall and
Walley Gave the Representatives the Oaths, &c. 64.
Councillors 26.   Winthrop, 82.   Russell, 84.   Hathorne,
71.   Elisha Hutchinson, 79.   Sewall, 83.   Addington, 77.
Brown, 86.   Phillips, 84.   Corwin, 78.   Foster, 81.   Hay-
man, 42.   Townsend, 80.   Higginson, 80.   Belcher, 74.

---

[1] As Savage's account of the Balstons is incorrect in part, we submit the
following sketch: There were three settlers of the name, William, who left
no son, James, and Jonathan.   The last was a merchant, and, by his wife
Mary, had sons John, Nathaniel, and Jonathan, daughters Mary, wife of
Isaac Vergoose, or Goose, Lydia Allen, and Prudence, wife of John Marion.
His wife died July 19, 1699, aged seventy-five, and he died June 6, 1706, aged
eighty-seven; both buried in the Granary.   His will (Suff. Wills, XVI. 156)
mentions all these children, John being deceased, leaving issue.   He seems
also to have had children, — Elizabeth, born Aug. 12, 1659; Elizabeth, born
Sept. 18, 1660; Robert, born Dec. 3, 1662; Benjamin, born Feb. 8, 1663–64;
all, probably, dying young.

As Captain Bozoun Allen had a wife, Lydia, we may safely consider her to
be the daughter of Jonathan Balston.   A grandson of Jonathan Balston
married Sewall's grand-daughter, as we have shown in the introduction to
Volume I. — EDS.

Legg, 70. Hunt, 53. Bromfield, 69. Stoddard, 56. Plimouth; Walley, 54. Thacher, 81. Winslow, 75. Pain, 80. Main; Hutchinson, 66. Hamond, 71. B. Brown, 71. Zag;[1] Lynde 53. Within the Province, Partridge 62, Samuel Appleton, 63. Debate about the Governour's Authority to Aprove or refuse the Speaker, made it late; so that twas past Eleven at night before the Election was finished. I advised the Gov[r] again and again to intermit the Debate, and considering the war, to let the election go on with a *Salvo Jure*, as to his Authority respecting the Speaker; Gave my Opinion, that in the clause of the Governour's Negative, General Court or Assembly, was no more than if it had been said Gen[l] Court: and that the House of Representatives was no where in the Charter, call'd Assembly. Gov[r] urg'd the Council to give their votes whether He had Authority to refuse the Speaker or no. Council pray'd it might be defer'd: But at last the Gov[r] prevail'd: And all were in the Negative except Higginson, Thacher, Lynde; 3 or four: and Higginson seem'd not to own his afterward. I said it was a point of great moment, and desired longer time; at present inclin'd to the Negative. Several sent in to the Deputies, I was almost forc'd in with them to persuade the Dept[s] to an Accomodation. First, Gov[r] told them He refus'd and directed them imediately to choose another. After an hour or more; Depts. sent a written vote asserting their Authority by Law and persisting, and shewing were ready to go on with the Election.[2] After this Message, sent to desire this Debate might be laid aside at present, and that might go on with the Election.

---

[1] This is Sewall's usual abbreviation of Sagadahoc. — EDS.

[2] Hutchinson, and other writers, mention this ill-advised attempt of Dudley to disallow the election of a Speaker by the House of Representatives. Hutchinson (Hist. II. 152) writes: "The prejudices against him [Dudley] were great. The people, in general, looked upon him as an enemy, even to the privileges of the new charter." — EDS.

Govr assented and wish'd us well with our work. Now twas Candle-Lighting: for went into Meetinghouse about 12. Mr. Easterbrooks made a very good Sermon. Twas four, or past, before went from the Anchor to the Townhouse.

May, 31. 1705. Govr, Major Brown, Sewall, Higginson, dine at Mr. Willard's with the Ministers. Brown, Sewall, Lynde go to Thank Mr. Easterbrooks for his Sermon and desire a Copy: He Thanks the Govr and Council for their Acceptance of his mean Labours and shews his unwillingness to be in print. When return'd found this paper on the Board:

GENTLEMEN, — I am very well satisfied of her Maj^s just Right and Prerogative to Allow, or disallow the Speaker of the Assembly of this Province, as well as the Council; being all elected by the Assembly. Therefore have proceeded as I have done, and as far as I can at present in that matter. But I have that just sense of the pressing Affairs of the War, that demand a very sudden Dispatch of this session, that will not consist with long Debates of any thing: And therefore shall not delay the Affairs necessary for the Security of the Province; which I desire may be first attended, Saving to Her most sacred Majesty Her just Rights as abovesaid, at all times.

This was comunicated to the Council and Assembly May, 31, 1705.[1]

per J. DUDLEY.

Note. Body was written by a scribe; Signing was the Governour's own Hand-writing.

In the forenoon pretty near Noon, Deputies sent in the Election by Major Converse, Capt. Checkly, Savage, Major Brown, Gardener. Govr gave us a very hearty wellcom to the Board, Sign'd the Bill, and 23. Took the Oaths before went to Diñer at Mr. Willard's.

Lord's Day, June, 10. 1705. The Learned and pious Mr. Michael Wigglesworth[2] dies at Malden about 9. m.

---

[1] The original is in Mass. Archives, Vol. CVIII. p. 30. — EDS.

[2] The Rev. Michael Wigglesworth was one of the most honored, eminent, and useful men of the early years of Massachusetts. Frequent mention is

Had been sick about 10. days of a Fever; 73 years and 8
moneths old. He was the Author of the Poem entituled
The Day of Doom, which has been so often printed: and
was very useful as a Physician.

July, 2. 1705. Lt Col. Thomas Savage dies about 6.
p. m̄.

July, 4. Com̄encment Day. I go by Water, with
Neighbour Deming, Green, Judd. Sail'd pleasantly till
came about the Capts Island,[1] then the wind and Tide
being against us, we went ashore and got over the Marsh
to the Upland; and so into the Rode and comfortably to

---

made of him in these pages in his twofold capacity as minister and physician. His gravestone, in the burial ground at Malden, commemorates him
in both these forms of professional service. In the time and circumstances
under which, both in Old and New England, the clerical and the healing
professions were often combined in the same person, Mr. Wigglesworth appears to have devoted himself, with equal earnestness and success, to each.
Though he was himself a life-long invalid, suffering from a mysterious disease, which compelled him for a season to suspend his ministry and to go to
the West Indies, he is credited with being a most helpful medical adviser to
others. Born in England, in 1631, he was brought, with his family, to Connecticut, in 1638. After graduating at Harvard, in 1651, he was a tutor
and a fellow of the College. Later in his life, in 1684, he declined the proffer
of the Presidency, on account of his health. He was ordained pastor of the
Church in Malden, which office he held nearly fifty years, till his death,
at the age of seventy-four. His son, Edward Wigglesworth, his grandson,
of the same name, and his great grandson, David Tappan, successively held
the Hollis Professorship of Divinity at Harvard for a period of more than
seventy years. Mr. Wigglesworth employed his leisure as an invalid in labors of the pen, especially in verse. The most famous, and at the time
popular and highly valued, of his productions, was his remarkable poem,
"The Day of Doom;" which, while it was the reward, must also have been
the terror, of the children of Puritan households, for whose use it was re-
produced in many editions, first published, in 1662. Another poem, which
he left in manuscript, was printed in the Proceedings of the Society for 1871.
"God's Controversy with New England." An elaborate memoir of Wigglesworth, by John Ward Dean, of Boston, is in print, the second edition bearing the date of 1871. — Eds.

1 Captain's Island is to be seen on Pelham's map of Boston and vicinity,
and is mentioned by Paige in his History of Cambridge, p. 13. It lies at
the westerly bend of the Charles River, below the Colleges, at the end of
Magazine Street. All the district was marshy, and perhaps overflowed at
high-water. — Eds.

Town.   Gave Gershom Rawlins a 20ˢ Bill.   Capt. Courte-
maruh¹ was there and din'd in the Hall.   In the morn.
Holyoke began that part of his oration relating to Mr.
Wigglesworth with, Maldonatus Orthodoxus.   Mr. Hutch-
inson² in his valedictory Oration Saluted the Justices of
the Superiour Court, and Councillors.   Came home in a
Calash with Col. Hutchinson and Mr. Penhallow: In the
Boat with Mr. C. Mather, Mr. Bridge.

July, 5.   Mr. Sol. Stoddard preaches the Lecture.   Col.
Savage buried about 7. p. m̄.   Companies in Arms: Bearers, Sewall, Foster; Walley, Lᵗ Coˡ Lynde; Townsend,
Belchar.   The Street very much fill'd with People all
along.

July, 16. 1705.   Mr. Barnabas Lothrop, of Barnstable,
visits me, with whom had much pleasant Discourse.   I
gave him Mr. Cotton Mather's sermon of the Lords Day,
and Letter to Govʳ Ashurst about the Indians, Mother
Hull's Epitaph.

July, 17. 1705.   I go a fishing in Capt. Boners³ Boat,
Joseph, Edw. Oakes and Capt. Hill with us; went out at
Pulling Point, between the Graves and Nahant, Catch'd
but 3 Cod.   I was sick and vomited; As came back went
to the Castle.   Neither Lᵗ Govʳ nor Capt. Tuthill there;
yet view'd the Works: Went to Governour's Island;
home.

July, 18.   The Deptford arrives.

July, 19.   Govʳ had a New Com̄ission read relating to
Pirats, and Queens Pleasure read for pardoning the sur-

---

¹ This name is utterly strange and mysterious. We have no clew to the
person intended. — EDS.

² William Hutchinson, A.B., 1702; A.M., 1705. — EDS.

³ From the rarity of this surname we are inclined to think that this was
John Bonner, father of the more famous Captain John Bonner (born in 1693),
whose map of Boston is well-known. It has been thought that the father
died abroad; but in the Heraldic Journal, II. 121, it is suggested that he
died in Boston, Jan. 20, 1725, aged eighty-four. The reference in the text
confirms this surmise. — EDS.

viving Pirats; and they in prison were sent for, and their
Pardon declared in open Court, Chains knock'd off; but
must go into the Queens service.

18. I visited the widow Hañah Glover, who is blind, is
just as old as Mrs. Rock to a few days. Father and
Mother Eliot [were?] married here.

July, 25. I went to Reading, and heard Mr. Pierpont
preach.

July, 27. I, my wife, Mary, Judith and Jane go to
Brooklin. Govr and Mr. White came to us there. July,
29. *Rimes apulit.*

July, 31. Went to Cambridge to keep Court. Augt 1.
Lodg'd at Mr. Brattles.

Augt 2. Court is finish'd. I visit Cousin Fessenden,
and dying Deacon Hasting. Augt. 7. Joseph goes to
Cambridge. Augt. 8. I and Mr. E^m Hutchinson go to
Noddles Island, visit Madam Shrimpton. Ride in the
Calash to Mr. Goodwin's: return to Madam Shrimpton.
Sup, Come home. Augt. 10. I visit poor Mr. Baily, sick
of the stone. Mr. Walter pray'd with him. Shew'd me
his new House which he goes into next week. Cousin
Moodey of York comes to us.

Augt. 15. I carry Mrs. Willard to Watertown Lecture and hear Mr. Gibbs preach excellently from John, 9.
4. — While it is Day — Din'd at Mr. Gibb's. When came
away were going to see Mrs. Sherman, and the Calash
fell backward and we both tumbled down; and twas long
ere could fit it again: so came directly home. *Laus Deo.*

Augt. 16. Mr. Walter preach'd the Lecture at Boston
in his Bro^r Mather's stead. Augt. 17th Cous. Moodey
goes away, I give him some folio of Calvin's Exposition.
Gave him a pair new Slipers.

Augt. 20. Went to Roxbury to wait on the Govr at
his going away to Connecticut, din'd there; went to Jamaica; Took Leave; went to Brooklin, to Cambridge, To
North Farms [Lexington] with Mr. Bordman and spoke

with Mr. David Fisk about Land of Nod: Came home late.

Augt. 22. Eliezer Moodey comes to us. Augt. 23. Judith is once thrown into the dirt above the stone-bridge; and the same day run over by a Horse; yet through God's Goodness receives little hurt. Mr. Sam. Melyen and his wife dine with us. I give him about 4. L. day, and 4. Baptistes.[1]

Augt. 24. I gave Mr. Rich'd Henchman Cooper's[2] Dictionary, cost 15^s, and Calvin on the Psalms cost 10^s, with these verses;

> *Mitto tibi Psaltem CHRISTUM et sua*
> *Regna canentem;*
> *Non erit ingratum dulce Poema tibi.*
> *Musicus hic lapides cithara sapiente trahebat;*
> *Et trahit: hinc Solymæ moenia celsa Novæ.*

Little Sam Green is buried; Bearers Sam. Gerrish, Mr. Eliott's Prentice, Mr. Campbell's Prentice, Sam. Smith. I, Hañah, Mary, Jane, at the Funeral.

Augt. 24. 1705. Mr. Samuel Myles[3] comes with his Bro^r before me; I bid him, Sam., sit down: but he quickly fell upon Nichols [the constable], the complainant against his Bro^r, and said by his Looks one might see the Gallows groan'd for him; I check'd him, and said it did not become a Minister so to speak. The constable ask'd me what weight the Money must be, 15. or 17. I answered there was no Money but 17^d w^t: but if Capt. Myles offer'd Bills of Credit he must take them. Mr. Saml Myles told me he complain'd of Nichols, but withall told me he was not ready to pursue it.

---

[1] We understand this to mean four copies of Mr. Mather's sermon on the Lord's Day, and four of "Baptistes, or a Conference about the Subject and Manner of Baptism," by the same author, published in 1704. — Eds.

[2] Probably "Thesaurus Linguæ Romanæ et Britannicæ," by Thomas Cooper, or Cowper, Bishop of Lincoln, and afterwards of Winchester, who died in 1594. — Eds.

[3] Rector of King's Chapel. — Eds.

Augt. 27. I sent Mr. Walter, Calvin on Hoseah by young Everden. Gave Mr. Pemberton Mr. Cotton on Ecclesiastes, and the Vials, having their double. He told me the evening before, He had little or nothing of Mr. Cotton.

Seventh-day; Sept.ʳ 8. 1705. Mrs. Mary Lake was buried at the North; Bearers, Sam. Sewall, Jnᵒ Foster; Eliakim Hutchinson, Sam. Checkley; John Ballentine, John Coney; Mr. John Cotton and his wife, Mrs. Lake's daughter, principal mourners: They got not to Town till the day after their Mother's death. Enock Greenlef dyed this day about 11 oclock.

Sept.ʳ 10. 2.ᵈ day. This morning I made this verse.

Oceani fluctus ANNA moderante superbos,
Euphrates cedit;[1] *Roma Relicta cadit.*

Faxit Deus! (See 8.ʳ 15.)

[In margin, *ut majestas tua palam apareat atque ejus sensu perculsa elementa cedant ac obtemperent.* Calvin, Isa. 63. ult.]

Sept.ʳ 10. In the Afternoon I went to speak to Mr. Allen that the Lord's Super might be celebrated once in four weeks, as it was in Mr. Cotton's Time and Mr. Wilson's: He was just come out of his house with Elder Bridgham, Elder Copp, Deacon Marion and Deacon Hubbard: I pray'd them to go back again, and open'd my mind to them. All save Mr. Hubbard plainly remember'd how it was in Mr. Wilson's days; and the Alteration upon the coming in of Mr. Davenport, upon his desire because he had it so at Newhaven: and seem'd inclinable enough to alter it. Then I went to Mr. Cooke, both he and Madam Cooke remember'd the change, and seem'd not displeas'd with my proposal. I discours'd with Mr. Pemberton, and told him it would be a Honor

---

[1] See Revelations, XVI. 2.

to Christ, and a great Privilege and Honor to Boston, to have the Lord's Super administerd in it every Lords Day: we having nothing to do with moneths now; Their Respect now ceases with the Mosaical Pedagogy. [Gal. III. 24.] It seems odd, not to have this Sacrament administred but upon the first day of each Moneth; and the rest of the Sabbaths always stand by.

Third-day 7ʳ 11ᵗʰ 1705. The Deputies send in their Answer to the Governour's speech dated this day, which begins, May it please your Excellency, and doth not end with, Sent up for Concurrence.[1]

This day 7ʳ 11ᵗʰ *mane*, Her Majesties Letter of the Third of May 1705. from Sᵗ James's, is read at the Board, wherein a new seal is order'd, and the old one to be defac'd: John Dixwell, the Goldsmith,[2] being sent for, cut it in two in the middle, with a Chisel.

In the evening I met with Mr. Cotton Mather's Letter which begins thus; Sir, your Distich entertains me. Both the Poetry and the prophecy of the vates, is very entertaining. I hope it begins to be a History &c. He had rather read CHRISTO, which I heartily agree; which besides Wars, takes in Storms and Tempests which Christ makes great use of in Governing the World; and in this He only is Moderator.

Friday, 7ʳ 14. I go to Newton, and hear Mr. Hobart. He has a Lecture once in Eight Weeks. Text was Levit. 26. 11. Doct. Obedience unto God, is the way to have the continuance of his Tabernacle; and to avoid the abhorrency of his soul.

Tuesday, 7ʳ 18. 1705. I went to Cambridge Court, where Col. Hutchinson, Tyng, Foster, Higginson, by a

---

[1] Apparently the document printed by Hutchinson. History, II. 150–152. — EDS.

[2] This was the son of the regicide, John Dixwell. This John left no male issue, but the name has been revived in his descendants in the female line, who changed their name from Hunt to Dixwell. — EDS.

special Comission, sat Judges of the cause between Charlestown and me [in margin, Land of Nod]; Jury brought in
for me Costs of Court: Court order'd judgment to be
entred : — Charlestown Comittee Apeal'd. Mr. Dudley
was my Attorney ; Hern and Valentine for Charlestown.
The chief plea they made was to the Jurisdiction of the
Court.

Sept.ʳ 20ᵗʰ Mary has a very sick turn, complains much
of the palpitation of the Heart.

Sept.ʳ 22. Set forward on my Journey towards Bristol,
with Col. Hathorn. Got to Wrentham an hour before
Sunset. Kept the Sabbath there.

Sept.ʳ 24. To the ship at Rehoboth, where din'd. Mr.
Newman piloted me to George Bairsto's, where saw him,
his wife, sister Gates. From thence Mr. Newman led us
the next way through the Neck. Then Mr. Pain accompanied us to Bristol. At Mr. Sparhawk's met with Col.
Byfield, his wife, Col. Taylor and wife, Madam Lyde and
her children. Major Walley and Leverett came late next
day; which made us almost lose the Forenoon. Thorsday din'd with Mr. Mackentash, Lᵗ Govʳ there, who came
up with Mr. Lyde. Col. Hathorne desired excuse, and
went homeward.

Friday broke up the Court and got to Rehoboth. Lodge
at Smith's, I got cold, and ventured not with the Company next morning being Rainy. But set out with Samˡ
Robinson about 11. m. when wether broke up. Dined at
Slack's: Got comfortably to Medfield, lodg'd at Mr. Bax-
ters, thô he not at home. Heard Mr. Jn° Veasy of Braintrey.

Octobʳ 1. Got home pretty early, about 12 or 1. (Mrs.
Fyfield and her daughter were at Medfield.) Drove a
Pin in the Ministers House which I found Raising; bolted
on the Raisers out of Bishop's Lane before I was aware.
Found my Family better than I left them. *Laus Deo.*
My horse fell with me this Journey, broke my crooper:

but I had no harm. Found Joseph at home, who on Satterday was a Bearer to Mr. Banisters child with Mr. Foster Stoddard. Heard of the childs death at Slack's.

Oct͏͏ᵣ 15. Three men are carried away from Lancaster
from Mr. Sawyers Sawmill [by Indians]. This day I made
this Distich;

> *Roma inhonesta jacet.*[1] *Sanctæ gaudete puellæ*
> *Vindicis et vivi Vivitis Urbe DEI.*

Gave them and two more to Mr. Phips at Charlestown
Oct͏͏ᵣ 16. Hear the bad news from Lancaster. Neighbour
Deming's House is Raised. Rainy day.

Octob͏ᵣ 17. very Rainy day.

Octob͏ᵣ 18. Dark and Rainy day.

Octob͏ᵣ 21. Several of the Fleet came in from Barbados. About Noon between Meetings, were several Claps
of Thunder, and Hail and Rain.

Feria tertia, Octob͏ᵣ 25. 1705. My Daughter Hirst is
Deliver'd of a Son, a little before Sun-rise. I staid there
till about 12 at night, then Mr. Hirst importun'd me to
come home. I prevail'd with my wife and Mary to go to
Bed (wife not well to go to her daughter.) Hañah and I
sat up to be in a readiness if any Messenger should come.
But the first we heard was this good News of a Son. *Laus
Deo.* As I sat up towards morning, I turn'd my Distich
thus

> CHRIST governing the mighty waves of the tempestuous Main:
> Euphrates turns,[2] and leaves old Rome to court Recruits in vain.

---

[1] *Mortua Moecha senex;* * &c. written 8͏ᵣ 21. 1715. on occasion of the
French King's death on the Lord's Day Augt. 21. 1715. [Sept. 1. N. S.]
Some say, he stunk alive.

[2] We copy, from Sewall's "Common-place Book," the following notes
which he had collected concerning this topic: —

"DE EUPHRATE. 'Dry up Euphrates and Babylon is taken with a wet
Finger.' Cotton's Vials, p. 96.

"'Ye shall have many Men serious of Reformation when the Lord shall

---

* This is the beginning of a Latin verse. The allusion, of course, is to the Eighteenth
Chapter of Revelations. — EDS.

At last I fix'd upon beginning, While CHRIST Com̄ands — that, according to our use, carrying more of the likeness of a Military Phrase: as our Governour is Com̄ander in Chief.

Seventh-day 8ʳ 27ᵗʰ These verses are printed off upon the side of the Almanack. This day we hear that James Blin is cast away. It seems the Castle is ordered to be call'd *Fort William;* and the Governour went down yesterday, and caus'd the inscription to be set up, a pretty many Guns fired. 8ʳ 27. as I was writing to my Brother, I ask'd the Govʳ; told me 'twas so, and directed me to tell my Broʳ that when he writt his account of Storey, he should style Salem Fort *Fort-Anne.* My wife went in the coach to see her daughter; 6ᵗʰ day, which is the first time since she Lay in, her Cold is so hard upon her.

Octobʳ 28. Little Samuel Hirst is Baptised by Mr. Colman; tis a very Rainy day.

Novembʳ This Distich finished

> *Desine Belshazzar Templo Omnipotentis abuti:*
> *Proxima fatalis nox sine fine tua est.*

Afterward this English

> Sound! Sound! the Jubilean Trumpet sound;
> Spread the Glad Tidings, Give the Word all round.

---

dry up the River Euphrates, that makes glad the City of Babel.' 116, 112, 127, 133. 'Some say that it's meant of Nations and People.' 89. 'Untill they have dryed up this River Euphrates, Hardness lyeth upon the Jews, but then all Israel shall be saved.' 94. ' This may serve to provoke us all earnestly to call upon the Lord, that He would stir up the Hearts of Princes to consider, and open their eyes to see how needfull their Attempts are to rise up against the Pope.' 95, 96.

"2 Esdras, 41, 42, 43. 'And they entered in at the narrow passage of the River Euphrates.' This place caused Mr. Ward, the Father, to conjecture that the Aborigines of America were descended from the ten Tribes; as Mr. Rowlandson told me Janʳ 22, 1696.

" ' By this time (it may be) we might have dried up Euphrates, I mean possessed the whole West Indies; which with little time and help from these parts may be accomplished.' H. Peters, Ap. 2, 1645, Sermon, p. 30." — EDS.

Novr 6th Super. Court. Novr 9th Tho. Odell Sentenc'd to pay a Fine of £300; suffer a years Imprisonment. Rochester, a Negro, sentenced to dye for firing Madam Savages Dwelling House in the night.

Novr 10. Ambrose Daws buried. Gillam and Mason arrive at Cape-Anne.

Novr 11th Hear of the Arrival, of Col. Hobbey being Knighted.[1]

Novr 12th New Comission for the Indian Affairs comes to hand. Brooklin is pass'd to be a Township by the Council. I go to Salem with Major Walley's Man. At Lewis's overtake Mr. Dudley, and have his company to Salem.

Novr 14. After the Court adjourned *sine die,* visited Rever^d Mr. Higginson, Madam Bradstreet, Bro^r Hirst. Novr 15. Had a very pleasant fair day to come home in. Baited at Sprague's. Visited Mr. Usher. He not at home, his wife entertain'd us. Found Mr. Willard at our house: He pray'd excellently with us. Have had a very comfortable Journey out and home.

Novr 21. Capt. Vech[2] and Mr. Wm Dudley come to Town from Cañada; came from thence last Friday was five weeks. Govr would not let them come till the Fleet sail'd for France.

Novr 24th Snow falls and covers the Ground. Has been very cold wether this week.

The College at Quebec was burnt the third time when

---

[1] Hutchinson writes (History, II. 152) of Hobby, that he "had been knighted, as some said, for fortitude and resolution at the time of the earthquake in Jamaica, others for the further consideration of £800 sterling." — EDS.

[2] Samuel Vetch (born in Edinburgh, says Drake) was charged soon after, with others, with supplying ammunition and stores to the French in Canada. The governor himself was accused of being concerned in this unlawful and treasonable traffic. In 1709, Vetch was colonel in the expedition against Canada, and became governor of Nova Scotia. He died in London, April 30, 1732. — EDS.

they were there; that set a small chapel at a distance, on fire; the chapel fired a high Cross with a Crucifix on it, so that it bowed and fell down. [Judges V. 27.]

Nov.ʳ 25. Mrs. Allen dies, 28, buried, 29. Snow. This day hear of Capt. Samuel Clark's death very suddenly at Sea, about 3 weeks ago: Sail'd from St. Thomas 2 or 3 days before. Was a good man, liv'd in our house more than Ten years, left one Son. The Lord fit me for my change. Dec.ʳ 1. made this Distich on the burning of the Quebeck Cross:

Crux atrox tandem flammam sentire jubetur:
Ipsa Salus fallax igne probata perit.

The bawdy bloudy Cross, at length
Was forc'd to taste the flame:
The cheating Saviour, to the fire
Savoury food became.

Dec.ʳ 1. Deputies send in a Bill against fornication, or Marriage of White men with Negros or Indians; with extraordinary penalties; directing the Secretary to draw a Bill accordingly. If it be pass'd, I fear twill be an Opression provoking to God, and that which will promote Murders and other Abominations. I have got the Indians out of the Bill, and some mitigation for them [the Negroes] left in it, and the clause about their Masters not denying their Marriage.[1]

Dec.ʳ 7. Went to Brooklin, set out about Noon, saw the Govʳ at his Fence, who invited me in to Diñer,

---

[1] The act to which Sewall refers was passed, and is chapter 10 of Acts of 1705-6. By it fornication between whites and blacks or mulattoes was forbidden, and the colored offender was to be sold out of the Province. Marriage between them was forbidden. A duty of four pounds per head was laid upon all negroes imported by vessel into the Colony, with a drawback if they were exported within one year. Sewall's benevolent clause is the fifth section. It reads: "And no master shall unreasonably deny marriage to his negro with one of the same nation, any law, usage, or custom to the contrary notwithstanding." — EDS.

stood with his Son Wm But I fear'd should lose visiting Mr. Bayley, and so pass'd on. [in margin — Carters
affront Governor]. After Diñer met the Govr upon
the Plain near Sol. Phip's; told me of what hapend
on the Road, being in a great passion; threaten'd to
send those that affronted him to England.[1] As I went

---

[1] We need hardly apologize for the length of this note since the subject-
matter occupies so much of the text. The trivial occasion of the dispute only
brings out more fully the almost insane rage of Dudley, and presents us with
a lively picture of colonial life. The two offending farmers belonged to
well-known and respectable families. Thomas Trowbridge, we presume,
was the son of Deacon James Trowbridge, of Newton. His son Edmund
was one of our most distinguished lawyers prior to the Revolution, and his
daughter Lydia was the mother of Chief Justice Dana. John Winchester, Jr.,
of Brookline, died in 1718, leaving issue. Jackson, in his "History of Newton," traces the descendants of Stephen, son of this John; among them was
the late Colonel William P. Winchester.

   Both were reputable citizens, and the Judges evidently felt that justice was
on the side of the defendants. Dudley was probably aware of his unpopu-
larity, and evidently took a morbid view of a presumed insult. At this time
the evidence seems to show that no offence was meant, but that a casual accident in a public road was rendered a serious matter solely by the position
of one of the parties.

   We are indebted to the kindness of Henry G. Denny, Esq., for copies of
the following affidavits in the case, the originals of which are in his possession. — EDS.

ROXBURY 23 Janu: 1705.

   REVERED AND DEAR SIR, — That you may not be imposed upon I have
covered to you my memorial to the Judges referring to the ingures offered mee
upon the road, which I desire you will communicate to the ministers of your
circle whose good opinion I Desire to mayntain, and have not in this matter
by any means forfeited.

I am Sir Your humble servant

J. DUDLEY.

   The Governour informs the Queen's Justices of her majestys Superior
Court that on friday, the seventh of December last past, he took his Journey
from Roxbury towards newhampshire and the Province of mayn for her
majestys immediate service there: and for the ease of the Guards had directed them to attend him the next morning at Rumney house, and had not
proceeded above a mile from home before he mett two Carts in the Road
loaden with wood, of which the Carters were, as he is since informed, Winchester and Trobridge.

   The Charet wherein the Governour was, had three sitters and three servants depending, with trunks and portmantles for the journey, drawn by

back, Jn° Bartlet, the middlemost Carter, shew'd me
the Ground where the three carts stood, which was a

---

four horses one very unruly, and was attended only at that instant by Mr.
William Dudley, the Governours son.

When the Governour saw the carts approaching, he directed his son to
bid them give him the way, having a Difficult drift, with four horses and a
tender Charet so heavy loaden, not fit to break the way. Who accordingly
did Ride up and told them the Gov.r was there, and they must give way:
immediately upon it, the second Charter came up to the first, to his assistance, leaving his own cart, and one of them says aloud, he would not goe out
of the way for the Governour: whereupon the Gov.r came out of the Charet
and told Winchester he must give way to the Charet. Winchester answered
boldly, without any other words, "I am as good flesh and blood as you; I
will not give way; you may goe out of the way:" and came towards the
Governour.

Whereupon the Governour drew his sword, to secure himself and command the Road, and went forward; yet without either saying or intending to
hurt the carters, or once pointing or passing at them; but justly supposing
they would obey and give him the way: and again commanded them to give
way. Winchester answered that he was a Christian and would not give
way: and as the Governour came towards him, he advanced and at len[g]th
layd hold on the Gov.r and broke the sword in his hand.

Very soon after came a justice of peace, and sent the Carters to prison.

The Justices are further informed that during this talk with the carters,
the Gov.r demanded their names, which they would not say, Trobridg particularly saying he was well known, nor did they once in the Gov.rs hearing
or sight pull of their hatts or say they would go out of the way, or any word
to excuse the matter, but absolutely stood upon it, as above is sayd; and
once, being two of them, one on each side of the fore-horse, laboured and
put forward to drive upon and over the Governour.

And this is averred upon the honour of the Governour.

J. Dudley.

I, Thomas Trowbridg of Newtown, being upon the seventh day of December 1705 upon the Road leading to Boston, driving my team, my cart being
laden with cordwood, as I passed through the town of Roxbury, in the lane
between the dwelling house of Ebenezer Davis and the widow Pierponts, in
the which lane are two plaine cart paths which meet in one at the descent of
an hill: I being with my cart in the path on the west side of the lane, I seeing the Governors coach where the paths meet in one, I drave leisurly, that
so the coach might take that path one the east side of the lane, which was the
best, but when I came near where the paths met, I made a stop, thinking
they would pass by me in the other path. And the Governors son, viz.
Mr. William Dudley, came rideing up and bid me clear the way. I told
him I could not conveniently doe it, adding that it was easier for the
coach to take the other path then for me to turn out of that: then did he

difficult place to turn; and the Govr had a fair way to
have gon by them if he had pleas'd.   Upon the Meeting-

---

strike my horse, and presently alighting his horse, drew his sword, and told
me he would stab one of my horses.   I stept betwixt him and my horses, and
told him he should not, if I could help it: he told me he would run me through
the body, and made severall pases at me with his sword, which I fended of
with my stick.   Then came up John Winchester, of Muddyriver *alias* Brookline, who was behind me with his loaden Cart, who gives the following
account.

I, John Winchester, being upon the road in the lane above written, on the
year and day above said, hereing Mr. William Dudley give out threatening
words that he would stab Trowbridge his horse, and run Trowbridge himself
through the body if he did not turn out of the way, I left my cart and came
up and laid down my whip by Trowbridge his team.   I asked Mr. Wm Dudley why he was so rash; he replyed "this dog wont turn out of the way for
the Governour."   Then I passed to the Governour with my hat under my
arm, hoping to moderate the matter, saying "may it pleas your Exelency,
it is very easie for you to take into this path, and not come upon us:" he
answered, "Sirrah, you rouge or rascall, I will have that way."   I then told
his Exelency if he would but have patience a minute or two, I would clear
that way for him.   I, turning about and seeing Trowbridge his horses twist-
ing about, ran to stop them to prevent damage; the Governour followed me
with his drawn sword, and said "run the dogs through," and with his naked
sword stabed me in the back.   I faceing about, he struck me on the head with
his sword, giveing me there a bloody wound.   I then expecting to be killed
dead on the spot, to prevent his Exelency from such a bloody act in the heat
of his passion, I catcht hold on his sword, and it broke; but yet continueing
in his furious rage he struck me divers blows with the hilt and peice of the
sword remaining in his hand, wounding me on the hands therewith: in this
transaction I called to the standers by to take notice that what I did was in
defence of my life.   Then the Governor said "you lie, you dog; you lie, you
divell," repeating the same words divers times.   Then said I, "such words
dont become a christian;" his Exelency replyed "a christian, you dog, a
christian you divell, I was a christian before you were born."   I told him
twas very hard that we who were true subjects and had bene allways ready
to serve him in any thing, should be so run upon; then his Exelency took up
my cart whip and struck me divers blows: then said I "what flesh and blood
can bear this:" his Exelency said "why dont you run away, you Dog, you
Divell, why dont you run away."

I Thomas Trowbridge, further declare that I seeing and hearing the fore-
mentioned words and actions, between his Exelency and said Winchester,
and seeing Mr. William Dudley make a pass at Winchesters body, with his
naked sword, I with my arm turned him aside, and he recovering himself, he
stabed me in my hip; then the Governer struck me divers blows with the
hilt of his sword; then takeing Winchesters driveing stick and with the great
end there of struck me severall blows as he had done to Winchester afore.

house hill met Mr. P. Dudley : I ask'd him how he got the men along, he said he walk'd them along.   Upon Satterday just at night Mr. Trowbridge and Winchester came to speak to me that their sons might be released out of Prison.   It being so late, I refer'd them to second-day Morning Decr 10. to meet at the Secretary's office.   Major Walley and I met there and Mr. Attorney, who desired Mr. Leverett might be sent for, being so near ; and writt a Letter accordingly in our Names, which was given to Mr. White.   Mr. Leverett came not till 3^d day xr. 11th Then in the Afternoon, we agreed to grant a Habeas Corpus, and I sign'd it, but Mr. Cook being at Charlestown-Court twas not seal'd till Wednesday morning.   The writt comanded them to be brought to the Court-Chamber in Boston on Friday morn, 9. aclock.   Twas put off till then that might have Mr. Leverett's company, whose business allow'd him not to be here sooner : And that Mr. Attorney [Paul Dudley] who was attending Charlestown-Court, might have oportunity to be present.

Sixth-day, xr. 14.   Mr. Leverett came, and Mr. Sheriff order'd the Prisoners to be brought : Mr. Attorney spoke against them : They had no counsil, could procure none. Justices withdrew into the Counsil Chamber, and agreed to Bail to the Super^r Court, 300£ Prisoners and 3 Sureties

---

Winchester told his Exelency he had bene a true subject to him, and served him and had honoured him, and now he would taked his life away for nothing.   The Governer replyed " you lie, you dog, you know that I intended you no harm."   When we spake of tarrying no longer but of driveing along our teams, his Exelency said " no, you shall goe to Goale, you Dogs ; " when twas askt what should become of our teams his Exelency said, " let them sink into the bottom of the earth."

JOHN WINCHESTER, jun^r.
THOMAS TROWBRIDGE.

The sequel to the matter seems to be given in the following extract from the Court records : —

At a session of the Superior Court Nov. 5, 1706, present Sewall, Hathorne, Walley and Leverett, both Winchester and Trowbridge " being bound by recognizance to this court, was discharged by solemn Proclamation."

each 100£. Examin'd the first and put it in writing.
And I sent Mr. Cook to Mr. Secretary to desire his Assistance, or presence, which he declin'd. Some would have
had five Hundred pounds and more sureties. I urg'd the
words of the Act, that saith regard is to be had to the
quality of the person; These men were not worth so
much. At last came to Three Hundred pound. I propounded Two Hundred, and Two sureties. Thomas
Trowbridge 300.£ James Trowbridge 100. Abraham
Jackson 100. and Capt. Oliver Noyes 100. John Winchester 300£, John Winchester the Father 100£, Josiah
Winchester, unkle, 100. Mr. John White £100. I
could hardly be brought to their being bound to their
Good Behaviour, because there was no Oath to justify
the charge laid in the Mittimus; and the Prisoners
pleaded their Iñocence. No Complaint in writing. A
little after Two aclock all was finish'd. I am glad that I
have been instrumental to Open the Prison to these two
young men, that they might repair to their wives and
children and Occasions; and that might have Liberty to
assemble with God's People on the Lord's Day. I writt
earnestly to Col. Hathorne to desire him, an experienced
Traveller, to help us to steer between Scylla and Charib-
dis: I mentiond it in Court. Mr. Willard sung 72 PS.
from the 4th v. two Staves — Poor of the People. — While
we were deliberating in the Council-Chamber, P. Dudley
writt a Letter, that would not Bail them yet; that would
be an error on the right hand; he would write to his
father Mompresson,[1] Mr. Secretary was not Settled in his

---

[1] This reference by Paul Dudley to "his father Mompresson" is inex-
plicable. Undoubtedly the person meant was Roger Mompesson, Judge of
the Admiralty Court for the northern district. Dudley married, in 1703,
Lucy, daughter of Colonel John Wainwright, by his wife Elizabeth, daughter of William Norton. Wainwright died July 30, 1708. As Dudley's
father and father-in-law were both living at this date.

Little can be found about the Mompessons in England. Sir Giles Mompesson is said to be the original of Sir Giles Overreach, in Massinger's play

opinion, Not one Gentleman present but thought they would not be Bail'd. Mr. Leverett shew'd me the Letter, writt an Answer and copied it on Mr. Dudley's. In publick I offer'd Coke's pleas of the Crown to be read, especially as to that clause of High Treason for killing the Chancellor &c. He declined having it read. I had the Statute Book there, Coke pleas Crown, and Reading on the Statutes, stuck to 31. Car. 2ᵈ, that Com̄ands all to be Bail'd that are not Committed for Felony or Treason.

Tuesday, Decʳ 18. Great Rain, which hinders my going to Roxbury-Lecture. This day Mr. Colman's sloop arrives; came from Plimᵒ Octobʳ 25ᵗʰ Brings news of a kind of Certainty that Sir Charles Hobby is to be our Governour.[1]

Decʳ 21. Cousin Noyes brings the News of Mrs. Coffin's death the 15ᵗʰ instᵗ, to be buried the 19ᵗʰ Went away suddenly and easily. A very good Woman of Newbury.

Decʳ 22. Very great snow.

xr. 24ᵗʰ I could not persuade Mr. Campbell to print my addition to the Quebeck Article, last [News] Letter: but now he does it:

---

of " A New Way to pay Old Debts." In Le Neve's Catalogue of Knights we find that Sir Thomas Mompesson was knighted in 1661, and was one of the Commissioners of the Privy Seal in 1697. In 1700–7 Charles Mompesson represented Old Sarum, and the family seems to have been settled in Wiltshire. Roger Mompesson was the adviser of Lord Cornbury, when Governor of New York, and left with his patron for fear of the results of his actions. — Eds.

1 Hutchinson writes (History, II. 153) that Dudley's enemies prevailed upon Sir Charles Hobby to go to England and solicit for the government. " He was recommended to Sir H. Ashurst, who at first gave encouragment of success. Hobby was a gay man, a free liver, and of very different behaviour from what one would have expected should have recommended him to the clergy of New England; and yet, such is the force of party prejudice, that it prevails over religion itself, and some of the most pious ministers strongly urged, in their letters, that he might be appointed their governor instead of Dudley; for which Ashurst himself, after his acquaintance with Hobby, reproves and censures them." — Eds.

Gallica Crux æquam flamman sentire coacta est:
Ista salus fallax, igne probata perit.
Iddum nihil est, restat de stipite longo
— Nescio quid cineris, quem capit urna brevis.

As soon as Mr. Green's daughter brought me a proof, I *deled the Title, In Obitum Crucis;* though I my self had put it in: because the English introduction seem'd to suffice.

I sent a Letter to Mr. Henchman, desiring we might pray that God would make the proud French Helper of the Antichristian Faction to stoop as Low as Quebeck Cross. Visited Mrs. Maccarty, sick Mr. Tho. Downs, and the solitary widow of Mr. Sam¹ Clark. Were very thankfull to me; especially Mr. Downs.

Writ to Govʳ Winthrop [of Connecticut], advising the Recᵗ of the Bond; enclos'd Letters of the day, Athenian Oracle, Selling Joseph.

Tuesday, Decʳ 25. Very cold Day but Serene Morning, Sleds, Slays, and Horses pass as usually, and shops open.¹ I just went into Town and visited Mr. Secretary, whose Indisposition has increased so much by a pain in his Back or side, that he has kept House from Satterday. Then went to Mr. Treasurers and Rec'd Bills of Credit for my Council, Attendance. I think the Govʳ was not in Town to-day; though tis said his Excellency came to Roxbury the night before. Capt. Belchar buried a Negro this day; his Coachman, a very good Servant. He was a Bearer to Cousin Savages Hagar. The Governour came not home till Tuesday, a very cold day; some think the coldest has been these many years, by the Vapor taken notice of at Nantasket. Decʳ 27. Govʳ warns a Council; reads the Letter that orders a Thanks-giving here: I mention'd the Thanksgiving in October had in general

---

¹ Every token of secular business in the Puritan town on the Church festival of Christmas was welcome to the Judge. — EDS.

mention'd the same thing : but the Govr would not hear of any thing but apointing a Day in obedience to the Queen. Before went out of the Council-Chamber — Capt. Belchar invited me to his Thanksgiving on account of his Son's preservation.

Sixth-day, Decr 28.   Mr. Pemberton prays excellently, and Mr. Willard Preaches from Ps. 66. 20. very excellently. Spake to me to set the Tune ; I intended Windsor, and fell into High-Dutch,[1] and then essaying to set another Tune, went into a Key much too high. So I pray'd Mr. White to set it; which he did well, Litchf. Tune. The Lord humble me and Instruct me, that I should be occasion of any Interruption in the Worship of God. Had a very good Diñer at three Tables. Had the Meeting ; and few else except Relations in Town, and me. The Lord accept his Thank-offering.

Jan^y .9.   Guns are fired at Boston upon the suposal of Mr. Belchar's [2] being married at Portsmouth yesterday : very cold wether.

Jany 10.   I corrected David for his extravagant staying out, and for his playing when his Mistress sent him of Errands.

Jany 11th   I visited languishing Mr. Bayley, carried him two pounds of Currants, which he accepted very kindly. Is in a very pious humble frame in submitting to the afflicting hand of God.

This day I met Mr. Leverett in the street at Boston, who told me, he had by the Governour's direction, written to Col. Hathorne to come to Town. I ask'd him, whether as a Councillor, or Judge ; he said both; the Governor had drawn up a Declaration relating to Winchester and

---

[1] From the context, we infer that to fall into High-Dutch was to sing at too low pitch. — EDS.

[2] This was Jonathan Belcher, Governor of Massachusetts from 1730 to 1741. He married Mary, daughter of Lieutenant-Governor William Partridge, of New Hampshire, who died Oct. 6, 1736. — EDS.

Trowbridge: I enquired whether it might not as well be let alone till the Trial: It seems Mr. Leverett's Letter went by the Post.

I call'd at the Governour's, only his Lady at home. Slander. It seems some have reported that I should say I saw Quarts of blood that run out of Trowbridges-Horses. I answered, I had never seen, nor thought, nor reported any such thing. Seventh-day, Janʳ 12ᵗʰ 170⅚. A Council is call'd to meet at eleven aclock. Govʳ call'd Maxwell, bid him go to Major Walley, and tell him the Govʳ and Council were sitting, and would have him there also. Maxwell answer'd that Major Walley was sick. Twas said also that Mr. Bromfield was sick. Mr. Leverett was call'd in, and bid to sit down. The Governour's Declaration was read as to the fray xr. 7ᵗʰ with Winchester and Trowbridge, Carters. The Govʳ said he did not know whether he should live to the time of the Court; bid Mr. Secretary keep it for the Court. Govr mention'd the Story of the blood, I said before the Council, as had said before. Govʳ said some Minister, mentioning Mr. Allen, had reported that he swore; whereas he said he was as free from Cursing and Swearing vainly, as any there. Made a Ridicule of Winchester's Complaint about Mr. Dudley's striking him last Monday. I mention'd Mr. Taylor's striking, which was inconvenient for a Justice of Peace. The Govʳ Answer'd, he did well. Brought that as an Argument for himself, his drawing his sword; A Justice of Peace might punish several offences against the Laws upon view. After diñer I went and told Mr. Willard what was Reported of himself and me. He said he knew nothing of it. Col. Hutchinson was not at Council. I laid down this as a position, That of all men, twas most inconvenient for a Justice of Peace to be a Striker. [Titus, 1, 7.]

Janʸ 12. Capt. Belchar apears at Council in his new Wigg: Said he needed more than his own Hair for his

Journey to Portsmouth; and other provision was not suitable for a Wedding. Jan.ʸ 13ᵗʰ apears at Meeting in his Wigg. He had a good Head of Hair, though twas grown a little thin.

Jan.ʸ 18. Sister Stephen Sewall, Son Hirst and his wife, dine with us; Major Walley droops with his Cold and Cough: He was not abroad on the Lord's Day, nor Lecture-day; wears plaisters or Poultices to his right side to ease the intolerable pain his Coughing causes him.

Lord's Day, Jan.ʸ 20ᵗʰ My Dame Mary Phipps, Lady Sergeant, *alias* Phipps, dies about Sun-Rise; Majʳ Genˡ tells me She was Dying from Satterday Noon. Has Bled excessively at the Nose. Mr. Sergeant was at Meeting in the Afternoon. Mr. Butchers son Alwin taken into Church and a woman; Mr. Ezek. Lewis dismiss'd from Westfield, and enter'd into Covenant with them.

Major Walley not at Meeting.

Jan.ʸ 20. Mrs. Jane Pembrook dies in the afternoon, was taken on Wednesday. Her Husband is at Coñecticut.

Tuesday, Jan.ʸ 22. Mrs. Jane Pembrook buried in the New Burying place. Saw no Minister there but Mr. Colman and Mr. Dallie [the French Minister]. I and Mr. Eᵐ Hutchinson went together; Capt. Legg was there.

Wednesday, Jan.ʸ 23. Storm of snow, for which reason the funeral of my Lady is put off to Friday.

Jan.ʸ 23. Mr. Jonathan Belcher and his Bride dine at Lᵗ Govʳ Usher's, come to Town about 6. aclock: About 20 Horsmen, Three Coaches and many Slays. Joseph came from College to visit us, and gave us notice of their coming before hand.

Jan.ʸ 24th. Comfortable day: Mr. Willard not abroad in the Forenoon by reason of pain; but preaches excellently in the afternoon. Mr. Broadhurst of Albany, Mr. Hirst and family, cousin Samˡ and Jonathan Sewall, dine with us &c.

Jan.ʸ 25ᵗʰ Friday, My Lady Phipps is laid in Mr. Ser-

geant's Tomb in the New Burying place. Bearers, Mr.
Winthrop, Cook; Elisha Hutchinson, Addington; Foster,
Belcher. Govr and Lt Govr there. Mr. Russel and I go
together. I had a Ring. Mr. Corwin and B. Brown
there from Salem. Mr. Holman married Cousin Ann
Quinsey a week ago.

Jany 26. I visit Mr. Sergeant, who takes my visit very
kindly, tells me, my Lady would have been 59 years old
next March, and that he was two Moneths older. It seems
Mr. Chiever buried his daughter Abigail, about an hour
before my Lady was entombed.

Jany 29th 170⅚. Col. Hathorn, Leverett, and S. hold
the Court at Charlestown; storm began by Noon; yet I
got home at night with difficulty. Jany 30. Extraordinary Storm; yet at Noon I rode to Jn° Russel's with very
great difficulty by reason of the Snow and Hail beating
on my forehead and Eyes hindering my sight, and the
extravagant Banks of Snow the Streets were fill'd with.
Waited 3 hours or more, and at last the Charlestown Boat
coming over, I went in that very comfortably; got thither
a little before four. Lodg'd at Capt. Hayman's with Mr.
Leverett.

Jany 31. Got not home till six at night, by reason of
much Ice in the River; fain to Land at the Salutation,[1]
having got below the Ice on Charlestown side.

Feb. 11. Mr. Jn° Marion, the Father, buried; Bearers,
Mr. Cook, Col. Townsend; Elder Bridgham, Copp; Dea-

---

[1] S. A. Drake, in his "Old Landmarks of Boston," states that the Salutation Tavern was on the corner of Salutation Street and North Street. The
tavern was the rendezvous of the North End Caucus in Revolutionary times.
As Mr. Drake repeats the idea that the term "caucus" was a corruption of
"calkers'" meeting, we annex the more plausible statement of Mr. J. Hammond Trumbull, made in 1872 to the American Philological Association.

He finds that the Indians have various words allied in sound and sense.
Thus "cau-cau-asu" means "one who advises," "a promoter," and he considers it most probable that our word is thus of Indian origin. In 1763, John
Adams spoke of the "Caucus-Club" and "those caucuses," showing that at
that date no one entertained the "calkers" derivation. — Eds.

con Tay, Hubbard.   Great Funeral.   I think Mr. Chiever
was not there.

Feb. 27.   My Neighbour Deming came to me, and
ask'd of me the Agreement between himself and Joana
Tiler; I told him I was to keep it for them both and could
not deliver it; he said he was going to Cambridge to ask
Mr. Leverett's Advice, he would bring it safe again.
When he still urged and insisted, I told him I would not
have him lose his time, I would not deliver it; I would give
him a copy if he pleas'd.   He said he was in haste and
could not stay the writing of it.   I said, You would not
take it well that I should deliver it to Tiler; no more
could I deliver it to him.   He said some what sourly, I
am sorry you have not more Charity for him.   And
going away, murmuring said, passing out of the Stove-
Room into the Kitchen, I have desired a Copy, offered
Money and am Deny'd: I was then more mov'd than
before, and said with some earnestness, Will you speak
false to my face?   He went away, and came not again,
but his son came, and I gave him a Copy of the Agreement, written with my own hand.   I thank God, I
heartily desired and endeavoured a good Agreement between him and his Neighbour as to the Bounds of their
Land: although he be thus out of Tune, upon my denying to grant his Unjust Petition.

Satterday, March, 2.   I visit my son and daughter at
Brooklin and little Rebecka: Visited Mr. Bayley as I came
home.   Most of the way over the Neck is good Suͫer
Travelling.

March, 4ᵗʰ   Cousin Duͫer and I take Bond of Mr.
Rust 30£, to prosecute his Sons Master, Jnᵒ Staniford, for
misusing and Evil entreating his Servant; Left Robert
Rust with his father in the mean time.   The invincible
fear of the Mother, who came from Ipswich on purpose,
and the high hand wherewith Staniford carried it, did in a
maͫer force it.   Mr. Jnᵒ Colman said, If his Servant should

answer so, he would trample him under his feet; afterward mention'd that Scripture, Obey in all things. Staniford said scoffingly before us: The Boy would do well
with good Correction; words were directed to the Mother.

Wednesday, March, 6. Council of Churches held at
Mr. Willard's. They advise that after a Moneth, Mr.
Joseph Morse cease to preach at Watertown farms. Adjourn'd to the First of May. Sharp Thunder the night
following. Mr. Gookin, Capt. Morse and Deacon Larned
dine with us. Cousin Noyes lodges here, and tells of
many Sheep being drown'd by the overflowing of Merrimack River. At the breaking up of the River, which was
furious by the Flood in Febr. The Ice jam'd and made a
great Dam, and so caus'd the River to Rise so much and
suddenly.

March, 6. 170⅚. At night, a great Ship, of 370 Tuns,
building at Salem, runs off her blocking in the night and
pitches ahead 16 foot. Her Deck not bolted off, falls in;
and opens at the Bows; so that twill cost a great deal to
bring her Right agen; and Capt. Dows thinks she will be
Hundreds of pounds the worse.

March 13ᵗʰ Mr. Torrey comes to Town; on Thorsday
even, Mr. Wadsworth came to visit him. Mr. Torrey told
him of his Elder Rogers's Carriage towards him; and
crav'd his pardon for chusing him; acknowledged his fault
and plainly seem'd to renounce that office.

March, 16. A Storm of Snow.

Friday, March, 22. Michael Gill arrives from Lisbon,
came out 11ᵗʰ Febʳ By him have News from London of
the 1. of Janʸ This day Mr. Jer. Cushing dyes at Scituat.
Jnᵒ Turner dies there suddenly p. m. — the same day:
He has the Character of a Drunkard, and Striker of his
Wife.

March, 23. Set out for Weymouth with Sam Robbi-
son, stop'd at Gibbe's to shelter our selves from a Gust of
Wind and Rain. Twas dusk before got to Mr. Torrey's.

I ask'd Mr. Torrey about laying the hand on the Bible in swearing: He said he was against it, and would suffer anything but death rather than do it.

March, 24. Mr. Torrey preach'd out of Amos, 8. 11. Four children baptised in the Afternoon.

March, 25, 1706. Din'd at Barker's; surpris'd the Sheriff and his Men at the Flat-house: Got to Plymouth about 1½ by Sun.

March, 26. Major Walley and Leverett come from Barker's.

March, 27.th I walk in the Meetinghouse. Set out homeward, lodg'd at Cushing's. Note. I pray'd not with my Servant, being weary. [A few lines unsuitable for publication are here omitted. In these Sewall relates a mortifying accident which befel him in the night. He regards his humiliation as a judgment upon him because, being weary, he had retired without calling his servant to prayer.] How unexpectedly a man may be expos'd! There's no security but in God, who is to be sought by Prayer.

March, 28, *mihi natalis*, got home about ½ hour after 12, dine with my wife and children.

Apr. 1. 1706. Col. Townsend, Mr. Bromfield, Burroughs and I went in the Hackny Coach and visited Mr. Thacher, din'd with him and Mrs. Thacher. Mrs. Niles is there to ly in; but saw her not. Got home well. *Laus Deo.*

Apr. 4, 1706. Last night I dream'd I saw a vast number of French coming towards us, for multitude and Huddle like a great Flock of Sheep. It put me into a great Consternation, and made me think of Hiding in some Thicket. The Impression remain'd upon me after my Waking. GOD defend!

Friday, Ap. 5. I went and visited Mr. Baily whose paroxisms are return'd to once every hour. Carried him two pounds of Currants which he accepted with wonderful kindness. When left him, went forward for Brooklin, and going up the Meetinghouse Hill fell in with the Governour's Coach with two Horses: in it were his Excellency and Lady, Madam Paul Dudley, and Madam Thomas Dudley. I follow'd the Coach mostly, especially at Mittimus Hill,[1] and observed, that the Coachman of his own accord took the Road next Boston, which was refus'd Decemb[r] 7, and nothing to incline to it but the goodness of the way. Took it also returning. Mrs. Kate Dudley, little Allen, and Capt. Gillam's little Maiden daughter rode in a Calash. Capt. Thomas Dudley rode on horseback.

Tuesday, Apr. 9. Mr. Dan[l] Oliver and I ride to Milton, and there meet with Mr. Leverett, and as Spectators and Auditors were present at Deacon Swifts when Mr. Leverett discours'd the Punkapog intruders. Dined at the said Swift's with Mr. Thacher. Seth Dwight waited on us.

Ap. 8. Monday, poor little Sam Hirst went through the Valley of the Shadow of Death through the op̄ression of Flegm.

Ap. 9. Wife takes Physick, has a comfortable night after it. *Laus Deo.* Brother visits us.

Ap. 14. Capt. Belchar is kept at home by the Gout.
Ap. 15. Abraham Hill arrives; makes us believe the Virginia Fleet is arriv'd.

Ap. 16. I first hear and see the swallows: They are now frequent. Mr. Banister says they were seen by him 2 or 3 days ago. Mrs. Gates lodg'd here last night. At

---

1 " The elevation beyond the Dudley estate has, from time immemorial, been known as ' Meeting-House Hill.' It was also called ' Roxbury Hill,' and just before the Revolution, from the fact of Isaac Winslow and other friends of the British government residing on or near it, it received the name of ' Tory Hill.' Putnam Street, its eastern limit, was given to the town by the First Church. Its western slope touched Stony River." F. S. Drake's History of Roxbury, p. 265.

As to Mittimus Hill, we find no other mention of it. Can it be a jocular perversion of Meeting-house Hill? — EDS.

night the Aer being clear, the Eclipse of the Moon was very much Gaz'd upon.

Tuesday, Apr. 23.   Govr. comes to Town guarded by the Troops with their Swords drawn ; dines at the Dragon,[1] from thence proceeds to the Townhouse, Illuminations at night.   Capt. Pelham tells me several wore crosses in their Hats ; which makes me resolve to stay at home ; (though Maxwell was at my House and spake to me to be at the Council-Chamber at 4. p. m̄.)   Because to drinking Healths, now the Keeping of a Day to fictitious St. George, is plainly set on foot.   It seems Capt. Dudley's Men wore Crosses.   Somebody had fasten'd a cross to a Dog's head ; Capt. Dudley's Boatswain seeing him, struck the Dog, and then went into the shop, next where the Dog was, and struck down a Carpenter, one Davis, as he was at work not thinking anything : Boatswain and the other with him were fined 10s each for breach of the peace, by Jer. Dumer Esqr : pretty much blood was shed by means of this bloody Cross, and the poor Dog a sufferer.

Thomas Hazard came in from Narragansett about the time should have gon to the Townhouse, said he came on purpose to speak with me ; so 'twas inconvenient to Leave him.

Midweek ; Apr. 24.   Privat Meeting at our House ; Read out of Mr. Caryl[2] on those Words, The Lord gives, and the Lord Takes,   Blessed — preface my Reading with saying, I will read now what read in course to my

---

[1] This may be the famous Green Dragon Tavern mentioned *ante*, Vol. I. p. 163.   It was the property of Governor Stoughton, and, in 1704, went to his niece, Mehitable Cooper.   The Castle Tavern (Vol. I. p. 196) was on the corner of Elm Street.   The Green Dragon, on Union Street, was famous in our local history, and its site is now indicated by a tablet set in the wall of a store. — EDS.

[2] Mr. Joseph Caryl, preacher at Lincoln's Inn, a member of the Westminster Assembly, and one of the Triers for Approbation of Ministers.   He was ejected from St Magnus, London, in 1662, and died in 1673.   He wrote a copious Exposition on the Book of Job. — EDS.

family because of the great and multiplied Losses, ——.
Cousin Savage and Capt. Hill pray'd, had a pretty full and
comfortable Meeting notwithstanding the much Rain and
Dirt. Sung 1 part and last v. of 48.ᵗʰ Ps. 119.

7th day, Apr. 27.ᵗʰ Joseph visits us, it seems he had a
Tooth pull'd out by Madam Oliver's Maid, on Mid-week
night.

Lords-Day, April, 28. Brief is Read. Bowditch Arrives.

Monday, Apr. 29. Cousin Gookin, his wife and son
Richard lodge here.

Tuesday, Apr. 30. I carry Capt. Belchar my Letter to
Mr. Bellamy, and he sends me the Comons votes. Note,
Lords Resolution is dated Dec.ʳ 6. Comons conferr'd with
them about it the 7ᵗʰ Agree to it Satterday xr. 8. Address upon it agreed to by the Comons xr. 14.ᵗʰ

Mercurii [Wednesday]. 19. *die.* Xr's 1705. [The Bill
for the better Security of Her Maj's person and Government,
and of the Succession to the Crown of England in the protestant Line, was read a second Time.   And Charles Cæsar
Esqr, upon the Debate of the said Bill, standing up in his
place, saying the Words following (which were directed
by the House to be set down in writing at the Table)

There is a noble Lord, without whose Advice the Queen
does nothing, who in the late Reign was known to keep a
constant Correspondence with the Court at St Germans.

Resolv'd, That the said words are highly dishonorable
to Her Majestys person and Government. Resolv'd that
the said Charles Cæsar esqr. be for his said offence
comitted prisoner to the Tower during the pleasure of this
House.] ¹

May, 1. 1706. Eclipse of the Sun, not seen by reason
of the cloudy wether.

May, 2ᵈ Mr. Penn Townsend junʳ dies about 10 m.

---

¹ The passage enclosed in brackets seems to be an extract from an
English journal. — Eds.

May, 3. ıs buried; Bearers Mr. Nathan¹ Williams, Major
Adam Winthrop, Capt. Oliver Noyes, Capt. Jnᵒ Ballentine junʳ, Mr. Habijah Savage, Mr. Elisha Cooke; all
scholars.

May, 2ᵈ, 1706. Capt. Stukely arrives from Barbados
in the Deptford, 3 weeks passage; was not suffer'd to
bring the Fleet with him, neither can they go for Salt;
but are embargod at Barbados. Tis much fear'd that
Nevis is Taken.

May, 4ᵗʰ Mr. Brattle and I send the School and College Deeds by Mr. N. Niles to be Recorded. Niles tells
me that Monotocott [Braintree] Meetinghouse is Raised;
he came that way, and saw it.

Mid-week, May, 15ᵗʰ 1706. Went to Brooklin, visited my
Daughter and little Grand-daughter. Visited Mr. Bayley.

May, 16. Capt. Benjᵃ Gillam buried about 7. p. m.

May, 20. Set out for Ipswich with Major Walley by
Winisimet; Rid in the Rain from Lewis' to Salem; staid
there, and assisted at the Funeral of Mrs. Lindal, Capt.
Corwin's only daughter, a vertuous Gentlewoman. Was
buried in the Tomb in a Pasture: Broʳ was one of the
Bearers.

May, 21. Set out early for Ipswich; got thither seasonably. Twas late ere Mr. Leverett came. Sarah Pils-
bury, Try'd for murdering her young Child, was Acquitted.

May, 23. Mr. Fitch preaches the Lecture: Companys in
Arms, Govʳ to view them; much fatigued by the Wet.

May, 24ᵗʰ Set out for Newbury with Major Davison:
visit Mr. Payson, and deliver him my wives present; I
hope he is recovering. Dine at Sister Northend's; Broʳ
Northend brings us going as far as Capt. Hale's. At Sister Gerrishes dismiss Major Davison: visit Broʳ and Sister
Tapan, Cousin Swett, cousins Jnᵒ, Henry, and Samˡ Sewall.
Lodge at Sister Gerrishes.

May 25ᵗʰ Saw the sheep shearing, visited Cousin Rolf.

May, 26ᵗʰ Mr. Tapan preaches. Deacon Cutting Noyes

Catechises in the Afternoon. In the evening visit Mr. Tapan.

May, 27ᵗʰ Col. Noyes invites me to his Training Diñer: Mr. Tapan, Brown, Hale and my self are guarded from the Green to the Tavern, Broʳ Moodey and a part of the Troop with a Trumpet accompany me to the Ferry. Sam. Moody waits on me. Get to Brother's in the night after nine aclock. Mr. Noyes had left his Verses for Mr. Bayley, which I carried with me next morning. Rested at Lewis' during the Rain.

Got home well, *Laus Deo.*

May, 29. Election-day, Winthrop 83. Russel, 80. (Cooke 50) Hathorn 68. Elisha Hutchinson, 80. Sewall, 83. Addington 79. Brown 76. Phillips 80. Corwin 75. Foster 75. Townsend, 78. Higginson, 69. Belcher, 80. Bromfield 55. Legg, 65. S. Apleton, 47. Partridge, 58. Thacher 79. Pain, 79. Winslow, 86. Cushing, 47. Eᵐ Hutchinson, 75. (Hamond 62.) Plaisted, 46. Leverett, 42. Walley, 37. Jnᵒ Apleton, 34.

June, 6. In stead of the Negativ'd[1] were chosen B. Brown, 55. Ephr. Hunt, 42.

Mr. James Taylor, Treasurer; James Russel esqr Comissʳ of the Customs.

This Court Mr. Lillie Prefer'd a Petition about his Reals not accepted by the Super. Court to go by Tale, which was Untrue in one material Article as to matter of fact, and the Justices much reflected on. Mr. Paul Dudley was Attorney for Mr. Lillie. I pray'd the Petition might be dismiss'd, or those Reflections abated: the Govʳ brake forth into a passionate Harangue respecting the Roxbury Carters. He might be run through, trampled on, &c no care taken of him. — Finally, at another time it was agreed that there should be a Hearing, only Mr. Lillie should

---

[1] Elisha Cooke and Joseph Hammond were the two negatived. Sewall has put their names in parentheses. — EDS.

first come into Council, make some Acknowledgment,
withdraw that Petition, and file another. The Govr was
very hot and hard upon me at this time, insomuch that I
was provok'd to say, It was a Hardship upon me that the
Governour's Son was Mr. Lillie's Attorney. At which the
Govr Storm'd very much. Some days after Mr. Lillie
came into Council. The Govr presently said, Sir, shall I
speak for you, or will you speak for your self, and so fell
a speaking —— at last Mr. Lillie said with a low voice, I
have prefer'd a Petition which I understand is not so satisfactory ; I did not intend to reflect upon the Judges, and
desire that petition may be withdrawn, and this filed in
the room of it. Withdrew, Govr ask'd it might be so, and
that the first petition might be Cast and Null. Secretary
whisper'd the Govr that the Petition had been read twice
in Council, whereupon the Govr took the pen and obliterated the Minute of its having been read on the head of
the Petition. And then after the Hearing before the
whole Court, when the Deputies were Returned, the Govr
bundled up the papers and sent them in to the House of
Deputies, without asking the Council whether they would
first go upon them, with whom the Petition was entered.
After many days, the Deputies return'd the papers agen
by Mr. Blagrove, expressing their desire that the Council
would first act upon them, seeing the Petition was entred
with the Secretary.

Some time after, the Govr sent in the Papers again, and
then the Deputies voted upon them and sent it in, but
before any thing was done in Council, the Court was prorogued to the 7th of August, &c., &c. Major Walley sick,
staid at home two Sabbaths. came out agen July 27th.

July, 28. 1706. Col. Hathorne comes to Town, Dines
and lodges at our House.

July, 29. Col. Hathorne, Major Walley, Sewall, ride
to Cambridge in the Hackney Coach. Mr. Sheriff, his
son, and the Steward of the College met us at Brooklin,

drank a Glass of good Beer at my son's, and pass'd on.
My case [In margin, Land of Nod] was call'd in the Afternoon and committed to the jury. I would have come
home but then Major Walley also would come; which
made me stay and send the Coach to Town empty.
Lodg'd at Mr. Brattles. July, 30. College Hall at Cambridge, The Jury brought in for me costs of Courts.
Charlestown Gentlemen and their Attorneys said not a
Word that I could hear. Col. Hathorne with Mr. Valentine, Charlest. Attorney, examined my Bill of cost and so
did the Clerk, and afterward Col. Hathorne shew'd it to
Maj^r Walley and Leverett, and then Allow'd it, subscrib-
ing his Name.

Augt 7. Genl Court meets. Augt 10, 1706. A Conference is held in the Council-Chamber, at the desire of the
Deputies. Mr. Speaker, The House is doubtfull whether
they have not proceeded too hastily in calling that a Misdemeanour, which the Law calls Treason; and are doubtfull whether this Court can proceed to Try the Prisoners.
Mr. Jewet, Comittee that were appointed to prepare for
the Trials, were doubtfull and unsatisfied that they had
called the crime of the Prisoners a Misdemeanour: If any
wrong steps had been taken, tis fit they should be retriev'd. Mr. Blagrove, If that which the Prisoners are
charg'd with, be made Treason by the Law of England;
this Court must not make Laws repugnant to the Law of
England.

The Governour answer'd, He had not seen the Papers,
and could not say that what they had done was Treason.
After this the Deputies sent in the Papers. And about
Augt 13. Govr put it to vote in the Council, whether the
prisoners should be Tried by the Genl Court according to
the order of last sessions: There were 17. at the Board
Nine Yeas, and Eight Nôs. Secretary was in the Negative as well as I.

Friday Augt. 16. Capt. Vetch was brought to his Trial

in the Afternoon, in the Court Chamber. Note. I came
home on Wednesday morn, and went not again till the
Govr and Council sent for me by Mr. Winchcomb Friday
morn. I went though I had a cold ; spake that a suit of
Cloaths might be made here for Mr. Williams.[1] Depts
would have had Mr. John Eliot, and Cousin Dumer M. A.
to have assisted Mr. Attorney : Govr did not consent :
they insisted so long that the Forenoon was spent, and I
fairly got home. Augt. 17. I am told Mr. Borland and
Lawson are brought to their Trial. Mr. Borland pleads
that he was a Factor in the management of this Affair.

Note. Govr would have had the Judges manage the
Conference, I declin'd it because was against the procedure. And so declin'd joining with the Judges to prepare
for it because I was against it. Col. Hathorne was at
Salem with his sick Son ; so that only Majr Walley, and
Mr. Leverett were active in the matter. And Mr. Leverett said at the Board that he did not interpret that Clause
in the Charter of imposing Fines &c. as if it did impour
the Genl Court to Try delinquents.[2]

Feria secunda, August 19th 1706. Went and visited
my son and daughter at Brooklin, and Dined there :
Went to Cambridge ; Gave Mr. Bordman, Town-Clerk,
Seven pounds in two Bills of Credit to help build the New-
Meetinghouse ; fourty shillings of it upon Consideration
of my ancient Tenant, the widow Margaret Gates, and her
family, going there to the publick worship of God. Gave
him also Ten Shillings for Mrs. Corlett, widow. Visited
Joseph, Mr. Flint, congratulated Mr. Whiting upon his
being chosen a Fellow. Went into Hall and heard Mr.
Willard expound excellently from 1 Cor. 7. 15, 16. It

---

[1] Rev. Mr. Williams, of Deerfield, then held as a captive by the French
and Indians, in Canada, for ransom. — EDS.

[2] The words in the Charter are, " The General Court, or Assembly, shall
have full power and authority — to impose fines, mulcts, imprisonments, and
other punishments." — EDS.

was dark by that time I got to Roxbury, yet I visited Mr.
Bayley, and gave him the Fourty shillings Mr. John Eliot
sent him as a Gratuity : He was very thankful for the
Present, and very glad to see me.   I told him, coming in
the night, I had brought a small Illumination with me.
Rid home; twas past Nine by that time I got there.
Found all well; *Laus Deo.*

Augt. 26. 1706. *feria secunda.* About 2 p. m. Mr.
Bromfield and I set out for Martha's Vinyard; got well to
Cushing's about Day-light shutting in.   27, to Morey's.
28, To Sandwich, 29, to Lecture at Pompesprisset;[1] on
the way thither, a small stump overset the Calash, and
Mr. Bromfield was much hurt, which made our Journey
afterwards uncomfortable.   30. rested : saw the Harbour,
Burying-place, Mill-pond.   31. Went to Succanesset but
could not get over.

Sept.ʳ 1.   Mr. Danforth preach'd there.   Lodg'd at Mr.
Lothrop's.

Sept.ʳ 2. embarked for the Vinyard : but by stormy
rough wether were forc'd back again to Wood's Hole.
Lodg'd at B. Skiff's, he shew'd me the Bay, and Mr.
Weeks's Harbour.   Sept.ʳ 3. Went to the Vinyard with
a fair wind, and from Homes's Hole to Tisbury and I to
Chilmark, to Mr. Allen's.   Sept.ʳ 4. to Gayhead, Mr. Dan-
forth, I, Mr. Tho. Mayhew, Major Basset.   Sept.ʳ 5.
Din'd at Mr. Mayhew's : went to Homes's Hole to wait

---

[1] Pompæsprisset was, probably, some part of Marshpee. Sewall was, before this, at Sandwich, and later at Succanesset or Falmouth. In Mass.
Hist. Soc. Coll., I. 231, we find it noted that there is a place in Marshpee
called Popponessit, and that "the place where Doctor Bourn's house stands,
about two miles up Manumit River, and near the Herring Pond, is called
Pumspisset."

Sewall next goes to Martha's Vineyard; stops at Holmes's Hole, in Tisbury; tarries at Tarpaulin Cove, in the island of Naushon, and thence goes
to Acushnet. Then, *en route* to Taunton, he stops at Assowamset, by which
we are to understand that part of Middleboro' called Lakeville since 1853. —
EDS.

for a Passage to Rode-Island, or Bristol. There lay wind-
bound. Sept.ʳ 8. Mr. Danforth and I go to Tisbury
Meeting, Mr. Josia Torrey preach'd forenoon: Mr. Dan-
forth after Noon. Return'd to Chases to Mr. Bromfield.
Sept.ʳ 9. Monday, embark'd with a scant wind; put in to
Tarpoling Cove: Mr. Bromfield not yielding to go to
Cushnet. There spake with Darby who shew'd us the
prisoners Fines: Spake with Mr. Weeks.

Sept.ʳ 10. Gave the Squaw that has lost her feet, Ten
pounds of Wool. When the Tide serv'd, sail'd for Cushnet, had a good passage; lodg'd at Capt. Pope's; he not
at home: borrowed six pounds of Mr. Pope; were well
entertain'd there. Sept.ʳ 11. Wednesday, Five Indians
carried Mr. Bromfield in a chair from Spooner's, to Assowamset, and so to Taunton. Twas near midnight by that
time we got there, where by Leonard, whom we accidentally met late at night, we were inform'd the Bristol
Court was not held for want of Justices; and that Maj.ʳ
Walley and Mr. Leverett adjourn'd *de die in diem*; Jury-
men murmur'd. This put me upon new Straits: but I
resolv'd to go to Bristol, and so did, next day, Sept.ʳ 12.
Thorsday, Capt. Hodges's son waiting on me: got thither
about 2. Saved the Afternoon. Mr. Blagrove is cast,
Asks a Chancery [1] in writing; Major Walley and Leverett
will by no means suffer it: I earnestly press'd for it. 13,
14. Court held, and then adjourn'd *sine die*. But twas
so late, there was no getting out of Town.

Sept.ʳ 15. Lord's Day, Mr. Sparhawk preaches forenoon;
Mr. Sever in the Afternoon. Sup at Mr. Pain's.

Sept.ʳ 16. By Mr. Niles's Importunity, I set out with
him for Narraganset. Din'd at Bright's: while Diñer
was getting ready I read in Ben Johnson, a Folio:

---

[1] See Province Laws, I. 373 (Sect. 4). Compare Province Laws, I. 285,
356. — EDS.

Wake, our Mirth begins to dye:
Quicken it with Tunes and Wine.
Raise your Notes; you'r out; fie, fie,
This drowsiness is an ill sign.
  We banish him the Quire of Gods
  That droops agen:
  Then all are men
For here's not one but nods.

Fol. 13.

Sejanus
——— great and high
The ☉ [world] knows only 2, thats Rome and I,
My Roof receives me not, 'tis Aer I tread
And at each step I feel my advanced head
Knock out a Star in Heaven ———

f. 144.

Howere the Age she lives in doth endure
The vices that she breeds above their Cure.

211.

I went to wait on Govr Cranston : but found him not at home. Ferried over, got to Narraganset shoar a little before sunset. Twas in the night before we got to our Lodging about 5. miles off the Ferry. Tuesday and Wednesday spent in settling Bounds between Niles and Hazard ; and the widow Wilson ; at last all were agreed. I was fain to forgo some Acres of Land to bring Niles and Hazard to Peace and fix a convenient Line between them. Thorsday 7^r 19. Forenoon I got Mr. Mumford, the Surveyor, to goe with us, and we found out and renew'd the Bounds of an 80 Acre Lot, just by Place's. Place went with us and assisted. After Diñer, went to Point Judith, was pleased to see the good Grass and Wood, there is upon the Neck. Just as we came there the Triton's Prise Pass'd by, all her sails abroad, fresh Gale, S. S. W., standing for Newport. News Letter, 7^r 30. — 8^r 4. Woman of the house sick ; House miserably out of Repair. Twas night by that time we got home. Friday, Septr 20. go into the Quakers Meeting-house, about 35. long 30 wide, on Hazard's Ground that was mine. Acknowledge a Deed

to Knowls, of Eight Acres, reserving one Acre at the Corner
for a Meetinghouse.   Bait at Capt. Eldridges.   From
thence to the Fulling-mill at the head of Coêset [Coweset]
Cove, and there dine; a civil woman, but sorrowfull,
dress'd our diñer.   From thence Niles brings me to Tur-
pins at Providence, and there Bait: From thence over
Blackston's[1] River, and there I send him back, and travail
alone to Freeman's, where I meet with Piriam, the under-
Sheriff, and Capt. Watts, whose company was helpfull to
me.

Satterday, Sept: 21.   Baited at Devotion's, who was very
glad to see me.   Din'd at Billinges; by Piriam and him
was inform'd of Mr. Bromfields being well at home.
Baited at Dedham.   Was Trim'd at Roxbury; my Barber
told me the awfull News of the Murder of Mr. Simeon
Stoddard,[2] in England, which much saddened me.   Got
home a little before Sunset: found all well, *Laus Deo.*

Sept: 25.   Mr. Bromfield and I took the Hackney
Coach to wait on the Govr: met his Excellency on this
side the Gate; went out of the Coach and Complemented
him, and then went on and visited Mr. Bailey.

Nov: 7th 1706.   I invited the Gov:, Col. Tyng, Mr. Sol.
Stoddard, Simeon, Mr. Pemberton, Capt. Belchar, Mr.
Bromfield, Capt. Southack.   I supos'd Mr. Stoddard had

---

[1] It is to be remembered that Blackstone's River, at Attleborough Gore,
was named after William Blackstone, the first settler at Boston.   In 1849,
the late L. M. Sargent printed some notes showing that, very probably, descendants of the emigrant, bearing the name of Blackstone, still survive. —
EDS.

[2] Simeon Stoddard, Jr., was born Oct. 20, 1682.   The following sermon
is in the Society's library: —

" The Just Man's Prerogative, a Sermon preached privately Sept. 27, 1706,
on a Solemn Occasion; for the Consolation of a Sorrowful Family, Mourning
over the Immature Death of a Pious Son, viz, Mr. Simeon Stoddard, who was
found Barbarously Murdered, in Chelsea-Fields near London, May, 14, 1706.
By. S. Willard. . . . Boston, N. E.   Printed by B. Green.   Sold by Nicholas Boone at his Shop, 1706."   16mo. pp. 28.   It contains no information
about Mr. Stoddard, or the circumstances of his death. — EDS.

preach'd the Lecture. Mr. Cotton Mather preach'd. He
did not pray for the Super. Court, or Judges in his first
prayer, that I took notice of: but in his last, mention'd
the Gen¹ Court, and any Administrations of Justice. I
invited him to dine by Mr. Cooke; He said he was
engag'd.

Nov.ʳ 8. There is a Hearing of Roxbury, Spring Street,
about another Meeting-house, and of Billericay proprietors and Farmers. Deputies Treat the Govʳ at Homes's.

Lords-Day, Nov.ʳ 10. Andrew Belchar, Nicholas Bows,
Debora Green, and Sarah —— are baptised by Mr. Willard.

Tingitur Andreas, Nicolaus, Debora, Sarah.

This morning Tom Child, the Painter,¹ died.

> Tom Child had often painted Death,
> But never to the Life, before:
> Doing it now, he's out of Breath;
> He paints it once, and paints no more.

Thorsday² 8.ʳ 17. Son and daughter Sewall and their
little Rebeca, son Hirst and his family, dine with us: all
here but Joseph. He keeps his Thanksgiving at Cambridge.

Friday, 8.ʳ 18. I visit Mr. Baily: as I enter, he saith,
I am even gon, even gon! said he had a Fever; the
night before and that day had subdued his Nature. In
his Paroxism said, Cutting, Cutting, Cutting all to pieces:
My Head, my Head; could not bear the Boys choping
without door.

---

¹ Thomas Child's will (Suff. Wills, lib. 16. f. 200) is dated Jan. 14,
1702, 1703; proved Oct. 13, 1706. He is termed painter-stainer. He makes
his wife, Katherine, his executrix, mentions his mother, Alice Martin,
"now living in Fryer Lane in Thames Street, London," and his "brother-
in-law, John Martin, now in Boston." Sewall's lines evidently imply that
he was a portrait-painter; and here may be the long sought-for artist who
preceded Peter Pelham. — EDS.

² These few entries in 8br., *i. e.*, October, seem to be misplaced. — EDS.

Tuesday, 8ᵣ 22. I go to Roxbury Lecture, Mr. Cotton Mather preach'd from 1 Jn° 5. 13. Concerning Assurance, with much affecting Solidity and Fervor. Went to see Mr. Baily, whose Mouth and Tongue were so furr'd, he could hardly speak at first: said he had been a long time in a storm at the Harbours Mouth, hôp'd he should not be swallow'd on Quicksands, or split on Rocks. God had not yet forsaken him, and he hop'd He never would. Said, Here I Wait!

Wednesday, 8ᵣ 23. Court meets; but the Govʳ has signified his pleasure that nothing be done till he come from Piscataqua: Adjourn till 3 p. m. after Lecture to-morrow. After Diñer I go and take the Acknowledgment of Mr. Nathan¹ Henchman and Aña his wife to a Deed to their Brother, the schoolmaster: She was lying on the Bed sick of a Fever; yet very sensible and set her hand to the Receipt.

Thorsday, 8ᵣ 24. Mr. Wadsworth apears at Lecture in his Perriwigg. Mr. Chiever is griev'd at it. Court meets, read Mr. Secretary's Letter to Mr. Constantine Phips; adjourn to Ten in the morn. This day I am told of Mr. Torrey's kinswoman, Betty Symmes,¹ being brought to Bed of a Bastard in his house last Monday night. I visit Mr. Chiever.

Feria Sexta, Novʳ 8, 1706. I visited Mr. Bayley; find his sister Cheyny² with him. He was very low at first;

---

¹ We refer to this misadventure merely to note the name. It seems that the widow of Captain William Symmes married Rev. John Torrey, of Weymouth, whose death is noted a few months later. — EDS.

² Daniel Cheney, of Newton, married Sarah Bailey in 1665, according to Jackson's History. Savage seems to be somewhat in doubt about this Rev. James Bayley, but from the names of his relatives it seems clear that he was the son of John Bailey, of Salisbury, by his wife Eleanor Emery. Sewall says he was born July, 1642; while Savage says Sept. 12, 1650, H. C. 1669. Sewall's date is hard to reconcile with the other births, and the year of graduating. Savage also considers that he was ordained at Weymouth, in 1703, and notes that the Roxbury record calls him Esquire. He seems to have never been settled long in any place, and perhaps was hardly recognized as a full "reverend," *though Italicised.* — EDS.

but after awhile revived and Spake freely; has been very
ill this Moneth; especially last Satterday and Sabbath day
night.   Desired his service to Bro^r, Sister, Mr. Noyes,
with much Thanks for his verses which had been a great
Comfort to him: To Mr. Higginson, Mrs. Higginson.   I
gave him 2 five shilling Bills of Credit to buy a Cord of
Wood, which he accepted with great thankfullness.   I
told him it was a time of great expense; he was in prison,
and Mrs. Bayley, in Fetters.   Upon my coming in, Mrs.
Bayley went to Sol. Phip's wife, who was hurt by a fall
out of her Calash.   I staid with him about 2 hours or
more, went from home at 3 and return'd past seven.

Novr 11th 1706.   Went to Salem with Mr. Dudley.
Novr 14th Return'd with Mr. Leverett, Mr. Dudley.
Had very comfortable Journey out and home.

Novr 15th   Midnight, Mrs. Pemberton is brought to
Bed of a dead daughter.   Her Life was almost despair'd
of, her Bleeding was so much, and Pains so few.

Novr 27.   Mr. John Hubbard comes in and tells me
Mr. Bayley is very sick, and much chang'd as he thinks;
is desirous of seeing me.

Novr 28, 1706.   Visited Mr. Bayley after Diñer; went
in the Coach.   I mention'd Heaven being the Christian's
Home: Mr. Bayley said, I long to be at home; why
tarry thy chariot wheels?   Told me twas the last time he
should see me.   Was born, July, 1642.

Decr 3.   I went with Col. Townsend, and Mr. E^m
Hutchinson, and visited Capt. Legg: He is in a low and
languishing Condition.   Then went and talk'd thoroughly
with Mr. Cotton Mather about selling Henchman's House;
He seem'd to be satisfied; tells me Mr. Williams is to
preach the Lecture.   Yesterday Mrs. Walker of the Neck
was buried, I follow'd for one; I saw none else of the
Council there.   Mrs. Hañah Oliver is to be buried tomorrow.

Decr 4, 1706.   I was at the Burial of Mrs. Hañah
Oliver.

Dec.ᵣ 5ᵗʰ   Mr. John Williams[1] Preach'd the Lecture.

Dec.ᵣ 6.   I went to Mr. Sergeant's and heard Mr. Pemberton preach from Ps. 4. 6.

Dec.ᵣ 7. 1706.   The Genˡ Court is prorogued to Wednesday the 12ᵗʰ of February, at 10. *mane.* I invited the Govʳ to dine at Holms's. There were the Govʳ, Col. Townsend, Bromfield, Leverett, Williams, Capt. Wells, Shelden, Hook, Sewall.

Midweek, Dec.ᵣ 11ᵗʰ I visited Mr. Bayley, find Mr. Walter with him; I moved that seeing Mr. Walter and I seldom met there together, Mr. Walter might go to prayer; which he did excellently; that Mr. Bayley and we our selves might be prepared to dye. Mr. Bayley is now, the night before last, taken with Pleuretick Pains, which go beyond those of the stone; New Pains: Cryes out, My Head! my Head! what shall I doe? Seems now to long, and pray for a Dismission. At parting I gave his Sister Cheyny a Ten-Shilling Bill for him, to help to buy somè Necessaries; I could not help them to watch. Mr. Bayley said he thought he should dye of a Consumption of the Lungs; by's Cough he found they were touch'd. When he mention'd the pain in his side : I said, twas sad for a Man to be circumvented with his Enemies : He answered pretty readily, He hôp'd there were more with him than against him. He desired me to write to his Brother Joseph to come and see him. Dec.ᵣ 13. I gave my Letter to J. Bayley to Mr. Simkins, who said he had one to send it by. Note. By reason of the Storm yesterday, the council met not; Govʳ was not in Town : but writt a Letter to the Secretary that the Council was adjourn'd to Friday; See Jan. 1, 17¹³⁄₁₄. I told the Secretary, the Council that met not, could not be adjourn'd; yet,

---

[1] Mr. Williams, who had been taken captive by the Indians in the burning of Deerfield, Feb. 29, 170⅘, was carried to Montreal, and being redeemed returned to Boston Oct. 25, 1706. — EDS.

Govr nominated Mr. Plaisted to be a Justice of peace in Yorkshire, and drove it throw, though he be a Dweller in Hampshire; and has a Brother Ichabod Plaisted, that is of the Council.

This day Mr. Melyen dies. Ætat. 67. Mrs. Mary Pemberton is very low, dangerously ill.

Decr 14th Joseph comes to see us, brings word that Wyth, the Mason, dyed yesterday at Cambridge. Goodman Swan is in a fair way to be Receiv'd into the Church again; was cast out in Mr. Oakes's time, in a very solemn mañer, in my sight and Hearing.

Decr 18. 1706. Bastian Lops the Elm by my Lord's Stable;[1] cuts off a cord of good wood. Mr. Sergeant came up Rawson's Lane as we were doing of it. Decr 19. *mane,* Maxwell comes in the Governour's name to invite me to Dine at Roxbury with his Excellency at one aclock tomorrow. Mr. C. Mather preaches the Lecture in Mr. Bridges Turn, from Gal. 3. 27 —— have put on Christ. Preach'd with Allusion to Aparel; one head was that Aparel was for Distinction.

Mr. Walter dines with us, and leaves with me £13.10.9. Roxbury Money. Mr. Sergeant marries Mrs. Mehetabel Cooper.[2]

Decr 20, *feria sexta,* very Rainy day; Mr. Winthrop, Russel, Elisha Hutchinson, E^m Hutchinson, Mr. Foster, Sewall, Townsend, Walley, Bromfield, Belchar Dine at the Governour's, Mr. Secretary. Go in Coaches. After Diñer I visit Mr. Bayley; Is in great Extremity, Paroxisms return

---

[1] We have already mentioned (Vol. I. p. 203, note) that Lord Bellomont, in 1699, was at a charge for a stable, besides his house. See Sewall's reference (I. 500) to Bellomont Gate. May it not be that Bellomont's stable kept its title, and that it was near the present Tremont House, towards the rear of Sewall's land? Rawson's Lane is now Bromfield Street. — EDS.

[2] Peter Sargeant, a very prominent citizen of Boston, married, secondly, the widow of Sir William Phips, and, thirdly, Mehetable (Minot), widow of Thomas Cooper. He died Feb. 8, 1714, and his widow married, thirdly, Simeon Stoddard. (See Vol. I. p. 163, *note.*) — EDS.

in about ½ hour; seem'd to desire death; and yet once I
took notice that he breath'd after some space and recovery
of strength before went hence : leave all to God's unerring
Providence.   He told me he heard Sister Short was dangerously sick : heard of by Jon.ª Emery.   Came home to
the Meeting at Mr. Bromfield's, Mr. Williams of Deerfield
preach'd : very Rainy, and dirty under foot.   When came
home, or a little after, had a Letter brought me of the
Death of Sister Shortt the 18.ᵗʰ Inst. which was very surprising to me.   Half are now dead.   The Lord fit me for
my Departure.   Dec.ʳ 21.   Not having other Mourning,
I look'd out a pair of Mourning Gloves.   An hour or 2
after, Mr. Sergeant, sent me and my wife Gloves; mine
are so little I cânt wear them.   See Jan. 20. 170⅚.   Mr.
Cooper's Son brought them, I gave him Dr. Mather's
Treatise of Tithes.

Dec.ʳ 23.   I visit Mr. Sergeant and his Bride; had Ale
and Wine.   Mr. Cook, Col. Hutchinson, Mr. Colman,
Adams, Capt. Hill, Mr. Dering were there.   After came
in Mr. Bromfield, and Cousin Dumer.

Dec.ʳ 24.   *Feria Tertia.*   My wife and I execute a
Lease to Mr. Seth Dwight, for 21. years, of the House he
dwells in.   Mr. Eliezer Moodey writt the Leases; and he
and David Sinclair were Witnesses: Twas transacted in
our Bedchamber.

Feria tertia, Dec.ʳ 24. 1706.   I went to Brooklin, and
visited my son and Daughter Sewall and little Rebekah;
Paid my son 30ˢ in full, and he is to send me 15. Foun-
tains, which are paid for in the mention'd Sum.   He has
been ill, and is not very well now.   Mr. Read, with whom
he has been, tells him he is Melancholy.   Din'd on Salt
Fish and a Spar-Rib.[1]

---

[1] There seems to be something peculiar about the word now spelled
" spare-rib."   In the Cutter Genealogy, p. 325, in a list of gifts to Rev.
William Brattle, in 1697, by his parishioners, we find: Mrs. Amsdal gave a
" ribspair of pork," also " Ribspaires of pork."   May not this suggest an

Visited Mr. Bayley as I came home; he has a very sore
Mouth. He tells me he has left off observing the distance
of his Fits, is tired and done. I gave him a Banberry
cake,[1] of which he eat pretty well, complaining of his
Mouth.

Mid-week. Dec.r 25. Shops open, carts come to Town
with Wood, Fagots, Hay, and Horses with Provisions, as
usually. I bought me a great Tooth'd Comb at Dwight's;
6ˢ.

Feria septima, Dec.r 28, 1706. A large fair Rainbow
is seen in the Morning in the Norwest. Madam Walley
call'd her Husband into the Shop to see it. The Gov.r
being indispos'd with the Gout, call'd a Council to meet
at Roxbury; and by that means I gain'd an Oportunity
to see my friend Bayley once again: He is now brought
very low by his Stone, Fever, Sore Tongue and Mouth;
could hardly speak a word to me. But he said, sit down.
His wife ask'd him if he knew me? He answer'd, with
some quickness, He should be distracted, if he should not
know me. He Thank'd me when I came away. I said
Christ would change his vile body, and make it like his
glorious body. And when the Coachman call'd, saying
the Company staid for me, I took leave, telling him God
would abide with him; Those that Christ loves, he loves

---

original form with which " spare " has no connection; and, if not, what
does " spare " mean in this place? Possibly it is a secondary form, suggested
by these being lean ribs, and may yet be a modern attempt to give sense to a
perverted and forgotten original. — EDS.

[1] Banbury, in Oxfordshire, has been long renowned for cheese, cakes, and
ale. Chambers (Book of Days) says that its cakes " are exported to the
most distant parts of the world, one baker alone, in 1839, disposing of
139,500 twopenny ones." Banbury was also famous for its Puritanism, and
this savor may have extended to its cakes.

It was in reference to this town that Braithwaite wrote the well-known
lines: —
        " To Banbury came I, O profane one!
        There I saw a Puritane one
        Hanging of his cat on Monday
        For killing of a mouse on Sunday."   EDS.

to the end. He bow'd with his head. His wife and sister
weep over him. He call'd for Mouth-Water once while I
was there, and then for his little pot to void it into : I
supos'd it was to enable him to speak. Though he doth
not eat at present; yet I left the Banbury cake I carried
for him, with his wife : And when came away, call'd her
into next chamber, and gave her two Five-Shilling Bills :
She very modestly and kindly accepted them and said I
had done too much already : I told her No, if the state of
my family would have born it, I ought to have watch'd
with Mr. Bayley, as much as that came to. I left her
weeping. Mark the perfect Man &c. When return'd to
the Governour's, I found the other Coaches gon; the sun
down some time. Major Walley, Col. Townsend, Mr.
Bromfield and I came home well together in the Hackney
Coach; though the ways are very deep by reason of the
long, strong southerly wind and Thaw. Serene day.
Wind W.

Dec.ʳ 31. 1706. Madam Dudley, and Mrs. Anne Dudley
visit my wife just a little before night, and inform of our
Son's illness, which they were told off at midnight : Will
send us word if he grow worse.

Mr. Salter makes us a little Chimney in my Chimney,
make a Fire in it to try it.

Midweek, Jan.ʸ 9th. visited Mr. Bayley. He is very
low, and the skin of his Hip now broken, and raw, which
is very painfull to him. He said I long to be gon, yet
with Submission to God's holy will : What I writt to him
out of Mr. Caryl was a cordial to him.[1] Met Sam, who
came to see us.

Feria Sexta, Jan.ʸ 10ᵗʰ Capt. Legg buried. Bearers,

---

[1] Of course Caryl's Exposition on Job, which was in two volumes folio,
consisting of upwards of six hundred sheets. " One just remark has been
made on its utility, that it is a very sufficient exercise for the virtue of patience, which it was chiefly intended to inculcate and improve." — EDS.

Govr, Mr. Winthrop; Mr. Cooke, Addington; Col. Byfield, Capt. Belchar. Councillors had Gloves, and many others.

Tuesday, Jany 14th Govr calls a Council, Propounds Mr. Danforth, Dorchester, and Mr. Belchar of Newbury to Preach the Election Sermon; Mr. Samuel Belchar is agreed on, Mr. Danforth having preach'd before.

Midweek, Jany 15th A great Storm of Snow; yet Danl Bayley breaks through, and brings us a Load of Walnut Wood. I had transcribed some choice sentences out of Calvin's Exposit. Mat. 4. 1, 2, 3, 4. and sent them by Daniel; Letter was just seal'd before he came, written and dated today. The Storm prevail'd so, that not one of our Meeting ventured to come to our House where it was to be. Mrs. Deming, and her daughter-in-Law, and Mrs. Salter came over; waited till six-a-clock, and then sung the 2 last Staves of the 16. Ps. Eat some Bread and drank. Gave Mr. Deming one of Mr. Higginson's Election Sermons; Daughter-in-Law, Greek Churches: Mrs. Salter, Greek Churches.

Friday, Jany 17. Mr. Tho. Bridge visits me. In Discourse I gave him my opinion that the Witnesses were not slain. Gave him one of Mr. Higginson's Election Sermons.

Satterday, Jany 18. Going down in the morning, I find David sick: tells me had been sick and vomited in the night: We have the Stove-room-Chamber fitted for him, and place him there; send for Mr. Oakes. Lords-day at even, Mrs. Plimly comes to nurse him.

Saturday morn, Jany 18th James Robinson, the Baker, coming from Roxbury, tells me Mr. Bayley dyed the last night 2 hours after midnight; one in Roxbury-street bid him tell me so.

Jany 20. Mr. Prentice gives me notice that the Funeral was to be on Friday, not before, because Mr. Bayley's Bro^r at Newbury, was to order it. Gave me notice to be a Bearer, Mr. Bayley had apointed it.

Friday, Jan.ʸ 24. 170$\frac{6}{7}$. I and Mr. John Clark, Mr.
Francis Burroughs, and Mr. John Bolt rode together in
Simson's Slay to the Funeral of Mr. Bayley. Were there
at One: Went about 3. Bearers Sewall, Bond; Fisk,
Walter; Clark, Noyes. Gov.ʳ was there; intended Mr.
Thacher, but the wether was bad over head, and under-
foot by reason of the snow in the Night, and Hail and
Rain now, and he was not there. Saw not Mr. Denison
there. Mr. John Hubbard, Mr. Daniel Oliver, and Mr.
Justice Lynde was there; Mr. Bowls. His Brethren Isaac
Bayley, and Joshua Bayly followed the Herse. The
Widow and her daughter Prentice rode in a slay. The
wether being bad, I took Leave at the Grave, our slay
being just at hand went into it, and got home by Four;
Laus Deo. I did condole and congratulat the Relations
upon our parting with our Friend, and his being gon to
Rest after a weary Race. Mr. Walter gave a very good
Character of Mr. Bayley. He was with him the evening
before he dyed, and pray'd with him: He answer'd perti-
nently, by Yes and No: thought he should dy that night,
of which was not afraid. Mr. Walter pray'd before we
went to the Grave.

Jan.ʸ 26.ᵗʰ I dream'd last night that I was chosen Lord
Maior of London; which much perplex'd me: a strange
absurd Dream!

Febr. 9.ᵗʰ Lord's Day; The latter part of the Night, and
this morn, we had great Lightening, and Thunder, Rain
and Hail.

Febr. 10. A pleasant, Serene, sun-shiny Day; sweet
singing of Birds.

Febr. 16, at night, Mr. Thacher of Milton is taken very
sick. Febr. 20, Sister Hirst, Sister Sewall of Salem, Mr.
Flint, Son and daughter Hirst, dine with us after Lecture.
Febr. 25. Mr. Colman, Sister Hirst, Sewall, Mr. Elisha
Coke jun.ʳ and wife, I and Mary dine at Son Hirst's.

After that I visit the widow Eliott, who dwells with her daughter Davis.[1]

26th A Fast is kept at Milton.

27th Dr. Mather was not at Lecture. Mr. Cotton Mather preached, Sung 10——14th 27th Ps. Mr. Dwight is much troubled about digging his Cellar; I get Mr. Cook and Capt. Clark to go to him after Lecture, and view the work and speak to Mr. Gibbins; they seem'd to be offended at Mr. Dwight's smart Replyes to Mr. Gibbins and his wife; and spake a little coldly, and told me it were best to agree. I went again near night, and Dwight told me, Mrs. Gibbins intended next day to make another Gateway, and hinder'd the workmen from digging home at that corner: whereupon I order'd the Men to digg it down, which they quickly did, at which Gibbins storm'd and ask'd me why I did not bid him pull down his House, if I did, they would do it. And Mrs. Gibbins spake many opprobrious words: But the men went on vigorously. Febr. 28. Gibbins orders Mr. Bernard's men to cutt another Gate-way, and with the Boards cut out nail'd up her own former Gate-way: then laid a Board, a door, over from the Cutt Gate-way over the Corner of the Cellar and pass that way, and the Negro said, This is our passage-way. I said little to it, but went in, and talk'd with Mr. Gibbins, his wife and son; and were ready to put it to Men to determin what should be; Mr. Dwight came in: and said he would not agree to put it to Men: I told Mr. Gibbins I would speak to him, and come again after Diñer. I went accordingly, and when I return'd found they had been Pumping Tubs of Water, and throwing them into my new-dug Cellar, to soften the Workmen's Corns, as they said, so that the men were forc'd to

---

[1] This was Mary (Wilcox), widow of Jacob Eliot, Jr., whose daughter Abigail married William Davis, and had a daughter Abigail, wife of Henry Lowder. — EDS.

leave off working. Several Tubs of water were thrown in while I sat in the House: I only call'd to Mrs. Gibbins and told her I saw she could not wait till I came. Durham came and dug through the Stone-wall into this little new Cellar, and I think that quell'd our antagonists: for our Cellar being a little higher than theirs, all the water would have run upon themselves. And after, the Select-Men, several of them viewing it, countenanc'd my Tenant; Mr. Secretary also look'd in upon us: and the workmen went on peaceably.

Friday, March, 7. 1707. Several Ministers prayed at the desire of the Court; began a little after Ten; Mr. Willard, Wadsworth, Bridge, Colman, Pemberton, C. Mather, Dr. I. Mather. Prayers were made with great Pertinency and Variety; I hope God will hear. Several pray'd that God would speedily, by some Providence, or one way other, let us know what might doe as to going against Port-Royal. Gave Thanks for the News of the 18. Indians kill'd, and one Taken last Tuesday; which heard of just after the Apointment of this Day. Sung the two first staves of the 20ᵗʰ Psalm, York Tune, which I set, Mr. Willard used my Psalm-Booke. Left off about ½ hour past Two. Council gave the Govʳ and Ministers a Diñer at Homes's.

Feria Septima, Martij 8ᵒ. 1707. *Anno Regni Annæ Reginæ Angliæ &c. Sexto.*

Nobilibus, causas quid præfers Angle latentes?

Annæ principium, Cæsaris annus habet.

> 'Till Annæ's Equal Reign begun,
> We ne'r could well begin the year:
> But now the Controversy's done;
> The Eigth of March can have no peer.

This day is rainy and dark, and the Govʳ came not to Town. Deputies sent in for going to Port-Royal to take it; if what was necessary in order to it might be provided

March, 8th. Having got Mr. Joseph Marion to write the verses fair, I gave them to Mr. Winthrop, in the Governour's absence, saying, I cân't drink the Queen's Health, *parvum parva decent*[1] —— Accept of a small essay for the honor of my Soveraign.

In the Afternoon Mr. Williams visits us, tells me he goes to Dearfield 14 nights hence, next Tuesday. I gave him a copy of the foremention'd verses. He tells me Quebeck Seminary was burnt the 20th of 7r 1705. our Style, Library burnt. His Narrative is now in the Press.[2] *Feria tertia,* March, 18th. Mr. Pemberton removes into the Churches House. March 20. I visit him, and wish him and her joy. March, 21. I give him a 20s Bill to help towards his House-warming, which he accepts kindly. Joseph comes to Town. March, 20. *feria quinta,* Mrs. Gibbs's Warehouse was burnt down in Lecture time. Meeting was disturb'd just as was coming to the particulars of Fighting against our Enemies and praying against them. After Mr. Colman had sat awhile, the people were quiet, and went on again.

March, 21. The Governour, Capt. Saml Apleton, Mr. Jno Williams, Mr. William Williams, dine with us in the new Hall.

Feria secunda, March, 24th. I set out in the storm with Sam Robinson, got to Barker's about 5, and there lodg'd, and dry'd my Coat, Hat, Gloves.

Feria tertia, March 25, 1707. Went to Plimouth, got thither about 10. m. Major Walley and Mr. Leverett came in after six; so that could only Adjourn the Court. March, 26. Mr. Josiah Torrey preaches the Lecture. March, 27. I go into the Meetinghouse. Hañah Parker is found guilty of Adultery. I spake with two of the

---

[1] Horace, Epis. I. vii. 44. — Eds.

[2] This is, of course, the well-known narrative by Rev. John Williams, entitled "The Redeemed Captive returning to Zion," &c., Boston, 1707; often since reprinted. — Eds.

Middlebury Men at Mr. Little's about Mr. Palmer, who is impos'd upon them as their Minister. Gave Mr. Little a pound of Chockalat. March, 28. 1707. Baited at Bairsto's; Din'd at Cushing's: Then I left the Company and went to Hingham; visited Mr. Cobb, Mr. Norton, cousin Hobart: Got to Mr. Torrey's just before sunset; He was very glad to see me. Read 17th Rev. Pray'd excellently. Pray'd excellently in the Morn. Visit Cousin Hunt, Quinsey; Got home about One and Dine there. Am well notwithstanding my journeying in the Rain, and find mine well; *Laus Deo!* March, 29. Mrs. Tucker, Mrs. Lothrop's Sister, is found dead in her apartment. March, 30. My wife goes out in the Afternoon. March, 31. *feria secunda,* I visit my Son, and dine with him; He is all alone. Visited Mr. Gibbs, presented him with a pound of Chockalett, and 3 of Cousin Moodey's sermons; gave one to Mrs. Bond, who came in while I was there. Visit Joseph; He pronounc'd his valedictory Oration March 28th. Heard Mr. Willard Expound from 1 Cor. 13. 8, 9, 10. Came home by the Ferry. Shall be Language in Heaven; but no need to Learn Languages as now; which is a fruit of the Curse, since the Confusion. Mr. Metcalf comes in late, and I ask him to lodge here; which he accepts: is going to Falmouth, where he preach'd last winter.

April, 5. Eclipse of the Moon: is seen in a serene Aer, Moon is of a Ruddy Colour when Eclipsed. April, 7. Mr. Sparhawk is again chosen to preach the Artillery Sermon. April, 8. I go to Cambridge and carry Joseph a small piece of Plate to present his Tutor with, Bottom mark'd, March, 5, 170$\frac{6}{7}$ which was the day his Tutor took Leave of them; price 39.^{s} 2.^{d} View'd his Chamber in the President's House, which I like. Came home and went to the Funeral of little Mary Bastian. Isaac Marion walk'd with me.

Midweek Apr. 9. I waited on Col. Hutchinson, Check-

ley, and others of the Comittee, as far as the last house
of Roxbury; came home by Mr. Wells's. Din'd at Mr.
Brewer's, about 3 p.m̅. It was a Frost, and Ice of half an
inch, or inch thick in the morn. Cold wind that I was
fain to wear my Hood. I got well home about Sun-set;
David stood at the Gate to take the Horse, and told me
the amazing News of Mr. Willard's dangerous Sickness.
He was taken at Diñer in his Study, so that he quickly
grew delirious. Some think he took cold at the Funeral
of Mr. Myles's child, the evening before. This day Mr.
Noyes preached his Lecture from Heb. 11th 32. 33. 34,
encouraging the Expedition to Port-Royal. April, 10,
1707. Mr. Bridge preaches our Lecture, from Psal. 149.
9. Encouraging the Expedition.

Feria Sexta Apr. 11th. I see a Swallow or two. 'Tis
Capt. Belchar's Meeting; Mr. Pemberton and he come to
propose to me, the begiñing at 3. aclock, and inviting the
Ministers to spend the Time in Prayer. Mr. Pemberton,
Colman, Wadsworth, Mather, Bridge. Dr. Mather pray'd
Excellently, Copiously. Dr. Mather, speaking of the
Port-Royal Affair, call'd it the uncertain Expedition;
Pray'd God not to carry his people hence, except He pros-
per'd them.

Apr. 12, *feria septima,* I see three Swallows together.
Mr. Willard grows more compôs'd. Lydia [wife of] William Lowder,[1] a young woman of 16 years, is deliver'd of

---

[1] The identification of this Lydia, wife of William Lowder, has been
difficult, owing to some remarkable coincidences of names. By Suff. Deeds,
lib. 24, f. 154, it is clear that she was the daughter of John Balston, who
had left, in 1709, a widow, Martha. This was Martha Bullard, whom he
married March 16, 1703. But there were two John Balstons; one a son of
James, the other a son of Jonathan. Each had a daughter Lydia. John,
son of James, had a Lydia born Aug. 25, 1691; but she must have died soon,
as he had a second Lydia born Nov. 16, 1695. John, son of Jonathan, was
a mariner, and by first wife, Anne, had Lydia, born June 22, 1688. This
must be the person meant in the text, although her age would be nineteen
instead of sixteen.

Prudence Balston, sister of this John, married John Marion; whilst his

a daughter, and dyes this morning; I think in the room where her Mother Balston dyed, and as suddenly.

Friday, April, 18. 1707. Just before Sun-set there is a Small piece of a Rainbow in the South-east and by south: I saw it out of our Chamber-window. Mr. Fisk tells me he saw it.

Monday, Apr. 21. Mr. Bromfield and I set out about 9. *mane*, to visit Mr. Torrey. Twas hot, and when were got to Braintrey, Mr. Bromfield grows weary, and chose to call at Cousin Fisk's, which we did; He is gon to Weymouth. This was about 11. m. Cousin Fisk would have us Dine; and while we were at Table, Mr. Fisk came in and told us Mr. Torrey was gon to Rest, dyed about Eleven aclock. So our journey was sadly determined. It seems the Souldiers go to Hull this day from Weymouth, there to imbark in the Port-Royal Expedition; Mr. Fisk pray'd with them. The Death of Mr. Torrey, a Laborious, Faithfull Divine, Excellent in Prayer, is a sad epocha for the Com̄encment of this Expedition.

Coming home, I turn'd off at Roxbury, and went to Brooklin; found my son and daughter gon to Boston. Look'd upon his Sheep and Lambs, and came home. Met Mr. Roberts on the Neck going to the Governour, I told him of Mr. Torrey's Death as had told the Gov^rs Maid before. His Excellency was gon to his Farm towards Dedham; and his Lady to Boston with my Son, but came not to our House.

Feria quarta, Apr. 23. 1707. Capt Nath! Williams and I ride to Weymouth, to the Funeral of Mr. Torrey: When were at Braintrey, the Guns went off; overtook Mr. Danforth, got to Cous. Hunt's about one, Din'd there at Two; went to the House of Mourning: Saml Sewall, Zech Whitman; Peter Thacher, John Norton: John Danforth, Joseph

---

sister, Sarah Marion, married the other John Balston. Hence numerous perplexities in trying to unravel these relationships. Probably these John Balstons were own cousins. — EDS.

Belchar, Bearers. Had a Table spread, which could not leave without offense. Mr. Whitman pray'd before the Funeral. Mr. Fisk craved a Blessing, Mr. Thacher Return'd Thanks. Mr. Fisk led the widow. Grave was caved in, Mr. Thacher and I let down the Head, Mr. Hugh Adams also put to his Hand under ours. Stood a pretty while before any apeared to fill the Grave, some words and enquiry was made about it: At length two Hoes came, and then a Spade. Set out to come home at ½ hour after Six: Baited at Miller's, Got home a little before Ten, before the Moon went down; *Laus Deo*. Besides Relations, I saw none at the Funeral from Boston, save S. S., P. Dudley, esqr. Capt. Williams, Seth Dwight.

May, 12. 1707. Mrs. Lydia Scottow buried; Bearers, Sewall, Addington; Hill, Williams; Ballentine, Coney. May, 13. Mr. Dan! Oliver, Capt. Tho. Fitch and I ride to Natick, and hear Mr. Gookin preach and pray to the Indians there: Din'd at Capt. Fuller's as came back: got home well. *Laus Deo*. May, 15. Govr moves in Council that Mr. Willard might be spared, because of his late sickness, and continued weakness; and that Mr. Will Brattle, and Mr. Flint might regulat the Comencement: Govr said, Sundry had spoken to him about it. Major Walley, Capt. Belchar, Mr. Bromfield and I were desired to go and speak to Mr. Willard.

May, 16. Mr. Bromfield and I wait on Mr. Willard: I took a fit oportunity to enquire when he would go to Cambridge; and He said next week, without any hesitancy: so reckon'd we were not to enquire any further. We went to Mr. Pemberton first, and his opinion was, we should not express our desires, or the desires of any other, of Mr. Willard's imediat giving over College-work, except he himself inclin'd to it.

May, 16. visit Madam Coke, Mr. C. Mather, Mr. Gibbs, who came to this Town this day señight to see if the change of Aer would mend him.

May, 19. Went with Robinson to Salem: got thither late by reason of Robinson's late coming from Cambridge, and Madam Leverett's illness. Neither Col. Hathorn nor the Sheriff did accompany me; went with Mr. Attorney Dudley to Ipswich, got thither a little before Nine aclock. Mr. Harris came to meet us, but heard we came not till next day, and went back. May, 20th Court rises about 7. Visit the widow Ap̄leton. May, 21. Looks like a storm; but breaks up; I ride to Rowley, dine at Bro^r Northend's. Essay to visit H. Sewall, who was gon from home. Bro^r and Sister Northend go to the Causey, and then return. Visit the poor Orphan Shortts, hear Jane and Mehetabel read; gave them Five Shillings. Went to sister Gerrishes; to Mr. Brown, but he was not at home, saw Cous. Noyes, Mr. Woodbridge.

May, 22. Thorsday, Mr. Coffin Trims me, reckon with Mr. Brown and take fourty shillings of him in full. Went to Cous. Pierce, and there eat sturgeon with Mr. Pike, Abr. Adams, Cousin Jn° Tap̄in's wife. Went to Bro^r Tappin's, visited Cousin Sweet, they have a lovely Son. To Jn° Sewall, saw his new House where he now dwells; saw the Ashes of the old House. Bro^r Tap̄in tells me of the death of Col. Saltonstall on Wednesday after Lecture. Went to Joshua Bayley, discours'd him about his Brothers debt, staid a long time there, then went to Byfield across the Woods. Bro^r Tap̄in left me. I desired him that if heard Col. Saltonstall was to be buried on Friday he should send an Express to me of it. Friday, 23. Bro^r Moodey and I see Mr. Hale, on Horseback, drink a Glass of Cider; look on Sister Mehetabel's Grave; ride to Topsfield, visit Mr. Capen who is very glad to see me. Went to Phillip's, dined there. Parted with B. Moodey at the Fulling-mill. Baited at Lewis's. Got over Charlestown Ferry about 8. Note, as came down Winter Hill saw a Rainbow, was so much Rain as to oblige me to put on my Riding Coat, but it prov'd very little Rain.

Midweek, May 28, 1707. Mr. Samuel Belcher preached,

from Mat. 6. 10. Thy Kingdom come. Shew'd it was the duty of all to promote the Kingdom of Christ. At Diñer Mr. Belcher crav'd a Blessing, Mr. Jn° Danforth return'd Thanks. Sir John Davie[1] dined with the Govr In the morn, Mr. Secretary, major Walley and I gave the Deputies the Oaths, 66. and after, five more were sworn in the Council-Chamber, which made 71. and Councillors 24. $\frac{24}{71}$

<u>95 votes.</u>

1	Wait Winthrop[2]	88	Plimouth	
2	James Russell	90	John Thacher	53
3	Jn° Hathorn	60	Isaac Winslow	84
4	Elisha Hutchinson	91	Nathan¹ Pain	81
5	S. Sewall	92	John Cushing	80
6	Isaac Addington	92		
7	Wm Brown	82	Main	
8	Jn° Phillips	75	Eliakim Hutchinson	69
9	Jn° Corwin	75	Benj^a Brown	72
10	Jn° Foster	79	Ichabod Plaisted	59
11	Penn Townsend	90	At Large	
12	John Appleton	61	Zagadahock	
13	John Higginson	78	Joseph Lynde	54
14	Andrew Belcher	78	[Leverett 30]	
15	Edw. Bromfield	82	At Large	
16	*Sam¹ Apleton*	53	Simeon Stoddard	44
	2^d Stroak		2^d Stroak	
17	*Sam¹ Partridge*	53	Ephraim Hunt	47
	3^d Stroak		[Walley 18]	
18	Peter Sergeant	45	[Leverett 12]	

[1] Sir John Davie was one of the three baronets, natives of New England, the others being Sir George Downing and Sir William Pepperell. Sir John Davie was son of Humphrey Davie, who was an assistant here in 1679–86. Humphrey was the fourth son of Sir John Davie, of Creedy, county Devon, who was made a baronet in 1641. The oldest son, John, was succeeded by his son John. Then the title passed to William, son of William, second son of the first baronet. On his death it passed to his cousin, then a resident in Groton, Conn. The male line ended in England, in 1846; but the heiress married General Henry R. Ferguson, who assumed the name of Davie, and a new baronetcy was created in his favor. — Eds.

[2] The Council records show that all the twenty-eight, to whose names are appended the number of votes, were duly elected. Jn° Corwin should be Jonathan Corwin, and John Cushing was the second Councillor of those names. — Eds.

Lord's Day, June, 15ᵗʰ I felt my self dull and heavy and Listless as to Spiritual Good; Carnal, Lifeless; I sigh'd to God, that he would quicken me.

June, 16. My House was broken open in two places, and about Twenty pounds worth of Plate stolen away, and some Linen; My Spoon, and Knife, and Neckcloth was taken: I said, Is not this an Answer of Prayer? Jane came up, and gave us the Alarm betime in the morn. I was helped to submit to Christ's stroke, and say, Well-come CHRIST!

June, 19ᵗʰ The measuring Bason is found with Margaret Barton just carrying of it to Sea, to Hingham; said she had it of James Hews, he gave it her to sell for him. Mr. Secretary sent her to Prison.

June, 21. Billy Cowell's shop is entered by the Chimney, and a considerable quantity of Plate stolen. I give him a Warrant to the Constable, they find James Hews hid in the Hay in Cabal's Barn, on the Back side of the Comon; while they was seising of him under the Hay, he strip'd off his Pocket, which was quickly after found, and Cowell's silver in it. At night I read out of Caryl on Job, 5. 2. The humble submission to the *stroke* of God, turns into a *Kiss* — which I thank God, I have in this Instance experienced. *Laus Deo.* See Jan. 10, 17$\frac{17}{18}$.

July, 1. A Rainbow is seen just before night, which comforts us against our Distresses as to the affairs of the Expedition, and the Unquietness of the Souldiers at Casco, of which Gideon Lowel brings word, who came thence yesterday.[1]

---

[1] This refers to the abortive expedition against the French. Massachusstts, Rhode Island, and New Hampshire sent a force on the 13th May, 1707, under command of Colonel March, to attack Port Royal. The naval force was only the "Deptford," man-of-war, Captain Stukeley, and the "Province Galley," Captain Southack. They arrived May 26th, had some skirmishes, and by June 7th re-embarked. Colonel Redknap (the engineer) and Colonel Appleton went to Boston for further orders, and the rest of the army to Casco Bay. (Hutchinson, Hist. II. 166, 167.) — Eds.

Midweek, July 2, 1707. Com̄encement Day is fair and pleasant. Jane and I go betime by Charlestown; set out before 5.; had a very pleasant journey; went from Charlestown in a Calash, Harris. Got Joseph a Table, and Bread, which he wanted before. Went into the Meetinghouse about 11. Mr. Willard pray'd. Mr. Wigglesworth began to dispute; before he had done, the Govr came; when the first Question was dispatch'd, the Orator was call'd forth: His Oration was very well accepted; I was concern'd for my son, who was not well, lest he should have fail'd; but God helped him. His Cous. Moodey of York had pray'd earnestly for it the night before; and gave Thanks for it in prayer the night after. My Son held the first Question in the Afternoon; *Anima non fit ex Traduce.*; by reason of the paucity of the Masters, being but two, Russell, and Mighill; for Mr. Dudley was in the Fleet bound for Port-Royal. Had oportunity to pronounce his Thesis. My Son was the first that had a Degree given him in the New Meetinghouse. The Desks were adorned with green curtains, which it seems, were Wainwrights. I could not hear one Word while the Degrees were giving. My wife durst not go out of Boston. Got home in good season, Jane and I by Charlestown again; Daughters in the Coach. Mr. Russell, Mr. Winthrop, Sewall, Major Walley, Col. Lynde, Mr. Eliakim Hutchinson, Mr. Bromfield, Mr. Stoddard, were there in the morn. Mr. Secretary and Capt. Belcher were there p. m̄. Mr. Willard made an excellent Prayer at Conclusion. Ladies there, Governours Lady, Madam Shrimpton, Madam Usher, Madam Walley, Madam Bromfield, Madam Stoddard &c. Mr. Whiting, Bilerica, Mr. Belcher, Newbury. Mr. Easterbrooks not there.

July, 3. *Feria sexta* Mr. Stoddard preached excellently from Mica, 1. 5 What is the Trangression of Jacob? is it not Samaria? and what are the high places of Judah? are they not Jerusalem? Said he could see no reason why

a papist might not *cross himself* Ten times a day, as well
as Minister cross a child once. —— Spake *plainly* in Several Articles against Superstition.   Spake against excess
in Com̄encem't entertainments.   Govr call'd at night
with Mr. Stoddard and told me I should cause them to
conclude.

   July, 4. 1707.   I printed
Feria Sexta; Quintilis quarto, 1707.

   CLAUDITE jam rivos, Pueri; sat prata biberunt.[1]

Gave to several Scholars, and order'd one or two to be
nail'd upon the Out-Doors.   Brought home my Son, Plate,
Clôths in Stedmand's Calash, 4^s Gave his Son a piece of
eight and bid him take the overplus to himself.   Did it in
remembrance of his Father's hard Journey to Martha's
Vinyard.   In the Ferryboat, heard the sad News from
Spain,[2] by Grant and the Loss of English ships.   Got home
before 9.

   Laus Deo.   This day I visited Mrs. Corlet who seems
dying: Mrs. Wigglesworth, who has the Jaundice; Madam
Oliver who is not well.   Note. Mr. Veazy [H. C. 1693]
of Braintry died the day after the Com̄encment, a young
hopefull Minister.

   July, 5th Go to Col. Hutchinson's to wait on him, Mr.
Leverett and others to the Water side.   Go off at Scarlet's
Wharf.   Gave three cheers, they 3. one from us.   After
Col. Townsend went off alone; — did the like by him.   The
Lord prosper them.

   Feria tertia, July, 8. 1707.   I bring Mr. Solomon Stod-
dard going as far as Watertown Mill; and there staid at
Churches till the Rain was over; then took Leave.   Mr.
Sampson Stoddard and I dined there.   In returning call'd

---

   [1] Virgil, Ecl. III. 111. — EDS.
   [2] This probably refers to the Battle of Almanza, in which the Allies were
defeated by the Duke of Berwick, April 25, N. S. — EDS.

upon Capt. Tho. Oliver, and drunk of his Spring in his Orchard. Look'd upon N. Sparhawk's Family: Call'd at my Son's at Brooklin; from thence Mr. Stoddard went to Cambridge, and I home. Note. In the morn, going down Roxbury Meetinghouse Hill, my Horse stumbled, fell on his Knees and there struggled awhile, broke his Crouper: I kept on and had no harm, not so much as a strain, *Laus Deo*.

I gave Mr. Stoddard for Madam Stoddard two half pounds of Chockalat, instead of Comencment Cake; and a Thesis.

Feria secunda, July, 14ᵗʰ 1707. Mr. Antram and I, having Benj. Smith and David to wait on us, Measured with his Wheel from the Town-House Two Miles, and drove down Stakes at each Mile's end, in order to placing Stone-posts in convenient time. From the Town-House to the Oak and Walnut, is a Mile wanting $21\frac{1}{2}$ Rods. Got home again about Eight aclock.

July, 23. 1707. Midweek, visited Madam Leverett; her son, Thomas Berry,[1] is afflicted with a sore under his left Arm ready to break: all else are well.

July, 29. 1707. *Feria tertia*, Major Walley and I walk to the Ferry. From Charlestown, Heaton carries us in his Calash, the Sheriff, Under-Sheriff, Mr. Bordman, Capt. Henry Phillips accompanying us. Finish'd the Court. Visited Madam Leverett, visited Mrs. Corlett, look'd upon her Grand-daughter Minott. Left a copy of Mr. Noyes's verses on Mr. Bayley; two Banbury Cakes, and a piece

---

[1] This lady was Margaret, first wife of President John Leverett. She was the daughter of John Rogers (President of Harvard College), and widow of Captain Thomas Berry, of Boston. Her son, Thomas Berry, was born in 1695; H. C. 1712, says Savage. John Leverett had a brother Thomas, called a barber on our town records. A curious attempt to mystify this statement is in the Leverett Genealogy (Boston, 1856), p. 149. The step-mother of John and Thomas Leverett, Sarah, widow of Hudson Leverett, was alive at this time, as she died in Roxbury, Dec. 16, 1714. — EDS.

of eight, with Mrs. Champney; Gave her a piece on Comͫ-
encem't day; both for her Mother.

Feria quinta, Aug: 7ᵗʰ 1707. Peter Weare set up the
Stone Post to shew a Mile from the Town-House ends:
Silence Allen, Mr. Gibbons's Son, Mr. Thrasher,——
Salter, Wᵐ Wheelers —— Simpson and a Carter assisted,
made a Plumb-Line of his Whip. Being Lecture-day, I
sent David with Mr. Weare to shew him where the second
should be set; were only two little Boys beside.

Monday, Aug: 11. 1707. Mr. Willard goes to Cambridge to Expound, but finds few scholars come together;
and moreover was himself taken ill there, which oblig'd
him to come from thence before Prayer-Time.

Tuesday, Aug: 12. between 6 and 7. I visited Mr. Willard to see how his Journey and Labour at the College
had agreed with him; and he surpris'd me with the above-
account; told me of a great pain in's head, and sickness
at his stomach; and that he believ'd he was near his end.
I mention'd the business of the College. He desired me
to do his Message by word of Mouth; which I did, Thorsday following, to the Govʳ and Council.

Quickly after I left Mr. Willard, he fell very sick, and
had three sore Convulsion Fits to our great sorrow and
amazement.

Thorsday, Aug: 14ᵗʰ When the Govʳ enquired after
Mr. Willard, I acquainted the Govʳ and council that Mr.
Willard was not capable of doing the College work, another year; He Thank'd them for their Acceptance of his
service and Reward. Govʳ and Council order'd Mr. Winthrop and Brown to visit the Revᵈ Mr. Willard, and Thank
him for his good service the six years past. Sent down
for Concurrence, and Depts to name persons to join in
the Thanks and Condolence. Depts concur and nominat
the Rever'd Mr. Nehemiah Hobart to officiat in the mean
time till Oct: next. This the Govʳ and Council did not
accept, and so nothing was done.

Satterday, 7: 6. 1707. Col. Hathorn and I go to Wrentham, Lodge at Wear's.

7: 7ᵗʰ Sat down at the Lord's Table with Wrentham Church.

7: 8ᵗʰ Went to Rehoboth, din'd at Mr. Smith's, invited Mr. Greenwood, who came and din'd with us; told us that Mr. Goodhue was sick of a Fever at his house: went to Bristol by the Bridge; at Carpenter's heard of the French Privateer in Marthas Vinyard Sound, and Rode-Islanders gon after him. Lodge at the ordinary with Capt. Leñard, Mr. Sparhawk's Indian Boy being sick of a Fever. 7: 9ᵗʰ at Diñer had the good News brought of the French privateer being Taken. Mr. Leverett came from Billinges just as were going to Diñer. 7: 10ᵗʰ Midweek, sentenced a woman that whip'd a Man, to be whip'd; said a woman that had lost her Modesty, was like Salt that had lost its savor; good for nothing but to be cast to the Dunghill: 7 or 8 join'd together, call'd the Man out of his Bed, guilefully praying him to shew them the way; then by help of a Negro youth, tore off his Cloaths and whip'd him with Rods; to chastise him for carrying it harshly to his wife. Got out of Town to Rehoboth.

7: 11ᵗʰ *feria quinta*, rid home very well. *Laus Deo.* Col. Hathorn and Mr. Leverett turn'd off to Cambridge from Jamaica.

7: 12. Mehetabel Thurston tells me Mr. Willard was taken very sick. I hop'd it might go off, and went to Diñer; when I came there, Mr. Pemberton was at Prayer, near concluding, a pretty many in the Chamber. After Prayer, many went out, I staid and sat down: and in a few minutes saw my dear Pastor Expire: it was a little after Two, just about two hours from his being taken. It was very surprising: The Doctors were in another room Consulting what to doe. He administred the Lord's Supper, and Baptiz'd a child last Lord's Day: Did it with suitable voice, Affection, Fluency. Did not preach: 7: 11ᵗʰ went to Lecture and heard Mr. Pierpont. At even seem'd much better than had been lately. Tis thought cutting his finger, might bring on this tumultious passion that carried him away. There was a dolefull cry in the house. *Feria secunda*, 7: 15th Mr. Willard is laid by his Tutor in my Tomb, till a new one can be made. Bearers, Dr. Mather, Mr. Allen ; Mr. Tho. Bridge, Mr. C. Mather ; Mr. Wadsworth, Mr. Colman. Fellows and students of the College went before. Mr. Pemberton Led Madam Willard. Gov[r] and his Lady had Rings: Bearers Scarvs and Rings. The Lady Davie, and Lady Hobbie were there. Son Sewall led his Sister Paul Dudley ;[1] he being gon to Plimouth Court. Very Comfortable Day.

Octob[r] 1. 1707. The five stone posts are set up in our Front. *Feria quarta*, I went to Brooklin, and chose some Aple-trees from which my Son is to send me Apples: Din'd with my Son and Daughter and little Grand-daughter; went to Amos Gates's; Went into the Cedar-Swamp Meadow. Gov[r] makes a Treat to day for Gov[r] Winthrop, Major Gen[l] Winthrop and Madam Eyre. Col. Paige, Madam Usher, Mr. Paul Dudley and wife.

Feria quinta, Oct[r] 2. Fast at the South church. Mr. Wadsworth prays, Mr. Pemberton preaches: Mr. Bridge prays and gives the Blessing. Capt. Atwood, Bernard, Gooding, Atkins go home with me at Noon. I give each of them one of Mr. W. Williams's [H. C. 1683] Sermons. p. m. Mr. Cotton Mather Prays, Dr. Mather Preaches, prays, gives the Blessing. Was a great Assembly.

Oct[r] 3. had a Meeting of the Church and Congregation : But very thin, Several came not because Mr. Pemberton said Gentlemen of the church and Congregation; affirmed they were not Gentlemen and therefore they were not

---

[1] Sewall, of course, means "his sister, Madam Paul Dudley; he [P.D.] being gone," &c. This phrase of " Madam Paul " occurs a few pages later. — EDS.

warned to come. Mr. Pemberton prayed, upon debate
apointed this day senight for the meeting.

Feria quinta, Octob.ᵣ 2. 1707. John Sewall, Sam.
Moodey, and Abrah. Tapin brought home Hañah Sewall,
Mary Sewall, and Jane Tapin from Newbury. Tis a fortnight since they went. Had a good passage thither by
water. *Laus Deo.*

Feria sexta, Octob.ᵣ 24ᵗʰ 1707. Capt. David Mason, Hol-
berton, Seers and Winter arrive from London in Boston
Harbour: Began to be in great fear about them lest they
were Taken; because they might have been expected before the Mast-Ships. Thanks were given on this account
at Mr. Willard's Meeting, which was kept at his widows
House this Afternoon; began between 1 and 2. Mr.
Wadsworth, Colman pray'd, Mr. Pemberton preach'd and
pray'd excellently.

Tuesday, Oct.ᵣ 28. 1707. The Fellows of Harvard College meet, and chuse Mr. Leverett President: He had
eight votes, Dr. Increase Mather three, Mr. Cotton Mather,
one, and Mr. Brattle of Cambridge, one. Mr. White did
not vote, and Mr. Gibbs came when voting was over.

Thorsday, Oct.ᵣ 30. The Man of War, and Physick arrive from Lisbon, bring News that the siege of Tholoun
[Toulon] was Raised.

Oct.ᵣ 31. Mr. John Jekyl was sworn Collector, and Mr.
Thomas Newton Controller: The Governour call'd for the
Bible for them to swear on.[1]

Nov.ᵣ 1. just about Noon the Govᵣ produces the Petition
sign'd by Mr. Higginson and others for his Removal: And
urges the Council to vote an Abhorrence of it. I pray'd

---

[1] This John Jekyll married Margaret, daughter of Edward Shippen, Jr.,
of Philadelphia, and probably left issue in Pennsylvania. In the Shippen
Family Papers, edited by the late Thomas Balch, it is stated (I. 19) that he
was a younger brother of Sir Joseph Jekyll, Master of the Rolls. But in
the annual register of the Sun Fire Office, London, where his death is recorded under date of 1733, he appears as a nephew of Sir Joseph. — EDS.

that it might be consider'd of till Monday, which the Governour would not hear of, but order'd Mr. Secretary to draw up a Vote : which with some alteration was pass'd. Said He had no Gall. After coming from Council I read the Book printed against the Governour in London. I had not seen it before.

Nov.ᵣ 8ᵗʰ Mr. Coffin of Nantucket is apointed by the Govᵣ and Council to have an oversight of the Indians there. I had mention'd Capt. Gardener, whom Capt. Belchar withstood about a week ago. Govᵣ mention'd Gifts as piety. Mr. Benja. Brown said Capt. Gardener was prefer'd before Mr. Coffin for Piety : then the Govᵣ said no more. I now mov'd that both might be apointed ; Capt. Belcher said ; then let there be three. I said Capt. Gardener was already apointed to receive what was sent from the Comissioners. The Govᵣ said it was all the better ; they would be a Check upon each other.

Nov.ᵣ 7. Mr. James Allen stood up, and said I was a Party, and therefore ought not to be a Judge in the Cause of Govᵣ Bellingham's Will. I had got of that Land in a wrong way ; which I resented ; for no Land on this side the water is mentioned except for Life, and my Fragment on the Hill is not mention'd at all.[1]

---

[1] This reference or excuse is not very plain, since Governor Bellingham's will had been set aside, as we will show ; and any title from his only son would seem to be free of flaw. The facts, as we find them, are as follows : —

Governor Bellingham's will (Suff. Wills, VII. 271) gives to his wife the rent of a farm, and also his dwelling-house, yard and field adjoining, " during her natural life." To " my only son and *his* daughter during their natural lives." Rents of two other farms to the relief of the daughter of Colonel William Goodrich, &c. After his wife's death, the farm she hath for life, and " after the death of my son and his daughter, my whole estate in Winnisimet " to church purposes, as set forth quite fully. His inventory mentions a pasture of 2½ acres at the south end, butting upon Angola's house, and joining the land of Mrs. Colburn, valued at £250 ; ground upon the hill, behind Mr. Davenport's, £30 ; dwelling-house, and ground belonging to it, and shop before it, £600. The four farms at Winnisimett were valued at £1,920. The total estate was £3,244 3 7. The General Court (Rec. V. 105) gave

Nov.ʳ 10ᵗʰ I received a Letter from Broʳ, who says Doctʳ Tapan fell off Mr. Titcomb's Wharf last Tuesday, was found by it on Wednesday morn : buried Thorsday in the Rain. Feria Secunda Nov.ʳ 10. 1707. I set out for Salem with Capt. Beñet; at Lewis's overtook Mr. Dudley, Valentine, Hern; from thence went together, had a very good Journey; got to Salem so early as to anticipat the sheriff; the wind being fair, went by Wiñisimet.

---

judgment "that said will is illegal, and so null and voyd in law," Sept. 6, 1676.

But the estate seems to have been the cause of much discord. Samuel, only son of Governor Bellingham, married in April, 1695, Elizabeth Savage, who came over here to arrange his affairs. She was drowned on her return voyage, and the following record is found here: —

Elizabeth, wife of Samuel Bellingham, made her will Nov. 1697, being bound on a voyage to London. (Suff. Wills, VIII. 283.) Her husband having conveyed to trustees for her use and disposal all lands, &c., in New England formerly belonging to Richard Bellingham, she gives her husband, for life, the rent thereof. Bequests then follow to Harvard College, Benjamin Woodbridge, Increase Mather, Samuel Willard, Cotton Mather, Nathaniel Thomas, Joseph Hiller and wife Susanna, Benjamin Hiller, all of Boston, Thomas Danforth, Samuel Sewall, Edward Mills. Mentions brother Edward Watts, of London, and sister Rebecca Watts, his wife; also their children, Samuel, Rebecca, and Elizabeth Watts. Sister Mary Smith, Rev. Samuel Slaughter, Edward Hull and John Shelton, all of London. Aunt Banniard, cousin Elizabeth Skibbow, cousin Elinor Bird, uncles Samuel and Edmund Hermer. Edward Watts, *alias* Bellingham Watts, the residuary legatee, to be succeeded by his brother Samuel, and sisters Rebecca and Elizabeth.

We have already shown (Vol. I. p. 61, *note*) that Sewall bought his lot from Mrs. Bellingham and her trustees.

The land at the south end of Boston, less the lot which Governor Bellingham gave to an Indian slave named Angola, for saving him from drowning in Boston Harbor (see Suff. Deeds, VIII. 298), were sold Jan. 7, 1710–11 (Suff. Deeds, lib. XXVI. f. 100), by Edward Watts, late of St. Buttolph's, Aldgate, London; Sawyer, and Rebecca, his wife, claiming to be the heir to Andrew Belcher. But July 8, 1712, Belcher thought it best to establish his title by also buying the same from Elizabeth Bellingham, of London, spinster, daughter and sole heir of Samuel Bellingham. The land was bounded east on Orange Street, south on land of Robert Sanders and of Thomas Walker, west by Benjamin Eliot, north by Benjamin Eliot, Andrew Belcher, Thomas Chamberlain, John Clough, and William Payne. (Suff. Deeds, lib. XXVII. f. 21.) — EDS.

Novr 13. Adjourn a little before night *sine die.* Visit Mr. Higginson the aged Minister; He can well and sensibly speak to us still, call'd me by my name; Mr. Leverett he did not hit off. Said he was sorry that his son should petition against the Govr Speaking of the Union, he repeated very well a verse of K. James.

Jam cuncti gens una sumus; sic simus in ævum.

His wife very decrepit and in pain; glad to see me. Visit Madam Bradstreet, Bro^r Hirst.

Novr 14. very good wether; Mr. Noyes Breakfast, prays with us: at taking Leave, I gave him a 20^s Bill in a paper writ on *Scalpellum* —— and verses on Mr. Goodhue. Had a very good Journey home by Charlestown, Mr. Leverett in company till parting.

Novr 15. Maj^r Genl sends my wife and me a pair of Gloves on account of his wedding the 13th. Novr 17 I and others visit Mr. Winthrop, and his Bride.[1] See 7.^r 19, 1707 in my Justices Book.

Novr 18. Daughter Sewall is brought to Bed of a Son at Brooklin between 5 and 6. *mane.* Danford told me of it; I gave him a shilling.

Novr 20. 1707. The Deputies not having voted as the Council did Novr 1., a Conference is agreed on: Col. Hathorne, Col. Hutchinson, Mr. Secretary Addington, Mr. Comissary Belchar are apointed to be Managers: others may speak as they see occasion.

Govr made a long speech begiñing from his father, who laid out one Thousand pounds in the first adventure, was Governour. —— He himself the first Magistrat born in New England.[2] Managers all spake in their order: Mr.

---

[1] Wait-Still Winthrop, the major-general and chief-justice, married, secondly, Nov. 13, 1707, Katherine, daughter of Thomas Brattle. — EDS.

[2] Palfrey writes (History IV. 308, *note*) that Sewall reports that Dudley calls himself "the first Governour born in New England." Palfrey adds: "If he did so, he must have flattered himself that the Court had forgotten

Blagrove spake on the part of the Deputies; said twas before the Queen and Council, not fit for us to intermeddle; Mention'd some Trade, as Nails, Pots, Sithes. Govr deny'd the quantity of Nails.

The Govr took an oportunity to say, he heard some whisper'd as if the Council were not all of a mind: He with courage said that all the Council were of the same mind as to every word of the vote. This gall'd me; yet I knew not how to contradict him before the Houses.

Novr 21. Depts vote again as to the Councils vote, and tis carried in the Negative. Conference about Vetch and Borland trading with French &c. Draw up a vote themselves shorter than ours, and vote it and send it in. Upon this, some began to be hot to send for the Book[1] wherein the Affidavits are, and Mr. M's Letter; and to burn it: others were for deliberation. Note. At the Conference the Govr had the Extract of many of Mr. C[otton] M[ather] Letters read, of a later Date than that in the printed Book and Observator, giving him a high character. See Decr 12. Novr 22. In the morn, I went

---

Sir William Phips. But I have observed no other report of such a declaration of his." But we have two other suppositions to make before convicting Sewall of error. The word in the text is "magistrate," not "governour." Did Dudley refer to the magistrates or assistants under the old charter? If so, the statement *may* be true, but the inquiry would be tedious and profitless. Or, again, is it certain that Phips *was* born in New England? We believe that there is no authentic record of Sir William's birth, and he may have been born before his father emigrated. — Eds.

[1] The reference is to a "Memorial of the Present Deplorable State of New England," to which there was a reply entitled "A Modest Enquiry," &c., 1707, and later, "The Deplorable State of New England," London, 1708. All these are fully described in the preface to the present volume. Palfrey, IV. 305, refers to the latter only. It is sufficient to state here that Governor Dudley was accused of connivance or participation in illegal trade with the enemy, the French, in Canada. Sewall's position was delicate, his son being the husband of Dudley's daughter. He took a manly part; but it is rather amusing to read his disgust at being praised therefor by the opposition. — Eds.

to Mr. Borland, and enquired of him whether the Govr knew of their Trade with the French. He said he order'd Capt. Vetch to acquaint him. I enquired whether he did it or no: Mr. Borland said, he did not hear him acquaint the Govr with it. By this I gather'd that Capt. Calley's Affidavit was true; and that the Govr did coñive at their Trading with the French, which has open'd a Tragical scene that I know not when we shall see the close of it.

Went to the burying of Mrs. Busby the widow.

Novr 23. Mr. Pemberton preaches more fully and vehemently against being cover'd in Sermon Time. p. m. Simeon Stoddard, the Son of A. Stoddard, is baptised. David Stoddard and others taken into Church.

Before family prayer, went to the burying of Capt. Thomas Dudley's Daughter: Sir Wainwright, and Capt. Southack's son Bearers. Govr was at the Funeral. About the middle of this Novr I dried up the Issue in my Left Arm; trusting to that of my Legg only.

Novr 23. 1707. My Son Samuel has his Son Samuel Baptised by Mr. Walter at Roxbury: Col. Partridge, who was present, inform'd me of it, Novr 24th.

Novr 25. 1707. The Govr read Mr. Cotton Mather's Letter to Sir Charles Hobby in Council, the Copey being sign'd by Mr. Povey, and animadverted on several paragraphs; When the Govr came to the *horrid Reign of Bribery:* His Excellency said, None but a Judge or Juror could be Brib'd, the Governour could not be bribed, sons of Belial brôt him no Gifts. Mov'd that Col. Hutchinson, Mr. Secretary, Col. Townsend and Mr. Cushin go to Mr. Cotton Mather with the Copy of his Letter to Sir Charles Hobby, and his Letters to the Govr, and speak to him about them: this was agreed to. I shew'd some backwardness to it, fearing what the Issue might be; and hinting whether it might not be better for the Govr to go to him himself: That seem'd to be Christ's Rule, except the Govr would deal with him in a Civil way.

Nov.ʳ 25. 1707. p. m. The Govʳ mov'd that Mr. Newton might be sent for; which was done; and the Govʳ minded him of the Confession he had made for signing the Petition against him; and Mr. Newton renew'd his acknowledgment of his misdoing, in some measure, and excus'd it by saying that he was surpris'd by being told that the Govʳ had written against his being Collector. When he was gon, the Govʳ order'd the Secretary to make a Minute of it, which was done. When this was over, I desired the Governour's patience to speak a word: I said I had been concern'd about the Vote pass'd Nov.ʳ 1. "At the Conference his Excellency was pleas'd to say, that every one of the Council remain'd steady to their vote, and every word of it: This Skrewing the Strings of your Lute to that height, has broken one of them; and I find my self under a Necessity of withdrawing my Vote; and I doe withdraw it, and desire the Secretary may be directed to enter it in the Minutes of the Council." And then I delivered my Reasons for it, written and sign'd with my own Hand; which were read. The Govʳ directed that it should be kept privat: but I think Col. Lynde went away before that Charge was given.[1] The Govʳ often says that if any body would deal plainly with him, he would kiss them; but I rec'd many a Bite, many a hard Word from him. He said I valued Mr. Higginson's *Reputation* more than his *Life*. When Mr. Newton was call'd in, Govʳ told him that the Court at N-Hampshire had voted an Abhorrence of the Petition; and the Council and Representatives here had voted it a scandalous and wicked Accusation. Just after our uncomfortable Discourse was over, and to help terminat it, a Master comes in from Virginia, who brings News that both Tholoun and Marseilles are Taken.[2] Note, before I Withdrew my Vote: The Govʳ took occasion to

---

[1] See these reasons printed in "The Deplorable State," &c. — EDS.

[2] The siege of Toulon was raised in August. Marseilles was not besieged. — EDS.

speak thus; " To say the best, The House of Deputies is out of Humour, though after all their search, all is as white as Chalk, as clear as the Driven snow; yet.

Nov.ʳ 26. Mr. Secretary reports the Discourse with Mr. Cotton Mather favourably; It seems they stay'd there more than two Hours; and Dr. Mather was present. Mr. Mather neither denys, nor owns the Letter: Think his Letters to the Gov.ʳ, and that to Sir Charles Hobbey, not so inconsistent as they are represented.[1] By Candle-Light before they went, It was debated whether Mr. Mather should be sent for before the Council; or whether the Gentlemen should go to him. Then I that had been backward to meddle in it before, plainly declar'd my mind that twas best for the Gentlemen to go to him; and so twas carried when put to the Vote. Mr. Secretary is well pleas'd that he went.

The Council invited the Gov.ʳ to Diñer to day; I drank to his Excellency, and presented my Duty to him. Col. Townsend drank to me. At Dinner Col. Hutchinson invited us to drink a Glass of Wine at Mr. Eliakim Hutchinson's by his order. We went some of us. And between 7. and 8. His son William and his Bride came; and Mr. Phips and his Bride; they were married privatly last Thorsday morn: and now both weddings are kept together.[2] Had Musick, Cake and Cheese to eat there, and bring away. They had a hard Journey from Rehoboth to Billenges yesterday in the Rain. Mr. Hutchinson told us

---

[1] The Council sent four of its members to confer with Cotton Mather. Council Record, quoted by Palfrey, IV. 319. — EDS.

[2] Eliakim Hutchinson was son of Richard Hutchinson, of London, and thus cousin of Colonel Elisha Hutchinson, of Boston. Eliakim died in 1716, when his will mentions only son William, grandson Eliakim Palmer, son of Thomas, and the children of daughter Elizabeth Phips. William had wife, Elizabeth, and died in 1721, leaving seven children. It seems quite evident that Elizabeth married Spencer Phips, though her surname is not given in Paige's History of Cambridge. His second child was born in 1710, and his fourth and eighth child received the name of Eliakim. — EDS.

the Bride was gon ill to Bed.   Govr Winthrop had a very
bad night.

This day the Govr apoints Wednesday Decr 3. for Nominating Officers; says He has only a Justice of Peace or
two on Essex side.

In the evening by Candle-Light I fell asleep in the
Council-Chamber: and when I waked was surprised to
see the Govr gone.

Col. Townsend ask'd me to withdraw my Paper, and put
it in my Pocket, pleasantly : I answered pleasantly, I
could as easily put him in my Pocket.

Friday, Novr 28. 1707.   The Govr puts forward to have
the vote of July 9. 1706. of the Representatives, the vote
of the Council of Novr 1., the vote of the Representatives
Novr 21., Printed, to prevent spreading false Reports : I
said I could not vote to it because I had withdrawn my
vote.   The Govr said, I pray God judge between me and
you !   Col. Townsend told me I was a Temporiser; I
hôp'd Mr. Higginson would be Govr, and endeavour'd to
procure his favor.   Prayer.   Lord, do not depart from me,
but pardon my sin ; and fly to me in a way of favourable
Protection !   Capt. Phips brings in Mr. Leverett Non-
Concurr'd.   Moves from the House that a suitable person
be thought of to take care of the College till May Sessions.
Col. Townsend tells me that my purpose to withdraw my
Vote was known a week ago ; Mr. Oaks mention'd it in
the House ; He was my Counsellor.   Whereas he really
knew nothing of it; and now tells me, he never mention'd
my Name.

Decr 1.   Our children visited their Sister at Brooklin.

Decr 4.   Mr. C. Mather preaches a very good Funeral
sermon.   Govr [Fitz John] Winthrop is buried from the
Council Chamber, Foot-Companies in Arms, and Two
Troops.   Armor carried, a Led Horse.   Bearers, Govr, Mr.
Russell ; Mr. Cooke, Major Brown ; Col. Hutchinson,
Sewall ; Mr. Secretary, Mr. Sergeant.   Father, Son, and

Grandson ly together in one Tomb in the old burying place.[1] Was a vast concurse of People.

Dec.ʳ 5. Dine at Holm's. I suppos'd the Council had Treated the Gov.ʳ, But the Gov.ʳ would pay. A Message is sent in to the Deputies about the College; whereupon they withdraw their Non-concurrence; rase out (Non) and turn it to Concur'd; And vote Mr. Leverett a Salary of One Hundred and Fifty pounds per añum out of the publick Treasury.

Dec.ʳ 6. Some desire that it may be put in the Bill that Mr. Leverett Lay down all his Civil offices; as Judge of Probat, and judge of the Superiour Court. And entirely to attend that service, was inserted, and Mr. Secretary carried it in to the Deputies, and took their Consent. Gov.ʳ has Two Hundred pounds given him. Col. Jn° Appleton, Hunt and I are sent in to speak to the Deputies about their denying any Reward to the commissioners to Port-Royal; Told them, denying all Remuneration was in a mañer to make them Criminals: Twas a burden God in his providence had laid on us, and to go about thus to shake it off, would be to his Dishonor. Spake also in behalf of Salem Fort and Marblehead. Upon this a Resolve was sent in to leave the consideration of it to another Sessions, being now a very thin House. Deputies had sent in a long Roll of Grievances to be Reform'd, as their Advice: Gov.ʳ would have had the Council advis'd the contrary in the whole: I opposed it, as inconvenient to vote against all together: and it was staid. And yet when the Deputies were come in, the Gov.ʳ took the paper and spoke to it; said he could not go according to it without having the Frontiers defenceless; said the Council were unanimously against it. Court is prorogued to the fourth of February.

---

1 This is, of course, the well-known tomb in the King's Chapel yard, very near the building of the Massachusetts Historical Society. A full description is given in Bridgman's Epitaphs. — EDS.

Dec.ʳ 10. Married — Hayward and Susaña Mills.

Feria quinta, Dec.ʳ 11ᵗʰ 1707. Thanks-giving-day, very serene, moderate, comfortable Wether. Mr. Pemberton preaches forenoon and afternoon. Yesterday I was told of a vast number of Pigeons in the Woods this Moneth. Capt. Mills at his Sister's Wedding says he saw an incredible Number at Woodstock last Friday.

Madam Usher, son and daughter Hirst and their family, Cousin Sam and Jonathan Sewall, Broʳ Wheeler and his wife, M—— and her daughter, dine with us. *Feria sexta*, Dec.ʳ 12. 1707. Just before the Funeral of Mrs. Eliot, I went to Mr. Borland, told him he had been at my House and I was not at home, so I now call'd at his. He seem'd to express some Concern that the Govʳ was troubled; and said they gave the Govʳ nothing. I told him what my discourse with him was the 22ᵈ Nov.ʳ He owns the substance of it now; and is confirm'd in it because he saw it in Capt. Vetches Petition at home. I desired to see the Petition but he declin'd it.

Bearers to Mrs. Eliot, widow of D. [eacon] Jacob Eliot: Sewall, Bromfield; Hill, Williams; Checkly, Mr. John Hubbard. Was buried from her daughter Davis's. At the Return to the house, I said to Mr. Holyoke, it was a happiness that our Condolance for the departure of our friend, was join'd with Congratulation for her being gon to her Rest and Reward. At parting with the Bearers, I told them we were often concern'd in Funerals; it would be well for us to pray one for another that God would prepare us for our own Dissolution.

Joseph return'd to Cambridge before the Funeral, last mention'd.

Feria septima, Dec.ʳ 13. 1707. I enquir'd of Mr. Jnᵒ Winthrop whether he had seen his Sister Sewall; he said not since her Lying in; I told him I would not impose upon him; but if he pleas'd, we might go together (he told me must go to Roxbury with the Coach and back

again); we rid together, call'd at Roxbury and took in
Madam Paul Dudley, and Mrs. Anne. Found my daughter
and her little Samuel well; his Father has a Cold. Little
Rebekah well. When return'd, went in again to the Gov-
ernour's, his Lady only now at home. Madam Paul
Dudley came home with us; had a comfortable Journey.
Laus Deo.

Feria Secunda, Dec.ʳ 15. 1707. The Governour calls a
Council, Reads a Letter of Mr. Bridger complaining of
Trees cut contrary to Charter and of a great Mast ship'd:
Now it seems Mr. Collins deals for Masts by the Royal
Authority, though his Powers are not shewn here: The
Govʳ press'd for a Proclamation as is emitted this day; I
express'd my self unready to vote for it; because twas
only Mr. Bridger's naked complaint, Without any Affidavit
to justify it. He had been here above a 12 moneth; and to
set forth a proclamation now, would be but to serve a Turn.
Ichabod Plaisted esqr. is of the Council, and, dwelling
in those parts, might inform the Board. I mov'd that Mr.
Mico might be sent for, who transacts for Mr. Collins: but
the Govʳ would not hear of it. I feared lest this proclamation should prejudice rather than forward the Queens
Interest, and therefore was against setting it forth. The
Govʳ was displeas'd, and said twas due to a Tinker, much
more to Mr. Bridger.

Feria tertia, Dec.ʳ 16. 1707. Mr. John Winthrop marries Mrs. Anne Dudley. Roxbury Lecture-Day.

Feria quinta, Dec.ʳ 18. Mr. Bridge apoints the 15ᵗʰ
Psalm to be sung: and takes Job. 15. 34. for his Text;
especially that clause, — Fire shall consume the taberna-
cles of Bribery: From which he preach'd an excellent
sermon. Mr. Pemberton's Cold suffer'd him not to be
abroad; Dr. Mather not at Lecture. Governour, and
Majʳ Genˡ Winthrop were there, notwithstanding the
Wedding.

Feria sexta, Dec.ʳ 19. 1707. Went to the Meeting at

Mr. Bromfield's.   Mr. Nath! Williams preach'd from 1 Cor.
7. 29.   The Time is short.   Mr. Stoddard tells me the
Govr has the Gout, and bespeaks my Company to visit
him to morrow.   Sent a Letter to my Bro^r to day by Mr.
B. Marston.

Feria septima, Decr 20.   Mr. Bromfield, Mr. Stoddard
and I ride together in Mr. Briggs's Hackney Coach and
visit the Govr, who keeps his Chamber; was taken ill on
Thorsday.   Wish his Excellency Joy of his Son and
Daughter Winthrop; gave the Bride Mr. Willard's, Blessed
Man.   Mr. Paul Dudley came home with us and fill'd up
the Coach.

Receive a Letter from my Bro^r, who says, the generality of thoughtfull people there aprove of my Mount
Etna Eruption : That's his expression.   Hopes to see us
in 10 days.   Mary is taken ill.

Decr 30.   Joseph goes home.   Brother comes to Town.

Jany 2.   Bro^r goes home in very cold windy wether,
lyes at Lewes's, then home 3.   Jany 8. 170⅞.   The Govr
apoints a Council to meet at Cambridge the 14th Inst for
the Installment of Mr. Leverett :[1] warns the Ministers of
the Six Towns[2] mention'd to be overseers of the College.
Midweek, Jany 14. 170⅞.   Went to Cambridge in Mr.
Brigg's Coach, with Col. Townsend, Mr. Bromfield, and
Mr. Stoddard.   Mr. E^m Hutchinson went in his own
Charet, taking Mr. Wadsworth with him.   Capt. Belchar
carried Mr. Secretary in his Calash.   Mr. Pemberton car-
ried his Bro^r in his Slay over the Ice ; Mr. Mico carried
Mr. Treasurer Brattle.   Mr. Colman there.   Maj^r Genl
Winthrop, Col. Elisha Hutchinson, Mr. Foster, Mr. Ser-

---

[1] This was the end of a long contest in which the Mathers, Increase and
Cotton, were very prominent.   They never forgave Dudley, and the reader
is especially desired to peruse the virulent letters addressed to him Jan. 20,
1707–8, printed in Mass. Hist. Society's Collections, 1st series, III. 126–134.
— EDS.

[2] Cambridge, Watertown, Charlestown, Boston, Roxbury, Dorchester:
Sex vicinis oppidis. — EDS.

geant, Dr. Mather, Mr. Cotton Mather, Mr. Bridge, Mr. Allen were not there. The day was very pleasant; Col. Phillips, Mr. Russel in his black cap, Col. Lynde met us from Charlestown; Mr. Bradstreet, Angier, there, Mr. Woodbridge of Meadford, Mr. Neh. Hobart. In the Library the Governour found a Meeting of the Overseers of the College according to the old Charter of 1650, and reduced the Number to seven; viz. Mr. Leverett President, Mr. Neh. Hobart, Mr. Wm Brattle, Mr. Ebenezer Pemberton, Mr. Henry Flint, Mr. Jonathan Remington, Fellows; Mr. Tho. Brattle, Treasurer. The Govr prepar'd a Latin Speech for Installment of the President. Then took the President by the hand and led him down into the Hall; The Books of the College Records, Charter, Seal and Keys were laid upon a Table running parallel with that next the Entry. The Govr sat with his back against a Noble Fire; Mr. Russel on his Left Hand iñermost, I on his Right Hand; President sat on the other side of the Table over against him. Mr. Neh. Hobart was called, and made an excellent Prayer; Then Joseph Sewall made a Latin Oration. Then the Govr read his Speech, and (as he told me) mov'd the Books in token of their Delivery. Then President made a short Latin Speech, importing the difficulties discouraging, and yet that he did Accept: Govr spake further, assuring him of the Assistance of the Overseers. Then Mr Edward Holyoke [1] made a Latin Oration, standing where Joseph did at a Desk on the Table next the Entry at the inside of it, facing the Govr Mr. Danforth of Dorchester pray'd. Mr. Paul Dudley read part of the 132 ps. in Tate and Bradey's version, Windsor Tune, clôs'd with the Hymn to the Trinity. Had a very good Diñer upon 3 or 4 Tables : Mr. Wadsworth crav'd a Blessing, Mr. Angier Return'd Thanks. Got home very well. *Laus Deo.*

---

[1] A graduate of 1705. President in 1737. — EDS.

Jan.ʸ 15ᵗʰ 170⅞. Mr. Bridge preaches; (Govʳ not at Lecture.) He speaks against Levillism, Buying and Selling Men. Council after Lecture: Col. Redknap had a Muster-Roll offer'd which the Council Refus'd. It seems he had Thirty pounds allow'd him at his embarking. This day Mr. Belchar brings me Squash-Seeds from Dedham. Jan.ʸ 16. 170⅞. Snow. I had a hard fall coming from daughter Hirst's, yet through the goodness of God, had little or no hurt. Tis very slipery under the Snow. Jan.ʸ 22. 170⅞. Mrs. Winthrop,[1] *vid.* of Mr. Dean Win-

---

[1] This reference brings up a formidable genealogical problem. Martha, second wife and widow of Deane Winthrop, was Martha Mellows. She was clearly the widow of John Mellows, Sen., because (Suff. Deeds, XX. 501), as Martha Winthrop, she released her interest in son John Mellows's house to her daughter-in-law, Sarah, relict of John, Jr. She is, probably, the Martha Mellows mentioned in 1652, in Reverend John Cotton's will, though there were then living her daughter Martha, and also Martha, widow of Abraham Mellows, of Charlestown.

The will of John Mellows, dated Sept. 15, 1674 (Suff. Wills, VI. 79), mentions wife Martha, sons John and Oliver, daughters Martha and Sarah, son John Chanterell. Witnesses to the will: Daniel Turell and John Conney; to a codicil, Conney and Martha Lue, who signs with a mark.

Jan. 21, 1703–4. Thomas Messinger, of Boston, and Elizabeth, his wife, one of the daughters of John Mellows, mariner, deceased, mortgage (Suff. Deeds, lib. 21. f. 458) "one full third (the whole in three parts to be equally divided) of the property of her late father John Mellows," between land of late Samuel Shrimpton and widow Turell, and the remainder therein, after the decease of Martha Winthrop, wife of Deane Winthrop, and mother of said Elizabeth. (Note. Martha Winthrop signs a deed July 31, 1678, in Suff. Deeds, XX. 225; an approximate date of her marriage.)

March, 19, 1706–7 (Suff. Deeds, lib. XXIII. f. 94), the Messingers sell this lot to Robert Ware, who also buys one third of the same of Thomas Winsor, "being land which I lately bought of Mary Chanterill, Martha Winthrop, and others." A third part, being one third of a lot in Coney's lane, forty-four feet front and sixty feet deep, bounded north on land of Mrs. Turell, deceased, east on Mr. Knox, south on the lane, and west on land of Samuel Shrimpton, deceased, was bought by Ware of Thomas Lee and Martha Winthrop.

We are sure that Mary Chanterell was a daughter of Mellows, and that Elizabeth Messinger was. The inference is unavoidable that Thomas Lee represented a third daughter. He was not the husband of a Mellows; for he married, at Salem, Deborah Flint, and had Martha baptized here in 1701.

throp, I supose, dines with us after Lecture. Gov' was at
Lecture.

Jan' 23. I go to the Funeral of Anne Needham, who
died in Child-bed : her former Husband was Lawson : her
first, Airs, to whom I married her Nov. 5. 1690. At first
I walk'd next the women with Mr. Wentworth : when had
gon a little way Mr. Cotton Mather came up and went
with me. Funeral was from Coñey's Lane,[1] to the new

His wife died in 1764, aged ninety years, seventy of which she " had employed
in the marriage state," as the newspapers stated.

Probably, then, Martha, the daughter of John Mellows (born Feb. 8,
1654), married a Lee, and was the mother of Thomas Lee. A Henry Lee
was admitted an inhabitant of Boston in 1655; Thomas Lee was taxed there
in 1681; John Lee, in 1687, 1688, 1691, 1695; and Joshua Lee, in 1688. —
EDS.

[1] In regard to Coney's Lane, we suggested, in our first volume, p. 37,
note, that it might be a part of Sudbury Street. We are indebted to Newton
Talbot, Esq., for the following references. (Suff. Deeds, lib. XXV. f. 116.)
Feb. 28, 1707-8. Thomas Odkins, and Elizabeth, his wife, the only child
of John Turill, mariner, deceased, and heir-in-law to the estate of said
Turill, sold, for £90, to James Codnor, all that old dwelling-house and land
situated towards the northerly end of the town, on Coney's Lane, being the
same lately belonging to Turill. It was bounded south on said Lane, forty
feet; west on land of John Mellows, deceased, now occupied by one Ware,
and Abiel Lawrence, sixty feet; north by Thomas Breden and George Bur-
rill, forty feet; and west on John Phillips, deceased, seventy-one and one-
half feet.

But new heirs appeared, and July 14, 1711 (Deeds, lib. XXVI. f. 42),
Daniel Oliver and William Welstead, attorneys for John Turill and William
Turill, sons of Samuel Turill, deceased, and grandson of John Turill, deceased, sell the same land to Codnor, by the same bounds, except that the
land fronts (south) on Cross Street, forty feet.

Cross Street was named in the Selectmen's vote of May, 1708, which date
is between the dates of these two deeds.

In our last note, we showed that the Mellows lot sold to Robert Ware was
bounded south on Coney's Lane, east by Knox, west by S. Shrimpton's, north
by Mrs. Turill's land, and was forty-four feet front and sixty feet deep.

(Suff. Deeds, lib. XXIII. p. 156.) Jonathan Gatchell, and wife, Martha,
only child of John Mellows, Jr. (having bought out the claims of her mother,
Martha Winthrop, in a house and land left to John Mellows by his father,
John Mellows, Sen.), sell the same to Abiel Lawrence, widow. It was
bounded N. W. by the four foot passage, running forty-one feet thereon
from the house of John Mellows, Sen., to land of Colonel Shrimpton, deceased, S. E. on the house and land of widow Turill forty-one feet, and is in

Burying-place. There Mr. Mather ask'd me to go with him to Madam Usher's, where we staid till past six. Speaking of death, I said twas a Hapiness to be so Conform'd to Christ, And it was a pleasure to take part with God in executing a righteous Sentence upon one's self, to aplaud his Justice —— Mr. Mather said that was high-flying; he would have such High-flyers be at his Funeral. Had been mentioning Mr. Dod's Will. As went thence told me of his Letter to the Govr of the 20th Ins^t and Lent me the Copy; intends to send another to Mr. Paul Dudley. Dr. Mather it seems has also sent a Letter to the Govr.[1] I wait with Concern to see what the issue of this plain home-dealing will be! I desir'd Mr. Mather to promote Col. Thomas's being brought into the Superior Court, if there was oportunity: the 12th Feb^r is apointed for a Nomination.

Jany 30. 170⅞ John Neesnummin [Indian Preacher] comes to me with Mr. R. Cotton's Letters; I shew him to Dr. Mather. Bespeak a Lodging for him at Matthias Smith's: but after they sent me word they could not doe it. So I was fain to lodg him in my Study.[2] Jany 31

width, from said Turill's house towards said passage-way, eighteen and one-half feet; S. W. on land late of John Mellows, Sen., now held by one Ware; N. E. on land late of S. Shrimpton, now of Anthony Blount.

In the Selectmen's order of May, 1708, "the way leading from the Mill Pond south-easterly by the late Deacon Phillips's stone house, extending down to the sea, *Cross Street*." "The way leading from the north-westerly end of Cross Street, passing northerly by Vearing's house, near the Mill Pond, *Old Way*." — EDS.

[1] These letters are noticed in our previous note. — EDS.

[2] There is a significance in this entry in the Journal which may not be obvious to the reader. It is illustrative of the strong antipathy felt by all those of English blood here, at that time, against coming into any close relation with the Indians on terms of social equality. The feeling of repulsion, which the first settlers brought with them, regarding the natives as heathens, was strongly intensified by subsequent relations with them, whether peaceful or hostile, till it generally resulted in contempt or disgust. Those who are well versed in our history are familiar with the many evidences of this antipathy, presenting themselves as long as any of the native race survived in this neighborhood. It was quite otherwise with the French, who came

p. m. I send him on his way towards Natick, with a Letter to John Trowbridge to take him in if there should be occasion. About half an hour by sun I went to the Funeral of my neighbour Sam Engs: I went first with Mr. Meers, and then with Mr. Pemberton, who talk'd to me very warmly about Mr. Cotton Mather's Letter to the Govr, seem'd to resent it, and expect the Govr should animadvert upon him. See Feb. 6. Said if he were as the Govr he would humble him though it cost him his head; Speaking with great vehemency just as I parted with him at his Gate. The Lord apear for the Help of his people.

Second-day, Feb^r 2. Council for passing Muster-Rolls. Somebody said, I think Capt. Belchar, That no man was admitted to be a Captain without giving the D. of Marl-

---

into terms of very free association and intimacy with the Indians, and never manifested, even if they felt, this antipathy of race. But "English stomachs" revolted from such fellowship. The same strong repugnance was indulged by them against social intimacy with the Indians, with which we are more familiar as felt towards negroes. The Jesuit Father and the French bushranger freely shared the loathsome lodging and food of the Indian, and came into hearty fellowship with him. Roger Williams, more than any other Englishman, struggled against this race antipathy. He says that he forced himself to lodge "in the filthy, smoky holes" of savages, that he "might win their language." But the wife of the good John Eliot, apostle as he was, carefully prepared some food for him to take with him when he mounted his horse to visit his red flock at Natick, and he tells us that he had partitioned off a lodging place and a bed in the loft of the Indian meeting-house for his private use. He reserved the closest fellowship with his converts till they should meet in heavenly regions, and would "all be changed," appearing in "celestial bodies." Judge Sewall, in his gentle kindness of spirit and his humanity of righteousness, proved himself far in advance of his contemporaries in his sympathy with negroes and Indians. Yet, as we read the above entry in his Journal, we present to ourselves his evident embarrassment. An approved Indian convert and preacher, on his way to professional service at Natick, calls on Sewall with letters from his friend Reverend Roland Cotton, of Sandwich, also a friend of the Indians, and a preacher to them. Sewall shifts off the intended lodger upon the keeper of a tavern open to very promiscuous guests. "They could not do it," writes the good Judge; "so I was fain to lodge him in my study." The hospitable guest chamber in the house was reserved for another class of lodgers. However, most of the citizens of Boston, at the time, would, if compelled to entertain an Indian, have given him a couch of straw and horse blankets in a barn. — Eds.

borough, or his Dutchess five hundred Guinys: the Gov[r] took it up, and said, What is that! Speaking in a favourable, diminutive way. And said that there had not been any admitted these thousand years but in a way like that; mentioning his own experience in the Isle of Wight.[1] His Excellency seems hereby to justify himself against those who charge him with Bribery. Gov[r] seem'd backward to grant, or say he would not grant the Chaplains &c, Unless Col. Hutchinson &c, had wages allow'd them.

Febr. 3. Went to the Funeral of Capt. Timothy Stephens of Roxbury. Mr. Walter pray'd, and tells me was a very good Christian, usefull Man, had great Assurance of the Love of God to him before he died; though he had much darkness before. Gov[r] and all his family there. Capt. Belchar, Mr. Bromfield, Mr. Stoddard and I there.

Feb[r] 4. Mr. Townsend, Bromfield, Stoddard, I, went and visited Mr. Leverett the President: I wish'd Madam Leverett Joy of the new Employment of her Husband. First din'd at Capt. Parker's. Visited Col. Foxcroft, who is abed with the Gout. When had paid our Reckoning at Capt. Parkers, rode to my sons chamber, sat awhile by his fire, Mr. Flint came to us. From thence came home slowly, which made us late. At Col. Foxcroft's was Col. Byfield, Taylor, Mr. Brattle, Cambridge. At coming from the President's Col. Townsend said he hop'd he should hear of his being in the Hall every day. He expounded the first of Matthew yesterday; Moderated the Bachelours Dispute to day. But we hear as if he intends to go into Hall but on some certain days.

Febr. 5. Mr. Colman preaches the Lecture in Mr. Wadsworth's Turn, from Gal. 5. 25. If we live in the Spirit, let we also Walk in the Spirit. Spake of Envy

---

[1] It will be remembered that Dudley, on his third visit to England, in 1693, was made Lieutenant-Governor of the Isle of Wight, and was a member of the House of Commons for the borough of Newton in that island. He seems to have obtained his title of Colonel at the same time. — EDS.

and Revenge as the Complexion and Condemnation of the
Devil; Spake of other walking: it blôted our sermons,
blôted our Prayers, blôted our Admonitions and Exhortations. It might justly put us upon asking our selves
whether we did live in the Spirit, whether we were ever
truly regenerated, or no. 'Tis reckon'd he lash'd Dr.
Mather and Mr. Cotton Mather and Mr. Bridge for what
they have written, preach'd and pray'd about the present
Contest with the Gov.ʳ   I heard not of it before, but yesterday Col. Townsend told me of Dr. Mather's Prayer
Janʸ 25, Wherein he made mention of One in Twenty-
Eight being faithfull; which makes many look on me with
an evil eye: supposing Dr. Mather ment my withdrawing
my vote of the first of Nov.ʳ   Feb.ʳ 6. Queen's Birthday,
I could not find in my heart to go to the Town-House;
because hardly anything is professedly there done but
drinking Healths. And Mr. Maxwell left his Message
with David; I saw him not. And I was entangled that I
could not conveniently go. I had written to Mr. Borland
earnestly desiring to see the Copy of Capt. Vetches Petition: and he sent me word he would wait on me this day;
which did in a manner bind me at home, lest I should be
out of the Way.[1] He came and told me with an air of
Displeasure, that I had made a bad use of what he had
told me. Afterward I ask'd upon what head he intended
I had made a bad use: He said little, but talk'd of making
a Flame. I had said in my Letter, I hôp'd he should not
have cause to complain that I had made a bad use of his
lending me the Petition till morning, or a less while, if he
pleas'd. Thus my neighbour Borland can take an oath
which is made use of to hide the Truth, and cause men to
believe a Lye; but he, with unjust reflection, refuses to
shew a Copy of a Petition for clearing the Truth of a con-

---

[1] There is an exquisite *naïveté* in the Judge's accumulations of the reasons
which made it proper for him to stay at home instead of going where he did
not wish to go. — EDS.

troverted matter of Fact: though the petition be publickly lying before the Queen and Council, and any one
may have a Copy for their Money. I said little to him;
but gave him the last of Mr. Wm Williams' Sermons.
Master Chiever his coming to me last Satterday Jany 31.
on purpose to tell me, he blessed God that I had stood up
for the Truth; is more Comfort to me, than Mr. Borland's
unhandsomeness is discomfort. But, above all, I hope I
have a good Conscience, and a good GOD to bear me out.

Second-day, Feb^r 9. 170⅞. Mr. D. Oliver, Capt. Keeling, Constable Loring and my self walk'd in the 7th Comp^a
to inspect Disorders. Found this to our Comfort, that the
widow Harman's daughter Ames is gon to her Husband at
Marshfield, which was a. gravamen for many years, I used
constantly to visit them and expostulat with them. I carried ½ Duz. Catechises in my Pocket, and gave them to
such as could read, Orphans several of them; Harman,
Hañah Dinsdal, Tho. Watson, Jno Phips, Hallowell, Odel.
That might not fail of meeting again, Din'd at Hobins's;
gave the Constable his Diñer, so it cost us 2^s apiece. Had
a very comfortable day overhead. The Apointment of a
Judge for the Super. Court being to be made upon next
Fifth day, Febr. 12, I pray'd God to Accept me in keeping a privat day of Prayer with Fasting for That and other
Important Matters: I kept it upon the Third day Febr. 10.
170⅞ in the uper Chamber at the North-East end of the
House, fastening the Shutters next the Street.——Perfect
what is lacking in my Faith, and in the faith of my dear
Yokefellow. Convert my children; especially Samuel
and Hañah; Provide Rest and Settlement for Hanah:
Recover Mary, Save Judith, Elisabeth and Joseph: Requite the Labour of Love of my Kinswoman Jane Tappin,
Give her health, find out Rest for her. Make David a
man after thy own heart, Let Susan live and be baptised
with the Holy Ghost, and with fire. Relations. Steer
the Government in this difficult time, when the Governour

and many others are at so much Variance : Direct, incline, overrule on the Council-day fifth-day, Febr. 12. as to the special Work of it in filling the Super. Court with Justices ; or any other thing of like nature ; as Plim^{o} infer Court. Bless the Company for propagation of the Gospel, especiall Govr Ashurst &c. Revive the Business of Religion at Natick, and accept and bless John Neesnumin who went thither last week for that end. Mr. Rawson at Nantucket. Bless the South Church in preserving and spiriting our Pastor ; in directing unto suitable Supply, and making the Church unanimous: Save the Town, College ; Province from Invasion of Enemies, open, Secret, and from false Brethren : Defend the Purity of Worship. Save Connecticut, bless their New Governour : Save the Reformation under N. York Governm^{t} Reform all the European Plantations in America ; Spanish, Portuguese, English, French, Dutch ; Save this New World, that where Sin hath abounded, Grace may Superabound ; that CHRIST who is stronger, would bind the strong man and spoil his house ; and order the Word to be given, Babylon is fallen. —— Save our Queen, lengthen out her Life and Reign. Save France, make the Proud helper stoop [Job. IX. 13], Save all Europe ; Save Asia, Africa, Europe and America. These were gen^{l} heads of my Meditation and prayer ; and through the bounteous Grace of GOD, I had a very Comfortable day of it.[1] The reading of Mr. Tho Horton's Sermon upon a Monethly Fast, before the House of Lords xr. 30. 1646. was a great furtherance of me, which was hapily put into my hand by Major Walley the

---

[1] We believe this is as minute and full a record — unless Cotton Mather's Diary may furnish more specific ones — of the method and use of a private fast-day, as observed by the devout worthies of the old time. The poet Whittier, in his beautiful ballad on Judge Sewall, represents him as annually setting apart such a solemnly kept day for mourning over his share in the dread proceedings about witchcraft. But, as there is no trace of any thing of the sort in the Journal, we must refer the conception to the imagination of the poet. — EDS.

latter end of last Moneth.   I rec'd a Letter from Mr.
Rawson at Nantucket about 2 p. m̅.

Feb.ͬ 12. 170⅞.   Mr. Bridge preaches from Hebr. 12.
17.   In his Explication and Exhortation put a great Emphasis upon *Afterward*, to stir up all presently to embrace
Christ, Instanc'd in the Misery of Judas returning his 30
pieces.   The Gov.ͬ was at Lecture.

The Business of the Council was not attended because
the Stormy Wether had prevented the Justices coming,
so that had but about 13.   None but from Boston and
Charlestown.   Adjournment is made to next Thorsday,
and persons to be Notified.

I went to the Gov.ͬ at Major Winthrop's after Lecture
and told him I could be glad Mr. Higginson might be
brought into the Superior Court.   Advis'd that Mr. Winslow [1] might be brought into the infer. Court at Plim.º and
Mr. Otis left out; Col Tho. son-in-Law.   Told him of the
fraudilent Deed complain'd of by Mr. Tomson of Middle-
borough; and that the said Otis's hand was to the fraud-
ulent Deed as a Witness, has now a part of what was
granted by it: and probably was the Adviser in the whole
matter.   Told the Gov.ͬ I intended to waite on his Excellency on Wednesday: but was hindered by the Storm.
Note.   The Gov.ͬ us'd to Tell the Councillors how acceptable 'twould be to him to be discours'd in privat about
such matters.

Febr. 13. 170⅞.   Though I walk in the midst of trouble,
thou wilt revive me; thou shalt stretch forth thy hand
against the wrath of my enemies, and thy right hand shall
save me. 138. 7.   I read the 137, 138 Psalms in course
this morn, and have noted this for Memory.

Feria Septima, March, 6. 170⅞.   Having the Company's

---

[1] Probably Isaac, son of Josiah, and grandson of Edward.   The Mr. Otis
mentioned seems to be Joseph Otis, of Scituate, who married, according to
Savage, in 1670, Dorothy, daughter of Nathaniel Thomas, of Marshfield. —
EDS.

Account [for Propagating the Gospel] written out; I went
to Col. Foster to pray him to be present to examin it;
went to the Maj^r Genl to acquaint him that I design'd a
Meeting at my house which he consented to: Then I went
to Maxwell to order him to warn the Comissioners; which
he imediatly took in hand. Then going up the prison-
Lane I met Mr. Sergeant, who told me of Mr. Arthur
Mason's Funeral,[1] which I knew nothing of before; neither
did I suspect it; thinking it would be defer'd till next
week for sake of Mr. Norton and his wife. But now I
could not go back for fear of losing my oportunity of finishing and sending my Accounts. As soon as ever had
Sign'd, left other important Business; and went all away
to go to the Funeral; but when we came to the School-
house Lane end, we saw and heard the Funeral was gon;
and so came back. I even despair'd of finishing my Account the Ships threatn'd to sail so soon; and I was taken
up so much with my Inventory. But by the Kindness of
God, I got well through it, made two fair Copies of the
Original, and had them Subscrib'd by the Comissioners
attesting their examination and Allowance of them. Not
one error discern'd. *Laus Deo Adjutori.*

Midweek, March, 10, 170⅞. The privat Meeting was at
Mr. Cole's, where Mrs. Noyes was, I read a Sermon of Mr.
Willard's. I went away a little before her but she overtook me near the New Meetinghouse; I saw the Glimpse
of her Light and call'd to her; spake a few words and
parted; feeling in my self a peculiar displeasure that our
way lay no further together.

March 12. She was at the Meeting of Maj^r Genl Win-

---

[1] From the notes to "Dunton's Letters from New England," pp. 90, 106,
we learn that Arthur Mason, a baker, died March 4, 1708, aged seventy-
seven years. He was the father of Joanna, who married, first, Robert
Breck, and, secondly, Michael Perry, and who was celebrated by Dunton as
" the very Flower of Boston."   Mason lived on School Street, and left seven
children. — EDS.

throp, where Mr. Adams preached. Presently after her getting home, she was seised with the Palsie, which took away her Speech. I heard of it at Scarlet's Wharf, March 13, as I was taking Leave of Mr. Jonathan Belcher, and Mr. Sam. Banister going aboard the Fleet ready to sail. Midweek, March, 17, 170$\frac{7}{8}$. my Country-man,[1] Mr. Josiah Byles, dyed very suddenly. *Feria quinta*,. March 18th the Fleet sails, though the Skie cover'd with Clouds.

Feria sexta Reginald Odell dies suddenly. Heard of it at Mr. Byles Funeral. About Candle-lighting, the day señight after her being taken, my old cordial Christian dear friend, Mrs. Sarah Noyes,[2] Expires. I saw her on Wednesday, she knew me, and ask'd how Madam Sewall did. She was Laborious, Constant at Privat Meeting, Lecture, Lords-Day. I am much afflicted for the Loss of her. Capt. Brattle tells me that a vertuous young Woman at Marblehead died in 4 or 5 Minutes after taken.

Feria secunda, March, 22, 170$\frac{7}{8}$. Mr. Zechariah Symmes, pastor of the church of Christ at Bradford, died in the morning. He was born at Charlestown, January 9. 1637. He was a Worthy Gentleman, Scholar, Divine. *Feria quinta*, March, 25, 1708. Intending to set out for Plimouth the 27th I went to the Major Gen^{ls} and to Mrs. Sergeant's to Receive their Bills if they pleas'd to pay them: found neither at home, and so went not in. Coming back, in the prison-Lane I met Mr. Sergeant. He ask'd me where I had been, I told him at his house: He said, What for, Money? I said Yes. At which he was angry, and said I was very hasty, I knew very little of that nature.

---

[1] We have here an example of "countryman," used for one of the same county. Josiah Byles, a saddler, came from Winchester, in Hampshire, married for his second wife Elizabeth Mather, and was father of the famous Reverend Mather Byles. — EDS.

[2] Probably this was Sarah, daughter of Peter Oliver, and wife of John Noyes, of Boston. Their son Oliver, H. C. 1695, was a prominent citizen. — EDS.

He would enquire how others paid me &c.   I told him I was going out of Town, this was the day,¹ and I thought it convenient to offer the Bills; he said he should not break; and at last call'd out aloud, he should not break before I came back again!   I know no reason for this Anger; the Lord sanctify it to me, and help me to seek more his Grace and favour.   This day was very stormy with Rain, and then with Snow; a pretty deal of Thunder.   Maj^r Cutler was with me in the morning.

March, 27. 1708.   Rode with Mr. Nehm. Hobart to Hingham, visited Madam Shepard by the way at Cousin Holman's, visited Mr. Fisk: visited Mr. Norton, who invited Mr. Hobart to preach next day.   Lodg'd at Cousin Hobart's.

March, 28.   See the Sermons in one of my Cover'd Almanacks.   Din'd at Mr. Norton's.   March 29. by 6. m. Gam! Rogers, the son, who had been sent Express in the night, came to my Lodging with an Adjournment of the Court to the 20th of April.   This as desired, I forwarded to Plimouth by Cous. David Hobart, who accompanied his Brother Mr. N. Hobart.   I agreed with Major Thaxter to run the Line of my 300. Acres of Land at Braintrey just by Milton.   Din'd with Cousin Quinsey, and engag'd him to meet me at Milton next Monday: Spake to Mr. Swift to assist me.   Call'd at the Governour's; came home well. *Laus Deo.*

April, 1.   Great Rain with Thunder.   Mr. Wadsworth preaches: Work out your own Salvation with Fear.

Feria Sexta, April, 2.   Last night I dream'd that I had my daughter Hirst in a little Closet to pray with her; and of a sudden she was gon, I could not tell how; although the Closet was so small, and not Cumber'd with Chairs or Shelves.   I was much affected with it when I waked.

Feria septima, Apr. 3.   I went to Cous. Dumer's to see

---

¹ The first day of the year, old style. — EDS.

his News-Letter: while I was there Mr. Nath¹ Henchman
came in with his Flaxen Wigg; I wish'd him Joy, i. e. of
his Wedding. I could not observe that he said a Word to
me; and generally he turn'd his back upon me, when
none were in the room but he and I. This is the Second
time I have spoken to him, in vain, as to any Answer from
him. First was upon the death of his Wife, I cross'd the
way near our house, and ask'd him how he did: He only
shew'd his Teeth.

Feria secunda, Apr. 5. Great Rain, whereby I am
prevented meeting Major Thaxter at Milton to run a Line,
as I intended.

Feria secunda, Apr. 12, 1708. I went and met Major
Thaxter at Miller's at Milton to run the Lines of the 300.
Acres bought of Mr. Stoughton; Cousin Quinsey, Mr.
Swift, Miller, White, Hunt, assisted us. Mr. William Rawson, having Land adjoining, was with us all day; Billing
a considerable while. Capt. Culliver and others peram-
bulating for Braintrey and Milton, went with us from B.
to C. which was measured, whereby the place we set out
from was ascertain'd to be the North Corner, of which
there was some doubt before: At C. the old white Oak
mark with H., we drank a Bottle of Madera together,
read the Queens Speech to the first Parliament of great
Britain,¹ and so took leave of the perambulators. Major
Thaxter, Cous. Quinsey, and White went quite through
the Swamp, marking Trees: southward of the Swamp is a
small Chestnut White-Oak; a little after that the Line
brushes by a Ledge of Rocks, touches them. At D. the
Oak upon the Rock is cut down injuriously, there it lyes
and no use made of it: by the Stump grows up a fine
little Chestnut Oak, which was prun'd; twas double and
one is cut away to make the other grow the better. In

---

¹ The first United Parliament of Great Britain (England and Scotland)
met Oct. 23, 1707. — EDS.

the Line from D to A found several Trees mark'd with H.
At A. we enlarg'd the Heap of Stones upon the Rock and
from thence, as all along, run by Compass and the an-
ciently marked Trees to C., where we begun; which
prov'd all the Work to be Right: There we made a large
heap of Stones upon the Stump of a Tree burnt down.

Paid to Major Thaxter	£0—8–0
To White 3ˢ Hunt for formerly, and now 3ˢ	0—6–0
To Miller for entertainment and Help	0–15–0
To the Widow Gray for my Horse	0—5–0
	£1–14–0

To Cousin Quinsey, Mr. Swift, and Mr. Lawson I am
oblig'd.

It is a Mercy that our work succeeded so well. Got
home before eight, and found all well. *Laus Deo.*

Apr. 11, 12, 13. Swallows proclame the Spring.

Feria Sexta, Apr. 16. I visit my daughter Hirst, and
finding her alone in her Chamber, pray with her. Afterward by Majʳ Genˡ Winthrop's direction I carry her a vial
of Spirits of Lavender. And of my self I join with it a
pound of Figs, that food and Physick might go together.
Leave her with Mrs. Hubbard.

Apr. 17. 1708. Col. Hathorne, Mr. Corwin and I set
out for Scituate. Lodg'd at Job Randall's. Apr. 18.
Heard Mr. James Gardener of Marshfield.

Apr. 19. To Plimouth, stay at Mr. Bradford's till Mr.
Attorney Cook came up. There the sheriff meets us.
Lodge at Rickard's. Apr. 22. Return'd.

May, 4. Daughter Hirst Deliver'd of a Daughter.
May, 7. Boston: Upon the Special Verdict, between Wats
and Allen, Sewall, Hathorne, Corwin for Watts; Walley
for Allen.

Feria secunda, May, 17, 1708. Major Walley and I set
out with a Coach and 4 Horses from Charlestown; Dine

at Lewis's; bait at Phillips's, Wenham, got to Mr. Rogers's before Sun-set.

Major Walley had a Fit or 2 of his Cholick, and yet by God's Goodness, came away about 3 p. m. May 21, got comfortably to Salem. Lodg'd at Brother's.

May, 22. set out about Eight m. Baited at Lewis's: Din'd at Cambridge, call'd at Brooklin, lighted at the Governour's. Got home well about 6. *Laus Deo.*

Midweek, May, 26. 1708. Mr. Secretary, Sewall, Eliakim Hutchinson administer the Oaths to the Representatives: 72 at first, and 2 more. 74 in all. Mr. Jno. Norton preaches a Flattering Sermon as to the Governour. Dine at the Exchange. Number of Councillors 25. Together, 99. Election.

Wait Winthrop	95	Plimouth *Cook and Pain Negatived.*	
James Russell	95	Nathan¹ Pain	88
Elisha Cook	57	Isaac Winslow	86
Jn° Hathorn	93	Jn° Cushing	74
Elisha Hutchins[on]	81	Jn° Otis	65
S. Sewall	98	**Main**	
I. Addington	94	Eᵐ Hutchinson	85
W. Brown	71	Ichabod Plaisted	86
J. Phillips	86	John Wheelright	45
J. Corwin	89		
[John] Foster	95	Zagadahock	
John Apleton	85	Joseph Lynde	65
[John] Higginson	91		
Peter Sergeant	82	At Large	
Samˡ Partridge	69	1 Vote None chosen.	
2ᵈ voting		2 Vote	
Ephraim Hunt	61	Edʳ Bromfield	64.
Nathanˡ Norden	52	3ᵈ vote Sam. Apleton	41
3ᵈ vote		which brought him in; the voters	
Andrew Belchar	54.	being now less in number.	

For Col. Townsend had 42. in the first voting for the Massachusets. Finished about ¼ past Ten.

May, 27. I was with a Comittee in the morn at Mr. Eᵐ Hutchinsons, apointed the 10. of May; and so by

God's good providence absent when Mr. Corwin and Cushing were order'd to Thank Mr. Norton for his sermon and desire a Copy. About 6. p. m̄. The Gov[r] bid the Secretary swear the Council: About 20. were sworn; Then the Deputies were sent for in, and the Gov[r] made a speech. When court was adjourn'd I enquired of Mr. Secretary what the Gov[r] had done with the Election; and he inform'd me that He had Negativ'd Mr. Cooke and Mr. Pain,[1] which was never done in this secret way before that I remember: but used to be done openly in Council.

May, 27. Mr. Joseph Noyes lodg'd at our House; I gave him the Broad Side of Boston streete, which came out this week: to shew him that he was in Newbury Street.[2] He pray'd with us very well. Is in the 71 year of's Age.

May, 31. The Gov[r] call'd a Council in the Morning, and had Capt. Chandler's Letter from Woodstock concerning Nenemeno, an Indian that went away ten years ago; He said the Gov[r] has a Crooked heart, he has taken away our Land, and now would send us to Salt Water. He first enquired after Ninequabben, who it seems was sent to sea upon Wages with his own Consent, and Taken. Gov[r] and Mr. Secretary writ what was convenient.

In the afternoon the Gov[r] went home indispos'd. Council pass'd an Act for altering the Style.[3]

---

[1] Sewall has given us the detail of the voting for members of the Council. In the place of Elisha Cooke and Nathaniel Paine, negatived by the Governor, there were chosen Daniel Epes and Joseph Church. — EDS.

[2] This broadside was doubtless an official description of the " streets, lanes, and alleys " of the town as bounded and named by the Selectmen May 3, 1708. The first item is " The broad street or highway from the old Fortification on the neck, leading into the town as far as the corner of the late Deacon Eliot's house, *Orange Street*." That is to say, Washington Street, from a little above Dover Street, to Boylston Street. — EDS.

[3] This was not to mark the change in dating the year from old style to new style, which was not to happen for nearly half a century, but only to notice the union of England and Scotland. The Queen's title was declared to be, " Anne, by the Grace of God, of Great Britain, France, and Ireland, Queen, Defender of the Faith," &c. See Province Laws, II. 622. — EDS.

Deputies sent in Capt. Savage, Capt. Hutchinson, Mr. Patch, with a Motion for a Comittee of both Houses to prepare a draught of an Address to Her Majesty; on several heads; viz. To Apologize for neglecting to Address so long, &c.

This day, May, 31, Mr. Crease removes to his own new shop next Mr. Sergeant's: Nothing now to be seen in his former empty place. Cousin Fisk must get a new Tenant.

About the 23 or 24ᵗʰ of June, Mr. Bromfield Rec'd a Letter without a name, putting him upon enquiring after Debaucheries at North's, the Exchange Tavern, and that he should ask my Advice. At last, June, 28. he got in writing what North's Wife and Maid had to complain of. I went to Mr. Sim. Stoddard's; he put it into my hand, and I read it first, being surpris'd to find my self unaccountably abused in it: I told Mr. Bromfield, I should not meddle in it, I must not be a Judge in my own Cause. At last when the matter was heard before Mr. Bromfield, Townsend, Dumer, by Mr. Banister's procurement, sundry Gentlemen were present, Capt. Tho. Hutchinson, Capt. Edᵂ Winslow, and others, at Mr. Bromfield's; They gave Mrs. North and her Maid their Oaths, fin'd Mr. Tho. Banister junʳ 20ˢ for Lying; 5ˢ Curse, 10ˢ Breach of the peace for throwing the pots and Scale-box at the maid, and bound him to his good behaviour till October sessions. At the latter end of the Court, I think about the first of July, the Dept's sent in for the Govʳ £200.; for Mr. Treasurer £225: at which the Govʳ was very angry, and said he would pass none of them, they would starve together. Sent for Mr. Taylor, Govʳ told him his Salary would not be pass'd, enquir'd whether he were ready to serve.

July, 2. Capt. Joseph Shelden dyes by reason of the great Heat.

July, 3, is buried at the publick charge, £21.6.1. Corps was set in the Deptˢ Room. In the afternoon I and Mr.

Comissary and one more were sent in with a Message to shew the Indignity of the Treasurer being above the Govr, and carried in both the Bills, and left them. In the way of argument I mention'd the vastness of the Gov^rs Authority; we could not lift up hand or foot or step over a straw; at which the house was mightily heated and said, They were slaves; I explain'd my self, that nothing could be pass'd but what the Govr Sign'd.

Tuesday, July, 6. The Treasurer is sworn; the Dept^s return the Bills without any alteration. The Govr orders the Secretary who draws up a vote to shew that the Council, having done all in their power to increase the Gov^rs Salary: but by reason of the length of the Sessions were necessitated to break. It was a Surprise to me. I said, I could not tell what Benefit it would be of. But when it was driven, I got it alter'd in the begiñing, to, having used the proper Means. Court is prorogued to the first of September.

July, 7. I go to Cambridge by Water with Mr. Tañan in Capt. Boñer; had a pleasant passage, wind and Tide for us. Boston Troop waited on the Govr, and Cambridge Troop, Capt. Goff, met his Excellency. Exercise was well entered before he came. Then the orator was call'd.

At Diñer I was surpris'd, being told my Son was ill and desired to speak with me. I went to him in a Garret in the old College, got Mr. Addington to us. After, Mr. Cooke came; cheer'd my son and staid with him; they left us. Note. Heard not a jot of the Singing in the Hall. I got a Calash, and brought my son home by Charlestown: so I saw nothing of the Afternoon Exercise, Disputes, Presidents Oration, Degrees. The Lord prepare me for Disañointments, Disgraces, Imprisonments.

July, 8. Mr. Pemberton comes with Mr. Stoddard into the Pulpit. Mr. Stoddard preaches a good Sermon against building on the Sand. Col. Foxcroft is made Judge of Probats in the room of Mr. Leverett.

Feria secunda, July, 12, 1708. Mr. Sol. Stoddard returns home. In the Afternoon the Govr holds a Council, and reads Two Letters from White-Hall, dated May, 1707, ordering the Union to be published in the most solemn mañer; and the Govr accordingly apointed Thorsday, the 22th Inst^t, for it. In the former part of the Letter, the Govr is order'd to write to the Lords an Account of Things here and persons; sign'd Stamford, Dartmouth, Herbert, Ph. Meadows, J. Poultney.

May, 3. The Queen gives an Instruction, that in absence of the Govr and Dep^t Govr, the eldest Councillor shall execute the Powers of the Governour. In passing the Muster-Rolls, It apeared that Capt. Turfrey was allow'd for wages at Saco when absent so as could not be answer'd: Govr said must be allow'd except would pull his Teeth out: Pleaded how many dead Souldiers, Military officers, were allow'd. I pleaded against that Lying way; and pleaded the poverty of the Country.

Maj^r Genl Winthrop came home from N. London July, 10. and was sworn and took his place at the Board this day July 12. 1708. He pleaded that what the Queen now orders, was so before: But I cant understand the Charter in that mañer. I believe we practis'd right.

July, 24, 1708. Mrs. Anna Fisk dy's a little before Sun-set.

July, 27. is buried at Braintrey in her Husband's Tomb. Govr and his Lady there. Bearers Mr. Peter Thacher, and Mr. Peter Thacher of Weymouth; Mr. B. Tomson, Mr. Belcher; Mr. Danforth of Dorchester, Mr. Flint. By reason of Cambridge Court I was not there. The wether was vehemently hot, My Coach was there. I rode to Cambridge with the Maj^r Genl in his Coach. Finish'd the Court; being but one civil Action; viz. Ephraim Savage against Major Swain. Savage Cast in his Review. Court held in the College Hall. Adjourned *sine die*. Visited Mr. President's Sick Anne; twas almost dark, and then staid so long at the Gov^{rs} that twas about 11. at night before got home; Madam Winthrop staid at the Gov^{rs} and came home with her Husband as went thither. Govr carried her to the Funeral.

Monday, Augt 9. 1708. I went to Brooklin, and Din'd there with my Son and Daughter; Saw little Sam well. Then went to the Funeral of Mrs. Wigglesworth. The Govr met me at my Sons Gate and carried me in his Chariot to Cambridge, in his way to Col. Paiges, and so to Ipswich. Bearers of Mrs. Wigglesworth, The President and Mr. Hobart; Mr. Thacher, Mr. Danforth Dorch^{r}; Mr. Brattle, Mr. Walter. Only Col. Phillips and I of the Council were there: Mr. Speaker was there.

Feria tertia, Augt 10. Mr. Fiske dies about Noon.

Feria quinta, Augt 12. I rode with Cous. Savage to Mr. Fisk's Funeral. Lighted at Cous. Quinsey's, whether came Mr. Wadsworth, Mr. Colman, and Mr. George. There we din'd. Bearers Mr. Whitman, Mr. Thacher; Mr. Danforth of Dorchester, Mr. Belchar; Mr. Wadsworth, Mr. Thacher of Milton. There was little Thunder and Rain; but near and at Boston, much Rain, Thunder; at Dorchester a Barn was burnt by the Lightening. Got home well about 8 a'clock, found all well; *Laus Deo*.

Feria sexta, Augt. 13. Mrs. Mary Stoddard dies;[1] The hot Wether occasion'd her being open'd, and two great Stones were taken out of her Bladder. She was a vertuous Gentlewoman, and one of the most kind Friends I and my wife had. Augt 17th *Feria Tertia*. Mrs. Stoddard is buried; being the day of Genl Council, they accompanied the Govr to the House of Mourning: Bearers, Sewall, Addington; Foster, Sergeant; Walley, Townsend. Was buried in a Tomb in the New-Burying place.

Feria quarta, Augt. 18. Yesterday the Govr comitted

---

[1] This was Mary, first wife of Simeon Stoddard, and mother of the young man whose death we have noticed, *ante*, p. 169. — EDS.

Mr. Holyoke's Almanack to me; and looking it over this morning, I blotted against Feb.ʳ 14.ᵗʰ *Valentine;* March, 25. *Annunciation of the B. Virgin;* Apr. 24, *Easter;* Sept.ʳ 29. *Michaelmas;* Dec.ʳ 25. *Christmas;* and no more. (K. C. mart) [King Charles Martyr] was lined out, before I saw it; I touched it not.

Feria quinta Aug.ᵗ 12. Mr. Chiever is abroad and hears Mr. Cotton Mather preach; This is the last of his going abroad: Was taken very sick, like to die with a Flux. Aug.ᵗ 13. I go to see him; went in with his Son Thomas, and Mr. Lewis. His Son spake to him, and he knew him not: I spake to him, and he bid me speak again: Then he said, now I know you, and speaking cheerily mention'd my Name. I ask'd his Blessing for me and my family; He said I was Bless'd, and it could not be Revers'd. Yet at my going away He pray'd for a Blessing for me.

Feria quinta, Aug.ᵗ 19. I visited Mr. Chiever again, just before Lecture; Thank'd him for his Kindness to me and mine; desired his prayers for me, my family, Boston, Salem, the Province. He rec'd me with abundance of Affection, taking me by the Hand several times. He said, The Afflictions of God's people, God by them did as a Goldsmith, Knock, knock, knock; knock, knock, knock, to finish the plate: It was to perfect them not to punish them. I went and told Mr. Pemberton, who preach'd.

Feria sexta, Aug.ᵗ 20. I visited Mr. Chiever, who was now grown much weaker, and his Speech very low. He call'd, Daughter! When his daughter Russel came, He ask'd if the family were compôs'd: They aprehended He was uneasy because there had not been Prayer that morn; and solicited me to Pray; I was loth, and advis'd them to send for Mr. Williams, as most natural, homogeneous: They declin'd it, and I went to Prayer. After, I told him The last Enemy was Death; and God had made that a friend too: He put his hand out of the Bed, and held it up, to signify his assent. Observing, he suck'd a piece of an Orange, put it orderly into his mouth, and chew'd it, and then took out the core. After dinner I carried a few of the best Figs I could get, and a dish Marmalet. I spake not to him now.

Feria septima, Aug! 21. Mr. Edward Oakes tells me Mr. Chiever died this last night.

Note. He was born January, 25. 1614. Came over to N–E. 1637. to Boston: To New-Haven 1638. Married in the Fall and began to teach School; which Work he was constant in till now. First, at New-Haven, then at Ipswich; then at Charlestown; then at Boston, whether he came 1670. So that he has Labour'd in that Calling Skillfully, diligently, constantly, Religiously, Seventy years. A rare Instance of Piety, Health, Strength, Serviceableness. The Wellfare of the Province was much upon his Spirit. He abominated Perriwigs.

Aug! 23. 1708. Mr. Chiever was buried from the School-house. The Gov', Councillors, Ministers, Justices, Gentlemen there. Mr. Williams made a handsom Latin Oration in his Honour. Elder Bridgham, Copp, Jackson, Dyer, Griggs, Hubbard &c. Bearers. After the Funeral, Elder Bridgham, Mr. Jackson, Hubbard, Dyer, Tim. Wadsworth, Ed" Procter, Griggs and two more came to me, and earnestly solicited me to speak to a place of Scripture at their privat Quarter-Meeting in the room of Mr. Chiever. I said, 'twas a great Surprise to me; pleaded my inability for want of memory, Invention: Said, doubted not of my ability; would pray for me. I pleaded the Unsuitableness, because I was not of that Meeting. They almost took a denial. But said one would come to me next night. Time is near, Lords-day Señight. Argued much because thereby a Contribution for poor Widows would be forwarded.

Aug! 23. *mane*, at Council, A Petition for building a

Quaker Meeting house[1] with Wood, pass'd by the Select-
men and Justices of the Town; was now offer'd to the
Govr and Council: I oppos'd it; said I would not have a
hand in setting up their Devil Worship. I pleaded that
Mr. Dudley had been at great Charge to Slate his House
Roof and Sides; Govr listen'd to that, and said, we always
enquired of the Neighbourhood to gain their Consent: so
Mr. Dudley should be spoken with.

Augt 23. 2. p̄. m. Go to Cous. Dūmer's, where Mr.
Wadsworth, Mr. Cotton Mather pray'd excellently: then
Mr. Bridge and Dr. Mather pray'd for Cous. Jer. Dūmer
going to England. Sung the 121 Ps. I set York Tune.
Went from thence to the Funeral. Mr. Allen and Mr.
Pemberton did not pray. Few there; their little Room
not full.

Augt 26. Mr. Henry Flint, in the way from Lecture
came to me and mention'd my Letter, and would have
discoursed about it in the Street: I prevail'd with him to
come and dine with me, and after that I and he discours'd
alone.

He argued that saying *Saint* Luke was an indifferent
thing; and twas cōmonly used; and therefore, he might
use it. Mr. Brattle used it. I argued that 'twas not
Scriptural; that twas absurd and partial to *saint* Matthew
&c. and Not to say *Saint* Moses, *Saint* Samuel &c. And
if we said *Saint* we must goe thorough, and keep the Holydays ap̄ointed for them, and turn'd to the Order in the
Cōmon-Prayer Book.

---

[1] Shurtleff shows that the Quakers first had a brick meeting-house,
twenty-four by twenty feet, on a lot sold in 1694 by Thomas Brattle to William Mumford. It was put into the hands of trustees, who sold it July 27,
1709. It was in "Brattle's Close," near the spot now covered by the Quincy
House. Jan. 5, 1708, Mumford bought of the heirs of Governor Leverett a
lot of land in Congress Street, opposite Lindall Street, about fifty by one
hundred and fifty feet in area. Here was their meeting-house and cemetery
till 1828. The Transcript building afterwards occupied the site. — EDS.

Aug.ᵗ 27. Mrs. Sarah Taylor, wife of Col. William Taylor, died last night. Col. Byfield gave her to him in Marriage.[1]

March, 2. 169⅞ He has now only one Child living; viz. Mrs. Lyde who has Children.

Feria Septima, Aug.ᵗ 28. 1708. Mrs. Taylor is buried in Mr. Stoughton's Tomb: Bearers, Col. Foxcroft, Mr. Palmer; Mr. Newton, Mr. Mico; Mr. Pain, Mr. Harris. Col. Byfield there and Mr. Lyde with three Children. Mr. Leverett and wife; Mr. Brattle and wife; Mr. Angier and wife. Mr. Sergeant and Col. Hutchinson were there with their wives as Relations.[2] Govʳ and his Lady, Majʳ Genˡ Winthrop and his Lady, Mr. Secretary, Sewall, Mr. Eᵐ Hutchinson, Belchar, Mr. Bromfield there; and many others. There was no Prayer at the House; and at the Grave Mr. Myles Read Comon-Prayer; which I reckon an Indignity and affront done to Mr. Stoughton and his Friends: There apears much Ingratitude and Baseness in it because twas Mr. Danforth's Parish, and Mr. Danforth's wife is Cousin German to Col. Taylor: and Col. Byfield and his deceased daughter dissenters as I supose. I was much surpris'd and grieved at it, and went not into the burying place. Majʳ Genˡ said, Mr. Stoughton heard them not. Mr. Leverett went not in. He spake to me about his Letter, desiring a Copy of his Memorial. I an-

---

[1] Concerning Nathaniel Byfield, the reader is referred to the Heraldic Journal, II. 126. He was born in 1653, at Long-Ditton, came to New England in 1674, married Deborah Clark, and had two daughters. One married Lieutenant-Governor William Tailer, and had no issue; the other married Edward Lyde; and her son, Byfield Lyde, inherited most of his grandfather's estate. — EDS.

[2] The text throws some light on various genealogies. Mrs. Deborah Byfield was daughter of Thomas Clarke, Sen., and his son, Thomas Clarke, Jr., had a daughter, who married Elisha Hutchinson. Peter Sargent's third wife (living at this time) was Mehitable (Minot) widow of Thomas Cooper. See *ante,* p. 174. We have already shown that Mehitable, and her sister Elizabeth Danforth, were own cousins of Lieutenant-Governor Tailer, on his mother's side. See Vol. I. p. 163, *note.* — EDS.

swered, I knew not who brought the Letter; I writt out
a Copy; but he neither came for it himself, nor sent any
body. He ask'd not for it now: but said he intended to
lay it before the Company. The Gov[r] seem'd to haste
into the burying place, when Mr. Miles's voice was heard.
Coming home Mr. Belchar told me that the widow Park,
a very good woman, in her 94th year, was buried last
Thorsday, at Roxbury.

Lords-day, Aug[t] 29. 1708. about 4 p. m. An Express
brings the News, the dolefull News, of the Surprise of
Haverhill by 150. French and Indians. Mr. Rolf and his
wife and family slain. About Break of Day, Those Words
run much in my mind, I will smite the Shepherd, and the
Sheep shall be scattered: What a dreadfull Scattering is
here of poor Havarill Flock, upon the very day they used
to have their solemn Assemblies. Capt. Wainwright is
slain.

Aug[t] 31. *Feria tertia,* I ride with Joseph, and visit Mr.
Hobart. I drove through Dana's Brook[1] to let the Mare
drink, and she lay down in it; so that Joseph and I were
fain to jump into the Water up to the ankles; and then
had much adoe to get her out. Din'd with Mr. Hobart,
Mrs. Hobart, Mrs. Jackson, Mr. Hobart's Daughter. Got
home with difficulty: but our Wellcome there at Newton
made amends for all. This day, Augt. 31. Mr. Rolf, his
Wife and Child, and Capt. Wainwright were buried in one
Grave, Several Ministers were there [Haverhill].

---

1 Although we have not located Dana's Brook, it must have been in
Cambridge, Brighton, or Newton. Undoubtedly it took its name from some
member of the family descended from Richard Dana. The family history
states that tradition says that the emigrant was the son of a Frenchman who
had been driven to England to escape religious persecution, and that the
name Dana is always a dissyllable, and distinct from Dane. As a strong
confirmation of this, we would state Agnew's "Protestant Exiles from
France" (London, 1871) mentions (II. 207, 208) that Elias Daney, advocate in the Parliament of Bordeaux, had a daughter, Anne, born in 1669,
who became a Huguenot refugee, and married in England. Other members
of the same family may well have shared her faith and preceded her in exile.
— Eps.

Sept: 1. Went to the burial of Mr. Simson's only daughter, 2 years and a few days old. Sept: 2. Mr. Colman preach'd from Numb. 14. 19. pardon — the iniquity of this people. — Mr. Colman said he would not declare what our iniquities were; but propos'd that a Synod Might be call'd to do it. At 3. p. m̄. the Council meets, from thence they goe to the Funeral of Mrs. Lyde, Col. Byfield's eldest daughter. Remembring what I had met with at her Sister's Burial at Dorchester last Satterday, I slipt from the Company up to my daughter's, and so went home, and avoided the Funeral. The office for Burial is a Lying, very bad office; makes no difference between the precious and the vile. Jer. XV. 19. They ought to return to us, and not we go to them by sinfull Compliances. Mrs. Lyde was in the Thirtieth, and Mrs. Taylor in the 26th year of her Age: born in January and February.

7: 3. I went to the Funeral of Mrs. Whetcomb's Granddaughter; who is also Grand daughter to Col. Townsend. I used to go to the same Room for the Sound of Mr. Brattle's Organs.

7: 5. Mr. Pemberton preaches, and administers the Lords Supper. 7: 6. I Train under Capt. Fitch, and by that means dine with Maj: Turner at North's. He was, I think, the only Guest. Mr. N. Williams pray'd in the field in the morn; and Mr. Allen at his own Gate, p. m̄. As were Shooting at the Mark, the Rain oblig'd us to put on our Cloaks. Went to Capt. Lieut. Ballentines; made an excellent Volley at Lodging the Colours, Mad: Ballentine rec'd them in at window. Mr. Hirst brings word that Mr. La Bloom has set up another Window on the partition-wall behind him and me, that stands half on my Ground. 7: 7th I view it, and advise about it; all say tis unjust. 7: 8th Last night we were alarm'd by Fire between 2 and 3. in the night. I look'd out at our South-east Window, and fear'd that our Warehouse was a-fire: But it proves a smith's shop, Hubbard's by Mr. Dastom's, and a Boat-builders Shed; 'Tis thought a Hundred pounds Damage is done. Blessed be God it stop'd there. Mr. Pemberton's Maid saw the Light of the Fire reflecting from a Black Cloud, and came crying to him under Consternation; suposing the last Conflagration had begun.

7ʳ 8 or 7ᵗʰ I order Mr. Hirst to speak to Mr. Labloom to take away his Window. 7ʳ 9ᵗʰ I meet the Workman by Mr. Pemberton's Gate, and forewarn him from making of it; and warn him off the Ground, and threaten to take away his scaffolding if he proceed. I speak to Mr. Pemberton that a Day of Prayer may be kept respecting his Health. It was mov'd last night at Mr. Josiah Franklin's [Father of Benjamin] at our Meeting, where I read the Eleventh Sermon on the Barren Fig-Tree.

Tis the first time of Meeting at his House since he join'd.

7ʳ 9. Mr. C. Mather Preaches from 2 Tim. 3. 15. In the end of his sermon gives a great Encomium of his Master Cheever. Mr. Hirst goes to Salem to-day.

Satterday, 7ʳ 11ᵗʰ Mr. Corwin and I set out for Wrentham. David waited on me. Visited Mr. Belchar who is Recovering. At Meadfield, Capt. Wear's son met with us in his way from Sherburn, and accompanied us to Wrentham, which was a great comfort to us; got thither before sun-set.

7ʳ 12. Heard Mr. Mann preach excellently. Mr. Corwin is much Taken with him. At Noon are told of Mr. B. Ruggles's death.

7ʳ 13. Capt. Weare accompanied us; At Rehoboth I visited Capt. Peck, who was very glad to see me; so much of the flesh and bone of his uper Jaw is eaten away with the Canker, that he has much adoe to speak so as to be understood; the want of the uper part of his Mouth disables him from making articulat Sounds. Din'd at Smith's; where Mr. Greenwood was, but could not stay, because of

Sick he had to visit.   Before got out of the Green, Mr.
Cooke overtook us.   Lodge at the Ordinary.

7ʳ 14ᵗʰ   Mr. Corwin, Dudley and I visited Col. Byfield
and Lady in a way of Condolance on account of the Death
of their Daughters.   Major Walley came not to Town till
past One ; By that time had din'd, being a little hindred
by Col. Byfield's employing the Sheriff to send Express of
the Privateer, was four p. m. before the Court was open'd,
which the people murmur at.   This Express brought News
of Major Brenton's Death ; in a Hospital, it seems, at Cam-
peche, where he was a Captive.   Col. Byfield, Mr. Sparhawk, Mr. Fisk dine with us.

7ʳ 15ᵗʰ   Mr. Sparhawk, Mr. Church, the Councillour,
Capt. Fyfield dine with us.   Court holds so late, that we
lodge at Bristol.

7ʳ 16.   The Sheriff and Capt. Davis bring us going to
the Ferry.

Dine at Rehoboth ; Bait at Devotion's : get to Billinges a pretty while after Sun-set, where we lodge ; viz.
Walley, Corwin, Sewall, Dudley.

7ʳ 17.   Friday, bait at Dedham, get home about One,
and dine with my wife and family, all well.   *Laus Deo.*

7ʳ 18.   Visit Cous. Dummer's wife, who lyes speechless,
was taken last Wednesday night ; which we heard of at
Billenges.

7ʳ 19.   Mary Winthrop is baptised, her Father held
her up : She bears the name of his Mother, who dyed in
June, 1690.   The child was born yesterday.   Madam
Dudley was hastening to the Travel as we came home ;
and was at our Meeting this afternoon, and Mr. Paul
Dudley.

Feria secunda, Septʳ 27. 1708.   I went to the Funeral
of Mr. John Wainwright, son of Col. Francis Wainwright ;
He was a Senior Sophister, in the 18ᵗʰ year of his Age.
What cause of humble Thankfullness have I, who liv'd 7.
years of my Life at the College ; had Leave to come away ;

and have liv'd 34. years since that! The Corps was set
in the College Hall. Gentlewomen in the Library: Bearers, Major Epes, Mr. Holyoke &c. Twas in a mañer dark
before got out of the burying place; yet I got home very
well in a Calash with the Wainwright that is prentice
with Mr. Harris. *Laus Deo.*

Sept.ʳ 28. A very pretty Boy of 4 years old, Son of
Samˡ Rand, grandson of Wᵐ Pain, was flourishing at Training this day; fell into a scurvy open Privy before night;
of which loathsom Entertainment he died in a day or two.

Sept.ʳ 30. Mr. Pemberton preaches the Lecture. Council for Appointmᵗ of a Judge for Bristol. The Govʳ gets
2000£ past for Capt. Belchar. Nominats Col. Church:
I said there was a letter: Govʳ said he could not name
him: He went from house to house to get Mr. Blagrove
chosen Deputy; that was the reason. The Govʳ made a
motion that the Genˡ Court might be prorogued further, past
the time of the Superiour Court's sitting: See News Letter, Oct. 25, 1705. Some objected the wether would
grow cold. Then the Govʳ mov'd that Boston Superiour
Court might be adjourn'd to the last Tuesday of Novʳ, and
Salem Court, to the first of Dec.ʳ Said he could not miss
the Judges in the Genˡ Court: So at the Governours Importunity the Council advis'd to it. Majʳ Genˡ is indispos'd and keeps his Chamber, I wait upon him with the
order the same Evening: He puts me in mind of the
Trial of Mr. Borland: and that Capt. Vetch is expected
with my Lord Lovelace: so that now I suppose I see through
the Governour's Dissimulation. Major Genˡ seems to decline signing a Writt for Adjournment because he shall be
absent at Connecticut during the time of the Court's Sitting.

Tuesday, Oct.ʳ 5. Went to Dorchester Lecture. This
day Cousin Elizabeth Noyes is buried at Newbury, died of
a Fever yesterday; is under 26 years of Age. Has left
3 sons and a daughter.

Oct.ʳ 7ᵗʰ   Mr. Cotton Mather preaches from Job, 37. 14.
on occasion of the victory[1] which heard of the 5ᵗʰ Inst.
Sister Hirst, Mrs. Betty Hirst, Mr. Thacher, Mr. Clap dine
with us.

8.ʳ 8ᵗʰ   Went to Newtown Lecture, din'd at Mr. Hubbard's; then Walked with him; Mrs. Jackson went on
foot. In sermon-time Govʳ and his Lady, Capᵗ Belchar
and his, Mr. Pemberton, Mr. Colman and theirs, came in.
Mr. Hobart preached excellently, from Luke, 17. 10. —
Say, we are Unprofitable Servants. — 113ᵗʰ psalm sung,
Y.[ork?] then 122 L. to delay the Sermon; the speaker
having conferr'd with Mr. Hobart just as was going to
begin.   I got home before Eight, about an hour before
the Coaches; I think twas before 7.

Feria Sexta, Octobʳ 15, 1708.   In the Afternoon I visited Capt. Nathanˡ Green, who is near 80. years old.   Has
been a Prisoner in his house almost two years by reason
of Sickness.   He was refresh'd with my Company.   He is
a Suffolk man.   His Mother brought him over about 9.
years old: serv'd his Time with old Mr. Graften of Salem;
has been married one and Fifty years.

Oct.ʳ 15.   Mr. Hirst, Sister Sewall, and daughter Susan;
my Daughter Hañah, and Cous. Betty Hirst go to Cambridge to see Joseph.

Octobʳ 18ᵗʰ   Mr. Bromfield, Stoddard, Sewall, Joseph,
ride in the Coach to Dorchester, to the Funeral of Elder
Samuel Clap, who is much lamented.   He was the first
man born in Dorchester, 74 years old.[2]   Saw Mrs. Wing
by the way; she lies in a very sad distracted condition.

---

[1] Probably the Battle of Oudenarde, July 11, N. S. — EDS.

[2] Concerning him, see the Memoirs of Captain Roger Clap, published
first in 1731, and several times since.   The Dorchester Antiquarian and Historical Society printed an edition in 1844, in which we read that "Mr.
Samuel Clap was born the eleventh day of October, 1634, when his mother
was but in the eighteenth year of her age. . . . He married Mrs. Hannah
Leeds, daughter of Mr. Richard Leeds, of Dorchester. . . . He died about
eight days after his wife, on Oct. 16, 1708, being about seventy-four years
old." — EDS.

Octob.ʳ 20. Capt. Anthony Checkley buried in a Tomb in the New Burying place. Bearers, Winthrop, Cook; Elisha Hutchinson, Sewall; Addington, Lynde of Charlestown.

Octob.ʳ 22. *Feria sexta,* I mentioned in full Council the Adjournment of the Super. Court to the last of November; That when twas advis'd by the Govʳ and Council Sept.ʳ 30. I was not aware that the Trials of Mr. Borland were to be brought on by order of Her Majesty; that May-Court was pass'd over already, and I doubted the Conveniency of adjourning the Court to a further day: especially because the Super. Court of Boston did not use to be adjourn'd by reason of the Genˡ Court's Sitting.

The Govʳ seem'd earnest that we should Adjourn; Several of the Council back'd the Gov.ʳ and no body Spake for holding the Court at the usual Time. Col. Hutchinson and Foster particularly, spake that the former Advice might stand. So that we saw if we held the Court, we must in a mañer do it *Vi* and *Armis.* And the Govʳ said plainly, that if we would not Adjourn the Super. Court, He would Adjourn the Genˡ Court. And it was considered, that the Governour was ordered by the Queen to bring forward the Trial of Mr. Borland; and if any thing should fail, the Governour would lay the blame upon the Justices of the Super. Court, for not observing his Advice in adjourning the Court: and Mr. Attorney being his Son, He had advantage in his hand to cast that blame upon us. So all, but Major Walley, agreed to adjourn the Court. He was not present at our Consultation. I advis'd Mr. John Clark of this a day or two before; to see if the Deputies would move. I mov'd that the Deputies might be advis'd; it concern'd them; that the Genˡ Court might give order about it; or at least the Deputies might signify their Liking of it. The Govʳ utterly refused.

Oct.ʳ 22. Mr. Samˡ Phillips's daughter of about 7 years old, is buried: Six Bearers. Mr. Sergeant and I walk'd together to the Funeral.

Octob.ʳ 23. We adjourn the Super. Court: Chief Justice and I sign for Salem Court, and send it by Mr. Epes to be sign'd by Col. Hathorne, and Mr. Corwine; they were slipt away. Chief Justice, Sewall, Walley sign for Boston Court; and about 3. p. m̄. I give the Warrant to Mr. Sheriff; and send an Advertisement to Mr. Campbell.

Wednesday, 8.ʳ 27, 1708. My wife is taken very sick as she was last April; taken with Shaking and intolerable pain in her Brest. Maj.ʳ Gen.ˡ visits her and she takes some of his powder; but is cast up so soon, that it works little. Great Rain. Dr. Noyes visits and administers: on Friday grows better, *Laus Deo.*

Monday, Nov.ʳ 1. Gov.ʳˢ best Horse dyes in his Pasture at Roxbury as goe to Dedham. Bouroughs, a worsted-comber, was at Mr. Colman's Meeting on the L. day p. m̄., went homeward towards Roxbury in the night; got beyond the Salt-ponds, and fell down a-cross the Cart path in the Mud, and there perished; was found dead on Monday morn, Nov.ʳ 1. And thô the Coroner did his Office in the Morning; yet the Corps lay as a sad spectacle, gazed on till late in the Afternoon.

Gov.ʳ calls and smokes a pipe with my wife at night 9.ʳ 1.

Nov.ʳ 4. Mr. Cotton Mather preaches from Jn.º 20. 19. Gov.ʳ not in Town. In the Evening Col. Checkly, L.ᵗ Co.ˡ Winthrop, and Major Savage came to me, and acquainted me that the Guards for the Prison would be dismiss'd to morrow; the Gov.ʳ sent them to tell me so. Now I objected to the Bill about Odell, that no mention was made in it of any Person at the Castle to receive him, and that might be oblig'd to have him forth-coming when the Court should demand him.

Friday, Nov.ʳ 5. At the Conference this day about weighing Hay, Measuring Boards, Searching Turpentine, &c. As the Maj.ʳ Gen.ˡ had desired, the Gov.ʳ mentioned Odell's business before the whole Court; and the chief

Justice said nothing could be done upon that Act, it did not direct the Justices what to do. I said I could not have a hand in sending a man to that place where a Habeas Corpus could not demand him. Deputies seem'd to incline to laying the Bill aside, and having him kept in the prison where he is; it should be made more strong. The Gov[r] plainly said before that the Justices might not send him thither; nor send for him thence: and he had them words added in the Margin — (in order to his being sent) — for fear it should be interpreted that the Justices sent him by the sheriff: The Gov[r] would give his order, without which it could not be. Chief Justice said at the Conference, The man would be put out of the Law; which he and I had discoursed of before.

Nov[r] 15. 16. Our Malt-House by the Mill-Crick is Raised.

Second-day, Nov[r] 15. 1708. Mr. Attorney Gen[l] enquired whether Odel might not have the Liberty of the yard upon Bail. I answer'd, I suῤos'd the Law was made only in favour of Debtors, not Criminals. And calling for the Law-Book, it plainly aῤear'd so to be by the preamble, and body of the Law, and Mr. Davenport also observ'd the Law was now Expired. It is to me amazing, that Mr. Attorney should speak of Bailing such a man as Odel,[1] who is in a mañer *Hostis Humani Generis! Quid non mortalia pectora cogit Auri sacra fames?*[2] Me thinks now I see the reason why the Govr desired to have Odel at the

---

[1] The warrant now preserved in Mass. Archives, lib. LXXI. f. 474, is "to commit to Castle William, Thomas Odell, now a prisoner in the Gaol under a sentence to twelve months' imprisonment, and to pay a fine of £300, for being concerned, with others, in counterfeiting and uttering false bills of credit on this Province." It seemed, also, that he had once broken prison and escaped, and was charged with since committing various thefts, and " being a very dangerous person." It was suggested " that some ill-minded persons were contriving again to work his escape." Hence he was to be sent to Castle William, " there to be straitly confined until he perform the above sentence," &c. — EDS.

[2] Virgil, Æn. III. 56. In the original it is *cogis.* — EDS.

Castle of his own sending thither; and so as a Habeas
Corpus might not affect him there.

Nov.ʳ 20. 1708.   Sent by Aspinwall of Brooklin, Three
Bushels of Salt; one for Madam Oliver, one for Mr. Brattle, one for the President.   Writt to Col. Higginson about
the Salt sold him, expecting an Answer by Monday.
Gave Madam Brown one of the Verses on Mr. Clap, for
her self, another for Mr. Benj. Brown.

Nov.ʳ 19.   Visited Madam Saffin, and rec'd of her 20ˢ,
towards Tiverton Meetinghouse.

Nov.ʳ 19.   A Ship wherein Mr. Bromfield is much concern'd is taken by a Sloop from Port-Royal, as she was
Turning out of the Cape-Harbour.   Had not notice of it
till Tuesday about 10. m : Order'd Capt. Southack to go
out after them in a sloop that outsail'd the other.

Nov.ʳ 24.   Joseph comes to Town.   25.   Mr. Pemberton preaches excellently.   Dine in my wives Chamber at
the great Oval Table; Sat down, My wife, Mrs. Betty
Hirst, Hañah, Elisa H., Mary, Mr. Hirst, Capt. Nathˡ Niles,
Joseph, Sam and Jonathan Sewall, my self; Eleven in all.
Nov.ʳ 26. is so windy, and Cold, that Joseph goes not
home till 27. with Sir Oakes.   I give Sir Oakes 20ˢ Cash
to buy some Necessaries, his father is so far off.

Nov.ʳ 28.   Mrs. Anne Winthrop is propounded, in order
to be rec'd into the Church.

Nov.ʳ 30.   *Feria tertia,* Last night Sir Charles Hobbey
comes home to his own house about eleven at night;
Came from Portsmouth about the 7ᵗʰ of Octob.ʳ   Lisle
not Taken; Sir William Ashurst and Mr. Higginson are
well.   Came out with the Queen of Portugal; and my
Lord Lovelace for New York.   I call'd upon Sir Charles
in the mornin and bad him Wellcom.

Dec.ʳ 5. 1708.   Mr. Nathanael Gookin preaches in the
forenoon; I think every time he mention'd *James,* twas
with prefixing *Saint:* about 4 or 5 times that I took notice of.   I suppose he did it to confront me, and to assert

his own Liberty. Probably, he had seen the Letter I
writt to Mr. Flint.. Spake also of Reverence in Gods
Worship; he may partly intend being Cover'd in Sermon-
Time : It had better becom'd a person of some Age and
Authority to have intermeddled in things of such a nature.
Quædam Confidentia non est virtus, at audacia.

Decr 6. Major Genl and I set out for Salem; had a
good passage over Winnisīmet Ferry, and Comfortable
Journey: yet setting out late, got not thither till about
6. in the evening.

Decr 7th Hold the Court. Note. Mr. Benjamin Brown
dyes just about three aclock p. m̄., Mr. Noyes being call'd
to him, Major Genl Winthrop and I followed, and heard
him pray with him, as he lay groaning. In the evening
were invited to see his Will open'd, and hear it read;
which we did at his house.

Wednesday, Decr 8. The Court is adjourned *sine die.*
Were fain to use Candles before we got out of Pratt's
Chamber. Note. This evening Mr. Noyes pray'd last,
and spake last, with the aged and excellent Divine, Mr.
John Higginson.

Feria quinta, Decr 9. Snowy stormy Wether. The
Maj^r Genl comes to Brothers, and tells me he would not
take his Journey that Wether, so I also agree to stay. As
we were at Diñer at my Brother's Paul Doliver calls Mr.
Noyes, saying his Grandfather slept so they could not
Wake him. Mr. Noyes answer'd, He would come as soon
as he had dined; (We din'd late) He and I went together:
but before we got thither, the good man was got to a
blessed State of Rest. He expired 2 or 3 Minutes before
we got into the room. Note. A good Christian Woman
of Salem, 92 years old, died the same day Mr. Higginson
did. I had sent home David in the morning with Mr.
Dudley, and Cook; and now I began to resolve to stay the
Funerals. I consider'd I had order'd my Brother to be
sure to send me Word of Mr. Higginson's Death; and now

I my self was one of the first Witnesses of it. Col. John
Higginson is at Boston, to whom an Express is sent.

Feria tertia, Decr 10. a very Cold day, and the ·snow
fiercely driven with the Wind. Maj^r Genl calls at my
Brother's, and tells me he was going home ; he thought his
Children would hardly come else : I told him he might
write to Mr. Sergeant, and he would bring them. When
I saw he would needs go, I told him his Courage exceeded
mine as much as the title of a Major Genl did that of
a Captain. He had a very hard difficult Journey, and
told some he met, he would not have undertaken it for
£100. if he had known it had been so bad.

Feria Septima, Decr 11.th Bro^r Hirst invites me to
Diñer, there dine also Mr. Noyes, Mr. Woolcot, and my
Brother. Sister Hirst, and Cousin Betty sat down. Bro^r
Hirst kept in the warm end of the House by the fire,
being sick of the Gout. Note. This day my dear Grand-
son, Samuel Sewall, was taken sick at Brooklin.

Lord's day, Decr 12. Mr. Noyes preaches in the forenoon from a Text he formerly had taken — He that sets
his hand to the plough and looks back. — Spake considerably of Mr. Higginson especially ; and of Mr. Brown.
Mr. George Corwin preaches in the Afternoon from Rev.
14. 13. Blessed are the dead. — Mr. Noyes put him upon
giving the Blessing. I dined at my Brother's.

Feria Secunda, Decr 13.th Had Fish for diñer at Brother's ; which was put by the 7.th day. I call'd for Honey,
and Mr. Noyes and all, seem'd to aprove of it. Mr. Benjamin Brown is buried ; Tho. Bernard came in the morning from his Master, Major Brown jun^r, and invited me to
be a Bearer. Bearers, Hathorne, Sewall ; Corwin, Jno
Appleton ; Col. Higginson, Maj^r Stephen Sewall. The
Ministers present had Scarvs. Was laid in his father's
Tomb at the Burying Point. Mr. John Winthrop told me
of my Grandson's illness.

Feria tertia, Decr 14. The Apletons, Mr. Rogers, and

Mr. Fitch dine at my Brother's. In the afternoon, the aged and Excellent Divine Mr. John Higginson is laid in Gov.ʳ·Bradstreet's Tomb : Bearers, Mr. Chiever, Mr. Noyes ; Mr. Shepherd, Mr. Gerrish ; Mr. Blowers, Mr. Green. Are all of that Association, and wear their own Hair. Was laid in the Tomb a little before Sunset, had a very Serene, and very Cold Aer ; And yet the Ipswich Gentlemen went home, having lodg'd in Salem the night before. Mr. Shepherd lodges with me.

Feria quarta, Dec.ʳ 15. I take leave of my Brother ; gave Margaret 10.ˢ, Susan, 5.ˢ, Jane 3.ˢ, Mehetabel, 1.ˢ, Mitchel, 1.ˢ, Henry, 1.ˢ, Stephen, 1.ˢ, Nurse, 3.ˢ, Scipio, 2.ˢ 6.ᵈ I and Mr. Corwin rode in Mr. Kitchen's slay to the Butts ; the Curtains defended us from the most Sharp, and Opposite Wind. At the Butts took our Horses and got comfortably to Lewis's, where Capt. Norden fell in with us ; a good fat tender Goose was ready rosted. Capt. Norden, Mr. Jno. Winthrop and his Sister, Col. Taylor, Mr. Lichmore there. Note. I crav'd a Blessing, and return'd Thanks, not thinking of Mr. Corwin till had begun to return Thanks, then I *saw* him, and it almost confounded me — I crav'd his pardon, and paid his Club, saying I had defrauded the Company. I intended to go by Cambridge ; but by the way I was told the Ferry was passable ; and so I alter'd my mind, and went with Capt. Norden, and Mr. Bayly to Charlestown : the Boat was ready, and had as comfortable a passage over, as if it had been September ; entred my own House about an hour before Sun-Set, found all well, *Laus Deo*. Privat-Meeting at our House. The Condition of my Grandson was com̄ended to God. Capt. Hill return'd Thanks for my safe Return home.

Dec.ʳ 16. very Cold and Lecture day, that I could not tell how to travail over the Neck so soon after my former Journey. Dec.ʳ 17. Court sits and only 3 Justices, which hindered my going to Brooklin. And Alas ! Alas ! seventh-day Dec.ʳ 18, News is brought that the poor Child is

Dead about an hour by sun *mane.* Alas! that I should
fail seeing him alive! Now I went too late, save to weep
with my Children, and kiss, and mourn over my dear
Grandson. My son desired me to pray with his family;
which I did. Madam Dudley, the Gov^{rs} Lady, Mrs. Kath-
arin, and Mrs. Mary came in while I was there; and
brought my little Rebekah with them. Call'd at the Governour's as came home. Seem to agree to bury the child
next fourth day. I mention'd its being best to bury at
Roxbury, for my son to keep to his own parish. Govr
said I might put the Child in his father's Grave if I pleas'd.
Got home well in my slay, had much adoe to avoid Slews.
Laus Deo.

My son perceiving the Governour's aversion to have the
child buried at Roxbury, writes to me of it. I go to the
Governour's on Tuesday, and speak about Bearers, He
leaves it to me; so does my son; as I come home I speake
for Sir Ruggles, Tim^o Ruggles, son of Martha Woodbridge,
my ancient acquaintance and Townswoman; and Col.
Checkley's son for the other. Wednesday, Decr 22, 1708.
My dear Grandson, Saml Sewall, is buried; Son and daughter went first: Then Govr and I; then Madam Dudley
led by Paul Dudley esqr; Then Joseph and Hañah; Then
Mr. Wm Dudley and daughter Hirst — Major Genl and
his Lady here with their Coach — Mr. Bromfield, Stoddard
&c. Gave Mr. Walter a Lutestring scarf, Bearers, Capt.
Noyes, Mrs. Bayley, scarves. Decr 30. Daughter Hirst
is much oppress'd with a Fear of Death; desires to speak
with me: I go to her presently after Lecture, and discourse with her, and she seems better compos'd. Seventh-
day, Jany 1. Is a very pleasant day. Jany 2. Cloudy
cold day. Mr. Bromfield is pray'd for, who is in much
pain by reason of his disorder'd great Toe; was very ill
last Lecture-day. Elder Bridgham lyes sick. Dr. Mather
is kept in by the Gout.

xr. 31. *Feria sexta,* Comittee meets for incorporating

the Town. Mr. Bridgham was absent, being taken sick
that day.

Midweek, Jan.ʸ 5. Mr. Cotton Mather visits me, then
(Mr. Mather not gon) Sir Charles Hobby visits me : While
they were [here] Capt. Chandler tells me in the entry
that elder Bridgham was dead; I come in and tell it the
Company.

Jan.ʸ 6ᵗʰ presently after Lecture, the Act of Parliament
regulating Coin,¹ is published by Beat of Drum and Sound
of Trumpet. In Council a Spaniard's petition is read
praying his Freedom. Govʳ refers it to the Judges. Mr.
Cook notifies Capt. Teat to apear to morrow. Jan.ʸ 7. Petition is read, Capt. Teat pleads the Govʳ told him he was
a Slave ; Capt. Teat alledg'd that all of that Color were
Slaves : Obliges to have the man forth-coming at Charlestown Court.

Jan.ʸ 8. My worthy friend Mr. Bridgham is buried :
Bearers Mr. Cook, Col. Hutchinson ; Elder Cop, Deacon
Jnᵒ Marion ; Deacon Isaiah Tay, Deacon Thomas Hubbard. Is buried in the Old burying place : Went up by
Mr. Dudley's House into King street, and so up between
the Town-house and Mr. Phillip's. He was a Righteous,
Mercifull, publick-Spirited man, very usefull in the Town :
was born the 17ᵗʰ Jan.ʸ 165½ The Lord sanctify this awful
sudden Stroak ; and help us duly to lay it to heart.

Note. Mr. Bridgham buried a Carolina Indian Man last
Monday ; and another the Monday before ; One about 30.
the other 40 years of Age, which he bought not a year
ago.

Feria tertia, Jan.ʸ 11. Dr. John Chip is buried in the
New burying place. Bearers, Deacon Hubbard, Mr. Pitts ;
Dr. Clark, Foyes ; Dr. Stephenson, Groundsill.

Feria quinta, Jan.ʸ 13ᵗʰ. 170⅘ Mr. Bridge preaches

---

¹ Probably 6 Anne, c. 30, " An act for ascertaining the rates of foreign
coins in her Majesty's plantations in America." This was to have effect
after the first day of May, 1709. — EDS.

from Gen. 12. 2.   Seem'd to make it with respect to Elder Bridgham; 112. Psalm sung; part of it.   Use.   Its a frown of God when such remov'd.   Should not succumb, but be more active.   Note. Mr. Colman went and sat in the pulpit this day.   It seems Deacon Avery, a very worthy man, died the last Moneth.

Jan.ʸ 24ᵗʰ I propound to Joseph to pray with his Mother and me for his Sister Mary ; he declines it and I pray, and was assisted with considerable Agony and Importunity with many Tears.   The Lord hear and help.

Jan.ʸ 28. I went to Mr. Hubbard's Lecture. He preach'd from Philip. 3. 3. Excellently.   It begun to rain as came out of the Meetinghouse.   So I took leave of Mr. Hubbard and came home well by Day-light, though there was a great Fogg.   *Laus Deo.*   John Trowbridge assisted me in setting up my Horse and helping me to him again when I came away.

Satterday, Jan.ʸ 29.   Our Tenant, Nurse Smith, is taken sick.

Jan.ʸ 31.   Mr. Spensar calls here, and I enquire of him about Mr. Gerrish of Wenham, what he should say ; He answer'd not directly ; but said his Cousin would come if he might have admittance.   I told him I heard he went to Mr. Coney's daughter.   He said he knew nothing of that : I desired him to enquire, and tell me.   I understood he undertook it ; but he came no more.

Feb.ʳ 2.   Note. Smith dyes.   3.ᵈ Sore Storm of Snow; Mr. Pemberton preaches.

Feb.ʳ 4ᵗʰ Nurse Smith buried.   Coming from the Grave I ask'd Mr. Pemberton whether S. Gerrish courted Mr. Coney's daughter ; he said No ; not now.   Mr. Coney thought his daughter young.

Feb.ʳ 5.   Storm of Snow, and I goe not out.

Feb.ʳ 6. is a Comfortable day.   Feb.ʳ 7ᵗʰ I deliver a Letter to S. Gerrish to inclose and send to his father, which he promises to doe.

Febr. 8ᵗʰ Sub-Comittee meets about drawing up a
Charter. Febr. 9th. Midweek, Mrs. Hañah Glover dies
in the 76ᵗʰ year of her Age; was widow of Mr. Habakkuk
Glover, daughter of Mr. John Eliot, who married here,
and this daughter was born at Roxbury in the Fall 1633,
just about the time Mrs. Rock was born. So that this
Gentlewoman, though born in N. E. pass'd not only 60.
but 70. years, and became a Great Grandmother in our
Israel.

Feria Sexta, Febr. 11ᵗʰ 170⅜ Mrs. Hañah Glover is
buried in a Tomb in the New burying place. Bearers,
Winthrop, Sewall; Addington, Sergeant; Fayerwether,
Checkly. Very Cold day.

Febr. 17. I receive Mr. Gerrishes Letter just at night.
Febr. 18ᵗʰ I leave Word at Mr. Gerrishes shop that I
would speak with him after Mr. Bromfield's Meeting was
over. He came and I bid him wellcom to my house as to
what his father writt about. So late hardly fit then to
see my daughter, apointed him to come on Tuesday, invited him to Super; I observ'd he drunk to Mary in the
third place. Febr. 23. When I came from the Meeting
at Mr. Stephens's I found him in the Chamber, Mr. Hirst
and wife here. It seems he ask'd to speak with Mary
below; her Mother was afraid because the fire was newly
made: and Mr. Hirst brought him up. This I knew not
of: He ask'd me below, whether it were best to frequent
my House before his father came to Town: I said that
were the best introduction: but he was wellcom to come
before, and bid him come on Friday night. Febr. 24. Mr.
Hirst tells me Mr. Gerrish courted Mr. Coñey's daughter:
I told him I knew it, and was uneasy. In the evening
daughter Hirst came hether, I supose to tell that Mr.
Gerrish had courted Mr. Coney's daughter: and if she
should have Mr. Stoddard, she would mend her market.
Friday, Febr. 25. Madam Winthrop, Oliver, and Mico
visit my wife. In the evening S. Gerrish comes not; we

expected him, Mary dress'd her self: it was a painfull disgracefull disapointment. Febr. 26. Satterday, Sam Gerrish goes to Wenham unknown to me, till Lords-day night Capt. Greenleaf told me of it. He was not seen by us till Wednesday March 2, David saw him. March, 5. Satterday, I go to Brooklin, and visit my son and daughter Sewall, who is sick. March, 7. I pay Mr. Minott his Account. March, 8. I visit Mr. Cotton Mather.

March, 9. Meeting at Mr. Stoddard's. Mr. B. Pemberton dyes. March, 10. Go to Mr. C. Mather's. March, 11ᵗʰ S. Gerrish calls here. March, 12. Mr. B. Pemberton buried; Bearers, Capt. Fitch, Mr. Harris; Mr. Cutler, Mr. Noyes; Mr. Edʷ Winslow, Mr. Wentworth. Simson, the Brickmaker, dyes. March, 14. The Reverᵈ Mr. Joseph Gerrish comes to our house in the evening. Dines with us March 15ᵗʰ Tuesday. At night his Son comes, and Mary goes to him. Mr. Gerrish goes home on Wednesday. His son comes and is entertain'd then also. Friday March 18. last night Mr. Thomas Downs fell into his own fire in the night and was burnt to death. Both his hands burnt off, and burnt to Ashes: His face so burnt away, that what remain'd resembled a Fire-brand.

Friday-night. S. Gerrish comes. Tells Mary except Satterday and Lord's-day nights intends to wait on her every night; unless some extraordinary thing hapen.

Satterday, March 19. I call at S. Gerishes shop; he was not within: but came in presently: I desired him to Bind me a Psalm-Book in Calv's Leather.

Lord's Day March, 20. Mr. Downs is buried in the old Burying place; Bearers Capt. Dumer, Dyer; Capt. Fayerwether, Foy; Mr. Tho. Walker, Timᵒ Clark.

March, 21. Mr. Cutler pulls out a Cheek Tooth of my right uper Jaw. It was loose and corrupted, and hurt me.

Satterday, March, 26. Col. Hathorne, Mr. Corwin, Mr. Taft and I set out for Plimouth, get to Job Randall's

about Sun-setting. March, 27ᵗʰ Mr. Eels preaches in the
Forenoon; Mr. Toft in the Afternoon: sup at Mr. Eels.

March, 28. Set out for Plimouth. Got thither before
any stress of Rain. Mr. Dudley and Cook came in very
wet. March, 30. I go into the Meeting-house. March, 31.
Col. Church goes with us p. m̄. Between Jones's River
and the old Rode my Horse falls; yet I fell not off; neither
had I any hurt. Lodge at Bairstos's.

April, 1. Breakfast at Cushings: Got home well about
3 p. m̄. *Laus Deo.* Mrs. Barthol. Green died the day
we begun our Journey.

Monday, April, 4. Genˡ Council, which prevented my
Training in the Artillery. I sent my Pike, and went my
self; and the Secretary follow'd me into Shrimpton's
Lane, and took me off. Mr. Pemberton had discouraged
me before, but I had thought to have Train'd this once;
had I not been thus call'd away.

Tuesday Apr. 5. I went to Roxbury Lecture.

Thorsday, Apr. 7. Mr. Neh. Hobart dines, and prays
with us. Friday, Apr. 8ᵗʰ Guns are fired at the Castle
76. Sconce, 24, and Flags hoisted half way the Staff on
account of the death of Prince George, the Queen's Consort. The Secretary had an Address of the Lord's to
Her Majesty on that head, dated Novʳ 20ᵗʰ. Govʳ is abed
sick of the Gravel. The Taking of several Vessels laden
with Provisions on the back of the Cape over against
Eastham last Wednesday, Apr. 6. 11. *mane*, makes the
Town very sad. Writts are gon out for an Assembly,
dated April, 6.

Apr. 8. Joseph takes purging Physick, which works
kindly.

April, 12. Joseph goes home. April, 11. Capt. Roger
Lawson dies. Apr. 13. buried; Bearers; Mr. James
Smith, John Campbell; Mr. George, Colman; Capt. Steel,
Mr. Joseph Wadsworth. Aged about 45. years. Mr.
Cook and I went together, next the Relations; then Mr.
Addington, Sergeant.

April, 15.   Madam Winthrop sends Mingo to invite me
to the Meeting at her House.   Mr. Pemberton preach'd
from Ps. 71. 16.   I will go on in the strength of the Lord
God.   Doctrine Believers sensible of the Danger and
difficulties that are in their Christian Course, Trust only
to the Strength of God.   Ps. 73. 23, 24. 25, 26.   Sung
S.t David's Tune, which I set.   Drunk Ale, Tea, Wine.

Apr. 22. 1709.   Went to Braintrey, visited Cousin's
sick wife: rid with him to Copeland's; to the farm he
hires.   Din'd with him, Mrs. Flint, Mr. Flint of the College: Came home to Mrs. Kate's Funeral.

Apr. 23.   Went to the Castle, and dined there upon
Col. Winthrop's Invitation.   Went from Scarlet's Wharf,
and Landed there agen about 5.   Mr. Russel, Hutchinson,
Addington, Sewall, Townsend, Hutchinson, Belchar, Stoddard, sat down with the Gov.r and Col. Winthrop.   Capt.
Tuthill, and Mr. Cutler, the Chaplain, sat at a little Table
by themselves.   Came away about four p. m.

Tuesday, April, 26.th visited Mr. Cotton Mather, who
has been indispos'd.

Wednesday, Apr. 27.   Mr. Cooke and I visited Mr.
Russell, who is very sick ; was taken on the Lord's Day.
He was glad to see us, and Thankfull; Visited Mr. Jenner.
Thorsday, April, 28.   Mr. Russell dies about 11. a. m.   He
was a good Christian, and right New-England Man ; is I
think the last of them chosen in the year 1680: about 68.
years old.

Friday, April, 29. 1709.   Town-Meeting to choose Representatives.   I was chosen Moderator.   Voters — 204.

John Clark esqr.	173.	Mr. Isa Tay — 53.	3.d voters	159.
Capt. Tho. Hutchinson	142.	Mr. W.m Clark 42.	Fitch — 82 chosen.	
Mr. James Barns	128	W.m Clark	35.	
		2.d voters	181.	
Capt. Tho. Fitch	73.	Fitch	78.	
Capt. Ephr. Savage	68	Savage	47.	
Col. Checkly	57	Checkly	45.	

Voted £100 to our Brethren of Rumney-Marsh to help build them a Meeting-house. Chose Jury-men for the Super.ʳ Court. I pray'd that God would not destroy the Town, twas a New Town : — dismissed about 2. p. m. Mr. Pemberton begun with Prayer.

Friday, Apr. 29. 1709. about 4. *post* $\overline{m}$. the Dragon Frigat arrives at Nantasket, in whom come Col. Nicholson, Col. Vetch, Mr. Jonathan Belchar, Mr. Giles Dyer, Mr. Bill, Mr. Walley, Capt. John Alden and others. First Mr. Dier tells me that Mr. Higginson was dead of the Small Pocks; but as to the time incongruously. Though it was now about 9. at night, I go to Mr. Belchar, who Confirms this Melancholy News. Saith he died in November, was buried in the night in Bow-Church: He was at his Funeral. Alas alas! that he should escape 1000. deaths in going to the East-Indies, dwelling there, and returning; and now to die so soon in London of the Small Pocks! The Lord help me not to Trust in Man; but in GOD.[1] They tell us St. John's in New-found-Land was Taken by the French last Dec.ʳ which is like to prove a great and surprising Evil to this place.

April, 30. The Queen's Letter is read in Council about the Canada Expedition, and Col. Vetch's Instructions, to which exact Obedience is comānded. Dine at North's. From thence go to Mr. Russell's Funeral. Bearers, Govʳ Dudley, Govʳ Nicholson; Mr. Cook, Hutchinson Elisha; Sewall, Addington; Phillips, Lynde. was buried in a Grave.

May, 2. Being Artillery day, and Mr. Higginson dead, I put on my Mourning Rapier; and put a black Ribband into my little cane. When I enter'd the Council-Chamber, the Govʳ with an Air of displeasure said, You are Chidden! pretending my late coming; though I think I was

---

[1] Sewall had heartily desired that Mr. Higginson should have been appointed Governor of this Province. — EDS.

there before eleven, and am, I think, the most constant attender of Councils.

I dined with the Artillery at Powells, whether Maxwell came and warn'd me to Council at 3. There I waited all alone, as many times I doe. At length the Govr came. When Col. Hathorne had his Quota 76. given him, he expostulated a little; upon which the Govr was very angry, and took him up with very smart words. I was on the same side of the board, and saw his Warrant. Then I went to my own, and seeing a number of Letters ly under the Secretaryes hand, I made a motion to see one which the Secretary declin'd: and the Govr taking notice of it with a very angry Air said to me, I will not be Govern'd by You!

May, 6th 1709. Mrs. Abigail Russell, widow of James Russell esqr. was buried. Bearers; Mr. Cook, Hutchinson Elisha; Sewall, Addington; Phillips, Lynde.

May, 7, 1709. About 6. or 7. p. m̄. Col. Lynde of Charlestown has his Malt-House and Dwelling house burnt down, Wind blowing hard at South-West, and very dry. One house more burnt. Mr. Leverett returns from New-York.

Monday, May, 9. 1709. Major Thomas Brown esqr, of Sudbury, was buried in the Old Burying place; Bearers, Cook, Sewall; El^m Hutchinson, Townsend; Jer. Dumer, P. Dudley. Scarvs and Gloves. Company Train; And a Declaration is read to encourage the Expedition to Canada. In the evening Mr. Williams of Derefield comes in to see me.

May, 16. 1709. Set out with David for Ipswich, Mr. Harris went over the Ferry with us, and went through. Dined at Salem, at Brother's. May, 19. Went to Newbury; visited Mr. Payson, sister Northend, Nelson, Mrs. Phillips. Got into the house of Abraham Adams where we staid during the Thunder shower. Lodg'd at Sister Gerrishes.

May, 20. visited Cousin Jacob Top̄an, laid a stone in
the Foundation of the Meetinghouse at Pipe-staff Hill.
3ˢ. Went home in the Rain to Sister Gerrishes; visited
my Cousin Gerrish, Pierce, Top̄an, Sweet; dined at Broʳ
Top̄an's. May, 21. visited Cousin Rolf: went with Broʳ
Moodey to Byfield, and lodg'd there.

May, 22. Went to Meeting at Byfield, din'd with
Cousin Hale: lodg'd at Broʳ Moodeys. May, 23. Set out
for Boston; Rid from Ipswich to Wenham in the Rain.
Din'd with Mr. Gerrish; and went not thence because of
the Rain. May, 24. it Rains much harder so lodge there
again. May, 25. Rise early, and set out for Boston. A
little before we came to Phillips's the Ipswich Gentlemen
overtook me; had the pleasure of their Company. At
Wiñisimet overtook Mr. Corwin, went over together; got
to Boston about ten. Heard Mr. Rawson preach the
Election sermon — Before your feet stumble upon the
dark Mountains. Dine at the Green Dragon. Mr. John
Clark chosen Speaker.

ELECTION.

Winthrop	82	Plimouth	
Hathorne	73	Winslow	82
Elisha Hutchinson	82	Pain	54
Sewall	84	Cushing	45
Addington	82	Otis	79
Brown	69		
Phillips	76	Main	
Corwin	77	Eᵐ Hutchinson	66
Foster	70	Plaisted	71
Sergeant	50	Wheelright	65
Townsend	51		
Jnº Ap̄leton	74	Zagadahock	
Higginson	82	Lynde	56
Partridge	69		
Belcher	54	At Large.	
Bromfield	57	Walley	42
Hunt	59	Norden	37
Epes	37		

Note.   The number of Voters at first was 86.   Council 19 } 86
                                                  Dep   67 }

Tuesday, May, 31.   Mr. S. Stoddard marries Madam
Shrimpton privatly. . See Aug. 13. 1708.   This week Mrs.
Blower dies, then her Husband : Capt. Sill, Mr. Lemon,
and Alas, alas! June, 3. The Rever^d Mr. Pierpont dies at
Reading ; a very great Loss!

June, 3.   Mary returns well from Wenham.   *Laus Deo.*

May. 26.   Mrs. Sarah Pemberton buried.   Bearers
Sewall, Sergeant; Walley, Checkly; Hill, Williams.

June, 6.   Artillery-day.   I went with Mr. John Wil-
liams, of Dearfield, to the Funeral of Mr. Pierpont at
Reading.   His Bearers were Leverett, Brattle ; Wads-
worth, Colman ; Green, Fox.   Mr. Jonathan Corwin and
I followed next after the Relations : None else of the
Council there.

Mrs. Wyllys dyed this day.

June 8.   Mrs. Wyllys buried.   Bearers Cook, Sewall ;
Phillips, Lynde ; Hill, Marion.

June, 22, 1709.   Going to visit sick Mr. Gerrish, Samuel; I met Dr. Mather, who tells me that yesterday, he
was 70. years old ; so was born June, 21. 1639.

June, 17. 1709.   Friday, I treat the Govr at Homes's :
had two dishes of Green pease : Sir Charles Hobbey, Mr.
Comissary, Mr. Leverett, Lt Col. Ballentine, Mr. Pemberton, Major Pigeon, Capt. of the Matroses, Eleven in all :
paid 36^s June, 24.   Elisa. Davis, Widow, is buried ; Mr.
Dering, Hill ; Williams, Meers ; Blish, Draper, Bearers.
They invited me and my wife by sending us good Gloves.

June, 27.   Col. Hutchinson, Townsend, Mr. Speaker,
and Col. Checkley meet at my house in the Afternoon to
discourse with Mr. Allen about Imprinting the Bills.   He
offers to doe it for 2^d a Plate ; he had 1½ last.

Midweek, July, 13. 1709.   N.B.   Last night, between 2
or 3 hours after midnight, my wife complain'd of Smoak ; I
presently went out of Bed, and saw and felt the Chamber
very full of Smoak to my great Consternation.   I slipt on

my Cloaths except Stockings, and run out of one Room into another above, and below Stairs, and still found all well but my own Bed-chamber. I went into Garret and rouz'd up David, who fetch'd me a Candle. My wife fear'd the Brick side was a-fire, and the children endangered. She fled thither, and call'd all up there. While she was doing this, I felt the partition of my Bed-Chamber Closet warm; which made me with fear to unlock it, and going in I found the Deal-Box of Wafers all afire, burning livelily; yet not blazing. I drew away the papers nearest to it, and call'd for a Bucket of Water. By that time it came, I had much adoe to recover the Closet agen: But I did, and threw my Water on it, and so more, and quench'd it thorowly. Thus with great Indulgence GOD saved our House and Substance, and the Company's Paper. This night, as I lay down in my Bed, I said to my Wife, that the Goodness of God apeared, in that we had a Chamber, a Bed, and Company. If my Wife had not waked me, we might have been consumed. And it seems admirable, that the opening the Closet-Door did not cause the Fire to burst forth into an Unquenchable Flame. The Box was 18 inches over, Closet full of loose papers, boxes, Cases, some Powder. The Window-Curtain was of Stubborn Woolen and refus'd to burn though the Iron-Bars were hot with the fire. Had that burnt it would have fired the pine-shelves and files of Papers and Flask and Bandaliers of powder. The Pine-Floor on which the Box stood, was burnt deep, but being well plaister'd between the Joysts, it was not burnt through. The Closet under it had Hundreds of Reams of the Company's[1] Paper in it. The plaistered Wall is mark'd by the Fire so as to resemble a Chimney back. Although I forbad mine to cry Fire; yet quickly after I had quench'd it; the Cham-

---

[1] Probably the paper belonged to the Society for Propagating the Gospel, for printing the Indian Bible. — EDS.

ber was full of Neighbours and Water. The smell of Fire pass'd on me very much; which lasted some days. We imagine a Mouse might take our lighted Candle out of the Candle-stick on the hearth and dragg it under my closet-door behind the Box of Wafers. The good Lord sanctify this Threatening; and his Parental Pity in improving our selves for the Discovery of the fire, and Quenching it. The Lord teach me what I know not; and wherein I have done amiss help me to doe so no more!

July, 21. A Council is warn'd to meet presently after Lecture before Dinner. The Govr took up Col. Vetch with him, who sat at the end of the Table leaning his Elbow on the Arm of the Gov^{rs} Chair; They both urg'd the sending a Flagg of Truce to Port-Royal, to fetch off Capt. Myles and others. Mr. Secretary and I oposed it as that that would expose us to be ridicul'd by our Enemies; they would detain our Flagg during their pleasure; the Canada Expedition being known to them. I mention'd the Suddeness of the Council. So the Govr adjourn'd it to Friday at 2. p. m.

Friday, July, 22. Maxwell warns me again to attend the Govr at 11. *mane* in Council. Govr and Col. Vetch sat as yesterday, and vehemently urged the sending a Flagg of Truce for poor Myles, as the Govr often spake. Mr. Secretary and I opos'd it. Mr. E^m Hutchinson said would doe no good. I mention'd that it might be laid before the Genl Court that was to sit on Tuesday. But the Govr first order'd that to be prorogued to the next week; however that was not so far gon but it might have been stay'd; for nothing was entred. I considered also the daily Expectation of the Fleet's arrival, where we might have further direction. I mention'd the parting with Men, Sloops, Provisions in vain. Col. Foster, with some Heat, said, He was ashâm'd to hear any mention Charge! Mr. Secretary hinted they would by our Flagg have notice the Fleet was not come. But all was rejected with disdain. Col. Vetch urg'd once and again, that if Capt. Myles were not sent for, it might tempt him to turn to the French, as Du Bart did. Twas urg'd that the Flagg was going when Col. Vetch, arrived; and that caused us unanimously to surcease, and to dismiss Col. Taylor. That was blown off as nothing. I spake against sending the Strong Beer to Supercass,[1] he had dealt basely at New-found-Land and at Port Royal. Col. Vetch urg'd, that if they deny'd to send our Captives, they should know how to Treat the French Prisoners: I answer'd, we knew already: The French had broke their Faith in not sending the Captives. Capt. Tuthill's Accounts.

In the evening, Mr. Mayhew and I bath our selves in Charles River behind Blackston's point.

July, 23. Mr. Mayhew goes to Natick to preach there to morrow. Between 4 and 5. p. m. is a great Gust of Wind and Rain.

July, 25. Mr. Banister dyes.

July, 26. Go to Cambridge Court with Major Walley by Charlestown, got thither before Col. Hathorne. Got home to the Funeral.

July, 27th lodge at Mr. Brattle's.

July. 28. Finish the Court, and get to Boston so as to hear great part of Mr. C. Mather's Fast-Prayer, and Dr. Mather's Sermon out of PS. 72. Amen, and Amen.

Aug[t] 5. The Gernsey arrives 4 weeks from New-found-Land, in whom comes Col. Moodey, the Gov[r] he brought thither. This morn, Madam Shepard dies, which I heard of at Charlestown, whither I went to Lecture. Mr. Brad-street preached from PS. 46. 1. a Present help &c.

Augt. 6. Saturday, Madam Shepard is laid in the

---

[1] Brouillan succeeded Villebon in the government of Acadie in 1702, and was himself succeeded, at his death, by M. Subercase. The latter successfully defended Port Royal from the Provincials under Colonel Marsh; but, as we shall see, was obliged, in 1710, to surrender to a new expedition. — EDS.

Tomb with her Excellent Husband and Son. Bearers Mr. Neh. Hobart, Mr. Peter Thacher; Mr. Angier, Mr. John Danforth; Mr. Colman, Mr. Bradstreet. She died at her Grandaughter Holman's at Milton and was brought thence to Charlestown by Water, and buried from her own House. I and Col. Phillips followed the Mourners, Capt. Belchar and the President next. But very few there besides Relations.[1]

Augt 9th Col. Hobbey's Regiment musters, and the Govr orders the Maquas[2] to be there and see them; and acquainted them there was not one of those Men in Arms they had seen at Roxbury. At night Sir Charles had a great Treat for the Govr, 5 Maquas, &c.

Augt 11th The Govr has the 5 Maquas to the Castle and Nantasket to shew them the strength of the Fort and of the Five Men of War. They spread all their Finery to set out their Ships. Note. As I came from Charlestown

---

[1] This was Anna (Tyng), widow of Rev. Thomas Shepard. Her daughter Anna (or Hannah) married Daniel Quincy, cousin of Mrs. Sewall. (See Vol. I. p. xxiii.) — EDS.

[2] These were, evidently, the five chiefs of the Maquas [Vol. I. 329] or Mohawks, then en route for England. Neal (Hist. of New England, p. 602) says they were *Teeyeeneenhogaprow* and *Sagayeanquaprahton* of the Maquas, *Elowohkaom* and *Ohneeyeathtonnoprow* of the River Sachem, and the Ganajohahore Sachem. He calls them "four Indian Kings of the Six Nations that lye between New England and Canada." In England considerable attention was paid them, and the Queen promised to send missionaries. In New York Documents, V. 224, is a note of a council held Aug. 19, 1710, at which Kaquendero was the orator, and he mentions "those of our nation who have lately been in England." In Notes and Queries, 2d S. VIII. 417, 455, we find mention of a letter written by these chiefs, dated Boston, July 21, 1710, directed to Archbishop Tenison, on occasion of their safe arrival. Two of the names are *Sagayouquaraughta* and *Etawacom*. Addison, in No. 50 of the Spectator, refers to them, and makes the third chief *E Tow O Koam*, "King of the rivers." It is mentioned that Matthew, Lord Aylmer, entertained them on board the Royal Sovereign in 1710; and that they were received by Her Majesty, Queen Anne, April 19, 1710, "in great ceremony." Major Pigeon, one of the officers who came over with them, read a speech, printed by Neal, p. 603. They sailed from Plymouth, in the "Dragon," May 7, 1710. — EDS.

Lecture I met Mr. Bernon[1] in Sudbury Street; he turn'd from me and would not have seen me; but I Spake to him. Quickly after I saw Col. Vetch in the Council Chamber, and said to him, Mr. Bernon is in Town, as I told you he would: He made light of it, and said he had bought Cider of him; he suppos'd he had business here. I observ'd he was at Sir Charles's Muster, and went round the Body with his Sword by his Side, follow'd the Gov[rs] Attendants. Aug[t] 12. At Council 'twas enquired whether Blew should go to Edgartown to convoy vessels there loaden with Bread: Col. Foster much opposed it, and some others; pleading we had Bread enough. I argued the Benefit of having Bread in time of War; and the great Hurt twould be to us, if it should fall into the Enemies Hands. At last it was agreed, that if at the foot of the Shoals, whether his cruise led him, he had a fair wind, he might goe. I had urg'd the Certainty of doing good if Blew went.

'Twas mention'd in Council, that 300 Eastern Indians, Men Women and Children, were gon to the 5 Nations to pray leave to dwell with them; and that others refusing them, they were gon to the Senecas: The Govr mention'd that the Gentlemen of Albany might be written to that they might be with the Maquas where they might [be] under Inspection. But the Council were of the mind, The further off the better; would more easily be apt to forget their own Country, and Less ready at so great a distance to añoy. And that twas best for us (they being Rebels) to say nothing about it.

---

[1] Gabriel Bernon was one of the Huguenot exiles who came to Boston, and was one of the commissioners of the English Corporation for Propagating the Gospel here. He was one of the persons naturalized Jan. 5, 1688, as recorded in a list published in Agnew's "Protestant Exiles" (London, 1871), I. p. 46–48. The same list was entered on our Suffolk Deeds, Lib. 14, fol. 212, "at the desire of Gabriel Bernon," July 20, 1688. The names of Abraham Tourtelot, Rev. Peter Fountain, and Isaac Converse, occur therein. — EDS.

Midweek, Augt 24. In the evening Mr. Pemberton marrys Mr. Samuel Gerrish, and my daughter Mary: He begun with Prayer, and Mr. Gerrish the Bridegroom's father concluded: Mr. Mayhew was present.

Augt 25. Mr. Cotton Mather, Mr. Pemberton and wife, and others, dine with us after Lecture. In the even I invited the Govr and Council to drink a Glass of Wine with me; About 20 came; viz. Govr, Winthrop, Hathorne, Elisha Hutchinson, Addington, Brown, Foster, Sergeant, Walley, Phillips, Townsend, Bromfield, Eliakim Hutchinson, Corwin, Higginson, Jno Apleton, Lynde, Hunt, Cushing, Norden, Epes. Gave them variety of good Drink, and at going away a large piece of Cake Wrap'd in Paper. They very heartily wish'd me Joy of my daughter's Marriage.

Septr. 10. Mr. Mayhew takes his Journey homeward, John Neesnumin, and James Printer[1] being gon before.

Septr 17. Mr. Green finishes printing Mr. Whiting's Oration.[2] Septr 21. When the Dept^s could not be brought into the Congress of the Governours; at last by some aplication they gave 80£ to bear the charges of the Govr and them that should go. I got away to the privat Meeting at C. Savages, when this was transacted. General Court rises.

Septr 24. Col. Hathorne, Mr. Corwin and I set out for Taunton. David waits on me. Dine at Morey's at Punkapôg. There Mr. Crossman meets us, and conducts us in the new Rode; rid near 14 miles without a house. Saw pleasant Winnicunnet Pond, and the River issuing out of it.[3] Got to Mr. Danforth's about 6. where we lodged.

---

[1] See Vol. I. p. 15, *note*. — EDS.

[2] We presume this to be a Latin oration which Rev. Samuel Whiting, pastor of Lynn, delivered at Harvard in 1649. The copy in our Society's Library contains sixteen pages, but lacks the title. — EDS.

[3] Winneconnet Pond is in the easterly part of the town of Norton, and receives the waters of Canoe River and Leach's Stream. It spreads over about one hundred and twenty-two acres. (Gazetteer.) — EDS.

Septr 25th   Lord's Day Mr. Danforth preached from Ps. 90. 14, 15, 16, 17, verses.   Work.   The Church-State, Worship and Ordinance, which were brought out of Egypt into Canaan to enjoy, are chiefly intended.   Doct. 1.   The great, and chief desire of the people of God, that which lyes upermost in their hearts is, that God's work may flourish in their Generation, and in succeeding Generations.   Doct. 2.   Every Christian should account it his Duty to put to his helping Hand, to forward God's Work in the World.   Every one should do something in bringing others home to Christ.

Septr 26.   We went to Bristol with Capt. Leñard, Mr. King.   Col. Byfield, Mr. Makentash, with the Sheriff and others, met us at Mr. Saffin's.   I lodg'd at Peter Reynolds's.[1]

Septr. 27.   Open'd the Court, empanel'd the Jurys, heard one Cause.   When came to Diñer found Major Walley come from Devotion's.

Septr 28.   Indians are Try'd for Murder and found Guilty.   29.   Mr. Saffin is Cast in his Action of Review against Mr. George.   Indians are condemned.   Court ends.

Friday, 7^r 30.   Col. Hathorn, Mr. Corwin, Cook ride out of Town early, near an hour before Sun-rising.   Major Walley and I set out about 9. a-clock.   Daniel and David waiting on us.   Call at Mr. Greenwood's, who is dangerously sick of a malignant Fever, to our great surprise.   Mrs. Greenwood at parting, with Tears, desired prayers for him; and that would leave word at Caleb Stedman's at Roxbury, to acquaint his Bro^r at Newtown.

---

[1] Robert Reynolds was one of the early settlers in Boston, and left only one son, Nathaniel, who moved to Bristol, R. I.   Peter was, doubtless, the son of the latter, born in 1670.   A century later a branch of this family returned to Boston; and one of them, Dr. Edward Reynolds, has been especially noted for his professional skill and his connection with public charities. — EDS.

Dine at Smith's; Bait at Devotion's. Lodge at Billinge's; Many stars were to be seen before we got thither. Cornil, a Quaker, in company. From Billings's writt to Mr. Man, enclosing an Oration. Left ten with Mr. Sparhawk and a 10ˢ Bill: a Douz ditto with Mr. Danforth. 8r. 1. Bait at Dedham. I go to Mr. Belcher's, where I drink warm chockelat, and no Beer; find my self much refresh'd by it after great. Sweating to day, and yesterday. Got home to Diñer about One. *Laus Deo.* My Horse went very hard, which made me strain hard on my Stirrup and contract a Lameness on my Left Hip of a Week's continuance, or more. If I might with Jacob prevail with GOD for his Blessing; and be surnamed Israel, how happy should I be! though I should go limping.[1]

Octʳ 2. Lords Suꝑer. Mrs. Rock and my wife there. I hope Christ welcomed us. Mr. Pemberton said he was glad to see me come home, 8ʳ 1. when I went to him to acquaint him with Mr. Greenwood's Sickness.

8ʳ 3. Govʳ calls a Council.[2] I acquainted the Govʳ with the Condemnation of the two Indian Men at Bristol for Murder, and the time intended for their Execution. Col. Vetch mutter'd somthing as if there was no malice prepense: I told him of the man's kicking his wife into the fire. He said he heard not of that. Capt. Blackmore

---

1 The reference is, of course, to Genesis xxxii. 24–31. — EDS.

2 It may be well to mention here that, during 1709, the Colony had been kept excited by warlike preparations. Colonel Vetch came over with instructions for a grand expedition against the French. Five regiments of regulars were to be sent over; Massachusetts and Rhode Island were to raise fifteen hundred troops, and the southern colonies twelve hundred men. Quebec and Montreal were to be attacked. The Massachusetts men were ready by.May 20th, and were kept ready till September, while the southern troops, under Nicholson, were encamped at Wood Creek. October 11 a vessel arrived at Boston with advices that the English troops had been sent to Portugal, but allowing the Americans to attack Port Royal if they judged proper. The fleet refused to join, and the Legislature desired the Governor to discharge the transports and disband the troops. (Hutchinson, Hist. II. 178, 179.) — EDS.

arrives this day and brings the Wellcom Orders for going on to print the Bible [Indian] and countermanding the selling any more of the Genoa Paper, with a considerable Remittance.

Oct.ʳ 4.ᵗʰ I shew the Letters to Dr. Mather and Mr. C. M.

Oct.ʳ 5. Midweek, Mr. Hirst and I take a Calash and meet Mr. Gerrish with John behind him. Son Gerrish, his wife and Hannah in a Calash. It was a little beyond Newhill's, who now keeps the Swan, that we met them. Din'd there, and there Mr. Gerrish would return, delivering up his Charge to me. As came homeward went over Charlestown Hill on the Neck of Land; and came into the Rode again by Mr. Emerson's. Got home very well, and I went to our Meeting at Mr. Thornton's. *Laus Deo.*

Octob.ʳ 6. 1709. Mr. C. Mather preaches from Prov. 14. 14. Backslider in heart shall be filled with his own Ways. Mention'd the indulgence of Adonijak; the prophet Micajah; not the prophet, but the King was hurt by his Estrangement.

Octob.ʳ 7. I read to Mrs. Rock; Mr. Allen came in and said I was Eyes to her. Octob.ʳ 28, 1709. In Council, Gov.ʳ said, They know nothing by me but what is of Honor. I have great faults, but they do not know them. Col. Nicholson is not yet Governour here, nor none of them, i. e. the Deputies. Said the Letter [1] sign'd by himself, Col. Nicholson, Vetch, was as good as that the Court had given to Col. Nicholson.

Friday, Nov.ʳ 4. 1709. The Gov.ʳ invites the Council and Representatives to Diñer at the Dragon. Mr. Secretary, and Mr. Wadsworth were at the other Table; The Gov.ʳ order'd Maxwell to say that he drunk to Wadsworth

---

[1] Palfrey (IV. 276) states that this letter, directed to Lord Sutherland, is in the British Colonial Papers. It is signed by Colonel Moody also. — EDS.

and his Brother Addington. And awhile after, in like
mañer, drank to Mr. Pemberton, and Capt. Belchar, coup-
ling them together; saying Capt. Belchar should answer
for him, as I understood it. Just before the Council, after
diñer, Mr. Comissary, and Mr. Pemberton walked together
upon the pavement below the Townhouse.

Nov.r 5. I walk'd at night with Col. Townsend, Mr.
Bromfield, Constable Williams, and a Man or two. Find
the Town quiet and in good order. Were jealous the 5th
Nov.r might have occasioned disturbance.

Nov.r 6th. Lord's day; Mr. Rowland Cotton preach'd in
the forenoon; Mr. Corwin in the Afternoon. Mr. Pemberton had propounded Hañah Butler to renew her Bap-
tismal Covenant; and now mention'd it, and said she had
sin'd scandulously against the 7th Comandment; read her
Confession imediatly, and by the silential vote restored
her. I think it is inconvenient, when persons have so
fallen, not to give the Church some previous notice of it;
that the Brethren may have Oportunity to enquire into
the Repentance. An ignorant Consent is no Consent.
And I understood Mr. Pemberton that he would not go in
that way again. Once before he did it, saying he knew
not of it when the party was propounded.

Nov.r 17. 1709. Deputies send in a Bill that the Secretary draw up an Address to the Queen, and that it be
presented by Col. Nicholson, or in his absence by Sir
William Ashurst.[1] The Gov.r was much displeas'd at it,

---

[1] The Ashursts were for a long time connected with our political affairs.
Henry Ashurst, of Ashurst in Lancashire, came to London in the seven-
teenth century, and was eminent for great benevolence, humanity, and piety.
He was treasurer of the Corporation for Propagating the Gospel in Foreign
Parts. He acquired a large property as a merchant, and died in 1680, leaving
four sons. The oldest son was Sir Henry Ashurst, Bart., of Waterstock,
County Oxford, M. P., whose son was the last baronet. A daughter of Sir
Henry married Sir Richard Allin, and had, with a son whose line soon ex-
pired, a daughter Diana, wife of Thomas Henry Ashurst. Sir William
Ashurst, Knight, brother of the first baronet, died January, 1719–20, leaving

and said, No Ashurst should doe any Business for him.
Mr. Secretary drew forth an Address he had prepared;
The Govr inserted Canada, interlining it: Twas for Nova
Scotia and Port-Royal before, I spake against Canada;
but twas carried and sent in. The Deputies sent it up
concur'd, and to be presented as they had signified in
their vote this day. The Govr express'd his Resentments
that should mention his Enemy: and put it not to vote.
Court is prorogued to the first of February.

Novr 18th Council meets about Capt. Hayman's Estate,[1]
Gives 30.£ more to Grace, and 12. to her Brother, to
come out of their Mothers Thirds now to be divided.

Capt. Teat, by his Letter, desired a License of the Govr
to work on his Ship on the Lord's day; the Ship was on
the Ground, and fear'd he should be nip'd: Govr argued
hard for it: Captain was Judge of the Necessity: I argued against it: He had time enough before, and had
time enough to come before the sailing of the Mast-fleet.
At the last the Govr collected the voices, and said it was

---

two sons, Robert, of Heveningham, County Essex, and Henry, Town Clerk
of London in 1700, who had two sons.

William Ashurst, uncle of Sir Henry and Sir William, was a member of
the Long Parliament, whose son Thomas had a son Thomas Henry Ashurst,
already noticed as marrying Diana Allin, grand-daughter and eventual heiress of Sir William. By this marriage Waterstock remained in the family
name. A son of this marriage was Sir William Henry Ashurst, a distinguished lawyer, whose grandson is now the representative of the family at
Waterstock. It seems extremely probable that valuable documents relating
to our history may be preserved in this family.

We see by the text that Dudley was at this time opposed to the Ashursts
Sir Henry was in feeble health, and his brother, Sir William, refused the
agency, recommending Jeremiah Dummer. Dudley preferred Henry Newman, the agent for New Hampshire; but Dummer succeeded in 1710.
(Hutchinson, Hist. II. 182, 183.) — Eds.

[1] From Wyman's Charlestown Records we learn that Major John Hayman, by wife, Grace, had a daughter Grace, wife of Thomas Berry, and
sons Samuel and Nathan. But Samuel lived till Dec. 15, 1712, and Nathan
died July 27, 1689. Hence this Captain Hayman was probably a son of
Nathan, as he had two sons, and a daughter Grace, who married Richard
Otis. — Eds.

carried by one : when I was ask'd, I said, I am dissatisfied, he ought not to be Licensed.

Nov.[r] 19. Very Cold;[1] Have the News of the great
Battel, eleventh 7.[r] N-style ; Confederats beat the French.[2]

Nov.[r] 21. I visit Mr. Lechmere and his Bride, Mrs.
Anne Winthrop.[3]

Feria quinta, Nov.[r] 24. 1709. Thanksgiving Day, Mr.
Pemberton preached forenoon and Afternoon, from Psal,
29. 3 latter part of the verse. In the afternoon he express'd his dislike of the Guns fired by the Ships and Castle, as not sutable for a Day of Thanksgiving.

Nov.[r] 25. *Theopolis Americana* is finished, the last
half-sheet printed off.[4] I stitch'd me up a Book, and sent
the Rev.[d] Author one to compleat his. And then Mr.
Mayhew and I went to the Funeral of his little Nathan[l],

---

[1] Hutchinson writes (Hist. II. 176) that "Tuesday, the 14th December,
was remarked as the coldest day ever known in the country from its first settlement." — EDS.

[2] This was the battle of Malplaquet, won by Marlborough and Prince
Eugene, over Marshal Villars. Lord Stanhope adds (Hist. II. 123) that a
rumor spread through France that Marlborough had fallen at this battle, and
that from the rumor appears to have sprung the famous ditty of

"Malbrough s'en va-t-en guerre." — EDS.

[3] This was Thomas Lechmere, Surveyor-General of the Customs for the
Northern District of America. He was brother of Nicholas, Lord Lech-
mere, of Evesham, a famous lawyer. He married Anne, daughter of Wait-
Still Winthrop, and died June 4, 1765, leaving two sons and two daughters.
(See N. E. H. G. Register, XIII. 302, and Heraldic Journal, IV. 43.) His
son Richard married Mary, daughter of Lieutenant Governor Spencer Phips,
and gave his name to Lechmere Point, in Cambridge. (See Paige Hist.
Camb. 168, 169, 173–178). — EDS.

[4] This is one of Cotton Mather's sermons, the full title being "Theopolis
Americana. An Essay on the Golden Streets of the Holy City. Publishing
a Testimony against the Corruptions of the Market-Place. With some Good
Hopes of Better Things to be yet seen in the American World. In a Sermon
to the General Assembly of the Massachusetts Province in New England.
3*d*. 9*m*. 1709. . . . Boston: Printed by B. Green. Sold by Samuel Gerrish
at his Shop, 1710." 12mo. Two pages dedication to Judge Sewall. pp.
4–51 "Pure Gold in the Market Place." Appendix, p. 2. The copy in the
Boston Athenæum is imperfect; but the Brinley Catalogue mentions a fine
copy. — EDS.

who dyed in the time of the Forenoon Exercise, which made his Father, Mr. Cotton Mather, take his Text from 1 Sam. 10, — therefore she wept and did not eat. At the Funeral I saw Mr. Bridge, and desired him to come to me at 7 a-clock, which he did. And I fully communicated to him my sense of Rev. 13th 18. desiring he would not disclose it without my Consent, which I apprehend he granted.

Decr 20. 1709. I went to Brooklin with my daughter Hañah in a Calash, and visited my little Grand-daughter Hañah Sewall who is this day eight weeks old; Had very comfortable Wether. Find all well there, and at home.

Decr 28. Midweek, Govr apoints Mr. Mackentash Judge of the inferiour Court of Bristol in the Room of Capt. Brown deceased.[1] Mr. Bromfield had a check for mentioning Mr. Pain, though of the Council, and a much fitter man. Col. Foxcroft's son is made his Register, as he is Judge of the Probat; which seems to me inconvenient.[2] I was not at the Council; my Cold kept me at home.

Feria septima xrs. 31.º I read Mr. Brightman's Excellent Epistle[3] to the British, German, and French Churches, out of Mr. E. Mayhew's English Book which lay in view. I was so pleased with it, that I read it in my Latin Book, *nec sine lachrymis*. This day Mr. Hubbard is taken sick after diñer.

Lords-day, January, 1. 170$\frac{9}{10}$. I read in course Mr.

---

[1] Henry Mackintosh succeeded John Browne, and held office till 1725. — EDS.

[2] The reader of this Journal will have noted with what a range of meaning and application Sewall uses the word *inconvenient*. It is made to signify the disability or pain coming from various bodily maladies; the impropriety of an act or a course of conduct; the wrongfulness of some measure of public policy, and various other disagreeable and objectionable matters. It is evident, too, that by its use he often softens the expression of very strong dissent or offence at what displeases him. The compass of the definition of the word in the dictionary, however, is a wide one. — EDS.

[3] This epistle was introductory to the author's " Revelation of the Apocalypse." Brightman died in 1607. — EDS.

Caryl on Job. 12. 22. from p. 311 to p. 319. The great Notice this great Divine takes of the Discovery of Columbina;[1] his Corollaries; Gloss on Mat. 10. 25, Encouraged me to publish, what I have long intended, on Rev. 10., Especially being usher'd in by Mr. Brightman's Epistle; and presently follow'd with Mr. Pemberton's Exhortation to a faithfull improvement of the Talents God has com̄itted to us, because He sees us — p. m̄, from Heb. 4. 13. The good Lord help me not to mistake! not to delay any thing He would have me now doe! Though the day were Cold, yet I found no Inconvenience by going to the Solemn Assembly.

Jany 2. Morât Salutes me with the Sound of the Trumpet. Govr warns a Council; but there was not a number: I go to Cous. Dumer's, where I read Cous. Jer. [Jeremy Dummer's] Letter of the 13th 7^r He writes that Col. Hunter is made Govr of New-York.

Sixth-day, Jany 6. James Hawkins dyes very suddenly, about 56 years old.

7th day, Jany 7th Mr. Exp. Mayhew goes to Natick.

Lords-day Jany 8. My old Friend Mr. John Hubbard dyes, in the forenoon, just before the Exercise began. Mr. Pemberton makes a pathetical mention of it in his Prayer, and that we might follow him so far as he followed Christ: mention'd him as a real Christian. Madam Hubbard put up a Note. *Alias* Leverett.

Jany 1. 170$\frac{9}{10}$. Mr. Gerrish was Bearer to a young hopefull Man, Hunt, the Turner's Son, who had been married about 6. weeks. The Lord help us to prepare to meet Him!

Jany 8. Lords day. The Matrosses apear in their Red Coats, 6 or 8 of them, at our Meeting.

---

[1] Caryl makes no reference to *Columbina* by name. It is probably a constructive inference by Sewall from Caryl's notice of the discoveries at the Antipodes. — EDS.·

Third-day, Jan.ʳ 10. Mr. John Hubbard is buried in
the New Burying place in a Grave near the Northwest
Corner of it.[1] Bearers, Sewall, Sergeant; Eliakim Hutchinson, Jer. Dumer; Capt. Thomas Fitch, Capt. Edward
Winslow. Govʳ was there, and the President and his
Lady: I saw none from Ipswich. Snow'd hard all the
way to the Grave and back.

January, 15, 17$\frac{08}{19}$. Mr. Benjᵃ Woodbridge died at
Medford: Thorsday, 19ᵗʰ buried. Mr. Parsons of Malden
preach'd the Funeral Sermon. Bearers, President, Mr.
Hubbard of Newton; Mr. Brattle, Mr. Bradstreet; Mr.
Parsons, Mr. Ruggles of Billericay. By reason that it
was Lecture-day, and Mr. Colman preach'd; and the Wind
very high and Blustering, not one Boston Minister was
there.

January, 24ᵗʰ I visited Mr. Habberfield about 5. p. m̅.
He is smitten with the Palsy on his right side. Was very
glad to see me, as I saw by his taking me by the hand;
but could hardly speak a word.

Jan.ʳ 28. 17$\frac{08}{19}$. I waited on the Govʳ and his Lady;
they entertain'd me very placidly. While I was there,
my daughter Sewall came in with her two little daughters,
Rebekah and Hañah. Hañah had never been there before. I suppose tis meant, not since the day she was baptised. I discours'd the Govʳ about giving a Deed of
Brooklin. Before I was got out of the House, Col. Vetch

---

[1] This was John, son of Rev. William Hubbard, of Ipswich, the historian. He married Ann, daughter of Governor Leverett, and had four sons,
three graduates of Harvard. Of them, Nathaniel was a Judge of the Superior Court from 1746 to 1748. Hutchinson (Hist. II. 147) refers to him;
but, as Savage remarks, makes him son, instead of grandson, of Rev. William.
It is worth notice that in the northwest corner of the Granary Yard there is
the tomb of Thomas Hubbard, 1742, with a coat-of-arms. He was, doubtless, son of Captain John Hubbard, who, with a brother, Zechariah Hubbard, were sons of Deacon Thomas Hubbard, by his wife, Mary Tuthill.
Deacon Thomas Hubbard died Nov. 17, 1717, aged sixty-three. As Savage
says that Rev. William may have had other children than he notes, this may
have been one of them. — EDS.

and Schyler came in. The Gov' told me of News from Albany, as if the French of Canaday were coming against us. The good Lord stop them!

Febr. 1. The Court meets, but the Deputies make not a House. Feb: 2. Make not a House.

Feb: 3. Friday, The Representatives have a Number, the Gov' sends for them in the Forenoon, and makes a Speech to them. Just at the time, I was taken with an irksome Flux, and was fain to go abroad: so that I saw nor heard any thing of this Solemnity.

Feb: 4. Now about the Gov' introduces Col. Schyler, and Major Pigeon to take Leave of the Council, as going for England. It was a Surprize to me; and I could not find that any body knew that Major Pigeon was going to England.

Feb: 6. the Queen's Birth-day. The Council Treat the Gov' at the Green Dragon, with Col. Vetch and several others. Mr. Tho. Bridge, Mr. Wadsworth, and Mr. Colman were there. Cost us 5ˢ apiece. After our Return to the Council-Chamber, Burnt near Six Thousand pounds of decay'd Bills. When the Candles began to be lighted, I grew weary and uneasy, and even slip'd away without drinking. When I came home, it was a singular Refreshment to me to read 2 Cor. 6. especially from the 14ᵗʰ to the end. See Mr. Pemberton's Sermon, March, 5ᵗʰ &c.

Feb: 7. Third-day, Col. Foster spake to me about a Bill for an Agent. I said I knew of none. He said there was one. It seems twas pass'd and sent in Feb: 6ᵗʰ as we had our Fire; and deliver'd to the Gov' who read it, and put it into the Secretary's hand, who laid it away, not knowing what it was. At last on this day it was read; and the Gov' spake against the thing largely and earnestly. Were now but a bare House. Refus'd an Agent the last Session when were full. To chuse Sir Willᵐ Ashurst was to cut him down, &c. Sir Wᵐ little at Court. I said He was Parliament Man for London. Gov' put it not to

Vote. In the Afternoon the Gov[r] had a great deal of warm discourse upon the same Theme. Said, Sir Henry had injuriously pursued him these twenty years; Sometimes no body follow'd him save Sir William; could procure none else. There were a great many men in England. Mr. Constantine Phips was their Agent had done them much good Service; would none serve but Sir William Ashurst? So the day was spent, and no Vote.

Midweek, Febr. 8. was Stormy with Snow: The Council meet, and show their Resolution to vote the Bill. Mr. Secretary receives a Letter from the Gov[r] that he could not come to Town: possibly he might in the Afternoon. Upon this the Question was put whether the Bill should be voted to in the forenoon, or wait till the Afternoon; and twas carried to waitt till the Afternoon, to see if the Gov[r] would come. Col. Hutchinson and Foster dine at Homes's.

Febr. 8. p. m. The Council met, but the Gov[r] came not. Maxwell was sent for the Secretary, who came and brought a large paper he had drawn up for Instructions, which was read at the Board. Then Col. Hutchinson and others spake that the Bill the Deputies had sent up, referring to an Agent, might be put to vote, which was done about four a-clock: There were Sixteen at the Board; Fifteen were in the Affirmative. Mr. Secretary said with a low voice so that I heard him, I cañot be of Advice in the matter. Representatives had often sent in to enquire what was done with the Bill for an Agent: Wherefore now the Council sent a Message to them to acquaint them the Council had pass'd it. Col. Townsend and Hunt were chosen by the Council; and about 4. of the Representatives to wait on the Gov[r] for his Consent. Capt. Buckminster went to Roxbury the night before, and brought a Letter from the Gov[r] next morning; upon which Mr. Secretary and Com̄issary went to Roxbury.

Febr. 9. 17$\frac{0\,9}{1\,0}$ *mane.* Soon after the Messengers from the Court went with the Bill, the Govr declin'd signing it; and sent a Letter, which follows.

ROXBURY, Febr. 9. 17⁰⁰/₈.

GENTLEMEN, — I have just now your Vote of yesterday referring to the Choice of the Honble Sir William Ashurst Agent for this Province. I am surpris'd at it, because this present House of Representatives, consisting of about 70 Gentlemen or more, in their last session, about three Moneths since, refused the Return of their own Committee recommending the Use of an Agent. And in this Session, which I understand consists of forty-one, this Vote was carried but by a Small Majority. So that I have not therein the Advice of the Majority of that House; three Counties being wholly absent; and two other Counties have but three between them, as I am informed. I am also sensible that it will be a great hardship upon Sir William Ashurst to stand against his Brother Sir Henry, who is Agent for Connecticut, who are at this time Complainants against us, to take away two or three Towns from us, and to lower their Quota of Men for the publick Service. Which Complaints are now lying before Her Majesty, as that Governour informs us. If the matter might be reconsidered, I am of Opinion it were better left to the Advice of a full Court; which if you desire [left incomplete].

March, 4, 17⁰⁰/₁₀. I went to Brooklin, and visited my son.

March, 10. I visit Bro^r Emons, who not only is kept within by his illness, but kept up; he cañot go to bed, but is oblig'd to sit in his Chair all night. Mr. Addington tells me of Mr. Pike's death, a good Man, and my particular friend. It seems he died March, 7.

Feria secunda, March, 13. 17⁰⁰/₁₀. General Town-Meeting. Mr. Cotton Mather went to Prayer; I stood in the Lobby, then went into the Council-Chamber; Constable —— came to me and surprised me with telling me that I was chosen Moderator. I went in; and they would have me sit in the Seat, which I did; After reading the Warrants, Law, Town-order, Chose Select-Men; Daniel Powning, 119. Isaiah Tay, 118. Samuel Marshal, 117. Richard Draper, 116. Capt. Ephraim Savage, 114. Joseph Wadsworth, 113. Jonas Clark, 108. James Barns, 109.

C. Timothy Clark, 86. Constables, Capt. Wentworth Paxton, Æneas Salter, John Pierce, John Savil, John Bulkley,
Timothy Prout, Joseph Kallender, Samuel Burnel; to
whom I administered the Oath belonging to their Office;
7 the first day, and Burnel, the 2ᵈ.

Seventh-day, March, 25. 1710. I set out for Plimouth
in Mr. Steadman's Calash, about ½ hour after 9. Lodg'd
at Cushing's.

March, 26. Went to Hingham to Meeting, heard Mr.
Norton from Psal. 145. 18. Setting forth the Propitious-
ness of God. In the afternoon Lydia Cushing, and Paul
Lewis were baptised. Din'd with Major Thaxter, Sup'd
with Mr. Norton, Mrs. Norton, and their sister Shepard,
who he says, is perfectly well. Return'd to Cushing's in
the night; it began to snow by that time we got thither.

March, 27. Am much disheartened by the Snow on
the ground, and that which was falling, there being a dismal face of Winter. Yet the Sun breaking out, I stood
along about 10. m. Every thing look'd so wild with Snow
on the Ground and Trees; that was in pain lest I should
Wander: But it pleas'd God graciously to direct, so that
I got well to D. Jacobs, and then call'd his Tenant Riply
to guid us over the Rocky Swamps to Curtis's. Din'd at
Bairstow's; from thence had the under-Sheriff Briant.
At Cook's the Sheriff met me. Mr. J. Cotton, Otis and
others with him. Got to Rickard's about Sun-set. *Laus
Deo.* Mr. Mayhew and Jnᵒ Neesnumin were got thither
before me by water. Mr. Little came to my Chamber
and Mr. Mayhew that evening.

Gave Mr. Little and his wife each of them a good pair
of Gloves. Little did I think that my worthy friend, Mr.
John Cotton of Hampton, was then dying.

Third-day, March, 28. 1710. I saw the Sun pleasantly
rising out of the Sea. Went to the Meetinghouse as I
had done in former years; but found it shut, to my disapointment. But quickly after my Chamber at Rickard's

was free; where I had Opportunity of solemn Secret Prayer; Two of the Articles were my Tenants and the Agency. Wrote out Mr. Moodey's Copy of Verses on a Minister's Imprisonment; and gave them to Col. Thomas.

About Noon, the Chief Justice Winthrop, and Major Walley came to Town from Bairsto's. Open'd the Court, and swore the Grand-Jury before we went to Diñer. Mr. Little, Mayhew, Josiah Cotton, Shurtlif dine with us. And Mr. Rowland Cotton, Mr. Robinson, and Mr. Thacher of Middlebury, at another time. March, 30, adjourn'd *Sine die.*

March, 31. 1710. Set out homeward, Din'd at Bairsto's; I lodg'd with Major Walley, at his Cousin Jacobs's; Mr. Winthrop went on to Weymouth.

April, 1. Visited Mr. Thacher at Weymouth, wish'd him Joy of his new House. Visited Cousin Hunt in her changed Habitation. Met Mr. N. Hubbard in Monotocot; ask'd, but he told me no News: As I was getting up Pen's Hill, Major Walley overtook me, and told me the dreadfull News of Mr. Cotton's Sudden Death; which was very surprising to me. Bait at Mills's; where I hear of Cousin Quinsey's being about 8 that Morning brought to Bed of her Son Josiah.[1] Mr. Smith and Walley told us of Madam Oliver's death, at Weymouth; The two Cousin Germans[2] were buried the same day; March, 31. Hampton, Cambridge. Got home about 2 p. m̄. found all well. *Laus Deo.* Took Leave of the Chief Justice, and Major Walley, at the Gate.

Lord's day, April 2, 1710. Mr. Pemberton finish'd his Discourse on 2 Cor. 6. 18. Took occasion to bewail the

---

[1] This was the first of six successive Josiah Quincys, five of them being noteworthy, and three conspicuously so. The youngest is yet a youth. — EDS.

[2] The cousins were Rev. John Cotton, of Hampton, whose mother, Dorothy Bradstreet, was aunt to Mercy Bradstreet (daughter of Samuel Bradstreet), wife of Dr. James Oliver, of Cambridge. They died only two days apart. — EDS.

death of Mr. Pike, and Mr. Cotton; of the last gave a
very August Character. Brought it in thus: If Believers
be God's Sons and Daughters, then their Death is to be
Regretted; especially the death of Ministers. Preached
forenoon and Afternoon.

Second-day, April, 3. The Gov[r] calls a Council. Mr.
Man's [1] 2[d] Letter of Refusal is read; The Choosing another
Minister is propos'd by the Gov[r] I thought twas not con-
venient now to go out of Town, or at least not far off. I
mention'd Mr. Brattle; Mr. E[m] Hutchinson, [mentioned]
Mr. Bridge; Gov[r] said he was a stranger. I think twas
Col. Lynde mention'd Mr. Angier. I did not think him
so Square and Stable a Man; and therefore propounded
Mr. Wadsworth, and Mr. Pemberton: The Gov[r] said
Mr. Pemberton, and all agreed to it. And finding a difficulty in apointing who should address Mr. Pemberton;
the Gov[r] said would have the Council meet there at 3.
Between 3 and 4. The Gov[r], Mr. Secretary, Sewall, Sergeant, E[m] Hutchinson, Major Walley, Mr. Comissary Belchar being there, the Gov[r] intimated that the Secretary
had a Message, would have him do it. He complemented
me; I replied, you are the most proper person. Then
Mr. Secretary did the Message. Mr. Pemberton disabled
himself: Mr. Secr. Answer'd. Then Gov[r] seem'd to beckon
me to speak. I said, The Council generally had regard to
Age in their Choice: We had a 1 and 2 Denial from Mr.
Man. It was Condescension in the Boston Gentlemen to
help us, when disapointed elsewhere: It would not be well
to venture abroad again; lest being balk'd we should give
those at home just Reason to say: *Cum nulli obtrudi
potest, itur ad me.* Mr. Pemberton said not much after.
I said I thought he had a clear Call. As we look towards

---

[1] Probably Rev. Samuel Man, of Wrentham. The sermon referred to
seems to have been the annual Election Sermon. In 1709 it was preached by
Grindal Rawson; in 1710, by Ebenezer Pemberton. — EDS.

the Artillery passing by, I said to Mr. Pemberton the passage of Ulysses,

Si mea cum vestris valuissent vota Pelasgi, —

Before we went away, word was brought that Dr. Mather was chosen to preach the Artillery Sermon. Mr. Pemberton said Must choose agen.

Third-day, Apr. 4. I had some Vines set by Bastian.

April, 13. 1710. Capt. Ephraim Savages wife dyes, about an hour after Lecture, to our great Surprise. She was at our Meeting at Capt. Hill's.

April, 14. I went to Charlestown Lecture, and din'd there with Mr. Hobart, and Mr. Brattle.

April, 16. About Sunset Mrs. Elizabeth Savage is buried. Bearers Winthrop, Sewall; Addington, Sergeant; Walley, Belchar.

April, 21. 1710. Sixth-day, I went to Newtown to Mr. Hobart's Lecture; and there met Son Sewall and his wife. This day Lydia Goose dyes after 14 weeks languishing. Joseph came home this day.

Apr. 23. Lord's Day Lydia Goose is buried; Bearers, Mr. Josiah Willard, Benj. Eliot; Jn° Foy, Joseph Sewall; Josiah Oakes, Sam. Clark.

Apr. 27. Mr. Cooke and I spake to Dr. Mather after Lecture to goe to the Schoolhouse on the 10th of May. He declin'd it. Understanding he went to dine at the Major General's, I hastn'd thither after I had din'd, and urg'd it there : He declin'd it; but mention'd Chimham.[1] As was going away, mention'd a Fast next Lecture for Rain. I said I was glad, or should be glad of it.

April, 30. Lord's day; In the Evening before the dismission of the Assembly; Mr. Pemberton said, The Ministers of the Town had appointed next Thorsday to be kept as a Fast for Rain; to turn the Lecture into a Fast;

---

[1] The reference is to 2 Samuel, xix. 37–40. — EDS.

and God's beginning to send Rain would not be a discouragement.

Note. Last night the Rudder of Capt. Rose's Ship was cut; The reason was Capt. Belchar's sending of her away Laden with Wheat in this time when Wheat is so dear.

Second-day, May, 1, 1710. Fourty or fifty Men get together and seek some body to head them to hale Capt. Roses Ship ashoar: but they were dissuaded by several sober Men to desist, which they did. This was about 5. m. I heard of it as I was going to Hog-Island to see my Tenant's Loss of Sheep. Went off about Nine, and return'd between 2 and 3.

May, 2. Mr. Pemberton prays; 5 Judges there. First Lieut Sam. Johnson was made Foreman of the Jury. May, 3. He pray'd to be dismiss'd by reason of sickness, which was granted while I was withdrawn into the Council-Chamber, and writing to Mr. C. Mather to dine with us; and Mr. Cumby was made Fore-man. At Noon Mr. Attorney objected against Cumby that he should say, Sure they cut the Rudder themselves, that is, Capt. Roses Men. Upon this Mr. Cumby was spoken to by the Court, and he in open Court desired dismission, or at least from being Fore-man. He was dismiss'd; and Mr. William Torrey was put in. Mr. Attorney and Capt. Belchar went to the Grand-Jury to forward the Bill against those that made the unlawfull Assembly. Just after Mr. Cumby was dismiss'd, Capt. Belchar made a motion that he might be sworn as a Witness. I look'd upon it as an indignity, he having been hardly enough dismiss'd from the Grand-jury: and nothing led to the calling him forth but his Situation. So I opos'd it, and it was not done. I insisted it most convenient to proceed with a few and not seek to inflame the Reckoning by multiplying Articles. And Col. Foster complain'd that twas almost like an Inquisition; the mañer of Capt. Belchars pursuing it in Council.

This Midweek morn, Mr. Pemberton stood in his Gate,

and occasion'd my going in with him. He spake very warmly about the Unlawfull Assembly : I said such motions ought to be supress'd; the thing should be thorowly and effectually dealt in. I said twas an ill office in Capt. Belchar to send away so great a quantity of Wheat (about 6000 Bushels besides Bread) in this scarce time. Mr. Pemberton said I cherish'd those evil seditious Motions by saying so. I said he unjustly charged me. He that withholds Corn, the people will curse him, though I did not affirm that Scripture Justified the Rioters. I mention'd something of God's people, that though they brought themselves into Straits by their own fault; yet God pitied and help'd them. Mr. Pemberton said, with much fierceness, They were not God's people but the Devil's people that wanted Corn. There was Corn to be had; if they had not impoverish'd themselves by Rum, they might buy Corn. I was stricken with this furious Expression. Mr. Pemberton also spake very sharply and upbraidingly, that he was invited to Diñer, and then not sent for at Diñer-time; was sick with waiting; lost his own Diñer; knew not where we din'd; 'twas indecent to ly lurking at the ordinary; wanted not a Diñer.

Midweek, May, 3. p. m̅. the Grand-Jury bring in *Ignoramus*, to my surprise. No order for the accused to pay Costs.

Mr. Cotton Mather din'd with us to day; Mr. Gookin of Sherbourn, yesterday. Spake not a word to Mr. Mather of any of the Causes, save of a Widow's that was past.

May, 15, 1710. Set out for Ipswich with Daughter Gerrish in my son's Calash, from Charlestown. At Lewis's Mr. Tim͞o Thornton overtook us, and accompanied us to Mr. Gerrishes at Wenham. There I leave my Daughter and proceed, Mr. Attorney rode with me from thence, Mr. Harris met me, and conducted me to Mr. Rogers's; find all well there. May, 17. I and Mr. Rogers visit Sis-

ter Northend, Mr. Rogers prays with Cousin Mehetabel
Moodey, who was hapily there. To comfort her, I told
her, God had given her a Visit: for Mr. Rogers and I
came to give her Aunt a visit; not knowing of her being
there. Went to Mr. Payson's Gate, and talk'd with him
a little, drank Cider, went to Ipswich; Night before we
got thither.

May, 18. Set out for Boston, Mr. Thornton in Company. Call'd at Bro^r Gerrish's; They expected son and
daughter Hirst, so went on to Salem, din'd at Bro^r Sewall's
who had a good Treat. Madam Hirst, Madam Colman,
Son Hirst and wife, Mrs. Betty, Mr. Sever there; we
join'd our selves to them, and made a good Diñer. Then
Mr. Thornton and I set forward, parted at the Wiñisiñet
Road, met Mr. Colman at Lin. Got home well; in the
night took Tom my driver with me. *Laus Deo.*

May, 31. Election-day; Major Walley, the Secretary
and Sewall gave the Representatives their Oaths; 70. before Sermon. Mr. Pemberton preached. Dine at the
Green Dragon. Election as last year.

Midweek July, 5th Comencement-day. I ride from
Charlestown with Cousin Hale in a Calash; Mr. Mayhew
has much adoe to get Mr. Short along; his Melancholy is
so prevalent. President is indispos'd, so that Mr. N. Hobart begins with Prayer. Sir Denison makes the Oration.[1]
The Bachelours Questions, and two of the Masters, were
dispatch'd in the forenoon. My son[2] concluded his Thesis
thus — *ideoque etsi inaudiatur Lugduni Batavorum; etsi
enarretur Lutetiæ Parisiorum; etsi audiant Nostrates
doctissimi, sive Oxonienses, sive Cantabrigienses; atta-
men Clamabo, Sabbatismus Septenarius existit jure Di-
vino, et immutabili.*

---

[1] John Denison, A. B. in 1710. He was Librarian of the College 1713–14.
— EDS.

[2] Joseph Sewall, A. B. 1707, would regularly take his Master's degree in
1710. — EDS.

Mr. Sol. Stoddard craved a Blessing in the Hall, and Mr. Williams of Hatfield return'd Thanks.

I came down a-foot in company of Mr. Wadsworth, and Mr. Hale; no Calash being to be hired: Neither Son Sewall, nor Hañah nor Betty were at the Comencement. Sam and Betty were sick. Note. The day was cool and pleasant, very little Dust by Reason of the Rain the day before.

July, 10. Mr. Jn° Marion and I went to Rumney-Marsh to the Raising of their Meetinghouse. I drove a Pin, gave a 5ˢ Bill, had a very good Treat at Mr. Chievers's; went and came by Wiñisimet.

July, 16. Mrs. Stoddard, Widow, is pray'd for. July 18ᵗʰ dyes about 7. m. Extream hot Wether. Mr. Cook, Bromfield and I goe to Rumney-Marsh in a Boat, to agree with Workmen to finish the Meetinghouse. Stowers is to make the windows. Got home well; *Laus Deo.* Several died of the Heat at Salem.

July, 19. Madam Stoddard buried, Bearers, Winthrop, Cook; Sewall, Corwin; Lynde, Cutler. Buried in the old burying place in Major Savage's Tomb.

Seventh-day, July, 15. 1710. As I was setting up a Column of Psalters, the 12ᵗʰ Column, about 11. m. I heard a Gun, and a while after another. Mr. Mayhew and Joseph run up to the top of the House, and saw two Flags hoysted at the Castle. Quickly after I went up, and saw the Flag hoysted at the Sconce, and two Guns fired; then presently the Drums beat and Alarm went through the Town. Some said, there was a Flag in the Main-Top; others said twas a broad Pendant. Twas Candle-light before Col. Nicholson got to the Council Chamber; where the Govʳ and Council waited. Col. Nicholson gave me a Letter from Cous. Jer. Dumer: and two more Packets were deliver'd me by an unseen hand, from Sir William Ashurst, wherein was a Letter to Mr. Secretary, Mr. Speaker, and Dr. Mather, wherein Sir William declines

our Agency, his Health being precarious; and saith he
has introduc'd Mr. Dumer into our Service, and Rec-
omends him to us as fit to be our Agent.

July, 16.   Mr. Jn° Emerson of New-Castle preaches for
Mr. Pemberton in the Forenoon.   Teach us so to number
our days.

July, 17.ᵗʰ   I deliver Sir Wᵐˢ Letter with my own
hand.

Now about a child of about 2 years old, having just
suck'd, was drown'd in a Tub of Water it toppled into.

In Council 'tis now mov'd that the Marines might be
brought ashore.   Col. [manuscript torn] the Castle because there might be more easily k[ept toge]ther.   I
mov'd that might be Landed at Hull where would have
much better Accomodation; and one of the Officers seem'd
to incline to it, and alleg'd a Guard might easily be kept
at the Neck.   I understood that was agreed to, and desired
Col. Townsend might go to facilitat their Reception; but
it seems the Officers would Land them at the Castle, as
Col. Townsend told me.

July, 24, 1710.   The Council Treats the Govᵣ, Col.
Nicholson, Col. Vetch, Sir Charles Hobbey, Col. Taylor,
Col. Redding, and the Sea-Captains at the Green Dragon.

July, 28.   Deputies Treat at the Green Dragon.   Govᵣ
Saltonstall came to Town yesterday.   This day the Deputies send in a Bill to chuse Mr. Jer. Dumer junᵣ their
Agent.   Dated July 27.   Govᵣ says, He will be drawn
asunder with wild Horses before he will be Thrust upon
as last year.   W. Winthrop esqr, much against Mr. Dumer
being Agent.

July, 28.   Mr. William Clark, Mariner, who served his
Time with Capt. Nathanˡ Green, made a Justice of peace
by Govᵣ Dudley :¹ is buried, Bearers, Mr. Cook, Sergeant;

¹ William Clark was made a justice of the peace June 18, 1706, with
Edmund Quincy, Samuel Sewall, Jr., and two others.   Hence, probably,
this mention. — EDS.

Walley, Stoddard; Dummer, Mico. Gov[r] Dudley, Col.
Nicholson, and many of the Council there; being the
time of the Gen[l] Court. I think all of the Government
had Gloves; I had a pair. Conference with the Council
of War, which lasted till 10. at night.

Satterday, July, 29th. last night John Saffin esqr. died.
He express'd to Mr. Pemberton an Assurance of his good
Estate 2 or 3 hours before his death.

Fifth-day, Aug[t] 3. 1710. Our little Grand-Daughter
Rebekah Sewall, born xr. 30. 1704. at Brooklin, died
about Eight or Nine this morn. We knew not of her
being Sick, till Dr. Noyes, as he returned, told us she was
dead. The Lord effectually awaken us by these awfull
Surprising Providences. My son and daughter got thither
before their Child dyed, and had Mr. Walter to pray with
her. She was sensible to the last, catching her breath till
she quite lost it.

Sixth-day, Aug[t] 4[th.] Rebekah Sewall is buried in at
Roxbury in the Governour's Tomb. Bearers, Daniel Allin,
Samuel Wainwright; Thomas Berry, Increase Walter.
White Sarsnet Scarvs and Gloves. Son and his wife fol-
low'd next the Corps; then the two Grandfathers; then
Madam Dudley and her son, Paul Dudley esqr; then Jo-
seph and his sister Hañah &c. Mr. Hirst and Gerrish were
there: their Wives were not well. Brother Sewall led
Madam Willard; his Son Sam. and Susan were also there.
Mr. Secretary Addington, Mr. Comissary Belchar, Mr.
Jno Leverett, president, and his Lady, Madam Rogers.
Mr. Walter, Mr. Mayhew, and many of Brooklin and
Roxbury.

This day, Augt 4. Nurse Elizabeth Johnson dyes.

Seventh-day, Augt 5. Is buried near the Entrance of
the old Burying-place; about 60. years old. I and Major
Walley follow'd next the Women, Mr. Pemberton, Hañah
and Cousin Jane Green were there.

Augt 10. Thanksgiving: Rainy morn [manuscript imperfect] at the beginning of exercise. Mr. Pemberton prea[ched] Madam Usher, Cousen, her Maid, son and daughter Hirst and their children and Nurse; son and daughter Gerrish and his Bro^r Paul and wife, cousins Sam, Jonathan, Susan Sewall, Jn° Gerrish dine here. Hill, Pierce, Johnson, Cornish, Wheeler, Plimly C° Green, Frost, Eaton, Hub^d; £1-4-6.

Augt 11. Sixth-day, I visited Mr. Tho. Brattle, who is very low and languishing; He express'd great respect to me : yet plainly told me, that frequent visits were prejudicial to him, it provôk'd him to speak more than his strength would bear, would have me come seldom. He told me his Thigh was no bigger than my Wrist. I said I hôp'd as the Wether grew Temperat, he might recruit which he seem'd to assent to.

Augt. 12. Mr. E. Mayhew carries his daughter Reliance to Braintry; intends to preach for Mr. Marsh tomorrow.

Monday, Augt 14. 1710. At a Town-Meeting, warn'd for that purpose, Fifteen feet of the old burying place Northward, and Ten feet Eastward, are granted to enlarge the Church.[1] Samuel Lynde esqr. was chosen Moderator.

---

[1] The records of the town have the following items Aug. 14, 1710: —

" A motion or Request in writing being presented and distinctly read at this meeting, and is as followeth, viz.

" The Request of the Honble Coll. Francis Nicholson together with the Ministers, Church Wardens, and others of the Church of England in Boston, sheweth — That the Church being too small to accomodate the congregation and Strangers that dayly Increase. And are desirous to Enlarge the same with the Approbation of the Selectmen and Inhabitants, but wanting Ground on the North Side and East end, Request that they may have a Grant of fifteen foot wide on the North side and Seventy four foot in length. And ten foot at the East end of the Church in Length, which is included in the said Seventy four foot. Reserving the same Liberty to all persons who have had any friends buryed in said ground which they enjoyed heretofore. Which Request being granted shall be ever acknowledged &c."

" Voted a grant to the said Gentlemen of this above said Request."

In the margin — " Grant of part of the Burying place for Enlargm^t of the Church." — EDS.

Col. Nicholson made a Speech before; And came in afterward and gave the Town Thanks for their Vote. Mr. Prout, the Town-Clerk, made some Oposition, because the Graves of his Ancestors would be thereby hidden.

Aug.ᵗ 15. p. m. I pray'd with Joseph in Cous. Dumer's Chamber, respecting his being call'd to preach for Mr. Pemberton the next Lord's Day at the South-Meeting-house. Then I read the 13ᵗʰ of Matthew, and Joseph concluded with Prayer. I hope God heard us.

Aug.ᵗ 18. Major Tyng is buried at Concord, where he had lien some time to be cured of his Wound.

Aug.ᵗ 19. Mr. Comissary Belchar tells me The news of the Taking Doway [1] is confirm'd. The Triton's Prize came out of Plimouth the 27ᵗʰ of June, and was spoken with at Sea.

Lord's Day, Aug.ᵗ 20. Mr. Joseph Sewall preaches for Mr. Pemberton, from Ps. 73. 28. But it is good for me to draw near unto God: stood a little above an hour. Before we went out of the seat, Maj.ʳ Gen.ˡ congratulated me on account of my Son; said he had done *Pie et Docte.* In the Afternoon, Mr. Pemberton traced much of his Discourse in his Prayer.

Aug.ᵗ 21. The Deacons come and deliver him 20.ˢ Col. Checkley very cheerfully Congratulated me on account of my Son's very good Sermon. Capt. Hill congratulated me, coming in first. In the Afternoon I visit my Daughter Sewall at Brooklin, and her little Hañah. I met my Son at Roxbury; and met him again with Mrs. Bayly behind him as I came home. Gov.ʳ tells me of Gen.ˡ Coddrington's Magnificent Legacies to pious uses.

Friday, 7.ᵣ 8. Col. Hathorn, Mr. Corwin, and Sewall set out for Bristow, by way of Punkapog: dine at Morey's; Get to Billinges before Sun-set.

---

[1] Douay capitulated to the allies on the 25th or 26th of June, N. S. — EDS.

7ͬ 9ᵗʰ ride in company with Mr. Henry Mackintosh junᵣ, Mr. Jnº Mills, undersheriff; his daughter; his Sister the Schoolmasters Wife, and their Son. We took up at the Ship; they went on to Bristol. Keep the Sabbath at Seaconk. Dine at Smith's, sup at Mr. Greenwood's.

Monday, 7ͬ 11ᵗʰ proceed to Bristol, are met at the Ferry by the Sheriff, Mr. Pain, Mr. Mackintosh, and others. Col. Byfield not there. Lodg at Peter Reynold's. 7ͬ 14. Journey homeward, Dine at the Ship with Mr. Newman. Note. The Mother of a Bastard Child condemn'd for murthering it. Lodge [manuscript imperfect] call at the Governour's [imperfect] him.

Octobᵣ At the first bringing in the Vote to make Mr. Dumer Agent, the Govᵣ grew very warm, and said he would be drawn asunder with wild Horses before he would be driven as last year.

Novᵣ 3. Friday Mr. Comissary Belcher and I are sent to visit the Govᵣ, being Sick, and to present the Council's Service. I carried the Vote for Mr. Dumer's Agency. Govᵣ was now more calm, being brought on anew. Said Mr. I. Mather was against it. Was by a Fire in his Chamber-closet. Went and came in Capt. Belchers Coach. Just as were ready to goe, Col. Higginson call'd earnestly for the Petition of Capt. Gardener and others, about a middle precinct for the Ministry, to be brought forward; which caused me to stay; and after reading papers and debates, at last they who were against the precinct, mov'd that a previous Vote might be put; whether would vote it now, or no;[1] and the Council was divided, so nothing was done. This many would have improv'd to hinder its being brought forward this Session. Whereas there was

---

[1] This is the old form of the Previous Question, which is still in use in England. Its object is, not to bring on a decisive vote, but to stave it off; the emphasis was on the word *now*. It was recognized in Jefferson's Manual, but is now out of date in this country. — EDS.

no Vote, and if there had been a Negative, twas only respecting that very evening intended.

Novr 10. 1710. Daughter Gerrish is brought to bed of
a daughter about 6. m. My wife being with her, I sat up
late and lay alone. This day with much adoe twas voted
that would Salem Middle precinct put to vote; and in the
Afternoon twas carried clear in the Affirmative. Mr.
Secretary stood firm for this. Though the Salem Gentlemen would not suffer Capt. Gardener and Company to
voted in Salem Town Meeting; they made no bones of
voting against them in the Council.

Novr 13. 1710. I visit Daughter Gerrish, and then
ride alone to Lewis's. From thence had Company, and
was met by the Sheriff.

Novr 14. Finished the Business of the Court, sitting a
little by Candle-light. Visited Madam Bradstreet, Bro^r
Hirst, Major Wm Brown.

Novr 15. Came home, fair Wether, and not very Cold.
Enquired of Mr. Gerrish as I came along concerning his
wife: He said she was something disorder'd; but I aprē-
hended no danger, and being just come off my journey,
went not to see her that night.

Novr 16. Thanksgiving. My wife sent my daughter
Gerrish part of our Diñer, which as I understood she eat of
pleasantly. But twas a Cold Day and she was remov'd off
her Bed on to the Palat Bed in the morning. After the
Evening Exercise my wife and I rode up in the Coach:
My daughter ask'd me to pray with her, which I did;
pray'd that God would give her the Spirit of Adoption to
call Him Father. Then I went away with Mr. Hirst to
his House, leaving my wife with my daughter Gerrish, till
she call'd to go home. After our coming home, the northern Chimney of the New house fell a-fire and blazed out
extreamly; which made a great Uproar, as is usual. An
hour or two after midnight Mr. Gerrish call'd me up acquainting us of the extream illness of his wife; All the

family were alarm'd, and gather'd into our Bed-Chamber. When I came there, to my great Surprise my Daughter could not speak to me. They had try'd to call up Mr. Wadsworth; but could not make the family hear. I sent for Mr. Mayhew, who came and pray'd very well with her. I put him [manuscript imperfect] again; Mr. Cutler the Physician said he [imperfect]. (Joseph pray'd at home with the family). [Near] four a clock after Midnight my dear child expired, being but Nineteen years, and twenty days old. When this was over, I advis'd them to take Mrs. Hubbard's Assistance; left Mr. Mayhew there and went home. When I entred my wife's Bed-Chamber, a dolefull Cry was lifted up.

Seventh-day, Novr 18th was the Funeral; Son Gerrish went first, then the two Grandfathers. Bearers, Paul Dudley esqr. Mr. Danl Oliver; Mr. Saml Phillips, Mr. Jno Winthrop; Mr. John Smith, Mr. Giles Dyer jun.^r Scarfs and Gloves. Note. Madam Pemberton was brought to Bed of a Son on the Thanksgiving-day during the Fore-noon Exercise.

Novem.^r 19. Mr. Pemberton preaches from Gen. 33. 5. And he said, The children which God hath graciously given thy Servant. Baptis'd his Son, having Named him William.

7th day, Novr 25th Dr. Increase Mather lays before me the first Libel, the Copy being of Sam. Sewall's writing; and mentions Mr. Bromfield, for me to consult with what to doe. When at Charlestown Lecture Novr 26th I writ a Letter to the president to invite him to Diñer the 28. that night goe to the Comissioners Meeting together.

Novr 27. Mr. Bromfield and I grant a Warrant to bring John Banister before us at 9. m. 9.^r 28.

Novr 28. I send my Son to invite Mr. Pembertón to dine with me and the President.

Novr 28. John Banister apears, sumond by Constable Kallender. I had desired Col. Townsend to be with us,

who came.   Mr. Tho. Brattle came of himself and pleaded
much in favour of the Libellers (for Aaron was brought in
too) and against the injured Doctors, which was the Cause
I invited him not to Dinner.   Fin'd Jn° Banister 20ˢ for
each Libel, Aaron Stuckey 20ˢ for publishing the 2ᵈ Bound
them to their good Behaviour.   Mr. Brattle argued hard
to issue it, and not Bind them over to the Sessions: and
had Dr. Cotton Mather's Letter in favour of Banister.
But he offer'd no Acknowledgment of his Crime in writing; so we took this middle way.

Novʳ 28. p. m.   When the President and Mr. Pemberton came to Diñer, I was in my Apartment, Mr. Mayhew
and my Son with me.   The President and Mr. Pemberton
being come to us; Mr. Pemberton quickly begun to say,
What you have been holding a Court to day!   Had it
over again; I was a little amus'd at the word Court; however, I began to relate what had been done.   Mr. Pemberton with extraordinary Vehemency said, (capering with
his feet)   If the Mathers order'd it, I would shoot him
thorow.   I told him he was in a passion.   He said he was
not in a Passion.   I said, it was so much the worse.   He
said the Fire from the Altar was equal impartial.   Up-
braiding me, very plainly, as I understood it, with
Partiality.   The President said, The Governour was barbarously Treated (meaning Dr. Cotton Mather's Letter to
his Excellency).   I answered; That was put to the Council.   Mr. Mayhew told me afterward, that I said his Carriage was neither becoming a Scholar nor Minister.   The
Truth is I was surpris'd to see my self insulted with such
extraordinary Fierceness, by my Pastor, just when I had
been vindicating two worthy Embassadors of Christ (his
own usual Phrase) from most villanous Libels.   And I
dônt know any syllable intimating that I had done Well.
As for the Letter, the Govʳ was not in humor to trust me
about it; because I just then Fil'd my Reasons for with-
drawing my Vote.   [In margin] Mr. Pemberton speaks

hard Words, and very reflecting. We went to Dinner, I sat
next Mr. Pemberton and ask'd him to crave a Blessing;
He also Return'd Thanks, the President declining it. Mr.
Sergeant came into our Company. The President walked
on his right hand to the Council-chamber; I and Mr.
Pemberton went next. In the Way Mr. Pemberton
charg'd me again, I was griev'd and said, What in the
Street! He answer'd, No body hears. But Mr. Sergeant
heard so much, that he turn'd back to still us. Mr. Pemberton told me that Capt. Martin, the Comadore, had,
abus'd him, yet I took no notice of it: I answer'd, you
never laid it before me. He said, You knew it. I said,
I knew it not. (For every Rumor is not ground sufficient
for a Justice of Peace to proceed upon; and Mr. Pemberton never spake word of it to me before). He said Capt.
Martin call'd him Rascal in the Street, and said had it not
been for his coat, he would have cân'd him. Mr. Pemberton said I excluded him, or he was excluded from
Dining with the Superiour Court by the Invitation of
Capt. Martin. I said 'twas with difficulty that his Company was obtain'd at our Diñer. The matter of Fact was
this: Upon Midweek Nov.ʳ 8., as I take it, twas nois'd that
General Nicholson was going out of Town to Pascataqua,
in order to his Voyage home: Hereupon the Justices
agreed to wait upon his Honor at his Lodgings; to take
Leave of him if going, to invite him to Diñer if he staid
in Town so long: (The Chief Justice was at New London),
Sewall, Hathorne, Walley, Corwin went in the morning to
the House of Mr. John Borland; When the Genˡ came,
and we had Saluted him, and understood his Honor staid
in Town that day; We invited him to Diner to the Green
Dragon; and Mr. Myles being there, I invited him; and
enquired of the Genˡ if there were any we should ask to
Dine with him? He mention'd Capt. Martin, the Comadore. Accordingly we sent, and for Major Handy. When
Mr. Pemberton had Pray'd, I desir'd him to Dine with the

Court, the Gen¹ was invited. Mr. Pemberton ask'd whether
Capt. Martin was to be there, I said yes; Then said Mr.
Pemberton, you must Excuse me! I reply'd, His Invitation was not of my proposal. And yet this was now thus
brought over again: Mr. Pemberton said the Council took
so little notice of Capt. Martin's Abusing him (though it
had been talk'd of in Council) that they invited him to
their Treat at the Return from Annapolis Royal.¹ This
concerns the whole Council, and therefore I have nam'd
it last, as in which I am least concern'd. But this is to be
said for the Council. The Fleet was a chief Mean of
Taking Port Royal; Capt. Martin was Comadore of that
Fleet, and therefore could not be separated from the Gen!
A personal Resentment of what had pass'd before the
going to Port-Royal, ought not to make a Balk in a Publick Invitation after God's granting Success; which had
been so much and Publickly pray'd for; and Thanks to
God Return'd. And if the Justices had sent for Capt.
Martin, I cânt tell what could have been made of the
Offence. Tis difficult medling with Captains of Frigats.
Reasons of State require the overlooking many grievous
Things. The Sons of Zerviah were too hard for David,
his calling them to Account. He was fain to leave Joab
to the Reign of Solomon.

These Things made me pray Earnestly and with great
Concern, that God would vouchsafe to be my Shepherd,
and perform for me what is mention'd in the 23. Psalm,
that He would not leave me behind in my Straglings; but
bring me safely to his Heavenly Fold.

Dec.ʳ 1. 1710. Mr. Neh. Hobart having invited Joseph
to Preach, I took him and his Sister Hañah in the Coach
and went to Lecture, and left Joseph there. The ways

---

¹ This name was substituted by the English for *Port* Royal at the
time (1710) of Nicholson and Vetch's Conquest. Hutchinson, II. 167. —
EDS.

were heavy; but being moderat wether, Hañah and I got home comfortably, though late.

Decr 2.^d Isaac Goose is buried; Bearers, Sewall, Belcher; Oakes, Checkley; Cutler, Welsteed. He was a very diligent and laborious man in his Calling, and I hope a Christian. I have heard he had a good Gift in Prayer; though his Speech at other times was something abrupt. Just at the same time a Considerable person that came from Barbados for his health, and died suddenly, was buried.

Lord's Day, Decr 3. 1710. I was enlarged in blessing God for answering my Prayer in Mr. Henry Flint's Sermon from Mat. 7. 24. In the Afternoon Mr. Pemberton order'd the 5 first verses of the 58th Psalm to be sung. I think if I had been in his place and had been kindly and tenderly affectioned, I should not have done it at this time. Another Psalm might have suited his Subject as well as the 5th verse of this. Tis certain, one may make Libels of David's Psalms; and if a person be abused, there is no Remedy: I desire to leave it to God who can and will Judge Righteously.[1]

---

[1] In doubt whether Mr. Pemberton used the Bay Psalm Book, or Tate and Brady's version, we give the reader the benefit of both.
The Bay Psalm Book renders verses 4 and 5 of Ps. 58, thus: —

> " Their poyson's like serpents poyson;
> they like deafe Aspe, her eare
> that stops. Though Charmer wisely charme,
> his voice she will not heare."

Tate and Brady's version is as follows: —

> " Speak, O ye Judges of the Earth
> if just your Sentence be:
> Or must not Innocence appeal
> to Heav'n from your Decree?

> " Your wicked Hearts and Judgments are
> alike by Malice sway'd;
> Your griping Hands, by weighty Bribes,
> to Violence betrayed.

Dec. 12. I went to Mr. Pemberton and Expostulated about his Treatment of me.

Nov. 28. Ask'd him whether the Mathers were not Embassadors of Christ and therefore ought to be vindicated; I might have expected his Escape.[1] As to Capt. Martin, the Comadore, when I had related the matter of Fact, he said he knew it not before. I visited Madam Pemberton, and gave the Nurse 3.

Dec. 14. Mr. Samuel Newman of Rehoboth dies; He sat in one Court as a Justice of Peace; was a very good Man: He dined with us at Smiths, as were coming home.

Dec. 17. 1710. Mrs. Jane Lindal, Mr. John Pole's only Child is buried.[2]

Dec. 29. Sister Jane Gerrish returns. My wife invited her earnestly to have staid all Winter. She came before Daughter Gerrish was brought to Bed. My wife gave her a Mourning Suit.

Second-day, Jan. 1. 17$\frac{10}{11}$. Mr. Mayhew returns, hav-

---

"To Virtue, strangers from the Womb
   their Infant Steps went wrong:
There prattled Slander, and in Lyes
   employ'd their lisping Tongue.

"No Serpent of parch'd *Afric's* Breed
   doth ranker Poison bear;
The drowsy Adder will as soon
   unlock his sullen Ear.

"Unmov'd by good Advice, and deaf
   as Adders they remain;
From whom the skilful Charmer's Voice
   can no attention gain."   —EDS.

[1] His way of evading the censure. — EDS.

[2] This was the first wife of Timothy Lindall, of Salem and Boston, H. C. 1695, Speaker and of the Council, Judge of the Common Pleas, &c. In his will he mentions his great-grandson, Thomas Lindall Winthrop, an example of the few links required to connect Sewall's times with our own. A good sketch of the Lindall family is in the N. E. Hist. Genealogical Register, VII. 15–24. — EDS.

ing with great Patience staid the finishing that Excellent work of Setting forth the Psalms and Gospel of John in English and Indian. He was abundantly Laborious in Skillfully revising the Translation, and Correcting the Press.[1]

Jan.ʸ 4. Mr. Wadsworth preaches Excellently, Doctr: They that are not Upright in heart are Rebels against God. I was much affected with the Sermon. About 4 weeks before at —— Bligh's Funeral, [I asked] whether Mr. Bridge and he administred the Lord's Super alternatly? He answer'd, they did, He did it last; which, as I take it, was the Lord's day before; I was inclin'd to go to the first church as sometime I had done, and partake with them; and this Sermon forwarded me in my design.

Lord's Day, Jan.ʸ 7. I goe to the first Church, and partake there. Mr. Wadsworth's Text was, 1 Cor. 10. 3 — And that Rock was Christ: made a good Sermon to my great Refreshment. Went also in the Afternoon and heard Mr. Bridge. It seems the Governour's Lady was very much affected with Mr. Wadsworth's Lecture Sermon, mentioned before; and fell sick; on the 9th of Jan.ʸ Mr. Paul Dudley told me they fear'd they should have lost her.

Jan.ʸ 11th I met Madam Willard going; she desired me to speak to Mr. Bridge to pray for her. I met with him in Mr. Buttolph's Shop, and did it; He pray'd for the Governour's Consort. After Sermon a Bill was read for her; so she was praid for twice Expressly.

Jan.ʸ 12th I goe to visit the Governour's Lady, sat with the Govʳ awhile; Mr. Paul Dudley, Capt. Chandler, Capt. Oliver Noyes, I should have mention'd before. Mr. Noyes spake so much of Madam Dudley's mending, that he said

---

[1] Massachusee Psalter, &c. See Brinley's Catalogue, Vol. I. No. 798. Printed by B. Green and the Indian, James Printer, 1709. Brinley had two good copies, and one imperfect, and at his sale, March 10–14, 1879, they brought large prices.

She was well; he had given her the Febrifuge several times. I went into Chamber and spake to her; She thank'd me for speaking to Mr. Bridge to pray for her: Hop'd she should praise God upon her Recovery.

January, 14. Lord's day, Mr. Sergeant tells me that the Governour's Lady was taken distracted, raving, in the night, and that she was dying.

January, 15th Lt Col. Quinsey's Barn is burnt down and all in it, as the Military Officers were taking the Oaths at Mills's. It came by a man's blowing out his pipe, who was swingling[1] Flax. 17. Widow Jn°son buried.

Jany 18th 5th day. Mr. Secretary and I give the Oaths to 24. Military officers of this Regiment, viz. Col. Checkley, Lt Col. Savage, Major Fitch, Capt. Jn° Ballantine, Capt. Samuel Keeling, Capt. Habijah Savage, Capt. Edw. Martyn, Capt. Edward Winslow —— Capt. Jonathan Bill &c.

Jany 20. Benj Larnell comes to my house at 3 or 4. p. m̄. with a Letter from Mr. Rawson, dated Jany 15th No man came with him to me, or gave. any account of him. Presently after his coming I went to the Funeral of Mrs. Boñer.

Jany 20. I was going to Brooklin, and Son Sewall came hither which prevented me. I sent the Govr ½ Duz. Consolations. Gave son ½ Duz. Sent daughter Sewall a Letter, and in it a 20^s Bill to buy her little Hañah a Coat. Very fair Warm day: Joseph went to Charlestown a little before B. Larnell came hither, to preach for Mr. Bradstreet to morrow.

Jany 22. Mr. Williams comes and examines Benjamin Larnell, and likes him.

Jany 25. I goe with him to School: in the way I meet Capt. Williams, who tells me of the death of Mr. Stoddard's Son, Solomon, last night.

---

[1] A good old English word for *beating*, the instrument used being called a *swingle*. — EDS.

Jan.ʸ 23. Mr. Pemberton visits us, and prays Excellently. Jan.ʸ 26. Council, which is adjourn'd to the first of February.

Jan.ʸ 27. I cut down the Elm that anoy'd the Coach-house Stable. Mr. Solomon Stoddard buried. Bearers, Major Dudley, Joseph Sewall; —— Hunt, Samˡ Shrimpton; Jn.ᵒ Walley, —— Borland. White Scarfs and Gloves.

Tuesday, Jan.ʸ 30. The Chief Justice, Sewall and Walley goe to Charlestown to keep Court; pleasant day, and no more sign of Ice in the River or Banks, than in the begiñing of April. Mr. Corwin met us there. Col. Hathorne came not. Gave away about 34. Consolations. Finish'd the Court by Candle-light.

Mid-week, Jan.ʸ 31. Went and heard Mr. Bridge, and Dr. Cotton Mather pray and preach, at the said Dr's House. Mr. Bridge's Text was about God's lifting up a Standard, when Enemy breaks in as a Flood. Dr. Mathers, The whole world lyes in Wickedness. Had Cake and Butter and Cheese, with good Drinks, before parting. As I went home, I heard Col. Vetch was arriv'd from Añapolis.

Feb.ʳ 1. As I go to Lecture, I wait on Gov.ʳ Vetch and congratulat his Safety; He thanks me for my Respect to him and to his Spouse.

At 3. p. m̄. The Council meets according to Adjournment. Upon Conference with Col. Vetch, the Expedition is set forward by Water. Mr. Secretary reads a paper given him by Col. Vetch, Certifying that the Government of Añapolis Royal had not Traded with the Indians as they were aspers'd, but with all in a vile mañer loading New-Engld with Calumnies; a spirit of Witchcraft, and now 7 fold a Spirit of Lying, haters of Monarchy, regretting Her Majesties success in Taking Port-Royal. I took it of the Secretary, and read it, and mov'd several of the Council that they would speak to it. I told them it would otherwise be taken as a tacit License to print it. When

no body spake, and Col. Vetch was going away, I pray'd
him to stay a little; and said I fear'd the reading that
paper without being spoken to, would be taken as a tacit
Licensing of it. I was for the Certificat so far as it vindicated their innocency; but was against the Reflections on
New-England, they would be dishonorable to Nova Scotia,
and New-England. I was against printing it with them.
Col. Vetch said, if it could not be printed here, he would
have it printed elsewhere; Copies of it were sent to England, I said it was Raillery unbecoming a Government.
When Col. Vetch was gon, I pray'd the Govr to forbid the
printing it unless those Reflections were first taken out.
The Govr said, he could not hinder it; they might take their
own way. And yet own'd twas Raillery. I don't know
but Col. Vetch may reckon that he has a tacit License to
print the Certificat just now read in Council. I am very
free the Substance of the Certificat, relating to their own
iñocency, may be printed: But to print the bulky Reflections would be dishonorable to Añapolis, and Boston.
And I can no way consent to it. I think it should be
spoken to.

Seventh-day, Febr. 3. 17¾¾. Col. Foster was taken with
an Apoplectick Fit as he was at the privat house about 8.
m̄. When he staid long they call'd, none answer'd; so
they burst open the door, and found him fallen down, and
Speechless.

Lords-day, Febr. 4th Mr. Joseph Sewall preaches for
Mr. Colman p. m̄ : prays for Col. Foster. Mr. Pemberton
Prays for him.

Febr. 5. Joseph returns to the College. I visit Deacon
Atwood, went to Col. Foster's and sat awhile with Mr.
Edw. Hutchinson, and Mr. Ruck; visited Elder Copp, Mr.
Gee.

Febr. 6. Maxwell calls not, so I go not out.

Febr. 7. A great Storm of Snow; yet I get to Bro^r
Thornton's, to the Meeting, and there read an excellent

Sermon out of Mr. Shepard, on the Ten Virgins; against Hypocrisy: should search for some Work wrought in us. Sung part of the 45ᵗʰ PS. Broʳ Manly invites for the first time; by which means it comes not to us till this day Moneth.

Febr. 8. Madam Usher and Cous. Rolf dine with us; by whom I sent 70 odd Sermons to Rowley and Newbury.

Febr. 9. Seventh-day, between 11 and 12 m. Col. John Foster expires.[1] His place at the Council Board and Court will hardly be filled up. I have lost a good Left-hand man.[2] The Lord save New-England! Now just half the Counsellours mention'd in the Charter, are dead; The good Lord prepare the rest, and me especially to follow after.

Now about I dream'd of being at the Comencment and seeing Mr. Leverett in Scarlet.

Thorsday, Febr. 15. John Foster esqr. is entombed. Bearers, Govʳ Dudley, Waitstill Winthrop esqr; Sewall, Addington; Walley, Belchar. Scarfs and Rings, Escutcheons. All of the Council had Scarfs; Col. Vetch. Many

---

[1] This was Colonel John Foster, an eminent merchant from Aylesbury, County Bucks, not to be confounded with any of the other distinguished families of the name here. His arms are given in Gore's Roll (Heraldic Journal, I. 120), and those of his widow, Abigail, whose death is noted under date of March 15th, following. She was Abigail, daughter of Captain Thomas Hawkins, and sister of Hannah Hawkins, who married Elisha Hutchinson, and had a son Thomas, whose wife was Sarah, daughter of Colonel Foster.

Mrs. Foster had been married twice before, first to Samuel Moore, — then to Thomas Kellond, who died July 12, 1686. As Foster's daughter married Thomas Hutchinson Dec. 24, 1703, it is *possible* that she was the child of this marriage, and thus own cousin to Hutchinson. Edward Hutchinson, half-brother of Thomas, married Lydia, the other daughter of Colonel John Foster, Oct. 10, 1706. It seems more probable that both were Foster's daughters by a first wife. By a curious blunder in N. E. H. G. Register, XIX. p. 16, line one, this Abigail Hawkins is included among the children of Elisha Hutchinson, when really she was his sister-in-law. Increase Mather preached a funeral sermon on the death of the Fosters. — EDS.

[2] The expression of a " good left-hand man " seems rather strange. At present the phrase would be a " right-hand man." — EDS.

great Guns were fired. Joseph Sewall came to Town, and was at the Funeral, had a pair Gloves sent him to our House. Son Samuel was at the Funeral, coming to Town to Lecture.

Febr. 18. Joseph preaches at the North [Meeting House].

Febr. 19. Returns to Cambridge. Capt. Atwood comes after his going away, brings 20ˢ.; speaks very favourably of my Son. It was night when had sat a little at the House of Mourning after return from the Grave. Mr. Stoddard carried me in his Coach, with Major Walley, Mr. Eᵐ. Hutchinson.

As I went to the Funeral, I call'd at Lᵗ Joseph Gallop's and left a Sermon with him for his wife. He surprises me by telling me she is very sick.

Febr. 20. Mrs. Elisabeth Gallop (first Alcock, then Dwight) dies last night. Bearers, Mr. Speaker, Capt. Southack; Capt. Giles Fifield, Jnᵒ Alden; Mr. Nichols, Wᵐ Alden. Mr. Pemberton and I went next the Women, Febr. 22.

Febr. 21. Mr. Jonathan Russell died last night, about 55. years old; an Orthodox Usefull Man: My ancient Friends and Acquaintance dye; tis not a year since excellent Mr. Cotton of Hampton dyed. Let GOD be my bosom Friend and Familiar, my *Amicus Necessarius!* [1]

Febʳ. 26. 17$\frac{1}{1}\frac{0}{1}$ Mrs. Wisewall widow, and Mrs. Allen dye. This day p. m̄. the Govʳ has the French Messengers from Canada in Council; Had the Councillors on his Left hand, Col. Vetch and them on his right; on the right also were Mr. Secretary and Mr. Com̄issary. Read their Credentials by Mr. Weaver the Interpreter. Reprimanded one Anthony Oliver for going to them at Meers's, and to the Frier without leave; made him take the Oaths, and subscribe

---

[1] This was, probably, Rev. Jonathan Russell, of Barnstable, H. C. 1675, four years after Sewall, and son of that Rev. John Russell, of Hadley, who concealed the regicides Goffe and Whalley for so many years. — Eds.

the Declaration.[1] Told the Messengers they should depart
that day señight, as had told the Council with some
Spirit, last Satterday: at which time Col. Vetch said the
people of N. E. were generally given to Lying; to which
the Govr said not a word.

Febr. 28. 17$\frac{10}{11}$ Midweek: This being my Marriage-
day, and having now liv'd in a married Estate Five and
Thirty years, notwithstanding my many Sins and Temptations, I spent some time in Meditation and Prayer in the
Castle-Chamber. I was much encouraged by reading in
Course the 32^d Psalm at family prayer without any fore-
sight of mine. And when I came to pray I was much
heartened to ask Forgiveness of God for my multiplied
Transgressions, seeing He had directed Peter a sinfull Mortal to forgive to 70. times 7. I hope God will forgive and
do as the matter may require. While I was thus employ'd
Maxwell warn'd me to Council; but I ventur'd to keep in
my Closet; and I understand by the Maj^r Genl they did
nothing in Council. Maj^r Genl and his Lady visited us
just before the Funeral. Bearers of Mrs. Allen were,
Elisha Hutchinson, Saml Sewall; Giles Dyer, Saml Checkley; John Cutler, Sam! Phillips: Scarves and Gloves.
Whiles I was Spending a little Fewel in privat Devotion I
was suply'd with a great Peñiworth of Bast[2] by Bastian,
and a Load of black Oak by Nathl Sparhawk.

March, 2. 17$\frac{10}{11}$ Joseph comes to Town; this morning
Mr. Pemberton's desire that he should preach for him was
told him by Mr. Flint, which he comply'd with, though he
was to preach at Mrs. Bridgham's in the evening.

March, 4. Lord's Day; To my aprehension God assists
my Son remarkably in prayer and preaching I hope tis
an Answer of my prayer last Midweek. Preaches again
in the Evening.

---

[1] See May 30, below. — EDS.
[2] The bark of the bass or lime tree. — EDS.

March, 5th Second-day. Mrs. Abigail Foster dyes between 11 and 12 at Noon.

March 6th Joseph visits Mr. Pemberton, dines at his Sister Hirst's, returns to Cambridge.

At the Meeting for the free School at Mr. Pemberton's; Mr. Bridgham declining to sign, saying it was not fit for him to sign with persons so much above him; I said pleasantly, We are at Foot-ball now; and then he presently Sign'd.

Fifth-day, March, 8th 1710/11. Mrs. Abigail Foster is buried at the North, in the Tomb of Mr. Kellond, her former Husband.[1] Bearers, Govr., Mr. Winthrop Chief Justice; Sewall, Addington; Walley, Belchar: the same that were for Col. Foster this day was three weeks. Scarvs, Rings, Escutcheons. Councillours and Ministers had Scarvs. Mr. Bridge made a funeral Sermon. (Those that weep as if they wept not.) Gave a honorable Character of Col. Foster and his Lady.

Lords-day, March, 11. 1710/11 Mr. Pemberton baptiseth Catharina Winthrop, Lucy Lechmere, Richard Hitchbourn. Takes Mrs. Elisabeth Partridge into the Church.

Feria secunda, March, 12. 1710/11 Añiversary Town-Meeting, Mr. Colman prays, and Col. Townsend is chosen Moderator: Will chuse Assessors distinct. 7 Select-men; viz.

		Assessors.	
Mr. Joseph Wadsworth	86	Mr. James Barns	65
Daniel Oliver	82	Tim° Clark	48
Addington Davenport	62	Francis Thrasher	46
Oliver Noyes	1	Dan¹ Powning	41
Thomas Cushing	57	Nathan¹ Oliver	41
Edward Hutchinson	48	Sam¹ Greenwood	39
Isaiah Tay	46	Jonas Clark	38

Martyn, Savage, Marshal quite left out. Thomas Lee, and George Bethune fin'd[2] for Constables. Eleazer Dorby

---

[1] See note on Colonel Foster, *ante*, p. 300. — EDS.

[2] Fined for refusing to serve. — EDS.

only Sworn.   Past 8. at night adjourn'd to 9. next morning.

About 150£ received for Constable Fines.

March, 17.   Gen¹ Court rises.

March, 22.   Council for Nomination of Officers aͬpointed
this day : but the Govͬ came not to Town; Secretary acquainted us from his Excellency's Letter, that twas adjourn'd to Friday, Mar. 23. at 3 p. m̄.   Friday, Mar. 23.
About 10. m. Maxwell comes to my house and warns me
to meet his Excellency in Council at 3 p. m̄.   About an
hour after comes again, and warns me to meet the Govͬ
presently.   After some other Business, the Govͬ nominated Mr. Tho. Brattle a Judge of the Infer. Court in the
room of Col. Foster; this pass'd in the Negative.¹   All
was over before the Arrival of the Time aͬpointed for the
Council.

Seventh-day, March, 24. 17¹⁰⁄₁₁ Mr. Corwin, Mr. At-
torney and I set out for Plimouth about 1 p. m̄.   Got to
Weymouth a pretty while before Sun-Set: I lodge at
Cousin Hunt's.

March, 25. 1711.   Hear Mr. Peter Thacher of Weymouth, who prays and preaches well ; though he had been
at Boston to see his new-married Sister, which might
occasion his preparations to be less full.   Sup at Mr.
Thacher's.

March, 26. proceed to Plimouth, Joshua Kibbe waiting
on me.   From Cushin's with Mr. Attorney, who kept the
Sabbath at Hingham.   Din'd at Bairstow's.   Were met
by the Sheriff a little on this side Cook's; got to Plimouth
before 5.   Quarter'd at Witherell's.   March, 27. Major

---

¹ After Brattle's rejection, the Governor nominated, for the fourth justice
of the Common Pleas of Suffolk, Samuel Lynde, April 2. He was rejected,
and the Council added: " It is their unanimous opinion That the three sur-
viving Justices, being a Quorum according to the Law, are legally qualified
to hold the said Court, and ought to hold the same accordingly, that the service of the Queen nor subjects be prejudiced for failure thereof." Finally,
June 11, 1711, Thomas Palmer was nominated and confirmed. — EDS.

Walley, who lodg'd at Cook's, comes to us seasonably.
Open the Court.

Martij 28. *mihi natalis, in Ædes intravi et ibidem Preces effudi.*

March, 29. Col. Byfield argues the Case of Prohibition; between Mr. Attorney and him, about three hours were taken up, from 11 to 2. Indian man charg'd with Ravishing an Indian Girl of 3 years old, was brought off, the principal Evidence being dead. Col. Thacher came to us; I gave him a Consolation to Mr. Lothrop. Artillery Sermon of Dr. Mather; to Mr. Little, and Mr. Sheriff Consolations. To many Question about marrying ones Wives own Sister.

Sixth-day, March, 30. Set out about 8. m: baited at Bairstow's, dined at Cushing's. Mr. Corwin rode away alone, and went out of his way towards Bridgewater; but got to Cushings. Baited at the half Moon at Miller's, came all together into Town; found all well. *Laus Deo.* God is the more to be acknowledged because I had more misgivings than at some other times.

Second-day, April, 2. Mr. Walter is chosen to Preach the Artillery Sermon. At a Council, the Govr Nominats Mr. Saml Lynde to be a Judge in stead of Col. Foster. I desir'd time of Consideration as Col. Foster us'd to doe. Council is adjourn'd to the 19th of April.

April, 3. I dine with the Court at Pullin's. Mr. Attorney treats us at his house with excellent Pipins, Anchovas, Olives, Nuts. I said I should be able to make no Judgment on the Pipins without a Review, which made the Company Laugh. Spake much of Negroes; I mention'd the problem, whether should be white after the Resurrection: Mr. Bolt took it up as absurd, because the body should be void of all Colour, spake as if it should be a Spirit. I objected what Christ said to his Disciples after the Resurrection. He said twas not so after his Ascension.

April, 4. Wadlin comes in from Salt-Tertuda [Tortugas],

in whom comes Mr. Josiah Willard,[1] who has been twice taken. Used civilly at first by the Privateer; but suffer'd hardship in Prison at Martineco. After, was going to Barmudas, was taken, Strip'd, and us'd Roughly.

Capt. Jn° Rainsford and Pulcifer are dead.

April, 13. Dr. Mather visited me, I return'd his little Book out of which I reprinted the Case of Conscience against a man's marrying his Brother's [?] sister.[2] He went into Chamber and Pray'd with my wife and family, particularly for Joseph, who was there. Joseph returns to Cambridge in the afternoon.

About 5. p. m̄. Richard Hobby, Son of Capt. John Hobby, a desireable youth of about 13 or 14 years old, was kill'd with the overthrowing of a Cart upon him near the N[orth] Meetinghouse.

April, 15. Mr. Pemberton is indisposed as was administring the Lords Super. Had so much of a Fever as to keep him at home in the afternoon, by which means Mr. Holyoke was alone.

April, 19. 1711. Council, present his Excellency the Gov.ʳ

Winthrop	Penn Townsend
Elisha Hutchinson	Joseph Lynde
S. Sewall	Eᵐ Hutchinson
Isa. Addington	Andrew Belchar
Petʳ Sergeant	Ed.ʳ Bromfield
John Walley	Nathan.ˡ Norden.

---

[1] This seems to be Josiah Willard, born 1681, H. C. 1698, for many years Secretary of the Province. The Willard Memoir, p. 369, says: "After leaving college, Mr. Willard became a tutor at that institution, pursued his studies in divinity, and began to preach; but, on account of an unconquerable diffidence, he soon relinquished the profession. He travelled abroad, to the West Indies and Europe; and, at one time, commanded a ship in the London trade." — EDS.

[2] In Brinley's Catalogue we find the following title: "An Answer of Several Ministers in and near Boston, to that Case of Conscience, Whether it is Lawfull for a Man to Marry his Wives own Sister?" pp. 8, 8vo. Boston: Bartholomew Green, 1695. Signed by Increase Mather, Charles Morton, James Allen, Samuel Willard, James Sherman, John Danforth, Cotton Mather, and Nehemiah Walker. — EDS.

The Govr Nominated Mr. Saml Lynde for a Judge of the Infer^r Court; which pass'd in the Negative. I observ'd but one for him; and that was Capt Norden in a mean way; as far as I could hear, he said he knew nothing against him. The Browns of Attleborough, Rehoboth, Swanzey pleaded before the Govr and Council about Wills and Lands bequeathed in Narraganset. I enquired what we had to do, to judge of Lands in the Narraganset Countrey? Mr. Secretary said, I was in the right. However, the Petition was dismiss'd, upon the head of the young men having offer'd equal Terms of Accomodation.

April, 20. 1711. Mr. S. Gerrish goes to Wenham.

April, 21. Plenty of Swallows. Note. Hannah Gerrish was taken very sick last night.

April 22. Lords Day, B. Gray calls me up at 1. at night: I find poor little Hannah Gerrish in an Agony, I went to Prayer; afterwards B. Gray read the 5th Rom. I found the Chapter so full of Comfort that awhile after I read it over again. About 6. m. Mr. Wadsworth came and pray'd with little Hañah. Mr. Gerrish her Father came home at ½ hour past Nine: put up a Note in the Afternoon, which Mr. Pemberton read coming out in his Gown.

April 23. I was call'd up between 2 and 3 at night, but my little Hañah Expired before I got thither. However, She had the Respect of one visit after death. She Expired about ½ hour after 2 at night. The Lord prepare me for my great Change.

Third-day, April, 24. Hañah Gerrish is buried. Bearers, Gillam Phillips, and Benj. Gray: white Scarvs. Was put into the Tomb just before Sun-set, several of the Council, Dr. Cotton Mather, Mr. Wadsworth, Colman there. Note. This day, about noon, John Kent of the Island had his Barn burnt by Tabacco, and Six oxen and four calves in it, and a Goose bringing young ones. The Oxen were heard to roar afar off: but the Flame was so rapid, the

Owners could not help them.   Carts, and Instruments of
Husbandry burnt.

Friday, May, 4. Mr. Charles Chauncey dyes. Mr.
Evans's Jury Acquit Pastre of Fornication, and Maria,
Mr. Wm Hutchinson's Indian woman, of Murdering her
Child, by letting it fall into the House of Office.

Seventh-day, May, 5. Capt. Oliver prevails with Joseph
to preach for Mr. Bradstreet to morrow p. m̅, that so Mr.
N. Williams may be releas'd to Succour Mr. N. Hobart of
Newtown, who is taken Sick yesterday.

May, 7. 1711. Mr. Chancy buried; Bearers, Mr. Daniel
Oliver, Mr. Francis Clark; Mr. Wm Welsteed, Mr. Grove
Hirst; Mr. Oliver Noyes, Mr. Anthony Stoddard. Many
of the Council there. His Excellency sets out for Pascataqua.

May, 8. The chief Justice Winthrop sets out for
New-London.

May, 9. Midweek. Town-Meeting to chuse Representatives; n° of Voters 173. Major part 87. Mr. John
Clark 161. Mr. Tho. Hutchinson 157. Major Tho. Fitch,
106. Davenport 74. Barns 68. 2^d Stroke, Voters 167.
Major part 84. Mr. Addington Davenport, 95.

The Town accepted my Proposals, and bought the upper
part of my Pasture to enlarge the North Burying Place.[1]

Agreed that the Select-men be impowered to Sell the

---

[1] Town Records, II. 325. " Voted that the proposall made by the Honble
Sam^ll Sewall, Esq. for sale of a parcell of Land for Enlargeing the North
burying place, at the price of One hundred and Twenty pounds, to abate
seventy pounds of the said purchase money, so that the Town please to Release an Annual Quit claim of Forty Shillings, Issueing out of a Ceadar
Swamp in his possession situate in Brooklyne, appropriated to the use of the
Grammar-School. Reported by the Com̅ittee, Be accepted. And that the
said Quit Rent of Forty shillings p. Annum be abated. The aforesaid
Sum̅e of Seventy Pounds to be drawn out of the Town Treasury and In-
vested in some Real Estate, or otherwise improved by the direction of the
Select men for the time being. The Yearly Rent or Profit thereof to be ap-
propriated to the use of the Free Grammar School, in lieu of the aforesaid
Quit Rent." See also Suffolk Deeds, lib. 26, fol. 97. — EDS.

Neck to Half-way pond to them that shall maintain the
way; leaving an Interval of 100. yards for Fortification;
I and Mr. White propos'd this; Mr. Paul Dudley opos'd
it much and got these words inserted, (or for other use):
reserved also a high way between the former Grant and
this.[1]   Mr. Wadsworth prayed; First I was Moderator;
which I declin'd, because of the Treaty that was to be
about the Burying Place.

Then Major Fitch was put up by the Select-men and
voted.   Not being present, he was sent to, and declin'd.
Then Col. Checkly was voted and serv'd.

May, 11.   Went to Charlestown Lecture: and then to

---

[1] The following entries explain this matter: —

Town Records, II. 326.   " Voted, that it is left to the Selectmen to
grant, sell, or dispose of the Townes Land on each side of the Highway on
the Neck, from the place where the Fortification formerly stood, as far as
the halfe way Pond, either by lease for term of years or by Grant of the Fee
thereof, as they shall think best; In order to secureing the Highway there,
(which is proposed to be left of a considerable breadth) Reserving a space of
about one hundred yards in breadth, across from sea to Sea, sutable for a
Fortification or any other use for the Service and benefit of the Town, Reserving also a Space for a Cross Highway next to the land formerly Granted
to Capt. Oliver Noyes and Company: and the said Selectmen are fully impowered to make and execute proper Instruments or Deeds for the same."

We infer, from the document next printed, that the grant to Oliver Noyes
and his associates began at Castle Street and extended south for some nine
hundred and sixty feet.   That would bring the southern limit to Dover
Street, or near that line, where there had been an old fortification, which was
then (1711) quite decayed.   In that year, another fort was placed there
(Shurtleff, p. 140) which stood "precisely in front of the southwest corner
of the Williams Market House."   This line of the "old fortification" is on
the maps down to the present century.

In 1785, Stephen Gore, John May, and others, had a grant of land and
flats, bounded south, on Malden Street, 900 feet, then north, on a causeway,
1400 feet long to a point 125 feet from Dover Street, then west on this line,
parallel to Dover Street, to the highway (now Washington Street), 132½ feet.
Also a similar strip, on the west side of the highway, 200 feet wide, the street
being 80 feet wide (Shurtleff, p. 141).

This limit, 125 feet from Dover Street, was, probably, the south line of
the strip of 100 yards reserved as above, within which the fort was placed.

During the siege of Boston, the British troops strengthened this fort, and
also built an advanced work, of which a view is in Drake's "Landmarks,"

Mr. Pemberton's Meeting: To me to live is Christ. Mr. Bradstreet Prov. 3. 34 — but he giveth Grace to the Lowly.

May, 13, 1711. Mr. Pemberton's Text, Beware of the leven of the Pharisees, which is Hypocrisy, was awfull to me; The Lord Create a Clean heart in me, and Renew a Right Spirit.

May, 14. Set out for Ipswich with Son Thomas. By reason of Letters from New-York by the Pacquet, I set out late, near Noon. Din'd at Brother's; Lodg'd at Mr.

---

p. 425. This stood between Dedham and Canton Streets, and crossed Washington Street from sea to sea.

The grant to Oliver Noyes is as follows (Suff. Deeds, lib. 24, f. 239): —

" Indenture made 30 Sept., 1709, *between*

1	Samuel Phillips, bookseller	(10)	6	Eliz. Pemberton, ex^r of Benj.	
2	David Jeffries, merchant	(9)		P., brewer	(4)
3	Thomas Savage do	(8)	7	Dr. Oliver Noyes	(2)
4	William Clark do	(5)	8	Elisha Cooke, gent	(7)
5	William Payne do	(3)	9	Stephen Minot, tailor	(1)
			10	John Noyes, goldsmith	(6)

holding, in common, upland, beach and flats to low water mark, and meadow, on both sides the highway to Roxbury, upon the Neck; extending from the northerly end of the pasture land now or late of John Bennett on the east side, and the land of Daniel Epes on the west side — so far south towards Roxbury as 24 feet beyond the new pavement on the said highway as it now is. Together with all right &c., on condition of keeping off the sea on both sides of the highway; as appears by an Indenture from the Selectmen of Boston, dated 31 Jany. 1708." [This is in vol. 24, f. 106; and adds that Bennett's land was bought of him by Samuel Lynde. The land reaches to the old fortification.]

They now make a division, reserving 48 feet for Orange Street, and lay out the lots across the territory from low-water mark. Stephen Minot has the first lot, " adjoining to the new highway called Castle Street laid out by the proprietors across the said neck on the north — the rest as above noted in the order of figures in parentheses. Lots to be 97½ feet broad on the east end on the flats, 96 feet on the east side of Orange street, 95 ft. 4 in. on west side of Orange street, except Minot's lot varies a little as specified. We also find that Castle Street was laid out in 1709, crossing Orange Street, and having, on the east side, the land of John Bennett, which he bought of Samuel Lynde, and on the west side, land of Daniel Epes. Epes bought, April 17, 1708 (Deeds, lib. 24, f. 147), of William Payne, his land being bounded south by the common, west by the sea or river, north by land of John Clough, and east by the highway. — Eds.

Gerrishes at Wenham.   Sun was down by that time I got over the Ferry.   Note.   When had enter'd Salem Bounds, a few Rods, my Horse being on a Hand-Gallop, fell upon his Nose and threw me off before him: There was danger of his falling upon me: but I freed my self as well and fast as I could; one Leg being under the Horse; Through the Goodness of God I had little or no hurt, when as [whereas] my Horse's Nose bled for it, and the Bitt of the Bridle was broken.

May, 15.   Col. Hathorne and Mr. Corwin call me at Mr. Gerrishes; get to Ipswich seasonably.

Govr comes to Town from Pascataqua; In the evening the Court waits on his Excellency at Madam Wainwright's. Went with Mr. Rogers to our Lodging about Nine.   Great Hail this day.

May, 16.   Adjourn *sine die*.   After the Rain set out for Salem; visited little Betty Hirst; went to Brother's; Saw the Funeral of Deacon Marston's daughter pass by the Gate.   Sup'd with Mr. Noyes and Mr. Attorney on Pickerill.   Meet Mr. Leverett's Letter encouraging Jonathan's procedure in Learning; and Mr. Rogers told me Mr. Payson had a Son as old or older, that was now return'd to School at Ipswich; upon this I encourage Brother, and tell him God's Time is the best Time, God's way the best way.   Left Jonathan my Distich transcribed by him at my bidding.

> *Vive, doce, regna, semper, mihi CHRISTE Sacerdos;*
> *Pendet ab Officijs Spes mea tota tuis.*

May, 17.   Ride home with Mr. Attorney; Have a fair Wind over Wiñisimet Ferry.   Find all well.   *Laus Deo.* Daughter Hirst lodges at our House to promote her Revival and strengthening.

Lords-Day, May, 20.   Rainbow about Six p. m̄.

May, 21.   Fair Serene wether after many days of Rain, Showery afterwards from transient Clouds.

May, 22, May, 23.   Fair Wether and Warm.

May, 24.   Great Rain.

May, 30.   Midweek, By a Dedimus, Col. Phillips, Major Walley and my self gave the Dept's the Oaths[1] and saw them and heard them Repeat and subscribe the Declaration: 72 before the Sermon.   Election as last year, save that Col. Noyes is put in the room of Col. Foster, deceased.

May, 27.   Mr. Pierpont preaches for Mr. Willard; Pemberton in the Afternoon.   Sung 2 last Staves 81 Ps.   Even I was much affected to think how we were fed with the finest of the Wheat, and Honey out of the Rocks Christ exhibited in the Gospel.   And coming home I look'd [in] Austin [St. Augustine], and found he allow'd the Meditation.

May, 30.   Col. Partridge brings News that Capt. Jo[s] Hawley died the 19. May, and was buried the 21. at Northampton.   Same time with Mr. B. Pierce.

May, 31.   Gov[r] dines with Mr. Wadsworth, And the Counsellours of the South Church, Dr. Mather, Dr. C. Mather, and many Ministers, and Mr. White; Mrs. Willard, Mrs. Cotton, widow, Mr. Belcher, Dedham, Mr. Joseph Sewall, and many young Students.

June, 3.   I goe to Mr. Bridgham's Quarter-Meeting and hear Mr. Bridge preach.   1 Cor. 8. 19.   Five pounds odd Money Collected.

Midweek, June, 6. 1711.   Col. Thomas Noyes Took the Oaths and subscribed the Declaration and then took his place at the Board.   When I went to salute him, the Gov[r] told him I was his father; Mr. Secretary was between me and the Gov[r] and I did not hear plainly and so could not take notice of the Complement; but I enquired of Mr.

---

[1] These are the oaths (of allegiance and supremacy) and the declaration (against transubstantiation) prescribed by the Province Charter, and borrowed from 1 William and Mary, Sess. I. c. 1.   The writ of *Dedimus potestatem* empowered certain persons to perform certain acts, as, for instance, to administer oaths in certain cases. — EDS.

Secretary, and did it at Holm's where we Din'd. I crav'd a Blessing and return'd Thanks.

Col. Jn° Appleton moves it, and we agree to invite the Govr, Friday, to dine with us at Holms's. June 7th Col. Apleton invites the Govr Sixth-day, June 8th m. At the Hearing between Dorchester and Bridgwater, Col. Townsend comes in, and says there was an Alarm at the Castle. Enter'd on another Hearing about a new precinct for Reading to the Northward of Ipswich River; but the Drums put us to Silence, and oblig'd the Govr to break off. At Dinner at Holms's in the lower room, one comes in, and says that Col. Nicholson was come; Two Men of War, two Transports, eight Weeks passage.[1] Comes up in

---

[1] This was the first part of the expedition destined for an attack on Quebec. The fleet consisted of fifteen men-of-war and forty transports, under the command of Sir Hovenden Walker, Knt., recently created an admiral. The troops were commanded by Brigadier-General John Hill (brother of Abigail, Mrs. Masham, the Queen's favorite), Colonels Charles Churchill, William Windresse, M. Kempenfeldt, Jasper Clayton, Percy Kirk, Henry Disney, and Richard Kane, of the British army; and Samuel Vetch and Shadrach Walton led two regiments of New England troops. In all, there were some seven thousand soldiers. The fleet was delayed by the difficulty in procuring stores, though the inhabitants alleged that it was no fault of theirs, but arose, mainly, from the secrecy preserved before the arrival of the forces. Captain Andrew Belchar, a rich merchant and contractor, was blamed, perhaps wrongly, as a speculator in these necessaries.

The fleet sailed July 30, and arrived at the mouth of the St. Lawrence, a river of which their Boston pilots knew little. The leaders became disheartened, a part of the vessels, with about eight hundred men, were lost in a storm, and, on September 16th, a council-of-war was held, which, as usual, decided to retreat. Soon after arriving at Portsmouth, England, the admiral's ship, the "Edgar," was blown up; and, although he was saved by being ashore, he lost, as he says, his books, journals, and charts, and the original of Sir William Phips's Journal of his Canada expedition.

In 1714, Admiral Walker was called upon, by the officials, for his accounts; soon after he was dropped from the lists entirely, and he died at Dublin, in January, 1726. His indignation prompted him to issue an account of the abortive expedition, entitled "A Journal, or full Account, of the late Expedition to Canada," &c. London, 1720, p. 304.

We extract therefrom a few items concerning New England. He lodged, at Boston, with Captain Southack (p. 67); he employed "two extraordinary divers" to examine the keel of one of his ships (p. 69); he visited the Gov-a Barge, and Lands at Butler's Wharf, where the Govr receives him with the Council. Enters the Council-Chamber between 5 and 6 p. m̄. Lays the Orders for the Canada Expedition before the Govr and Council. Regiment dismiss'd. I observ'd that has Authority to draw Bills on the Massachusetts Treasury, and Col. Vetch is to Com̄and our Men, and leave whom of them he pleases at Añapolis, to Relieve that Garrison. Gracious Queen Anne pays the charge of the Garrison since the Taking of Port-Royal. Col. Nicholson comes in the Leopard, Capt. Cooke.

Monday June 11. Mr. Palmer is propounded and voted a Judge. I voted not, but said I knew not that twas a Council for such a purpose.[1]

Tuesday, June, 12. No prayer is in the Council. Mr. Bromfield tells me he sent to Mr. Pemberton and he says, Tis not his Turn; sends to Mr. Colman, and he says, Tis not his Turn; so none comes. I told Govr of it about 11. m. This day the Proclamation for the War is pass'd. I carried it to the Printer at Noon. Vessel from Annapolis. Between 6 and 7., A very glorious Rainbow appears, being compleat, and of long continuance.

Midweek, June, 13. Serene.

June, 14. Dr. Cotton Mather Preaches from those words, That which is Crooked cañot be made Streight. Genl Nicholson sat in the Gallery: Govr not at Lecture.

June, 17. Great Heat, Much Rain p. m̄.

---

ernor, at Roxbury (p. 75); and he consulted "Mr. Nelson, of Long-Island, a person of good sense." He was much troubled by desertions, and he prints (pp. 229–234) various proclamations issued against harboring such criminals. He gives on p. 245, a list of vessels taken for the service as transports; on pp. 264–266, a list of deserters; and, in various places, he mentions the names of the Massachusetts men engaged as pilots.

Palfrey (IV. 280–287) says that this unfortunate expedition was the favorite plan of Secretary St. John, afterwards Lord Bolingbroke. He refers to a series of letters, still preserved, showing St. John's "interest in what he hoped to make the crowning exploit of his administration, and a title to his permanent supremacy in the national councils." — EDS.

[1] See note, ante, p. 304. — EDS.

June, 18. I waited on his Excellency to take Leave at his Departure; excus'd my not being at Council on Satterday: Not discerning when his Excellency went away, I knew not of the Adjournment. There was told of the death of the Emperour, and Mr. Harley's[1] being made Treasurer, and Lord Mortimer. Col. Partridges Son that came now from England, was there. We are told also that the Dauphine is dead.[2] The Monmouth and Swiftsure that came from Spit-head the 2ᵈ May, arriv'd at Nantasket this day June, 18ᵗʰ 1711. are part of the Fleet for Canada. Mr. Partridge came from Torbay the 26. April. Are told also that Col. Taylor is our Lt Govʳ. Dr. C. Mather said twas impossible. I read to Mrs. Rock of the Greatness of GOD. "The Vine and Figtree think it no great matter to reign over the trees: but to the Bramble this seems a great matter. Jud. 9. 8–15. Great minds are not much affected with injuries, Gal. 5. 12." P. 138. Abridgem't. Towards night Mr. Berry acquaints us Joseph was very sick; desired to have the Coach sent for him.

June, 19. I goe in the Coach my self; set out at Six and got home between 11 and 12. In the afternoon [Joseph] had a Tooth drawn and is better. Mr. Pemberton visits us and prays. This day Mr. James Oliver and Sam Banister come to Town from Piscataqua; came in Chr. Taylor. I went over at night, Mr. Banister says he saw Col. Taylor's Comission for Lieut Govʳ.[3] says he came to Town with Col. Partridge. Reports that Sir Henry Ashurst is dead.

---

[1] The Emperor Joseph died April 17 (N. S.), 1711. Harley was created Earl of Oxford and Earl of Mortimer on the 24th May (O. S.). He is better known by the former peerage. — EDS.

[2] This was not true. — EDS.

[3] William Tailer was appointed during this year, and arrived Oct. 3, 1711. Nov. 9, 1715, he became acting Governor, and held till the arrival of Governor Samuel Shute, Oct. 4, 1716. Then he was superseded, as Lieutenant Governor, by William Dummer. He was appointed a second time, April 14, 1730, and died in office, March 1, 1731–32, aged fifty-five. — EDS.

June, 22. Sixth-day, Mrs. Mary Dyer is brought to Bed of a Son.

June, 23. Tis known in Town, that the Fleet were seen off of Cape Sable upon Wednesday the 20th Inst^t. Council agree that Mr. Secretary, Mr. Comissary and I should goe down to meet Brigadeer Hill. Sabbath, June, 24. I read Isa. 40. Comfort ye, Comfort ye, my people. After the Forenoon Exercise the Signal is given, Mr. Secretary sends for me ; As I was going I meet with that sad News from Añapolis which much damp'd me.[1] Went down from Butler's wharf ; Mr. Maryon went in another Boat ; order'd the Col. not to make an Alarm till we sent to him, or made a Signal. Went on board the Dunkirk, Capt. Butler, just come to an Anchor ; He could give little news of the Fleet. Met two Transports full of Souldiers. Return'd, saw the other Ships coming in. Gen. Hill arrives.

June 25, 1711. Went down again ; Mr. Secretary, Mr. Comissary, Borland, Sewall ; Mr. Maryon. At the Castle sent for Capt. Tuthil, who told us the Devonshire and Dunkirk were arrived. we saw a Boat going up in which was Col. King, Hail'd him : He came to us, who told us he was going from the Genl to the Senat ; we told him we were sent by them ; then he came into our Boat and sent up his own. Went on Board the Devonshire, saluted and wellcom'd the Genl. Gave us Bread and Sack. After awhile came off Genl and Flagg in one Pinace ; we in our own. Finding the Tide not made, we Land at the Castle ; eat Rusk and drank. Saluted at Landing and Returning with 21. Guns. By Capt. Tuthill. Landed at Scarlets Wharf, went into Town, Turn'd by the Dock, and went up King-street in the Front of the Regiment to the Council-Chamber. Then to Johns's to Diner. Mr. Wadsworth

---

[1] This probably refers to the loss of a part of the garrison, cut off, on an expedition from the fort, by the Indians. — EDS.

crav'd a Blessing; Mr. Colman return'd Thanks. Note. When Spake with Col. King order'd Capt. Tuthill to give the Signal.

Tuesday, June, 26. 1711. Mr. Secretary, Mr. Com̄issary [Belchar] and I wait on the Gen¹ at Mr. Borland's, to pray his Excellency's assistance in sending a Man of War to Añapolis, apprehending the Garrison to stand in need of it; the enemy being flush'd, and grown insolent and daring since their late Success.

Midweek, June, 27. Govʳ Dudley comes to Town, being return'd from New-London. About Two aclock p. m̄. the Transports come up, which make a goodly, charming prospect. A Sailer beaten last night, and threatened to be carried on Board the Weymouth; which the Watch prevented.

June, 28. 1711. Mr. Bridge preaches from Psal. 72. 17. mostly from the latter part of the verse; draws it down to the present Canada Expedition. Govʳ Dudley not at Lecture, nor I think any of the Fleet or Army. After Lecture the Govʳ had up the Gen¹, Admiral, Quartermaster Gen¹, Paymaster Gen! Govʳ set the Gen¹ at his right hand at the end of the Table; Admiral sat above, Mr. Secretary next the Govʳ, Paymaster up̄ermost on the other side. Admiral had sharp discourse about the Merchants offering but Twenty per cent for exchange, threaten'd to be gone somewhere else with the Forces. At last the Govʳ call'd for a vote of the Council to Lend Two Thousand pounds at the Representation of the Paymaster Gen! I mov'd it might be at the Motion of the Gen¹: which was conceded: and Mr. Secretary mov'd that something might be done in writing, which was agreed. Mr. Secretary drew it and the Gen¹ sign'd it, with a Promise to give his Bills. The whole was a surprise to me, and the vote call'd for in the presence of the mentioned Gentlemen. Govʳ would make the Gen¹ goe out before him; though he much resisted it.

June, 29. Gov[r] Treats the General.

June, 30. Seventh-day, Gov[r] sets the Gen[l] and Admiral at the Council-Table, as yesterday.

Mrs. Sarah Banister, widow, dyes between 3 and 4. p. m̄, being drown'd with Dropsie. News comes that Capt. Carver is Taken by two Privateers. Just as had written this I went to look of the Rain at my East-Chamber window, and saw a perfect Rainbow. I think the setting of the Sun caus'd its Disappearance. *Laus Deo.*

July, 3. 1711. Mrs. Sarah Banister, aged about 57., is buried. Bearers, Sewall, Belchar; Draper, Kilby; Capt. Tim° Clark, Mr. Colman.

July, 4. Went to the Com̄encem't by Water in a sloop; cous. Hale with me; Mr. Shepard, Mr. Myles, Chaplain of the Humber, one that was a Fellow of New-College &c. had them to my Son's chamber. The Friar sat with the Fellows. I dined at Fissenden's because there were many Strangers. Rains hard p. m̄. The President makes an Oration, wherein he highly aplauds the Gov[r], his Integrity &c., the Gen[l], Admiral:[1] makes a honorable mention of Col. Nicholson though absent. This night his little son dyes.

July, 7. The Gov[r] sends in Mr. Secretary and me to the House of Deputies, and there by the Govr[s] order Mr. Secretary Prorogues them to the 18th current. Mr. Shove comes to our house.

July, 8. Joseph preaches at Charlestown. Mr. Williams, of Hatfield, with us. Cous. Shortt, at Attleborough.

---

[1] Admiral Walker mentions this visit (Journal, p. 83); he adds, under date of July 7, that Captain Bonner came to him with a chart of Canada River; and as he had " the general character of the best Pilot, as, indeed, he appeared to me to be, I told him he should be abord that Ship when I hoisted my Flag; notwithstanding he was very instant with me to be dispensed with, and for an Excuse alledged his Age."

July 18, Walker was visited by General Nicholson, who had with him a Sachem and several other Indians from Connecticut, who performed their war-dance. — EDS.

July, 12.   I send the Gen[l] 12. Salmon Trouts by Jane
Boston.

Dr. Cotton Mather preaches on the Rainbow, from Rev.
10. 1.   Many Chaplains at Meeting.

July, 13.   Capt. Nathan[l] Holms is buried: Bearers,
Capt. Fayerwether, Capt. Williams; Mr. Tay, Darby;
Mr. Gallop Merch[t], Tilly.   I and Mr. Deringe went together first; then Mr. Pemberton went with me.   None
of the Council there but I.   But a very few days are
pass'd since he came from the Lee-ward Islands.

July, 16. 1711. m.   Two Proclamations order'd; one
for a Fast July 26, and Augt. 30.

In the afternoon was great Thunder, Lightening, Rain.
The beginning of it put in Mr. Jn[o] Williams into our
house.   The discourse of Capt. Torrey put me upon asking Mr. Williams to pray with us, who did it excellently,
and thank'd God for the Opportunity.

July, 17. 1711.   I go to Brooklin and visit my son and
Daughter; Gave my little Grand-daughter an English
shilling, Cakes.   The Rain seems to have been more vehement at Roxbury than at Boston, has much confounded
the High way near Capt. Ruggles, Stop'd up the Mill
Canal that could not Grinde: Were clearing of it.   Lightening burn'd the widow Drapers Barn with a considerable
quantity of Hay in it.   Barn might be 40. feet long.[1]

Aug[t] 3. 1711.   Col. Francis Wainwright dies at his own
house at Ipswich.   Left Salem for his last July 25, the
day before his first-apointed Wedding-day; which Appointment was remov'd to the last of July.   He was

---

[1] Walker notes (Journal, p. 104), under date of July 23, that General
Nicholson came on board with some chiefs of the Five Nations, called Mo-
hocks.   They danced in their fashion, viz.: " each in his turn sung a Song
and danced, while the rest sate down and hum'd and hollow'd at distinct
Periods of his Dance, with a Tone very odd and loud, but yet in Time."
They expressed themselves as hostile to the French.

Walker then reprints the "Boston News Letter," No. 379, giving an
account of his forces. — EDS.

taken Sick at Ipswich on the Lords-Day, July, 29. and
died on the Friday following at 10. m; his Bride being
with him.[1] Tis the most compleat, and surprising Disapointment that I have been acquainted with. Wedding-
Cloaths, to a Neck-cloth and Night-Cap laid ready in the
Bride-Chamber, with the Bride's Attire : Great Provision
made for Entertainment; Guests, several come from Boston, and entertain'd at Mr. Hirst's; but no Bridegroom,
no Wedding. He was laid in a new Tomb of his own
making lately; and his dead wife taken out of another,
and laid with him.

Tuesday, Augt. 7.   Bearers, John Apleton esqr., Col.
John Higginson esqr; Daniel Epes esqr., Stephen Sewall
esqr; Lt Col. Savage, and Mr. Daniel Rogers. Mrs. Betty
Hirst, the Bride, was principal Mourner.

Augt. 9.   Mr. James Barns buried.

Augt. 11.   Mr. Elizur Holyoke dies;[2] Tuesday, Augt
14th buried : Bearers, Sewall, Addington; Townsend, Dr.
Clark; Col. Checkley, Mr. La Bloom. As were passing
along in Middlestreet; One of the Porters stoop'd to take

---

[1] Wainwright was the son and grandson of distinguished citizens bearing
the same two names. The lady he was to have married was, doubtless,
Elizabeth, sister of Grove Hirst, Sewall's son-in-law. If so, she married,
in 1711, Walter Price, as his second wife, according to Savage. — EDS.

[2] Elizur Holyoke is often mentioned by Sewall, being a son-in-law of the
second Jacob Eliot, and thus one of that south-end neighborhood for which
Sewall seems to have had a special affection. He was sixty years old at his
death, and his widow died Feb. 2, 1720–21; both being buried in the Granary
yard. Their children were: John, Rev. Edward, of Marblehead, Samuel
(a brewer), Jacob (a merchant), Hannah (Charnock), Mary (wife of William Arnold), and Sarah, who married her cousin, Deacon John Eliot, sta-
tioner. These children all owned parts of the old Eliot estate.

June 4, 1740 (Suff. Deeds, lib. 69, f. 63), the Eliot heirs laid out Eliot
Street, still known to us, and also a street at right angles thereto, from Frog
Lane (now Boylston Street) to Hollis Street, to be called Holyoke Street.
This was the beginning of our Tremont Street. But in Price's map, of
1743, it was called Clough Street, from John Clough, who owned the land
where the Hotel Boylston stands; and this name, continuing for some fifty
years, entirely extinguished the pious intentions of the first projectors. —
EDS.

up his Hat, by which means the Corps was lower'd so that
the Head of the Coffin jounc'd upon the Ground; but
was retriev'd; the widow was much disturb'd at it; went
to the South-burying place.

Friday, Augt. 10. Alarm is made by reason of advice
from Plimouth, Marble-head, Man-of-War at Nantasket.
Had apointed this day to visit my daughter at Brooklin,
whose little daughter Mary is now 3. weeks old. My
wife goes with Hañah and Judith. Augt. 11. Satterday,
I fetch her home. Augt. 19. 1711. Mrs. Perry is buried,
a good woman, aged 68. Aug.ᵗ 21. Samuel Greenwood,
an honest christian, North-burying place. 65. Midweek,
Augt 22. Mrs. Abigail Whippo, after the Rain and Rainbow; she was Capt. Hamond's daughter; Mr. Collins
was her Grand father. New Burying place. See her
Marriage Febr. 25, 169½. She was Luke Greenough's
widow.[1]

Augt. 24. 1711. Sharp debates about the Province
Gally. Deputies sent in a first vote Earnestly to desire
the Govʳ to send her out in defence of the Coast infested.
Afterward sent a 2ᵈ, wherein twas Resolv'd that the Galley, being built at the Province charge, for defence of the
Coast, cânt be put to any other use without Consent of
the Genˡ Court. No forwardness in putting either of these
to vote. But Mr. Secretary suddenly drew up a vote,
That it being Her Majesties express and positive Comand
that the Galley should go in the Expedition; a Sloop
should be taken up and Man'd. This was non-Concurr'd
in the House of Deputies. Rejected Fire-Ships, and Hulk
to Sink.

---

[1] Savage says that she was the daughter of Captain Lawrence Hammond
by his second wife, Abigail (Willet), daughter of Deacon Edward Collins, of
Medford. She married Luke Greenough in 1690, by whom she had an only
daughter, and then married, in February, 1692, at Boston, James Whippo,
or Whipple, of Barnstable, as his second wife. By him she had nine children. — Eds.

Seventh-day, Augt 25. about one a-clock, Gov͏ͬ sent in
Mr. Secretary, Phillips, Sewall to Prorogue to Sept͏ͬ 26. at
10 m., which was done.

Capt. Matthews arrives Augt. 25., a little before
Sunset.

Monday, 7͏ͬ 10. 1711. Major Walley, Mr. Pemberton
and I set out in the Coach for Bristol, Lion drove: Daniel
Hasting rode by us; intended for Rehoboth; but our
Axel-tree, that complain'd before, and we mended at
Calef's, broke quite off by that time we got to Caperons:
Lodg'd there: Fish'd [1] on a piece in the morning; set out
about 10. m., got to Bristol about 4 or 5. p. m. open'd the
Court and put the Grand-jury upon Business.

Friday, 7͏ͬ 14. Went to Newport to speak with Mr.
Brenton. Twas night before I got thither: Sent Mr.
Brenton word by his Housekeeper, but he neither came
nor sent to me, though I staid there till 3 or past. Mr.
Clap and Pemberton dine with me at Mr. Melvills, where
I lodg'd. I visited Capt. Ellary, he not at home; gave
Mrs. Ellary one of Mr. Willard's Meditations of the Lord's
super. Saw Mrs. Pelham's Grave, buried a few days be-
fore. From the Ferry sail'd in Burden's Boat to Bristol.
7͏ͬ 16. Lord's Day, Mr. Sparhawk preaches a. m. Mr.
Pemberton p. m̄. Dine at my Land Lords. 7͏ͬ 17͏ᵗʰ Mon-
day, set out for Boston: Mr. Mackintosh, Col. Pain, Capt.
Davis, accompany us to the Gate. Dine at Miller's,
Rehoboth, where we are stun'd in hearing the Defeat
of the Canada Expedition. [2] Baited at Caparon's; got

---

[1] This word, in the sense of strengthening, or splicing, is still in use
among seamen. — EDS.

[2] Hutchinson says (Hist. II. 199): " Although the principal object of
this expedition was not obtained, yet, in all probability, Annapolis-royal
was saved by it from falling into the hands of the French."

The garrison had become very small, and the people were rebellious and
daring. Walker (Journal, p. 147) left four hundred troops there, under
Colonel Vetch, Governor, and Colonel Cawfield, Lieutenant-Governor. The
Admiral, just before leaving Spanish River (Journal, 150) finding a cross set

well to Billenges about an hour after Sun-set, where we lodg'd.

7.ʳ 18.ᵗʰ Third-day, set out for Boston; Baited at Dedham. Refresh'd our selv's at Mr. Belcher's: Got well home a little after Diñer time: we recreated our selves with Mr. Watt's Poems, going and coming. *Laus Deo Servatori.* About 7 or 8 aclock of the night between the 2ᵈ and 3ᵈ of October, a Dreadfull Fire hapens in Boston;[1] broke out in a little House belonging to Capt. Ephraim Savage, by reason of the Drunkenness of ―― Moss: Old Meeting House, and Town-House burnt. Old Meeting-

---

up by the French, while " the island had been always in the times of Peace, used in Common, both by the English and French for lading Coals, which are extraordinary good here, and taken out of the Clifts with Iron Crows only, and no other Labour," set up a cross in opposition, claiming the country for the English. Then he sailed away. — EDS.

[1] The great fire of 1711 is fully described by our historians. " It broke out in an old Tenement within a back Yard in Cornhill, near the First Meeting-house, occasioned by the carelessness of a poor Scottish Woman, by using Fire near a parcel of Ocum, Chips and other combustible Rubbish." (News Letter; Drake, Hist. p. 541.) Drake adds that the woman was called Mary Morse. Hutchinson (II. 200) says it began in or near Williams's Court; " All the houses on both sides of Cornhill, from School Street to what is called the stone-shop in Dock-square, all the upper part of King-street on the south and north side, together with the Town-House, and what was called the Old Meeting-house above it, were consumed to ashes."

Drake says the " stone-shop in Dock-square " was probably " Colson's stone House," at the intersection of Brattle Street and our Cornhill. The old Cornhill was a part of our Washington Street, and the fire reached School Street.

Increase Mather improved the occasion in a sermon entitled " Burnings Bewayled, In a Sermon Occasioned by the Lamentable Fire which was in Boston, October 2nd, 1711. In which the Sins which Provoke the Lord to Kindle Fires are Enquired into." In it he revealed the cause as follows : —

" But has not God's Holy Day been Prophaned in New England? Has it not been so in Boston this Last Summer, more than ever since there was a Christian here? Have not Burdens been carried through the Streets on the Sabbath Day? Have not Bakers, Carpenters and other Tradesmen been employed in Servile Works on the Sabbath Day? When I saw this . . . . my heart said, Will not the Lord for this Kindle a Fire in Boston?" — EDS.

house had stood near 70. years. I had a house burnt, wherein Mr. Seth Dwight was Tenant, who paid me Twenty pounds per añum. Oct. 3. The Lt. Gov.ʳ Taylor arrives. He saw the Fire 20 Leagues off.

Octob.ʳ 11. Fifth-day, Fast. A Collection was made for sufferers by the Fire; Two Hundred Sixty odd pounds gathered at the South church, the oldest Meetinghouse in Town.

Note. Octob.ʳ 7. Mr. Pemberton stays the Church, who vote to have the Pastors of the First Church to officiat with us alternatly in Preaching and administering the Sacraments: and to be recompenced as our Minister.

Octob.ʳ 17. Gen¹ Court meets. About the 24. The Gov.ʳ will have it voted that one instruction to the Comittee be that they Address the Queen to bring forward a New Expedition to Canada. I spake against it, but the Govʳ press'd it vehemently; said with a Hectoring Aer, that he must bring in the Frontiers; put the Vote himself. I think but two besides my self in the Negative. Col. Townsend said twas a matter of such moment, and so sudden to him, he could not vote.

Octobʳ 23. Mrs. Mary Ardel buried;[1] Bearers, Elisha Hutchinson, Sewall; Mr. Oakes, Capt. Hill; Mr. Baker.

---

[1] Her tombstone, in the Granary yard, is inscribed: "Here lyes buried the body of Mary Ardel, Aged 72 years, Died October the . . 1711." In the Lane Papers (N. E. H. & G. Reg. xi. 234), Job Lane writes, in 1695, to his correspondent in England: "I have received the ten pound you paid Mrs. Ardell's sister, viz. Frances Thompson." . . . "Direct your letters to me, to be left for me at Mrs. Mary Ardell's, at her house in the Town Dock, over against Mr. Thomas Clark, brazier, in Boston."

Savage notes that William Ardell, Boston, 1687, merchant, removed to Portsmouth, and was made, in 1699, sheriff of New Hampshire.

We learn, from Suff. Wills, lib. 22, f. 15, that Captain John Barrell married Abiah, only daughter of Mrs. Mary Ardell, and had children. He states that Mrs. Ardell gave them three tenements on Cornhill, which he had mortgaged to build brick houses upon. Then he sold them, and had a balance of £165 in hand for his children. To secure them, he mortgaged, to the probate judge, certain land of his own at the south end. It was between

Octob.^r 28. 1711. Joseph preaches for Mr. Colman, who is at Salem; Reads the Scripture. Mr. Pemberton prays largely for the Lieut Govr, that God would make him a Blessing like his predecessor, meaning Mr. Stoughton. Mr. Wadsworth p. m. pray'd for the Govr, Lt Govr, and all in Authority; Baptis'd 2 children; Charles and Mary.

Octob.^r 26. a Man falls from a Scaffold at the church of Engl'd[1] into the Street, and is stricken dead. Octob.^r 27. Mrs. Bridge is buried; Sam. Bridge the carpenter's wife.

Octob^r 26. Treated Col. Nicholson at the Dragon: Treated Lt Govr there about a week before.

Midweek, 8.^r 31. Mr. Sheriff Dyer Treats the Govr, Col. Nicholson, Capt. Wade, Justices at his house. In Council I mov'd for Direction where to hold the Superiour Court. Govr aprov'd of Mr. Pullin's.

Fifth-day, Novr 1. Col. Nicholson sits in the Gallery, Lt Govr in his Pue.

Govr not at Meeting because Dr. C. Mather preach'd.[2] Feasted Col. Nicholson, Lt Govr, C. Studly at his house: They went after Lecture.

Second-day Novr 5. Major Genl Winthrop came to Town with Madam Winthrop and her Daughters, from Dedham, having kept Sabbath there. See May, 8.

Seventh-day, Novr 10. 1711. Mr. John Pole died. Novr 7th, Was buried this day in a Tomb in the old Burying place.[3] Bearers, Winthrop, Sewall; Addington, Cor-

---

his barn and Mr. Sheaf's Lane, bounded west, in front, on a lane twelve feet wide, to be forthwith laid out, one hundred and fifty-seven feet; from front to rear, fifty feet, seven inches; bounded south on William Pollard, and north in said lane. — EDS.

[1] This was in connection with the enlargement of the original chapel, an edifice of wood. The work was protracted from 1710 to 1713. — EDS.

[2] The bitterness continued between the Governor and the divine. — EDS.

[3] This was, doubtless, John Poole, son of William Poole, of Boston, whose tombstone is in the old, i. e., the King's Chapel Yard. We give a

win; Walley, Higginson. The Govr and many of the Council, there. Mrs. Rebekah Clark, Mr. Eliott's Granddaughter, is dead.

Lord's day, Novr 11. Mrs. Sarah Walley, wife of John Walley esqr., died last night.

Novr 12. Mr. Attorney and I set out for Salem in Mr. Austin's Calash, overtake the President and his Lady in a Calash : Sit together a pretty while at Lewis's.

Novr 13th Third-day, only I and the Salem Justices at the opening the Court.

Novr 14th, Mr. Noyes made an excellent Sermon from PS. 77. 20. Thou leddest thy people like a Flock, by the hand of Moses and Aaron. Mr. President mistrusted the cloudy Lowering day, and return'd before Lecture. Had the councillors and Ministers at Diñer. Mr. Noyes crav'd a Blessing, Mr. Green return'd Thanks excellently.

That we might finish, we held the Court by Candle-Light, and adjourn'd *sine die:* When came out found a Considerable Snow on the Ground. Went to Pratt's and made up Accounts. Visited Madam Bradstreet.

Novr 15. 5th day, Stormy morn, but set out about Ten, got home Comfortably. Made up at Austin's before Sun-set. At the Mill-bridge met Col. Lynde with a Scarf;

---

transcript of what can be read, from a copy made by the late Thomas B. Wyman, as Bridgman's copy is imperfect: —

"[Illegible] . . . . of John Poole aged 7 . . . .

" Here lyes ye body of . . . . . aged . 0 years . . . . .

" Here lyes ye body of Elizabeth Poole, late wife to John Poole, daughter of Governor Brenton, esq^r aged 44 years died Octr ye 17, 1694."

"Here lyes ye body of Jane Lendall, late wife to Timothy Lendall, dau^r of John and Elizabeth Poole, deceased December ye 15th 1710 in ye 29 year of her age."

" William Poole, aged 2 months, died March . . . . William Poole, aged 8 months, died Sepr 12, 1679, children of John and Elizabeth Poole."

" Mary Lendall aged 3 weeks, died Aug. ye 1 . 17 . . Elizabeth Lendall died Decr y^e . . 1710 in ye 5th year of her age. Poole Lendall died June . . 1710 in ye second year of his age. . . . . . Lendall aged 3 months and . . . . Died . . . . 1710, ye children of Timothy and Jane Lendall." — Eds.

I ask'd him what Funeral, he said Mrs. Walley.   Nov.ʳ 16.
Major Walley sends Jnº Roberts to me with a good Lutestring Scarf and Ring, Gloves.   Madam Walley's Bearers
were, Wait Winthrop esqr, Elisha Hutchinson esqr; Addington, Sergeant; Belchar, Stoddard.   All the Councillors had Scarvs.   Nov.ʳ 19.   Capt. Thomas Matthews beats
Alexander Tulloh, Capt. John Alden's Mate; sends him
by force a-board the Chester and there whips him twenty
Stripes; which lawless action greatly disturbs the Inhabitants of the Town.

Nov.ʳ 29.   Thanksgiving;   Madam Usher, Mr. Odlin,
Mrs. Kay, and her daughter dine with us.   Mr. Bridge's
Prayer and Preaching was excellent.   Mrs. Hañah Walley
died last night, aged better than 30. years.

Nov.ʳ 30.   Mrs. Margaret Corwin died last night.   Dec.ʳ 1.
Mrs. Sarah Walley buried.   Bearers, Major Wᵐ Dudley,
Mr. Joseph Sewall; Mr. Benj. Walker, Mr. Jnº Foy;
Mr. David Stoddard, Mr. James Walker.   White Scarvs
and Rings.

To day or yesterday, Mr. Bromfield in Council again
moved the Govʳ in behalf of Alexander Tulloh.   The
Govʳ answered him sharply, and Comanded him to speak
no more about it.   Because The Chief Justice and Major
Walley did not agree with me to write it as I desired; I
now said to the Govʳ in Council, It highly concerns the
Honor of the Government, the Safety and Wellfare of
Her Majˢ Subjects of this Province, that your Excellency
suffer not your Order in Writing under your hand to
Capt. Matthews, for bringing Alexander Tulloh a-shore,
to be disobey'd, and your Authority as Govʳ of this Province and Vice-Admiral, to be contemned.

I said also, That confining Capt. Matthews for this Contempt was not Suspending him.   At this the Govʳ was
touch'd, and said with some displicency, you come with
your Logical Distinctions!

Second-day, Dec.ʳ 3.   Mrs. Margaret Corwin, Mr. Jnº

Corwin's Widow, Maiden name Winthrop, is buried in
Govr Winthrop's Tomb.[1]   Bearers, Cooke, Sewall; Addington, Joseph Lynde esqr; Eliakim Hutchinson esqr.,
Andr. Belchar esqr.   Neither Govr Dudley, nor Govr Saltonstall there.   They came to give me a visit, and were
here when the Time call'd me to the Funeral, upon account of which I was oblig'd to go away.   Govr said What
Funeral?   I would have had them stay; but they went
away also.   Gave each a Rainbow.[2]

Decr 5th   Lt Govr returns from visiting the Fronteers.

Decr 6.   Cousin Moodey dines with us and his son
Joseph, whom he brings to send to school at Cambridge.
Cous. Fissenden, the Schoolmaster, dines too.   I give
cousin Moodey 3. silver spoons, marked S. $\frac{S}{L}$. 1711. of Mr.
Edwards, cost 41.^s   Cousin married Lydia Storer.

Novr 7th   Gave Cous. Moodey a Rainbow, and one for
Cous. Lydia.   Cousin goes to Cambridge.

Sixth-day, Decr 7th   Mr. Hirst and son Joseph set out
for Salem in Brothers Calash, Jonathan drives; get
thither about 6.; comfortable moderat Wether.

Sabbath, xr. 9th   Serene moderat Wether.   Margaret
Smith is baptised; I supose for sake of her Grand-mother
Corwin.

xr. 10. 1711.   I read Major John Livingston's account[3]
of the number of Frenchmen and Indians in Canada;

---

[1] John Corwin, or Curwin (son of George Corwin, who came from Work-
ington, County Cumberland), married Margaret, daughter of Governor John
Winthrop, of Connecticut. — EDS.

[2] Probably the sermon by Cotton Mather: "Thoughts for the Day of
Rain: Two Essays, I. The Gospel of the Rainbow. II. The Saviour with
his Rainbow." B. Green, 1712, pp. (2) VI. 64. See Brinley's Catalogue,
Nos. 1246, 1220. — EDS.

[3] Hutchinson says (Hist. II. 185) that he had Livingston's journal.
Walker says (Journal, 88) that Livingstone was to go, in July, to Quebec,
carrying copies of the manifesto to scatter around; then to await, near Quebec, the arrival of the fleet, and bring it all the news he could. He went to
Port Royal, thence to Castine's house, on the Penobscot, and finally to
Quebec. He brought back only a disclaimer from Vaudreuil of any unusual
atrocity in conducting the war. — EDS.

Frenchmen, 4070: Indians 830. Great Guns, 145. Pettararos,[1] 22. Went from Añapolis to Penobscot by water. Octob.ʳ 15. 1710. Reach'd the first houses of Cañada, Dec.ʳ 5. 1710. Got back to Albany, Febr. 3.ᵈ following; and at Boston, 23.

Fifth-day, xr. 12. Son Joseph, and Mr. Hirst return from Salem very comfortably in a Slay. Joseph Preach'd on the Sabbath at the new Precinct; and yesterday, Mr. Noyes's Lecture, My Peace. *Laus Deo.* This day, xr. 12. Mr. Bridge preached excellently from Heb. 11. 33., who through Faith wrought Righteousness; shewing that working Righteousness in our several stations — was a very noble Effect of Faith. Mr. Chiver of Rumney-Marsh, Mr. Josiah Oakes, and Cousin Margaret dined with us: The Governour not at Meeting.

Dec.ʳ 15. 1711. Mr. Josiah Oakes goes to Needham to preach. I visit Major Walley, who has his left foot bound up in a cloth, tells me he went not to Bed the two nights before but sat up by the fire in a chair, by reason of the Twinging pain. Visited Mr. Pemberton, who spake to me that it might be well to come to a choice of some person for the South-Church, notwithstanding the Pastors of the Old Church were with us.

Lord's-day xr. 16. Four persons were taken into church. Mrs. Frances Bromfield and Marshal's Negro woman, two of them. Their Relations very acceptable. Mr. Wentworth's son dies at ——

Dec.ʳ 17. visit Mrs. Beatrice Bosworth, 88. years old. At her daughters Request I pray'd with her: She entertain'd me with great Respect, and enquired after my wife and Son.

Dec.ʳ 19. Mr. Shurtliff tells my Son that the Lᵗ Govʳ has a Comission to be Capt. of the Castle; goes thither to morrow.

---

[1] Pederero, a kind of swivel gun, used for discharging stones. — EDS.

Dec.ʳ 20. Meet with the Justices and Selectmen to determin what they shall have that had their houses blow'd up :¹ voted 230£ and the enlarging the Highway where the Houses have been burnt down.

Dec.ʳ 21. Broʳ calls in to see us, goes over with his Daughter to Mistick.

Dec.ʳ 22. I visit Major Walley, who is now in a mañer wholly confin'd to his chair. Visit Mr. Joseph Parsons.

Dec.ʳ 23. very sharp Weather; yet Serene, and had a comfortable day : Mr. Pemberton administred the Lords Super. Mr. Bridge baptised John Grice.

Third-day Dec.ʳ 25. 1711. I took with me Joseph, Hañah, and Judith; and went to Brooklin in Mr. Simson's slay to see little Mary, 5. Moneths old; taken with Convulsions last Lords day night : comforted my Son and daughter what I could, pray'd with them and took leave; got home a little after sunset, *Laus Deo.* We had much ado to get along for the multitude of Sleds coming to Town with wood, and returning. Sixth-day, xr. 28. Went with Mr. Daniel Oliver to Newtown, Isaac Williams drove the Slay. Visited Mrs. Hobart,. very sick a-bed; went to Lecture, and so home. Din'd at Mr. Hobart's. Mrs. Elizabeth Parrot, Mr. Bridge's eldest daughter, about 24. years old, dyes in child-bed xr. 29ᵗʰ. 1711.

xr. 30. Joseph preaches for Mr. Walter at Roxbury.

xr. 31. Joseph returns to College. Major Walley has Prayer at his house respecting his Foot;˙began between 2 and 3 p. m̄. Mr. Pemberton first, Mr. Bridge, Mr. Colman, Mr. Wadsworth, Dr. C. Mather. Mr. Wadsworth insisted pretty much, that several in the room might dy before Major Walley; all of them might. Dr. C. Mather very near the Conclusion of his Prayer, said, Probably, some remarkable person in the room might dye before

---

¹ To arrest the progress of the fire, on October 2 previous. — Eds.

Major Walley. Major Walley was easy all the time of the exercise, had not one Twinging pain.

Jany 2. 17$\frac{11}{12}$. Set up the Clock in our Bed-Chamber.

Jany 4th. Sixth-day; Joseph and I retired into the Castle for 3 or 4 hours, to ask direction from GOD about his Call to the new Precinct at Salem.

Decr 31. 1711. When I return'd to my own Chamber I met with Brothers Letter of Jany 3.

This sixth-day, Jany 4th Major Walley's Left foot is opened underneath, and found to be very hollow, and spungy: Mr. Pemberton told me of it at the Funeral of Mrs. M. Atkinson,[1] born in New-England, aged 73. years, buried in a Tomb in the New-burying place, from her son, Mr. Lyde's house, Jany 4. Bearers, Col. Elisha Hutchinson, Sewall; Addington, Stoddard; Dumer, Col. Checkley.

Jany 5th I went to Cambridge and consulted with the President and Mr. Brattle; who treated me very candidly, and told me, they at first propounded to Capt. Gardener — Mr. Flint, Mr. Whiting, Mr. Stephens. They objected against Wiggs, and upon their motion, as I understand, Consented to my Son's going, cautioning them with the difficulty might hapen in obtaining him; If they would have it so, they must run the venture of that Neither of them advised my Son's going to them.

Jany 7th A considerable Snow fell last night. I visit Major Walley, who seems much impaired since the opening of's foot; the taking away so much dead or rotten flesh, Loss of blood do weaken him. One of the Servants told me he was Light headed the day before.

Third-day, Jany 3. Capt. Gardener Junr, Mr. Holton, and Mr. Foster come to see Son J. from the new precinct of Salem, to receive his Answer, which he gives with Regrett in the Negative; and they receive with great sad-

---

[1] Theodore Atkinson married, as second wife, Mary, daughter of Rev. John Wheelwright, and widow of Edward Lyde. — Eds.

ness. Dine with us on boil'd Beef and Roasted Pork. I gave each of them a Rainbow, and one for Capt. Sam¹ Gardener.

Midweek, Jan.ʸ 9. I visit Major Walley, who is much worse, and seems to be hastening to his Long home. Desired of Mr. Wadsworth the continuance of his Prayers. Rec'd of Col. Checkley £83–13–3. for my proportion, for my Labour in signing and numbring Bills of Credit. Receiv'd in the small plate, No. 1600, £55.

Sixth-day, Jan.ʸ 11. 17$\frac{11}{12}$. Major John Walley dies. I was at prayer with him last night. Mr. Pemberton pray'd excellently. He was a good Neighbour, a publick spirited Man, a Purchaser and principal Settler of Bristol.

Mrs. Beatrice Bosworth is buried, aged 89. years.[1] Her first husband's name was Joclin, by whom she had her daughter Stephens.

Second-day, Jan.ʸ 14ᵗʰ 17$\frac{11}{12}$ William Pain, Joyner, dies in his Chair of the Tissick. Writ to Dr. Increase Mather, and inclos'd three 4ˢ Bills, Thanking him for his many Favours. To Dr. C. Mather two 5ˢ Bills, *ditto.*

Fifth-day, Jan.ʸ 17. There is an overseers Meeting in the Council Chamber after Lecture, and Mr. Joseph Stevens is confirmed Fellow of Harvard College. Order'd a Hundred Men to strengthen Derefield and other Fronteers.

Went to the Funeral of Major Walley; Bearers, Winthrop, Sewall; Addington, Sergeant; Belchar, Mico. Tomb in the new Burying place.

Jan.ʸ 18ᵗʰ Went to the Funeral of Wᵐ Pain. Bearers, Col. Checkley, Capt. Jn° Alden; Capt. Mason, Mr. Mills; Mr. Eustace, Mr. Ellis Chirug[eon.]

Jan.ʸ 21. Second-day, Gave Mr. Bridge, Pemberton,

---

[1] She married, first, Abraham Jocelyn, and, secondly, Nov. 16, 1671, Benjamin Bosworth, of Hull, as his second wife. Her daughter, Rebecca, married, successively, John Croakham, Thomas Harris, and Edward Stevens. (See Savage.) — Eds.

Colman, Wadsworth, each of them, a Rainbow with 10^s Bill inclos'd.

Third-day, Jany 22. Council, Mr. Chiever, of Marble head, order'd to preach the Election-Sermon; the Govr seem'd to decline Mr. Walter and begin to hover over Mr. Anger. Visited the Major Genl, sick of a Cold.

Jany 29. Went with the Chief Justice in a Slay to the Ferry, went over comfortably. Mr. Justice Corwin coming this day from Salem, twas about an hour after Noon before he got to Charlestown, yet Gave the Grand-Jury their oaths; Mr. Saml Sparhawk Foreman. Found the Bill against Mingo, alias Cocke Negro, for forcible Buggery, Arraign'd. As came over at night, Pendleton, the Japañer, making more haste than good, from the Stairs to the Causey, where the boat lay, jumping from a Sloop broke his Legg; twas sad for us to see him and hear his Cryes.[1]

Midweek, Jany 30. Rode again with the Chief Justice, met Jno Usher esqr. who insulted us about keeping the 30th Jan^y [2] Try'd the Negro, GOD furnish'd the Court with such a series and Frame of evidence that was brought in Guilty. Not one word spoken on his behalf. Condem'd.

Jany 31. Mr. Pemberton preaches from Job, 31. 14. Govr not at Lecture.

Febr. 2. Are invited to dine at the Governour's next Midweek, by Maxwell. Govr said nothing to me.

Febr. 6. Went in Capt. Tho. Hutchinson's Coach, with Col. Hutchinson. The Lt Govr, Sir Charles Hobby, Col. Vetch, and many Officers there. I saw not Mr. Bromfield,

---

[1] This was, probably, Roger Pendleton, japanner, who seems to have died of his injury, as administration on his estate was granted to Richard Pullen, innholder, of Boston, Feb. 9, 1711, 1712. (Suff. Wills, lib. 17, f. 388.) — EDS.

[2] This was, of course, the anniversary of the execution of King Charles I., a day devoutly commemorated by Cavaliers, and as strongly repudiated by Puritans. — EDS.

Col. Adam Winthrop, Mr. Jn° Clark. No Chaplain. Got
home seasonably to go to the Meeting at Capt. Savages.
I carried a Rapsodie, and spake to Capt. Savage to read
Dr. J. Mather's Sermon on the Fire and then gave him
the book, Meditations Lords Super, &c Two Legs broken
in Town this day, Frank Homes, by his Horse falling on
him, and Labourer, by a Lump of frozen Earth falling on
his Legg as was digging in C. Jn° Gerrishes Cellar; I met
him carried in a Chair and crying out, as I went to the
Meeting. Brother comes hither. Febr. 8ᵗʰ returns.

Febr. 8. I read the death of pious Mr. Brett

"Bridgewater; Janʸ 14. 1711–12. Last Sabbath, yesterday, we
had a solemn breach made upon us here: our Justice Brett got up
well, by what apear'd, early in the morning; and having been at his
barn upon necessary occasions, came into his dwelling house, sat down
in a chair, being about to take some repast, fell down dead, dead in
an instant. O that this very sudden and awfull death may be sanctified to this people, and to me in particular, who have so many Warn-
ings of the near approach of death.——James Keith."¹

And, after a postscript,
Janʸ 28. 17¹¹⁄₁₂. Inclosed in the same Letter to Dr.
Cotton Mather.——" have not dared to make any apearance for a vindication. But having now some confidence
of my Son's innocence; I am willing to venture for him,
as far as may be lawfull and expedient "——

Friday, Febr. 8. A Duel is fought between Lᵗ James
Douglas, and Lᵗ James Alexander, near the new Burying
place.

Friday, Febr. 15ᵗʰ Went to Charlestown, and heard
Mr. Bradstreet from Prov. 24. 32. He brought it down
to the Condemned Malefactor then present; had pray'd
excellently for him before: executed presently after Lect-

---

¹ Rev. James Keith, of Bridgewater, educated at Aberdeen, was settled
here in 1664. He had a large family, and numerous descendants. We are
unable to trace the reference in the next paragraph to his son's troubles, but
suspect it may have been ecclesiastical. — EDS.

ure. Mr. Brattle pray'd at the place of Execution. This day before Noon a man falls between the new wharf and a ship, and with the blow on's head dyes instantly; buried at night. This day Mr. Howell's child buried. Joseph was at Charlestown Lecture, and comes over to preach for Dr. Incr. Mather.

Satterday, Febr. 16. Mr. Jonathan Belchar comes to me with Mr. Bromfield, and tells me the near approach of Lt James Alexander's Death; I think this was after Noon. I went to the chief Justice who declar'd his opinion, that twas fitter for other Justices to meddle with than the Judges. I went to Dr. Clark as the next Justice and a Chirurgeon, whom I found indispos'd and keeping house. Lt Alexander Douglass, the Dueller, lodg'd at Barnsdell's near Scarlet's Wharf. I call'd again at Mr. Bromfield's who inform'd me, Alexander, aprehensive of death, was just going to receive the Sacrament. I went home, (twas now Sun-set) and writ a Letter to Mr. Attorney, telling where I had been and what I had heard; and desir'd him to take some order about it. About 7 aclock he sent for me, I went to the chief Justice, and there sign'd Warrants to the sheriff &c., and Mr. Weaver, an Admiralty Warrant; Franklin made Constable Oliver his Deputy. Sent Mr. Deputy Dyer and him to Barnsdell's; and order'd him to go to Nantasket as soon as the Wether would admit (for the wind now was intolerable as to its height and cold). Came home, Benj. Larnell lighting me.

Monday, Febr. 18. 'Twas mention'd in Council, that Govr Vetch might be spoken to to send Douglass from Añapolis hither. It was reported he was gon thither in Capt. John Alden. Lt James Alexander dyed, on Satterday night about 10. aclock. The Govr's Answer was, Let Warrants be first granted out; and then 2 or 3 days after, Let a Motion be made to Govr Vetch from the Council-Board. A Warrant was drawn by Mr. Secretary to all the sheriffs and Constables in the Province, and

given to Dept. Dyer. Mr. Joseph Gerrish comes to Town;
I write to him to invite him to Diñer to morrow. A Let-
ter is written to the Govr to regulat the Funeral of L^t
Alexander, and prevent its being Great.

Tuesday Febr. 19. I go to Charlestown and visit Col.
Phillips, who was very glad to see me.

Write to Jonathan Kendal to pay 6.^s for his Ferry-
man that swore profanely Febr. 15th and would add no
more charge. Dine with Mr. Gerrish, son Gerrish, Mrs.
Anne. Discourse with the Father about my Daughter
Mary's Portion. I stood for making £550. doe: because
now twas in six parts, the Land was not worth so much.
He urg'd for £600. at last would split the £50. Finally
Febr. 20. I agreed to charge the House-Rent, and Difference of Money, and make it up £600.

Febr. 21. I buy two caps at Mr. B. Walker's and give
Mr. Gerrish one. Cost 7.^s apiece. Mr. Addington draws
Mr. Gerrishes Release.

Febr. 22. Mr. Gerrish comes, Signs, Seals, and delivers
it to me in presence of Barthol. Green and Thomas
Crump: I then put it into Mr. Gerrishes hand to Acknowledge it before Mr. Secretary Addington, and give it
me again. Before Executing it, I gave him Cousin Quinsey's Bonds, offering to do any thing that might be necessary for his demanding what was due on them, and gave
him my Note to pay the Remainder.

Gave Cous. Wm Gerrish 10.^s to buy a Candlestick, with
Exhortation to imitate his Grandmother who dyed in the
house he is to live in. Be diligent in General and particular Calling; Save himself and his intended wife.

Febr. 22. p. m̄. Mr. Pemberton comes to see me, and
comūnicats to me the Mock-Sermon and mentions my
going to Mr. Secretary, which I doe; but twas night before could concert Measures. He not being at home at
first. Agree to goe to Dr. Clark's, his house being in the
midst of the Persons concern'd.

Febr. 23. Mr. Secretary and I go to Dr. Clark's between 8 and 9. m. in the Rain; Recover three copies of the Mock Sermon which was pronounced the Tuesday 4 night before, in presence of Col. Townsend, Capt. Savage and others; I motion'd and prevail'd to send away Russel for an Original and his own Copy; before Green came: He happily recover'd both, and brought them in with which we stop'd Green's Lying Mouth. Bound him over to the Sessions in £50. to answer for making and pronouncing a Mock-Sermon full of Monstrous profaneness and obscenity. Got home about one a-clock. I heard nothing of this till Mr. Pemberton shew'd it me.

Febr. 26. I go to the Town-Treasurer, from him to Dr. Clark, and propounded to send for the other persons, we sent not for on Satterday. He declin'd it; said twas in vain: he knew not but there might be 40. Copies, one gon to New-york.

Midweek, Febr. 27. Fast at the South-church in order to call a Minister. Mr. Colman began with Prayer, Mr. Pemberton Preach'd excellently; Mr. Wadsworth pray'd. p. m̄. Dr. Cotton Mather pray'd Excellently : Dr. Incr. Mather preach'd a very good sermon, Mr. Bridge pray'd, Sung 2 first Staves 67. Ps. Dr. Mather gave the Blessing. Great Auditory. Mr. Pemberton very sharply Reprov'd the Mock-Sermon, pronounc'd in the *face of Government*. Son not in Town, nor any from Cambridge that I took notice of. Mrs. Hobart was buried yesterday. Bearers, Mr. Leverett, Brattle; Mr. Thacher, Anger; Mr. Danforth, Belchar. Both my Sons were there. I heard not of her death till Monday-night, and then had apointed Business on Tuesday p. m̄. that held me in Town; to hear Capt. Joseph Swaddle, as to his being accessory to the death of John Johnson one of his Sailers.

This day, Midweek, Febr. 27. Joseph Bailey of Newbury, introduc'd by Mr. Myles, Mr. Harris, and Mr. Bridger, Presented a Petition to the Gov᷑, sign'd by Abraham Merrill, Joshua Brown Sam. Bartlett, John Bartlet, Sam. Sawyer, Joseph Bayley &c., 22. in all, declaring that they were of the pure Episcopal Church of England, would no longer persist with their mistaken dissenting Brethren in the Separation; had sent to their Diocesan, the Bp. of London, for a Minister, and desired Protection.[1]

Fifth-day, Febr. 28. Great Storm of Rain: This day the Govr Dates his Letter to the Episcopal church of Newbury. At night the Rain falls vehemently with Thunder and Lightening.

Sixth-day, Febr. 29th The Govr orders this Petition to be read in Council: and ask'd the Council's Advice upon it. It was answer'd, It was not directed to the Council. Govr said He must have our Advice notwithstanding. I said, for my part I would say nothing to it; Others were so far of the same opinion, that Nothing was said to it. I ask'd the Govr to take a Copy of it: He said No, It should remain yet in Petto, and so took it off the Council-Table and put it in his Pocket, and carried it away.

Midweek, February, 27. 17$\frac{11}{12}$ Cous. John Sewall, a very pious young Man, is buried at Newbury. He died the Monday before.

March, 3. Joseph comes to Town.

March, 5. returns. We have our privat Meeting, I read out of Mr. Flavel, his preparation for Sufferings. Sung 27, 28, 29, 30, 39, 40, 41, 42, 55, 56.[2]

March, 6. Mr. Hobart of Newtown visits us in the

---

[1] Coffin (Hist. Newbury, 175–184) has much to say about this affair, with copies of the petition and Dudley's reply. It seems that a minority in the parish wished to build a new meeting-house in a spot disliked by the majority. The General Court forbade, though not until the house was built. Then, "in a pet," the minority took the advice of John Bridger, "surveyor of the King's woods," an Episcopalian, and said that they would also conform. Dudley promised his countenance, and they wrote to the Bishop of London for a minister. A Mr. Lampton seems to have been sent accordingly. When, as is proposed, Sewall's Letter Book is printed, more will appear on this subject. — EDS.

[2] Probably verses of a Psalm. — EDS.

morning, and din'd with us after Lecture, and Cousin Moodey of York. Cousin Moodey left a Guiney with me to buy him a Booke.

Seventh-day, March, 8. $17\frac{11}{12}$ Went to the Castle and din'd with the Lieut Govr. Many Healths were drunk, and Guns fired at drinking them: Ld Treasurer, Col. Nicholson. Last of all, I think, the Govr said, call Capt. Campbell, we will drink the Duke of Argyle's Health;[1] when Capt. Campbell was found twas done. When came off, The Govr, Col. Vetch, Sir Charles Hobbey, Capt. Campbell went in one Boat to the Neck; There the Govr took Col. Vetch and Capt. Campbell into his Coach, and left Sir Charles to goe up in the Boat alone. Col. Hutchinson, Mr. Secretary, Mr. Sergeant, Mr. E^{m} Hutchinson, Capt. Belchar, Mr. Bromfield, Col. Townsend, and Sewall, went in the other Boat. Gave the Cock-swain 18^{d} apiece, 12^{s} all.

Before I came off, I gave Capt. Tuthill Mr. Tompson's, Heaven the best Country, with my Distich;

Auris, mens, oculus, manus, os, pes, munere fungi
Dum pergunt, præstat discere velle mori.

Gave Mr. Shurtliff, the Chaplain, a Rainbow.

Midweek, March, 19th. Church Meeting; each gave in one vote: I alleg'd twas fit to give two votes, seeing Two were to be Nominated; But Mr. Pemberton stood for the first, and twas carried: Mr. Joseph Stephens had 19. Written Votes; Mr. Joseph Sewall 44. Mr. Flint, 4. Mr. Holyoke, 2. Before Voting, Capt. Belchar mov'd it might be kept secret what Number each had; I opos'd it as a

---

1 The Duke of Argyle is, of course, the head of all the Campbells. In 1712, the peer was John, second duke, a soldier of distinction. He left five daughters, and was succeeded by his brother, Archibald, who died *sine prole* in 1761. The title passed to John Campbell, son of his cousin John Campbell, of Mamore. This John had other children, and, possibly, Captain Campbell was of this branch. — Eds.

Novel [novelty]; and should not know whether any had above two votes; some others seconded me; and that was best.

7ᵗʰ day, March 22. 17$\frac{11}{12}$ Daniel Hasting waits on me; Col. Hathorne, Mr. Corwin, with Capt. Cushing set out for Plymouth. Majʳ Genˡ stays at home. Set out between 10 and 11. Din'd at Mills's, Baited at Cushings, Got to Job Randal's about Sunset, where we were kindly receiv'd.

Lords Day March 23. Heard Mr. Eels. Rain'd hard last night and somthing this day; Thin Meeting.

2ᵈ day, March, 24. The under-Sheriff, Joseph Briant, being our Guide, we went over Bisby's Ferry, 2ᵈ Horse, and Man, the North River Bridge being down. Rain'd at our first setting out. Got comfortably to Cook's where we din'd. While there it Hail'd pretty much, Thunder'd, though I heard it not. When had been there about 2 Hours, Mr. Sheriff came with his Guard. Went to Plimouth: Snow'd all the way. Got to Mr. Witherel's about 4 p. m̄. *Laus Deo.*

3ᵈ day, March, 25. 1712. About 10. m. Col. Thomas arrives, and brings a Letter and Packet from Mr. Cooke over, shewing his incapacity of attending the Court; whereupon the Justices aꝑointed Major Russel, Clark; Mr. Little was in doubtfull circumstances by reason of the Gout and sickness of which was scarcely recover'd.

John Rickard, Ordinary-keeper, our quondam Landlord dyes this day.

Midweek March, 26. Oyster Island is by Review Confirmed to Nathan and Zacheus Wicket, Indians, &c.

Hittee, an Indian Girl, found Guilty of Burning her Master Little's Dwellinghouse. Adjourn'd to the Meetinghouse by reason of the Press of people, and there the Negro Betty was Try'd for Concealing the death of her Bastard-Child: Found Guilty.

March, 27. 5ᵗʰ day, Col. Byfield and Mr. Valentine were

heard upon the Prohibition to the full before Diñer. Col. Thomas, Col. Byfield, Col. Otis, Capt. Cushing, being invited, Din'd with us. Ministers. Col. Byfield would have some time set for attendance next Court: I said should not be call'd before Noon of the second day of the Court: could not before hand fix a day.

Betty Condemn'd. Hittee's Master pray'd she might not be Condemn'd; was under sixteen years old. Upon this she was remanded to Prison, and the Court adjourn'd to Six a-clock next morning.

Sixth-day, March, 28. Court met: order'd Oyster-Island not to be sold; but the Attorney, Mr. Parker, to represent the state of it at the next Term. Upon reading Hittee's Indenture (which was now brought), Left her in Prison uncondemned; and order'd Col. Otis her first master, and Major Basset, to take Affidavits concerning her Birth. Adjourn'd *sine die*. Left my Statute Book with Capt. James Warren. Came homeward; Rain'd hard quickly after setting out, went by Mattakeese Meeting-house, and forded over the North-River. My Horse stumbled, in the considerable body of water, but I made a shift, by GOD'S Help, to sit him, and he recover'd and carried me out. Rain'd very hard that went into a Barn awhile. Baited at Bairsto's. Din'd at Cushing's. Dryed my Coat and Hat at both places. By that time got to Braintry, the day and I were in a mañer spent, and I turn'd in to Cousin Quinsey, where I had the pleasure to see GOD in his providence shining again upon the persons and Affairs of the Family after long distressing Sickness and Losses. Lodg'd in the chamber next the Brooke.[1]

7th day March, 29. Rode home, Mr. Rawson overtook me and accompanied me on the Neck; Got well home

---

[1] This old Quincy mansion is still in good preservation. "The chamber next the Brooke" — which still flows, is known as Tutor Flint's chamber. — EDS.

about Noon; found all well. *Laus Deo.* Mr. Colman,
the father, died last Thorsday night.[1]

Lords-day March, 30. Wrote Mr. Pemberton some
passages of my Journey, and of Lt Wood, of Little
Compton, his burying Six children in Eight days, two and
two in a Grave; youngest twelve years old.

Midweek, April, 2. Congregational Meeting at South-
Church. What the Church had done in their Nomination, was by a Silential Vote Approved. The Money left
in Æneas Salter's hand, is to be improv'd in making a
Tomb for the South-church Ministry. I was not at the
Meeting; because Some had given out they would have
both the persons Nominated. I went to Mr. Pemberton's
before-hand and intimated to him; that Such debates
might hapen[2] that I might not know well how to de-
mean my self, and therefore had thoughts of not being
at the Meeting. Speaking of Mr. Eels, and enquiring how
he preach'd, I Comended him; and Mr. Pemberton upon
it, with a very remarkable Aer Said, his Pupils could do
worthily, he was one of them. I gave no occasion at all
for that Air.[3] Mr. Colman was entombed after the Meeting, I went to it. The Rain and Snow of Monday, and
Tuesday hindred it's being done before.

Seventh-day, April 15. I visited Mr. Comissary Belcher, sick of the Gout. Capt. Papillon arrives.

---

[1] William Colman, of Boston, father of the well-known clergyman, Rev.
Benjamin Colman, was the son of Matthew and Grace Colman, of Satterly,
near Beccles, County Suffolk. Baptized there, Aug. 31, 1643. In Turell's
" Life of Benjamin Colman " (p. 210), it is stated that, " after the Decline
of his Father's worldly Estate, he cheerfully afforded him all needful Assistance, and did every Thing that lay in his Power, to render his Age easy and
agreeable." His father's life was " continued down to the year 1712." He
came from London, and settled in Boston not long before Benjamin's birth,
Oct. 19, 1673. — Eds.

[2] His son Joseph being a candidate. — Eds.

[3] It will be noticed, in subsequent references in the Journal, that Mr.
Pemberton was not earnest, at least, for having Joseph Sewall as his col-
league in office, and that the father was sensitively observant of the fact. —
Eds.

Midweek, April, 9ᵗʰ Capt. Paxton reviles Mr. Jonathan Belchar upon the Parade, calls him Rascal, many times, strikes him with his Cane: Mr. Dudley upon his view fines him 5ˢ. He carried it insolently, and said, He would doe so again. Twas about Noon.

Feria quinta, April, 10. Mr. Wadsworth preaches very Seasonably and Excellently from 2 Cor. 1. 9. After Lecture was a Council; and the Govʳ hankered after its being agreeable to the Charter. Not to have a new Court at the Election-day. I spake against that Notion. Govʳ pleaded, he could not be 40 days without a Court, Her Majesties Affairs might be such. Col. Hutchinson said, Writs might go out for the New Court, sitting the Old. Mr. Secretary express'd him self of a Contrary Opinion. Finally the Court was further prorogued to the 24ᵗʰ April, the day of the Genˡ Council. Madam Gerrish dines with us. Benj. Larnel and I prune the 4. Elms set this Spring, and the other Trees at Elm-pasture.

Sixth-day, April, 11. I saw Six Swallows together flying and chipering very rapturously.

Went to Charlestown Lecture, heard Mr. Bradstreet from Ps. 71. 3. Shew'd what an invaluable privilege twas to have GOD our strong Habitation: None but the Regenerat, God's Children, had it. Din'd at his house with Mr. Flint, Madam Brattle, Mrs. Martha Foxcroft. Visited Capt. Timᵒ Phillips, very dangerously sick of a Cancer; about a week since tis broken out into a large Sore on the left side of his Neck, hollow'd like a Saucer in his Swell'd Neck; can scarce speak. Visited Adam Winthrop as I went; and Capt. Fayerwether as I came home. Had quite lost it that the Meeting was at Mr. Stoddard's. I rather thought it had been at Mr. Sargent's. I was invited after I went out which was at 11. I met the Scholars. I was weary and the time past when I got home.

Lord's Day, April, 13. Joseph preaches for Dr. Incr.

Mather, and in the Evening for young men who meet at Matthias Smith's.

Second-day, April, 14. I lay'd a Rock in the Northeast corner of the Foundation of the Meetinghouse. It was a stone I got out of the Comon.[1] Gave Kates a 3ˢ Bill. Tis the first stone is laid. This day Capt. John Fayerweather dies, born in Boston, Sept? 1634. A good Christian Member of the old Church.

April, 15ᵗʰ 1712. Go to Hog-Island to view the old Barn, blown down yesterday, and to Consider of building a new one. Had a very Comfortable passage thither, and home. Joseph returns to College before I come home. Cousin, Mrs. Moodey, of York, here. Gave Mrs. Belcher Mr. Willard's Meditations on the Lords Super: young Mrs. Belcher, Dr. C. Mather's Sermon of Children·Walking in the Truth. Her Son Joseph, 14 years old, Mr. Quick's Answers.

Fifth-day, April, 17. Dr. Mather mentions Capt. Fayerweather[2] with Honor; He has been a Select-man, Comissioner, and Captain of the Castle. Buried between 6 and 7. Bearers, Cooke, Elisha Hutchinson; Sewall, Bromfield; Howard, Burroughs.

April, 18. Went with Mr. Daniel Oliver to Mr. Hobart's Lecture; visited Deacon Trowbridge, who was very glad to see us, overcome with Affection. At Mr. Hobart's after Lecture, Mr. Porter told me of Joseph's indisposition. April, 19. Send Ben. to him.

Apr. 20. Lords-Day, send David.

Apr. 21. I visit him my self, go by Charlestown.

Apr. 22. His broʳ Gerrish visits him, by whom he inti-

---

[1] There are many intimations in our old records that Boston Common once afforded boulders and foundation stones, which were turned to account for cellars and walls. — EDS.

[2] John Fairweather was a very noted citizen, and, by his will, mentions children and grandchildren. It seems that he was quite rich. He commanded the Castle at the time of Andros's overthrow, and had charge of the prisoners sent there by the victorious rebels. — EDS.

mats some inclination to have a Coach sent for him; which Message Madam Clark also brings. This day last Capt. Rouse, in the Saphire, brings in his Spanish Prize, which has a Considerable quantity of ps. ⅜ [Spanish milled dollars] and Silks.

23. Midweek, Mr. Hirst and I visit him [Joseph].

24. Sam¹ Sewall, *de Stephano*, goes with the Coach and brings him home; has a bad night.

Sixth-day, April, 25ᵗʰ Church-Meeting in the Afternoon: Mr. Pemberton enquired whether were ready to proceed; Answer'd Affirmatively. Whether would goe by a Majority, or two Thirds: were for a Majority as the usual way. Voted by papers; Mr. Joseph Stevens had Twenty votes; Mr. Joseph Sewall, Forty Seven. Mr. Pemberton pray'd earnestly for them both. Mr. Comissary sent his vote seal'd up. Major Gen¹ is at New-London.

April, 26. Mr. Pemberton prays with Joseph.

April, 27. Mr. Wadsworth prays very much for him as Elected; and Mr. Pemberton p. m̄.

28. 29. Joseph sleeps well: Mr. Bridge steps in to see him. Mr. Thair, Oakes. 29. Went to the funeral of Mr. Peter Oliver. Apr. 30. Sent Dr. I. Mather a Psalter bound in Turkey Leather, which He sent me from Webber; The French that took him gave him my Booke again. Essay'd to goe to Brooklin, but was stop'd by the Rain.

May, 1. 1712. Capt. Williams (79 PS.) reads *The vengeance of thy Saint's blood shed*, too soon skiping the foregoing Line; and consequently omitted it in its proper season; so that I was forc'd to Read it, to prevent a Blunder. Mr. Bridge from Isa 4. 4. Exhorts to the study of prophetical Scriptures: Fall of Babylon certain: Jews shall be call'd.

Mr. Thacher dines with us. Mr. Hobart visits Joseph and prays with him. Treats him with great Respect and

Kindness. I give him Virgil on account of the Poem he has gratify'd me with. Virgil with an Index, *in usum Delphini*.

Friday, May, 2. The Gov.ʳ sets sail for Portsmouth.

Seventh-day, May, 3. The Lᵗ Gov.ʳ holds a Council, wherein Lᵗ Brett is order'd to goe in the Province sloop. (Capt. Matthews will furnish 100. Men) and convoy the Provision Fleet. p. m. I go to Brooklin, and invite my Son and Daughter to come next week and perfect the Deeds.

Lord's Day, May, 4.ᵗʰ 1712. Mr. Pemberton speaks to the Congregation, and by a Silential Vote, Mr. David Jeffries, Col. Thomas Savage and Capt. John Gerrish are apointed to join with the Churches Messengers to acquaint Mr. Joseph Sewall with his Election.[1]

Monday, May, 5.ᵗʰ I lay a stone at the South-east Corner of the Town House and had Engraven on it S. S. 1712.

May, 6, Col. Hathorne, Mr. Corwin and I hold the Court.

May, 7.ᵗʰ Col. Townsend, Mr. Bromfield and Mr. Danforth of Taunton, dine with us.

Between 6 and 7. Mr. Sergeant, Mr. Bromfield, Capt. Hill, Capt. Williams, Col. Checkley, Major Fitch, Lᵗ Col. Savage, and Capt. Gerrish, come and acquaint my Son with the Churches Election. He acknowledges the Honor done him, sensible of the weightiness of the Work, and asks time to consider of it.

May, 8.ᵗʰ Mr. Cooke, Col. Hutchinson, Mr. Secretary, Mr. Sergeant, Mr. Belchar of Dedham, Capt. Moss, dine with us. I also paid for the Sheriff and Mr. Dudley. I told Mr. Dudley, I invited him as the Governour's Eldest son. Could not have the Lᵗ Gov.ʳ Capt. Paxton had en-

---

[1] The members of a church, that is, the communicants, according to the usage of the time, took the initiative in the election of a minister, and the members of the congregation voted subsequently. — EDS.

gaged him. At night, Dr. Increase Mather married Mr. Sam¹ Gerrish, and Mrs. Sarah Coney;¹ Dr. Cotton Mather pray'd last. PS. 90. 13 —— 2½ staves, I set Windsor Tune. Had Gloves, Sack-Posset, and Cake. Mr. Gerrish, the Minister, and Mr. Pemberton were there. Joseph went to Lecture, but was somewhat faint after it, being the first of his going abroad after his sickness, and was not there. The whole family was Invited.

May, 9. Sixth-day Rainbow ——

May, 10. Went a-foot to Roxbury, and bought Mr. Tomson's Gravel, and discours'd Mr. Dimond.

May, 13. 1712. My Wife visits the Bride and Bridegroom at Mr. Coney's; and visits Madam Checkley, who has been so long confin'd.

Midweek, May, 14. I goe to Concord in Austin's Calash. Set out from my own house at five m., got to Mr. Whitings, at Ten. Exercise began about half an hour past eleven, ended about ¼ past one. Great Assembly, Mr. Whiting pray'd, and preach'd from 1 Tim. 3. 1. Mr. Nehemiah Hobart Ask'd if any had to object, 1. of the Church. 2. of the Congregation. 3 of all the present Assembly. Declar'd that the Elders and Messengers of Churches had apointed him to give the charge; Mr. Anger, Brattle, Hancock to join in laying on Hands. Mr. Hobart pray'd excellently, and so gave the Charge, one Word in it was Diligence or Labor, or to that purpose; pray'd again. Declar'd that Mr Anger was to give the Right Hand of Fellowship; which he did. Sung the Forty-Seventh Psalm, G. Mr. Whiting Bless'd the people. Went and Din'd at young Mr. Prescott's. Set out to come home about half an hour after three; went and told Mr. Hutchinson of his Daughters having, by a fall

---

¹ It seems (*ante*, pp. 249–251) that Mr. Gerrish had been attentive to Captain Coney's daughter before his marriage with Sewall's daughter. It appears, however, that this second marriage was countenanced by the Sewalls. (See Vol. I. p. xxxviii.) — EDS.

from her Horse, broken her Arm, one of the bones just above the Wrist.

Return'd into my own House a very little before Nine. *Laus Deo.* Govr returns this day.

Fifth day, May, 15th. Dr. Cotton Mather preaches from PS. 51. 18. Build thou the Walls of Jerusalem. Sung the 147th PS. : the six first verses of it, O. I could not perceive that in either of his prayers he did one jot mention the Building the South-church has in Hand in Settling another Minister. Let the Gracious GOD be in the way, to be found, Near at hand; And even be found before we Seek, Hear before we call! Let the Bountifully Gracious GOD take away the filthy Garments from me, and from my Son, and give us Change of Rayment![1]

May, 19. Set out for Ipswich from Charlestown with Daniel Hasting; Had the company of young Mr. Stephen Minot. Din'd at Lewis's : By Mr. Gerrishes importunity, I lodg'd at his House, and rode in the Rain next morning to Ipswich; only 3 Judges, Hathorne and Corwin.

Midweek, May, 21. Adjourned *sine die.*

May, 22. The morning being Rainy till about 11., I resolv'd to stay Lecture; and visited the languishing Widow Appleton, who was very glad to see me, as she was bolster'd up in her Bed. After Lecture went to Salem; Lodg'd at Brother Hirst's.

May, 23. Went home by Wiñisimet, Brother brought me going.

May, 26. The Govr invites Col. Hutchinson by name to come and eat Salmon with him Election-day morn, and all generally invited.

May, 28. Election-day, the Governour not having apointed me to give the Deputies their oaths as for many years formerly, I went with my Coach to Roxbury. Col.

---

[1] Sewall's sensitiveness to every seeming lack of sympathy in any of his clerical friends to the new relation of his son, which so engaged his own paternal feelings, is significant of some disturbed tranquillity. — EDS.

Vetch, and Bro' went with me. Col. Hutchinson surprises us by bringing Mr. William Dumer, whom I knew
not Arrived May 27. at Marblehead, about 4 Weeks passage from Milford Haven. Tells me of Cousin Stork's
death, last winter. Coming to Town the Gov' took Gov'
Vetch; and I had ˙Bro˙, Mr. Williams of Dearfield, Mr.
Sam. Lynde.

Note. Before Sermon was done, My Son Joseph was
by Sickness oblig'd to go home! which I knew not of till
between 9, and 10, when went home after the Election.
Which holds, vomiting grievously, hinders his preaching
June, 1. as was apointed, and hinders his giving his Answer to the Church. This Disapointment is very hum-
bling.

June, 2. Mr. Thacher of Weymouth preaches: I refrain going to Diner; because of my Son's incapacity to
feed, I refus'd to Feast. Mr. Sam. Carter din'd with us at
home.

Midweek, June 4ᵗʰ Council day for Apointment of
officers: Col. Hathorne resigns his Judge's place. I went
to the Governour a. m. at Mr. Dudley's. Acquainted Him
that Col. Townsend, Col. Higginson, and Mr. Jnº White
would be acceptable to me. And so far as I was to be concern'd hop'd the Government would provide better for
me, than I for my self; chose to be at home; Had a Consultation of Physicians for my Son; viz. Mr. Cooke, Oakes,
Cutler, Williams, Noyes. Col. Thomas and Mr. Thomas
Brattle are Apointed Judges.[1] Mr. Brattle denys serving,
had not rid 20 miles in 20 years.

June, 5. Mr. Pemberton preaches from Kings being

---

[1] The two vacancies on the Supreme Bench were caused by the death of
John Walley, and the resignation of John Hathorne " by reason of his great
hardness of hearing." Brattle declined, requesting the Secretary " to return
his thanks to the Governor and Council for their respect shown him, and,
withall, to acquaint them that his bodily infirmities and unacquaintedness
with the Law, will not allow of his acceptance of the office of a Justice of the
Superior Court." Council Records. — EDS.

Nursing Fathers, &c. [Isaiah, 49. 23.] Mr. Benjamin
Lynde of Salem is made Judge, although the Govr objected to me yesterday that twas not convenient to have
so many Judges from Salem. Mr. Epes acquainted me
with it, said all the Council except his father Brown, voted
for him: Gave a good Comendation of him as a good Man,
of the church, keeping good Order in's family.

June 11th Mrs. Mercy Wade sends her complaint against
Jonathan Willis,[1] her daughter Dorothy's Husband, for his
Inhumane Actions; Hatefull Expressions, as well as Mur-
derous Threatenings towards his wife. Order for Willis's
Apearance was dated June, 5th serv'd June, 9th I mov'd
twas fit the person complaining should be present. At
last several Witnesses were Sworn, and Dorothy Willis,
the wife, her Declaration sign'd with her Hand was read;
Mr. Wade mov'd a Justice of peace might give her her
Oath; At last the Govr order'd an Adjournm't to Friday,
and that then she should apear. Willis gave in an Answer against the Complaint, it should have been his wive's
Complaint; Crimes general &c. and therefore pray'd it
might be dismiss'd.

June, 12. Govr not in Town. Dr. C. Mather preaches
from [Psalm] 110. ult. Sam Takes a Vomit. He was
taken sick of the Fever and Ague last Tuesday; was fain
to leave the Court and come home

June, 13. 1712. The Govr is very hot in his Nieces
Cause. I would have had it put whether the petition
should be dismiss'd, as the Respondent pray'd; several
seconded me but the Govr refus'd. Council carried it
against Dorothy, the wife, taking her oath; Col. Apleton

---

[1] Jonathan Wade, Jr., of Ipswich and Medford, married Deborah, youngest daughter of Governor Thomas Dudley, and her youngest daughter, Deborah, married Jonathan Willis, of Medford. He was the son of Stephen and
Hannah (Eliot) Willis. His mother was the daughter of Francis Eliot, and
he was thus the second cousin of Joseph Eliot, of Boston, whose daughter
Mary he married for his second wife, according to Morse's genealogy. — EDS.

alleg'd they did not admit Abigail Emery to her Oath.
The wife Dorothy is admitted to indorse the Complaint of
her Mother, Mrs. Mercy Wade. Hearing is adjourn'd to
this day Moneth.

I am put upon a Comittee about Volunteers; Col.
Pynchon pleads mightily for it : 12ˢ a week besides Subsistence : I argued, I fear'd it might become a Trade;
what we did now might be drawn into Example afterward; knew not who might be our Capt. General. If
persons should not be spirited by Love to their wives,
Children, Parents, Religion, twas a bad Omen : fell below
the heathen Romans. At last brought it to 12ˢ 6ᵈ Wages
and Subsistence; and I prevail'd that stand, forces, Marching and in Garrison might have the same Encouragement
as to Scalp Money, their danger being as great or greater.
Skin for Skin. I sign'd as Chair-man. Council would have
had Subsistence and £100 Scalp-money.[1] But Deputies
insisted on their own vote; till this Return of the Comittee of both Houses, which they comply'd with. As soon
as twas pass'd, the Govʳ propos'd to set up two Captains
in each County; which startled me; I said, Will not that
be too much ? His Excellency Laugh'd, and said, would
drop those that could not raise a company. Said among
others, My Eaton !

June, 14. Depts. brought it £200. for the Judges, to be
proportion'd according to their Attendance. When Depts.
brought in £50. for the Dep. Govʳ, Governour said, I
wish it had been £150. Govʳ apoints Mr. Secretary and
me to Prorogue the Court to July, 16. Midweek 10. m.

Col. Thomas accepts of a Judges place, by Letter.[2]

June, 17. I ride home with my Eldest Son, find all
well at Brooklin. Tom brings me back almost to the

---

[1] The exigencies of Indian warfare had induced the authorities to allow a
scale of bounties for the bringing in of Indian scalps. — Eds.

[2] The editors have received the following letter, by Judge Sewall, from
Mr. Edward E. Salisbury, of New Haven, Ct. It was copied by him from

Fullingmill; I visit Mrs. Ruggles, who tells me her Sister Aṗleton dyed the 9ᵗʰ June. About Calef's, Mr. Coṁissary took me into his Chariot, Mr. White Condescending to ride before, sitting hardly. Carried me to Mr. Pemberton's, where paid 10ˢ to the Charity School.

Midweek, June 18. Danˡ Hasting brings Joseph's Books, a Trunk, Desk &c. from Cambridge. Just before Sunset is a very noble Rainbow, one foot was between the Wind-

---

the fly-leaf of a manuscript volume of theology in the Library of Harvard College. — Eds.

"BOSTON, June 14ᵗʰ, 1712.

"REVEREND SIR, — I have yours pr. Mr. Ashly, for which I thank you. I herewith send you Sermons just come out of the Press, which I doubt not but you will find valuable, and specifick for you, in your high Calling. I understand you have the News-Letters at Westfield, and so I can send you little News. The Act of Parliament tolerating Episcopacy in Scotland is a matter of great Consequence. The General Assembly of Scotland in their Recesses aṗoint a Coṁittee to obviat any Evil during that time. This Coṁission (as they call it) made a very thorow and close Representation to Her Majesty, to prevent the passing of it. But it did not prevail. One thing they complain of is that the Draught for the Act gives up the Church of Scotland Authority over those of their persuasion, which imports an Exemption of the Episcopalians; which they fear will tend to very pernicious Confusion and Disorder.*

"My Son Joseph Sewall should have preached at the South-Church the first of June; but on the Election-day he was seised with an intermitting Fever, which oblig'd him to quit the Meetingh. before the Sermon was done. Has been followed with vomiting, is now slowly recovering. On Tuesday last my eldest was taken here with the Fever and Ague. I hope he grows better. I desire your Prayers for them Respectively. They both present their humble Service to you, desiring your Prayers. Tis a very weighty work Joseph is called to, and especially need your Remembrance of him to the giver of all grace. The Major Genl who was lately the first of our Council, was taken sick at New-London the 5ᵗʰ cur't. If he should dye, New England would lose a very worthy Patriot. Madam Winthrop took her journey towards him last Thorsday. Desiring your Earnest Prayers that I

---

* "The official changes following the Union brought a few English families to Scotland who were desirous of attending Episcopal Service after the forms to which they had been accustomed. . . . Gradually clergymen of the Church of England crept into the country." But these are not to be confounded with the remnant of the deposed Scottish hierarchy. The act mentioned by Sewall was intended to protect the new Episcopal clergy in the performance of their ceremonies. See Burton's History of Scotland, VIII, 218-227. Edition of 1873. — Eds.

mill, and the Lazar house; [1] other, on Dorchester Neck.
This Afternoon rode with Joseph and his Mother in the
Coach round the Comon. Note. In the Address to Her
Majesty this Court, the Committee had said these Words,
We are well satisfyed with the Laying out of our Money.
These words the Deputies obliterated, which the Gov[r] re-
sented, and order'd Mr. Secretary to go in and expostulat
with the Deputies; saying, The Council were surpris'd at
it. If it had never been in, it had not been so much.
But I think it was not alter'd.

June, 19. 1712. There was a great uproar in the S.
Meetinghouse just as Mr. Colman was opening his Text,
because he was zealous for his GOD. Col. Townsend's
Kitchen fell a-fire. But twas presently out, and the As-
sembly rallyed. I was not got out. Had an excellent
Sermon. After Lecture, before Diñer, the Govr held a
Council; ordered the payment of the G. Court's Allow-
ances, Several Muster-Rolls. Just before night I visited
Cousin Duñer, and wish'd her Joy of her Son's safe Ar-
rival.

Sixth-day, June, 20. rode with my wife and Joseph in

---

may be strengthened in Watching and keeping my garments, that my Walking naked, and men seeing my shame may be prevented, I take Leave who
am Sir,   Your loving friend and humble serv[t]

"SAMUEL SEWALL.
"My service to Madam Taylor."

[In another hand.]

" SIR, — I have as I see sent you enclosed Things which you sent for and
hope they will suit you.

"For the Reverend Mr. EDWARD TAYLOR
       At Westfield."

[1] We find no distinct reference to a lazar or pest house. Aug. 19, 1702,
in a case of sailors taken with small-pox, the Selectmen voted to quarter
them "in the house of widow Salter, at the sign of the Roebuck, nigh the
South Battery." Again, April 17, 1710, they voted to instruct "the nurses
to attend the man sick of the small-pox at the house on Fort Hill," evidently the one which the town owned there. Probably the reference in the
text is to one of these. — EDS.

our Coach Dorchester Road, almost as far as the first Brook. Brigs's Indian drove us.[1] Mr. Pemberton, and Mr. Abiel Walley visit Joseph.

June, 21. Plentifull Rain.

June, 22. Wallis's House was in danger of being burn'd down last night by a candle.

The Post brings word that the Maj[r] Gen[l] is better. Mr. Pemberton joins him and Joseph together in his Prayer. My Wife at Meeting p. m̄.

Midweek, June, 25. I go in a Calash with Mr. Josiah Oakes to Reading, to the Ordination of Mr. Richard Brown. Mr. Green, of Salem Village, began with Prayer, Mr. Brown preach'd well from Act. 20. 28., pray'd. Mr. Jer. Shepard ordain'd, pray'd. Mr. Tappan Gave the Right Hand of Fellowship. Mr. Parsons of Maldon pray'd, sung the 122 psalm, York Tune, Mr. Brown gave the Blessing. Got home before 9. *Laus Deo.*

Midweek, July, 2, 1712. Went with Mr. Hale to the com̄encement; at Charlestown fell in with Dr. Cotton Mather, went above a Mile before we got a Calash, and then paid full price. Intended to have staid a Considerable time at Sir Berry's Chamber: but as were going in were inform'd that the President —— were gon into the Meetinghouse: upon this I went directly thither: was in the Pue before the President begun his Prayer. Dispute, when the Govr and Govr Saltonstall came in the Orator was call'd for, Sir Cooper, who Saluted very well, Govr, Govr Saltonstall, Lt Govr his Kinsman.[2] At Diñer Col. Waldron

---

[1] This phrase strikes us strangely. Sewall had left college four years before King Philip's war broke the power of the Indians, and yet he lives to write: "Brig's Indian drove us." It seems a most sudden change in the character of the dreaded savage enemy to find him installed as the family charioteer. — EDS.

[2] Lieutenant-Governor Tailer, as we have shown (Vol. I. p. 63), was own cousin of Mrs. Mehitable Cooper, mother of Rev. William Cooper, the graduate of 1712. (Register, Vol. 18, 289.) Mr. Cooper published a funeral sermon on his kinsman in 1732. — EDS.

sat next me on the out-side. Mr. Shepard was call'd by
the Gov[r], and Return'd Thanks. Mr. P. Dudley set the
Tune: At *Gloria Patri*, our L[t] Gov[r] stood up, alone.

P. meridiem. After the Dispute was over Mr. Barnard
made an Oration in Latin. And the President made a
Latin Speech, taking the Whistonian Notion about the
Flood.[1] Gave the Degrees, Pray'd. Went to the President's house, came home with Mr. Cooke and Mr. Brattle,
got over the Ferry very well, being early: Saw a man
play Tricks on a Rope on board the Man of War.

July, 5. Mr. Solomon Stoddard, Mr. Williams, [of] Hatfield, Mr. Pemberton Dine with us. Mr. Stoddard crav'd
a Blessing, Mr. Pemberton return'd Thanks, Mr. Williams
pray'd Excellently; Joseph came down and was present.

July, 9, 1712. Daughter Hirst is brought to Bed of
her son William.

13th Baptis'd by Mr. Colman. Joseph intended to
have gone abroad to day; but was prevented by his Ague
that seis'd him quickly after Diñer, which also was a means
to hinder my presence at my little William's Baptisme.

July, 15. I and Mr. Gerrish went to Hog-Island and
saw the Barn Rais'd, Twas a very Hot Day, yet accomplish'd the work comfortably. I carried over a Jugg of
Madera of Ten Quarts. Went in Langden's Boat. We
took water to come home when twas almost dark: past
Nine before we Landed; having a Contrary Wind.

I drove a Pin, and gave a 5[s] Bill in Mr. Thacher and
Danforth's Book.[2] Gave a Book to my Tenant Belchar,

---

[1] Probably the work of Rev. William Whiston (born in 1667, died in
1752), an able scholar both in theology and science. He is now, perhaps,
best known as the translator of Josephus. For several years he was professor of mathematics in the University of Cambridge. Before his appointment
to that place he had published " A new Theory of the Earth, from its Original to the Consummation of all things." This work contains " A Solution
of the Phænomena relating to the Universal Deluge." — EDS.

[2] This mention may serve for a note to identify the book on Consolations,
which Sewall gave away so freely the previous year. (*Ante*, p. 298.) It was,

his Brother Bill, Mr. Baker of Linn.　Mr. Chiever Crav'd
a Blessing and Return'd Thanks.

July, 17.　Thunder and Lightening: about 4. p. m.
The House of Wm Morean at Brooklin was miserably Shat-
ter'd and Maul'd, Timbers broken yet no person kill'd.
Com̅issioners met at Dr. Cotton Mather's; Rain'd hard
going and coming.

July, 21.　Rain falls very plentifully which I hope
Soakes the Ground.　Gave Govr Saltonstall 18. Cata-
logues.

July 22.　Dr. C. Mather, Sir Charles Hobby, Major
Fitch and I set out for Natick.　At Mills's the President
meets us, Fisher conducts us, Mr. Deming in company,
Benj. Larnell waited on us.　Murat was there with his
Trumpet.

[This volume of the original Journal closes with the following memoranda.]

July, 13, 1709.　Fire in my Closet.
Mitto tibi P　　　　　　　　　Augt. 1705.
Oceani fluctus —— 7^r 10. 1705.
Saml Hirst born Octob^r 23. 1705.
The bawdy bloody Cross at length —— Novr 25, 1705. Decr 24.
Tingitur
Tom. Child had often painted death Novr 10. 1705.
Mr. Jacob Melyen dyes Decr 13. 170.
Sister Short dyed xr. 18. 1706.
Mr. James Baily *moritur* Jany 18. 170$.
Nobilitus　　　　　　　　　　March, 8. 170$.
House broken up, June, 16, 1707.
Mr. Willson dies 7^r 12 1707.
Jn° Jekyl esqr sworn 8^r 31.
M. Winthrop marries Mrs. Eyre Novr 13. 1707.
French Trade, Novr 20.

doubtless, the one entitled "Nehemiah.　A Brief Essay on Divine Consola-
tions, how great they are; and how great the regards to be paid unto them,
with an application thereof to some frequent cases, especially the Death of
Relatives.　Offered at the Lecture in Boston, 30 *d.*, 9. *m.*, 1710.　By Cotton
Mather, D. D. . . . . . Boston in New England.　Printed by Bartholomew
Green, 1710." sm. 4to, pp. 24.　It is dedicated to Sewall. — Eds.

Gov: Fitz John Winthrop's Funeral Dec: 4.
Mr. President Leverett Dec: 5. Install'd Jany 14th
Marriage Mr. Jn° Winthrop, Mrs. Añe Dudley xr. 16, 1707.
Arthur Mason buried March, 6. 17⅚.
Dr. Dumer　　　　　　 ⎱
Indifferent Flynt　　　 ⎰ Augt. 23–27–1708
Col. Tailer's wife buried ⎰ Sept: 2. Mad^m Lyd
Haverhill insulted Augt. 29.
Mr. Chiever's Funeral Sermon, 7: 9th
Mary Winthrop baptised, 7: 19. 1708.
Cous. Elisa Noyes dies Oct: 5. Maiden name was Tapan.
Elder Clap buried Oct: 18.
Capt. Checkly, 20–1708.

Friday, July, 25. 1712. Went to Cambridge in the
Castle Barge with the Lt Govr, Mr. Sergeant, Mr. Eliakim
Hutchinson, Mr. Benjamin Lynde ; to a Corporation Meet-
ing. In the Library the said Lynde disabled himself in a
Speech; and then took the Oaths and subscribed the Dec-
laration. Rec'd his Comission, and Mr. Secretary admin-
istred the Oath belonging to a Judge of the Superiour
Court, to him. Barnard, Eustace and others view'd the
Roof of the Colledge which S. Andrews built, and judg'd it
necessary to be taken down, by reason of the Rain and
Rottenness the Gable-Ends had convey'd to the Timbers.

His Excellency held a Council to hear Stimson complaining of Col. Foxcroft, the Judge of Probat ; Present,
Lieut. Govr, Sewall, Addington, Sergeant, Townsend, E^m
Hutchinson, Joseph Lynde, Andrew Belcher Esqrs. Had
a very good Dinner ; Mr. Justice Lynde din'd with the
Overseers. Mr. Colman went down with us in the Barge :
only Mr. Bridge and he were there of the Boston Ministers : Mr. Bridge return'd Thanks.

Seventh-day, July 26. I went to enquire whether Col.
Thomas was come to Town, and his daughter-in-law Thomas
inform'd me that he was sick, like to dye the last Lord's
Day.

Lord's Day July, 27. Mr. Joseph Sewall goes to Meeting in the Fore-Noon: Note was, Joseph Sewall being, after long Sickness, in some good measure Restored, desires Thanks may be given to GOD: and begs Prayers, that he may profit by the Affliction; and may have his Health perfected and Confirmed.

July, 29. Went alone to the Ferry in the Coach, Capt. Sam¹ Gookin, the under-Sheriff, met me at Charlestown, and Mr. Bordman the Steward. Before Mr. Lynde's Com̄ission was read I said, Although the Court be not so full as we could have desired, yet through the good providence of GOD there is a Court, a Court consisting entirely of such as have been brought up in the Society happily founded in this place by our Ancestors: Our Alma Mater will Grace us; it behooves us that we do not disgrace our Alma Mater. One worthy Member of this Court has been removed by death. Another has given us a further Instance of his Integrity by resigning his place because he apprehended himself incapable of sustaining it by reason of the Infirmities of his Age, (hardness of hearing). The Government have appointed two worthy Gentlemen to sustain these places; Col. Thomas, last Lord's Day was Señight, was Sick likely to dy, which prevented his Attendance. In the Gentleman present I hope we shall have an Instance of the Advantage of an Inns of Court education superadded to that of Harvard College.¹ To shew that he has Right to sit here, his Commission shall now be read to you. Note. Mr. Brattle pray'd Excellently.

July, 29. The Adjournment was so late, that I lodg'd at Mr. Brattle's.

July, 30. Mr. Steadman brought me home round: I

---

¹ Benjamin Lynde, who was graduated at Harvard in 1686, studied law at the Temple. He succeeded Sewall, as chief justice, in 1728, and held that post till his death, January 28, 1744–45. His son Benjamin was appointed to the bench at that date, became chief justice in 1771, but resigned the same year. — EDS.

visited my Son and Daughter, and Grand-Children at Brooklin. This day Mr. Wm Pain's Negro Woman cast her self from the Top of the house above, 40. foot high. I went to the old Church Lecture: Mr. Bridges Text —— we are members one of another.

July, 31. Williams calls me to the Tomb, I go into it to view the order of things in it. Mr. Willard was taken out yesterday, and laid in the new Tomb built by the South-Congregation.

Augt. 1. Enlarge the number of Steps by adding one more. Dug a hole in the North-East Corner and there buried the scattering bones, and buried the pieces of Coffins in Mrs. Willard's Grave.

Augt 2. Shut up the Tomb. Went to the Funeral of Rebekah Dudley, not a fortnight old; laid in Mr. Allen's Tomb.

Wednesday, Augt. 6. Meeting at Bro^r Cole's: I concluded with Prayer. Went from Mr. Comissary's; he offered me his Chariot for my Son to ride out.

Augt. 7. Dr. C. Mather preaches a sermon on occasion of the Heat, out of Rev. —— sun nor heat. Cousin Storke dines with us and Mr. Webb.

Friday, Augt. 8. p. m. Very hot words pass'd between the Lt Govr and Mr. Comissary; each said he was barbarously Treated. Mr. Comissary said he sat in Council upon equal terms with the Lt Govr, which Col. Tailer took very hainously. Govr said Queen had but 3 officers here; Govr, Lt Govr, and Secretary. Council is to meet again next Monday.

Lord's Day, Augt 10. 1712. Joseph goes to Meeting forenoon and p. $\overline{m}$. Mr. Pemberton prays very particularly for him. No Baptisme.

Augt. 16. I bring daughter Hirst to her Mother in a Calash, and carry her home. When return, I visit Mr. Wadsworth, desire his Prayers for Joseph, D[aughter] Hirst, Jno Stuckey. Give a verse to him and to Mr. Pemberton of Mr. Wadsworth.

Augt. 17.   Mr. Pemberton goes to the Castle to preach;
Hear nothing particular in Mr. Wadsworth's prayer, only
for this Flock.   On Satterday Mr. Pemberton spake of
my Son's riding in Mr. Comissary's Charret; Mr. Comissary had spoken to me of it; spake as if he would go
with him to Cambridge.   Augt. 19.   I visit my little
Grand-daughter Mary Sewall at Brooklin; sick of a Fever
and Flux; had Mr. Bridgham's company; From thence to
Roxbury Lecture; Mr. Walter's Text, Mat. 26. 28.   Many
of Boston there: visited the Gov. Mr. Paul Dudley and
his Sisters, Mrs. Kath^a and Mary, set out this morn for
New-London.   Left the Govr two of Mr. Hobart's verses.
Went to go to the Funeral of Mr. Wm Pain's Son, about
4 years old; but when I came to B. Walker's Corner understood the Funeral was gon to the North-End; so desisted.   Mr. Pemberton and Mr. Comissary and son walk'd
a considerable time together on the Parade;[1] I went to
them to see if Capt. Belchar would say any thing of riding
out; said nothing.

Augt. 20. 1712.   Madam Elisa. Whetcomb, 57. years
old, buried;[2] Bearers, Cook, Sewall; Addington, Belchar;
Bromfield, Borland.   Neither Govr nor Lt Govr there.

---

[1] Of course this was not our Parade Ground on the Charles Street Mall,
that being but recently recovered from the sea.   But, as B. Walker's corner
was on Boylston Street, we may fairly presume that some neighboring part
of the Common had already obtained the name. — Eds.

[2] Mrs. Elizabeth Whetcomb was, presumably, the second wife of the
James Whetcomb whose will, dated Nov. 7, 1686, is in Suffolk Wills,
Vol. XI. fol. 55.   He was a merchant, and, by wife Rebecca, had James,
born Nov. 30, 1662; Peter, March 1, 1664; Peter, Dec. 7, 1666; Joseph,
Nov. 26, 1667; Rebecca, June 20, 1671; Richard, May 3, 1673.   By wife
Elizabeth he had William, born April 21, 1680; William, Sept. 9, 1681;
Elizabeth, April 2, 1683.

His will mentions son James, daughters Jane and Rebecca, wife Elizabeth, and "those dear babes, William and Elizabeth, which God hath given
me by her."   Also he bequeaths "my father's and mother's pictures."
Also he mentions his uncle Edward Willys.

Thomas and Rebecca Whetcomb had James, born Aug. 31, 1669; Samuel
Whetcomb married Abigail Champney, April 24, 1701. — Eds.

Went as soon as ever· the Court rose. Gave Mr. Colman
one of Mr. Hobart's verses. Augt. 21. Could not perceive that Mr. Bridge pray'd for my Son.

Augt. 22. Finish the Act that in part takes off the en-
tail of Jn° Clark esqr. his estate. Augt. 21. My Son
brings us word that Mr. Hobart was dangerously sick. I
tell Mr. Bridge and Pemberton of it and he was pray'd
for publickly. Augt. 33. The Govr speaks with some
earnestness that we should not give the Ordinary Court
the go-by, in taking off Entails; it was in their power to
take off Entails.

Augt. 24. Son sends Tom with a Letter to acquaint
me that his daughter Mary died about 1 or 2 aclock last
night; his wife sick.[1] p. m̄. I send the Letter to Mr.
Pemberton. Both Mr. Bridge and Pemberton pray very
Expressly for my Son as call'd to the south-church. I
goe to the Funeral of Capt. Oliver's child. Bearers, Mr.
Jn° Walley, Mr. David Jeffries. Mr. Pemberton deliver'd
me my Son's Letter at the house of Mourning.

Second-day, Augt. 25. Between Roxbury, and Brooklin I met a youth of Newtown, who told me Mr. Hobart[2]
dyed about Sun-rise this morning. Proceeded and waited
on Madam Dudley in her Charret to Brooklin. So soon
as I could get the Coffin, I had little Mary nàil'd up in it,
and brought my dear Grand-Child to Town in my son's
Calash, leaving my Horse for him. The Rain overtook
me near the Governour's, yet I proceeded, and got to my

---

[1] From the note-book of Samuel Sewall, Jr., we extract the following: —
" Dec. 23, 1711. Daughter Mary had a convulsion fitt and continued to
have them till Tuesday noon following, being 25th instant; in which time
she had 14 fitts. January 29. Daughter Mary had a fitt about sundown and
continued to have them till Thursday afternoon following, being 31 of January; in which time she had 22 fitts. Feb. 1. 1711–12, putt daughter Mary
to neighbour Gleason for to suckle her: suckled her a month. March 2 had 4
fitts; April 4th, four fitts at nurse Pike's; April 16 brought her from nurse
Pike's after been there a month, and April 17th had 2 fitts." — Eds.

[2] Rev. Nehemiah Hobart, H. C. 1667. He was a Fellow of the College.
— Eds.

House, just about Two a-clock. About sun-set, or a little after, little Mary Sewall, born July, 20, 1711, was born to the Tomb by Mr. William Cooper, and Mr. Appleton, Mr. Dan¹ Oliver's Aprentice. The Father follow'd alone, then the Gov' and I. The Grandmothers rode in the Governour's Charret.

Tuesday, Augt. 26. I went with my Son and Mr. Nichols in a Calash to the Funeral of Mr. Hobart. Mr. Comissary carried Mr. Pemberton in his Charret. The Gov' went with four Horses. Bearers, President, Mr. Thacher of Milton; Mr. Danforth of Dorchester, Mr. Brattle of Cambridge; Mr. Belcher of Dedham, Mr. Pemberton; Mr. Flint, Mr. Barnard, and Mr. Stephens led the three Daughters. Gov', and Sewall; Mr. Comissary and Bromfield follow'd next after the Mourners. A great many people there. Supose there were more than Forty Graduates. Was inter'd a little more than an hour before Sun-set. Mr. Danforth went to Prayer; mention'd his having been there more than Forty years. Got home well about eight.

Midweek, Augt. 27. I went to Hog-Island with Latherby to see how the Workmen finished the Barn. Saw two Sloops go away with Hay; Turn'd down with them against the Wind. Visited Dr. Increase Mather. He is touch'd with the Gravel. Benj. Larnell kick'd Joshua Gee.

Aug⁺ 28. I went to his Father and ask'd his pardon. Mr. Pemberton preaches a Funeral Sermon on Mr. Hobart, My father —— [2 Kings, 13. 14.]

Augt. 29. My Son and I go to the Meeting at Mr. Phillips's. Mr. Pemberton preach'd excellently. Mr. Phillips spake very kindly to Joseph. Yesterday visited Mrs. Hatch and her new married daughter, Davis; Went to the Funeral of Mrs. Lillie's Son, about 8 years old.

Tuesday, 7r. 23. 1712. Had a Meeting of the Comissioners at my house to adjust the Affairs of the Journey to Martha's Vinyard; That very night I fell sick of a Fever.

7r. 25. Am kept at home by my illness: go to Bed, Vomit: p. m̄ am visited by Mr. Wadsworth, Mr. Clap, Dr. C. Mather and others.

7ʳ 27ᵗʰ It plainly shews it self to be the Fever and Ague. Madam Wharton died last night, 2 hours past midnight.

7ʳ 28. Sit up all the night after the Sabbath and take a vomit, which works well. Mr. Oakes sits with me. My Fits do not yet leave me but are only Burning without any discernible preceding Cold. 7ʳ 30. Madam Wharton buried; Bearers, Mr. Cooke, Sergeant; Eᵐ Hutchinson, Belchar; Mr. Nelson, Borland. I was sent [for] to be a Bearer, but my sickness disabled me. Octobʳ 4. Satterday, About 4 p. m̄. Cousin Green is brought to Bed of a Son. Sam. Kneeland told me of it, to whom I gave a shilling. Octobʳ 5. Mr. Pemberton baptiseth this little son, whom his Father named Samuel. Now about my Fever ceaseth.

Monday, Octobʳ 6ᵗʰ. Mr. James Meers [1] dieth, about 67. years old, born in Boston. I have eaten many a Diñer of his Dressing.

Octobʳ 7ᵗʰ. The Govʳ sets out for Pascataqua.

Octobʳ 8ᵗʰ. Mr. Meers buried: Bearers, Dering, Capt. Williams; Mr. Cutler, George, &c.

Satterday, Octobʳ 11. The Mast Fleet arrives, in which comes Capt. Keeling, Mr. Newton's son, Mrs. Vallentine. William my Barber told me of it first. Mr. Clark of the Comōn, [Commissioner] Mr. Alford.

Lord's-day, 8ʳ 12. The Norwest Wind blows so hard, and Cold, that I venture not abroad. This day Mr. Joseph Sewall's Answer to the Church and Congregation's Call, was read to them.

---

[1] James Meers, or Meares, was a caterer in the town. He was one of the original members of the Brattle Street Society. — Eᴅs.

Midweek, 8ʳ 15ᵗʰ 1712. Mr. Pemberton visits us, staid
a good while, was very placid. This day the Lᵗ Govʳ,
Col. Townsend, and my Son S. S. come home from the
Vinyard.

Sabbath, Octobʳ 19. I am restored from sickness to the
publick Celebration of the Lords day; for which I put up
a Note, that GOD may have the Praise, and that He would
teach me to profit by my Afflictions. Mr. Wadsworth
pray'd Excellently for me and Mr. Secretary recovering.
Third-day, 8ʳ 21. Dr. Mather, Mr. Walter, I and my
Son Joseph ride in the Coach to Newtown, to assist in
keeping a Fast there, to Pray GOD'S Direction of them
in Calling a Minister. Mr. Walter prays, Dr. C. Mather
Preaches and Prays. Sup with Mr. Hobart's Daughters.
Got home well. *Laus Deo.*

Octʳ 22. Court sits. Octʳ 23. Mr. Colman preaches
from [Ps.] 132. 7. Dr. C. Mather, Mr. Bridge, Brother,
Mr. Rawlins &c, dine with us.

Sixth-day, Octobʳ 24, 1712. The Queen's Proclama-
tion[1] for Cessation of Arms, is brought by Capt. Thacher
from Newfoundland; Read in Council, and in the House
of Deputies; sent to the Press. Note. 8ʳ 23. at night,
Broʳ Sewall, Sister Northend, Cousin Hañah Moodey of
York, Cousin Pain of the Great Island, Son Sewall of
Brooklin, cousin Jnᵒ Northend Sup with me, my wife, Son
Joseph Sewall and Daughter Hañah.

Octobʳ 24ᵗʰ Son J. S. and I go to Mr. Pemberton's
privat Meeting. Made a good Thanks-giving Sermon
from PS. 116. 9.

Octobʳ 25. Mrs. Wells, widow, of Salem, dies 70. years

---

[1] In August, "Bolingbroke and Torcy signed a suspension of arms for
four months, — a term afterwards prolonged, — and which was not, like the
former, confined to the armies in the Netherlands, but extending to all parts
of the world, both by land and sea. From this moment, it may be said that,
in effect, peace was re-established between the two nations." Stanhope's
Reign of Queen Anne, Ch. XV. The proclamation was issued on the 18th
of August. — Eds.

old.   Octob.[r] 28. Tuesday, at Noon, Mr. Robert Kitchen
dies, aged 56.

Octob.[r] 29. Hearing before the Court as to Salem middle precinct.

Octob.[r] 30. Council voted in favour of the Precinct,
asserting their having worthily performed their Promise
in Building a Meeting House &c. Deputies Concur.
Day of very sore Rain. Dr. Cotton Mather preaches
from Luke 21. 36. That you may be accounted worthy
to escape.

Octob.[r] 31. Order for Thanksgiving is past. The Secretary writ *Peace;* the Gov.[r] added *Happy;* which I objected against; because we saw but one side, we saw not
what the French had reserved for themselves.[1] Voted it
not. I would have had it plentifull *later* Harvest; because the Wheat and Rye were much blasted; the Barly
much diminished: but I prevail'd not. Sister Northend
returns.

1712, Nov.[r] 1.   Gov.[r] Saltonstall comes to Town.

Nov.[r] 2.[d] Lords-Day; Gov.[r] Saltonstall and Col. Thomas
come to the South Assembly: Mr. J. Sewall preaches
a. m. Mr. Bridge p. m̅.

1712, Nov.[r] 3. I procure Col. Thomas to be sent for
before the Gov.[r] and Council, where he takes the Oaths,
Subscribes the Declaration, and receiv's the Comission
from the Governour. The Bill[2] for forcing the Bills of
Credit to be accepted in all payments for the future, was
again read, debated : and a Conference order'd upon it on
Tuesday morning. Tuesday, Nov.[r] 4. Mr. Jonathan Belchar comes to me and speaks very freely for passing the
Act about Bills of Credit ; said I should do well to be out
of the way rather than hinder so great a good ! I went

---

[1] This was the famous peace of Utrecht, signed March 31st, 1712. — EDS.

[2] See Palfrey, Hist. of New England, IV. 333, 334, and the authorities
cited by him. — EDS.

to the Court at Pullin's; when we were busy in our Work Maxwell was sent to call us to the Conference, which was unexpected. When came there the Govr sur-pris'd me by saying that I and Mr. E^m Hutchinson were apointed to manage the Conference. However, I, after many had spoken, Spake to this effect. " I was at mak-ing of the first Bills of Credit in the year 1690: They were not made for want of Money; but for want of Money in the Treasury. If the Government pass this Act, they Comand and Compell men to Lend them that value. None are oblig'd to take them. He that has Bills may want every thing else. Mr. Comissary gave me occasion to mention the sad effect such a like Act had at Barbados. Govr said they were ready to knock one another in the head.

" The Government may make a vast Quantity of Bills of Credit, and leave them with us in Exchange for our Estates.

" If money be wanting, Twere a better expedient to oblige Creditors to take Wheat, Indian Corn, Salt, Iron, Wool at a moderat valuation, as twas of old: Then there would be *Quid pro Quo;* whereas now privat Creditors are forc'd to take the publick Faith for payment for their Comodity. The Merchants that complain of the scarcity of Money, tis they that have sent it away, and do send it away." [1]

Return'd to the Super^r Court; Dr. Cotton Mather dines with us.

Thorsday, Novr 6. Make a considerable Entertainment.

---

[1] This act will be found on pp. 700, 701, of Vol. I. of the reprint of the Province laws. It is Chap. VI., and is entitled " An Act to prevent the oppression of debtors." Referring to " the great scarcity of money and the want of other adequate media," it provides that all debts incurred between Oct. 30, 1705, and Oct. 30, 1715, " specialties and express contracts in writing always excepted," may be paid in " good and lawful bills of credit on this province." It was a " legal-tender act." — EDS.

Have the Govᵣ, Govᵗ Saltonstall, Lieut Govᵣ, Major Pigeon, Mr. Whiting out of Captivity; Mr. Secretary, Mr. Comissary, Mr. Pemberton.

Friday, Novᵣ 7ᵗʰ Bill passes, was read 3 times this day with the Deputies. This is the date of Mr. Harris's preface against Dr. Increase Mather.

Satterday, Novᵣ 8. ·I went not to Court because I was unwilling to be present at Reading the Engrossed Bill.

Friday Novᵣ 7. I visited Broᵣ Belknap on his Sickbed; said he was hoping in the Free Grace of GOD. Mr. Wadsworth Dines with us, Mr. Speaker, Col. Hutchinson, Townsend.

Novᵣ 9. Lords day. Mr. Wadsworth couples Mr. Pemberton and my Son in his prayer.

Novᵣ 10. Ride to Salem in a Calash with Mr. Dudley.

Novᵣ 11. Col. Thomas comes to us. Capt. Norden and Mr. Speaker were Justices specially assign'd for the cause between Marston and Brown.

Midweek, Novᵣ 12. Mr. Blower preaches a very good Sermon — whether present or absent may be Acceptable to Christ. Ministers dine with us, Major Brown, Higginson, Epes.

Thorsday, adjourn *sine die*, just at night. A great Snow falls, that were fain to leave our Calash at Lewis's. Spar'd Mr. Corwin our Horse back; met him at Lewis's going and coming. Got home comfortably. *Laus Deo.* Met with my Wedding Gloves and Bride-cake from Govᵣ Saltonstall.[1]

Novᵣ 17. My Son and I visit Govᵣ Saltonstall and his Bride.

19. Midweek, very high Tide.

18. Tuesday. Mr. Belknap buried. Joseph was in-

---

[1] Bond says that Governor Gurdon Saltonstall, of Connecticut, was thrice married. His second wife, Elizabeth Rosewell, died Sept. 12, 1710; and he married, thirdly, Mrs. Mary Clarke, daughter of William and Mary (Lawrence) Whittingham, and relict of William Clarke, of Boston. — EDS.

vited by Gloves, and had a scarf given him there, which is the first. Mr. Pemberton is not well.

20. Joseph preaches in the Forenoon, Mr. Pemberton not abroad.

22. Satterday. About 30 Horsmen come and accompany Mr. Thair[1] to Roxbury: He is to be ordain'd next Wednesday.

Nov.ʳ 22. My desire of seeing foreign Countries was incomparably abated, by considering that at Home I might visit GOD, in whom all Perfection of Goodness is Centred.

Midweek 9.ʳ 26. Mr. Thair is ordain'd; Mr. Danforth, Dorchester, gave the Charge, Mr. Walter the Right Hand of Fellowship. Mr. Short tells us he was ordain'd the 12. 9.ʳ Mr. Gr[indall] Rawson gave the Charge, Mr. S. Danforth Right Hand Fellowship.

Nov.ʳ 26. 1712. Mrs. Sarah More died last Satterday night, was buried this day. Bearers, Elisha Hutchinson, Sewall; Oaks, Barnard; Gilbert, Shipreve. Aged 80 years. Dr. Incr. Mather said her death was like a Translation, wish'd he might dye so. She was a very loving familiar friend of ours. Buried in the Old burying place.

27. Dr. Cotton Mather preaches from Heb. 13. In a few words. Mr. Thacher, Blower, Shortt &c dine with us.

In the evening in the Street Mr. Pemberton spake to me whether some further step should not be taken about Joseph. Spake of the church's Thanking him for his Answer and desiring his readiness to assist. I told him, I left it to him. Three persons buried to day; Capt. Oburn,[2] Mr. Edwards's infant Son, widow Flack.

---

[1] Ebenezer Thayer, H. C. 1708. — Eds.

[2] James Oborn, of Boston, made his will Nov. 15, 1712, which is not recorded, but is on the files (No. 3460). In it he mentions his wife Abigail (he married Abigail Winslow May 11, 1702), and gives £100 to his daughter Abigail when eighteen or married. He uses as his seal one bearing the Sheaffe arms, and Jacob Sheaffe was one of the witnesses. See the Heraldic Journal, IV. 81, where the name is wrongly printed Osborn. — Eds.

Nov.ʳ 28.   Major Livingston and Armstrong arrive in Waters from Añapolis.   Weeks passage.

Friday, Dec.ʳ 12.   Gov.ʳ, Mr. Pemberton, Brother, his son Sam, dine with us.

17.   Sam sails in Cap.ᵗ Sunderland for Barbados.

18.   Mr. Wadsworth preaches of the Talents, and our Accountableness.

A little while ago Capt. Belchar presents me with half a Quintal of Fish.

Dec.ʳ 18.   After Lecture, and Diñer I go to the Funeral of Capt. Sam.ˡ Hayman, aged 70. years.   Bearers, Col. Elisha Hutchinson, Sewall; Addington, Sergeant; Eᵐ Hutchinson, Belchar.   He was at Boston Lecture this day Señight, and died on the Lords-day night.   He was a Lover of New-England.

Dec.ʳ 19.   Benj. Larnell's Books and Bedding are carried to Cambridge by Tho. Hutchins.

20.   He visits the School, presents his Master, Submaster, and the Scholars, each a copy of verses.   I added two to the last.

> *Erroresque meos mihi condonate perosos;*
> *Absentique mihi precibus succurrite semper.*

Very cold blustering day; we have 3 cords wood brought into yard that came from Hog Island yesterday.

Febr. 3. 17$\frac{1\ 2}{1\ 3}$ Madam Elisa. Hutchinson dies about 9. *mane;* Suddenly.

Febr. 4.   privat Meeting at our house, pretty number of Men; Mr. Tilly here; tis the first Meeting he has been at since his Sickness.   Sung 3 Staves 27ᵗʰ Ps. W[indsor] v. 1, 2, 3, 4, 5, and the last 4 Lines of the 9ᵗʰ verse. Cousin Savage was here with his new wife.

Febr. 5ᵗʰ   Mr. Bridge gives Madam Hutchinson a great Character, as to her Piety and Charity, Exact Walk.

Febr. 6.   My son visits us from Brooklin.

Febr. 7.   7th day.   Madam Hutchinson is buried; Bearers, Cooke, Sewall; Addington, Townsend; Bromfield, Belcher; came to the South-burying place. Col. Hutchinson by reason of his Sore Toe was fain to ride in the Coach. Mr. Edward Hutchinson, and Madam Woolcot were the principal Mourners; Son and Daughter by Freak, and Hutchinson.[1]

Febr. 9. Council at Roxbury; Mr. Secretary, Bromfield, Sewall, Belchar ride in his coach.

Tuesday, Febr. 10. A vehement storm of Snow. Mr. Stoddard sent his Coach to fetch me to the Comissioners Meeting at his House. When return'd could scarce get in at my door for a great Drift of Snow blown up there; were fain to Shovel it away first.

Wednesday, Febr. 11. Mr. Aaron Porter[2] is ordain'd pastor of the church at Meadford. Mr. Angier gave the charge; Mr. Hancock, the Right Hand of Fellowship. The storm foregoing hinder'd my Son from being there. And Mr. Jonathan Belchar made a Splendid Treat for Mr. Wainwright, to which my Son was invited on Tuesday; were many more people there than the Meetinghouse would hold.

Febr. 12. Sam. comes not to Town as he intended. In the Afternoon Devotion informs my wife of his very uncomfortable Circumstances, and of the Necessity of fetching him to Boston.

Friday, Febr. 13. Joseph and I ride in Mr. Stoddard's Coach to Brooklin, got thither at Eleven a. m: find Sam abed. In a little while got him up, din'd there, came away. I was somwhat afraid, by reason his [Joseph's] Pulse was disorder'd. But the Coach being close, Harry drove us home well about 4. p. m̄. At Brooklin I saw the Lambs, encourag'd Tom. to be faithfull in his Masters business, which he promis'd. Told him he could not obey

---

[1] This was Elizabeth, second wife of Elisha Hutchinson. She was daughter of Major Thomas Clark, and married, first, John Freke. — EDS.

[2] Graduated H. C. 1708. — EDS.

his Master without obedience to his Mistress; and *vice versa;* bid him take that as a Rule. Gave him a Two-shilling Bill of Credit. When my daughter alone, I ask'd her what might be the cause of my Son's Indisposition, are you so kindly affectioned one towards another as you should be? She answer'd, I do my Duty. I said no more.[1] At parting I pray'd God to be with us going, and with them staying. Son gave Hañah a piece of Silver.

Satterday, Febr. 14. Cousin Moodey of York comes in the night; which made me think of those words; The Lord that comforteth all those that are cast down, comforteth us by the Coming of Titus.

Febr. 16. Mr. Moodey departs about noon. Brill calls just at night, From the Gov.ʳ enquires of my Son's Well-fare.

Febr. 17. Great Snow. Tom comes for Meal. I give him half a Bushel of pease home with him, of our best. All well at Brooklin. I enquired of my daughter, Hañah, and the whole family.

Febr. 19. Lecture-day, son S. goes to Meeting, speaks to Mr. Walter. I also speak to him to dine. He could not; but said he would call before he went home. When he came he discours'd largly with my Son; I also spake to him: His advice was, that Ilsly should be put away; some Friends talk to them both and so come together again. My Son was very helpfull to me in copying out Dr. Mather's Circular Letter.[2]

Febr. 21. Satterday, Daughter Sewall calls and gives us a visit; I went out to carry my Letters to Savil's, that

---

[1] In our first volume (Introd. p. xxvii) will be found the result of this domestic disturbance. It culminated, two years later, in a separation which lasted for three years. Judge Sewall's delicacy, in his references to the alien-ation between his daughter-in-law and his son, exhibits one of the winning traits of his character. — EDS.

[2] This Circular Letter probably was not printed, as it does not appear in Sibley's list of the works of Dr. Increase Mather, nor in the brief list of Cotton Mather's publications. — EDS.

were to be carried by Mr. Crocker to Barnstable. While I was absent, My Wife and Daughter Sewall had very sharp discourse; She wholly justified her self, and said, if it were not for her, no Maid could be able to dwell at their house. At last Daughter Sewall burst out with Tears, and call'd for the Calashe. My wife relented also, and said she did not design to grieve her; Son carried his daughter to the Calash, and desired her to send Tom. with the Horse for him on Friday.

Febr. 25. Sore Storm of Rain. Brill comes to Town, and acquaints that the Gov.ʳ was taken with a sore Fit of the Gravel last night; so cânt be a Council to day.

Febr. 27. Friday, A Council is held at the Governour's, who is now below Stairs. Saw my Son, but spake not to him. When the business of the Council was over, and pipes were call'd for, I slipt into Kitchen; but my Son was gon; sat with Madam Dudley alone a pretty while; She said nothing to me; I gave her my Silk-Hand-kerchief, which I bought last Satterday for my daughter, but was prevented giving it to her, she being just gon before I got home. Yet this occasion brought her not to speak; Ask'd kindly after my Wife. Went to the Govʳ agen, Took leave, came home as went, with Capt. Belchar, Bromfield, Norden.

Febr. 28. Amos Gates comes to Town, and says my Son is better.

March 2. Monday, Madam Elisa. Addington dyes, aged 76 years; died ¼ after one p. m̄. By accident I call'd in and pray'd God to accompany him in his Solitude. Went to meet Col. Townsend and go with him to Col. Hutchinson to certify about a Counterfeit Bill; knowing nothing of this Death. Had been married 46. years.[1]

---

[1] This was Elizabeth (Bowen), wife of Secretary Isaac Addington. He married again, Nov. 19th following, Elizabeth, widow of Hon. John Wainwright. — EDS.

Note. James Peñiman was buried last Lord's-day night;
Bearers, Mr. Cutler, Creese; Beñet, Brisco; Ellis, Steward.
Mr. Bridge and Wadsworth were there, being I suppose in-
vited, and to comfort the Relations. He had been such a
Drunkard and Idler that I went not to the Funeral, hav-
ing no heart to it. My son preaches at Mr. Bridgham's
Meeting Lord's day night.

March 3. m. Am sent for to Mrs. Fifield, as dying. I
went, staid some time, and Mr. Pemberton came and
pray'd with her; spake very little, Breath'd hard. I
came away, Quickly after was told she was dead. Died
between 9 and 10 in the morning; a good friend of ours,
as her Ancestors before her. She was a diligent, frugal,
Chaste Woman.

March, 4. Capt. Whiting tells me of his Father's death
last Satterday, an hour before Sun-set. To be buried on
Thorsday.

March, 5. A very severe cold Night and day. Mr.
Bridge preaches from Isa. 63. 5: show'd that when the
set time was come, GOD would destroy Babylon, though
expected helpers fail'd. Before last prayer, acquainted
the Congregation with Mr. Whiting's death, to be bewail'd, and the Church sympathiz'd with. After Lecture,
Madam Addington buried. Bearers, Lt Govr Tailer, Sewall;
Sergeant, E^m Hutchinson; Belcher, Bromfield. Buried
in a brick Grave in the Old burying place.

March, 6. Mr. Sever calls in to see us. p. $\overline{m}$. Mrs.
Mary Fifield is buried in the New burying place;[1] Bearers,
Oakes, Howard; Tim^o Clark, Cutler; Tilly, Jno Foster.
Aged 45. years the 11th February. Gave my son a Scarf.

---

[1] In the Granary Yard is a broken stone, probably of this person. It
reads: "Here lyes ... body of M ... Fifield, wife ... Richard Fifie ...
Aged 45 yea ... 22 dayes."

Richard Fifield married Mary Drew Aug. 25, 1701. A Richard Fifield,
of Boston, mariner, made his will July 18, 1716 (Suff. Wills, Vol. XXI.
fol. 386), and leaves his estate to wife Maria. — EDS.

After this son and I visited Govr Saltonstall's Lady. Mrs.
Laurence was there. Mrs. Mary Saltonstall came in after,
and sat with us.

March 17th Govr Saltonstall comes to Town.

March, 24, 17$\frac{12}{13}$. Spake to Mrs. Chaney.

March 25, 1713. J. S. went to visit Mr. Walley, but
found him not at home. Went to Neighbour Fifield;
Mrs. Mehit. Thurston not within.

March, 26. Mr. Pemberton preaches 1 Pet. 1. 17 —
pass the time of your sojourning here in fear. Made a
very good sermon. 2^d p^t 39. Ps. sung, M. Mr. Saml
Danforth visits us in the evening. Has hopes of Mr. Jno
Williams's daughter at Canada; may be as when Samson
married a Philistin. I mention'd the Omen of her Name
Eunice, *Bene litigans*.[1]

---

[1] Eunice Williams, daughter of Rev. John Williams, of Deerfield, was
carried to Canada in 1704, at the age of ten years. She married an Indian,
probably named De Rogers, by whom she had a son and two daughters.
Sarah, her daughter, married Dr. Williams, said to be a son of a Bishop of
Chester, and their son Thomas was father of the notorious Rev. Eleazer Williams, the "Dauphin." At least, this is the story told by him and printed
in the "Williams Genealogy," pp. 92–96.

The case of Eunice Williams was one which, at the time, excited
much interest in this community, and engaged a warm sympathy for her
father. If she was ten years old when she was taken by the French and Indians as one of the captives in the destruction of Deerfield, in 1704, O. S.,
she was at this time eighteen. Her father, in his famous book, "The Redeemed Captive," and other writers of that period, give very full accounts
of the zealous efforts made by the Jesuit priests in Canada to convert prisoners, especially young persons, taken thither after the furious raids on our
frontiers. Eunice Williams yielded to the influence exerted upon her for
this purpose, and became a convert. She was left at Montreal when many
of the captives were ransomed and brought to Boston in 1706, and she could
not be induced to return to her home and friends. Some time after, dressed
in the full Indian garb, she made a visit, with her husband, to Deerfield,
where her father had resumed his ministry, but no entreaties would prevail
with her to resume a civilized life. She was one among very many of those
born in New England, in Puritan families, as well as of a much larger number of the French, who were so fascinated by the charms of a wild life with
the natives in the woods as to renounce their own race and homes. A more
famous example of this "reversion" was that of Mary Jemeson, the so-
called "White Woman." Competent authorities tell us that, in all the

Court prorogued to the 15th April.

March, 28, 1713. Mr. Justice Corwin, Lynde, and Sewall set out on our Plimouth Journey. Baited at Mill's; Din'd at Cushings. Baited at Bairstow's. From thence got to Capt. Joshua Cushing's a little before Sun-set. Pembrook. Mr. Daniel Lewis, their Minister, preaches twice.

March, 30. Visit Abigail, Momontaug's widow, at Mattakeese,[1] a pleasant Situation by great Ponds. Din'd at Cook's, whether came Mr. Justice Thomas, Mr. Attorney, Cook, Vallentine. Mr. Sheriff Lothrop, with his Guard, conducted us to Plimouth, where we Arriv'd early.

March, 31. Held the Court.

April, 1. Went into the Meetinghouse and Spent some Time in Prayer in the new Addition, in the Gallery.

April, 2. Court adjourns by Candle Light, *sine die.* Note. Mr. Thacher of Milton din'd with us twice.

April, 3d 6th day. Rain keeps us at Plimouth. Only just before night rode to Cook's to shorten our Journey.

April, 4th. Pleasant serene weather; bait at Bairstow's. Dine at Hingham, Cushing's; Bait at Mill's; Got well home about an hour by Sun. *Laus Deo.*

April, 5. Mr. Wadsworth preaches Excellently, on the sovereignty of God.

April, 6. Little Billy Hirst dyes 10 at night, 9 months old.

April, 8. I visit Mrs. Betty Walley;[2] thank her for her

---

relations, peaceful or hostile, between Indians and Europeans on this continent, more than one hundred of the whites have been " Indianized " to each single Indian who has been civilized. — EDS.

[1] Duxbury was called Mattakeeset by the Indians; but Winsor's history says nothing of this Abigail. The nearest sachem was Josiah, or Chickatabut, whose son was Josiah, father of Jeremy, father of Charles Josiah, the last of the race. (Winsor, p. 75.) — EDS.

[2] This is about the beginning of the courtship of Rev. Joseph Sewall, who married Elizabeth, daughter of John Walley. A brief sketch of the family is in Bridgman's " Granary-yard Inscriptions," pp. 34-35. Samuel

favour to my son, desire the continuance of it. She
Treats me with Apples and Wine. Son goes at night and
presents her with a Portuguese piece of Gold, 4000. [reis ?]
1704. I had given her Dr. C. Mather's Treatise against
Antinomianism [*Adversus Libertinos*], just come out.

April, 9. Mr. Colman goes on with 1 Jn? 3. 1. How
unreasonable are we ; that God should make offers of his
Son to us, to be our Husband ; and we no more fill'd with
Humble Thankfull Admiration ! O that I could Loath
my self for this Criminal Omission so long as I Live !

Friday, April, 17. Madam Elizabeth Stoddard dyes
about 4. m : reckon'd a vertuous Gentlewoman ; Has lan-
guish'd a long time.[1]

April. 18. I visit Madā Cooke, who seem'd very glad
to see me. Has been confin'd a long time; tells me she
accounts her self older than Madam Stoddard rather than
else. I told her in pleasancy She and I were in the same
year of our Age. She was born Apr. 26. 1651. I was
born March 28. 1652.

Lords Day, April, 19. Mr. Wadsworth preaches at the
South, Excellently ; and with Great and very obliging
Affection Took Leave of the South church. Pray'd for
Joseph in the 2ᵈ Prayer. *Post meridiem*, Dr. Increase
Mather preaches 1 Tim? 2. 1. Excellently, vigorously.
Prays for Joseph, mentioning his having been made a
Blessing. Pray'd not a 2ᵈ time because was Baptisme.
Mr. Pemberton preach'd for the Dr. in the Forenoon, by
which means Mr. Wadsworth was alone ; but now had all
Three. Mr. Pemberton pray'd for Govʳ Saltonstall re-
moving with his family ; and very largly for his Lady,
that God would bless her, and make her a Blessing. Dr.

Hurd Walley was a member of Congress in 1854 and 1855, Speaker of the
(State) House of Representatives, 1844–46, &c. — EDS.

[1] This was Elizabeth, second wife of Col. Simeon Stoddard. Much genealogical information about the family is to be found in Sumner's " History of
East Boston." See Vol. I. p. 424, *note*. — EDS.

Mather and Mr. Wadsworth pray'd expressly for Govr Salstonstall as removing. I visited Mr. Pemberton in the Evening; told him I endeavour'd to visit him before I went to Plimouth, and after my return. Said he heard not of it. The Swallows have come; I saw three together, April 19. Backward spring.

Tuesday, Apr. 21. Govr Saltonstall sets out for New-London; Col. Townsend, and I on Horseback. Mr. Comissary and Pemberton in his chariot. Mr. . Rogers and many others accompany to Dedham. Madam Saltonstall, Mrs. Mary Saltonstall, and Mrs. Martha Rogers ride in the Coach. Govr goes from Roxbury. After Diñer set out for Meadfield, rather before four. Very good day. Mr. Comissary paid the Reckoning; of which the Govr paid 40^s. I paid 15^s. Twas in all £4. odd. Got home very comfortably.

Midweek, Apr. 22. Madam Stoddard buried; Bearers, Govr Dudley, Lt Govr Tailer; Lt Govr Usher, Saml Sewall, Peter Sergeant esqr. All the Ministers had Scarves, and Joseph had one. It seem'd inconvenient presently to throw off Mr. Stoddard's Scarf, and not wear it once as was like to be, if had gone to Salem.

Apr. 23. I went to the Funeral of Mrs. Martha Patteshall;[1] Bearers, Cooke, Sewall; Dumer, Treas^r Taylor; Col. Checkley, Capt. Hill. This took me off from going to the Castle, which I was glad of. No body ask'd me to go to Salem, I consider'd Madam Bradstreet had been a Widow there Sixteen years, and was loth to intercept any Respect might be now shown to the Gentlemen there. Five of the Council at Salem; Col. Apleton is of Ipswich, of which Town the Relations are, Madam Wainwright, &c. *This Invitation* fell in Thorsday morn unexpectedly.[2] Mr.

---

[1] She was the wife of Richard Patteshall, of Boston. By her son Robert she was grandmother of Rev. Richard Patteshall, who died in 1768. (See N. E. Hist. and Gen. Register, Vol. XVII. p. 237.) — EDS.

[2] There is some confusion in this paragraph. The explanation may be

Wadsworth preached Excellently from Ps. 146. 10. Concluded with Philip. 1. 21. To me to live is Christ, and to dye is Gain. Sung the last Two Staves and half of the 146 Ps.

Mr. Marsh, Wigglesworth, Tuft, Rawlings dined with us.

Friday, Apr. 24. Mr. Pemberton calls at my house; Hañah went to the door, and suposing me at the Town-meeting said I was not within; whereas indeed I was, but in the Chamber. Mr. Pemberton said his business was with me, and declin'd coming in. When I understood it, I went to Mr. Pemberton's the same morning. He not within, I sat some time with Madam Pemberton: Ask'd her what people thought of my Son's Courtship; She spake well of it; Said Mr. Alford had done ungentlemanly by her, and she thought at the time of it, she would have a better Husband; comended Mrs. Betty. I told her I would call again about 3. p. m. I went again, she crav'd my pardon, said she had forgot to tell Mr. Pemberton what I had said of calling. He was gon out.

April, 25. Satterday, About 4 p. m. as soon as I could get my book finish'd, I went to Mr. Walley's. Neither of the Sisters within. At last Mrs. Lydia came in, and sat with me. I gave her Mr. Walter of CHRIST, very well bound in Calvs Leather, to give Mrs. Betty. I had written her Name in it. When had staid about half an hour or little more, I came away.

April, 26. Mr. Bridge[1] signifies to the scattered Flock their intention to meet in their new built Meeting-house,

---

that Sewall was glad of an excuse for not going to the Castle for the celebration of Queen Anne's Coronation Day, by the firing of cannon, the drinking of healths, &c. He had expected, but did not receive, an invitation to attend Mrs. Bradstreet's funeral, at Salem, so he accepted the invitation to be a bearer to Mrs. Patteshall. — EDS.

[1] Rev. Thomas Bridge was minister of the First Church from 1705 to 1715. Their building was destroyed by the fire, and was succeeded by a brick one on the same site. — EDS.

the next Lords-day; Took Leave in very pathetical, obliging Terms. Pray'd much for Mr. Pemberton, acknowledging the Gifts with which God had adorn'd him. In second Prayer pray'd for that other worthy person call'd to assist [Joseph Sewall] — that his Settlement might be hasten'd, might be a lasting Blessing.

April, 27. The first Court was open'd in the New Townhouse. I was present. Mr. Colman pray'd Excellently. It was a damp to me that the first thing was done was the calling out the monstrously profane John Green.[1] p. m̄. Waited on the Court at the Green Dragon, with Capt. Tim? Clark, to inform against Richard Vince, who is more like a wild-Cat than a man. From thence went to Dr. Increase Mather. Thank'd him for the Perseverance of his Love to my Son Joseph : agreed to call a Meeting of the Com̄issioners at the Town House at 4. p. m. next Thorsday.

Tuesday, April 28. I waited on Mr. Pemberton. Mr. Wisewall was there. Mr. Marsh of Braintry came in. Mr. Pemberton spake very fiercely against the Govr and Council's meddling with suspension of Laws, respecting Church of England men not paying Taxes to the dissenting Ministers. Spake very fiercely in dislike of the overseers,[2] that nothing had been done; would chuse others. I think this was before Mr. Marsh came in. At the Gate said what I did twould be reckon'd my Son did; intimat-

---

[1] Doubtless this was the Green previously mentioned (*ante*, p. 337) as concerned in the matter of the Mock Sermon. By a comparison of dates that sermon seems to have been delivered on Shrove Tuesday, and the whole matter was perhaps exaggerated by Sewall's immoderate fear of popery or prelacy. — EDS.

[2] By the "Overseers" seems to be meant the committee who had charge of annually assigning the seats in the meeting-house. This was sometimes a perplexing and invidious duty, exciting personal jealousies. The hint given to Sewall to release himself from the responsibility implied that he might be charged with being influenced by his son, the new pastor, if any charge of favoritism was made. — EDS.

ing as I conceive, twere best for me to lay down my Overseers place. Post m̄ went to Roxbury Lecture with Mr. Thair and Josiah Oakes. Mr. Walter preach'd excellently from Ps. 41. 4. I saw Samuel; It is yet dark wether at Brooklin.[1] Came home with Thair and Oakes. Thair went off at his Brother's; Oakes and I visited the Bride Adams, they were married last Tuesday morn before Gov' Saltonstall went out of Town.

Midweek, April 29. Council held at 11. a. m̄; ordered so many to attend the Gov' Eastward as to make a Council there. Sam¹ Penhallow's Petition read,[2] as to importing Indians contrary to Law, craves relief; Gov: urged the Council vehemently: Mr. Com̄issary question'd the Council's power. I said if Mr. Secretary would admit him to his oath, I should not blame him. If he could not do it lawfully, the council could not make it Law. Voted not for it. Gov' would have had the Council order'd the Sheriff to have Took them out of the hands of those they were sold to at Plimouth. p. m̄. Son and I visit Mr. Stoddard, who treats us kindly; speaks with great Affection of his deceased wife. I go to the Meeting at Mr.

---

[1] Referring to the unhappy domestic relations of his son. — EDS.

[2] This refers to the Act passed in 1712, " prohibiting the importation or bringing into this Province any Indian servants or slaves." Province Laws, I. 698. The preamble to this Act is so emphatically worded that we here copy it: —

"Whereas divers conspiracies, outrages, barbarities, murders, burglaries, thefts, and other notorious crimes and enormities, at sundry times, and especially of late, have been perpetrated and committed by Indians and other slaves within severall of her majestie's plantations in America, being of a malicious, surley and revengeful spirit, rude and insolent in their behaviour, and very ungovernable, the over-great number and increase whereof within this province is likely to prove of pernicious and fatal consequence to her majesties subjects and interest here, unless speedily remedied, and is a discouragement to the importation of white servants, this province being differently circumstanced from the plantations in the islands, and having great numbers of the Indian natives of the country within and about them, and at this time under the sorrowful effects of their rebellion and hostilities . . . " — EDS.

Franklin's.[1]   Pray, read Mr. Doolittle's Morning Lecture about Leading of the Spirit. Visit daughter Hirst who has a Swell'd face. The Lord Heal her!

Note. At the Council an Order was made to restore the Lecture to the new built Meetinghouse, as accustomed; and the place most Central.[2]

Lord's-Day, May 3. 1713.   In the forenoon Mr. Wadsworth preaches the first Sermon in their New-built Meetinghouse, from Haggai 2. 9. The glory of this latter House.[3]

Monday, May 4. I wait on Mr. Pemberton at his desire. Mr. Sergeant and Col. Checkley there: Mr. Pemberton declares a Necessity of adding to the number of the Seaters. Would have us nominat at least. I said I would venture to mention one, Mr. Daniel Oliver; then Major Fitch was nam'd, whom Mr. Pemberton much applauded; I and all lik'd him very well. Then Mr. Pemberton enquired whether it might not be convenient to apoint one of the Congregation; we came into it. Mr. Jeffries was mention'd, whom all approv'd. I desired Mr. Pemberton to assist at opening the Court to morrow; He wholly declin'd it upon the account of his Lecture this week, and his great Indisposition. Mention'd my son. But I chose to call Dr. Cotton Mather in the evening. He readily undertook it, and appointed to be at Mr. Phillips his shop.

Tuesday, May 5, 1713. *mane.* Dr. Cotton Mather makes an Excellent Dedication-Prayer in the New Court-Chamber. Mr. Pain, one of the Overseers of the Work wellcom'd us, as the Judges went up Stairs. Dr. Cotton

---

[1] The son, Benjamin, was then in his eighth year, and may have had the privilege, then enjoyed by children, of sitting quite still at the meeting. — EDS.

[2] We notice here the official character and sanction attached to the famous Thursday Lecture, established by John Cotton, and which faded away into a shadow before its quite recent disuse. — EDS.

[3] There appear to have been no special dedication services on the occupancy of a new meeting-house in those days. — EDS.

Mather having ended Prayer, The Clark went on and call'd the Grand-Jury: Giving their Charge, which was to enforce the Queen's Proclamation, and especially against Travailing on the Lord's Day; God having return'd to give us Rest. [In the margin. My speech to Grand jury in new Court House.] I said, You ought to be quickened to your Duty, in that you have so Convenient, and August a Chamber prepared for you to doe it in. And what I say to you, I would say to my self, to the Court, and to all that are concern'd. Seeing the former decay'd Building is consum'd, and a better built in the room, Let us pray, May that Proverb, Golden Chalices and Wooden Priests, never be transfer'd to the Civil order; that God would take away our filthy Garments, and cloath us with Change of Raiment; That our former Sins may be buried in the Ruins and Rubbish of the former House, and not be suffered to follow us into this; That a Lixivium may be made of the Ashes, which we may frequently use in keeping ourselves Clean: Let never any Judge debauch this Bench, by abiding on it when his own Cause comes under Trial; May the Judges always discern the Right, and dispense Justice with a most stable, permanent Impartiality; Let this large, transparent, costly Glass serve to oblige the Attornys alway to set Things in a True Light, And let the Character of none of them be *Impar sibi;* Let them Remember they are to advise the Court, as well as plead for their clients. The Oaths that prescribe our Duty run all upon Truth; God is Truth. Let Him communicat to us of His Light and Truth; Let the Jurors and Witnesses swear in Truth, in Judgment, and in Righteousness. If we thus improve this House, they that built it, shall inhabit it; the days of this people shall be as the days of a Tree, and they shall long enjoy the work of their hands. The Terrible Illumination that was made, the third of October was Twelve moneths, did plainly shew us that our GOD is a Consuming Fire: but

it hath repented Him of the Evil.   And since He has declar'd that He takes delight in them that hope in his
Mercy, we firmly believe that He will be a Dwelling place
to us throughout all Generations.

The Church Meeting was begun before I could get to it;
Major Fitch and Mr. Oliver Nominated.   Then were
chosen by lifting up the Hand.   Then Mr. Pemberton
call'd on them to Nominat another ; Som body said, Capt.
Savage (I understood it of Ephraim) ; but Capt. Habijah
Savage stood up and disabled himself because of the Dispute between his Unkle and him about the Pue.   Then
some body mentioned Mr. Phillips.   After awhile, I said,
Some have thought it might be convenient to have one of
the Congregation.   Mr. Pemberton assented.   Mr. Jeffries
was Nominated and voted.   Mr. Pemberton said, Mr. Phillips was Nominated ; but I had carried it over to the Congregation : whereas 'twas what he himself had introduc'd
at the Meeting of the Overseers at his House.   And I
reckon'd Mr. Phillips not so fit because of the Controversy
about the Pue.   Concluded with Prayer : Pray'd that my
son now call'd to more Constant Work might be blessed
of GOD.

May, 6.   Dr. Cotton Mather Pray'd again.   Sir Ch.
Hobby dines with us.   Court adjourns without Day.

May, 7.   Mr. Pemberton preaches the First Lecture in
the New-built Meeting-house, from 2 Chron. 6. 18.   But
will God in very deed dwell with Men —— very good
Discourse.

10.   Lord's day.   Joseph preaches again.

Tuesday, May, 12, 1713.   Joseph prays at the head of
the Regiment : entertain Mrs. Elisa. Walley, her Bro.ʳ and
Sisters, Mrs. Kath. and Bethiah Eyre and Mr. Jeffries &c.

May, 14.   Dr. Cotton Mather preaches the Lecture
Excellently.

May, 18, 1713.   Col. Thomas and I set out for Ipswich
by Winnissimmet, Benj. Smith waits on me.   In the Butts

Brook¹ my Horse lies down, but I kept on his back, and had no hurt but wetting my feet, and breach of the Crooper. Din'd at Brother's; visited Col. Hathorne, who seems not to expect to go out of Salem any more. Visited Broʳ and Sister Hirst. Call'd at Brother Gerrishe's and refresh'd till company came up. Got well to Ipswich in Season.

May, 19. Mr. Rogers prays at opening of the Court. Din'd at Smith's. At Noon Brother and I persuaded them of Artichoke precinct,² to Agree. I gave Lᵗ Moodey Five pounds, and Jnᵒ Emery gave five pounds, and Moodey and others let fall their Review; went into Court, and said, They are Agreed. The Agreem't was made in Smith's Garret. Adjourned *sine die*. As the Post went along, he told us of Mr. Brattle's Death. He died between 11 and Twelve, 2ᵈ day a. m.

Midweek, May 20. The Rain hinder'd my Return. Visited Dr. Hale at Beverly who, opress'd with Melancholy, was a-bed at. 5. p. m. Visited Mr. Blower. Got to Brother's at Salem about 7. and lodg'd there. By this means I was not Entangled with the Riot³ Comitted that night in Boston by 200 people or more, breaking open Arthur Mason's Warehouse in the Comon, thinking to find Corn there; Wounded the Lᵗ Govʳ and Mr. Newton's Son; cry'd Whalebone. Were provoked by Capt. Belchar's sending Indian Corn to Curasso. The Select-men desired him not to send it; he told them, The hardest

---

¹ We have not been able to identify this brook. It was, evidently, on the road from Chelsea to Salem. — Eds.

² Artichoke River is in Newbury, and the reference is obviously to the dispute about the Episcopal Church there. (See *ante*, pp. 337, 338.) — Eds.

³ We find no other mention of this tumult, the only " bread riot," probably, that Boston has ever witnessed. Belcher had exported grain before in a time of scarcity, just previous to the arrival of Admiral Walker's fleet. Oct. 14, 1713, the Selectmen voted to petition the Legislature for an act prohibiting the export of grain; and when a cargo arrived, December 10, it was apportioned among the bakers. So the scarcity was real. — Eds.

Fend off! If they stop'd his vessel, he would hinder the coming in of three times as much.

May, 21. Went to Boston, Lit at the Meeting-house door, and heard Mr. Colman's Lecture; had just begun Prayer.

May, 24. Joseph preaches again.

May, 27. Col. John Appleton and I administer the Oaths &c. to the Deputies. Mr. Samuel Treat preaches the Election Sermon from PS. 2. 8. Ask of me.——— Encourag'd Rulers to be Faithfull; Christ would meet them with better Revivals and Refreshm'ts than Melchizedec met Abraham with. Gave this advice as to choice of Rulers, whatever other accomplishments were; yet, *Si profanus* is to be avoided. Din'd at the Green Dragon. Went late to the Election. 102 Voters at first: Mr. Addington had all but his own, 101. Col. Hutchinson and I had 97. each. But tis to be lamented that Maj^r Genl Winthrop had but 46. and was left out. He was the great Stay and Ornament of the Council, a very pious, prudent, Couragious New-England Man. Some spread it among the Deputies, that he was out of the province, and not like to Return. (Has been absent ever since April, 1712. but through Sickness.) Lieut Govr said he was a Non-Resident. Staid the Election; but voted not, said 'twas against his principles; the Councillors ought not to vote. Said of voting by papers, It was a Silly way! I took no notice of it. Thus Mr. Winthrop is sent into Shade and Retirem't while I am left in the Whirling Dust, and Scorching Sun.

> So falls that stately Cedar! whilest it stood
> It was the truest Glory of the Wood.[1]

May, 28, 1713. The Four Churches[2] Treat the Minis-

---

[1] It will be seen that Mr. Winthrop was soon restored to his place. See August 6. — EDS.

[2] The four churches were the First (Mr. Bridge's), Second (the Mathers'),

ters, and Councillors in Town at the Exchange Tavern. Mr. Marion invited me.

Thorsday, May, 28. All the Councillors are sworn except Major Brown, who was not in Town. In the Afternoon I declar'd to the Council, that Prayer had been too much neglected formerly; we were now in a New House, we ought to Reform; without it I would not be there. Mr. Secretary assented, and I was desired to see it effected. I rode with Col. Hutchinson in his Coach, and earnestly solicited Dr. Increase Mather to begin, and give us the first Prayer: He disabled himself by his Indisposition; He must take Pills. I press'd him, and came away with some hope; obliged Cuffee to call for him; Col. Hutchinson promised me; I went to his Master also, Capt. Thomas Hutchinson, for fear of failing.

May, 29. Dr. Increase Mather prays Excellently in the Council. Lt. Govr at the Castle. Went to Dr. Cotton Mather, and engag'd him.

May, 30. 1713. Dr. Cotton Mather prays very Excellently. Adjourn'd to June, 2. because of the Artillery.

June, 1. Mr. Stoddard of Chelmsford preaches the Election sermon, 1 Sam. 2. 30. Them that honor Me, I will Honor: made an Excellent Discourse.

June, 2. Mr. Veisy[1] of Braintry, and Constable Owen

---

the South (Pemberton and Sewall), and Brattle Street (Colman's). The Quakers', King's Chapel, and Baptist, were not counted.

We find here the recognition of a usage which gave origin to what is known in Boston as " Anniversary Week," though it is now but the shadow of what it once was. The May meeting of the General Court was chosen as the occasion on which the ministers of the country towns, thawed out from the isolation of a long winter, made an annual visit to Boston, where they found genial hospitality in friendly homes. " The Convention of Congregational Ministers " was formed to bring the pastors together mainly for a sermon and for a charitable collection for the widows and orphans of the brotherhood. On a day of " Election Week " the Congregational societies " treated " the ministers to a public dinner. This generous courtesy was continued till less than forty years ago. — EDS.

[1] Mr. Veazie claimed to be of the Church of England, and objected to being taxed for the support of the Congregational Minister. He had been fined, in 1696, " for plowing on the day of Thanksgiving, &c." — EDS.

are heard ; about his distraining for a Rate of 26.ˢ toward
Mr. Marshes Salary, when the Gov.ʳ and Council had
order'd him to forbear, till the Gen.ˡ Court, which order
was sent by Veisy himself, who would not let Owen take
a copy of him, and provok'd him, whereupon Owen took
a Cow of Veisy pris'd at £4.0-0., offer'd Veisy the overplus before Witnesses, which Veisy refus'd. The Gov.ʳ put
the Vote whether the Cow should be return'd, which pass'd
in the Negative. I said, The Gov.ʳ and Council had not
Authority to rescind the Laws, by nulling an Execution.
Mr. Secretary seconded me. Then the Gov.ʳ put it whether
he should be bound over to the Sessions ; which was Voted.
Gov.ʳ directed £50. But 'twas brought to £10. and £5
each Surety.

It was afterward thought advisable to dismiss this Bond,
Chide him and let him go, which was done next day, upon
his Submission and petition to be dismiss'd.

June, 4. Mr. Wadsworth preaches an excellent Sermon [1] from Mal. 2. 16. — therefore take heed to your Spirit,
that ye deal not Treacherously. Apointment of Officers
was adjourn'd to Friday 2. p. m̄.

June, 5. Gov.ʳ Nominates Officers before Diñer ; L.ᵗ
Col. Spencer Phips made a Justice, and Capt. Cary of
Charlestown. Mr. Daniel Parker is made Justice of the
Inferiour Court instead of Col. Thacher deceased. Mr.
Jewet a Coroner. Done of Billings-Gate ; [2] Worth of Ed-
gartown, Justices. Charlestown Lecture being over, Col.
Phillips came p. m. and found the Nomination over. He
had spoken for my Classmate Capt. Sam.ˡ Phips to the
Gov.ʳ, that would Nominat him for a Justice. Supōs'd it

---

[1] The first Monday in June is now, and has long been the occasion, in
Boston, for the preaching of a sermon before the Ancient and Honorable
Artillery Company.— EDS.

[2] Billingsgate precinct, in Eastham, was incorporated in 1763 as a town,
and named Wellfleet. The origin of the first name is patent, but that of the
second has remained a profound mystery. — EDS.

had been done; and the Govr in a bantering way extorted Thanks from him.

Satterday, June, 6.   The Rain-water grievously runs into my son Joseph's Chamber from the Window above. As went out to the Barber's I observ'd the water to run trickling down a great pace from the Coving.   I went on the Roof, and found the Spout next Salter's stop'd, but could not free it with my Stick.   Boston went up, and found his pole too big, which I warn'd him of before; came down a Spit, and clear'd the Leaden-throat, by thrusting out a Trap-Ball that stuck there.¹   Thus a small matter greatly incomodes us; and when God pleases, tis easily remov'd.   The Rain that fell the two Nights and Lords-day following was in such Abundance, we had been almost Drown'd, if the Spout had not been cleared.

Satterday, June, 6.   Am Chair-man of the Comittee for Lt Tuthill's Accounts: I express'd to him my dislike of his reflecting on Capt. Homes; if he were dead he would not be willing to be so serv'd.   From 3ˢ 9ᵈ advanced his allowance to 4. 6ᵈ¼ per week for a man.   Note. He said he did not reflect; and yet when I mention'd *the drinking water*, Tuthill answer'd, it was sworn by two men.

June, 7.   Lord's Super, I could not discern that Mr. Pemberton pray'd for my son; observ'd not so much as the ordinary prayer for him that is to preach in the Afternoon.   The Lord Help!²

June, 8.   Mr. Bridge comes to our house, I accompany him to the Council-Chamber, and there he prays 3 p. m. After Adjournment, Govr goes to Mr. Comissaries, who

---

¹ It is refreshing to be able to presume that the small boy of Puritan times played ball, and then, as now, threw or struck the same into places not intended to receive it; but how many householders of to-day would be moved thereby only to a strictly pious reflection? — Eds.

² We note again the sensitiveness of Sewall on a matter which so engaged his paternal and his devotional feelings. — Eds.

Treats with Wine, Walnuts, Raisins. I was there. It seems the Provinces Sloop is stricken with the Lightening, Mast, and two Planks of the Deck; They write from Piscataqua, that the Indians will not meet the Gov.̣ Govr. Vaudrel advises them to the contrary.[1] Third day, June, 9.

June, 10. Last night Mr. Sergeant and I Walked about the Town from about 10. to 2. Had Constable Howell with us, Sam. Greenlef, and Mat. Smith's Dupee. This day Mr. Pemberton comes to our House, desires me to take my Letter again; would not have me resign my Seaters place now. I took it. Would have Joseph ordain'd in August; Marry first, that might lose no time. I again express'd myself desirous that it might be before changes from England. Best to be fix'd before such Temptations arrive.

As I came from Mr. Stephens's Meeting, Mr. Pemberton join'd himself to me. Told me of the Governour's vehement pressing that Col. W.m Dudley might be made College-Treasurer.

June, 11.th Thorsday, Dr. C. Mather preaches the Lecture. Gov.r dines with the Lieut-Gov.r I at Mr. Hirst's, where was Mr. Willoughby. Now about the Gov.r procures a Letter to be written to the Gov.r of Rhode-Island, that Comitties might from this Governm.t and Coñecticut, with one from Rode Island Lay out the Rodes in the Narraganset.[2] Spake of his being president there once.

June, 12. Capt. Moodey of Casco-Bay is in Town, and

---

[1] Though this was a time of peace between the home governments, the influence of the French in Canada and in Acadia, under the prompting of the Governor (and of some of the Jesuit Priests, as was, with apparent good reason, believed), was strongly employed to inflame and excite the eastern Indians against the English settlements. There is no question but that the "infamous" Father La Loutre was an effective agent of mischief in the years that followed. — EDS.

[2] Hutchinson (Hist. II. 201–206) dwells upon the settlement, which was made in 1713, of the boundary between Massachusetts and Connecticut. — EDS.

contradicts what Mr. Penhallow writ about the Indians refusing to come and meet the Gov.ʳ

June, 13. Court is adjourn'd to Monday 15. p. m. Tom brings a load of Faggots from Brooklin, and tells us of their Health.

Lords-day, June, 14. Dr. Incr. Mather preaches for Mr. Pemberton p. m. Prays very much for Mr. Pemberton that God would continue him long a great Blessing : for Joseph thus, that other Servant upon whom their eyes are that God would fit him and furnish him.

Friday, June, 12. I went to Mrs. Betty Wally¹ to persuade her to marry before ordination. Madam Pemberton was at our House this day, staid a considerable time which I knew not of till I came home at night.

June, 29. Went with Mr. Bromfield to the Funeral of Col. Hunt. Bearers, Govʳ, Sewall ; Townsend, Bromfield ; Cushing, Quinsey.

June, 26. Mr. Stoddard of North-Hampton, and Mr. Jnᵒ Williams. About 9 Captives come from Canada by way of Albany. Mr. Schyler could not prevail with Mr. William's daughter to come away.

July, 1. Went to Comencement with my son and Cousin Hale. I observ'd no strangers save Mr. Pitkin, and Col. Whiting, the Connecticut Comissioners. Sir Hall made the Oration very well. President crav'd a Blessing in the Hall, and Mr. Stoddard return'd Thanks. Came home with Dr. C. Mather, and his Son Increase² in a Calash. Son came over in the same Boat.

July 2. Mr. Thair marries his Unkle Townsend's eldest Daughter. Mr. Secretary thinks Col. Townsend Married them.

July 2ᵈ Mr. Stoddard preaches the Lecture. Dine

---

¹ Joseph Sewall's intended bride. — EDS.

² This was the youth whose ill courses were so grievous a sorrow to the father, and of whom, when the father hears of his death abroad, he makes in his Diary the pathetic entry: " Increase, My Son! My Son!" — EDS.

with us, Mr. Webb, Mr. Moses Hale, Mr. Lorin, Mr. Metcalf, Mr. Rawlins, Cous. Tho. Sewall.

July, 4. 'Tis known that Lt Saml Williams died at Derefield last Tuesday night to the great grief of his Father.

July, 5. Thunder and Rain at Noon. Mr. Stoddard preaches p. m̄. Prays for my Son that God would prepare him, and that he might live long to be a Rich Blessing. At the close apoint 1½ staff in the first part 40th PS. I try'd to set Low-Dutch Tune and fail'd. Try'd again and fell into the tune of 119th Psalm, so Capt. Williams read the whole first part, that he might have Psalm to the Tune. Partial Rainbow in the evening.

July, 6. Major Genl Winthrop comes to Town being sent for by Express by reason of Madam Winthrop's Sickness.

July, 12. Comes to Church p. m̄., puts up a large Note, and Mr. Pemberton prays accordingly. Was not at Church in the Forenoon, when my Son preached.

July, 28. At the Superior Court at Cambridge, the Chief Justice, and the four other Justices were present; made a full Court. Mr. Brattle pray'd. I gave the President and him the reading of Mr. Sewell's Answer to the Bp. Salisbury's new preface;[1] which Answer is very sharp. Gave each of them Maroll's[2] Martyrdom, Marbled. Concluded the Court that day, went and came in the Chief J.'s Coach: Col. Thomas accompanied on Horseback. Call'd at the Governour's and my Son's going; and at the

---

[1] The then Bishop of Salisbury was Gilbert Burnet. The "new preface" seems to be that to the Third Part of his History of the Reformation. The answer was by William Sewel, the historian of the Quakers. Possibly this Sewel was one of the family connections mentioned by the journalist on his trip to England. — EDS.

[2] Louis de Marolles, a persecuted Huguenot. The history of his sufferings (translated from the French) appeared in 1712. It was republished by Dr. Priestley, and may be found among the tracts in the collection of his works. — EDS.

Governour's again coming home, though late at night.
Govr, Mr. Comissary and others went to Notimy [Menot-
omy, now Arlington] this day a-fishing.

Augt 5.   Genl Court meets, Makes not a House.

Augt 6.   Govr makes his Speech.   In the Afternoon
Maj^r Genl Winthrop is chosen into the Council in the
room of Col. Hunt, deceased.

Augt 7.   Takes the Oaths, and his place at the Board,
which I look at as a great Blessing of GOD.   The Deputies will not vote an Address on the head of the Peace,[1]
but only to be finished and Signed, when it is here proclaimed.

Augt 8.   Court Rises.

Augt 12.   Wednesday, Mr. Sheriff [Giles] Dyer dies,
after long Languishing, about 6. M.   Church-Bell rings just
before the School Bell, so both ring together.   I went to
Dr. Increase Mather to ask when he would have a Commissioners Meeting; He inclin'd to Monday.   Dr. Cotton
Mather not having answer'd my Letter nor look'd upon
me on his Lecture day last Thorsday; I was in a strait
to know what to do, as to the disposal of my Proposals;
and let none go.[2]   Now Dr. Incr. Mather spake pleasantly

---

[1] Of the treaties which collectively bear the name of the Peace of Utrecht,
that which was concluded between France and Great Britain bears date of
March 31, 1713, O. S., and April 11, N. S. — Eds.

[2] This was Sewall's book entitled "Proposals touching the accomplish-
ment of Prophesies humbly offered by Samuel Sewall, M. A., and sometime
Fellow of Harvard College, in New England . . . . Massachusetts; Boston,
Printed by Bartholomew Green, 1713. Pp. 12." At the end are certain
verses upon the new century, a part of which we have already printed (ante,
p. 28); but as Sewall here adds three more stanzas we reprint the whole: —

"Wednesday, January 1, 1701, a little before Break-a-Day, at Boston of
the Massachusetts.

> "Once more! Our God, vouchsafe to Shine:
> Tame Thou the Rigour of our Clime.
> Make haste with thy Impartial Light,
> And terminate this long dark Night.

to me ; of his own accord thank'd me for my book, said his Son had shew'd it him ; I was fond of America. After I came home I sent him Two Duz. by Bastian about 2 a-clock. At 3. or 4. p. m̄. Council was held. Mr. Sturgis and Thacher made Justices at Yarmouth, Mr. Hubbard at Braintrey, Col. Wᵐ Dudley at Roxbury.

Thorsday, Augᵗ 20. is ap̄ointed for another special Council for Nomination of a Sheriff ; and the Capt. Savage, the Coroner, is directed to officiat in the mean time. I accompany Mr. Addington to the Funeral of Col. Winthrop's John, 6 months old. After this I went to Cous. Dumer's. He not being at home I gave his wife 6 Proposals : She gave her sister Coney one ;[1] I gave her another for Mr. Coney. Then went to Mr. Pemberton and

---

"Let the transplanted English Vine
Spread further still : still call it Thine :
Prune it with Skill : for yield it can
More Fruit to Thee the Husbandman.

"Give the poor Indians Eyes to see
The Light of Life : and set them free ;
That they Religion may profess,
Denying all Ungodliness.

"From hard'ned Jews the Vail remove ;
Let them their Martyr'd Jesus love ;
And Homage unto Him afford,
Because He is their Rightfull Lord.

"So false Religions shall decay,
And Darkness fly before bright Day ;
So Men shall God in Christ adore ;
And worship Idols vain, no more.

"So Asia and Africa,
Europa with America :
All Four, in Consort join'd, shall Sing
New Songs of Praise to Christ our King." — Eds.

[1] Jeremiah Dummer married Hannah Atwater, and her sister Mary (widow of John Clark) married John Coney, of Boston. — Eds.

gave him four; prayed his favourable Acceptance; He
might have as many more as he pleas'd. *Copia errandi.*
Mr. Pemberton spake of some Gen[l] Meeting to morrow
night in order to call a Church Meeting referring to
Joseph's ordination, said I need not expect any other
Notice: I said I needed not.

Aug[t] 13. Mr. Colman preaches from PS. 132. 8., his
2[d] Sermon: Shew'd that a due worshiping of God was a
people's Strength and Safety. Spake much of the Sab-
bath. Bewail'd that the Word of GOD was not publickly
honoured by being Read to the Assemblies on the Lords
Day.[1] A little after 7. Met at Mr. Pemberton's, Winthrop,
Sewall, Sergeant, Bromfield, Stoddard, Sim. Hill, Williams,
Checkley, Mr. Nathan[l] Williams, Schoolmaster,[2] Major
Fitch, Mr. S. Phillips, Mr. Borland, Mr. Dan[l] Oliver, Capt.
Winlow, Mr. Campbell. Conferred about the Ordination
in order to have the Churches' Aꝓrobation. Propounded
Wednesday, the Sixteenth of September, That Mr. Pemberton should give the Charge, as Mr. Willard gave him.
Twas debated whether Joseph should preach, or some
other. Some thought it was better for some other to tell
Joseph and the people their Duty: Others said, His Duty
would be told him by the Charge. Finally, twas left to
the Church Meeting which is to be next Tuesday at 10.
m. in the Meetinghouse. One Bell to be Rung. Churches
to be sent to, Old, North, Colman, Cambridge, Charlestown, Roxbury, Dorchester, Milton, Weymouth.

Aug[t] 14. Am invited to be a Bearer to the Sheriff. I
enquired of Mr. Secretary, who was a Bearer, whether
there was a Sermon, he told me yes, Mr. Harris was to

---

[1] It will be remembered that one of the distinctive principles on which
Mr. Colman's church in Brattle Street was founded was that the Scriptures
should be read at each service. This was not the usage in the other churches,
in which the Scriptures were read only in connection with comments. —
EDS.

[2] Son-in-law and successor of the famous Master Chiever. — EDS.

preach; [1] and seem'd to make no doubt of [my] going to hear him : I now begun to be distress'd : Jn° Roberts told me the Governour excus'd himself from being a Bearer because of his inability to go. In the evening, I sent one to call out Jn° Roberts, and told him it so fell out, I could not be a Bearer; and bid him drop such a word that I had rather wear a pair of Gloves for his sake.

Aug.ᵗ 14. Joseph and Jn° Gerrish bring home Hañah and Judith. Are both well. *Laus Deo.*

Aug.ᵗ 15. I have a pair of Gloves sent me. Bearers are Sir Charles Hobby, Col. Hutchinson ; Mr. Secretary, Mr. Edward Lyde ; Mr. Robt Howard, Mr. Thomas Newton. Col. Hutchinson was put in stead of the Gov.ʳ, and Mr. Lyde in stead of me. Gov.ʳ went in his Coach. L.ᵗ Gov.ʳ and Major Gen.ˡ Winthrop follow'd the Relations ; Mr. Cooke and I next. All seem'd to be, for going to hear the Sermon, except the Major Gen.ˡ and I. Went in to Col. Townsend's ; when had drunk, the Maj.ʳ Gen.ˡ and I went away. I call'd at the Maj.ʳ Gen.ˡ, and read the order for holding a Special Court. Then went and visited Capt. Belchar, sick of a Fever.

Lord's Day, Aug.ᵗ 16. In the Afternoon, after Sermon and Prayer and Contribution, Mr. Pemberton Warn'd a Church-meeting next Friday, at Ten in the morning at the Meetinghouse, One Bell to be rung. To agree about Mr. Sewall's Ordination, the Time and Circumstances of it.

Aug.ᵗ 17. Went to the Funeral of Mr. Elisha Cook's little Daughter, near a year and half old. In the forenoon, the Chief Justice, Mr. Lynde, Sewall apointed Wednesday Aug.ᵗ 26. for the Trial of David Wallis, comitted for Murther, Mr. Cook, our Clerk, and the Attorney Gen.ˡ were with us.

---

[1] Giles Dyer was a warden of King's Chapel, and the funeral sermon was by Rev. Henry Harris, of that church. Hence Sewall's desire to avoid attendance thereon. — EDS.

Tuesday, Augt 18. 1713. Mr. Hirst, his wife, daughters Mary and Hañah, went to Salem; I tooke leave of them at the Salutation.[1]

Augt 19. The president visited me, and discours'd about Mogungug Lands;[2] I gave him Six Proposals. He says Mr. Flint Studies the Revelation. When I got home from Mr. Tilly's Meeting, I found B. Larnell there: Mr. Rawson sent him with a very pathetical Letter, sent his son John with him. Mrs. Elisa. and Lydia Walley were here to see my wife, intending to journey towards Bristol next day.

Augt 26. A Special Court of Assize is held at Boston by all the Justices, and Dr. Cotton Mather pray'd at opening the Court. Grand-jury brought in *Billa vera* against David Wallis in the Morning, he was arraign'd and remanded to prison till after Dinner; and then Tried; Capt. Thomas Gilbert foreman of the Jury; as Mr. Joshua Gee was of the Grand-Jury. They brought David Wallis in Guilty. Being ask'd what he had to say, He Beg'd a little Time. The Chief Justice pronounced the Sentence.

Septr 5. Mr. Justice Corwin, Lynde, Sewall set out for Bristol. The two former lodge at Frenches, I at Dagget's. In the morning I ride to Attleborough Meeting and hear Mr. Shortt, who preaches well. I dine, and lodge at his house.

7.^{r} 7.th I ride with Hasting to Rehoboth; from thence with Corwin and Lynde, to Carpenter's at Swansey. Dine there. Was met at the Gate by the Sheriff, Col. Pain, Mr. Mackintosh, Capt. Davis, and others.

---

[1] This tavern was on the corner of North Street and Salutation Alley. The sign, usually representing two friends accosting each other, is common in England, and has been traced back to some Biblical scene as the original. — EDS.

[2] Undoubtedly in Hopkinton, formerly called Quansigomog. A hill there was named *Megonko*. See *post*, p. 416. — EDS.

7r. 8.   Mr. Sparhawk prays Excellently at opening the Court.

7ᵣ 11ᵗʰ   Mr. Mackintosh has us in his Coach to his house to Suꝑer: had a splendid Treat.   Adjourn'd till morn.

7ᵣ 12.   Capt. Churches Review goes against him.   Adjourned *sine die*.   Breakfast at Mr. Newgate's.   We set out for Rehoboth about Noon.   Mr. Mackintosh, Sheriff, Mr. Pain; son and one or two more accompanied us part of the way.   Baited late at Rehoboth.   Twas dark before we got to Dagget's.

7ᵣ 13ᵗʰ   Rode to Wrentham, and there kept the Sabbath.   Mr. Man Preach'd upon the Subject of the high Wind, from Ps. 107. 25.   For he comandeth, and raiseth the Stormy Wind.   To stir us up wisely to observe and improve this providence of God.   PS. 28. 5.   Dine at Mr. Man's.

7ᵣ 14ᵗʰ went home; had Mr. Belchar's company at Fisher's.   Got home about 5. p. m.   found all well, *Laus Deo*.

Just about Sun-set Mr. Secretary brings me the Govrˢ Letter about David Wallis, Chief Justice being sick.

7ᵣ 15.   Cloudy, raw Wether, so that I fear'd a sore N. E. Storm next day: but it Rain'd great part of the Night, and clear'd in the morning, and was a very comfortable day.   7ᵣ 16ᵗʰ for thé Ordination.   Began a little after Ten m.

Dr. Cotton Mather begun with Prayer, Excellently, concluded about the Bell ringing for Eleven.   My son preached from 1 Cor. 3. 7.   So then neither is he that planteth any thing, nor he that Watereth; but God that gives the Increase.   Was a very great Assembly; were Elders and Messengers from 9 Churches viz. North, Old [First], Colman, Cambridge, Charlestown, Roxbury, Dorchester, Milton, Weymouth.   Twelve Ministers sat at the Table by the Pulpit.   Mr. Pemberton made an

August Speech, Shewing the Validity and Antiquity of New English Ordinations. Then having made his way, went on, ask'd as Customary, if any had to say against the ordaining the person. Took the Churches Handy vote; Church sat in the Gallery. Then declar'd the Elders and Messengers had desired the Ministers of Boston to lay on Hands (Mr. Bridge was indispos'd and not there). Dr. Increase Mather, Dr. Cotton Mather, Mr. Benjamin Wadsworth, Mr. Ebenezer Pemberton and Mr. Benjamin Colman laid on Hands. Then Mr. Pemberton Pray'd, Ordain'd, and gave the Charge Excellently. Then Dr. Increase Mather made a notable Speech, gave the Right Hand of Fellowship, and pray'd. Mr. Pemberton directed the three and Twentieth Psalm to be sung. The person now Ordain'd dismiss'd the Congregation with Blessing. The chief Entertainment was at Mr. Pemberton's; but was considerable elsewhere. Two Tables at our House, whereat were Mr. Gerrish of Wenham, Mr. Green, Mr. Graves, Mr. Holyoke, Mr. Robie, &c. &c. At night Mr. Pemberton was taken very ill with his old distemper, that could not sit down, took little or no[thing]. On the Sabbath 7^r 20. Mr. Rowland Cotton preaches for Mr. Pemberton, and will preach in the Fore-noon, that may preach at the North p. m. Felix trembled &c. J. S. preach'd p. m. from Jno 1. 29. Behold the Lamb of God which taketh away the Sin of the world. Spake well to the Condemned prisoner, who was in the Assembly. Baptiseth Thomas Robinson,[1] great Grand-son of Mr. John Woodbridge by his daughter, Martha Ruggles; this was the First; baptis'd also Deborah Simson, and John Merriwether.

---

[1] Rev. John Woodbridge, according to Savage, bred at Oxford, came here in 1634, and died in 1695. His daughter Martha married Samuel Ruggles, July 8, 1680, and her daughter Patience married James Robinson, July 3, 1711. These were the parents, we presume, of the child here mentioned. Mrs. Ruggles lived until 1738. — EDS.

Tuesday, 7ʳ 22. I go to Roxbury, wait on the Govʳ with the Letter of Mr. Justice Corwin, and Lynde. Govʳ tells me a sad story of Sam, as if he were disguis'd with Drink in the Salt-Marsh; His wife comes in with little Hañah: I sit a little while, and go away to Brooklin, find Sam very hard at Work mowing up Stalks.

7ʳ 23. Sam. comes to our house, goes home late after the Rain that Tom might come to the Execution as tis promised him.

7ʳ 24. Very vast Assembly. Mr. Colman preaches excellently, PS. 51. Deliver me from Blood-guiltiness. Condemned Wallis present. In the Fore Seat were only Sewall, Sergeant, Lynde of Charlestown. Mr. Peter Thacher of Milton. Mr. Mix and White of Glocester dine with us.

About 3 or 4. p. m̄. Wallis is executed to general Satisfaction. Training warn'd.

7ʳ 25. A great number of Guns fired on account of Mr. Jnᵒ Geffries marrying Mr. Clark's daughter.[1] p. m. I walk a-foot to Roxbury and talk largly with Mr. Walter about Sam.

Lord's Day, 7ʳ 27. a. m̄. Mr. Pemberton still kept in by Sickness, his Collegue preaches from Philip. 2. 8. Being found in fashion as a Man, he humbled himself to death, even the death of the cross. Administred the Lords Supper to good Satisfaction. Mr. Bromfield and Mr. Sergeant congratulated me upon it: p. m. Mr. Flynt preaches. Thomas Hatch baptised.

---

[1] John Jeffries, son of the emigrant David Jeffries, married Anne, daughter of Thomas Clarke, by his second wife. Her half-sister, Jane Clarke, married Rev. Benjamin Colman. Mr. Clarke was very wealthy, and Mr. Jeffries, by inheritance and otherwise, acquired a large estate. He was town treasurer for many years, and lived on Tremont Street, where the Albion is, being, of course, a near neighbor of Sewall. He had an only daughter, who died young, and his heir was his nephew, David Jeffries, in whose line the name is perpetuated. A few years ago, a number of papers belonging to this John Jeffries were discovered in the ceiling of a room in Faneuil Hall. — EDS.

Octob.ʳ 1. Fifth-day, Dr. C. Mather preaches Mrs. Rock's Funeral Sermon, from PS. 25. 13. His Soul shall dwell at ease.[1] Sam was here, I invited him to come to us on the Lords Day; The Lords Suꝑer being administred at both churches in Roxbury, and he under disadvantages to partake.

Octob.ʳ 4. Mr. Jnᵒ Barnard[2] preaches a Sermon too much savoring of Arminianisme. p. m. Son preaches from ps. 37. 37. on occasion of Mrs. Rock's death. Samuel Eliot, son of Andrew Eliot, Baptis'd. Sam. here all day. Sup'd here. went home about 7.

Second-day, 8.ʳ 5.ᵗʰ I goe to Brooklin, meet my daughter Sewall going to Roxbury with Hañah, to dine with her Broʳ Winthrop. Sam. and I dined alone. Daughter return'd before I came away. I propounded to her that Mr. Walter might be desired to come to them and pray with them. She seem'd not to like the motion, said she knew not wherefore she should be call'd before a Minister! I urg'd him as the fittest moderator; the Govʳ or I might be thought partial. She pleaded her performance of Duty, and how much she had born. Mr. Hirst came in and smok'd a pipe and we came away together. I gave Sarah a Shilling. Hañah ditto and cake, the sick Indian Boy a cake, Tom. a Shilling.

Got home a little before 7.; visited Mr. Sergeant confin'd to his house: was not abroad on the Lords Day.

8.ʳ 6. Sam. comes to Town on account of his Sick Boy.

---

[1] This sermon was printed. In S. Mather's list it is called "An Essay upon a Soul at ease; a funeral sermon for Mrs. Mary Rock." — EDS.

[2] This eminent man, one of the first of the New England clergy who relaxed the rigidness of its Calvinism, was born in Boston, in 1681. For a while he assisted Dr. Colman, in Brattle Street, was chaplain and historian of the expedition to Port Royal, in 1707 went to London, where he received much respect, and declined, as a non-conformist, a chaplaincy offered him by Lord Wharton, returned home, was ordained Minister of Marblehead in 1716, and died in 1770, seventy years after he had graduated at Harvard. — EDS.

8ʳ 8ᵗʰ   Din'd with the Court which sits the longest of any; had 147. Actions, 98. New.   Jury not dismiss'd till Satterday 8ʳ 10ᵗʰ near Sun-set.

Octobʳ 12.   Col. Townsend and I prepare to set out in our Journey to the Vinyard.   But my Horse is taken out of the Stable and gon; and cânt be recover'd: and the day doubtfull.   While were thus Bustleing, Capt. Wade's Guns were heard, in whom comes Col. Nicholson : and are by Maxwell warn'd to Council.   I call to see sick Mr. Sergeant by the way.   While there it Rain'd very hard; was held there by it awhile.   Then proceeded, and with Col. Townsend, Stoddard, Capt. Moodey went to the Governour, who was waiting upon the New wharf, and waited hours in a Warehouse.   At last Col. Nicholson came ashor; Cheers, Guns from Capt. Wade, Capt. Brown, Ships, North, South Battery.   Capt. Clark's Guns spake very audibly, and the wind favour'd their Report.

Went to the Town-House; From thence to Homes's, to Diñer.   None with him that I see but Mr. Net-maker, who is his Secretary.   At my motion Mr. Colman was sent for, and crav'd a Blessing.   Mr. Myles came in, and the Govʳ desired him to return Thanks.   Col. Nicholson said to me, He was glad that I held out so well.

Octobʳ 13. 1713.   *Feria tertia.*   Last night was very Tempestuous, with Lightening, Thunder, Rain.   Morning Cloudy : A Council was warn'd, which made us too late to Charlestown.   Mr. Stevens ordained.   Mr. Stephens was in his Sermon — from Danˡ 12. 3.   The Seats were so fill'd that I went into Col. Phillips Pue, and Mr. Secretary follow'd, where had good Hearing and View.   Mr. Bradstreet Pray'd; and declar'd that Dr. Increase Mather was desired to Ordain, and be Moderator in the Affair, which he perform'd.   He, Dr. Cotton Mather, Mr. Bradstreet, Mr. Brattle, Mr. Barnard of Andover laid on Hands.   Dr. Incr. Mather pray'd, Ordain'd, Charg'd, pray'd; Declar'd Mr. Stephens to be a Minister of Christ and a pastor of

the Church in that place. Dr. Cotton Mather made an
August Speech, shewing that the Congregational Churches
early declar'd against Independency, that all the Reformation of the Continent of Europe ordain'd as New England
did ; shew'd that their Ordination had no other Foundation.
Declar'd what was expected of the Ordained person, what
of the church, and then gave the Right Hand of Fellowship. 3 last Staves of the 32ᵈ PS. sung. Capt. Phips set
the Tune, and read it. Col. Hutchinson and Townsend
sat in the Pue next Col. Phillips. Capt. Belchar, and Mr.
Bromfield in the Deacon's Seat. Govʳ came over afterward, He and Genˡ Nicholson went into the Fore-Seat, Lᵗ
Govʳ Taylor into the Fore-Seat.

Wednesday, Octobʳ 14th. Genˡ Court meets About
4. p. m. Govʳ sends for the Deputies in, makes his
Speech.

Thorsday, 8ʳ 15ᵗʰ About 9. m. a portentous Birth at
the North-end in Prince street. Mr Bridge preaches, 112.
PS. To the Upright Light ariseth out of Darkness.
Pray'd for Col. Nicholson, who sat in Mr. Addington's
Pue. Govʳ not at Meeting. p. m̄. Lᵗ Govʳ propounds
me, Col. Jnᵒ Ap̄leton, and Col. Higginson to join with
Capt. Hutchinson, Capt. Oliver and Mr. Mather, a Com̄-
ittee to consider of Grain, to prevent its Exportation. I
shew'd it the Govʳ when he came in, who ap̄rov'd.

The Deputies made a Motion to Congratulate Genˡ
Nicholson's safe Arrival. Govʳ Nominated Mr. Addington, Mr. Eliakim Hutchinson, Col. Higginson, Capt. Belcher To Congratulate, and to say *they were ready to receive Her Majesties Com̄ands, and to do their Duty so soon
as they knew them.*

But the Deputies drew up another, leaving all out but
Congratulations. Their Names were, Mr. Clark, Davenport, Gill, Porter. I observ'd Two Leather Chairs were
set at the end of the Council Table, and the Elbow Chair
set aside : But when Genˡ Nicholson staid not to sit down

they were remov'd, and the Governour's Arm'd Chair took place again.

Octob.ʳ 16. 1713. I went to see the portentous Birth; it seems to be two fine Girls to whom an unhapy Union has been fatal. The Heads and Necks, as low as a Line drawn from the Arm-pits, are distinct. A little below the Navel, downward again distinct, with distinct Arms and Legs; Four of each. I measured across the perfect Union about the Hips and found it to hold about eight Inches. Oh the Mercies of my Birth, and of the Birth of Mine! *Laus Deo!* Dr. Cotton Mather introduc'd me and Mr. John Winthrop to this rare and awfull Sight.[1]

Octob.ʳ 19. Mr. Winslow of Marshfield comes to Town; Set out so long before Sun-rise that he was here about 3. p. m̄. and in the Council-Chamber, in his own Hair.

Octob.ʳ 20. He appears with a Flaxen Wigg, I was griev'd to see it, he had so comly a head of black Hair.

Octob.ʳ 21. Now about two Leather Chairs are set at the end of the Council Table, and Genˡ Nicholson sits at the Governour's Right Hand. Govʳ speaks of sending Mr. Williams and Mr. Stoddard to Canada.[2]

Octob.ʳ 22. I go to Salem, visit Mrs. Epes, Col. Hathorne. See Mr. Noyes marry Mr. Aaron Porter and Mrs. Susan Sewall, at my Brother's. Was a pretty deal of Company present; Mr. Hirst and wife, Mr. Blower, Mr. Prescot, Mr. Tuft Sen.ʳ and jūn.ʳ, Madam Leverett, Foxcroft, Goff, Kitchen; Mr. Samuel Porter, Father of the Bridegroom, I should have said before. Many young Gentlemen and Gentlewomen. Mr. Noyes made a Speech, said Love was the Sugar to sweeten every Condition in the married Relation. Pray'd once. Did all very well. After the Sack-

---

[1] A more prosaic generation has in these days, this year, exhibited for money, a few rods from Sewall's door, a similar combination, under the name of the " Double-headed Nightingale, Millie." — EDS.

[2] About negotiating the redemption of prisoners. — EDS.

Posset,[1] &c. Sung the 45th. Psalm from the 8th verse to the end, five staves. I set it to Windsor Tune. I had a very good Turky-Leather Psalm-Book which I look'd in while Mr. Noyes Read : and then I gave it to the Bridegroom saying, "I give you this Psalm-Book in order to your perpetuating this Song : and I would have you pray that it may be an Introduction to our Singing with the Choir above." I lodg'd at Mr. Hirst's.

Octobr 23. I set out for Boston a little before noon, Cousin Henry accompanys me to Lewis's; gave him half a crown. Mr. Leverett and Pemberton at the head of Schoolstreet. Mr. Pemberton welcom'd me from the Wedding. Mr. President enquired after his wife. Got home a ¼ of hour before Sun-set. Being weary with Journy, I went not to the Meeting at Madam Willard's, where my Son preached. Meeting was Thin.

Octobr 24. I go to Council. I help'd Mr. Secretary to compare the Bill for Medway, the new Town on the West of Charles River.

Octobr 25. In the Night after 12. Susan comes, and knocks at our chamber door, said she could not sleep, was afraid she should dye. Which amaz'd my wife and me. We let her in, blew up the Fire, wrapt her warm, and went to bed again. She sat there till near day, and then return'd; and was well in the morning. *Laus Deo.* I was the more startled because I had spilt a whole Vinyard Cañ of water just before we went to Bed : and made that Reflection that our Lives would shortly be spilt.

Octobr 26. I visit Dr. Increase Mather, who is sick upon his Bed, has not been abroad since Mr. Stephens's Ordination. Tells me he hears Col. Banks is like to be our Governour.[2]

---

[1] " Sack-Posset " appears not to have been a beverage to be drank from a glass, but a compound of milk, spirit, and other ingredients, partaken of with a spoon. — EDS.

[2] We are unable to identify this Colonel Banks. There was, at the time,

Octob.^r 27. Have a Meeting of the Comissioners in the Evening at the Council Chamber. This day Joseph Homes, father of Capt. Nath! Homes, is buried with a very thin Funeral.

Octob.^r 28. Privat Meeting at Bro^r Thornton's joining to the Draw-Bridge that was. I think have not Met at his House since the Fire till now.

Octob.^r 29. Ipswich Hamlet petitions the Genl Court to give them the Powers of a Precinct. Dr. Cotton Mather preaches. Genl Nicholson not at Meeting; Judg of Admiralty at New-found-Land sits in Mr. Addington's Pue. In the Evening Mr. Ebenezer Pemberton marries my Son Joseph Sewall, and Mrs.^l Elizabeth Walley. Wait Winthrop esqr., and Lady, Samuel Porter esqr., Edmund Quinsey esqr., Ephraim Savage, esqr. and wife, Madam Usher, Mr. Mico and wife, Jer. Dumer esqr., Cousin Sam. Storke, Cous. Carter, and many more present. Sung out of the 115.th Ps. 2½ staves from the 11th to the end. W. which I set. Each had a piece of Cake, and Sack-Posset. Mr. Pemberton craved a Blessing and Return'd Thanks at eating the Sack-Posset. Came away between 9 and 10. Daughter Sewall came in the Coach with my Wife, who invited her to come in and lodge here with her Husband; but she refus'd, and said she had promis'd to go to her Sister Wainwright's, and did so.

Friday 8.^r 30. Sam. and his Wife dine here, go home together in the Calash. William Ilsly rode and pass'd by them. My son warn'd him not to lodge at his house; Daughter said she had as much to doe with the house as

---

a family of the name settled at Revesby Abbey, co. Lincoln, the head of which was Joseph Banks, M. P. for Grimsby. His great-grandson and representative was Sir Joseph Banks, Bart., the distinguished president of the Royal Society. — Eds.

¹ It hardly needs to be mentioned that the appellation of " Mrs." or " Mistress " was, by courtesy, attached to the names of maidens of high social station, as well as to those of married women. — Eds.

he. Ilsly lodg'd there.[1] Sam. grew so ill on Satterday, that instead of going to Roxbury he was fain between Meetings to take his Horse, and come hither; to the surprise of his Mother, who was at home. Lord save him and us! Mr. Jn° Williams preached for my son in the morn, and went at Noon to preach for Mr. Walter. About 9. on Satterday night, Mr. Bridge was taken with another paralytick Fit, was in danger of falling into the fire.

Joseph and his Bride sat in Mr. Walley's Pue.

Nov.‍ 2. Sam. is somthing better, yet full of pain; He told me with Tears that these sorrows (arising from discord between him and his wife) would bring him to his Grave. I said he must endeavour to be able to say, O Death, where is thy sting? O Grave, where is thy victory? He is refresh'd by discoursing with Simon Gates of Marlborough, and Amos Gates. They tell us that Mr. Sam! Sparhawk is like to dye at Cambridge. I visit the Bride-Groom and Bride, and Mr. Bridge.

Nov.‍ 5. I first see Col. Tho. Noyes in a swash Flaxen Wigg; At Dinner I told him, in going home he must keep Ipswich Rode and not goe to Salem; his cousin would take him to doe.

Nov.‍ 6. The Council invite Col. Nicholson to diñer at Mr. Davenport's, house ½ Mile from the Town House; so the Super-Court kept their Diñer at the Exchange Tavern.

Nov.‍ 8. Mr. Flint preaches for my son.

Nov.‍ 9. I set out for Salem with David about 10. m. Had a very good passage to Winnisimet; Got to Salem near an hour before Sunset; At the parting of the ways Mr. Attorny fell in with me.

Nov.‍ 10. Finish'd the Business of the Court by Candle-light; visited Major Brown, Bro.‍ Hirst.

---

[1] We seem to get a hint here that jealousy had something to do with the junior Sewall's domestic troubles. The Ilsleys were a Newbury family, the emigrant being a William. We have no means of identifying the one named in the text. — EDS.

Novr 11. Came home, Visited Cousin Porter sick of the Measles. Got home about 4 p. m̄. Went to the Funeral of Mrs. Mather,[1] who died last Monday; Bearers, Col. Hutchinson, Mr. E[m] Hutchinson; Mr. Dallie,[2] Wadsworth; Pemberton, Colman. Visited Hañah Parkman.

Novr 12. Mr. Pemberton preaches Forenoon and Afternoon. Between Meetings, Mr. Bromfield and I go to Genl Nicholson, and desire him to forbear the intended Bonfire : He Treats us very Civilly, and sends for Col. Redknap, who he said was the Engineer, and agreed to it; we took leave with Thanks. When I came home from Salem found Mr. Mayhew here, come from New-London. Goes to Roxbury to keep Thanksgiving for fear of the Measles. Gov[r] sends his Coach for his sons Dudley, and Wainwright to Dine with him. Sam went to Meeting.

Nov[r] 15. Sam. goes to Meeting, Mr. Mayhew also goes.

Tuesday, 9[r] 17. Sam. rides home though the wether were bad.

9[r] 19th. Mr. Mayhew goes homeward before Lecture. Mr. Wadsworth preaches. Elder Cop pray'd for as dangerously sick. Mr. Addington marries Madam Wainwright at Col. Winthrop's before Mr. Colman.

---

[1] This was the second wife of Rev. Cotton Mather, of whom his son Samuel writes: " She was one of finished Piety and Probity, and of an unspotted Reputation; one of good sense, and bless'd with a compleat Discretion in ordering an Household; one of singular good-Humour and incomparable Sweetness of Temper; one with a very handsome engaging Countenance ; and one honourably descended and related. 'Twas Mrs. Elizabeth Hubbard, who was the Daughter of Dr. John Clark. She had been a Widow four Years, when Dr. Mather married her, which was Aug. 18, 1703. He rejoiced in her as having great spoil, and in finding her found great Favour of the Lord. They lived together in perfect Content and Harmony ten Years: She died Nov. 8, 1713, with Willingness: the Fear of Death was extinguished in her: She committed herself into the Hands of her Saviour, and in the same gracious Hands She left her Children. She was much beloved and greatly lamented." — EDS.

[2] It is pleasant to notice that the minister of the Huguenot congregation in the town was in such fraternal relations with the other pastors as to be asked to this service. — EDS.

9ʳ 20 p. m̄. Elder Cop dies. Meeting at Mr. Pemberton's.

9ʳ 21. Very Cold; Sam. comes to Town on foot. Capt. Arthur Savage arrives, 5 weeks passage.

Novʳ 22. Very Cold Wether; Sam. partakes at the Lord's Super.

Novʳ 23. I visit Mr. Addington and his Bride at Col. Winthrop's.

Novʳ 24. Went to the Funeral of Elder David Cop, aged 79 years; was buried in the North.[1] Bearers, Mr.

---

[1] It would be inexcusable to pass over the name of Copp without a note. Copp's Hill is a part of the history of the town; and, though we cannot enter upon full details, the following facts may be of use: The emigrant was William Copp, whose wife is called Goodith by Drake (Hist. p. 549), and Judith by Savage. His will (Suff. Wills, Vol. VIII. f. 32), dated 1662, proved 1670, mentions sons David and Jonathan, daughters Lydia and Ruth, and daughter Tewksbury. Undoubtedly a daughter Joanna married Samuel Norden; Ann married Herman Atwood, and Martha married, first, William Harvey, and secondly, Henry Tewksbury.

Of these Jonathan left issue probably; and David certainly, by wife, Obedience Topliff, had four sons, David, Jr., and Samuel, of Boston, and Jonathan, of Stonington, and John, of Norwalk, who divided his estate, March 29, 1714. (Suff. Deeds, Vol. XXIX. f. 118.)

William Copp had, originally, as appears by the Book of Possessions, " one house and lot of half an acre in the mill field, bounded with Thomas Buttolph south-east, John Button north-east, the marsh on the south-west, and the river on the north-west."

May 1, 1706 (Suff. Deeds, Vol. XXII. f. 531), certain depositions were made by David Copp, David Copp, Jr., and David Farnum, to the effect that about 1674 or 1675, Jacob Willett, merchant, of London, took into his hands all the estate of Mr. Thomas Broughton, except a part of a house and garden actually occupied by said Thomas Broughton. When Willet went away, he left these affairs in the hands of said David Copp, Sen.; and this estate " is now and has been for some years in the use and possession of Joshua Gee, shipwright."

June 13, 1689 (Suff. Deeds, Vol. XXII. f. 1), Joseph Osborn, of East Hampton, Long Island, and wife, Elizabeth, sold to David Copp land at the north end of Boston, bounded north-east on the street from the North Meeting-house towards Centre Haven, 103 feet; north-west, on the old highway, next the Mill-Pond, 150 feet; south-west, by Osborn, 27 feet; south-east, by Osborn, 101 feet. This land David Copp gave, Aug. 31, 1704 (Suff. Deeds, Vol. XXII. f. 2), to his grandchildren, William and Anne Cobb, children of son William, deceased, mariner; he gives the same

Thomas Oakes, Mr. Thornton; Capt. Atwood, Mr. Maryon; Deacon Tay, Deacon Hubbart. Follow'd the Mourners, Mr. Cook, Hutchinson; Sewall, Col. Lynde; E^m Hutchinson, Col. Townsend; Dr. C. Mather, and Mr. Wadsworth there. A pretty many Men but few Women. Mrs. Boon and Feño buried this Afternoon. I could be at neither of the Funerals, because of this.

Tuesday, 9: 24. Joseph visits us after his sickness of the Measles; dines with us. David brings Susan's Mother from Braintrey to tend her.

25th Henry Farwell of Dunstable talks with me about a Meeting at Woburn of the Non-residents.

Decr 23. at Noon. Great Rain, I went not to the Meeting.

26. Dr. Mather preaches. I could not discern that he return'd any Thanks for Joseph's Recovery, though he knew he was at Lecture. Return'd Thanks Expressly for Mr. Bridge. Mr. Thacher of Milton, Son of Brooklin, and Cousin Quinsey din'd with us.

27. I get a Grist of Wheat among the many that were pressing for it.[1] I think tis this day that Mr. Edw. Hutchinson buries his only child, a daughter of $\frac{1}{2}$ year old: The Lord comfort him and his wife. Very cold day.

28: Sam. comes to Town from Brooklin, dines with us, comes to keep the Sabbath with us. I visit Mr. Pemberton. Very cold day. John Gerrish has the Measles at Mr. Lowder's.

Decr 6. Sam. keeps Sabbath with us.

---

bounds, except that the Osborn land appears to be in the hands of Joshua Gee.

We do not learn when the name of Copp's Hill first appears in use. It is on Page's map, of 1775, and is there applied to the whole elevation, over which various streets extend; but forty years later it seems restricted to the triangle bounded by Snow-hill, Prince, and Commercial Streets. The deeds of David Copp and his sons (Suff. Deeds, Vol. XXIX. ff. 118–121, and Vol. XXX. f. 170) do not give us sufficient data to establish the oldest limits. — EDS.

[1] We have already noticed the scarcity of wheat at this time. (*Ante*, p. 384.) — EDS.

Dec.[r] 6. 1713. Sun is Eclipsed just about the begin-
ning of the Fore noon Exercise; when well enter'd many
Guns are Fired by Capt. Brown Going down to Nantasket.
Mr. Holyoke observes the Eclipse in the Town House
Turret. Very clear day. I saw it plain as I came home
at Noon.

xr. 8. Major Fitches son Thomas died last night, of
a Relapse after the Measles.

xr. 9. Nurse Hañah Cowell buried, Bearers, Mr. Odlin,
Tho. Walker; Deacons Maryon, Hobart; Brother Wheeler,
Foreland. Was a very pious Woman, and a true Lover
of the first Ways of New-England. Col. Hutchinson,
Sewall, E[m] Hutchinson, Townsend, Mr. Wadsworth, Col-
man, followed after the Mourners.

Thorsday, xr. 10. Mr. Wadsworth preaches in Mr.
Bridges Turn; PS. 69. 5. Mr. Bridge not abroad. Mr.
Francis Burroughs[1] buried after Lecture; Bearers, Mr.
Winthrop, Townsend; Belcher, Bromfield; Checkley, Bal-
lantine. He is Lamented as having been an intelligent
Exemplary Christian. Buried in Mr. Heath's Tomb, New
burying place.

Dec.[r] the Eleventh. Mr. Thomas Fitch his son Thomas
buried:[2] Great Funeral; Bearers, Major W[m] Dudley, Capt.

---

[1] This was the merchant from London whom John Dunton found here,
and who furnished the necessary security that Dunton should not "be chargeable to the town." He married here, as his second wife, Dec. 29, 1709,
Elizabeth (Gross), widow of —— Heath. His daughter Sarah married Captain John Brown, of Salem. — EDS.

[2] Thomas Fitch, who died June 23, 1736, *vide* "News Letter," was a
very distinguished citizen. He was Colonel of the Boston Regiment, Captain of the Ancient and Honorable Artillery Company, Representative and
Councillor for nearly twenty years. His name is also closely connected with
Boston Common. May 21, 1714 (Suff. Deeds, Vol. XXVIII. f. 107), he
bought, of George Waldron, land at the south end of the Common or Training Field, bounded east by land of Edward Bromfield 300 feet, north by the
Common 261 feet, west by the Common 361 feet, south by Frog Lane 438
feet. June 9, 1757, Andrew Oliver, Jr., and wife, Mary, sold (Suff. Deeds,
Vol. LXXXIX. f. 64) to the town land east 320 feet on land of Mrs. Martha

Josiah Willard, Mr. Borland.   White Scarves and Rings;
Govr, Lt Govr, Genl Nicholson, Col. Vetch had Scarves.
Ministers.   I had Gloves sent.   Was laid in Mr. Wilson's
Tomb old Burying place.

Allen; south on Frog Lane 321 feet, north on the Common 189½ feet, west
on the Common, on a bevelling line, 355 feet.

Oliver also bought, May 5, 1755, from Mrs. Allen (Suff. Deeds, Vol.
LXXXVII. f. 21) her lot, bounded east, on the highway, 324 feet; north,
on the Common, 324 feet, 5 inches; west, 302 feet, 3 inches; south, 281
feet, 9 inches.   Thus Fitch's heirs must have bought all the land on the
north side of Boylston Street.   As we have seen, Oliver sold the burying
ground lot to the town, and the remainder he sold to William Foster,
March 25, 1780; and Foster, Oct. 6, 1787 (Suff. Deeds, Vol. CLXII. f. 125),
sold it to the town.

As to Thomas Fitch's pedigree, we find, by his will (proved June 30,
1736, Wills, Vol. XXXII. f. 459) that he left a daughter, Martha Allen, and
grandson, Andrew Oliver, *alias* Thomas Fitch Oliver; daughter-in-law,
Martha Fitch; wife, Abiel; sister, Sarah Warren; nephew, Jabez Hunt;
nieces, Priscilla and Mary Hunt, and Sarah Watts.   These Hunts were the
children of Thomas and Mary Hunt; Thomas Warren married Sarah Fitch,
Dec. 14, 1694.

Hence we conclude that he was the son of Thomas and Martha (Fiske)
Fitch, of Boston, who had Martha, born Nov. 9, 1656; Mary, Feb. 17, 1658;
Sarah, June 14, 1661; Elizabeth, Aug. 2, 1664; and Thomas, Feb. 5,
1668–69.   Administration was granted to Martha, widow of Thomas Fitch,
Aug. 21, 1678.   He left considerable property, his house being valued at
£250.

Colonel Thomas Fitch married Abiel, daughter of Rev. Samuel Danforth,
of Roxbury (Suff. Deeds, Vol. XXI. f. 537), and had Mary, born April 21,
1695; Thomas, Sept. 21, 1697; Samuel, Aug. 31, 1703; Martha, Sept. 25,
1704; Mary, Oct. 28, 1706; John, Oct. 19, 1709.   The sons seem all to have
died before him, administration being granted July 1, 1735, to James Allen
and Andrew Oliver, on estate of their brother-in-law, John Fitch, merchant.
(Suff. Wills, Vol. XXXII. f. 197.)   Mary Fitch married, June 20, 1728,
Andrew Oliver, afterwards Lieutenant Governor, and had three children,
of whom only Andrew lived.   This Andrew, Jr., was the progenitor of the
Salem line, which took the popular side, and remained here at the Revolu-
tion; the children of Lieutenant-Governor Oliver, by his second wife (Mary
Sanford, sister of Mrs. Hutchinson), nearly all were refugees.   Dr. Fitch
Edward Oliver has a good portrait of his ancestor, Thomas Fitch.

We have not been able to trace the Fitches back of Thomas Sen., but it is
very probable that he was son of Zachary Fitch, of Reading, and brother of
Jeremiah and Benjamin, both of Boston.   They seem not to be related of
the Norwalk family, of which one Thomas Fitch was Governor of Connecticut, 1754–1766. — Eds.

Dec.ʳ 12, Great storm of Snow.

Dec.ʳ 13. Mr. Bridge preaches again.

Dec.ʳ 14. Several Ministers pray with and for Mr. Sergeant; Mr. Danforth of Dorchester, Mr. Wadsworth, Pemberton, Colman, Sewall. Began between 1 and 2 p. m̄. Candles were lighted before Mr. Pemberton had ended.

This Afternoon Mr. Matthew Skinner (A young Merchant of about 32 years old, Capt. Keeling's partner, Mr. Eᵐ Hutchinson says has Good Friends in London), was buried. Died by a Fall from his Horse, Nov.ʳ 11ᵗʰ, near Lyndsey's, coming from Salem. Was brought to Town last Friday. That very day I Travelled from Salem home by Charlestown, and rec'd no Hurt. *Laus Deo!*

The widow Gibs's Eldest Son was buried this day.

Novemb.ʳ 17. Thorsday is a Cloudy and very Cold Day, which made the Fast-Assemblies the thinner in the 4. Congregations in Boston; yet the Work was carried on. Two Sermons. In the Afternoon £103. was gather'd at the South Church, 68. at the old, about 70. at Mr. Colman's, £126. at the North.

Satterday, Nov.ʳ 19. A Council is call'd; Sit round the Fire: Genˡ Nicholson blames the observing a Fast without the order of Authority; the Queen was Head of the Church: seem'd to be Warm. The Lieut Governour seem'd to intimat that their Church [King's Chapel], the members of it, were Treated as if they were Heathen. Genˡ Nicholson mention'd it as graviminous that the Shops were shut up. The Governour said, Twas voluntary; none was order'd to shut up his Shop. Country-men brought wares to Town as on other days; that he himself came to Town as supposing the Episcopal Church had observ'd the Fast: when he saw they did not, he went to Mr. Colman's; I was surpris'd with this uncomfortable Talk, and said Nothing! At length a Motion was made, I think by Genˡ Nicholson, that there might be a Genˡ Fast. I was of Opinion there was great need of it, and readily voted for it. The Govr pitch'd upon the 14th January.

Decr 20. The weather is much more moderat: my Son administers the Lord's Super.

Decr 22. Mr. Secretary reads the Order for the Fast, which is pass'd in Council, and bears Date this Day.

Decr 23. Midweek I went to Cambridge in a Calash, visited Mr. Brattle, who has been very sick. Gave him an Angel[1] to buy him and Madam Brattle a pair of Gloves. I din'd there in his Study.

xr. 24. Dr. C. Mather preach'd of God's Punishing Sin with Sickness. After Lecture I went to the Funeral of Mrs. Bodin,[2] Mr. Jn° Campbell's eldest Daught, of about 26 years old: a vertuous Woman.

Decr 25. Being moderat weather, A great abundance of provisions, Hay, wood, brought to Town; and Shops open as at other times. In the Afternoon I went to the Funeral of Mr. Francis Clark's daughter Hañah, between 9 and 10 years old, a desirable Child. Were 3. Funerals in the South-burying place together.

Decr 31. Stormy Weather; the Govr not at Lecture, nor Lieut-Govr No Council for Nominating Officers.

Friday, Jany 1. There is a Council. Govr propounds Officers. — Goreham, a Sheriff for Barnstable. I humbly offer'd my Advice that there was not a Council to such

---

[1] The angel was a coin whose value, probably, differed at times. Worcester pronounces it worth six shillings, eight pence; but Coles, in 1701, called it worth ten shillings. — EDS.

[2] This enables us to make certain Savage's conjecture that Sarah, wife of James Bowdoin, was the daughter of John Campbell. The first of the name was Pierre Baudouin (see Andros Tracts, III. 79, 80), a Huguenot refugee. The oldest son, James, settled in Boston, and his descendants have been famous here, though the name is now extinct in the male legitimate line. Another son of the emigrant was John, who went to Virginia, where his descendants continued the name. As additional proof of this branch, it may be noted that in Massachusetts Archives, Vol. LXIII. f. 210, 224, are business letters, &c., from John Bowdoin, of Williamsburg, Va., dated in 1712, in which he refers to his brother, James Bowdoin, of Boston. — EDS.

purposes. Govr said He had adjourn'd the Council. I
answer'd, The Council did not meet yesterday, and therefore could not be adjourn'd. However the Govr went on.
I think were but just 7. I mention'd Lothrop as a fit
person: but I voted for no body, as knowing there was
no Council for that purpose.

Tuesday, Jany 5. I go to the Funeral of Capt. Beñet's
daughter Butler;[1] is said to be the most desirable of his
daughters, but about 25 or 6. years old. Cousin Moodey
strikes in, and I go in the middle between him and Joseph
S. Mr. Saml Moodey of York lodges here.

Jany 6. I visit Cousin Mrs. Anna Dumer. In the evening, Mr. Walter, Cousin Moodey and I had discourse about
my son at Brooklin, his Circumstances. Yesterday after
Mrs. Butler's Funeral, I visited Mr. Pemberton, who has
Sore Eyes.

Fifth-day, Jany 7th, Son J. Sewall preaches the Lecture,
which is the first Sermon he has preached in the old
church. 1 Cor. 6. 19. 20. Was invited, and din'd with
the Court at Holms's. Was a very great Fogg all day.
Rain'd toward night. Visited Mr. David Stoddard[2] and his

---

[1] The Boston records say that Joanna, wife of Stephen Butler, died
Jan. 3, 1713 (*i. e.*, 1713–14). When Stephen died a few years later, administration was granted (Suff. Wills, Vol. XIX. f. 145, 175) to John Bennet,
gent., on the estate of "his son-in-law," Stephen Butler, blacksmith, at the
request of the widow, Mary Butler. The only relative mentioned is his
mother, Tabitha Butler; but we may presume that he was a grandson of
Stephen Butler, of Boston, who had several sons.

John and Joanna Bennet had Peter, born June 17, 1687; *Joanna*, Jan. 7,
1688–89; James, Sept. 4, 1694. There were, at least, two Johns, at this
date, in Boston. One John married Hannah Denison, June 17, 1703 (perhaps he had married Elizabeth Gilman, May 15, 1701), and had Mary, born
June 23, 1707; William, March 19, 1709–10. But John and Sarah Bennet
had Jonathan, born May 14, 1701; and John and Ruth had Jonathan, Oct. 16,
1701, and Mary, July 5, 1704. A John Bennet died Nov. 17, 1717, but left
no will. Very possibly these are grandchildren of Samuel Bennet, of Lynn
and Chelsea. — EDS.

[2] David Stoddard married Elizabeth (Richardson), widow of Samuel
Shrimpton, Jr., and had three daughters. — EDS.

Bride, who was married privatly last Wednesday was 14 night, by Mr. Colman. Visited Mr. Sergeant, who is very feeble and lame of his Right foot and Thigh.

Sixth-day, Jany 8th. Went to the Funeral of Mrs. Mary Phillips,[1] widow, who was born at Sea, is within a few Moneths of 80 : a good Woman. Bearers, Mr. Cooke, Elisha Hutchinson ; Mr. Addington, Townsend ; Mr. Dumer, Ephraim Savage.

Seventh-day, Jany 9th. very great Storm of Wind and Snow last night, and today. About ½ hour past 8 m. was considerable Thunder and Lightening.

Jany 14th. Fast-day, Mr. Sergeant is so weak that he keeps his Chamber ; where to my surprise I find him at Noon. Mr. Saml Moodey takes Leave in the evening, intending to sup at Mr. Hirst's, and Lodge at Tim^o Green's that may be near the Ferry, and forward the folding and Stitching 100. of his Sermons now wrought off.

Jany 15th. Goes homeward by Charlestown. Now about Mr. Secretary reads a Petition in Council upon the Act for shortening the years for Marriage from 7. to 3.[2] whereas

---

[1] The will of widow Mary Phillips, dated July 2, 1709, proved Jan. 30, 1713–14 (Suff. Wills, Vol. XVIII. f. 233), mentions her daughters Mehitable, wife of Thomas Savage, and Elizabeth, wife of Benjamin Sweetser, her sons Timothy and Samuel (but Timothy did not live to administer), grandsons Henry Phillips, Eleazer Phillips, and John Phillips, Jr., grand-daughter Anne Bly, and all her great-grandchildren who should be alive at her death: cousin Sarah Fausdicke. House and land in Pudding Lane are bequeathed.

These data enable us to identify her as Mary, daughter of John Dwight, and third wife of Henry Phillips, butcher, of Dedham and Boston, who died in February, 1686. The above items also add considerably to Savage's note on this family. The Dwight Genealogy, I. 97, states that Mary is called, on the Dedham record, "the first child born in Dedham," which conflicts with Sewall's statement that she was born at sea. — EDS.

[2] This Act, passed in 1698, "in addition to and explanation of" an act of 1694, reduces, from seven to three years (in the sole case of the supposed loss of a vessel bound on a voyage of not more than three months), the term of absence of either husband or wife, after which the remaining party may marry again. In such case the Governor and Council are authorized to grant a license. Sewall's point seems to have been that the clause "or shall only

the Man sail'd from hence but November was 12 Moneths :
I quasht it, saying our Laws must not be so sham'd ; Sec-
retary said was more in the Law ; viz. or so heard of.
But I said the 3 years must precede : The Govr and Coun-
cil had nothing to doe with it. It was dismiss'd. Lord's
Day, Jany 17. Mr. Sergeant makes his Will.

Jany 18. Great Snow falls last night. I pay Sir
Charles Hobby Fifty pounds. He asks to see the Commission from the Corporation, I shew'd it him. Then he
ask'd to carry it away to copy it ; that I refus'd, saying
it was comitted to me. He began to huff ; but I per-
sisted.

Jany 14. Tuesday. There is a Meeting of the Trustees
for Mr. Edward Hopkins's Legacy,[1] upon due Warning.
Present Joseph Dudley esqr. Wm Tailer esqr. Isaac Addington esqr. Wait Winthrop esqr. S. S. Bromfield, E^m
Hutchinson, P. Townsend, S. Stoddard, Dr. Cotton Mather,
Mr. John Leverett, Jer. Dumer Esqr. Mr. Danl Oliver,
Mr. Thomas Fitch, Mr. John Burhil. A Letter to my
Lord Chancellour,[2] and another to Sir William Ashhurst,
pen'd by the President, were voted with some Amend-
ments. After this Meeting I consulted with the Comissioners about giving Sir Charles the mentioned Comission ;
a copy of it : None appear'd to allow it save Dr. C. Mather ;

---

be heard of under such circumstances as may rather confirm the opinion,
commonly received, of the whole company's being utterly lost," could not
have the effect to reduce the period of three years, even if such circumstances
became known before the end of that time. (Province Laws, I. 171, 354.) —
EDS.

[1] Quincy (Hist. Harvard College, I. 205) states that, after more than fifty
years from the death of Edward Hopkins, the college took steps, in 1709, to
claim the legacy left it. In March, 1712-13, a decree in Chancery gave it
£800, which was placed in the hands of trustees. When Quincy wrote, the
fund, despite various accidents, amounted to nearly thirty thousand dollars.
— EDS.

[2] The letter to Lord Chancellor Harcourt is probably the one printed in
Quincy's History, I. 521. — EDS.

many spake against it; all concluded twas not to be done without calling a meeting.

Jany 20. 17$\frac{1 2}{1 4}$. Mr. Sergeant speaks very passionately against Capt. Tim^o Clark and his judgm't for storehouse Room of 100. Barrels of powder; and against Mr. Dudley and Nowell's Arbitration concerning his wives portion in her Bro^r Shrimpton's Hands. Desir'd me to deal honestly as to the Stable he had built; he had laid out Sixty pounds. I have many times ask'd for the Writing I gave him, the Agreement; that I might take a Copy of it: But it cañot yet be found. When I first went in, he said he was just going; I answer'd, I hope to Canaan. Meeting, that has been a Considerable time discontinued by the sickness of the Widow Emons, was now held at Mr. Stevens's beyond the Bowling Green.[1] I read the Priestly and Prophetical Offices of CHRIST out of Mr. Jer. Burroughs,[2] which Discourses were very refreshing to me. Christ can teach the heart, teach them that are of Weak Understandings.

Jany 21. Dr. Cotton Mather preaches; 1 Jno. 5. 16. Sin no more — tells us will finish this time Six weeks. Govr not at Meeting. Mr. Secretary Sick a-bed, was taken about 9. last night when had scarce finish'd Essecombewit's Submission. In Council I spake against the Submission in my Ld Bellomont's time, Autumn 1699.

Jany 22. Mr. Secretary Recovers.

---

[1] Drake says the Bowling Green was, in 1722, the space between Cambridge Street, the Mill Pond, and Sudbury Street. That is, the space bounded by the present Bowdoin Square, and Court Street line, extending to Pitts Street, and extending northerly to the water's edge as it then was. In the lists of streets in 1708, we find "the way leading from Emmons's corner, passing by Justice Lynd's pasture, extending from thence westerly to the sea, Cambridge street." — EDS.

[2] Rev. Jeremiah Burroughs, who died in 1646, was an eminent non-conformist, "an excellent scholar, a good expositor, a popular preacher." He was one of the small number of "Dissenting Brethren" in the Westminster Assembly. — EDS.

Jany 24. Mr. J. Sewall baptiseth John Butler; the Grandfather, Capt. Ephra. Savage; holds it up.

January, 25. I watch'd last night with Mr. Peter Sergeant; was with him from 9. at Night to Seven in the morning.

He slept a great part of the night: is pretty free from pain. Takes only Liquids; and them he presently Vomits up. Madam Sergeant sat up till past one; and from thence Nurse Wheeler and I manag'd the Task.

January 25. 17$\frac{13}{14}$. Judge Thomas visits me; he came to Town last week. I gave him Cousin Moodey's Warning.

Jany 26. 1713. Rode in Wardell's Slay with the Chief Justice, Mr. Justice Lynde, and Mr. Attorney, to the Ferry; pleasant comfortable Weather for holding the Court; Mr. Bradstreet and Stephens dine with us. This day my son, Mr. Joseph Sewall, Removes into the Church's House and Lodges there.

Midweek, Jany 27. As I pass along I call at my Son's, and wish the Blessing of Winthrop, Norton, Willard, Pemberton to come upon him.[1] Judge Lynde was with me, coming out from Mr. Sergeant's just as I came by in the Coach; says Mr. Sergeant had a Fainting Fit yesterday.. Issue the Court by Candle-Light and get over well and home in the Coach.

Jany 28. Mr. Bridge preaches from PS. 27. 11. — because of my Enemies, Observers. Capt. Belcher and I write a Letter to Genl Nicholson, giving Account of the Contribution for St. Christophers.

Jany 29. Great Storm of Snow began about 3. p. m̄. yesterday: Last night, about Midnight, was a dreadfull Cry of Fire; was stop'd at Mr. Blunt's Work-house where it begun. *Laus Deo*. This day I sent Joseph my Pole's Synopsis Criticorum. I have enjoy'd them one and Thirty

---

[1] All of whom had resided on the site. — EDS.

years; and now have the pleasure to bestow them on a worthy Minister, my Son. O the patience, Longe Suffering, and Goodness of GOD !

Jany 30. 17$\frac{13}{14}$. Serene Cold Weather. Last night Ephraim Becon, going over the Neck with his Sled, Wandered to the Left hand, towards Dorchester, and was frozen to Death. One of the Horses is found dead. I presented my Son and daughter with six silver spoons, cost about 21^s a piece, bought of Capt. Winslow this day: and 6. Alchimy[1] spoons, of Mr. Clark, cost 3. 6.^d Before diñer, the chief justice, S. S. and Mr. E^m Hutchinson sign'd the Letter to my Ld Chancellor, and another to Sir William Ashhurst. About 4 p. m̄. I procured Mr. Sergeant to Sign them, after I had read them to him. Went to the Funeral of Mr. Calf's only son, about 2 years old. Last night Dr. Noyes's House was in danger of being burnt.

Seventh-Day, Feb^r 6. I went to the Town-house on the occasion of the Queen's Birthday; Mr. Bromfield and I sat a-while in one of the windows, Table being full; afterward sat in. A little before Sun-set I went away. Mr. Eliakim Hutchinson seeing me about to rise up, Said we would go and see Mr. Sergeant; I went with him. Mr. Sergeant took my Hand and held it with great Affection. My neighbour Colson knocks at our door about 9. or past to tell of the Disorders at the Tavern at the South-end in Mr. Addington's house, kept by John Wallis. He desired me that I would accompany Mr. Bromfield and Constable Howell thither. It was 35. Minutes past Nine at Night before Mr. Bromfield came; then we went. I took Æneas Salter with me. Found much Company. They refus'd to go away. Said were there to drink the Queen's Health, and they had many other Healths to drink. Call'd for more Drink: drank to me, I took notice

---

[1] Alchimy or occamy is a term for an inferior mixed metal, probably alloyed with copper. — EDS.

of the Affront to them. Said must and would stay upon
that Solemn occasion. Mr. John Netmaker drank the
Queen's Health to me. I told him I drank none; upon
that he ceas'd. Mr. Brinley put on his Hat to affront me.
I made him take it off. I threaten'd to send some of them
to prison; that did not move them. They said they
could but pay their Fine,[1] and doing that they might stay.
I told them if they had not a care, they would be guilty
of a Riot. Mr. Bromfield spake of raising a number of
Men to Quell them, and was in some heat, ready to run
into Street. But I did not like that. Not having Pen
and Ink, I went to take their Names with my Pensil, and
not knowing how to Spell their Names, they themselves
of their own accord writ them. Mr. Netmaker, reproach-
ing the Province, said they had not made one good Law.

At last I address'd my self to Mr. Banister. I told him
he had been longest an Inhabitant and Freeholder, I expected he should set a good Example in departing thence.
Upon this he invited them to his own House, and away
they went; and we, after them, went away. The Clock
in the room struck a pretty while before they departed.
I went directly home, and found it 25. Minutes past Ten
at Night when I entred my own House. About 5. in the
Morning there was a cry of Fire; Bells rung. Son J.
Sewall came to our Chamber door and acquainted us.

---

[1] Referring to Chap. XXII. Province Laws, Acts of 1692–93, an Act "for
the better observation and keeping the Lord's Day." It inflicts a fine of
five shillings on every person remaining in a public house, "drinking, or
idly spending his time on Saturday night, after the sun is set, or on the
Lord's Day, or the evening following." Other provisions prohibit travelling
on that day by any persons "except they were belated and forced to lodge in
the woods, wilderness, or highways, the night before, and in such case to
travel no further than the next inn or place of shelter."

Also magistrates were "to restrain all persons from swimming in the
water, unnecessary and unseasonable walking in the streets or fields in the
town of Boston or other places, Keeping open their shops or following their
secular occasions or recreations," on the Lord's Day, the evening before, or
that following that day. — EDS.

But quickly after our rising, the Bells left off ringing, and I saw no Light. Mr. Webb's Malt-house, near Mr. Bronsdon's, was burnt down. Twas a great Mercy that the Fire was not spread all over the North-End. Part of the house of Mr. Bronsdon, the Landlord, began to burn.

Lord's Day, Febr. 7. A Note is put up for Mr. Sergeant in the morning, to pray for him as near his End, which my Son read, and pray'd Excellently for him.

Monday, Feb. 8. Mr. Bromfield comes to me, and we give the Names of the Offenders at John Wallis's Tavern last Satterday night, to Henry Howell, Constable, with Direction to take the Fines of as many as would pay; and warn them that refus'd to pay, to apear before us at 3. p. m̄. that day. Many of them pay'd. The rest appear'd; and Andrew Simpson, Ensign, Alexander Gordon, Chirurgeon, Francis Brinley, Gent. and John Netmaker, Gent., were sentenc'd to pay a Fine of 5ˢ each of them, for their Breach of the Law Entituled, An Act for the better Observation, and Keeping the Lord's Day. They all Appeal'd, and Mr. Thomas Banister was bound with each of them in a Bond of 20ˢ upon Condition that they should prosecute their Appeal to effect.

Capt. John Bromsal, and Mr. Thomas Clark were dismiss'd without being Fined. The first was Master of a Ship just ready to sail, Mr. Clark a stranger of New York, who had carried it very civilly, Mr. Jekyl's Brother-in-Law.

John Netmaker was fin'd 5ˢ for profane cursing; saying to —— Colson, the Constable's Assistant, God damn ye; because the said Colson refus'd to drink the Queen's Health. This he paid presently. Then Mr. Bromfield and I demanded of the said Netmaker to become bound in a Bond of Twenty pounds, with two Sureties in Ten pounds a-piece, to Answer at the next Genˡ Session of the Peace for Suffolk, his Contempt of Her Majesties Government of this Province and vilifying the same at the house of John Wallis, Innholder in Boston, last Satterday night. Mr. Banister declin'd being bound; and none else offer'd

(To imbarrass the Affair as I conceiv'd). Upon this Mr. Netmaker was dismiss'd, giving his Word to apear on Tuesday. at 10. m̄. that he might have Time to provide Sureties.

Tuesday, March, 9th. Mr. Bromfield and I waited till past 11. and dismiss'd the Constables Howell and Feño, suposing No body would come. Constable met Mr. Netmaker at the door, and came back again with him: He came all alone. Mr. Bromfield and I spent much time with him to bring him to some Acknowledgment of his Error, but all in vain. Offer'd not so much as his own Bond: which constrain'd us to Write a Mittimus, and send him to Prison. Angry words had pass'd between him and Const. Howell; he Threatn'd Const. Howell what he would do to him; or his Servants for him. For this reason I dismiss'd Constable Howell; sent for Mr. John Winchcomb, and gave him the Mittimus, out of respect to Mr. Netmaker; and he took it kindly. This about ¼ past 12. at Noon by my Clock. Went into Town; Mr. Wᵐ Pain spake with me near the Townhouse; express'd himself concern'd that Mr. Netmaker was in prison; he would pay his Fine that he might be releas'd. I told him there was no Fine. Went on, visited Hañah Parkman, saw the place, where the Malt-house was burnt down. As I return'd, went to the Funeral of Mrs. Green. There, Mr. Secretary (who was a Bearer), Told me, a Council was Warn'd to meet after the Funeral. Accordingly I went. Present, Govʳ, Lᵗ Govʳ, Winthrop, Elisha Hutchinson, Sewall, Mr. Addington, Townsend, Eᵐ Hutchinson, Belchar, Bromfield. It was late and Duskish, and Col. Elisha Hutchinson went away before any thing was Voted. Sat round a little Fire; I hapen'd to sit next Genˡ Nicholson. He aply'd himself to me and Mr. Bromfield, ask'd whether did not know that he was here with the Broad Seal of England? I answer'd, Yes! Ask'd whether did not know that Mr. Netmaker was his Secretary? I answer'd, Tis generally so receiv'd. Then with a Roaring Noise the Genˡ said, I demand JUSTICE against Mr. Sewall and Bromfield for sending my Secretary to prison without acquainting me with it! And hastily rose up, and went down and walk'd the Exchange, where he was so furiously Loud, that the Noise was plainly heard in the Council-Chamber, the door being shut. The Governour vehemently urg'd the Discharge of Netmaker; argued that Genl Nicholson was as an Embassador; his Servant ought to have been delivered to him. I said, Mr. Netmaker was upon his Parole from Monday to Tuesday; in which time he might have acquainted Genl Nicholson with his Circumstances. The Govr said, Mr. Bromfield and I ought to have acquainted him our selves. Would have had the Vote so Worded. Would have had us that committed Mr. Netmaker to have released him. I objected to that; saying, we had comitted him: but I did not know that we had power to release him. Then the Keeper was sent for with the Mittimus, which Mr. Secretary read by Candle-Light, in these words;

MASSACHUSETTS,

(Seal.)   SUFFOLK ss.

(Seal.) To the Keeper of Her Majesties Goal in Boston, Greeting,

We herewith send you the body of John Netmaker, Gent: who being Order'd by our selves, two of Her Majesties Justices for Suffolk, to give Bond with Sureties, to appear at the next General Sessions of the Peace to be held for the County of Suffolk, to make Answer for his Contempt of Her Maj' Government of this Province, and Vilifying the same at the house of John Wallis, Innholder, in Boston in the Night Between the Sixth and Seventh of this Instant February: Refus'd so to doe;

You are therefore in Her Majesties Name required to receive the said Netmaker, and him safely keep till he be discharged by due course of Law.

Given under our Hands and Seals in Boston, this Ninth day of February 17$\frac{13}{14}$ *Annoque Regni Annæ*, Reginae Magnae Brittanicae &c., Duodecimo,

SAMUEL SEWALL.

EDW. BROMFIELD.

Upon reading this, Mr. Secretary drew up an Order, importing that those general Words would not hold him, and order'd his Discharge. The Governour Ordered the Keeper to discharge Mr. Netmaker, and the Secretary should give him a Copy of the Council's Order. And order'd Mr. Secretary to Copy it out, and wait upon Gen¹ Nicholson with it in the Morning. They that voted being hardly drawn to it. Some of them, were Lt Govr, Mr. Addington, Eliakim Hutchinson, Penn Townsend, Andrew Belchar; Mr. Winthrop was in the Negative; said he understood not how it belong'd to the Council to meddle with it. Sewall and Bromfield were the parties complain'd of. If they had withdrawn, there had been no Council left; but the Govr charg'd that none should withdraw. This was pretty hard, seeing a General Council was to meet the next day; and the Bond required, was but Twenty pounds the principal, and Ten pounds a piece two Sureties.

Lords-Day, Febr. 7th. My son preaches the first Sermon after the New Watch being set up. Mr. Pemberton Preach'd not by reason of his Lame Legg.

Fourth-day, Febr. 10. The New Capt., Stephen Minott, new Lieut, Gyles Dyer, &c. bring the Govr to Town. Mr. Banister open'd his sashes, to whom the Govr made a deep bow as he rode along. The Gen¹ and Lieut. Govr visited the said Banister last Lords-Day when the Afternoon Exercise was over.

Febr. 11th. Mr. Colman prays.

Sixth-day, Febr. 12. The Storm of Snow is so violent, that Jn° Roberts gives notice Mr. Sergeant's Funeral will not be to-day.

7th day, Feb^r. 13. Serene pleasant Weather. Mr. Sergeant interr'd. Bearers, Winthrop, Elisha Hutchinson; Sewall, Addington; Townsend Belcher; Scarvs, Rings, Gloves Escutcheons. Laid in his Tomb in the New Burying place a-while before Sun-set.

Third day, Febr. 16. My Son, Mr. Joseph Sewall, Prays at the opening of the Council, which is the first time [Prays?], 17. 18. 19. 20.

Febr. 23. 24. Dr. Cotton Mather prays. This Court a large Township, of 12 miles square, is granted near Wadchuset, out of which my 1000. Acres are excepted. I was surpris'd, not having seen it, till twas pass'd by the Deputies. Govr is uneasy till the Word *Associats* be inserted. Will have it call'd Rutland: I objected because that was the name of a shire. The chief Justice said 'twas not convenient except the Land was Red. But the Govr would not be diverted. I suppose the Quantity might be one thing inclin'd his Excellency to this Name. Westfield Petition is granted as to a small addition of Land for the sake of Wood, and Building-Stone.

March, 27. 1714. Mr. Corwin and I set out for Plimouth: David waits on me. Mr. Lynde meets us at Braintrey. Rode in the Rain from Weymouth to Cushing's. Mr. Corwin was so weak and faint with his Cold that he kept in his Quarters on the Lords Day, March, 28.

March, 29. Mr. Corwin returns homeward, Mr. Thacher accompanying him. We pass on to Plimouth.

March, 30. Court open'd.

March, 31. *Ædem intravi.*[1]

April, 3. Set out for Sandwich.

April, 5th for the Vinyard with Major Thaxter, had a very prosperous Journey through the Goodness of God. See my Journal.

[Among the MSS. of Judge Sewall in the Cabinet of the Society is a small parchment bound volume, with a strong brass clasp, on the cover of which is inscribed, "Magunkaquog, Octob. 11, 1715."

---

[1] It will be noticed that it was Sewall's custom, when away from home, at some hour on his birthday, March 28, or on one as near to it as was convenient, to go alone into the meeting-house of the place where he might be, for a private religious exercise. We cannot suppose that he regarded the edifice as peculiarly sacred, but that he merely sought privacy. — EDS.

The word is the Indian name of Hopkinton. It contains a most miscellaneous collection of entries, chiefly abstracts of sermons which he heard while absent from home, also sketches of conversations, brief references to cases before the courts, accounts of money loaned, or disbursed, &c. Probably he carried this little volume with him, on his longer journeys, instead of his larger volume of journal for the time being, in which to make entries, though he did not transfer them to the latter on his return home. It is evidently to this little supplementary volume that he refers in the words: "See my Journal." We are thus enabled to supply from it the narrative of his very interesting journey for the performance of his official duties as a commissioner of the English Society for the Propagation of the Gospel among the Indians.

The extracts made from the Magunkaquog volume will begin and close between asterisks. Some entries made previous to the account of the journey are copied as they stand on the pages.]

* April 3. 1714, Expended,

At Morey's		0. 4. 2.
At Newcomb's, Sandwich		0. 8. 6.
7ʳ 11ᵗʰ 1714. Bristol Circuit Dedham		0. 4. 0.
7ʳ 12. Billings		0. 5. 6.
Contribution		0. 5. 0.
7ʳ 13. Wear		0. 6. 4.
Rehoboth, Millar		0. 1. 4.
Swanzy, Carpenter		0. 2. 10.
7ʳ 15. Bristol Barber		0. 1. 2.
„ 16. Postage 2 Letters and the News Letter		0. 1. 2.
„ „ Lantern		0. 0. 5.
„ 17. Osburn		1. 13. 0.
Mr. Hale		1. 0. 0.
Lantern		0. 0. 6.
„ 18. Mrs. Osburn		0. 2. 0.
Barber		0. 1. 0.
Reynolds		0. 13. 4.
Ferriage to Febt		0. 0. 6.
Millar		0. 2. 6.
19. Attleborough		0. 7. 8.
20. Slack		0. 12. 6.
25. To John Cornish for himself and Horse		3. 0. 8.
		9. 1. 5.

9. 1. 5.
3. 13. 4. Received.
5. 8. 1.*

* Dr. Calamy, 2ᵈ volume of the Ejected Ministers, p. 222. Plymouth: Mr. George Hughes, B. D. Born in Southwark, 1603. His Mother was then 52 years of age, and had never a child before, though she had three Husbands before Mr. Hughes's Father. And her Age was as remarkable afterwards: for she lived to her 96ᵗʰ year. He was entred in Corpus Christi College, in Oxon, 1619.

The Elector George Lewis born May, 28. 1660; Hanover. The Electoral Prince George Augustus, Duke and Marquis of Cambridge, Earl of Milford Haven, Viscount Alerton and Baron of Tewksbury, born Octob. 30. 1683. He gives the greatest Hopes of himself that we or any people on Earth can desire. The present Prince of Brunswick, his son, born Jan. 30, 1706.

Honᴮᴸᴱ Sirs, His Excellency has intimated a General Council to meet at the Council Chamber in Boston upon Thursday, the Seventh of April next, for Consideration and Settlement of Civil Officers, and other the important necessary Affairs of Government. Your Presence in Council is then expected and desired, and that you will not fail of attending on this extraordinary occasion accordingly.

I am your Honor's most Humble Servᵗ

Jos. HILLER, Cler. Coun.

Jⁿᵒ Cushing and Isaac Winslow, Esqʳ
on His Majesty's Service. To the honorable Jⁿᵒ
Cushing, Esq. Situate. To be communicated.

Instructions for the Honourable Samuel Sewall, Esq. and Penn Townsend, Esq. Agents for the Company for Propagating Religion among our Indians, employed now by their Commissioners in a Journey to Martha's Vinyard for the Regular Disposing of the Land lately purchased by the Honourable Corporation for the Service of the Indians there.

I. The Gentlemen are to enquire of them, whom they take to be the most capable of advising them, among the Inhabitants of the Island, and hear what Advice they may offer concerning the best Methods for the Settlement and Improvement of the Land at Gay-Head and elsewhere; that it may answer the Ends of the Honourable Company in Purchasing it.

II. Competent and Convenient Portions of this Land, are to be by them assigned unto the Indians for to be Inhabited and Cultivated by the Indian Families. Each of the Families to know their own Allotments. But whether they shall be Equal Allotments, or proportioned unto the Condition of the several Families, tis left unto the Discretion of the Agents when they arrive upon the place.*

* III. That part of the Land which will remain after the Indians have their Portions allotted unto them, shall be Leased out unto Tenants, at such Rates and for such Terms, as by the Agents may be thought most Reasonable, that so there may be something of a Revenue from thence towards the Support of Schools, and other good Interests among the Indians of that Island. And the Indians are to be fully informed that what Revenues doe arise from this Land Will be wholly applyed for their Benefit and Advantage.

IV. There should be some suitable Factor for the Commissioners left on the Spot, who may after the Return of the Agents go on with such Things as they may be forced for want of Time to leave unfinished; and pursue such Directions as the Commissioners may from time to time Transmit unto him, about agreeing with Lessees and receiving of Rents, and other Points that may call for the Management of some Discreet person there. The Commissioners will rely on the Nomination which these their Agents may make for this purpose.

By Order of the Commissioners,

PETER SERGEANT.[1]

BOSTON, September the 21st 1713.*

---

[1] In Judge Sewall's Letter Book, the publication of which it is proposed by the Society shall follow that of the Journal, will be found abundant evidence of the interest, zeal, and devotion which he gave to his official duties as a commissioner of the corporation having in view the civilizing and converting of the Indians. He took a most warm, humane, and Christian interest in every thing that was attempted or done for the welfare of the natives. As he came into manhood just at the period when the havoc, desolation, massacres, and burnings on our frontiers in "King Philip's War," threw all the colonists of New England into a panic of dismay over the horrors and apprehensions of the times, he, of course, sympathized with, and took part in, the measures and warlike acts to which the community had recourse, either for protection or vengeance. But he still reserved a place in his feelings for considerate pity, and for works of mercy. The Benjamin Larnell mentioned in previous pages was an Indian young man in whom Sewall took such an interest as to provide for his education and to send him to Harvard College; but he proved a failure, and died early in his course. From the experiences of that fearful crisis in the almost desperate fortunes of New England, is to be dated a manifest change in the feelings of the great mass of the people towards the Indians, precisely like that which showed itself, nearly a century afterwards, among the frontier settlers of Pennsylvania and Virginia, during the direful atrocities of Pontiac's war. A degree of toleration and commiseration had previously been exercised towards the Indians. The General Court of Massachusetts had proposed and enacted some measures for their protection and just treatment. Some considerable interest — but by no means so

* *Feria Sexta*, April 2, 1714. Plimouth. I went up the Burying Hill to take a Prospect, 6. m. and saw the Land all round about covered with Snow. The Quantity of it on the Ground everywhere *

---

considerate, extensive, sympathetic, and practically generous, as has been often supposed — was taken in the attempts to civilize the Indians. Eliot, Gookin, and others of the most devoted laborers in this work, do not conceal their regret that so few of their brethren were ready and hopeful in it, and that from many they received slight and discouragement. Still the work had progressed, — advanced, mainly, as is soon to be stated, by aid from abroad, — and showed some fair prospect of success, till the dread crisis just referred to came with its appalling shock upon the people, especially those in the farming towns of our frontiers. From that period an embitterment of feeling, contempt, disgust, and rage, became widely entertained here against the Indians; and, as has since been noticed on our frontiers, with each successive belt of advance of civilization over our continent, those who had had experience of Indian warfare came to regard the natives simply as vermin and wild beasts, to be exterminated.

From Sewall's Letter Book, from the Records of the Commissioners of the United Colonies, from the small publications by Eliot, the Mayhews, Gookin, and others, relating to their labors in behalf of the Indians, may be gathered information which might, perhaps, surprise some who are but slightly informed about the history of those times. They might learn, from those sources, to how great an extent a work which was done here for the Indians, and for which our own colonists have had the credit, was prompted, encouraged, sustained, and actually paid for, by influence and funds from abroad. In fact, no earnest and vigorous efforts were made here in behalf of the Indians till rebukes and reproaches from friends of the colonists in England, censuring the indifference and neglect of our magistrates and ministers in the cause, had provoked them to áction. Then the Corporation, formed in England in Cromwell's time, and revived by Charles II., furnished wise counsels and generous pecuniary grants and salaries to carry on the work. Incidentally, too, the New England Colonies, and Harvard College especially, received valuable helps from the Corporation in objects not always limited to the Indians. The first edifice of brick in the College Yard was built from the funds of the Society, intended for the accommodation of twenty young Indian scholars; but it very soon served other uses. A printer, fonts of type, and paper, were sent over by the Society, for printing Eliot's Bible, primers, catechisms, tracts, &c. Eliot, and other preachers and schoolmasters to the Indians, received regular salaries from England. As the Indian village in Natick was about reaching its most hopeful stage, the Society sent over a cargo of tools, household and farm implements, &c. The vessel was cast away on Cohasset Rocks, but some of its valuable cargo was sáved. The pious and strong-hearted Eliot cheered his neophytes in their dismay over such a baffling providence, by telling them that, though Satan, in his rage, to withstand a holy enterprise, had wrecked the vessel, God, in his mercy, had saved some of her lading. — EDS.

* makes the dismal face of Winter like February. Major Thaxter, who came to us yesterday, says he saw a man Sledding. The Out [East]-Wind has prevented a hard Frost.

Last night at Mr. Thomas's had Discourse about the Body. Mr. Dudley maintained the Belly should not be raised, because he knew no use of it. I maintained the Contrary, because Christ saw no Corruption. Saints shall be conformed to Him. The Creator in his infinite Wisdom will know what use to make of them.

Dudley. What use of Tasting, Smelling?

Sewall. Tis possible the bodies of the Saints may have a Fragrancy attending them.

Dudley. Voice is Laborious.

Sewall. As much Labour as you please, the more the better, so it be without Toil, as in Heaven it will be. I dare not part with my Belly, Christ has Redeemed it; and there is danger of your breaking in further upon me, and cutting off my Hand or Foot. *Obsta Principiis.* Wee'l Continue this Action to the next Term.[1]

This morning comes to my mind. I can't believe the blessed Womb that bore our Saviour, will always be buried. Her Son, her Father, her God will Redeem it from the prevailing power of the Grave.

David Toby, Brother-in-Law to Amos Sipson, moves to have their Charges that they may go home.

To Jocelyn — Twenty Shillings, £1. 0. 0.

Seventh-Day, April 3, 1714. Mr. Thomas' Daughter Mary, of 3 years old: his only Daughter, died last night, a little before Break of Day. We saw her in her Mother's Lap last Thorsday night when we were there. It grieves me the more that it should be just after we had been so kindly Treated there. Cloudy Morning. When left Plimouth, about 9 or 10 m, I had in my Bills of Credit —— £35. 7. 0.

Major Thaxter and I rid to Sandwich accompanied by Mr. Justice Parker, Capt. John Otis, our Pilot, Mr. John Denison our Chaplain. It did not Rain, but Wet, being an Out-Wind. But part of the Way the Sun appeared through the Clouds, and the Weather was Comfortable. Got to Newcomb's, where we Dined. I treated the Barnstable Gentlemen. Mr. Cotton came to us and invited Major Thaxter and me to his House. He had invited me at Plimouth. Mr. Justice Lynde returned homeward, having Mayo for his Pilot. Mr. Cooke *

---

[1] We have in the biographies of English and American judges and lawyers many graphic sketches of the manner in which they occupied leisure hours on a circuit. But this discussion between Judge Sewall and the Attorney of the Province, Paul Dudley, Esq., may be regarded as unique. — EDS.

* intended to keep the Sabbath with his Kinsman, Counsellour Winslow.

In the Evening Mr. Cotton made a short Speech of God's Mercies in the Week past, Sung part of the 103 Ps. W. Pray'd.

Lord's Day, April 4. Mr. Cotton [in the family] reads the 29th of Deut., sings the 12. 13. 14 verses of the 19 Psalm, Y[ork] *memoriter*.

[As Judge Sewall wrote in his little book abstracts of the two Sermons which his host, the Rev. Rowland Cotton, Minister of Sandwich, preached on this day, one of them, that of the afternoon, is here copied.]

Post meridiem. Ps. 118, 4th part, D.

2 Corin. 4. 4. In whom, the god of this ☉ [world], Man is undon by Sin. Christ is the only Helper; the Gospel directs how we may come at it; yet men don't; men won't regard it.

Doct. That the reason why the Gospel is hid to many to whom it is revealed, is, because the god of this ☉ has blinded their Eyes.

First, though the Gospel be granted, many do not believe. All men have not Faith. Who hath believed our Report?

Use. To persuade all to take care that it may not be said of them, They believe not.

2. They that live under the Gospel and yet don't believe. The reason is because the god of this ☉ has blinded their Eyes. Query, Who is the god of this ☉? Answer. It is certain the Lord Jehovah is the God of the whole Earth. He made all, and is the Proprietor. What men's desires rest in is said to be their god. But the Devil is here intended. *This World* is usually in Scripture taken in an ill sense. John 12. 41. Prince of this world: 14. 40. Prince of this — Ephes. 6. 12. 96 [Psalm?] 5. Idols, 106 [?] 47. Idols, Devils, 1 Corin. 10. 20. Sacrificed to Devils, 1 John, 5. 19. He rules in the Children of Disobedience. Ephes. 1. 2. Men of this ☉ prefer him before Jesus Christ. Is not any god by right of Creation, but by the Wickedness that is in the hearts of men. Taken Captives by him at his will.

Query. How comes he to blind men?

God may permit men to be blinded. Isai. 6. 10. Make the ☉ (heart of this people fat) 1 Kings 22. 2 Thess. 2. 11. God sends them strong Delusions, to believe a Lye. Devil blinds several ways.

(1) By keeping men in Ignorance. Men are naturally gone out of the Way. Hinders Children from learning their books. Keeps men from attending the public worship.

(2.) By leading men into Error. Revel. 16. 14. 2 Corin. 11. 14. Into an angel of light: his suggestions are taken for great beams of light: presents men with errors suiting their Constitutions.*

* (3). By taking advantage of what mens Affections are set on. Matt. 19. 22. rich young man. How can you believe who seek honor one of another? What to think of parting with all for Christ! Covetous, Ambitious, Voluptuous.

(4) By prejudicing men against those that teach them the Truth. Undervaluing the Ministers of the Gospel.

Use 1. Those under the Gospel who do not believe may truly be said to be under the dominion of the Devil. Isai. 49. 4. Christ delivers the Lawfull Captive. In Baptism God becomes the Guardian of the Baptised. All are naturally under the Kingdom of Satan, till rescued by Christ. Covenant for Substance is the same. Not a word said to forbid the baptising Children. Suffer little children to come to Me.

Use 2. Since not ignorant of this let us beware we be not deceived with the Devices of Satan.

Eldad Tupper and John Osburn were baptised. 103 [Ps.] 17. 18. W.

Second-day. April 5. 1714. We pass on to Fishe's by a brave Pond, where we bait our Horses. Then proceed to Falmouth, to Capt. Lothrop's. Got thither about Noon. William Basset was our Pilot. Din'd there on Bacon and Eggs. Mr. Metcalf with us. Mr. —— Butler; but I neither saw him nor knew him, and so missed speaking with him. He lost his Anchors in the Sound. Went to the Ferry. Mr. Metcalf and Capt. Lothrop accompanied us, and our pilot. At Weeks' I saw Mr. John Robinson, who waits there for the calling of a sloop to take a family and him in to carry them to Coñecticut. Is about 74 years old. I gave him my Ten Biskets and 5ˢ.

In our Passage we were becalmed, and the Tide against us [so] that were 2½ hours getting over. Were fain to row to the west side of Oukakemy Bay, where we landed, the Sloop coming to an Anchor. Our Horses were forced to leap into the Sea. By that time had tackled them was duskish.

Major Thaxter discovered some men and Horses, as he thought, upon the Beach, at a distance. When came to them found Thomas Paul, a Lame Indian, on Horsback with his Net on his shoulder, to catch Fish by Night. Upon my speaking to him to Pilot me, he left his Net and did it very well. We were ready to be offended that an Englishman, Jonathan Lumbard, in the Company spake not a word to us, and it seems he is deaf and dumb. Got to Mr. Allen's a little before 9. at night.

Third-day, April 6. I am somthing indispos'd; resolved not to goe abroad. Mr. Thomas Mayhew, Mr. Allen, Father, Mr. Haws,*

* and others come in to see us. Mr. Mayhew writes a Letter in Indian to Saul, which I subscrib'd, to notify the Indians of the Gay Head to come together somthing before Noon. I would speak with them after Mr. Mayhew's Lecture. I writ a Letter to Mr. Mayhew of the same import. Sent them by Mr. Haws, who is going to Nomans Land. Discours'd Mr. Mayhew largely of the Indian Affairs. I was glad to hear that the Gay Head Indians had of their own accord met together and run a Fence across the Neck. Mr. Mayhew had advised them to it many years agoe, but they did it not till this Spring. Mr. Mayhew was with them at their Consultation. He tells me that a Ditch four foot wide and two deep which he effected the last, will cost but 6ˢ per Rod. Mr. Torry and Cathcart dine with us, and Mr. Homes, who boards at Mr. Allen's, to teach School.

In the Evening Mr. Ralph Thacher and his son Ralph çall in and Wellcom me to the Island. They tell us of a Governour coming over for us; had been gone three Weeks: to take Ireland in his way. They had this News from Mr. Otis, of Sandwich. They reckon a Ship is come in from England. Mr. Otis read the Letter. They lodg'd at Fish's last Monday Night. After they were gone, Mr. Experience Mayhew came in to see me, and invited us to Dine or Sup with him after the Lecture, in our Return home.

Midweek, April 7. 1714. Very Serene, Sunshiny Morning, the most pleasant we have had since we came from home.

Memorandum. If any of the Gay Head be to be Leased out, Mr. Ebenezer Allen, our Landlord, desires he may have the first Refusal of some Pasturage, if it may stand with the Main design of benefitting the aboriginal Natives.

Indian Boy, Josiah Hassit, jun'r. Psalm Book.

Abel Sacuchassauet, Promised, sent a New Testament, July 5. 1714. Major Thaxter and I went to the Gay Head, accompanied by Mr. Thomas Mayhew, Mr. Josiah Torrey, Mr. Ebenezer Allan, Mr. Robert Cathcart, Mr. Benjamin Haws, Mr. John Denison, Mr. Robert Homes, David Sinclar. Major Skiff, and Mr. Experience Mayhew, we took in our Way. About one Hundred Men and Women were gathered together besides Children. Mr. Mayhew directed Joash Pannos, Minister of Gay-Head, to begin with Prayer; then Mr. Mayhew preached from Ephes. 1. 11. — who worketh all things after the Counsel of his own Will. Sung 4 verses of the 111ᵗʰ Psalm. Mr. Torrey set the Low-Dutch Tune. Mr. Mayhew gave us the heads of his Sermon in English; a good Discourse. Isaac Ompane concluded with Prayer. I enquired if any could read English; proclamation was made. At last only two young men were produced. I set him *

* to read in my Psalm-book with red Covers, and then gave it him. Promised a Testament to the 2ᵈ

Fifth-day. April, 8. 1714, at Mr. Ebenezer Allen's, in Martha's Vinyard; sent for Mr. Benjamin Mayhew, who has Land adjoining to the Gay-head Neck. I informed him that the Gay-head Indians have made their Half of Fence, on the side towards the Sound, and desired him to make his Half, that the Neck might be closed; which he agrees to. And he is promis'd that his so doing shall not alter any Lease he has of Sam. Osowit for about 10 or 12 Acres just within the Neck. To Sarah Japhet, widow, 12ˢ, to help Fill her Land. Bethiah, Nicodemus' widow, who died at Port Royal, is her daughter, and dwells with her. Bethiah has one son, of 22 years old, who is helpless by reason of Sickness; have one Servant 17 years old.

April 8. 1714. Jonas Aosoe, saith that he took up with Govᵣ Dungan's [Dongan] Terms, brought a Red-Ear of Indian Corn to Mr. Thomas Mayhew to signify it. Terms were to pay a Peck of Wheat yearly for a while, and then to pay a Bushel of Wheat *per annum*, which Conditions he has not perform'd. Yet he expects to hold the Land, because his House is there, and that is the place Major Mat. Mayhew assign'd him. Dont understand he has any Evidence of it. He also gave Elezer Sonamog three pounds and Ten shillings for his Forty Acre Lot at the Gay-head Neck, which Sonamog took up as he, the said Jonah, took up his.

In answer to Thomas Paul, of Christian Town, who is angred that Isaac Ompane, of the same Town, lives in the Town's English House Rent-free. It is directed and Ordered, that Isaac Ompane for the future pay Twelve Shillings *per* annum Rent for the said House so long as he dwells in it, which shall go towards reimbursing the Widow Abigail's Lease. And it is very necessary that the Town speedily join together as one Man, and pay what is owing to the said Widow. And then the Twelve Shillings *per* annum shall be employed in some other public use of the Town, and shall be paid accordingly to the Select-Men thereof by Isaac Ompany, who has been a principal Doer and Sufferer in Recovering the same. Sewall, Thaxter, Thomas Mayhew, Esq. Benjamin Skiff, Esq. April 8. 1714. This day, April 8, was exceeding dark at one Time in the morning. I have hardly seen such Thick Darkness. Great Rain, considerable Lig. tening and Thunder before Night.

Sixth-day, April 9. 1714. Fair Wether; Cold Northerly Wind. Visit Abel's Widow. Go to the top of Prospect Hill, from thence to the Sound, and by Mr. Thomas Mayhew's direction view'd the River falling into the Sound, and the Shoar all along to the end of the 327 *

*Rods which extends Southward to the middle Line, containing about 1000 Acres which belongs to the Corporation.

CHILMARK, April, 9. 1714.   Receiv'd of Samuel Sewall Twenty Shillings in full of all Demands for Services done by me as under-Sheriff, or otherwise, in Recovering some Lands of Oukakemy to the Indians.   I say, received in full by me,

THOMAS TRACY.

5. I give further to my daughter Hanah and my Grandson Jno. Harlock all such Land or Lots of mine, which are not mentioned in this my last Will, and I add to my daughter Hañah half the Whale at Natyk which I had forgot.

June 16. 1681.   THOMAS MAYHEW.

Samuel Sarson's Patent.   8ʳ 18. 1687.   To pay 25th March yearly, One Bushel of Wheat, and at the death of the Tenant, or entring of every new Tenant, for ever, such sum as the above demised premises would or might yield if to Farm-Letten for the Term of one full year.

Thomas Lothrop, One Hundred Acres, Nov. 24, 1704.   One Ear of Corn yearly, and every 21st year the full Value of One Year's Rent.

CHILMARK, April 10, 1714.

GENTLEMEN, — I intend, God Willing, to go off the Island this Day.   Desire and order you to take Mr. Benjamin Mayhew with you and Repair to the Entrance of the Gay-head Neck and Stake the Line between the Honble Corporation and him, the said Benjamin Mayhew, and then Call upon him speedily to make up his Part of the fence towards the South-Sea, that the Corporation Gate may be set up and the Neck Closed, and then let a Ditch of four-foot Wide and two foot Deep be made all on the outside of the Hedge, and set within Thorns or Barberries all along the top of it this Spring, or the Next, if it prove too late now.   In consideration of the whole Ditch being made on Mr. Mayhew's Side, I will be at all the Charge of making it at the first, and Mr. Benjamin Mayhew shall keep his part in Good Repair from time to time.   I hope the advancing Spring will Quicken your dispatch.

This is what Major Thaxter and I have Agreed upon and Ordered, and have accordingly set to our hands.

SAMUEL SEWALL.
SAMUEL THAXTER.

To THOMAS MAYHEW, ESQ. and Mr. EBENEZER ALLEN.
    In Chilmark.*

* April 10. 1714.   The Wind being excessive high we did not goe to Homes' Hole, but viewed Watsha Neck all over, being conducted by Mr. Simon Athern and B. Haws: find much of it good for Herbage and Tillage.   Sat awhile in the Wigwam where Elisabeth, Stephen Spoko's Widow, dwells: eat roste Alewive and very good Hasty Pudding.   Gave the Widow at coming away 10ˢ.   Get to Mr. Worth's between 3 and 4.   Demanded Rent of Mrs. Worth for the Neck.   Went to Mr. Mat. Mayhew for a Copy of another Letter of Attorney of his Father.

Seventh-day, April 10. 1714.   The last night was very Cold. Plenty of Ice was to be seen in the Road between Mr. Allen's and Cathcart's, past Ten a clock in the fair sun-shine.

Edgartown; April 11ᵗʰ 1714.   Serene Day.   Ps. 90. 1-6. L.   By Mr. Samˡ Wiswall, A. M.

Eccles. 9. 10.   Whatsoever thy hand findeth to do, do it with thy might, for there is no work, nor device, nor knowledge, nor wisdom in the Grave, whither thou goest.

This Life is our season for design, counsel, work.   This a time of Probation.

Doct.   Men ought with the utmost diligence to prepare for the Eternal Estate while this Life lasts, because this is the only time to prepare in.

Prop. 1.   This Life is a space of probation and preparation for Eternity.   If we are irreligious here, we must needs be miserable for ever.   We are here upon our good Behaviour.   Eccles. 3. 26.   Spirit of a man goes upward, is immortal.   Heaven is a state of Eternal Blessedness, Hell of Eternal Misery.   Rom. 2. 7.   Dan. 12. 2.   Thes. 1. 9.   Do not rightly acknowledge these Truths except we give them agreable Entertainment, Govern our Lives by them.

Prop. 2.   It is a work of the greatest Importance to prepare for Eternity.   Believe in Christ, Repent of our Sin, fly from the Wrath to come.   One thing is Necessary.

Prop. 3.   This Life is the only opportunity to prepare for Eternity in.   Heb. 9. 27.   Apointed to all men once to dy, and after death the Judgment.   Lazarus died and his Soul Convoyed to Abraham's bosom, to the Society of the Spirits of Just men made perfect. Dives — [the Judge leaves a gap here.]

Our Life is very short, Ps. 90., 70 years soon cut off, and we fly away.   Those who live the longest very short in itself, compared with those before the flood.   Especiall if we compare it with the Eternal Abode in the next life, which is consequent upon it.

(2) Tis very Uncertain, compared to a Shadow, Prov. 27.   Boast not thyself of tomorrow; James 4. 13. 14. 15.   What is your Life? *

* Prop. 4. We ought to use our utmost Diligence in preparation for Eternity. This is the whole Duty of man. Deut. 32, 46, 47. It is your Life. Engage our Souls most intense Resolution, most industrious Endeavours. Work out our Salvation with Fear and Trembling. If we are not prepared, if Death surprise us, we are Everlastingly Undone.

[Of course there was an afternoon service, and the Judge has notes of the Sermon, which was a second part of the morning discourse, but we omit it.]

Contribution. Mr. Jonathan Duñam made a short pithy prayer, and then pronounced the Blessing, taking in that the Priests were to give. He seems to breathe a Spirit of Holiness.

In the evening visited Mrs. Lothrop. As we went we met Capt. Dogget and Mr. Mat. Mayhew coming to see us. Mrs. Lothrop has eight Children. They are all well. Mr. Wiswall eat with us between 4 and 5, p. m. Their Custom is not to dine. Capt. Dogget expresses a great desire that Mr. Wiswall may continue, with fears lest he should be discouraged and remove. Would have me endeavour to persuade him to stay among them. Two Sloops sailed yesterday; One for Boston, the other for Wood's Hole.

Second-day, April 12. 1714. Major Thaxter and Mr. Denison go to Mr. Mayhew for the Letter of Attorney and an extract of the Deed. Yet our Landlady scruples paying Arrears. Thinks I may be able to demand only what has grown due since my Lord Lymerick made conveyed [sic] his Lands and Lordship to the hon^{ble} Company whereof Sir William Ashurst is Governour.

Mr. Samuel Sarson left two Daughters that are now living, viz: Anne Sarson and Jane Sarson, who are descended from Mrs. Jane Sarson, Widow of Mr. Thomas Mayhew,[1] Minister, lost in Garret, whom Mr. Richard Sarson[2] married, and by her had Samuel Sarson, brother by the Mother's side, to Major Matthew Mayhew; and Mehetabel Sarson, (now Lothrop.) To S. W[iswall] 10ˢ

Rode to Homes's Hole accompanied by Mr. Jnᵒ Worth, Capt. *

---

[1] This was Thomas Mayhew, Jr., son of Thomas Mayhew, the pioneer English settler at Nantucket, the founder of an honored family. The son was well educated, a good classical scholar, and a devoted friend of the Indian, to whom he was the first English preacher in their own language. He was in his thirty-seventh year, when, in 1657, on a voyage to England, he was on board a vessel the fate of which was never known. — Eds.

[2] Savage enters Richard Sarson under the head of " Sansom," though he corrects it in the *errata*. He was made a Justice of the Peace, Dec. 8, 1692, and acted until 1697. He seems also to have been a special Justice of the Court of Common Pleas for Duke's County. — Eds.

* Doggett, Mr. Matthew Mayhew, Benj. Haws, John Tolman. Came off about 25 minutes past 10. m. To Job Soumauau, Schoolmaster, at Christiantown, Ten Shillings. Had a good passage over with young Mrs. Dagget of Attleborough. Wood's Hole, left with young Mrs. Weeks, for Rachel Pepeena, who has no feet, Five Shillings. Din'd at Capt. Lothrop's. It began to Rain, [so] that I would have had the Horses set up again. But Mr. Thaxter and Mr. Denison were for standing along. Capt. Lothrop accompain'd us to the River. Baited at Fish's, where were sundry Indians; had brought Elisha Sonamog going in his way homeward. He administer'd the Lord's Super yesterday at Mashpan. Rain'd hard, yet being warm, and not Driving, got comfortably to Mr. Cotton's a little before Sunset. Mr. Cotton is gon to Boston. Madam Cotton tells us that Mrs. Maria Mather died April 4. Mr. Attorney sued by Col. Nicholson in an £1800 Action. Governour bound for him. Mr. Stoddard and Davenport, Sureties.

Sandwich, April 13. 1714. Cold Storm of Rain and Snow.

To Caleb Papmoŭet   £0. 4. 0.

To Mouniment Peter, a pair of Pumps 0. 4. 0.

To Mr. Jnº Denison, Forty Shillings.

The Rain ceasing we set out from Sandwich about 2. p. m : got well to Plymouth a little before Sunset, just as men were returning from the Funeral of Lieut. Samᶦ Bradford, who was buried this day at Duxbury, 46 years old; is Lamented. Col. Thomas says Mrs. Maria Mather should have been buried on Thorsday; but the Stormy weather hinder'd, and she was buried on Friday. Col. Fr. Wainwright's daughter lay dead at Mr. Addington's. Visited Mr. Thomas and his Wife, to condole the Loss of their Daughter.

In the Night, long before we went to Bed, twas fear'd Sam. Toon, an Indian, was drown'd. He was Servant to Capt. Church, and our Landlord Willard. They gave £24 for him. The dead Corps was found before. Somebody sent him to fetch 2 Fish from a vessel, and tis conjectur'd miss'd in stepping from his Canoe to the Sloop. Was about 26 years old. Every body says he was in no way disorder'd with Drink.[1] Mr. Sheriff shows me the Proclamation for dissolving the General Court, dated April 6.*

---

[1] The poor and forlorn condition of the scattered remnants of the Indian tribes in the region visited by Sewall officially, may be taken as illustrating the fate of many others of the aboriginal race at the time, and of those that survived soon after, till all of them vanished as now from the soil of New England, except the few still left on the Penobscot, in westerly Rhode Island, and in occasional patches of our territory. In the volumes of the earlier series of the Collections of the Society are found many fragments of history

* Midweek, April 14. 1714.   Between 6 and 7 I went on board the
Sloop Success, John Davis Master, burdened about 42 Tuns, Loaden *

---

of biography, and of local descriptions, and sketches of missionary effort for
the Indians, which give evidence alike of the conscientious attempts, at much
cost of patience, money, and hard labor, in their behalf, and of the discour-
agements and failure which shadowed and saddened the results.   Primers,
catechisms, tracts, and Bibles, were printed in their own languages.   Schools
were established for Indian children.   Tools and implements for agriculture,
and for household thrift, were generously furnished.   Guardians and overseers were sent into the bounds reserved for the Indians to teach them agriculture and profitable industry.   About the time of Sewall's visit to Martha's
Vineyard and Nantucket, there were a score of graduates from Harvard who,
as preachers, were capable of conducting religious services in the language
and dialect of the natives, while eight of the red men had been trained and
ordained to the work of the ministry to their own people.   But contact and
intimacy with the white man and with civilization, in almost every case, de-
moralized the Indians, robbing them of such wild manhood as they might
have had in their savage condition and in their forest life, and making them
degraded and humiliated in the presence of a superior race.   No community
of Indians, in New England at least, has ever advanced much beyond a stage
of semi-civilization, and it is very rarely that a single one is now to be seen
among us of pure, unmixed, native blood: while in the vast regions of our
western and northwestern territory it is estimated that a very large proportion of the Indian tribes are half-breeds, chiefly of a French mixture; and
while such tribes in the Indian Territory as the Creeks, the Choctaws, the
Chickasaws, the Seminoles, and the Cherokees, as have made the most advance in civilization, show a commingling of the blood of all European na-
tionalities, as well as of the African.   The negro blood predominates among
those who represent the natives in New England.   The sketches from life
given in the papers in our Collections, above referred to, though showing the
devotedness of such hopeful friends of the Indians as Shepherd, the Mayhews,
Eliot, Gookin, Cotton, and others, were regarded by contemporaries as over-
stating and over-coloring the real truth.   The prevailing opinion was the
cheerless one that labor, in behalf of the Indian, was wasted.   An abject
demeanor, a spiritless dejection, a squalid mode of life in a hovel so sur-
rounded with mud and filth as to be more forbidding than a smoky wigwam,
and subsistence on the dole of pauperism, marked the aspect and condition of
the former lords of the soil in presence of those who supplanted them.   The
kind-hearted Sewall distributed among those whom he saw his private
gifts, and gave, or promised, religious books to the children, who he thought
would value what he so prized.   The poor waif whose sad fate by drowning
— under the relieving qualification that he might not have been intoxicated
— he relates so sympathetically in his Journal, was one of many of his race
at the time scattered over our farming towns, who did laborious and menial
service for the whites for a bare subsistence, showing how complete was the
transformation from their natural state, in which they refuse and despise all
work. — EDS.

* with Wheat, Rye, Barley, Pork, &c. They that carried me aboard saw the Indian's Canoo upon the Beach, Lanch'd it and Tow'd it to Town with them. Just as I came to the Wharf Mr. Thomas, the Coroner and Jury were viewing the body of the poor Indian. Thus I, in many respects, a greater Siñer, am suffer'd to go well away, when my poor namesake, by an unlucky Accident, has a full stop put to his proceedings, and not half so old as I.

Dine with Pork and Pease. I had my New York Biscuit to eat, and a Bottle of Wine. Four Men in the Sloop : John Davis, Thomas Davis, Timothy Mulford, of East Hampton, Owners, and John King whom they hire to go with them. The Owners speak very well of Mr. Hunting, the Minister.

Cargo: 600 Bushels of Wheat : 280 Barley : 40 Rye : 40 Indian : 50 Oats, to Mr. Jekyl : 70 Barrels of Pork, 40 Barrels of Beef, 16 firkins Butter, 19 Boxes Candles, about 80 pounds a Box, Some Tallow and Bay-Berry Wax, 500 Weight, Few Feathers, Furrs. They clear at New London, and we drunk New London Water. They have a privilege of late that the East End of Long Island may clear at New London.

Got up with the Castle just about Sunset. Were becalm'd, and Collins and Marshall, coming by in a small Boat, landed me at the Long Wharf. I visited my Son, who very heartily welcomed me. He had been taking Physick. Got into my own House just about Eight, and found all well. David complains of the Heat of the Day, which confirms me I did best to come by Water. *Laus Deo.*

April 16. To Mr. Stedman for David's Horse to the Vinyard and home, 30ˢ *

Return'd to my own home April 14, 1714. By water from Plimouth. *Laus Deo.* Mrs. Maria Mather was buried in my absence.

INDEX.

INDEX.

NOTE. — This index contains chiefly the names of persons only. It is intended hereafter to furnish a complete index of persons, places, and subjects for the whole Diary. The numbers with an asterisk added, which numbers are at the end of each group of references, refer to the Introduction. As that part occupies over one hundred pages, it was deemed inexpedient to use the Roman style of pagination. The usual Arabic figures were used with a distinguishing mark. — EDS.

A.

Y.

Z.

University Press, Cambridge: John Wilson & Son.

RESEARCH LIBRARY

OF

COLONIAL AMERICANA

An Arno Press Collection

Histories

Acrelius, Israel. **A History of New Sweden; Or, The Settlements on the River Delaware** . . . Translated with an Introduction and Notes by William M. Reynolds. Historical Society of Pennsylvania, MEMOIRS, XI, Philadelphia, 1874.

Belknap, Jeremy. **The History of New Hampshire.** 3 vols., Vol. 1— Philadelphia, 1784 (Reprinted Boston, 1792), Vol. 2—Boston, 1791, Vol. 3—Boston, 1792.

Browne, Patrick. **The Civil and Natural History of Jamaica.** In Three Parts . . . London, 1756. Includes 1789 edition Linnaean index.

[Burke, Edmund]. **An Account of the European Settlements in America.** In Six Parts . . . London, 1777. Two volumes in one.

Chalmers, George. **An Introduction to the History of the Revolt of the American Colonies:** Being a Comprehensive View of Its Origin, Derived From the State Papers Contained in the Public Offices of Great Britain. London, 1845. Two volumes in one.

Douglass, William. **A Summary, Historical and Political, of the First Planting, Progressive Improvements, and Present State of the British Settlements in North-America.** Boston, 1749–1752. Two volumes in one.

Edwards, Bryan. **The History, Civil and Commercial, of the British Colonies in the West Indies.** Dublin, 1793–1794. Two volumes in one.

Hughes, Griffith. **The Natural History of Barbados.** In Ten Books. London, 1750.

[Franklin, Benjamin]. **An Historical Review of the Constitution and Government of Pennsylvania, From Its Origin** . . . London, 1759.

Hubbard, William. **A General History of New England, From the Discovery to MDCLXXX.** (*In* Massachusetts Historical Society, COLLECTIONS, Series 2, vol. 5, 6, 1815. Reprinted 1848.)

Hutchinson, Thomas. **The History of the Colony of Massachusetts Bay** . . . 3 vols., Boston, 1764–1828.

Keith, Sir William. **The History of the British Plantations in America** . . . London, 1738.

Long, Edward. **The History of Jamaica:** Or, General Survey of the Antient and Modern State of that Island . . . 3 vols., London, 1774.

Mather, Cotton. **Magnalia Christi Americana; Or, The Ecclesiastical History of New-England From** . . . the Year 1620, Unto the Year . . . 1698. In Seven Books. London, 1702.

Mather, Increase. **A Relation of the Troubles Which Have Hapned in New-England, By Reason of the Indians There From the Year 1614 to the Year 1675** . . . Boston, 1677.

Smith, Samuel. **The History of the Colony of Nova-Caesaria, Or New-Jersey** . . . **to the Year 1721** . . . Burlington, N.J., 1765.

Thomas, Sir Dalby. **An Historical Account of the Rise and Growth of the West-India Collonies,** and of the Great Advantages They are to England, in Respect to Trade. London, 1690.

Trumbull, Benjamin. **A Complete History of Connecticut,** Civil and Ecclesiastical, From the Emigration of Its First Planters, From England, in the Year 1630, to the Year 1764; and to the Close of the Indian Wars . . . New Haven, 1818. Two volumes in one.

Personal Narratives and Promotional Literature

Byrd, William. **The Secret Diary of William Byrd of Westover, 1709–1712,** edited by Louis B. Wright and Marion Tinling. Richmond, Va., 1941.

Byrd, William. **The London Diary (1717–1721) and Other Writings,** edited by Louis B. Wright and Marion Tinling. New York, 1958.

A **Genuine Narrative of the Intended Conspiracy of the Negroes at Antigua.** Extracted From an Authentic Copy of a Report, Made to the Chief Governor of the Carabee Islands, by the Commissioners, or Judges Appointed to Try the Conspirators. Dublin, 1737.

Gookin, Daniel. **An Historical Account of the Doings and Sufferings of the Christian Indians in New England in the Years 1675, 1676, 1677** . . . (*In* American Antiquarian Society, Worcester, Mass. ARCHAEOLOGIA AMERICANA. TRANSACTIONS AND COLLECTIONS. Cambridge, 1836. vol. 2.)

Gookin, Daniel. **Historical Collections of the Indians in New England.** Of Their Several Nations, Numbers, Customs, Manners, Religion and Government, Before the English Planted There . . . Boston, 1792.

Morton, Thomas. **New English Canaan or New Canaan.** Containing an Abstract of New England, Composed in Three Books . . . Amsterdam, 1637.

Sewall, Samuel. **Diary of Samuel Sewall, 1674–1729.** (*In* Massachusetts Historical Society. COLLECTIONS, 5th Series, V–VII, 1878–1882.) Three volumes.

Virginia: Four Personal Narratives. (Hamor, Ralph. *A True Discourse on the Present Estate of Virginia . . . Till the 18 of June 1614* . . . London, 1615/Hariot, Thomas. *A Briefe and True Report of the New Found Land of Virginia . . .* London, 1588/Percy, George. *A Trewe Relacyon of the Proceedings and Ocurrentes of Momente Which Have Happened in Virginia From . . . 1609, Until . . . 1612.* (In *Tyler's Quarterly Historical and Genealogical Magazine*, Vol. III, 1922.)/Rolf, John. *Virginia in 1616.* (In *Virginia Historical Register and Literary Advertiser*, Vol. I, No. III, July, 1848.) New York, 1972.

Winthrop, John. **The History of New England From 1630–1649.** Edited by James Savage. Boston, 1825–1826. Two volumes in one.

New England Puritan Tracts of the Seventeenth Century

Cobbett, Thomas. **The Civil Magistrate's Power in Matters of Religion Modestly Debated** . . . London, 1653.

Cotton, John. **The Bloudy Tenent, Washed, and Made White in the Bloud of the Lambe** . . . London, 1647.

Cotton, John. **A Brief Exposition with Practical Observations Upon the Whole Book of Canticles.** London, 1655.

Cotton, John. **Christ the Fountaine of Life:** Or, Sundry Choyce Sermons on Part of the Fift Chapter of the First Epistle of St. John. London, 1651.

Cotton, John. **Two Sermons.** (*Gods Mercie Mixed with His Justice* . . . London, 1641/*The True Constitution of a Particular Visible Church, Proved by Scripture* . . . London, 1642.) New York, 1972.

Eliot, John. **The Christian Commonwealth:** Or, The Civil Policy of the Rising Kingdom of Jesus Christ. London, 1659.

Hooker, Thomas. **The Application of Redemption,** By the Effectual Work of the Word, and Spirit of Christ, for the Bringing Home of Lost Sinners to God. London, 1657.

H[ooker], T[homas]. **The Christian's Two Chiefe Lessons,** Viz. Selfe Deniall, and Selfe Tryall . . . London, 1640.

Hooker, Thomas. **A Survey of the Summe of Church-Discipline** Wherein the Way of the Churches of New England is Warranted Out of the Word, and All Exceptions of Weight, Which Are Made Against It, Answered . . . London, 1648.

Increase Mather Vs. Solomon Stoddard: Two Puritan Tracts. (Mather, Increase. *The Order of the Gospel, Professed and Practised by the Churches of Christ in New-England* . . . Boston, 1700/Stoddard, Solomon. *The Doctrine of Instituted Churches Explained, and Proved From the Word of God.* London, 1700.) New York, 1972.

Mather, Cotton. **Ratio Disciplinae Fratrum Nov-Anglorum.** A Faithful Account of the Discipline Professed and Practised, in the Churches of New England. Boston, 1726.

Mather, Richard. **Church Covenant:** Two Tracts. (*Church-Government and Church-Covenant Discussed, in an Answer to the Elders of the Severall Churches in New-England* . . . London, 1643/*An Apologie of the Churches in New-England for Church-Covenant, Or, A Discourse Touching the Covenant Between God and Men, and Especially Concerning Church-Covenant* . . . London, 1643.) New York, 1972.

The Imperial System

[Blenman, Jonathan]. **Remarks on Several Acts of Parliament Relating More Especially to the Colonies Abroad** . . . London, 1742.

British Imperialism: Three Documents. (Berkeley, George.
*A Proposal for the Better Supplying of Churches in our
Foreign Plantations, and for Converting the Savage
Americans to Christianity by a College to be Erected in the
Summer Islands, Otherwise Called the Isles of Bermuda . . .*
London, 1724/[Fothergill, John]. *Considerations Relative to
the North American Colonies.* London, 1765/*A Letter to a
Member of Parliament Concerning the Naval-Store Bill . . .*
London, 1720.) New York, 1972.

Coke, Roger. **A Discourse of Trade** . . . London, 1670.

[D'Avenant, Charles]. **An Essay Upon the Government of the
English Plantations on the Continent of America** (1701).
An Anonymous Virginian's Proposals for Liberty Under the
British Crown, With Two Memoranda by William Byrd.
Edited by Louis B. Wright. San Marino, Calif., 1945.

Dummer, Jeremiah. **A Defence of the New-England Charters** . . .
London, 1721.

Gee, Joshua. **The Trade and Navigation of Great Britain
Considered:** Shewing that Surest Way for a Nation to
Increase in Riches, is to Prevent the Importation of Such
Foreign Commodities as May Be Rais'd at Home. London,
1729.

[Little, Otis]. **The State of Trade in the Northern Colonies
Considered;** With an Account of Their Produce, and a
Particular Description of Nova Scotia . . . London, 1748.

Tucker, Jos[iah]. **The True Interest of Britain, Set Forth in
Regard to the Colonies:** And the Only Means of Living in
Peace and Harmony With Them, Including Five Different
Plans for Effecting this Desirable Event . . . Philadelphia,
1776.

SCHOOLCRAFT
COLLEGE LIBRARY